CW01545091

MARINERS, MERCHANTS AND OCEANS
Studies in Maritime History

MARINERS, MERCHANTS AND OCEANS

Studies in Maritime History

Edited by

K.S. Mathew

MANOHAR

1995

The publication of this book has been financially supported by the Indian Council of Historical Research and the responsibility for the facts stated or opinions expressed is entirely of the author and not of the Council.

ISBN 81-7304-075-3

First Published 1995

© K.S. Mathew

Published by
Ajay Kumar Jain
Manohar Publishers & Distributors
2/6, Ansari Road, Daryaganj
New Delhi - 110002

Lasertypeset by
A J Software Publishing Co. Pvt. Ltd.
305, Durga Chambers,
1333, D.B. Gupta Road,
Karol Bagh, New Delhi - 110005

Printed at
Effecient Offset Printers
215, Shahzada Indl. Complex
Delhi - 110035

CONTENTS

PREFACE

Because of geographical and historical reasons the Department of History, Pondicherry University has been showing great interest in maritime studies right from its inception in December 1987. The University has academic jurisdiction over the erstwhile French colonies of Yanam, Pondicherry, Karaikal and Mahe besides Andaman and Nicobar Islands in the Bay of Bengal and Lakshadweep in the Arabian Sea. Several research scholars from various parts of India registered their names for doing in-depth studies in maritime history. The University Grants Commission, Indian Council of Historical Research, Indian Council of Social Sciences Research and Society for Indian Ocean Studies came forward to help us in organising an international symposium on maritime history in February 1989. Eminent historians from various parts of Canada, Europe, Australia, Southeast Asia and India participated in the symposium. The selected papers were brought out in 1990 under the title *Studies in Maritime History*.

The response of the participants of the first inter-national symposium and the reception given to the publication encouraged us to organise the second international symposium with a wider catchment area. Professor A. Gnanam, the second Vice-Chancellor of Pondicherry University graciously sanctioned the seed money for organising the symposium. The Indian Council of Historical Research as well as Society for Indian Ocean Studies came forward to co-sponsor our endeavour. Seasoned scholars from Canada, United States, United Kingdom, Belgium, the Netherlands, Germany, France, Hungary, Portugal, India, Sri Lanka, Singapore, Taiwan, Australia and the Philippines participated in the symposium conducted in December 1991. The selected papers of the second international symposium are brought together in the present volume.

We place on record our indebtedness to all those who contributed the papers and helped us in organising the symposium. Special thanks are due to Dr. S. Babu who assisted in bringing out this volume. The painstaking efforts of Miss M. Joyce and Mrs. C. Sumathi in computerising the proceedings are remembered with gratitude. The services extended by Mr. G. Sivasubramanyan in the preparation of the final draft are acknowledged gratefully. The efficiency of Manohar Publishers & Distributors in publishing the work on time is greatly appreciated.

K.S. Mathew

Pondicherry
8 December 1994

CONTRIBUTORS

Professor Ajit Neogy
Department of History
Visva-Bharati University
Santiniketan
West Bengal
India

Professor Aniruddha Ray
Department of Islamic History & Culture
University of Calcutta
Calcutta
India

Professor S. Arasaratnam
Department of History
University of New England
New South Wales
Australia

Professor Ashin Das Gupta
Flat B/3
32 Ballygunge Circular Road
Calcutta
India

Professor Bertram E.S.J. Bastiampillai
Department of History & Political Science
University of Colombo
Colombo
Sri Lanka

Ms. Bhaswati Bhattacharya
C/o Centre for European Expansion
Leiden University, Leiden
The Netherlands

Professor Gerald E. Panting
Maritime Studies Research Unit
Memorial University
St. John's Newfoundland
Canada

Professor Lewis R. Fischer
Maritime Studies Research Unit
Memorial University
St. John's Newfoundland
Canada

Professor Haraprasad Ray
C.E.A.L.
School of Languages
Jawaharlal Nehru University
New Delhi
India

Professor John G. Everaert
Seminaire voor Koloniale &
Overzeese Geschiedenis
State University of Gent
Gent, Belgium

Professor Juan R. Francisco
Asian Centre
University of the Philippines at Diliman
Quezon City
Philippines

Professor Karel Degryse
Faculteit Van de Letteren en Wijsbegeerte
Rijksuniversiteit
Gent
Belgium

Dr. A.R. Kulkarni
Vice-Chancellor
Tilak Maharashtra Vidyapeeth
Gultekadi
Pune, India

Dr. Luis Frederico Dias Antunes
Universidade Nova de Lisboa
Lisboa, Portugal

Dr. Madhais Yasin
N-480, Sector 25
Noida
Ghaziabad, Uttar Pradesh
India

Dr. Man-houng Lin
Research Fellow
Institute of Modern History
Academia Sinica
Taiwan

Mr. Mark Vink
1458, N. Cleveland Avenue
St. Paul, MN 55108
U.S.A.

Professor K.S. Mathew
Department of History
Pondicherry University
Pondicherry,
India

Dr. Ng Chin-keong
Department of History
National University of Singapore
Singapore

Dr. Ranabir Chakravarti
Department of History
University of Calcutta
Calcutta,
India

Dr. Remco Raben
Institute for the History of European Expansion
Leiden University
The Hague, The Netherlands

Ms. Rose Marie Gräfin Fugger
Prinzregentenstrasse 144
D-8000 München 80
Germany

Vice-Admiral M.K. Roy
Nehru Fellow
New Delhi
India

Professor G.V. Scammell
Department of History
Pembroke College
Cambridge
United Kingdom

Dr. Tansen Sen
Department of Oriental Studies
School of Arts and Sciences
University of Pennsylvania
Philadelphia
U.S.A.

INTRODUCTION

K.S. Mathew

A scientific approach to maritime studies covering the Indian Ocean regions is an appropriate means to reconstruct the history of India in its various dimensions. India, right from the dawn of her civilisation in the prehistoric period, had long- distance maritime contacts, as evinced by the archaeological findings of the Harappan sites. The Harappan cities, which came into existence towards the middle of the third millennium B.C., seem to have had commercial relations with Mesopotamia by sea. A number of typical seals from the Indus Valley civilisation are found in Sumer, at levels going back to 2300 to 2000 B.C. These seals, which were found in large numbers in Mohenjodaro and Harappa, are believed to have been used to mark the ownership of property. Every merchant or mercantile family, according to scholars like A.L. Basham, had a seal. A number of typical Indus seals were found in Mesopotamia, besides several products of the Indus regions. The archaeological findings in Mesopotamia, prompted some historians to conclude that people of the Harappan civilisation (2500-1750 B.C.) had trade and commerce with Sumeria. Cotton, the staple item of export from India, was presumably taken to Mesopotamia. Scholars like B.B. Lal and R.S. Sharma subscribe to the view that the trade the people of the Harappan civilisation conducted with Mesopotamia was seaborne. This suggestion is based on the findings of the excavation conducted in Lothal, not far from the Gulf of Cambay, which was the inlet of the Arabian Sea on the Gujarat coast. A dockyard, 216 metres long (north to south) and 37 metres wide, situated to the east of the township of Lothal, one of the city sites of the Harappan civilisation, was discovered by the archaeologists.

A channel connected the dockyard of Lothal with Bhogavo river; and the boats entered the dockyard through this channel during high tide. B.B. Lal is of the opinion that the structure, located near the dockyard of Lothal, could be a warehouse where commodities of exchange were stored. The opinion that Lothal had maritime trade contacts with other parts of the world is strengthened by the discovery of seals and sealings of the Indus style at Ur, Susa, Umma, Lagash and Tell Asmar in West Asia. Of special importance is the discovery of a sealing at Umma, which was associated with a bale of cloth—evidently an export from India. A seal found in Lothal, more or less the same as those discovered at the contemporary sites of Barbar, Ras-al-Qala and Failaka in the Persian Gulf region, confirms the view that the commercial relations between the sites of Harappan civilisation and West Asia were, at least partly, maritime. A.L. Basham also subscribes to the view that the merchants of Harappan civilisation resided in Mesopotamia and that there were maritime trade contacts with West Asia, which is now proved in the light of the findings at Lothal. D.D. Kosambi and R.S. Sharma are of the view that the merchants of the Harappan period had trade with Dilmun, which can be identified with Bahrain on the Persian Gulf. This could have been through maritime routes.

Bharukachcha (Broach) in Gujarat was the chief port during the period between 600 and 320 B.C. catering to India's maritime trade with the West. An early *Jataka* story mentions ships sailing from the port of Bharukachcha to Baveru, identified as Babylon. Sopara near Bombay was another port of great importance in India's seaborne trade in the pre-Christian era. By the Mauryan times (321-185 B.C.), Tamralipti (Tamluk), situated in the Ganges delta, became the main seaport of the Ganga basin, from where ships sailed to Sri Lanka, Southwest Asia and Indonesia.

India's seaborne trade reached great heights during the period between 200 B.C. and A.D. 300, especially on account of the trade conducted by the seamen of Roman Egypt. The Roman trade with India was facilitated by the Roman conquest, in A.D. 115, of Mesopotamia which was made a Roman province. The Roman emperor Trajan conquered Muscat and explored the Persian Gulf. The use of monsoon, known to the Arabs from the mid-first century B.C., was discovered by Hippalus by the beginning of the first century A.D. This was used by the Romans for trade with India. The seaman's guide, compiled in Greek by an anonymous writer at the end of the first century A.D., *Periplus Maris Erythreae*, was used by the merchants and seamen of Roman Egypt. The three important ports of peninsular India, namely Musiris known as Cranganore in the kingdom of Ceras on the Malabar coast, Korkaiin the land of Pandyas not far from the modern Tuticorin on the eastern coast of India, and Kaveripattinamat the mouth of Kaveri in the kingdom of the early Colasare mentioned in Ptolemy's *Geography.* Strabo speaks of the embassy sent by the ruler of Pandyas to Augustus at Athens about 20 B.C. The early Colas profited greatly out of the seaborne trade, especially the one based on Kaveripattinam, their headquarters. The famous cotton products of Uraiyur found their way to various parts of the world through this port town, which was built up by the Cola ruler Karikala, who flourished around A.D. 100. He founded Puhar and constructed an embankment of 160 km length along the Kaveri. A number of foreign merchants resided in this port town. Tamil literature of the period, called *Sangam,* describes the layout of the city of Kaveripattinam, especially the two different sections occupied by the Indian and foreign merchants and the marketplace situated in between. The boats built at the coastal towns of the Colas were used for long-distance voyages to Malaya and Southeast Asia. The Roman demand for spices drove the merchants of the Cola territory to Malaya, Java, Sumatra, Cambodia and Borneo. They acted as middlemen for the Romans. Merchants from Kalinga and Magadha intensified their commercial activities in Sri Lanka and Burma, besides the trade on the eastern coast of India during the period 200 B.C.-A.D. 300.

Another important centre of India's maritime trade from the first century B.C. to the second century A.D. was Arikamedu, known to Periplus as Poduke, near modern Pondicherry. The extensive excavations conducted in 1945, and recent ones by a group of scholars from United States in collaboration with the Archaeological Survey of India in 1989, 1990 and 1991 unearthed a lot of material related to the commercial activities centred on Poduke. Besides being a port of call en route to Malaya and China, Poduke comprised a Roman settlement where certain commodities like muslin were manufactured. Pottery, glassware, arretine and other wares, wine amphorae and gold were brought to Poduke. The report of the excavations at Poduke written by Wheeler, Krishna Deva and Ghosh, was published in *Ancient India*, 2, 1946. The findings of the recent excavations will be available in the forthcoming work by Vimala Begley.

Muziris, on the Malabar coast, had a flourishing trade with the Romans. Two Roman regiments were said to have been kept at Muziris to protect their interests. It is concluded by the archaeologists that the Romans built a temple for Augustus at

Cranganore. Scholars like R.E.M. Wheeler and E.H. Warmington have written on the Roman trade with India.

The other port-towns that had commercial relations with Rome during the Satavahana period (A.D. 106-220) were Amravati and Nagarjunakonda, on the eastern coast of India.

Even after Roman trade with India declined, seaborne trade of the subcontinent continued to flourish during the period A.D. 300-700. The commercial contacts established with the Southeast Asian regions in the wake of Roman demands gave the opportunity to Indian merchants to continue the pursuit. The missionaries carrying the message of Indian religions were joined by the merchants. Indian settlements came up in Thailand, Cambodia, Java and Malaya. Ships from Tamralipti and Amravati were said to have sailed for Burma, Martaban and Indonesia. The South Indian ports sent vessels to Tenasserim, Trang, Straits of Malacca and Java. Indian ships crossed the China Seas often. Besides Tamralipti, Ghantashala and Kadura on the eastern coast were the centres of trade of North India with Southeast Asia. Commercial relations with the Mediterranean, Western Asia and the eastern coast of Africa developed during this period. Broach, Chaul, Kalyan and Cambay were the important ports that had trade with these regions. Spices, pepper, sandalwood, pearls, precious stones, perfumes, indigo and herbs were exported from India to the West, in return for which horses from Arabia, Iran and Bactria were brought to India. Ivory from Ethiopia and Chinese silk in great volume were imported to the subcontinent. It is concluded by historians like Thapar and Basham that Indian merchants had contact with Zanzibar and Madagascar during this period.

The economic prosperity, and subsequently hold on society achieved by the merchants during this period, must have, presumably, compelled Brahmins to object to travelling overseas, which was considered a taboo even later on. It was concluded by the lawmakers that by going overseas, the caste Hindus would come in contact with *Mlechcha* (impure) people and contract contamination. Ludovico di Varthema, who came to India in the sixteenth century, makes mention of this taboo.

The Pallavas of South India, beginning with Mahend-ravarman I (600-630), developed a navy and built dockyards at Mahabalipuram and Nagapattinam on the Coromandel coast. The navy assisted in the maritime trade with Southeast Asian regions such as Kambuja

(Cambodia), Champa (Annam) and Srivijaya (Southern Malaya peninsula and Sumatra). South Indian merchants were frequently found in these kingdoms. Arab merchants began to occupy an important position on the western coast of India, and Indian merchants became mere suppliers to the Arabs.

The later Colas under Rajaraja I (A.D. 985-1014) and his successor Rajendra provided an environment conducive to maritime trade. Rajaraja attacked the alliance between Kerala, Sri Lanka and the Pandyas with a view to breaking the monopoly of western trade. He destroyed Anuradhapùram, the capital of Sri Lanka. Rajendra conducted an overseas campaign against the kingdom of Srivijaya in Southeast Asia. Thapar is of the opinion that this campaign might have been for the protection of Indian commercial interest from the interference of the kingdom of Srivijaya. The Cola king himself might have had his investment in trade with China, which was going to be imperilled by the ruler of Srivijaya. His intention was to keep his territory as one of the end-points of the trade, so that he could get the profits. The ships from South India used to pass through the seas held by the kingdom of Srivijaya to China. According to Thapar, if the campaign of the Cola ruler were only on account of "the desire for overseas empire, this would have been followed up with Indian colonisation of the areas annexed and an attempt to conquer more of the hinterland". Since this did not take place, the Cola enterprise was considered forming part of the commercial interest.

Marco Polo, who visited the Pandyan kingdom in 1288 and 1293, left a detailed narrative of the trade of South India, especially maritime trade. As described by him, Mahabalipuram, Kaveripattinam, Shaliyur and Korkai on the east coast, and Quilon on the west coast, controlled the seaborne trade to the East and the West. Siraf on the Persian Gulf was the entrepot of the westward trade, reaching up to Persia and Arabia. Trade with China was at its peak. Formosa is believed to have had Indian settlement during the thirteenth century. South India exported textiles, spices, drugs, jewels, ivory, horn, ebony and camphor to China and to West Asia. Horses in large numbers were imported to South India from Arabia and Persia, as noted by Marco Polo. The maritime trade of peninsular India was controlled by merchant guilds like *manigramam* and *valajiyar*. Some guilds like *Nanadeshi*, with bases in South India and Sumatra, were quite rich and influential.

Chinese contact with South India during the period starting with the fourteenth century is being studied by scholars like Roderich Ptak and Haraprasad Ray. Their sources are Chinese, especially the details furnished by the participants of the Cheng Ho missions. The importance of Quilon, Kayankulam and Calicut on the western coast of India in the Sino-Indian trade relations is brought out very well in their reports. Chinese contacts with Rander near Surat and Diu, north of the Gujarat coast, are referred to in Portuguese writings of the first quarter of the sixteenth century. Similarly, the Karimi merchants of the Red Sea areas, specialising in the trade of pepper and spices, had their own establishments in Calicut and other ports of the western coast. Based on contemporary sources, S.D. Goiten and Fischel brought out interesting details about the commercial contacts of the Karimi merchants with the western coast, especially the Malabar coast. Calicut and Diu were the chief emporia of coastal western India in the East-West axis of the emporia trade connecting Malacca and Venice before the sixteenth century.

Indian merchants were found on the East African coast when Vasco da Gama, on his way to Calicut, anchored off the coast. The Gujarati merchants trading there offered to the Portuguese large supplies of pepper and spices from the Malabar coast on the port towns of East Africa. More than a thousand Gujarati merchants with their own *shabandar* were permanently involved in trade in Malacca. In addition, four to five thousand traders used to visit Malacca every year from Gujarat. This was by the end of the first decade of the sixteenth century, when the Portuguese reached Malacca.

The Europeans, bent on finding a direct sea-route connecting the spice-producing areas of the Orient with Europe and thereby avoiding intermediaries, reached India at the end of the fifteenth century. Invoking the papal authority, a couple of legal presumptions and by force of arms, the Portuguese wanted to keep their monopoly over the Indian Ocean regions. The Turks, Venetians, commercially minded governors of Gujarat and Indian rulers deprived of their income by way of taxes on the traders, set up a common front to oust the Portuguese from India in the first decade of the sixteenth century itself. But the Portuguese mariners proved their mettle and established themselves firmly in the Indian Ocean regions.

The lure of Indian trade did not permit the other European powers to watch the developments silently. Finally, Indian Ocean regions became an object of scramble for the Dutch, the English, the French and the Danes. Every one wanted to have a share in the trade of the subcontinent of India. The English delegation waited at the court of Akbar to get permission to start factories in India. The Dutch obtained, from the ruler of Golconda in Deccan, permission (*farman*) to open a factory in Masulipatnam in the first decade of the seventeenth century. The Danes got a place from the ruler of Tanjore to build a factory in Tranquebar. The French, too, established themselves first in Surat and then in Pondicherry.

The English establishment at Madras was a threat to the French at Pondicherry. The English and the French crossed swords in South India for realising their ambition to acquire territories, wherefrom they could raise local funds for trade and commerce. The Dutch diverted their attention to Southeast Asia and intra-Asian trade. Finally, the French and the English fought vigorously for territorial possessions and embroiled themselves in local politics. The English brought to an end the imperial ambitions of the French, who were compelled to confine their activities to Chandernagore, Yanam, Pondicherry and Karaikkal on the eastern coast, and Mahe on the western coast. They further obtained *diwani* rights from the Mughal emperor, suppressed the expansionist attempts of the Marathas and did away with the roaring Tiger of Mysore, Tipu, who was the last straw of hope for the French. The English became the colonial masters of India while the French and the Portuguese remained content with their small territories on the coastal regions. All these colonial powers continued their "missionising" activities till the subcontinent of India, which was the first target of their maritime attempts right from the end of the fifteenth century, was brought to the group of "third world" countries. The amazing story of maritime trade from the period of commercial revolution till the full "development of underdevelopment" could be studied in its various ramifications.

The long history of the maritime activities of India attracts the attention of scholars in various fields. The study of the techniques of navigation, especially the indigenous haven-finding art, knowledge of oceanic currents, the method of calculating the depth of water, the direction and nature of oceanic currents before the use of western techniques, would throw light on the technological achievements of the Indian navigators. Of late, scholars like Arunachalam have taken up admirable studies in this direction. The stagnation of the technology in the wake of European domination can be easily assessed by scientific studies of this nature. If Indians could reach safely the East African coast in the west and Malacca in the east with their commodities of exchange even before the Portuguese arrived, the Indian navigators must have attained thorough knowledge of the various aspects of navigation in the Indian Ocean. Vasco da Gama, when on the East African coast, took them to his ship to show the navigational instruments used by the Portuguese. The Portuguese writers remarked that the Indian navigators did not evince any admiration, since they were used to these techniques in their ships crossing the Arabian Sea and going to the East African coast as well as Malacca. This degree of achievement, made by Indians in navigation of the pre-Portuguese era, suffered a setback in the colonial period, as they could not keep pace with the progress in technology.

Shipbuilding, tonnage of ocean-going ships, and the various activities connected with the production of a seaworthy vessel constitute a few other aspects that may draw the attention of historians of science and technology. As reported by the Portuguese writers, iron nails were not used in the manufacture of ships in India; coir and wooden nails were used in plenty. The Portuguese were fully aware of the qualitative superiority of the ships constructed in India and of the timber available. In course of time, several ships for the Portuguese were manufactured in Bassein, Calicut, Cochin and Goa. Presumably, they must have used Indian artisans for the work. Even some of the rulers of West Asia purchased the ships manufactured in India under the supervision of the Portuguese in the first half of the sixteenth century.

Life on board ships coming to India from Europe, covering almost three quarters of a year, presents an interesting subject of study. The treatment for various diseases contracted by the navigators, the type of entertainment they had, and a host of other aspects of the social life of the male-dominated society deserve the special attention of scholars. There were theatrical performances on board. The psychological and religious attitudes of the mariners on the high seas, depending on natural energy and exposed to the fury of storms, were totally different from those on land. The same could be said of the coastal and island communities vis-a-vis the people living away from the sea front. Development of urban or trade centres on the coastal regions on account of maritime activities could be studied in detail in connection with capital accumulation, organisation of accessories of trade, banking, habitational patterns, hinterland-foreland relations and also production in the secondary sector.

The flourishing maritime trade of India through centuries points to the surplus of produce both in primary and secondary sectors. Cotton, pepper and spices were exported from India in large quantities to various parts of the world. This naturally presupposes increase in the production of cash crops and new relations of production. Similarly, export of large volume of textiles from the Coromandel and Gujarat coasts indicates steady growth in production in the secondary sector and also expertise in the production of high-quality textiles which were taken to Europe. This would have definitely brought about a situation in which readjustments in production were to be made to the neglect of some other items not required for export but needed for day-to-day life. Coromandel coast and Goa were important centres of the export of pearls, diamonds, precious stones and saltpetre to various parts of the world. This speaks for the development of extractive industry. In short, scholars of economics find a vast field of study in connection with maritime activities.

The participation of Indian entrepreneurs in India's maritime trade through the centuries provides ample avenues for indepth study of local investment and the role of indigenous merchant magnates. Persons like Malik Gopi, Malik Ayaz, Khwaja Sofar, Vriji Vohra of Gujarat, Marakkars of Cochin, Khwaja Shamsud-din Giloni of Cannanore, Malai Chetty, Kasiviranna, Periathambi Marakkar and Ananda Rangapillai of Coromandel and a host of others played a significant part in the European trade with India. The Marakkars of Cochin provided even men to fight for the Portuguese on the Coromandel coast.

The mingling of various races in and outside wedlock, especially in the *Estado da India Portuguesa*, is well known. The cultural domination or assimilation in such associations attracts the attention of historians and sociologists alike. Similarly, the spread of some species of plants from far-off lands in the context of maritime activities is studied by scholars of life sciences and historians. It is surmised that even tapioca, very commonly used in South India, was the same as *casata* found in Mexico when America was discovered and this was later introduced into Africa and finally to India. The same is true of potato, sweet potato, corn (maize), tobacco, cashewnut, red chilly and a number of other items that began to be cultivated abundantly in India in the wake of Portuguese contacts with India. Thus we could address ourselves to a huge array of problems in the context of maritime studies which will definitely help us reconstruct history in its various dimensions.

Ashin Das Gupta tries to give a theoretical framework in his paper under which discussions on various aspects of maritime history could be conducted. Moreland's attempt to conceive Indian Ocean regions as a single unit and economic activities in a Eurocentric view are evaluated against the background of the hypothesis propounded by J.C. Van Leur. Das Gupta suggests that the Indian Ocean cannot be considered a single unit and trade in the Indian Ocean should not be conceived as a separate entity. In fact, he points out, the connection of the littoral with the hinterland should be taken into account while dealing with maritime activities. The author is of the opinion that Moreland relied chiefly on the official documentation to the total neglect of private collections and documents in various other languages, both oriental and western. This study provides useful insight on various aspects of maritime trade in the medieval period.

Tansen Sen in his article discusses the maritime contacts between China and the Cola empire from the second half of the ninth century. Archaeological evidence from the coastal areas of both China and South India is used. The documents in the Chinese language are skilfully used by the writer to throw light on the trade in pearls, ivory, frankincense, camphor and cotton. He is of the opinion that the maritime activities between coastal India and China provided a congenial environment for the exchange of culture, especially the expansion of Indian culture to South China. The writer holds the view that Srivijaya played an important role in the contact between China and India. Considerable light is thrown on the relation between Srivijaya and the Imperial Colas, especially based on the Srivijaya inscription where Kulottunga is depicted as Lord of Srivijaya. He concludes that the Imperial Colas, with the help of a strong navy, extended their influence to Sri Lanka, Bay of Bengal and even Southeast Asia.

Juan R. Francisco highlights the relations between India and the Philippines, which became quite prominent between the tenth and fourteenth centuries. He traces the origin of the contact to the third century B.C. Archaeological findings of the Manila area are brought to light to substantiate his arguments regarding the maritime relations of India with the Philippines in the pre-colonial period. He is of the opinion that Srivijaya played an important role in the course of "Indianisation" of Southeast Asia in general and the Philippines in particular. The author analyses some Sanskrit words which are used in the Philippines, which had been accepted in the local language, especially in connection with trade and commerce. He adds that the seafarers from the eastern coast and the Malabar coast of India left cultural vestiges in the Philippines.

The importance of two maritime centres, namely Mottupalli and Visakhapattanam during the early medieval period, is brought out by Ranabir Chakravarti in the subsequent study. He argues that maritime historians, because of the availability of documentation, lay emphasis on the period after 1500, though India in the period before the opening of the sea route by the Portuguese had kept up very important maritime relations. The writer describes the rise of Visakhapattanam under the Colas and that of Mottupalli under the Kakatiyas. He discusses the emergence of Nagapattinam in the Kaveri delta replacing Mamallapuram, which occupied an important position during the Pallava times. The attempts made by Kulottunga to maintain Chinese contacts are also discussed. To buttress his arguments, he refers to the inscriptions at the Taoist monastery temple at Canton. The successors of Kulottunga diverted their attention to the south, especially on account of the Pandyas of Madurai, who were the arch-rivals of the Colas. Therefore, Visakhapattanam could not be sustained. He traces the rise of Mottupalli which came into prominence in the thirteenth century because of the interest shown by Ganapati (1199-1261), a Kakatiya ruler. The Charter of Security (*abhayasasana*) issued by him extending protection to the traders abroad facilitated the development of Mottupalli as an international port for long-distance trade. The author highlights the fact that the policies followed by the Colas and Kakatiyas were chiefly responsible for the development of the port towns of Visakhapattanam and Mottupalli.

Bastiampillai, in his study, focuses attention on the connection of Sri Lanka with the countries east and west of the island from the early years till the arrival of the Portuguese. Archaeological evidence is made use of to throw light on the maritime contacts of Sri Lanka with West Asia. The strategic importance of Sri Lanka for the trade in the Indian Ocean regions is clearly brought out. The chief sources related to Sri Lanka's international contacts are discussed scientifically.

The sudden disappearance of the Chinese from the Malabar coast since the mid-fifteenth century and its causes are discussed by Haraprasad Ray in the next study. He argues that even though China's official trade with India came to an end, the unofficial trade continued. The failure of State-sponsored trade with India is brought out very clearly. He states that cessation of State-controlled trade gave way to the emergence of private trade in South and Southeast Asia on account of the manipulations of the influential individual merchants with the connivance of the Government. Even the court officials participated in the private trade, he adds.

The beginning of the sixteenth century provided ample opportunities for those who were interested in accumulating capital by way of trade and commerce. This was the period of the rise of merchant capital, which served as a transitional phase from feudal to capitalist mode of production. The merchant's capital began to have sway over distant regions. The Fuggers are an example of merchant capitalists who made capital out of the situation. The emergence of Hans Fugger from a simple peasant to a great merchant financier who wielded significant influence with the Roman Emperor, Popes, kings of Spain, Portugal, Hungary, the Netherlands and England is traced in this study. The firm of Fugger dealt in spices, copper, silver, quicksilver, bills of exchange and bonds whereby they amassed great wealth, excelling all other merchant financiers of the world by the sixties of the sixteenth century. The details of the rise and decline of the Fuggers are discussed by Rose Marie Gräfin Fugger, a descendant of the famous family.

With the opening of the direct sea route connecting India with Europe, an opportunity was offered to many Europeans to move out from their own native country. Exiles, renegades and outlaws reached Asia after 1500. A cosmopolitan crowd at the court of Akbar was witnessed by the Jesuits. Refugees and rejects of the western society came from many parts of Europe. Most of them were expatriates and deserters from the service of western maritime powers. By the seventeenth century there were many Portuguese renegades in the service of the Persian rulers. Economic disaster, poverty, religious bigotry, intolerance, oppression and lack of opportunity at home drove the ambitious or disgruntled Europeans to Asia. They performed a lot of economic functions during their stay in the Orient. The details about European renegades and their activities are discussed by Scammell.

The Portuguese came to India primarily to conduct trade and derive profits out of this. Gradually, they found it difficult to raise the required funds in their own country to conduct trade with India. Consequently, they had to rely on the financial help extended by foreign merchants and capitalists. Further, they devised ways and means to generate money locally in India through taxation. To justify their claim for revenue from different sectors of production and exchange like the primary, secondary and tertiary, they developed several theories. Some of the theoretical discussions were based on papal bulls and legal titles. Various sources of income from the East and juridical explanations given by them to justify their claim are presented by K.S. Mathew in the article on taxation in the coastal towns of western India during the sixteenth century.

The period after the close of the fifteenth century witnessed mercantile battles waged by Portugal, Spain, the Netherlands, Britain and France. They chose Macao, which is strategically very important, as a colonial base to extract commodities from China. Traffic in manpower and opium provided enormous profit to the colonial powers. Portugal occupied Macao, which was considered to be a gate to the great country of China, illegally. The battles waged by the Europeans accelerated the disintegration of the feudal system in China. The details of the commercial battles based chiefly on Macao, and the after-effects, are discussed by Deng Kaisong.

With the arrival of the Mughals in Bengal, Bihar and Orissa in the seventh decade of the sixteenth century, the banks of the Hooghly became unsafe on account of the continuous warfare among the advancing Mughals and the Afghan powers. Therefore, there was a shift of population from western Bengal to the safer banks of the Padma and Brahmaputra in East Bengal. New urban settlements came into existence along with *zamindars* of different types. The Portuguese began to be powerful in the Bay of Bengal from the third decade of the sixteenth century. Contemporary revenue records indicate the growth of Bengal's revenue from 1595 onwards. Based on Persian and other contemporary sources, Aniruddha Ray throws light on the coastal society in Bengal in the context of mercantile enterprise and urbanisation during 1575-1608.

Scholars of maritime history have dealt in detail with trade in spices, textiles, precious metals and diamonds. Very little attention is paid to trafficking in slaves. According to Arasaratnam, slave trade assumed great proportions in the seventeenth century. There were several sources for the supply of slaves: slave-raiding, capture and voluntary sale in slavery through destitution. During famines and natural calamities, many sold themselves to moneyed persons who traded in slaves. The Dutch and Asian traders involved themselves in large-scale slave traffic. Acheh was an important market for slaves. Large numbers of slaves were collected from the region of Burma and Bengal through the activities of the Arakkanese, Mughals and Portuguese. Arasaratnam discusses, in the subsequent chapter, the details of slave trade in the Indian Ocean in the seventeenth century.

Remco Raben dwells on the ethnic residential pattern of two colonial cities of the Dutch East India Company from 1600 to 1800, that is, Colombo and Batavia. The material available from census reports is the basis of his study. He deals with segregation based on racial, religious, political and economic factors in these two cities. However, the writer states that the social separation of the Europeans from the Asians could not be complete on account of the practice of mixed marriages and the economic interest of the Company. A complicated system of social regulations emerged out of the criss-crossing of several interests. Even the Asians themselves were separated from each other. He singles out the Spanish practice in Manila where all non-Europeans were directed outside the walled inner city, disregarding the unity of faith. He mentions that the Portuguese did not insist on segregation. A lot of statistical data are provided by the author.

The Portuguese established several fortresses and factories on the western coast of India in the sixteenth century. They employed several well-equipped vessels to keep watch on the movement of the ships in the Arabian Sea. By the time Shivaji began to consolidate the Maratha power, he realised that without a strong navy he might not be able to resist the Portuguese power on the Konkan region. So he constructed a few marine forts like those of Vijaydurg or *Gheria*, Kolaba, Sindhudurg, Ratnagiri, Anjanwel and Yashwantgad. He developed a system of administration of forts.

Shivaji had warships as well as mercantile ships. M. Yasin sheds light on mercantile ships of various types and Shivaji's naval exploits.

A substantial change in the composition of commodities exported from India is seen in the seventeenth century, especially with the arrival of the English on the eastern coast of India. Textiles from Coromandel, chiefly piece goods, were in great demand by the English, who sent them to Southeast Asian regions. The cotton textiles available on the Coromandel region were cheaper than those of Surat. Moreover, the nearness of the Coromandel coast to the Southeast Asian regions prompted the English to have larger quantity of textiles from here. The textiles of various types exported by the English from the Coromandel regions and the various aspects of the trade are discussed by S. Babu in his study on commodity composition of the English trade on the Coromandel region.

During the age of European expansion, the non-western world was gradually incorporated into a global economy based on maritime exchange. Indigenous trading networks on the various continents, however, did not automatically wither away when confronted with the "Modern World System". On the contrary, in many cases the old commercial routes showed signs of remarkable endurance, for instance, the overland trade between Malabar and the Coromandel coast. From the arrival of Vasco da Gama at Kozhikode in 1498 to the capture of the chain of Dutch forts in 1795 by the English, the Indian merchant more than held his own against the European competition. Mark Vink throws light on the several stages of the overland tradeproduction, transportation and marketing—between the west and east coasts of India in the pre-industrial 'age of competition'.

Banyans constituted an important section of Gujarati society involved in trade and commerce. They came in contact with the Portuguese, who established their foothold in Bassein, Diu and Daman in the sixteenth century. Some of the Banyans migrated to East Africa on account of the Portuguese contact with the Dark Continent, especially Mozambique. They traded chiefly in ivory, gold and slaves. The process of settlement of the Banyans in Mozambique was rather gradual and later they were allowed by the authorities to have contact with the mainland. In the later part of the eighteenth century, their Company was legally extinguished. However, their indispensable role in commercial activities of the State is highlighted by Luis Frederico Dias Antunes in his study.

In the subsequent study, Ajit Neogy throws light on the role played by the early *Mudaliars* in the commercial enterprises of the French in Pondicherry, especially Tanappa Mudaliar and Naniappa Pillai as agents of the French East India Company. He states that the interference of the Jesuits in the commercial activities of the Company spoiled François Martin's dream of transforming Pondicherry into a chief entrepot on the Coromandel coast between 1707 and 1720. The able Naniappa Pillai had to face the constant hostility of the Jesuits and ultimately he became a victim of conspiracy hatched by them.

Karel Degryse in his paper discusses the various aspects of social life and tensions on board the eighteenth-century ocean-going vessel, *Ostend Chinamen* (1718-35) based on two important recent publications, *The Wooden World* and *Between the Devil and the Deep Blue Sea.* Not only has the author used the archival sources of the Ostend Company but also notarial records, lawsuits and a very original ship's journal written by a company spy to highlight life in the "Wooden World".

The Dutch monopoly over certain goods in the later decades of the seventeenth century in the Bay of Bengal was challenged by other European and Asian traders. The *Chulias* or *Maraikkayars* of the Coromandel coast posed a serious threat to Dutch Company trade in the late eighteenth century. They traded with ports under indigenous rulers, avoiding those under Dutch control, and exploited their age-old commercial links with Southeast Asia, amassing huge returns. In the absence of an effective naval fleet, the Dutch failed to check this traffic. Aware of this limitation, the Dutch Governor at Nagapattinam favoured freedom of trade. The commercial enterprises of the *Chulias* are brought out by Bhaswati Bhattacharya in her study.

The Dutch-born Willem Bolts, a veteran of the Dutch East India Company in Bengal (1759-68), made an attempt along with the Antwerp merchant banker Charles de Proli, to form an "Asiatic Association" with a view to reopen indirect East India trade. A mission was sent to the Maratha court in Poona to establish networks of trade, which did not bear any fruit. Subsequently, their attention was diverted to the Malabar coast, where spices, dye-wood and rice were available. Negotiating with Haider Ali Khan, Bolts established the main factory in Mangalore and a satellite settlement in Karwar and Baliapatnam. The concessions could not, however, be fruitfully used because of the military confrontations between the Sultan of Mysore and the British. Bolts also tried to organise country- trade campaigns in collaboration with the Portuguese and the English from the west coast of India to Africa. By combining his own experience in India with the financial backing of the Antwerp company, Bolts established indirect maritime traffic between southern Netherlands and the East. But the political situation in India and the crippled organisation of the home company did not permit him to reap fruits. John Everaert throws light on Bolts' trade-related activities.

An attempt has been made by Lewis R. Fischer and Gerald E. Panting to study the experiences of European vessels, especially those of the British moving in the Indian and Pacific oceans, with special emphasis on those that entered Indian ports on the return voyage. Further, they examine quantitatively the patterns of tramp sailing vessels reaching Indian ports before the turn of the twentieth century. The authors are of the opinion that some vessels came to the subcontinent in search of return cargos, and in due course the pattern changed. Indian ports acted as an "alternative source" of supply of cargo for Europe-bound ships.

Chinese scholars are of the opinion that the import of Indian opium led to the drain of silver from China. In her paper, Man-houng Lin, by and large, subscribes to this view generally accepted by economic historians of the nineteenth century. There was, however, flow of silver into China despite the increased receipt of opium. Production of silk and tea was enhanced to avoid the drain of silver. Also, the inflow of silver from Latin America into the international market helped the Chinese to retain the white metal in their own country. The recession of 1810-50 is reckoned to be another cause for the slump in the movement of precious commodities.

Ng Chin-keon analyses the details of the transhipment of *coolies* from China under the Treaty of Nanjing signed between Britain and China in 1824. Amoy in China was the major port of embarkation for thousands of contract labourers until 1850. This human cargo was carried by the British agents stationed in Amoy. Though illegal under Chinese law, the local Chinese officials connived at it. But after a riot in 1852, the *coolie* trade began to decline drastically. The outcry among the public has been expressed in a number of Chinese and English literary sources.

A.R. Kulkarni highlights the geopolitical setup of the port town of Malwan and its hinterland as a background to the study of socio-economic aspects in the nineteenth century. He traces the history of the Konkan, in which lies the Malwan port, and the Marathas' interest in navy. Great emphasis is laid on the different sections of the people dwelling in this area, and their profession, with statistical details. The author discusses the trade, communication and industry of the region to assess the role played by the people of Malwan in India's seaborne trade. He concludes that the coastal society of the region, having its roots in the medieval period, started disintegrating in the nineteenth century when the British took over South Konkan. Overseas trade declined, and the harbours were neglected.

Mihir Roy points out that fourteen of the seventeen conflicts of the 1990s were centred on the Indian Ocean and laments that only thirteen per cent of India's defence budget is set apart for naval defence. The Bay of Bengal and the Arabian Sea are being converted into a refuse bin for oil spillage, detergents and sewage disposal, he points out. He appreciates the development of maritime technology in the last decade, though this has affected the nature of war at sea and naval force in its various dimensions. The expanding activities in the Indian Ocean have created tension among the people bordering on the ocean in the context of boundary disputes, smuggling and grabbing of islands. The author suggests developing a national maritime policy based on a correct understanding of the emerging relations between India and the Indian Ocean. Maritime resources are yet to be tapped adequately by the people of India.

MORELAND HYPOTHESIS

Ashin Das Gupta

I wish to present a general idea before you, knowing fully well that most of you do not like general ideas. Research in maritime history in recent times has emphasised the need for concrete case studies. This is the case, if I may say so, in all fields of history, this country and maritime history being no exceptions. As we all know, there is a close connection between ideas, general and particular. General ideas have to be more tentative than anything in particular. We call such general notions hypotheses and we do our case studies only in the light of such general beliefs. Naturally, we have a few of these general notions, specially Indian Ocean studies. I know from my own experience, as you know from yours, that broad notions do not apply very well if one is going into details. I have found that even terms which we are always using are not so useful when we go deep. Thus, the 'Indian merchant', round whom I like to write, does not exist in quite the same manner as that term would suggest. There were different kinds of people, all of whom you can call 'the Indian merchant'; and you have to stand some way off from your documents for this general term to become meaningful. So, we cannot do our case studies except with the help of general ideas, and these general ideas do not seem appropriate when we are testing them out. It is in the light of this peculiar relationship between the general and particular in maritime history that I bring an old general idea before you. You know it well; only, there are so few of these ideas floating around in the Indian Ocean, that it is worthwhile to look again and take our bearings.

The first point about William Moreland, whose ideas about India's external trade I wish to remind you of, is what most of us still think of him—that he was a very fine historian, in fact one of the best who have written on Indian history. It may be that, as a historian, he was concerned to show the superiority of the British Empire over anything which had gone before; but we are not concerned here with that. There was a central sanity about Moreland, there was a fairness in whatever he wrote, which we all admire. We may not share his opinions, we may disagree with his conclusions, but we all feel that Indian history has seldom been written better. He has been very popular in India and abroad; so much so that he is still taught in Indian schools and colleges. Much of Indian history, if it touches any of the themes which Moreland made his own, would be footnotes on his work—or counterblasts against what he was doing. The legacy still persists. Sometimes we know what we are doing, sometimes we do not. It is important for us to understand Moreland precisely because of this legacy. But it goes without saying that he was not constructing a hypothesis to explain the Indian Ocean. Some of what he wrote dealt with India's foreign trade; and the ideas I now discuss are from there. This work was done in the 1920s, and of course discussed only the Mughal Empire. There was much that was not known then—and there is a great deal to be said for the period before the Mughals and after. But with all these limitations, Moreland taught us a great deal; and we have to look back and see what we are reacting against.

Moreland was saying something which, to my mind, set him against Karl Polanyi. And in it, he prepared the way for Van Leur. He was against the notion of administrative trade although he paid much attention (some of it misguidedly) to elements in the administration who had an adverse effect on trade. He made no mistake about the fact that, whatever can be said about the Dutch and English merchants, they were unable to affect the Indian market. They penetrated the market and they strengthened it, but they did not dominate it. The Indian market was dominated by the Indian merchant, who was financially as skilful as his European counterpart; and the financial instruments which he used were as sophisticated as any in his contemporary world. Prices in the market in which the Indian merchant operated were fixed by demand and supply and by stiff competition. There was never any question of the administration fixing the prices, although some officials could and did establish monopolies from time to time. It may be that Polanyi was looking at a much earlier period; but from the sixteenth century onwards, Moreland's views still hold the field. If we now take a look at all the period together, it may be that we shall be able to firm up a succession of these general ideas; and in this progression Polanyi, because he dealt with the ancient period, may be seen as a precursor of Moreland. What the consequences of such a firming up process will be in the study of the Indian Ocean will be futile to speculate now. Researchers will certainly take a closer look at the linkages between what has been called the ancient and medieval periods: and the habit may spread. It is certain that Moreland was not merely taking up a position which would eventually go against Polanyi and his disciples. He was saying two things of significance which would be taken to their logical extreme by J.C. Van Leur, the disciple of Max Weber. One was that Asian trade was highly developed and there was no distinction as between the Indian merchant and his European counterpart in this period. The other thing he was saying was that if we are studying India, it is advisable to go to India. It is true that Moreland did not follow these ideas to where they would lead: this work would be done by J.C. Van Leur in the 1930s. But that is another story.

We are now following the trends of Moreland's thought; and the thing to notice there is the unitary concept of the Ocean. This is crucial in much that Moreland wrote. We use it ourselves although not quite like Moreland. It may be that in using the expression 'Indian Ocean' we are guilty of the suggestion that this vast stretch of water is one. Moreland certainly wrote as if the coast from the Cape of Good Hope to Japan belonged or ought to belong to the same system and could be controlled from one centre. It may be that the role of the British Navy in policing the Indian Ocean in the nineteenth century suggested this idea to him. This led to the idea that there was supremacy over the Ocean and that this supremacy could be transferred—that Arab supremacy yielded to the Portuguese, the Portuguese to the Dutch, the Dutch to the English and so on. Once we are committed to this 'one ocean' idea, there is no possibility of thinking of the Indian Ocean as a plurality comprising discrete bodies of water and different systems. We may think of an overarching civilisation and we may think of linkages. It is easy to slip into meaningless slogans, specially if we follow the trail of unity in diversity in the Indian Ocean. This is something Moreland never did. There is enough evidence of plurality in what he wrote. But he went resolutely for naval encounters. Which State had the dominating navy in the Indian Ocean, is Moreland's question and we keep repeating it. If the Portuguese navy defeated everything in the Indian Ocean, it would follow that Goa would 'control' the Ocean. If the Dutch and the English would, in their turn, defeat the Portuguese, then they would 'control' the Indian Ocean. We know now that it is one thing to defeat a naval force at a point of the Ocean, it is another to make sure that no merchantman escapes your net in the wide stretch. But the naval preoccupation has come to stay; and I believe it comes mainly from the 'one ocean' idea.

There is nothing wrong, of course, in the naval historian going for the navies, provided we know the nature and limits of this curiosity. To Moreland, there was no distinction between the seaborne empire set up by the Portuguese and the later empires of the North Europeans, because, I suppose, all of them relied on naval power. There was, however, an important difference. The Portuguese never left the coast in search of trade and the North Europeans did. The Dutch and the English invested their money in inland cities like Ahmedabad, Burhanpur and Agra. When they did this, their investments came under the land power of the Mughals and some kind of balance was established. It was not a moral balance; a balance of blackmail, you may call it. The English and the Dutch were strong at sea and they did not mind playing the pirate from time to time. The Mughal would retaliate as a bandit on land without any scruple. The Indian merchant, if there was such a creature, was sandwiched between the two and acquired an adroitness in playing off one against the other. The Portuguese had no such problems as they remained coastal throughout. This difference between them and the North Europeans is likely to be missed if we go strongly for the naval encounters.

Quite apart from this idea of a unitary ocean and the emphasis on navies (both of which we have inherited), Moreland used to think that eastern conditions were such that colonial empires became inevitable. There is some force in this contention; but if we harp too much on 'eastern conditions', we are in some danger of missing an important truth. If we are looking at the stretch of water to the east of the Cape of Good Hope and the human beings on it at a time when the colonial empires had not yet divided them beyond retrieval, we have a composite picture before us. There is a little bit of the West mixed with the East in the picture. We have caught on to it now, and we tend to think of the West influencing the East or the other way round. We have left Moreland's 'eastern conditions' behind and we think we are safe. If we do that, however, we tend to miss the European logic which became a part of the Asian landscape. The matter will become clear if we consider one example of how it happened. When the Portuguese came round the Cape, they brought a great deal of their own experience with them. They had inherited a century-old struggle against Islam. The Portuguese who came with the first shipping tended to be violent. They would trade, but political power would be a part of this trade. Eastern conditions were not at the root of the developments which flowed from this experience. You cannot argue that this is 'the West' which is going to influence 'the East'. We should rather think of it as specific Portuguese experience and it was going to be part of whichever area of the Indian Ocean the first Portuguese touched. Similarly with the Dutch. When they came round they were at war with Spain, and this war had nothing to do with Asia. The Dutch, quite deliberately, decided to fight the Portuguese wherever they were found. Asia had nothing to do with this decision but the consequences were all part of Asian history. Then, they decided to have a much stricter monopoly specially over the spice trade than the Portuguese ever had. They wished to exclude the English from Southeast Asia possibly as a consequence of this decision. You cannot call such things 'eastern conditions', and you cannot call this process as 'the West' influencing 'the East'. This was the European logic, and by the beginning of the seventeenth century, it was very much a part of Asia.

I shall be through with this European logic with one more example which may show how the Indian merchants took advantage of customs they did not know. If you only recall the custom of lending a flag, a navigator or a pass, you will see what I mean. If there is a British, French or Danish flag on an Indian vessel, the Dutch would think twice before they did anything to it. If the Indian vessel 'belonged' to a European enclave, it was unlikely to be touched. This might cause complications in Europe and Indian merchants were happy to take the protection of this habit. But it was a European habit and it formed a part of European experience which was being imported into Asia. You will see that such labels as Europe and Asia get mixed up in these waters. By substituting European influence for Moreland's 'eastern conditions', we may be following him more than we know. Then we come to Moreland's conclusion about the seventeenth century. You know this better than I do: Moreland argued that though a case can be made out for European participation having increased Asia's trade, you should not argue like that till you know that this was no replacement. Asia had a great deal of trade of her own. Were the Europeans edging out some of the Asians or were they adding to the total? This was Moreland's question; and it still remains with us although we know a great deal more now than he did. Basically, we are arguing from impressions, as was Moreland. You cannot do anything else if you are arguing about Indian trade and you have only European documents. We believe that Indian trade was doing very well in the seventeenth century: Moreland thought that the seventeenth century showed no such progress. The answer now seems to depend on which set of impressions are better. This may be one reason why we seek an escape in case studies.

But the additional knowledge we have picked up since the 1920s: does it stand us in good stead in countering the thoughts of Moreland? He was relying on British documents published in his time on the early seventeenth century. He was depending on the travellers, but basically there was no archival work. We know now that one company's version may be compared to another company's. There has been much work on the Portuguese, the Dutch and, of course the English. This can and should be expanded. We know the travellers much better now. For many years now, we have become aware of the private version; and we know now that we may not rely too much on the official version which, in Moreland's day, was simply the truth. We are now going deeper into India and we are seeking explanations of Indian history in countries beyond India. It would be rash to deny that we are adding to our knowledge and understanding. But Moreland with his questions still remains, and it is good to come back to him as to our source.

MARITIME CONTACTS BETWEEN CHINA AND THE COLA KINGDOM (A.D. 850-1279)

Tansen Sen

Merchants played a major role in ancient Sino-Indian relations. They not only paved the way for the very first diplomatic and religious contacts, but also played an important role in the exchange of ideas and information.[1] While the Silk Road through the perilous deserts of Central Asia formed the main overland route from China to northern India, the coasts of the two countries were linked by the maritime route through Southeast Asia. Unfortunately, research on ancient maritime contacts between India and China has been overshadowed by the studies on the Silk Road. Sino-Indian maritime contacts after the tenth century increased so rapidly, mainly due to the decline of trade along the Silk Road, that they deserve more attention. In the following pages, I discuss the maritime contacts between China and the southern coast of India during the ninth to the thirteenth centuries. I shall focus on the relations between the powerful Cola kingdom of South India (A.D. 850-1279) and China during the Sung dynasty (A.D. 960-1279).

THE COLAS IN CHINESE RECORDS

As Chinese records form the primary source for this study, it might be fair to start with a brief survey of some important Chinese notices on the Colas. One of the earliest records on the Colas in the Chinese sources comes to us from the work of Hsüan-tsang (600-664). Hsüan-tsang, during his pilgrimage to India in the seventh century, wrote of a country called Chu-li-yeh as follows:

> The kingdom of *Chu-li-yeh* is about twenty-four to twenty-five hundred *li* in circuit. Its capital is little more than ten *li* in area. The country is deserted and filled with marshes and jungles. It is scarcely populated, crime is common and the climate is hot

> and moist. People are wild in nature and follow 'foreign' religion. The Buddhist monasteries are in ruins and only a few of them have monks. There are tens of Deva temples, most of which are of 'foreign' religion.[2]

As Hsüan-tsang's record dates from the seventh century, and since the area he was travelling through was along the southern-central Andhra Pradesh, the Colas in his record, most probably, were one of the branches of the Telugu Chodas.[3]

Some five centuries later, the first record of Cola-China diplomatic and commercial contacts comes to us from the work of Chou Ch'u-fei, known as the *Ling-wai tai-ta* (Information on what is Beyond the Southern Passes [hereafter *LWTT*]). Written in 1178, the *LWTT* records the Colas as the kingdom of *Chu-lien*. A part of the record was incorporated in a later work called *Chu-fan chih* (Descriptions of the Barbarous People [hereafter *CFC*]) written by Chao Ju-kua in 1225. In 1319, Ma Tuan-lin included the notice on the kingdom of *Chu-lien* in his encyclopedia called the *Wen-hsien t'ung-k'ao* (General History of Institutions and a Critical Examination of Documents and Studies [hereafter *WHTK*]). *Sung shih* (Dynastic History of the Sung [hereafter *SS*]), compiled by T'o-t'o in 1345, also has a notice on the kingdom. Records on the Cola kingdom in *CFC* and *WHTK* have been translated into western languages by F. Hirth and W.W. Rockhill, and Hervey de Saint Denys respectively.[4]

Another aspect which should be discussed here is the compilation of these records. Unlike Hsüan-tsang, none of the authors of the above mentioned works had the opportunity to visit India. Most of the Chinese records on the Colas, we may presume, were based on hearsay accounts. How and from whom did the Chinese writers get their information ?

Since the records in *WHTK* and *SS* are based on *LWTT* and *CFC*, I will discuss here only the possible sources for Chou ch'u-fei and Chao Ju-kua's records on the Cola kingdom. Chou Ch'u-fei was an Assistant Sub-Prefect of Kui-lin (Kuang-hsi province). As pointed out by Hirth and Rockhill, Chou Ch'u-fei might have collected the information on maritime trade and foreign countries while he was passing through Canton on his way to Kui-lin.[5] Canton, as we know, was a leading seaport of medieval China. Foreign royalty, merchants, and monks had settled down in this port city. Special areas known as *Fan-fang* (foreign quarters) were established to look after the growing population of foreigners. To administer the foreign trade, an office called *Shih-po ssu* (Bureau of Maritime Trade) was established (some of its duties are discussed below). Chou Ch'u-fei could have easily gathered the information on foreign trade and countries from the foreigners settled in Canton, and perhaps also from Chinese merchants who were engaged in foreign trade.

Chao-Ju-kuo was in a much better position to gather information on foreign countries and trade. He was a "descendant of the Emperor Tai-tsung (of the Sung dynasty), in the eighth generation through the Prince of Shang, a younger brother of Emperor Chen-tsung (998-1023)".[6] During the *chia-ting* period (1208-24) he held the post of *ti-chu shih-po shih* (Superintendent of the Bureau of Maritime Trade). His duties included levying taxes from seafaring merchants, inspection of incoming and outgoing ships, taking care of tributary envoys, etc. He was in charge of receiving the foreign envoys; inspecting their official documents; inquiring about the size, strength and the distance of the envoy's country from China; and making a list of all the tribute to be presented to the court. Chao Ju-kua, therefore, could have got his information on the Cola kingdom from the traders and envoys coming from South Asia.

Another interesting fact about collection of information on the Cola kingdom may be found in the *Sung Hui-yao* (Collection of Important Documents of the Sung [hereafter *SHY*]). The work records that in 1016 Chang Fu, the Supervisor of the Court of Diplomatic Reception, was ordered to compile a chart of the customs and clothings of the Cola kingdom and present it to the emperor.[7]

We may therefore conclude that the Chinese notices on which this study is based, were collected both officially, like that by Chang Fu, and unofficially, like by Chou Ch'u-fei.[8] These Chinese writers, as we have seen above, mostly got their information on the Cola kingdom from the seafaring merchants who frequently came to the Chinese ports.

SEA ROUTE FROM THE COLA KINGDOM TO CHINA

According to the Chinese records, the first Cola envoys of 1015 started their voyage from Na-wu-tan-shan (Nagapat-tinam?). The mission passed through So-li hsi-lan (Ceylon?), Chan-bin (Jambi? in Sumatra), I-mo-lo-li (near the banks of river Irrawaddya in Burma?), Ku-lo (in Java?), Chia-pa (in the Langkwai islands), Kou-pu-lao

(Cham?), Chou-pao-lung (near river Salat Sembilan in Singapore?), San-fo-Ch'i (Srivijaya), Man-shan (Muntok in the Banka islands?), Tien-chu shan (Pulo Aor in the Malayan peninsula), pin-t'ou-lang shan (Panduranga in southern Vietnam), Yang shan (Pulo Gambir in southeastern Vietnam) and Chiu-hsing shan (near Hong Kong or Macao). The mission reached Canton after a voyage of 1,150 days.[9]

A direct route to the Far East (or at least to Southeast Asia) from the Coromandel coast seems to have been known to the Colas. The Cola navy, which raided Srivijaya in 1025, as recorded in a Tamil inscription from Tanjore, passed through the Nicobar islands and the Malaya peninsula.[10] From the discussions below, we shall see why the Cola mission of 1015 took the longer route to China, when they could have taken the shorter route through the Nicobar islands and the Malay peninsula.

TRIBUTARY TRADE BETWEEN THE COLA KINGDOM AND CHINA

Chinese sources record four separate Cola missions to China. The first mission, according to the Chinese records, was sent by Rajaraja I (985-1014) on 16 October 1015. The mission had fifty-two people including the Chief Envoy Sa(P'o)-li-san-wen, Vice-Envoy P'u Chia-hsin (Abu Kasim?), Staff Weng-wu and Embassy Guard Ya-Ch'in-chia. The Chinese court seems to have known about the arrival of the mission from the Cola kingdom, because between 21 May and 18 June the court had ordered Shih Yu-chih, the Imperial Aide (Kung-feng kuan) Usher at Imperial Audience (*K'o-men chih hou*), to act as a Lesser Lord of Diplomatic Reception (*Hung-lu shao-ch'ing*) and escort the Cola embassy to the Chinese capital.[11] The Cola envoy was given the status of the kingdom of Ch'iu-tse, a tributary state of China. The envoy presented the Emperor with 800 kilograms of pearls, sixty pieces of ivory, sixty pounds of incense and 3,300 pounds of perfumes.[12]

The second Cola embassy reached China on 29 February 1020. P'a-lan-te-ma-lieh-ti, the chief envoy, fell ill and died in Canton before he could reach the Chinese capital. The other members of the mission were given a banquet and return presents.

The third Cola mission arrived in China on 15 November 1033. This mission, according to the Chinese sources, was sent by Rajendrachola I (1012-44). P'u Ya-t'o-li (Abu Adil?) was the chief envoy. To demonstrate barbarian etiquette (*i-li*), he scattered pearls from a silver container below the throne and retired. Between 22 February 1034 and 22 March 1034, titles were granted to the Cola ambassadors.

Kulottunga I (1070-1120) is supposed to have sent the fourth Cola mission to China. The mission, which included chief envoy Ch'i-lo-lo, vice-envoy Nan-pei-p'a-ta, and Staff Ma-t'u-hua-lo, reached China on 26 June 1077. On 29 June, the envoys had an audience with the emperor and performed the ritual of scattering pearls and ripe camphor below the throne.

Although the Chinese sources record the missions as 'embassies from the Colas', we should be cautious in concluding that the envoys were all natives or officials of the Cola kingdom. The Cola missions seem to have also consisted of Arab nationals. The names of some envoys, like P'u Chia-hsin (Abu Kasim?) and P'u Ya-t'o-li (Abu Adil?), are of Arab origin. Both of them seem to have represented other countries as well. P'u Chia-hsin (Abu Kasim?), for example, in 1004 and 1019 visited the Chinese court as an envoy from Arabia, while in 1011 he represented Oman.[13] It is, however, not surprising that the Chinese records include Arabs in the list of foreign envoys. Maritime trade on the Indian Ocean during that period, as we know, was mostly in the hands of Arab traders. It is not unlikely that the Cola envoys sailed on Arab ships which were on trading missions. This would explain why the embassy of 1015 took 1,150 days to reach China. These Arab traders, on reaching the Chinese port, might have presented themselves as envoys from the Cola kingdom.

The following study of some of the tributes presented to the Chinese emperor by the Cola 'envoys' further proves that the Cola 'embassies', including the one in 1015, were on a trading mission rather than on a diplomatic one. Things like pearls, frankincense and camphor, as we shall see, were commodities imported by the Chinese and were levied under high import duties.

PEARLS

CFC records:

> As a general rule a pearl is considered valuable if it is perfectly round; the test for its absolute roundness is, that it will not cease rolling about all day when put on a plate. Foreign traders (coming to China) are in the habit of concealing pearls in the

> lining of their clothes and in the handles of their umbrellas, thus evading the duties leviable upon them.[14]

Pearls (Skt. *mani* or *mukta*) found in the Palk Straits were exported to northern India, Far East and Rome and Greece by the Pandyas during the first few centuries of the Christian era.[15] *Periplus of the Erythraean* Sea records:

> From Comari [Cape Comorin] (towards the south) the country extends as far as Colchoi (Korkai), where the fishing for pearls is carried on. King Pandion (king of Pandyas) is the owner of the fishery. To Colchoi succeeds another coast lying along the gulf having a district in the interior bearing the name Argalu (Uryaiur). In this single place are obtained the pearls....[16]

Ptolemy and Pliny also record of pearl fishery in India and their export to Rome.

Like South India, Ceylon too was engaged in pearl trade. The fact was noticed by Fa-hsien in the fifth century. Later *CFC* records Ceylon as one of the main exporters of pearls to China. In the tenth century, after Ceylon was conquered by Rajaraja I, the Colas might have monopolised the trade of pearls in the Indian Ocean.

IVORY

Ivory, according to Chao Ju-kua, came to China from Arabia, Champa and Annam. On the duty and restrictions applied on ivory *PCKT* records:

> Ivory tusks of thirty catties weight or over, and gum olibanum, besides paying the 'clearance dues' must be disposed of exclusively at the official market, since they are 'licensed articles' (i.e., sold only to those having received licences to import them). Merchants who have rather large ivory tusks (and those who wish to sell them elsewhere) must cut them into pieces of three catties or less to escape the official markets. All prices on the official market are low, and other varieties of goods are so greatly undervalued on it that the merchants are displeased (or 'injured') thereby.[17]

Indian ivory was exported to Persia, Greece and Rome. Indians monopolised the ivory market until Ptolemy II introduced African ivory. In the tenth century, India continued to export ivory to the Far East. *CFC* mentions ivory as a native product of the Cola kingdom, but does not mention India as an exporter of ivory to China.

FRANKINCENSE

Frankincense, the Arab trader Soleman writes, was a principal import into China.[18] According to *CFC*, Arabia was the major exporter of frankincense to China. Indians also imported frankincense from Arabia. Frankincense was "used at a rate of several thousand tons a year" in China for making incense, and medicines for toothaches, ulcers, sore eye, etc.[19] As Robert Hartwell has shown, Srivijaya monopolised the re-export of frankincense to China.[20]

India, too, was an importer of frankincense. The frankincense carried by the Cola missions might have come directly from Arabia, or was picked up on the way in Srivijaya. But the fact that frankincense was presented to the Chinese emperor as tribute, once again tells us that the Cola 'envoys' were aware of the commodities which were in demand in China.

CAMPHOR

Chou Ch'u-fei lists camphor as a native product of the Cola kingdom. Paul Wheatley suggests that the record is incorrect. "All the genuine Barus Camphor", he argues, "imported into China undoubtedly came from the lofty dipterocrap *Dryobalanops aromatica* Gaertn., which is indigenous in parts of Sumatra, the Malay Peninsula and Boreno".[21]

The Arabian trader Soleman notes that camphor was a principal import of China. The 'white plum-blossom camphor' presented to the Chinese Emperor by the Cola mission might have come from Southeast Asia.

COTTON

Tamil literature records cotton fabrics as a native product of Kaveripattinam and Madurai. According to *Silappadhikaram*, on the streets of Puhar (Kaveripattinam) were seen weavers dealing in fine fabrics made of silk and cotton.[22] *Periplus* records that Indian cotton was known as *monache* and was exported to East Africa.[23]

The most durable and the strongest cotton, according to Chau Ju-kua, was *Tou-lo mien*. Paul Wheatley describes the word as a "composite coinage from Sanskrit *tula* = 'cotton' and Chinese *mien* = 'downy'".[24] *CFC* records it as a native product of the Cola kingdom.

Other commodities involved in the Cola-China trade might have included corals, rose water, putchock, mica, indigo and jack fruits. Chinese porcelain, lapislazuli and peach might have entered Cola markets since these products, which were exported to African and Arabian countries, might have been carried by the Arabian merchants through the Coromandel coast.

ARCHAEOLOGICAL EVIDENCE FOR COLA-CHINA CONTACTS

Most of the above discussion has been based on Chinese records. Unfortunately, they do not tell us about the role of Tamil traders in the Chinese trade. They also provide no information on Chinese traders in South Asia. Fortunately, archaeology has provided us some clues for the possible presence of Tamil merchants in South China, and Chinese merchants on the Coromandel coast. In the city of Ch'üan-chou, in the Fukien province in South China, about two hundred pieces of Hindu relics have been discovered. These relics include sculptures of Hindu gods like Vishnu, Krishna and Hanuman; a lingam; and various works of Hindu mythology.[25]

The lingam, known to the Chinese as 'stone bamboo shoot' (*shih-sun*), seems to have existed during the Northern Sung period (970-1127). The *Chin-chiang hsien-chih* (Local History of the Chin-chiang Country) records that the "stone bamboo shoot" broke into two in the fourth year of *Ta-chung hsiang-fu* (1077), and was repaired during the *Cheng-hua* period (1465-87) of the Ming dynasty.

These relics indicate that at least one Hindu temple of a considerable size existed in the city of Ch'üan-chou. The discovery of a pair of bilingual stone tablets in 1957, moreover, has connected the possible existence of a Hindu temple with Tamil merchants. The stone tablets, which are in fact two pieces of one large tablet, have inscriptions in Tamil and Chinese. The Tamil part, translated by T.N. Subramaniam, reads as follows:

> Obeisance to Hara (Siva). Let there be prosperity! On the day (having) the Chitra (asterism) in the month of Chittirai of the Saka Year 1203 (April 1281), the Tavachechakkaravattigal alias Sambandhap-perumal caused, in accordance with the *firman* of Chekachai-Khan, to be graciously installed the God Udaiyar Tirukkandalisvaram Udaiya-nayinar, for the welfare of the illustrious body of the illustrious Chekachai Khan.[26]

This Tamil record is followed by twelve Chinese characters plus at least one missing character. The characters, when put in the form of a sentence, seem to make little sense. A rough translation may be: Lu-ho-chih-jih, [who was] good in Chinese [language], compiled the sutra of the Great Mountain (Mahameru?) without the help of a teacher (Guru).

Tamil inscriptions and Hindu sculptures are also found in Southeast Asia. A Tamil inscription from Pagan, for example, records donations from merchants from the Malabar coast for a Vishnu temple.[27] On the significance of Indian temples in Southeast Asia and China and their relationship with the Indian merchants, Stanley J. O'Connor Jr. writes:

> As there can be no question of Cola sovereignty over Burma, the significance of the inscription is probably that, in preponderantly Buddhist Pagan, the Hindu merchants found necessary and desirable to build their own temple. Similarly, the twelfth or thirteenth century South Indian statues discovered in a Chinese temple at Ch'üan-chou, on the China coast opposite Formosa, do not indicate any Indian political role in China. But they suggest a parallel to the Pagan temple, showing that the guilds erected Hindu temples and statues in countries where the prevailing religion was Buddhism or some other non-Hindu religion.[28]

T.N. Subramanian has persuasively argued that the installation of the image of the Hindu god mentioned in the Tamil inscription from Ch'üan-chou was done by an envoy from the son of the last Cola ruler, Rajaraja III.[29] Since the inscription only records the installation of the image, and not the erection of a temple, we may presume that a Hindu temple existed in Ch'üan-chou before 1281. The existence of a Hindu temple, perhaps, also indicates the presence of

Indian merchants on the southern coasts of China. It is not clear what connection, if any, they had with the Cola kingdom.

Discovery of Chinese coins on the Coromandel coast, on the other hand, has provided us with clues to the presence of Chinese merchants in South India. Eight hundred and thirty-eight Chinese coins, dating from the *Yüan-ch'u* period of the Han dynasty to *Hsien-hsun* period of the Sung dynasty (1265-1275) were found in the Tanjore district of Tamil Nadu in 1944.[30] Pointing out the possible presence of Chinese sailors in the Cola kingdom, P.C. Bagchi writes:

> When Chau Ju-kua wrote his famous work, the Chu fan che (*CFC*) in the beginning of the thirteenth century, the Chinese sailors were better acquainted with the Cola dominions than with any other part of India. The coins had apparently been collected from the Chinese sailors but it is difficult to say how the coins of such varying ages as the eighth and the thirteenth centuries could have been brought together. They might have belonged to the collection of some temple in which the coins of such a long period could be possibly preserved.[31]

Bagchi seems to have overlooked the fact that Chinese coins from earlier periods were still in use during the later periods. The coins could have been deposited together on the Coromandel coast after (or during) the last dated coin. Moreover, the coins could have been deposited by the Arabs or the Srivijayans who were in continuous contact with China and India. However, a notice about a Chinese pagoda in the Cola port of Nagapattinam in a fourteenth-century Chinese work, and its existence recorded by a British officer in the nineteenth century, supports the view of possible presence of Chinese merchants in South India.

The *Tao-yi chih lüeh* (Brief Account of the Barbarian Isles), written by Wang Ta-yuan in 1350, notes a Chinese pagoda built in 1267 at the port city of Nagapattinam. Later, Sir Walter Elliot seems to have been describing the same pagoda in 1846. Five Buddhist images, four of them of bronze and the other, according to French accounts, of a mixture of porcelain and clay, were excavated from an adjacent brick chamber in 1856.[32] John Guy suggests its possible similarity to the Chinese glazed ceramic Buddha image of the qingbai-type, produced in Ching-de chen during the late Sung and Yuan periods.[33] Unfortunately, the pagoda was demolished by the French Jesuit missionaries in 1867.

ROLE OF SRIVIJAYA IN COLA-CHINA RELATIONS

The study of Sino-Indian maritime contacts during the ninth to the thirteenth centuries will be incomplete if we do not discuss the role played by Srivijaya. Maritime trade route from India to Far East, before the fifth century, was through the Isthmus of Kra. Later, by the end of the fifth century, the route shifted to the Straits of Malacca. "Out of this development", Kenneth Hall writes, "rose the classic maritime state of Srivijaya".[34] The rise of Srivijayans is also attributed to the rule of Sailendras, who unified the small states in the Malay archipelago and the Malay peninsula. The Sailendras developed a strong naval force and pursued highly diplomatic relations with both China and India.

The naval expedition of the Cola kingdom on Srivijaya in the eleventh century; the mention of Cola kingdom as a vassal state of Srivijaya in *WHTK*; and a puzzling Srivijayan inscription, mentioning Kulottunga as the "Lord" of Srivijaya, found in Canton, point to a complicated triangular relation between the Cola kingdom, Sung China, and Srivijaya.

Some scholars have suggested Srivijaya's intervention in the Cola-China trade as the reason for the Cola raid of 1025.[35] George Spencer opposes this view, and suggests that "a more likely possibility is that as the Cholas gradually widened their diplomatic horizons, coming into closer contacts with China and various kingdoms of Southeast Asia, they were tempted to intervene in local situations that they sought to exploit to their own advantage".[36] Although George Spencer's suggestion is both reasonable and persuasive, the possibility of a 'trade war' cannot be completely ruled out. According to *CFC*, the Srivijayans were preventing foreign ships from passing the Straits of Malacca without first stopping at the Srivijayan ports. The ships which resisted were attacked and destroyed by the Srivijayan ships. It is, therefore, possible that the Srivijayans created problems for the Tamil merchants engaged in the Far East trade, which could have ultimately led to a military confrontation with the Colas.

Further involvement of the Srivijayans in the Cola-China relations can be seen from a notice in the *WHTK*, which records that the Cola kingdom was a vassal state of Srivijaya. *WHTK* records that in order to receive an envoy from Pagan in 1106:

> the Emperor at first gave the order to receive them and treat them as they treated the envoys of the Chu-lien; but the President of the Council of Rites said: 'The Cola is subject to San-foch'i, this is why in the years *hsi-ṇing* (1068-1077), we were content to write to the king of this kingdom on strong paper with an envelope of plain stuff. The King of Pou-gan (Pagan), on the contrary is a sovereign of a great kingdom of the Fan....[37]

SS too records the kingdom of Cola as "subjugated by a foreigner from Srivijaya".[38] Although these statements are not recorded in the chapters on Colas and Srivijaya, they seem to have affected the treatment of the Cola 'envoys' when they arrived at the Chinese court. The Cola 'envoys', according to the Chinese records, were given the lowly status of the kingdom of Ch'iu-t'zu, a vassal state of China.

The discovery of a Srivijayan inscription in a Taoist temple in Canton has further complicated the issue. The inscription, translated by Tan Yeok Seong, records that a large sum of money was donated by Ti-hua-kia-lo, the "Lord of Land" (of Srivijaya), for the repair of the Taoist temple.[39] Ti-hua-kia-lo, who is also mentioned in the *SS*, was supposed to have sent the Cola envoy of twenty-seven people in 1077. The names of the Cola ambassador and judge, Ki-lo-lo and Mo-t'u-hua-lo, are also found in the inscription. The Srivijayan envoy, according to the inscription, reached China during the reign of Emperor Chih-ping (1064-67).

Pointing to the similarity between the Srivijayan inscription and the Chinese records, Tan Yeok Seong concludes that Kulottunga I was the ruler of both Cola and Srivijaya. George Spencer, however, rejects this theory, and suggests a possible marriage alliance. "It was", he writes, "after all, very common for the Colas to establish such alliance with both defeated adversaries and potential rivals, so a marriage alliance with the kings of Srivijaya, as a result of Rajendra's conquest or even under other circumstances, would not have been out of character".[40] Both Tan Yeok Seong and George Spencer seem to have overlooked a simpler explanation. Ki-lo-lo and Mo-t'u-hua-lo could have been seafaring merchants engaged in the South Asia-Far East trade. They might have come to China as the envoys of both the Cola kingdom and Srivijaya.

Kulottunga I could not have been responsible for sending the Srivijayan envoy because he came to the throne only in 1071. He could, however, have sent the Cola envoy of 1077. T-hua-kia-lo, according to *SS* and *SHY*, was an envoy from Srivijaya. He came to the Chinese court in 1077 and 1088. He is supposed to have died in China on 3 July 1089.[41] Kulottunga I, on the other hand, died in 1120 in India. Ti-hua-kia-lo and Kulottunga, as we see, were two different persons; therefore, the transcription of Kulottunga as Ti-hua-kia-lo was possibly a mistake.[42]

CONCLUSION

Archaeological evidence, like the relics of the Hindu temple and Tamil inscription from Ch'üan-chou, and Chinese coins found on the Coromandel coast, have provided us some important clues for the contacts between China and the Coromandel coast. This archaeological evidence points to the possible presence of Tamil merchants in China and Chinese merchants in South India. Records from the Cola kingdom perhaps could have told us more about the role of Tamil merchants in China-Cola relations, and about the Chinese commodities which might have entered the kingdom. Unfortunately, I am not aware of any Cola record which tells us about the contacts of the Coromandel coast with China during the ninth to thirteenth centuries.

The Chinese records, on the other hand, tell us about the geography, customs, and native products of the Cola kingdom. They also provide us information on the tributary trade between China and the Cola kingdom. As noted above, the tributes from the Cola kingdom were mostly carried by Arab merchants. Both the Chinese government and the tribute carriers benefited from the tributary trade. The foreign tribute, as Robert Hartwell has shown, formed an important source for the Sung imperial privy purse.[43] Tribute bearers, on the other hand, could make a huge profit because they were allowed to bring, free of duty, prescribed quantities of goods for resale. This might be one reason why the Arab traders were so much involved in the tributary trade. They could, as tribute carriers, make a huge profit by selling part of the tribute in the open market.

The Chinese records on the geography and customs of the Cola kingdom still need to be studied. These records, as discussed above, were mostly based on hearsay accounts. Only through comparative study of the Chinese notices and archaeological evidence from the Coromandel coast can we prove or disprove these records. But of one thing we may be sure: the Chinese, even though in some distorted form, were aware of the existence, the rulers, and the customs of the Cola kingdom. We are still not sure what the Colas knew about the then "most populous" and "wealthiest" nation of the worldChina.

LIST OF COLA MISSIONS AND TRIBUTES PRESENTED TO THE CHINESE COURT

DATE OF MISSION	MAIN ENVOYS	TRIBUTES
5/21/1015 To 05/10/1016	(Chief) Sa(P'o)-1i-san-wen (Vice) P'u Chia-hsin (Staff) Weng-wu (Embassy Guard) Ya-ch'in-chia	Elephant tusks; Frankincense; Pearls
02/29/1020 To 02/29/1020	P'a-lan-te-ma-lieh-ti	Rosewater Rhinoceros Horn; Frankincense; Putchuck; Cloves; Borax; Barus Camphor; Pearls; Brocade Opaque Glass; Plumflower Camphor
11/15/1033 To 03/22/1034	P'u Ya-t'o-li	Elephant Tusks; Pearls
06/26/1077 To 06/29/1077	(Chief) Ch'i-lo-lo (Vice) Nan-pei-p'a-ta (Staff) Ma-tu-hua-lo	Rosewater; Frankincense; Rhinoceros Horn; Elephant Tusks; Cloves; Pearls; Borax; Barus Camphor; Opaque Glass; Plumflower Camphor; Brocade

Data from Robert Hartwell (1983), pp. 188-90.

NOTES

[1]Chang Ch'ien, an envoy sent to Central Asia by Emperor Wu of the Han dynasty, found out that commercial relations between India and China existed even before the Chinese court became aware of the existence of India. See Burton Watson's translation of *Shih-chi* (Record of the Grand Historian) as *Records of the Grand Historian of China, Translated from the Shi-chi of Ssu-ma Ch'ien,* New York, London: Columbia University Press, 1961 p. 269.

[2]See Thomas Watters' (1906) translation of *Ta-T'ang Hsi-yü chi* (The Record of the Western Regions during the Great T'ang [dynasty]) as *On Yuan Chwangs Travels in India,* London: Royal Asiatic Society.

[3]See Chi Hsien-lin, et al., annot. *Ta-T'ang Hsi-yü chi chiao-chu* (Annotation of the Records to the Western Regions [during the] T'ang [dynasty], Beijing: Chung-hua shu-chu, 1985.

[4]See F. Hirth and W.W. Rockhill, *Chau Ju-kua: His Work on the Chinese and Arab Trade in the Twelfth and Thirteenth Centuries, entitled Chu-fan-chih,* St. Petersburg: Printing Office of the Imperial Academy of Sciences, 1911; Hervey de Saint Denys, *Ethnographie des peuples entrangers a la Chine par Ma-Touan-lin,* Geneve: Meridionaux, 1883. Both these translations can also be found in Nilakanta Sastri's *Foreign Notices of South India: From Magasthenes to Ma Huan,* Madras: University of Madras Press, 1972.

[5]Hirth and Rockhill, *op.cit.*, p. 22, n. 2.

[6]*Ibid.*, p. 35.

[7]*Sung-hui-yao* (hereafter *SHY*): Fan-yi(FY) 7.20b; Robert Hartwell, *Tribute Missions to China, 960-1126,* Philadelphia, 1983, p. 188.

[8]These records were later used as primary sources by Ma Tuan-lin and T'o T'o. But neither acknowledges the fact that his record on the Cola kingdom was based on the information collected by Chou Ch'u-fei or Chao Ju-kua. Hirth and Rockhill (1911) point out that this was typical of most Chinese writers, p. 36.

[9]According to *SS*, the mission reached the Chinese port of Ch'üan-chou.

[10]See George Spencer, *The Politics of Expansion: The Cola Conquest of Sri Lanka and Srivijaya,* Madras: New Era, 1983, pp. 139-40.

[11]See Robert M. Hartwell, *op.cit.*, p. 188.

[12]Hervey de Saint Denys correctly concludes that these figures are exaggerations.

[13]*SS* 489.11b and *SHY*: FY4.9b; see also Robert Hartwell, *op. cit.* (1983).

[14]See tr. by Hirth and Rockhill, *op. cit.*, pp. 229-30. According to *P'ing-chou k'o-t'an* (hereafter *PCKT*) a duty of 10 per cent was levied on pearls.

[15]See Clarence Thomas Maloney, "The Effect of Early Coastal Sea Traffic on the Development of Civilization in South India", unpublished Ph.D. dissertation, University of Pennsylvania, 1968, pp. 6-17.

[16]*Periplus Maris*, p. 59; tr. by J.W. McCrindle in R.C. Majumdar, ed., *The Classical Accounts of India*, Calcutta: Firma KLM, 1960, pp. 288-312.

[17]See tr. by Hirth and Rockhill, *op. cit.*, p. 21.

[18]J.T. Reinaud, *Relations des voyages faits per les Arabes et les Persans dans l'Inde et a la Chine dans le IXe siecle de lere chretiene*, Paris: Imprimerie royale, 2 vols., 1845, 1:13 and 33-35.

[19]See Robert Hartwell, *op.cit.*, p. 455.

[20]*Ibid.*, p. 456.

[21]Paul Wheatley, "Geographical Notes on some Commodities involved in Sung Maritime Trade", *Journal of the Malayan Branch, Royal Asiatic Society*, 1959, 32.1:4-140, p. 101.

[22]V.R. Ramachandra Dikshitar, tr. *Silappadikaram*, Madras: Oxford University Press, 1938, p. 92.

[23]*Periplus of the Erithrean Sea*, p. 6.

[24]Paul Wheatley, *op.cit.*, p. 59.

[25]See Ananda K. Coomaraswami, "Hindu Sculptures at Zayton", *Ostasiatische Zeittschrift*, 1933, 9:5-11; T.N. Subramaniam, "Tamil Colony in Medieval China", in R. Nagaswamy, ed. *South Indian Studies*, Madras: Society for Archaeological, Historical and Epigraphical Research, 1978, pp. 1-52.

[26]T.N. Subramaniam, *op.cit.*, p. 8.

[27]See E. Hultzch, "A Vaishnava Inscription at Pagan", *Epigraphia Indica*, 1902-3, 7:197-98.

[28]Stanley J. O'Connor Jr., *Hindu Gods of Peninsular Siam*, Switzerland, p. 56.

[29]T.N. Subramaniam, *op.cit.*, pp. 40-3.

[30]See P.C. Bagchi, "Report on a New Hoard of Chinese Coins" and "Chinese Coins in Tanjore", in *Indological Studies: A Collection of Essays*, Santiniketan: Visva-Bharati Press, 1982, pp. 110-17.

[31]*Ibid.*, p. 116.

[32]For a detailed discussion on the Chinese pagoda, see John Guy, "The Lost Temples of Nagapattinam and Quanzhou", Paper read at the UNESCO Ch'üan-chou International Seminar on China and the Maritime Routes of Silk Route, 1988.

[33]*Ibid.*

[34]Kenneth R. Hall and John K. Whitmore, "Southeast Trade and the Isthmian Struggle, 1000-1200 A.D.", in Kenneth R. Hall and John K. Whitmore, eds., *Explorations in the Early Southeast Asian History: The Origins of the Southeast Asian Statecraft*, Ann Arbor: Michigan Papers on South and Southeast Asia, 1976, p. 303.

[35]See Nilakantha Sastri, *op.cit.*, p. 214.

[36]George Spencer, *op.cit.*, p. 144.

[37]*WHTK*, 332:2612.

[38]*SS*, 248:14087.

[39]See Tan Yeok Seong, "The Sri Vijayan Inscription of Canton (A.D. 1079)", *Journal of South East Asian History*, 1964, 5.2:17-24.

[40]See George Spencer, pp. 146-7.

[41]*Hsu Tzu-chih t'ung-chien ch'ang-pien (HCP)*, 427.14a; Robert Hartwell, op.cit., p. 177.

[42]Nilakanta Sastri (1973) also points out that the restoration of Ti-hua-kia-lo as Kulottunga is impossible.

[43]Robert Hartwell, "The Imperial Treasuries: Finance and Power in Song China", *Bulletin of Sung Yuan Studies*, No. 20:18-89, 1988.

SANSKRIT IN PHILIPPINE LANGUAGES: REFLECTIONS ON PRE-COLONIAL TRADE AND TRAFFIC

Juan R. Francisco

INTRODUCTION

Maritime trade in the pre-colonial Philippines may be understood in terms of the pattern of archaeological finds, or more appropriately sites, in the archipelago. At least, we have been witness to the most spectacular finds in the Manila area, particularly that on which the present Sta. Ana church stands (Fox and Legaspi 1977). The Bolinao finds (Legaspi 1974), the Calatagan excavations (Fox 1959), the Butuan (Peralta 1980) and also the Cebu discoveries (Hutterer 1973) further attest to the pattern of trading in a period earlier than the advent of colonial rule. Indeed, the Jolo-Zamboanga axis in the south might have proved to be very rich in archaeological evidence of pre-colonial trade, if further work had been done in the area beyond what Alexander Spoehr (1973) had done. Other areas of substantial evidence of that trade in pre-colonial times may be seen in the Masbate pottery finds made famous by Wilhelm G. Solheim II, who perpetuated these by the name Kalanay pottery (1958). Certainly, there are a dozen or more areas or ports in the contemporary Philippines which could have been important trading centres in the past (also Hutterer 1973).

Within the last two years, two instances put the Philippines again in the limelight of pre-colonial contact with India, through the intervening Southeast Asian regions: one was a bronze image of Rama and Hanuman, back-to-back in execution, which was found among the Philippine collection of Captain J.D. Dow, U.S. Coast and Geodetic Survey, who gifted these to the Smithsonian Institution, U.S.A (Francisco 1991); the other was a copper plate inscription believed to have been discovered in the Laguna de Bay area in southern Luzon (Postma 1991). These latest data will not be discussed here because they will be given full attention on an appropriate occasion.

Accounts emanating from the Chinese dynastic records, as well as those travellers who may have traded in the Philippines, if these could be firmed up by other corroborative data, can help us draw a clear picture of that pattern of trade during the period before the advent of colonial rule. A theory that looms large in the full understanding of the advent of Arab culture—nay, read Islam—in the Philippines is the trade theory (Majul 1962). It is, perhaps, the most plausible and widely accepted view; for Islam made deep impact upon the societies of Southeast Asia, even as the Arabs, antedating Prophet Muhammad, had already made important trade contacts in this region (Nilakanta Sastri 1949, 1966).

INDIA AND THE PHILIPPINES

Perhaps, the most heavily documented pattern of contacts between the Southeast Asian regions and the most important cultural resource in the past was India. India's presence in this region has been documented to as early as the second century A.D. (Majumdar 1927, 1937-38; Coedes 1968), although there are indications that this could go as far back as the third century B.C. (*ibid.*). The evidence is overwhelming to a point that anyone could speculate as to the deepest, or more appropriately the earliest period Indians had reached these regions.

As to the Indian presence in the Philippines, my works on the subject may be taken as a gauge of the extent of that cultural encounter (Francisco 1964, 1969, 1971, 1973, 1988, 1991; Postma 1991).

But it would be worthwhile to refer here to areas in which India made her presence felt in the Philippines. These are art (Francisco 1983, 1991), systems of writing (Francisco 1973), and language and literature (Francisco 1961, 1972). In art, we have only a few religious artifacts; in writing, or systems of writing to be more exact, the earliest known systems in the Philippines were borrowed from the South Indian scripts, through their developments in Southeast Asia, particularly northern Sumatra.

Perhaps the most important Indian cultural element known in the Philippines is the Maranaw version of the great Indian epic, the *Ramayana*. Discovered in 1968, and published in 1969, it put the Philippines into the world of *Rama* scholarship (Francisco 1969).

The Philippine languages had somehow come within the ambit of Indian cultural impact.

At this point, it is important to refer to the date of Indian 'influences' in the Philippines. In this, I have set it on the basis of datable evidence: the images of significant religious worth discovered in various archaeological sites in the country belong to the period ranging from the tenth through the thirteenth centuries. These dates have been further corroborated by those adduced to be the date of the introduction of the systems of writing in the country, i.e., the tenth through the fourteenth centuries. These datings could stand some refinements, given more data to work on.

SRIVIJAYA AND THE PHILIPPINES

The view that Srivijaya had political control over the Philippines at the height of its power between the seventh and thirteenth centuries has somehow been institutionalised in the minds of Filipinos. This has been the work of H. Otley Beyer (1929) and others who dominated the Philippine history textbook writing industry in pre-1941 years to the present (see Agoncillo and Alfonso 1948; Agoncillo and Guerrero 1968). This view was rejected in a paper I published in 1961, but the view still persists in current textbooks on the subject.

It is not the purpose here to dwell on this very controversial issue. Rather, Srivijaya is brought into the discussion in view of its role in the process of 'Indianisation' of Southeast Asia in general, and of the Philippines, in particular. The view of Srivijaya's political control over the Philippines has been rejected with, strong evidence. The influx of Indian cultural elements, however, certainly occurred at the height of Srivijaya's power; and such elements reached the Philippines via trade and traffic. In other words, the filtering of Indian elements at a period it is believed to have occurred was during the height of maritime interchanges between and among the peoples of Southeast Asia. The goods exchanged were not just material goods, but also intellectual goods, like concepts having to do with the universe and belief systems. The kind of power that Srivijaya is believed to have wielded at that time generated trade which expanded as far west as India (see Beyer and de Veyra 1952) and as far north as China (ibid.), with the Philippines providing 'entrepot facilities' particularly between its capital in

Palembang and the southern Chinese ports. It must be understood, however, that Srivijaya was the entrepot par excellence between China and India (see Coedes 1948, 1968). Hence, it may not be ill-considered to advance the view that the influx of Indian cultural elements into the Philippines was generated by the trade and traffic that emanated from/through Srivijaya.

TRADE AND TRAFFIC: THE LANGUAGE DATA

Among most important goods exchanged or adopted by a given locality in the process of trade and traffic is language. Srivijaya, being highly 'Indianised', certainly had access to the language of the elite, that is Sanskrit. As such, it might have used the language in various of its activities, ritual as well as secular, including its main source of economic power, that is, trade and traffic.

Thus, some Philippine terms have been identified to reflect activities in trade and traffic with localities beyond its boundaries, and these are in Sanskrit.

Traffic, trade or commerce (Ilk. *banyaga*, Ceb. *baligya*, Dib. Mand. *baligaya*, 'sale, peddling', Sans. *vanijya*, 'traffic, trade, commerce') may have been conducted in 'frame sheds made of palm leaves' or 'outhouses', which in Ilk. is commonly known as *bangsal*, which could be Sans. *vanijya*, 'trade' + *sala*, 'hall' on the suggestion of R.O. Winstedt (1957) by his derivation of Mal. *bangsal*, 'cooly lines, shed', e.g. (1) Bengali *bankasala*, Sans. *vanija* +*sala*; and/or (2) Sans. *bhandasala*, Malm. *pandisala*, 'a storehouse, magazine'.

Merchants and traders (Tag. Ilk. *banyaga*, Ceb. *mabaligyaon*, Sans. *vanijika*, 'merchant, trader', Mal. *beniyaga, berniaga,* Jav. *banyaga*, etc.'), either singly or with business (Tausog *kreja*, Sans. *karya*, 'work, business to be done') partners (Tag. *banig*, Sans. *vanija*, or Tag. *sama*, Sans. *sama*, 'equal'), exchanged goods (Tau. *arta*, 'articles, goods', Sans. *artha*, 'substance, wealth'). Currency may have been in use, if *Pardo de Tavera's* (1887) derivation of Tag. *salapi*, 'money' from Mal. *usa* or Tag. isa, 'one' compounded with Sans. *rupya*, 'the Indian currency' were correct.

The goods that may have been exchanged or sold were Tag. sulta, 'silk thread', Ceb. *sukla*, 'silk', Sans. *sutra*, 'a thread, yarn', ornaments, perfumes and other precious metals, e.g. Ilk. *tanikala*, 'chain, golden chain', Tag and Bis, *talikala*, 'chain, bond', Sans.

srnkhala, 'fetter, chain'. Minerals may have been part of the trade or traffic, e.g. Tau. *sendawa*, 'saltpetre', Sans. *saindhava*, 'a kind of rock salt, salt'. Cf. Tag., Ilk. and Ceb. *tumbaga*, 'copper, brass', ?Sans. *tamraka*, 'made of copper, copper colour' (Mal. *tembaga*, Jav. *tembaga, tembagi,* OJav. *tambaga*, 'brass, copper'); Tag. tingga and Tausog *tenga*, 'lead', ?Sans *tankana*, 'borax, lead' (Mal. *tinkal*, 'lead'). Other objects of trade were certainly ornaments of precious stones.

Sans. *petaka, petika*, 'little basket, basket' provides a name for Mar. 'pocket-book, bill-folder, purse' and Ilk. 'bag, wallet', e.g. *pitaka* (Mal. *petaka*, 'book').

A widely spread Sans. loan-word relating to trade is *argha*, 'value, worth, price', Tag., Ceb., So. Mang. *halaga*, Tausog *halga*, Mar. *arga*, 'price, value, cost, charge, rate', Mag. *haraga*, 'value'. Tag., Tagb. and Ceb. *mahal*, 'expensive costly, of an exorbitant price' is known in Bik. and So. Mang. as *mahal* also, but with a different meaning, e.g. 'dear, holy, dignified, precious'. Sometimes, Tag. *mahal* means 'good, fine, excellent' and hence, 'beautiful, expensive'. The word may be Sans. *maharha*, 'very worthy, or deserving, very precious or valuable' (cf. Sans. *maha*, 'great'). But, Sans. *mahargha*, 'high priced', seems closely related to Tag., Tagb. and Ceb. *mahal*, like Mal. *mahal*, 'of an exorbitant price'.

The word in both Tag. and Ceb. always refers to 'price or cost' and rarely in Tag. to mean 'esteemed', e.g. *Kay mahal mo sa akin*, 'you are very dear to me' (or, 'much esteemed by me').

It is likely that the intermediate forms in Mal., *laba*, 'profit', and *lebeh*, 'more (than)' [Sans. *labha (labh*, 'to gain possession'), 'profit, gain, excess'] may have developed in Tag. and Ceb. as *laba*, 'profit, benefit, gain, winnings' and in Tausog *lebi*, 'to exceed', respectively. Cf. this word with Mag. guna, 'profit', Sans. *guna*, 'good quality, merit, virtue' (?Mal. *guna*, 'benefit' and Jav. *guna*, 'benefit, profit').

Sans. *bhanda*, goods, wares, merchandise, capital, income becomes, in various forms, in four Philippine languages, a term for 'wealth, etc.': Tag. and *Pamp, bandi,* 'estate, a piece of land to let, wealth, security', Ceb. *bahandi*, 'furniture, household, goods, prob. treasure, wealth'. But, Bik. *bahandi*, 'jewels' may be Sans. *bhanda*, 'ornament, gem?'. It is doubtful whether Mal. *benda*, 'thing, article, object, material, treasure, riches' is San. *bhanda*, through which the Philippine term may have developed.

Ilk. dondon, 'fine, a redemption of something lost and found or of a mortgage', Mag. *dinda*, 'fine', Sans. *danda,* punishment, 'fine', via Mal. *denda,* archaic, penalty, a fine' (Jav. *denda*, 'fine' and TBt. *dandan,* 'fine, sum paid by the loser' is more akin to Ilk. than Mal. However, the Mal. form is closely related to Mag.

While Pardo de Tavera (1887) seems to be convinced that Tag. *upa,* 'pay, salary, rent' (Ilk. and Pang. *upa,* 'wages, rent') is Sans. *utpatti,* 'products, production' (*ut-pat,* to be produced) with Mal. *upati,* 'tribute, tax, contribution' as the intervening form, there seems to be no other evidence to confirm his derivation. R.O. Winstedt (1957) does not list Mal. upati, in his Dictionary: instead he lists *upah,* 'payment for work done or for special service' (i.e., wages, fee, expenses, commission). He derives this word with caution from Sanskrit. He lists *upeti,* 'tribute (to a more powerful state)'. Jav. opah, and epah apparently show closer affinity with the Philippine forms. But the question arises whether or not the Jav. has its origins in Sans.

Sans. *bhaga* (bhaj), 'to divide, to distribute, division, allotment', provides a similarly widespread terminology in the islands like Sans. *argha.* Tag. and So. Mang. *bahagi,* 'share, portion, division, sharing', Ilk. and Mar. bagi, 'share, part' and Tausog *bahagi,* var. *bhagian,* 'to distribute, to divide, a division, separate'. It may be assumed that Tausog, Tag. and So. Mang. are probably Mal.; Ilk. and Mar., Jav. Bik. shows very doubtful origin. Cf. this word with Ceb. *sagala,* 'piece, part, fragment', though isolated seems to show Sans. origin, e.g. *sakala,* 'fragment, piece'.

Certainly, trade and traffic through the vast expanse of the seas also introduced the early Filipinos to Sanskrit terms denoting natural phenomena and/or cosmic bodies. Sans. *surya,* 'sun', is known in Tau. as *surya,* which naturally recalls to us Sans. *megha,* 'cloud'. Sans. *vayu,* 'strong wind', could possibly be Tag. Ilk., and other Philippine languages, *bagyo,* 'storm'. All these are known in Malay and Javanese, both being highly Sanskritised.

The terms used to identify the three quarters of the universe seem to have been known—Sans. *uttara,* 'north': Mag. *utara*; Tau. *utala*; Sans. *udaya,* 'the east': Ilk., *daya,* Jav. and Mal. *udaya*; and Sans. *daksina,* 'south': Mag. Mal. and Jav. *daksina.*

Most interesting, however, are numerals in the Philippine languages of high value, which indeed could only be recognised in terms of extensive trade and traffic relations.

The lesser numerals in the Philippine languages are Malayo-Polynesian. The lowest numeral, two (Ilk. *dua*, Bik. *duwa,* Ceb. *duha*, Tagb. *duwa*, and Tag. *dalawa*), shows an Indian origin. This may be assumed through the presupposition of an Indian contact, which actually occurred at a period early enough for the languages of the Indian archipelago to assimilate the numeral within a reasonable time. But it has been pointed out that the word is "derived from Austronesian 'DUWA' (Jav. ro, *Hova rua, Fiji,* Futura and Samoa, lua) which has been treated by Otto Dempwolff (1934, 1937, 1938) as a "native Austronesian word". A reconstruction of *duwa* or *dewha*, 'two' has been attempted by Isidore Dyen (1947).

The numerals that were actually borrowed from Sanskrit begin with 'ten thousand' and reach the highest possible figure of 'one hundred million'. Pang., Ilk., and Tau. build the highest numerals'one hundred thousand' and 'one million'; and 'ten million' and 'one hundred million' in Pangupon the lower numeral, 'ten thousand'. 'One hundred thousand' in Hil., Pang., Ilk., and Tau. for instance, is 'ten ten thousand'; 'one million' in Hil. Pang. and Tau. is 'one hundred ten thousand' and 'ten thousand ten thousand', respectively. Tag. and Mar. do not build their two highest numerals upon the lower. 'One million' in Tag. is built upon 'one hundred thousand'. It would then be, literally, 'ten one hundred thousand'.

Sans. *ayuta*, 'ten thousand', *laksa*, 'one hundred thousand', and *koti*, 'ten million' either reduce or increase their values in the Philippine languages. Sans. *koti*, retains its value in Tag. *kati*, but becomes one-tenth of its value in Mar. *sakati* (*isa* or *usa*) 'one million'. Sans. *ayuta* is increased in value ten times in Tag. *sang yuta* (*isa ng yuta*), 'one hundred thousand'; in Mar. *sajuta*, a similar increase is observed. It is increased in Mal. *juta*, 'one million' by a hundred times. The increase is also observable in Pamp. *sangyota*, 'one million'. Sans. *laksa* undergoes reduction of value in Mal. and Jav. *laksa*, 'ten thousand' (Bat. *loksa*, Mak. *lossa*, and Day. *laksa*, 'id'). This becomes the basis in some Philippine languages. Mag. had *laksa*, 'ten thousand', and *yuta*, 'one million', that undergo similar decrease and increase of value from Sans.

'One hundred million' is expressed in Pang. by *ni laksa laksa* 'ten thousand ten thousand' (a reduplicated form with prefix ni-). F.R. Blake (1919) suggests that the prefix may be the Pang. ni- which is used instead of the infix-prefix -in-/in-expressing similarity before 'l' or 'y' initials, or it may be the Sans. prefix ni-, which is used with certain higher numerals, e.g. *niyuta*, 'one hundred thousand', *nyarbuda*, 'one hundred million' and nikharva, 'one hundred billion'.

Ornaments that adorn the body, and scents that make a person of agreeable odour had names that may be identified as Sanskrit.

Tau. has *manik-manik,* So. Mang. *manik*, 'beads'. Tag. manik, 'glass beads, beadwork'; Mal. *manek* or *manik*, 'bead', which could possibly be Sans. *manika*, 'jewel, pearl, precious stone, any amulet or ornament' (Jav. *manik*?). The Tag. and probably the Zambali *maniknik* may be the various species of palaquim and other genera of *sapotaceae*, the brilliantly polished seeds of which are used as beads.

Sans. *mutya, mukta* or *muktika*, 'pearl' develops in the Philippines through the Mal. *mutiya, mutiá* 'pearl, mother pearl', var. *mutika*, 'precious stone', Mag. and Ilk. *mutia*, 'pearl, charm, precious stone, amulet', Bik. *mutya*, 'pearl, gem', Ceb. *motya*, 'pearl, jewel', Mar. *montia*, 'jewel, gem'. Tagabili *mutia*, 'charm stone', So. Mang. *mutya*, 'besoar stone, amulet', and Tau. *mucha*, 'pearl' (cf. OJav. *mutyara*, OMad. *mutyara*, Osund. *mutiara*, Bug. and Mak. *mutiara*).

Tau. has a term generally applied to 'gem, jewels': *pamata*, var. *permata, parmata*, which is probably Sans. *paramata*, 'excellence' (Mal. *permata*, 'jewel, gem').

Sans. *kaca*, 'glass', which Pardo de Tavera translates as 'crystal or quartz used as an ornament' tag. *kasa*, 'bracelet or green and gold stones'. Ceb. *katya*, 'glass, crystal', and Tau. *kacha*, Mag. *kacha*, 'glass, bottle' may be Sans. *kaca* (Mal., Jav., Sund., Mak., Bug., Day. *katcha*, 'id'). Cf. Igt. *kanching*, 'brass (?glass beads)' which may be Sans. *kancana*, 'gold' (Mal. *kanchana*, 'id').

Mag. *gantang*, 'bell' may have been also an article of trade, and the name may be Sans. *ghanta*, 'a plate of iron or mixed metal struck as a clock, bell(?)'. (Jav. *genta*, Mal. *genta* 'bell').

'Silk or silk thread' is in Tag. *sulta*, Ceb. *sukla*, Tausog *sutra* or *sutla*, and So. Mang. *sutla* which developed from Sans. *sutra*, 'a thread, a yarn, a string'. The intermediate forms in Mal. *sutera*, 'silk', Jav. and Sund. *sutra* (Bat. *suntura*, Mak. and Bug. *suntara*, 'id') show definite borrowing from the Sans. It could, however, be the Jav. from which the Philippine forms were developed, judging from the very phonetic structures.

Of the scents, Sans. *kasturi*, 'musk' is found in Tag. *kastuli*, Ceb. *katsuli*, and Ilk. *kastoli*, 'musk, a kind of musk' (Jav. *kasturi*, 'musk (name of the animal that produces musk), civette', Mal. *kesturi*, 'id').

CONCLUDING REMARKS

These notes do not have a conclusion because the subject as discussed above is still in the process of being probed. If I have been rather arbitrary or dogmatic in my presentation, it is quite understandable in terms of the very glaring errors in the presentation of our pre-colonial past, which have been interpreted with so many implications in our national life, particularly the view of a 'Srivijaya period' of Philippine history (Beyer 1952) which really did not exist. It is perhaps more acceptable that that period in Philippine pre-colonial history was an age of emerging commercial interchanges between very active economies within the region and equally viable economies beyond the western seas. I would not argue for a static Philippine economy during pre-colonial times. Rather, the Philippine society was dynamic and pulsating, contrary to the view so successfully put forward by other students of the Philippine society and culture.

POSTSCRIPT

In assessing the impact of Indian culture in Southeast Asia, particularly in the Malay Peninsula and Indonesian and Philippine archipelagos, it needs to be noted that the people on the Coromandel coast or northern Bengal Bay coast were not the only seafaring people who plied their trade with the lands beyond the seas. The people of the Malabar coast would not have been less intrepid, hence they must have crossed the oceans for trade and traffic. If they did—and I am sure they did—vestiges of their culture after long centuries of contact through trade and traffic with the people of insular and peninsular Southeast Asia should be found.

The question may, however, arise: why did they leave only (the) Brahmanic/Buddhistic elements of their culture, and not elements of their own culture? To illustrate this with language—Why didn't they leave behind 'Tamilisms' or 'Malayalamisms'? With the exception of three Tamil inscriptions found in Sumatra and northern Malaysia, in the Isthmus of Kra, there is no evidence enough of that impact—if we can call it impact—and to impart significance on a broad perspective or high level influence. Of 'Malayalamisms' we certainly have no evidence.

Earlier works on the South Indian impact on trade and traffic in Southeast Asia provide no material evidence of Kerala's influence in the Southeast Asia region. I would still believe, however, that there were trade and traffic contacts between the Malabar coast and the Southeast Asian regions.

I would advance the view that 'Malayalamisms', and indeed 'Tamilisms', are not found in these regions on account of one very significant event in South India itself. That is, during this period—the period of trade and traffic contact, South India was at a period of high saturation of Brahmanic and Sanskrit traditions, acceptance of which was deep and wide-ranging. The enthusiasm that the Tamils and Malayalees had for the traditions extended beyond their own physical borders. As a result, instead of imparting their 'indigenous' cultures to the people of Southeast Asia, they imparted the new culture as a legacy of their contact with the Malayo-Indonesian—and hence with the Filipino—people of early times, whose cultures had been permeated with Brahmanic, if Sanskritic, traditions. In the Philippines, the coastal and the riverine people received the greatest bulk of that tradition; and through them all other people of the archipelago received their share of that tradition.

All this is pure speculation, and I shall stand corrected in the face of substantial material evidence that shall may be discovered later on. I would not, however, be surprised if this evidence tends to support my view.

BIBLIOGRAPHY

Agoncillo, Teodoro A and Oscar Alfonso. *A Short History of the Filipino People,* Quezon City, University of the Philippines, 1958.

Agoncillo, Teodoro A. and Milagros Guerrero. *A Short History of the Filipino People*, Quezon City, University of the Philippines, 1968.

Beyer, H. Otley. *Early History of Philippine Relations with Foreign Countries...*, Manila, National Printing Company, 1948.

Beyer, H. Otley and Jaimen C. de Veyra. *The Philippine Saga*, Manila, Capitol Publishing Company, 1952.

Blake, F.R. "Contribution to Comparative Philippine Grammar", *Journal of*

American Oriental Society, 23, Part 2, 1906-7.

______"Reduplication in Tagalog", *American Journal of Philology,* .38, 1917.

Brandstetter, R. *An Introduction to Indonesian Linguistics,* Royal Asiatic Society, London, 1916.

Coedes, Georges. *Les Etats Hindouises d'Indonesie d'Indochine,* Paris, Histoire du Monde, VIII, 1948.

Dempwolff, Otto. *Vergleichende Lautlehre der Austronesischen Wortschatzes,* Berlin, 1934, 1937, 1938.

Dyen, Isidore. "The Tagalog Reflexes of Malayo Polynesian D", *Language,* 23, 1947.

Fox, Robert B. "The Calatagan Excavations", *Philippine Studies,* VII, August 1959.

Fox, Robert B. and Avelino Legaspi. *Excavations at Santa Ana.* National Museum of the Philippines, 1977.

Francisco, Juan R. "Sri Vijaya and the Philippines: A Review", *Philippines Social Sciences and Humanities Review,* 26, Part 1, March 1961.

______*Indian Influences in the Philippines,* Quezon City, University of the Philippines, 1964.

______*Maharadia Lawana,* Quezon City, Philippine Folklore Society, 1969.

______*The Philippines and India,* Manila, National Book Store, 1971.

______"Sanskrit in Philippine Language and Literature", *Studies in Indo-Asian Art and Culture,* vol. 2, New Delhi, International Sanskrit Conference, 27-31 March 1972.

______*Philippine Palaeography,* Quezon City, Linguistic Society of the Philippines, 1973.

______"The Iconography of Indian Images in the Philippines", *SEAMEO Project in Archaeology and Fine Arts,* Jakarta, 1983.

______"The Rama-Hanuman Bronze Image from Manila, Philippines", Paper presented to the 12th Conference, International Association of Historians of Asia (IAHA), University of Hong Kong, 24-28 June, 1991.

Hutterer, Karl. *An Archaeological Picture of a Pre-Spanish Cebuano Community,* Cebu, University of San Carlos Publications, 1973.

Legaspi, Avelino. *Bolinao: A 14th-15th Century Burial Site,* National Museum of the Philippines, 1974.

Majul, Cesar Adib. "Theories on the Introduction and Expansion of Islam in Malaysia", Proceedings. 2nd Biennial Conference, IAHA, Taipei, 6-9 October 1962.

Majumdar, R.C. *Ancient Indian Colonies in the Far East,* I-Champa, Lahore, 1927.

______II - Suvarnadvipa, 2 Parts, Calcutta, 1937-38.

Nilakantha Sastri, K.A. "A Tamil Merchant in Sumatra", *Tijdschrift voor*

Taal- Land- en Volken-Kunde, 72, 1932.

______"Takuapa and its Tamil Inscription", *Journal of the Royal Asiatic Society*—Malayan Branch, 22, 1949.

Pardo de Tavera, T.H. *El Sanscrito en la Langua Tagalog*, Paris, 1887.

Peralta, Jesus T. "Ancient Mariners in the Philippines", *Archaeology*, New York, 1980.

Postma, Antoon. "The Laguna Copper Plate Inscription", *National Museum Papers*, 2 (1), pp. 1-25, 1991.

Solheim II, Wilhelm G. "The Kalanay Pottery Complex in the Philippines", *Artibus Asie*, 20, 1959.

Spoehr, Alexander. "An Archaeological Approach to Ethnic Diversity in Zamboanga and Sulu", *Sulu Studies*, 2, 1973.

Windstedt, R.O. "Sanskrit in Malay Literature", *Bulletin of the School of Oriental and African Studies*, 20, 1957.

______*Malay Grammar*, Oxford, 1957.

ABBREVIATIONS

Bhind.	Bahasa Indonesia
Bik.	Bikol
Bug.	Buginese
Ceb.	Cebuano
CCNeg.	Central Cagayan Negrito
Dib.Mand.	Dibabaon Negrito
Hil.	Hiligaynon
Igt.	Igorot
Ilk.	Iloko
Inib.	Inibaloi
Jav.	Javanese
ModJav.	Modern Javanese
OJav.	Old Javanese
Mag.	Magindanaw
Mak.	Makassar
Mal.	Malay
Mar.	Maranaw
Pamp.	Pampanga
Pang.	Pangasinan
Phil.	Philippine(s)
Pkt.	Prakrit
Sans.	Sanskrit
SoMang.	South Mangyan
Sp.	Spanish
Sund.	Sundanese
Tag.	Tagalog
Tagb.	Tagbanua
Tagi.	Tagabili
Tau.	Tausog
TBt.	Toba Batak

RULERS AND PORTS: VISAKHAPATTANAM AND MOTTUPALLI IN EARLY MEDIEVAL ANDHRA

Ranabir Chakravarti

I

A recent bibliographical survey of the trends of historical research in South Asia by Burton Stein tells us of some "stunning developments" in South Asian historical studies during the 1980s.[1] He traces these developments in the historiography of early medieval India, of 'late pre-colonial' period, in the emergence of the 'subaltern team' and in the Euro-American scholarship on the eighteenth century. While it is perfectly valid and understandable that one has to leave out many issues—important as well as trivial—when one takes a bird's-eye view of the trends of decadal historical research, it is rather surprising that the state of the subject, known as Indian Ocean studies (or more precisely, the historical role of South Asia in the Indian Ocean), fails to make the grade for Stein's bibliographical survey. The present essay takes a close look at an interesting aspect of India's overseas trade in the Indian Ocean during early medieval period of Indian history.[2] This, however, requires one to take into account the perspective of Indian Ocean studies, even in its bare outline, without which the exercise is hardly possible.

With the focus of power gradually shifting from Europe since the 1940s, the Eurocentric view of history has slowly taken a back seat. The emergence of new nations in the 'Third World', following decolonisation, has immensely encouraged scholars to appreciate the role of non-Europeans in their historical development. An evident impact of this shift in emphasis and perspective is in the growing importance of Indian Ocean studies. Pierre Chaunu thought that "the Atlantic in practice is the oldest ocean on a human scale, the first that has been regularly crossed, the first to be located at the heart of an economy, even of a civilization."[3] In the context of recent studies on the Indian Ocean, Chaunu's claim cannot pass muster. One may in fact say, following Franz Broeze, that a long-term perspective, for instance over the last two millennia, would project Asia and not Europe as the leading maritime continent of the world.[4] Such a perspective and vigorous recognition of the importance of the Indian Ocean has certainly helped the spurt of in-depth research on India's maritime history with the Indian Ocean as the general unit of study.[5]

Historians of maritime India, however, largely concentrate on the period from A.D. 1500 onwards. It does not necessarily indicate lesser significance of the pre-1500 days in India's maritime history. The historian's enquiries into this age are often severely thwarted by the acute shortage of data. The meagre information available is essentially impressionistic and rarely offers any statistical details. The other major stumbling block is the extreme paucity of indigenous documentation. The historian has to fall back regularly upon the accounts left behind by foreigners, the very nature of which source puts considerable limitations on the historian's search. A careful culling of data from early Indian documents—when judiciously combined and compared with non-indigenous materials—may help us build up at least a workable knowledge of India's participation in the Indian Ocean commerce during the pre-1500 days. These shortcomings notwithstanding, Genevieve Bouchon and Denys Lombard urge us to unravel the mystries of the maritime situations in the Indian Ocean during the thirteenth, fourteenth and fifteenth centuries.[6]

An immediate problem is concerning the origin and the earliest use of the expressionthe Indian Ocean. M.N. Pearson opines that the expression is derived from a translation of the Arabic term *al bahr al* Hindi.[7] He traces back the antiquity of the expression to early medieval Indian history. So far, the earliest known use of the term belongs to Pliny (death in c. A.D. 79), who says: "Here begins the Indian race, bordering not only in the Eastern Sea, but on the Southern also, which we have designated the Indian Ocean (*mare Indicum*)".[8] Since it does not figure in the *Periplus,* written before Pliny's *Natural History,* the expression 'Indian Ocean' seems to have been coined in the second or third quarter of the first century A.D. As Pliny differentiated the Southern Sea (equated with his *mare Indicum*) from the Eastern Sea, his definition of the Indian Ocean differed considerably from its present connotation. The map of the Indian Ocean, published by the National Atlas and Thematic Mapping Organisation, places this maritime space up to the Cape of Good Hope in the west, to Antarctica in the south, and includes the Red Sea, the Persian Gulf and the Bay of Bengal, but leaves out the Java and China Seas.[9]

Maritime historians of India and the Indian Ocean appear to have been largely inspired by Fernand Braudel's seminal researches on the Mediterranean Sea.[10] As Braudel repeatedly stressed the unity and coherence of the Mediterranean,[11] he was the first to name a civilisation after a sea. Taking the cue from Braudel, India's maritime historian does not look at the Indian Ocean primarily in terms of naval battles and tactics or from the nationalistic stance[12] or to champion the cause of a strong navy in modern India.[13] As a historian 'at sea', he would very much like to focus on the broader Braudelian concept of the unity between the land and the sea.

Ancient and medieval terms like *mare Indicum* and *al bahr al Hindi* leave little room for doubt that such terms came into existence because of India's continuous long-distance overseas contacts with various parts of Asia. While the earliest definite knowledge of such long-distance trade of the subcontinent goes back to the time of the Harappan civilisation (c. 2300-1750 B.C.),[14] India's regular participation in overseas international commerce emerged probably first during the age of Indo-Roman commerce (c. late first century B.C.-middle third century A.D.).[15] The subsequent period witnessed India's growing commercial ties in the eastern Indian Ocean; harbours of the western littorals also appear to have reaped some advantage out of the trade in the Persian Gulf in which the Sasanids of Iran were vitally interested.[16] The rise of Islam in the seventh century and its subsequent spread must be seen as a major landmark. The definite orientation of Islam towards trade and urbanisation provided a tremendous fillip to long-distance maritime commerce in the Indian Ocean.[17] Two terminal points of Asian seaborne trade emerged: China in the east and Basra (under the Saldjuk and the Abbasid realms) and later Egypt (under the Fatimid Caliphate since the later part of the tenth century). As movements of vessels in this vast maritime space were largely guided by the patterns of monsoon winds, harbours on both the seaboards of the Indian subcontinent became indispensable as stopovers, transhipment points, gateways and entrepots. 'West'-bound Muslim pilgrims for *hajj* had to start or tranship from Indian ports.

Indian harbours also facilitated the leap-frogging of Islamic preachers along maritime Asia.

Other preliminaries should be taken into account. Most studies on India and the Indian Ocean have an unmistakable thrust on the western sector of the Indian Ocean. Recent researches by S. Arasaratnam, Sanjay Subramanyam, Om Prakash, Louis Philippe Thomaz, etc. have enlightened us on many unknown aspects of seaborne commerce in the Bay of Bengal during the period 1500 to 1800.[18] But here, too, the situation before 1500 is only dimly known.

II

In view of the desiderata in Indian Ocean studies in general and the gap in our knowledge of the Bay of Bengal trade in particular, an attempt is made here on one aspect of India's maritime history before 1500, namely ports and rulers. The present essay is a case study of two early medieval ports of the Bay of Bengal, viz. Visakhapattanam and Mottupalli. Both ports were situated on the Andhra littoral (ancient Vengimandala), washed by the Bay of Bengal, which was designated as *bahr al Harkand*[19] in early medieval Arab accounts.

Geographers have drawn attention to the strong contrasts between the western and eastern littorals. The latter is a much wider coastal plain than its western counterpart; the coastal lowlands, as a rule, are softer than those on the western seaboard. There is a clear climatic variation on the 1,200 mile (1,930 km) long east coast, particularly seen in the fluctuations of the rainfall pattern from the northern to the southern part of the coast (60"-40" of annual rainfall). The coastal areas of present Andhra Pradesh run from Srikakulam in the north to Nellore in the south.[20] While Visakhapattanam was situated in between two major deltas of the eastern seaboard, namely those of the Mahanadi and Godavari, Mottupalli stood between the deltas of the Godavari and the Krishna. The rainfall pattern around 40" (conducive to rice cultivation), the fertile deltas and two major rivers (the Godavari and the Krishna) provided the Andhra coast with a sound agricultural basis. The proximity to the sea naturally encouraged activities 'at sea'.

The Vengi littoral came into prominence in the early centuries of the Christian era. Agricultural prosperity is indicated by the toponym *dhanya-kataka* (rice bowl); seaborne commerce clearly figures in the classical accounts and archaeo-logical materials speak of flourishing urban centres and Buddhist sites.[21]

The Bay of Bengal assumes considerable importance in the contacts between the eastern littoral of the subcontinent and Sri Lanka and Southeast Asia. This is especially visible since the rise of the Coromandel coast[22] during the Pallava and Cola times. The Colas, though never a coastal power, harboured definite interests in the affairs of the Bay of Bengal. The remarkable success of Cola naval power over Sri Lanka and several Southeast Asian islands during the reigns of Rajaraja (985-1014) and Rajendra (1012-1044) led scholars to view the Bay of Bengal as a 'Cola Lake'.[23] That the Cola embassies to China—obviously reaching their destinations by maritime voyages—had commercial significance, has been ably brought out by Nilakantha Sastri[24] and Hall.[25] The port of Mamallapuram stole the limelight as a regular point of voyages across the Bay of Bengal during the Pallava times. The Cola period witnessed the arrival of a new port, Nagapattinam (in the Kaveri delta), which replaced Mamallapuram.

All this gives an impression of the overall supremacy of Colamandala and the apparently subordinate position of Vengimandala. The Vengi coast possessed, however, the harbour of Visakhapattanam. The homonymous modern port (Vizagapatam or Vizag) stands between the 1600' Kailana ridge to the north and the 1100' Yaroda to the south and it is sheltered by the Dolphin's Nose.[26] The exact location of ancient Visakhapattanam is uncertain, but it probably stood more or less where modern Vizag stands. The very suffix *pattana/pattinam*[27] shows that Visakhapattanam must have been on the coast. The earliest epigraphic reference to Visakhapattanam goes back to the second half of the eleventh century. A Telugu inscription of Saka 990 (= A.D. 1068), from Draksharam near the Godavari delta, mentions the gift of a lamp to a temple by a merchant of Visakhapattana (pattana).[28] The epigraph hints at contacts between Visakhapattanam and Draksharam.

The port figures once more in an inscription of Saka 1012 (= 1090) in the Vizagapatam taluk. Significantly, the port is called Visakhapattanam alias Kulottungacolapattanam,[29] probably named after the reigning Cola monarch Kulottunga Cola I (c. 1070-1120).[30] The renaming must have occurred sometime between

1068 and 1090. It is a unique case where an existing port was renamed after a Cola ruler, while retaining its original name. The Colas applied their names to temples, towns and even deities; but this is a solitary case where an existing port was renamed after a Cola king.[31] It must be underlined that Kulottunga attached his name not to a Colamandala harbour in the core region of the Colas, but one situated in the Andhra littoral, suggesting official recognition of the growing importance of a harbour on the Vengimandala coast. The situation may be better appreciated in the perspective of the changing economic and political conditions within the Cola realm, in Sri Lanka and in Southeast Asia.

Kulottunga I's accession to the Cola throne signified the rise of rulers who belonged not to the main line of the Colas of Thanjavur proper but to Vengi. A matrimonial alliance ensured Kulottunga's accession to the throne, and paved the way for closer linkages between the heartland of the Colas and the Andhra coast, which had hitherto been under the control of the Eastern Calukyas of Vengi. Kulottunga's two expeditions in Kalinga region[32] (in 1095, and the next at the end of his reign) were undertaken to consolidate his reign over a region adjacent to coastal Andhra. That Kulottunga strove for the administrative integration of coastal Vengi with the core area of the Colas is clearly illustrated by the epigraphic reference to the presence of two Tamil officers, Karunakaracaryan and Madhurantaka Brahmaraya at Simhachalam in 1099.[33] Another crucial evidence is the issue of the 'Eastern Calukya' type of coins by Kulottunga I. A particular coin type bearing the title *Calakhurayana* (emended as *Calukyanarayana*), but having a central device typically like that of the Colas is logically attributed by B.D. Chattopadhyaya to Kulottunga I.[34]

All this speaks of the growing importance of the Andhra coast and measures taken by Kulottunga to use its potential. The record of 1090, cited above, mentions a *perumballi* or a Jaina temple, at Visakhapattanam constructed under the patronage of *Ainnurruvar,* the famous Tamil mercantile guildthe 500 *svamis* of Ayyavole. This celebrated commercial guild not only made its presence felt in various areas in South India and the Deccan, but was also active overseas, particularly Sri Lanka and Southeast Asia.[35] The inscription, besides proving the presence of the guild at Visakhapattanam, also signifies that this Andhra port was the northernmost point of the distribution of this vigorous Tamil trading group.[36] The other interesting point is the reference to the presence of a merchant (*vyapari*) belonging to another trading group *Anjuvanattu*.[37] Like the 500 *svamis* of Ayyavole, *Anjuvanattu* also came to Visakhapattanam from outside Andhraprobably from Karnataka.[38] The reference to two commercial guilds—neither local, but figuring in a local Telugu inscription—at Visakhapattanam amply demonstrates the interest of these groups in the port. The official recognition of Visakhapattanam as a leading Cola port must have helped its rise to prominence.

Kulottunga's reign is also well known for his policy of abolishing tolls and custom duties. His records of years twenty-eight and thirty-two (1098 and 1102) refer to this particular administrative measure (*Sunganadavirtta-solanallur*).[39] A study of a textual commentary led K.A. Nilakantha Sastri to identify the term *sunga* with tolls and customs.[40] The policy of abolishing tolls and custom duties was launched obviously to attract trade, especially foreign trade, to the Cola domain. The Kavilayadavalli hoard, Atmakur taluk, Nellore district in Andhra has yielded a particular variety of Kulottunga's gold coins. On their obverse appears the Tamil legend *sung*, for *Sunganadavirtta-solanallur* or the abolisher of tolls; on the reverse of some of these species is the word Ne = Nellur (Nellore).[41] The numismatic evidence, coupled with the epigraphic data, leaves an impression that the Andhra coast, including the Nellore region, came within the scope of the operation of the new policy of remitting tolls and customs. There is a distinct possibility that Visakhapattanam, the leading Cola port on the Andhra coast, reaped considerable advantages out of this policy.

Kulottunga I's accession to the Cola throne in 1070 marked the final overthrow of the Cola occupation of Sri Lanka by Vijayabahu. Besides being a territorial loss, it meant a major economic setback, as the island was a principal trading zone in the long-distance commerce in the Indian Ocean. Southeast Asian islands, too, had less to fear from a Cola naval raid in the last quarter of the eleventh century than during Rajendra's reign, despite some vague references to Kulottunga's successful naval operations against Kadaram in the *Kalingattupparani*. The Cola interests in the occupation of Sri Lanka and spreading their influence in Southeast Asia were linked up with their urge to maintain contacts with China which, we have already mentioned, was the easternmost terminus of the Asian maritime commerce in pre-1500 times. Hall has ably pointed to the intermediary role of Southeast Asian islands to reach China from the west.[12] The loss of Sri Lanka and the Colas' decreasing influence in the Bay of Bengal could have spelt some problems in maintaining the Chinese connections.

Kulottunga seems to have been fully alive to the need for maintaining the Chinese contacts. In 1077, the king of Chu-lien (Cola) Ti-hua-kia-lo (identified by Nilakantha Sastri with Kulottunga) sent a commercial embassy to the Chinese court.[13] A Taoist monastery temple inscription at Canton, dated 1079, refers to the Cola king,[14] most likely Kulottunga. But in view of the decrease of Cola naval power in the Bay of Bengal and Southeast Asia, there was, in all probability, a need for an alternative intermediary between the Cola realm and China. Chau-Ju-kua states that one way to reach Chu-lien or the Cola country from China was through Pu-kan or Pagan.[15] Pagan, one of the nine fortified towns of the Pyu kingdom, derived its importance as a central point on the north-south and east-west routes in Burma. The eleventh century witnessed the rise of Pagan as the centre of the Burman kingdom. During Anawratha's reign, Pagan's power spread to Pegu and Thaton in the south and to Arakan in the west. Janice Stargardt has made exhaustive studies of the overland routes which connected Pagan with Chu-ko liang, wherefrom the route continued to Yung-ch'ang and Ta-li, the capital of Nanchao. Attention has been drawn to the route from Yunnan in China to the Irrawaddy in the vicinity of Bhamo, onward to the Chindwin valley. This route was connected with Kamarupa, located around modern Guwahati in Assam. Anawratha's interests in maintaining contacts with India, Sri Lanka and Thailand were continued by his son and successor Kyanzittha (1077-1122).[16]

The Shewsandaw inscription of Kyanzittha informs us of the contacts—apparently cultural—between Kyanzittha and a Cola king.[17] Kulottunga I was the contemporary Cola king. Beneath the cultural communications between the Cola ruler and his Paganese counterpart can be discerned material interests, especially in the light of Pagan's emergence as an intermediary between the Cola and the Chinese realms. It may be that, with Kulottunga's accession, contacts with Pagan opened up a new avenue of commercial intercourse between China and the Cola realm. In this context, the discovery of a type of Kulottunga's copper coin from Arakan[18] is significant. Kulottunga's coin could have reached the Arakan coast by overseas voyages.

Overseas contacts with Pagan could be established more conveniently from a Vengimandala port than a port like Nagapattinam in the Kaveri delta. As early as the first century A.D., the *aphaterion* or the departure point of ships bound for Chryse Khora/Chryse Khersonesis (i.e. *Suvarnabhumi* or *Suvarnadvipa*) was in Maisolia/Masalia[49] country, i.e. Vengi. A port like Visakhapattanam could have been an ideal and preferred port to reach the Burma coast, which lies just across on the eastern shore of the Bay of Bengal. There are grounds to infer that the Cola ruler enhanced the status of an Andhra harbour and shifted his focus to some extent from the Colamandala port to the Andhra littoral, with a view to encouraging trade with Pagan.

The opening of dialogue with Pagan seems to have closely coincided with the renaming of an existing port in coastal Andhra and the remission of tolls and customs. The three events, if judged cohesively, suggest a possible solving of the puzzle about the emergence of the Andhra coast as the main point of contact with Pagan, the new intermediary between China and the Colas, in the latter half of the eleventh century.[50]

Kulottunga I was the last of the great Cola emperors. His successors appear to have been more intensely involved in the affairs of the far south where the Pandyas of Madurai, arch rivals of the Colas, began to emerge to political prowess. Lesser attention to Vengi inevitably led to the desuetude of Visakhapattanam. Local powers like the Telugu-Codas, successors of the Colas in that area, were not up to using Visakhapattanam as a port of consequence in the long-distance overseas network of the Bay of Bengal. Visakhapattanam, despite its immense potential, gradually faded away from the maritime history of pre-modern India.

An inscription from Visakhapattanam dated 1121 Saka (= A.D.1199) refers to the port which still had its second name Kulottungacolapattanam. The Jaina temple (*perumballi*), known at least since a century, was still patronised by the mercantile guild, the 500 *svamis* of Ayyavole.[51] After about five decades, another record (A.D.1250) from the same place once again mentions Visakhapattanam along with its second name. It refers to a merchant at this port who was a native of Pandalayani Kollam, i.e. Quilon in Malabar.[52] One can hardly miss that in the middle of the thirteenth century Visakhapattanam had contacts with a faraway area, the Malabar coast on the western seaboard of India. Information regarding the continuity of this contact in later times is, however, lacking.

The memory of the enhancement of the status of the port of Visakhapattanam by Kulottunga remained alive for nearly two centuries, but the mere epithet was perhaps not enough to sustain the position. As the eastern Deccan was no longer politically integrated with the Colamandala soon after Kulottunga's reign, Visakhapattanam gradually lost its relevance. This could have spelt serious economic problems for a coastal region like Vengi, but for the emergence of another port in coastal Andhra namely Mottupalli, in the forties of the thirteenth century.

III

Eastern Deccan experienced some degree of political stability under the Kakatiyas of Warangal. The new dynasty rose on the ruins of the Western (Kalyani) Calukya kingdom who, like the Kakatiyas of Warangal, were interested in consolidating their power over the coastal eastern Deccan. The Kakatiyas emerged as a formidable power of the Deccan under the greatest ruler of the dynasty, Ganapati (1199-1261).[53] A dynasty that had their power firmly rooted in the interior and were never a coastal power, the Kakatiyas nevertheless showed a lively interest in the affairs of Vengi.

An inscription of A.D. 1231 shows Ganapati in occupation of Divi, i.e. *Dvipa* (modern Divi Point just below Masulipatnam, 81^{0}E long. and 16^0 N lat.) which lay at the junction of Kṛṣṇaveni (i.e. Krishna) and the Salt Sea (or the Bay of Bengal).[54] The deltas of the Godavari and the Krishna and the land between the two rivers remained very fertile. The Pithapuram pillar inscription of Pṛthvisvara (1186) describes the region between two rivers (obviously the Godavari and the Krishna) as possessing all kinds of grains and abundance of fruits.[55]

Kakatiya interests in Vengi largely contributed to the rise of the port of Mottupalli in Baptala taluk, located just below and to the southeast of the Krishna delta. The earliest definite notice of the relationship of this area with the Kakatiya ruler is dated to 1231 when a land grant was made to a local temple by Siddayadeva Maharaja, a subordinate ruler under Ganapati, for the merit of his overlord.[56] This hints at an attempt to integrate the coast with the stronghold of the Kakatiya power on the mainland. Motupalli has so far yielded no less than twelve epigraphic records. These, when examined along with the account of the Venetian traveller Marco Polo (1295), bear eloquent testimony to the importance of this harbour on the Vengi coast.

Fourteen years after its incorporation into the Kakatiya realm (1231), the most important point in the history of Mottupalli took place in 1245. In that year "by the glorious Maharaja Ganapatideva the following edict (assuring) safety (*abhayasasana*) has been granted to traders by sea, starting for and arriving from all continents, islands, foreign countries and cities".[57] Such an *abhayasasana* in early medieval India is a rarity and naturally merits a closer scrutiny. The royal proclamation guaranteeing security to maritime merchants surely suggests that previously traders had enjoyed little safety in carrying commercial activities in and around Mottupalli. And the *abhayasasana* exactly demonstrates this. "Formerly kings used to take away by force the whole cargo, viz. gold, elephants, horses, gems, etc., carried by ships and vessels which after they had started from one country or other, were attacked by storms, wrecked and thrown on the shore." Several other contemporary (or nearly so) sources confirm that this nasty practice of looting ships which fell victim to storms and shipwrecks, was rampant in both seaboards of the subcontinent.[58] Such a predatory policy was hardly conducive to the free and uninterrupted flow of commerce, especially long distance trade.

The charter of security did not make vague promises to merchants at bay: it spelt out a concrete policy. According to the charter, nothing else than fixed duties (*klptasulka*) would be levied on those "who have incurred the great risk of a sea voyage with the thought that wealth is more valuable than even life". This is a remarkably perceptive attitude of a ruler to seaborne traders, more so because of the essentially land-based character of the Kakatiya kingdom. On all exports and imports (*ekkumati-dikkumati; egumati-digumati* = exports, imports, shipping and unshipping)[59] a fixed duty of one in thirty would be levied. Other items were levied in cash, e.g. sandal (*srigandhamu*), camphor (*karpura)*, Chinese camphor (*cinikakarpura*), pearls (*mutyalku*), rose-water (*pamniru*), ivory (*dantamu*), civet (*javadi)*, camphor oil (*karpura taila*), zinc (*tagaramu*), lead (*sisamu*), silk thread (*pattunulu*), corals (*pavadamu*), perfumes (*gandhadravya*) and pepper (*miriyala*).[60]

The range of items levied at Mottupalli is quite impressive, consisting of not only luxury, high-value items, but also low-value bulks like copper, arecanuts and pepper.

The taxes in cash refer to two coin-terms, ga, an abbreviated form of *gadyana* (also called *pagoda*) and a symbol indicating *r/ru.* i.e. *ruka.* Ruka is same as *pana/fanam,* meaning gold coins. *Pana/fanam/ruka* was generally struck on a gold weight standard 5.2 grains. Ten panas normally equalled one *gadyana,* which means the *gadyana* would have been struck on a weight standard of fifty-two grains, though there were variations. In fact, the Kakatiya *gadyana* or *pagoda* coins often weighed up to 61.2 grains.[61]

The rate of levies was:

(a) On one tola of sandal 1 *gadyana* 1/4 *pana* (*ru*).
(b) On 1 *gadyana's* value of camphor, Chinese camphor and pearls 3/4 and 3/8 *pana.*
(c) On 1 *gadyana* value of rose water, ivory, civet, camphor oil, copper, zinc, lead, silk threads, corals and perfumes $1^{1}/_{4}$ and 1/8 *panam.*
(d) On all silks $5^{1}/_{2}$ *pana* per bale.
(e) On every lakh arecanuts 1 *gadyana* and $3^{1}/_{4}$ *pana.*

The Kakatiya charter of security pushed up Mottupalli virtually from a nonentity into a major harbour. Its impact is best seen in Marco Polo's account on Mutfili, i.e. Mottupalli.[62] Polo's description is dated around 1293—nearly half a century after the issue of the *abhayasasana*—when Ganapati's daughter, Rudramba (1261-95) was the sovereign. Two products find special mention in Polo's account, namely diamond and textile. According to him, diamonds of the best quality were available and exported to the court of the Great Kaan (=Kublai Khan of the Yueh dynasty in China). Mutfili also had "the best and the most delicate bucrams and those of the highest price: in sooth they look like the tissues of spider's web". Polo uses the term Mutfili to denote the entire Kakatiya kingdom itself, signifying how, in the eyes of a foreigner, a port city became the focal point of an inland kingdom.[63]

During the fourteenth century, the Kakatiyas' attention seems to have shifted from the coast back to the interior, mainly because of their protracted hostilities with the Yadavas of western and central Deccan. Malik Kafur's South Indian campaign (1307-13) dealt the Kakatiyas a crushing blow. The Vengi coast under such circumstances passed out of their hands to the local Reddi rulers who were firmly rooted to Vengi.

It appears that political uncertainties and dynastic upheavals in the interior Andhra adversely affected the affairs in its littoral, especially in and around Mottupalli. This probably necessitated the Reddi king Annapotta (also spelt as Annabotta) to issue another charter at Mottupalli (now called Mukula) in 1358, laying down fixed rates of duties on various items. The charter was signed on behalf of the ruler by minister Somayamatya.[64] This record, reminiscent of Ganapati's *abhayasasana* issued more than a century earlier, once again highlights the administrative backing of this harbour. Merchants were offered settled lands, obviously to induce them to make their stay permanent in and around the port. "They were given full liberty in the manner of conducting trade." Merchants were exempted from transferring to the ruler their heirless property. There was also a remission of duties by one-third on the import of sandalwood. The charter assures that commodities would not be detained in the warehouses. The fixed duties were as follows:

(a) goods coming from the southern side—three packages on every 100 packages; every 100 cloths for export—two coins.
(b) on goods coming from the north—on every package three coins and on every 100 packages of cloth for export three coins.
(c) on cloth for export three coins per 100 packages, and seven coins per 100 pearls.

The practice of raising commercial levies both in cash and kind continued from the days, at least, of Ganapati. But the more significant point is that the charter is trilingual: Telugu, Sanskrit and Tamil. In fact, the Tamil version contains greater details than its Telugu counterpart. One may reasonably infer the presence of a handsome number of Tamil merchants in this Vengi port. Offers of inducements of land and remission of some taxes were, in all probability, meant for these Tamil-speaking merchants. In this respect, both Mottupalli and Visakhapattanam appear to have thrived and prospered if and when the Vengi coast had close interactions with the Tamil-speaking merchants of far South India.

By the later part of the fourteenth century, Mottupalli was incorporated within the Vijayanagara empire. Epigraphic records from Mottupalli during the Vijayanagara period make this clear. One such record of the time of Devaraya I speaks of the presence of *Colamandalavyapari* at Mottupalli.[65] This once more draws our attention to the continuity of the interests of Tamil merchants of far south in the commerce of Mottupalli and also the seemingly uninterrupted linkages between the Vengi coast and the Colamandala area. Epigraphically speaking, Mottupalli is probably last heard of in a record dated 1390, when the port was still under the Vijayanagara realm, the ruler being Devaraya Udaiyar, son of Harihararaya.[66] The commercial importance and the revenue yielding potential of maritime trade at Mottupalli are borne out by the fact that import duties on corals and 'sealed goods' continued to be levied at this port at the close of the fourteenth century. Mottupalli does figure in subsequent times in early European documents.[67] But the references to Mottupalli therein are only off and on and are beyond the purview of this essay.

Which areas had commercial links with Mottupalli? This vital question cannot be satisfactorily answered and only guesses can be offered. The products mentioned in the *abhayasasana* of 1245 do not figure in Marco Polo's account as items produced locally. Textiles and diamonds, according to Polo, were local products of Andhra. So those products figuring in the record of 1245 were, in all likelihood, imported to Mottupalli. Some of these items also figure in a more or less contemporary Chinese text by Chau-Ju-Kua (1225) who was also well aware of the Indian situation.[68] Gleanings from Chau-Ju-Kua may not therefore be irrelevant. Sandal was found at various places, including Malabar in India, but that from San-fo-ts'i (Palembang) was especially famous.[69] Camphor was available from several areas of Southeast Asia, particularly P'o-ni and Pin-su identified respectively with Borneo and Sumatra.[70] Pearls could be brought to Mottupalli from the Gulf of Mannar area, known for its pearl fisheries.[71] Ivory appears to have been normally brought from an area noted for its supply of elephants. This brings to our mind the availability of elephants in Burma, wherefrom ivory too could be procured.[72] Copper seems to have reached India from Japan (Ji-pon) via China and Southeast Asian islands.[73] Silk thread, in all probability, was imported from China for which it was justly famous. Coral is also mentioned by Chau-Ju-Kua as a precious item of trade. The country of Pi-no-ye of the Ta-shi was noted for coral. This is generally located in West Africa—Mo-kie-la (el Maghreb).[71] Pepper must have been brought to the Andhra coast from Malabar, for which it was internationally famous. Arecanuts too were Indian products, being imported from Karnataka and adjacent areas. It is quite plainly visible that many of the products either originated in Southeast Asia or passed through these areas. We have already pointed out that harbours on the Andhra littoral were particularly suited for long-distance trade in the Bay of Bengal, especially with Burma and mainland/maritime Southeast Asia. Imports to Mottupalli largely came from Southeast Asia—a fact not only evident from the record of A D.1245, but also from the inscription of 1358. The combined testimony of inscriptions from Mottupalli and Marco Polo's account would also indicate that textile products were a staple item in the export trade from Mottupalli.

IV

The above study may help us fill up some gaps in the history of ports and maritime commerce on the Andhra coast before 1500. It also highlights that indigenous dataădmittedly handfulwhen compared and supplemented with the contemporary extra-Indian ones may yield encouraging results regarding the rise and fall of harbours of pre-1500 times. On the basis of what may be called the forerunners of later port documents, it is nearly impossible to present a reliable biography of these ports; but these may at least prompt us to take a close look at the changing fate of some harbours on a particular coast of India.

Visakhapattanam and Mottupalli seem to have shared certain common characteristics, in addition to the obvious one that they were situated in the same littoral. Both attained their prominence rather suddenly, mainly as a result of the support of the then political powers in the interior. An integration of Vengimandala with Tamil coast, politically and/or commercially, was a vital factor for the rise of these two ports to prominence and prosperity. This would suggest that the fate of the ports was considerably shaped by the politics of the hinterland. Eastern Deccan, the immediate hinterland of both Visakhapattanam and Mottupalli, was often a bone of contention between the rulers of Vengi and those of the central Deccan, western Deccan and Karnataka. Ever since the Eastern Calukya kingdom was established in the first half of the seventh century in Vengi, it was involved in protracted rivalry against the Rastrakutas, the Western Calukyas of Kalyani and the Colas. This rivalry continued during the Kakatiya occupation of Vengi; the Kakatiya hostilities with the Yadavas and Hoysalas[75] could have rarely generated the vital stability, so badly needed by the harbours of Vengi. The hinterland, often disturbed politically, yielded virtually only one important exportable commodity, namely textiles. All these factors probably led to the rather heavy dependence of Visakhapattanam and Mottupalli on some political powers which acted as the principal scaffolding of the two harbours.

Here probably lies a crucial difference between these two and the ports in Gujarat and Malabar. Ports in Gujarat and Malabar not only stood on major international maritime routes and reached out to faraway forelands, but also had extensive hinterlands and offered valuable transhipment facilities.[76] The Gujarat and Malabar ports seem to have outrun the Andhra ports like Visakhapattanam and Mottupalli on these scores. This may explain why Visakhapattanam and Mottupalli, despite considerable administrative propping and despite their early promise, did not finally attain their full potential. The uncertainties about a stable political support did not allow Visakhapattanam and Mottupalli to enjoy sustained commercial success like some of their more illustrious counterparts on the western littoral like Cambay, Cochin and Calicut.

It is tempting to suggest that these features of the two Andhra ports appear to have continued later even in the celebrated harbour of Masulipatnam. Arasaratnam finds that the success of Masulipatnam in the seventeenth century, too, depended "largely on the politics of the hinterland",[77] namely the kingdom of Golconda. The principal product its hinterland could offer was once again textiles, which largely catered the markets of mainland and maritime Southeast Asia. There were, of course, two major departures from the past tendencies. First, Masulipatnam had a thriving westward trade with the Persian Gulf, which must have contributed to the "rise of Masulipatnam to some position of significance in Oceanic trade".[78] And second, Europeans made their presence felt in the Bay of Bengal. But these developments and expansion of Masulipatnam's commerce notwithstanding, "it did not take on an extrepot role similar to Surat in relation to Coromandel exports and imports."[79] And when the Mughal conquest of Golconda unsettled the hinterland, it triggered off a series of administrative crises in the Andhra coast. Seen from such a perspective, one may perhaps hear in the affairs of pre-1500 Visakhapattanam and Mottupalli, the footsteps of Masulipatnam, and discern the shape of things that were to come in coastal Andhra during the seventeenth century.

NOTES

[1]Burton Stein, 'A Decade of Historical Efflorescence', *South Asia Research*, X (2), Nov. 1990, pp.124-38; the comment appears in the first paragraph of the essay.

[2]There has been a well-known debate on the significance of trade in early medieval economy of India. While D.D. Kosambi, R.S. Sharma, B.N.S. Yadava, D.N. Jha, etc. have culled material to suggest a slump in trade, 'monetary and urban anaemia' in the wake of the feudal social formations in India, D.C. Sircar, B.D. Chattopadhyaya and B.N. Mukherjee cite evidence, to the contrary, to the expansion of trade, regular use of different media of exchange including coins and the 'third urbanisation' in Indian history. See, for a recent statement of the debate on the nature of early medieval economy, B.D. Chattopadhyaya, 'Trends of Research in Ancient Indian Economic History', *Journal of Ancient Indian History*, XVIII (1-2), 1988-89 (1991), pp.109-31.

[3]Pierre Chaunu and Huguette Chaunu, *Seville et Atlantique,* VIII, pp. 1, 5 quoted in Ashin Das Gupta and M.N. Pearson (eds.); *India and the Indian Ocean*: 1500-1800, Calcutta, 1987, p. 8 (hereafter *IIO*).

[4]Franz Broeze (ed.), *Brides of the Sea,* Kensington, 1989, p. 8.

[5]For a general understanding of the Indian Ocean studies, vide K.N. Chaudhuri, *Trade and Civilization in the Indian Ocean from the Rise of Islam to the Seventeenth Century,* Cambridge, 1985; Satish Chandra (ed.), *The Indian Ocean: Exploration in History, Commerce and Politics,* Delhi, 1987 and *IIO.*

[6]Genevieve Bouchon and Denys Lombard, "The Indian Ocean in the Fifteenth Century", *IIO,* pp. 46-70.

[7]M.N. Pearson, "The State of the Subject", *IIO,* pp. 9-10.

[8]Pliny, *Naturalis Historia,* tr. J. Rackham, London, 1942, p. 381. The text reads: *Indorumque gens incipit, non Eoo tantum mari adiacens verum et meridiano quod Indicum appellavimus*" (VI.XXI. 56). I am deeply indebted to Prof. B.N. Mukherjee for kindly drawing my attention to this passage and also for allowing me to use his unpublished notes on this passage.

[9]The chart produced by the Royal Australian Navy Hydrographic Office in 1980, entitled, "Australia and the Adjacent Waters: Limits of the Oceans and Seas" had "created a Southern Ocean, girdling the world around Antarctica". Thus this chart places the southern limit of the Indian Ocean to the north of the Southern Sea; *IIO*, pp. 9-10.

[10]Fernand Braudel, *The Mediterranean and the Mediterranean World in the Age of Philip II,* English translation in two volumes by S. Reynolds, London, 1972.

[11]*Ibid.*, p.14.

[12]K.M. Panikkar, *The Geographical Factors in Indian History,* Bombay, 1955.

[13]K. Hariharan, *A Maritime History of India.*

[14]Bridget and Raymond Allchin, *The Rise of Civilisation in India and Pakistan,* Cambridge, 1982, pp.183-90; Shireen Rutnagar, *Encounter: Westerly Trade of the Harappans,* Delhi, 1981.

[15]E.H. Warmington, *Commerce between the Roman Empire and India,* Delhi, 1978 (reprint); R.E.M. Wheeler, *Rome beyond the Imperial Frontiers,* London, 1954; U.N. Ghoshal, 'Economic Conditions' in K.A. Nilakantha Sastri (ed.), *The Comprehensive History of India,* vol. II, Calcutta, 1957.

[16]David Whitehouse and Andrew Williamson, "Sasanian Maritime Trade", *Iran,* XI, 1973, pp. 29-49.

[17]K.N. Chaudhuri, *op.cit.*

[18]For a brief but clear account of the Bay of Bengal studies, see Ashin Das Gupta, *Vangopasagara* (in Bengali, the Bay of Bengal), Calcutta, 1989.

[19]*Hudud al 'Alam,* tr. V. Minorsky, London, 1937, p. 87. The term Harkand is obviously derived from Harikela, a country which generally denoted the south-easternmost littoral area of present Bangladesh, namely Chittagong, Comilla, Noakhali. The name of the area, i.e. Harikela goes back to at least seventh century A.D.

[20]O.H.K. Spate and A.T.A. Learmouth, *India and Pakistan, a General and Regional Geography,* London, 1967, p. 728ff.

[21]H. Sarkar, "Emergence of Urban Centres in Early Historical Andhra", B.D. Chattopadhyaya and B.M. Pande (eds.), *Archaeology and History,* vol. II, Delhi, 1987, pp. 631-41.

[22]The expression Coromandel coast generally denotes a major portion of the eastern seaboard, embracing areas up to the Andhra coast. The expression used here is synonymous with ancient *Colamandala,* i.e. the core area of the Colas in the Kaveri delta.

[23]K.A. Nilakantha Sastri, The Colas, Madras, 1955; G.W. Spencer, *Politics of Expansion: The Chola Conquest of Sri Lanka and Sri Vijaya,* Delhi, 1983.

[24]K.A. Nilakantha Sastri, *ibid.*

[25]K.R. Hall, *Trade and Statecraft in the Age of the Colas,* New Delhi,

1980.

[26]O.H.K. Spate and A.T.A. Learmouth, *op.cit.*, p. 734.

[27]K.R. Hall, "International Trade and Foreign Diplomacy in Early Medieval South India", *Journal of the Economic and Social History of the Orient* (*JESHO*), XXI, 1978, p. 81.

[28]V. Rangacharya, *A Topographical List of the Inscriptions of the Madras Presidency,* (*RTL*), 1991, Vol. II: 724, No. 92.

[29]*RTL,* vol. III: 1674, No. 63.

[30]K.A. Nilakantha Sastri, *op.cit.*, pp. 301-41.

[31]Later epigraphic evidence from the Pandya country in South India refers to naming of ports after the reigning king or queen. Thus Ulagamadevi Pattinam was named after the Pandya queen Ulagamadevi, *South Indian Inscriptions* (*SII*), Vol. VII: 214-15, No. 404. Similarly Virapandyapattinam and Kulasekharapattinam bear names of the Pandya kings Virapandya and Kulasekhara. Sonadukondan, an epithet of Maravarman Sundarapandya (A.D. 1216-41), is associated with the name of the port Sonadukondapattinam, *Annual Report of the Indian Epigraphy,* (*ARE*), 311 of 1964. Also see, P. Jayakumar, "Identification of Some Pandyan Ports", *Quarterly Journal of the Mythic Society,* LXXXII (3-4), 1991: 28-31.

[32]K.A. Nilakantha Sastri, op.cit., pp. 321-23. The account of the campaign is available in the *Kalingattupparani.*

[33]*ARE,* 1935-36, pt. II, para 2.

[34]B.D. Chattopadhyaya, *Coins and Currency Systems in South India,* 225-1300, (*Coins and Currency System*), Delhi, 1977, p. 57.

[35]Meera Abraham, *Two Medieval Guilds of South India,* Delhi, 1988. The presence of this mercantile guild in Southeast Asia is clearly attested by two inscriptions from Takua-pa (ninth century) and Loboe Toewa (late eleventh century). See K.A. Nilakantha Sastri, *South India and South East Asia,* Mysore, 1978, pp.172-7 and 237-47.

[36]Meera Abraham, *op.cit.*, pp. 62-3. That the Andhra coast attracted merchants of the far south is indicated by the renaming of the port of Ghantasala as *Colapandyapura.* It is quite evident that merchants from Cola and Pandya countries used to come fairly regularly at this ancient harbour near Masulipatnam. Vide, M. Krishna Kumari, *The Rule of the Chalukya-Colas in Andhradesa,* Delhi, 1985, p.169.

[37]*SII,* X, p. 651.

[38]The term *anjuvannattu* closely corresponds to *anjuvannam.* D.C. Sircar, *Epigraphia Indica* (*EI*), XXXV, pp. 291-2 shows that the term stood generally for a professional body, consisting of several types of craftsmen. The term, according to Sircar, had nothing to do with *hamjamana* or Parsi communities. Meera Abraham, *op.cit.*, p. 25 shows that the *anjuvannam* also included merchants. But it would be difficult to agree with Abraham that the term denoted Arab-Persian merchants, at least in the context of the Andhra coast. Early medieval Andhra did not have regular settlements

of Muslim merchants like those in Gujarat, Konkan, Malabar and Maabar (Coromandel) of the Arab chronicles. See, S.M.H. Nainar, *The Arab Geographers' Knowledge of South India,* Madras, 1942. That the *anjuvannattu* merchants came to the Andhra coast from Karnataka can be suggested on the basis of frequent references to them in inscriptions from Karnataka. Vide, K.V. Ramesh, *A History of South Kanara,* Dharwar, 1970.

[39]*ARE,* 374 of 1908.

[40]K.A. Nilakantha Sastri, *op.cit.,* p. 331.

[41]B.D. Chattopadhyaya, *op.cit.,* p. 60.

[42]K.R. Hall, *op.cit.; JESHO,* XXI.

[43]K.A. Nilakantha Sastri, *op.cit.,* p. 316. Also Chau-Ju-Kua, *Chu-fan-chi,* tr. Friedrich Hirth and W.W. Rockhill, St. Petersburg, 1911, p.100, note 6.

[44]Andre Wink, *Al-Hind,* vol. I, Delhi, 1990, p. 334.

[45]Chau-Ju-Kua, *op.cit.,* p. 95.

[46]Janice Stargardt, "Burma's Economic and Diplomatic Relations with China from Early Medieval Sources", *JESHO,* XIV, 1971, pp. 38-62.

[47]*Epigraphia Birmanica,* I, No.8, p.165.

[48]B.D. Chattopadhyaya, *op. cit.,* p. 262, serial No. 267.

[49]Claudius Ptolemy, *The Geographike Hupegesis,* tr. E.L. Stevenson, New York, 1932, vol. VII, 1.15.

[50]Though K.R. Hall is aware of Visakhapattanam as a Cola port (*op.cit.*), he mainly focuses his attention in the *Colamandala* region on Cola trade. Hence affairs in the Andhra coast are of marginal importance to him. But both Janice Stargardt (*op.cit.*), and Andre Wink (*op.cit.*) say nothing about the port and how Visakhapattanam rose to prominence in the long-distance trade of the early medieval Bay of Bengal.

Cola aggressive designs outside their core area have been seen by Burton Stein, *Peasant State and Society in Medieval South India,* Delhi, 1980 as the political activities of a segmentary State which could hardly integrate peripheral regions to the core because of the lack of a bureaucracy, the substitute of which was the ritual sovereignty of the Cola monarchs. George W. Spencer (*op.cit.*), following Stein, explains the Cola expansion and aggressive designsincluding the naval designs in Sri Lanka and Southeast Asiain terms of plunder dynamics and 'push' and 'pull' factors. The concept of the 'segmentary State' as applied in the case of the Cola realm has generated lively scholarly debates. For a critique of this formulation, see B.D. Chattopadhyaya, "Political Processes and Structures of Polity in Early Medieval India: Problems of Perspectives", Presidential Address, Section I, *Indian History Congress,* Burdwan Session 1983; also, R. Champakalakshmi, "Peasant State and Society in Medieval South India: A Review Article", *Indian Economic and Social History Review (IESHR),* XVIII, 1981. The discussion on the significance of the renaming of Visakhapattanam after Kulottunga may suggest that the Cola interests in the faraway Vengi country were deeper than that reflected by the theories of plunder dynamics and ritual sovereignty.

It may be of some significance that Kulottunga was shown a beautiful stone as a curious object (*Katchi*) by the king of Kamboja (Khmer). Similiarly, the king of Srivijaya in Southeast Asia requested in 1090 to grant villages to two *viharas* at Nagapattinam, the celebrated Cola port in the heartland of Cola territory. Is it possible to infer that Southeast Asian kings became interested in cultivating friendly relations with Kulottunga at a time when Kulottunga was trying to raise the status of Visakhapattanam and opening cultural/commercial dialogues with Pagan, the new intermediary area between the Colas and China?

[51]*RTL*, III, 1674, Inscription No. 61.

[52]*Ibid.*, Inscription No. 62.

[53]G. Yazdani (ed.), *Early History of the Deccan*, vol. II, London, 1960, Chapter on Historical Geography.

[54]*EI*, III, pp. 82-93. The passage reads "*Krsnaveni lavanabdhisamge dvipam*".

[55]*EI*, IV, pp. 32-54. The passage reads, "*Sindhuyugmantara desamccasesasasyaphalayutam*".

[56]*RTL*, II, Baptala Taluk, Inscription No. 107.

[57]Mottupalli Pillar Inscription, edited by E. Hultzsch, EI, XII, pp.188-97. "*Sakala dvipamtaripa desamtara pattanesu gatagatam.... samyatrikebhyah*".

[58]Shipwrecks as a result of terrible storms and cyclones were not at all uncommon in earlier times. O.H.K. Spate and A.T.A. Learmouth, *op.cit.*, pp.736-7 refer to a devastating cyclone in 1864 which killed 30,000 lives at Masulipatnam and ruined the prosperity of the port. For a general understanding of the practice of plundering ships that fell victim to storms etc., see Ranabir Chakravarti, "Horse Trade and Piracy at Tana (Thana, Maharashtra): Gleanings from Marco Polo", *JESHO*, XXXIV (2), June 1991, pp.159-82.

[59]*EI*, XII, p.197, fn.

[60]*Ibid.*, pp.195-7.

[61]B.D. Chattopadhyaya, *Coins and Currency Systems*, pp. 80-5; A. Appadorai, *Economic Conditions in Southern India, 1000-1500*, vol. II, Madras, 1936, pp. 701-27; B.N. Mukherjee, *The Indian Gold*, Calcutta, 1990, p. 20 states that "there is a superficial proximity" of the weight standard of 65-68 grains—which approximates the weight standard of 61.2 grains—"to the Arabic (Islamic) gold dinar (of c. 65-66 grains)".

[62]H. Yule (tr.), *The Book of Ser Marco Polo*, vol. II, London, 1903, pp. 295-98.

[63]Marco Polo similarly used the term Tana, i.e. Thana to denote the

whole of the northern Konkan. Ranabir Chakravarti, *op.cit.; JESHO*, pp.189-92.

[64]*RTL*, II, Baptala Taluk, Inscription Nos. 102-103; *ARE*, 601-602 of 1909. Mottupalli apart from being known here as Mukula, was also termed as *Desyuyakkondapattana* in the record of Ganapati, vide *EI*, Vol. XII, p.196, line 169.

[65]*RTL*, II, Baptala Taluk, Inscription No. 111.

[66]*Ibid.*, Inscription No. 111A. For a list of epigraphic records at Mottupalli, see *RTL*, II, pp. 757-9.

[67]S. Arasaratnam, *Merchants, Companies and Commerce on the Coromandel Coast*, 1650-1740, New Delhi, 1986.

[68]Chau-Ju-Kua was a government officer in charge of external trade and hence his account can be handled with some amount of certainty.

[69]Chau-Ju-Kua, *op.cit.*, p. 208.

[70]*Ibid.*, pp.193-94.

[71]A. Appadorai, *op.cit.*, vol. II, pp. 464-66.

[72]*The Culavamsa*, tr. W. Geiger and C. Mabel Rickmers, Colombo, 1929-30 refers to the importation of Burmese elephants to Sri Lanka.

[73]Chau-Ju-Kua, *op.cit.*, pp.170-5, particularly 171 and 172.

[74]*Ibid.*, p. 226, also fn.

[75]For a general account of these endemic wars, see, G. Yazdani (ed.), *op.cit.* and K.A. Nilakantha Sastri, *A History of South India*, Bombay, 1966 (3rd ed.).

[76]V.K. Jain, *Trade and Traders in Western India, 1000-1300*, Delhi, 1990 enlightens us on many aspects of the seaborne trade and ports of early medieval Gujarat. Malabar's advantageous position is eloquently described in Marco Polo, Ibn Battuta and Rashi-i-uddin. See K.A. Nilakantha Sastri, *Foreign Notices of South India from Megasthenes to Ma-Huan*, Madras, 1939. Malabar's Jewish connections are now better understood, thanks mainly to the stupendous research by S.D. Goitein, *Letters of Medieval Jewish Traders*, Princeton, 1973.

[77]S. Arasaratnam, "India and the Indian Ocean in the Seventeenth Century", *IIO*, p.116.

[78]*Ibid.*, p.103.

[79]*Ibid.*

MARITIME RELATIONS OF SRI LANKA (CEYLON) UP TO THE ARRIVAL OF THE WESTERNERS

Bertram E.S.J. Bastiampillai

Sri Lanka, known earlier as Ceylon, has been called by different names at different times by different people. It illustrates the fact that, as an island it came to be known widely, mainly because of its strategic location on the Indian Ocean. It is placed a few miles off the southern tip of India, separated from the subcontinent by a shallow stretch of water, the Palk Straits.

Greek and Roman accounts of Sri Lanka provide singular evidence of the history of the island's maritime contacts with ancient Europe. The earliest substantial foreign written sources relating to the country, are fragmentary, imprecise and repetitive. Consequently, those classical accounts have engendered speculation and interpretation.

The seafaring Greeks had discovered the island around the fourth and third century B.C. Among the earliest literary references found are the accounts of Onesicritus, who served in the army of Alexander the Great (350-23 B.C.); records of Megasthenes, the envoy of Seleucus I Nikator (321-280 BC) to the court of emperor Chandragupta Maurya (322-298 B.C.); and references made in the writing of the geographer Eratosthenes of Cyrene (267-196 B.C.). These accounts are founded on second-hand sources such as the material gathered by Onesicritus, Megasthenes and other sojourners from the Greek world; and merchants and envoys in ancient northern India with which Sri Lanka enjoyed relations during the latter half of the first thousand year B.C.,[1] across the sea.

Many of these earliest accounts are not available in their original versions but have been reproduced from other sources such as the *Geography* of Strabo and the *Natural History* of Pliny the Elder (A.D. 23-79). The *Geography* of Ptolemy (c. A.D. 150) gives a later and comprehensive account from the classical period while Cosmas Indicopleustes (c. A.D. 540) provides an extensive post-classical record. Over forty Greek and Latin writers have mentioned Taprobane, an earlier name given to Sri Lanka.[2]

These classical notices concentrate on details, giving lists of products, measurements of distances, coordinates of longitude and latitude and exact placement of ports, cities and areas in relation to faraway countries such as Sri Lanka. Also, Greek and Roman maps throw light on lands like Sri Lanka. In this respect, the map and description of Sri Lanka by Ptolemy are remarkable. Although the shape and size of the island are wrong, the data display substantial awareness of its existence, its coast, topographical features such as rivers and mountains, cities, towns and ports—material of interest principally to ocean-going venturers.

The Ptolemaic map, like the world map of Eratosthenes, and the later Arabic maps like those of the geographer Al-drisi, indicate Sri Lanka as a vital geographical entity of the Indian Ocean. It was depicted as an island of note off the South Asian coast, an utmost isle. These maps were constructed out of the knowledge conveyed by mariners and sea travellers and were meant to inform their patrons. Sri Lanka obviously was of significance for early maritime venturers across the ocean. To the classical world, the country seemed fascinating from a navigational and economic point of view.

Later on, during the time of Cosmas Indicopleustes, the island had definitely become the midway of the Indian Ocean, both for travellers from the west and for merchants. It was also an eminent entrâpot in those later times: its products comprised local articles and items brought for transhipment from eastward regions and other distant places.

Archaeological evidence, unearthed in older cities like Anuradhapura, a capital of early Sri Lanka, and Mantai, a port city of the early period, corroborates the evidence furnished by classical writers on the seaborne commerce and contact that the island enjoyed with the European world. The maritime intercourse of the classical world with Sri Lanka occurred at a time when the island's civilisation, culture and achievement were developed.

Mantai is one of the few surviving identified urban port centres when Anuradhapura dominated life on the island. This port city consisted of a raised mound with a horseshoe shaped plan, demarcated by earthen ramparts and a double moat. The site covered an area of about 125 acres. The area inside the moats was the place of main settlement; but evidence shows that even the area outside was inhabited and that there were roads outside. Trade and communication were important in the formation of the urban port city of Mantai, as archaeological study reveals.

The popularity and the use of Mantai as a major port from early times are evident from several and continuous references to this port discernible in different records and chronicles. The importance of Mantai—also known as Mantota, Mahatitha, Mattotom and by other names—in early maritime commercial and cultural interaction arose from the fact that Sri Lanka was a vital port in the Asian mainland's south. The island lay almost on the equator where navigational winds and monsoonal impact altered directions. It was the midway centre between the two great early empires of Rome and Peking.[3]

With such an advantageous position in the Ocean, Sri Lanka became an unavoidable point of call for anchorage, for ships awaiting the correct winds for onward journey, and for collecting victuals and supplies needed on voyages. Traders found in Sri Lanka a suitable place for the transhipment of goods and exchange of produce that formed the ware of commerce between the distant imperial centres of Rome and Peking, and the island.

Studies on the ports and the past capital cities of Sri Lanka, and discovery of foreign artefacts at such sites indicate close transoceanic links between the island and the wider world. Roman coins have been unearthed in Jaffna in the north, Kataragama in the south and in several other places of past importance, proving trade with the West. Likewise, Chinese ceramics and coins have been found at places like Jaffna, Mantai in the north and Galle and Tissamaharama in the south. Such discoveries confirm that there was lively commerce with China. Sri Lanka with its ports at the mouths of rivers meeting the sea, offered strategic and safe havens for commercial intercourse. No doubt, Mantai looms large in early maritime history as one of the finest ports, until the shallow water course later hindered larger vessels from berthing.

Many ancient sources have delineated the navigational routes reaching the island, having reckoned its geographical and geological conditions. The *Milindapanha* (1st century A.D.) details the lines of communication through the Straits of Mannar, connecting China with the Red Sea. An Egyptian scholar, Huzayyin, mentions that communication between Aden and the Malabar coast was never abandoned since it received a stimulus by the rise of

Ceylon. The route of early sailors, described by Dionysius Perigotes, speaks of the great island of Colias, Taprobane, mother of Asian-born elephants; elephants were an object of maritime trade. Fa-hsien, the Chinese scholar who engaged in the sedulous pursuit of truth, observed in A.D. 411 that the northeast winds had taken him to Sri Lanka from Tamralipti near Calcutta. From China there came later in 1405-7, the Grand Admiral Cheng Ho on his first expedition to the southern ports of India and Sri Lanka, with a fleet of 317 ships which docked in Beruwala in the southwest.

During the early centuries, the Mannar Channel off Sri Lanka was taken by the Greeks and Romans of the classical times, and Arabs and Persians of later times from the west; and the Indians, Burmese, Malayans, Indonesians and Chinese from the East. Ships from the west had apparently called at the old port of Kudiramalai. It was from here, then called Hippuras, that Annius Plocamus, the Roman Commander of a vessel, was welcomed by the Sri Lankan king's representatives who embarked as envoys to Claudius Ceasar (A.D. 41-54). Ships coming in from the east also touched Mahatitha, the ancient port.

The ships called at the ports in Sri Lanka to collect provisions and water, which were needed on long voyages. Sri Lanka, midway in the Indian Ocean, has several roadsteads and havens on the coast; and a fertile and developed hinterland naturally made it offer facilities for callers across the sea. In the eighth century, a pilgrim traveller monk saw that there were thirty-five Persian vessels at Mahatitha on their way to China.

Huzayyin confirms that the growth of navigation between West Asia and East Asia handled by the Persians, Arabs, Indo-Malaysians and Chinese made it possible for mariners to chart a still more direct course from Ceylon to Malacca or Java and thence to the ports of Tong-King and South China. He also affirms that during the sixth century, Sri Lanka enjoyed intimate relations with Ethiopia and was noted as a halfway station between Southeast and Southwest Asia. Apparently, the outward crossing of the Indian Ocean between Ceylon and the Gulf of Aden was more direct than the crossing from the island to the Gulf of Oman.

Trade was the principal concern that lured foreign vessels to the ports of Sri Lanka in the early times. The thirty-five Persian vessels en route to Canton had bartered some of their ware for Sri Lankan precious stones. According to a quaint Chinese record of the seventh century, Sri Lanka was situated in the middle of the southwest seas and the island had a surfeit of treasures: these were traded for money with the merchants who came in boats. The Greek writer Cosmas Indicopleustes, commenting on trade in Sri Lanka, pointed out the significance of the island as an emporium. Since Sri Lanka's position was central, it was the haven for ships from India, Persia and Ethiopia. Likewise, ships set out from the island. From China and other emporia Sri Lanka received silk, cloves, clove wood and other products which in turn were despatched to other places such as Male. Exports from other emporia were received in Taprobane and exchanged elsewhere along with the island's own produce. Sri Lanka, placed in the middle of the Indian Ocean, received goods from all nations and distributed them, thus emerging as a great emporium.[1]

Warmington thinks that South Indians controlled much of this trade. In the sixth century, trade tension between Sri Lanka and the Sassanid empire had been high. Hamzah-al-Isfahani noted that Emperor Cosroos-Nounchirwan despatched a fleet to subdue Sarendeeb island (Sri Lanka). During the later decades of the thirteenth century, Sri Lanka endeavoured to build up its trade with Egypt. Exports sent from Sri Lanka were pearls, gems, chank shells, tortoise shell, pepper, cinnamon, cloves and herbs, according to Warmington. War elephants and even birds were exported while horses were imported from Persia. Clearly, the trade of those times was in luxury goods.

As much as trade, evidence suggests that religious interests, too, inspired foreign contact with Sri Lanka from the early years of Buddhism. The Chinese scholar-monk Fa-hsien lived for two years (412-13) in Anuradhapura to collect Buddhist scriptures, to be used in China. After collecting the sacred texts, which were not available in the land of Han, he took them aboard a large trading vessel that could carry more than 200 people. A stern was fastened to a small vessel to insure against the perils of an ocean journey and damage to the larger vessel.

Especially for China, Buddhism and commerce seem to have been the two factors that stimulated its maritime contacts with Sri Lanka in those centuries. The Buddha image grew popular in China in the fifth century, when a Sri Lankan sculptor, Nante, visited the country with his articles and stayed behind to teach the craft. From Sri Lanka in the fifth century, Buddhist nuns were introduced to China.

Buddhism accounted for much of Sri Lanka's maritime contact with neighbouring lands. The mission of Mahindra, the son of Asoka, who introduced Buddhism into the island, came via the sea. Later on, a Sri Lankan Buddhist fraternity (*vihara*) was founded at Nagarjunakonda in southern India in the second century, at Buddha Gaya in the north in the fourth century, and in Ratubaka (Indonesia) in the eighth century. On these occasions, Sri Lankan monks went out on their mission across the seas.

A Sri Lankan Buddhist pilgrim assisted in constructing a railing at Buddha Gaya in the third century B.C. Similarly, repairs at the Amravati vihara were carried out by a Sinhalese monk from the Gadaladeni vihara. A king of Kashmir is said to have sought retirement at the Abhayagiri vihara in the fifth century. A minister in the fourteenth century from Sri Lanka, Sena Lankadhikara, sent money and men to set up a Buddhist shrine at Kanci, in southern India. Religious links prevailed between Siam and Sri Lanka in the eighth and fourteenth centuries. All these contacts, inspired by Buddhism, took place across the seas.

Sri Lanka also had political ties with its neighbours. Envoys and embassies were despatched across the seas. Between India and Sri Lanka on the one hand, and China and Sri Lanka on the other, maritime intercourse on account of politics had been common in the early centuries. There were several visits of political emissaries to China, particularly in the fourth, fifth, sixth and eighth centuries. Records also indicate that Sri Lankan envoys visited the Roman court during the first century A.D. Evidence of such Sri Lankan contacts made across the seas with foreign lands can be found in demi-official reports, trade news, travellers, tales, cartographers, notes, tales of pilgrims and travellers and legends. The trade news which throws interesting light on maritime contacts, deals with information on tariffs, taxes, tolls and the costs of articles available for sale or for barter. These data reveal the sophisticated and complex nature of maritime commercial intercourse between the island and foreign countries during the early centuries.

Information concerning trade and sailings to and from Sri Lanka seems to have been available to South Indian traders from Pandya country and merchants from China, Egypt, Burma and Indonesia. Accounts of travellers can be gleaned from writers like

Strabo, Onesicritus, Pliny the Elder, Cosmos Indicopleustes, Marco Polo and Ibn Battuta. Cartographers had drawn maps and made useful notes on Sri Lanka which would serve well the needs of mariners. Among the early cartographers who spent their effort on charting maps of Sri Lanka are Ptolemy and Idrisi, while among the better known religious travellers who wrote of the island are Fa-hsien, Hsuan-tsang, I-tsing and Vajrabodhi; some of these accounts, however, were based on second-hand information. There were several settlements of foreigners in Sri Lanka in those early times. The inhabitants were traders and merchants hailing from Persia, Arabia and other distant lands.[5]

The spread of Buddhism to Sri Lanka and religious interrelations thereafter, yield interesting and valuable information on the sea routes to Sri Lanka.[6] Buddhist influence during the Maurya era, specifically in the reign of Asoka, came along the eastern sea route from Tamralipti to Jambukolapattana. In the trek to and from India, the land route, too, was used in the early times, but yet, the Palk Straits had to be crossed in simple and ordinary local craft.

Influence from southern India came along the commonly used sea route from Andhra or used by traders from Kancipuram and Kaveripattanam in Tamil Nadu. While trade was always a motive for sea voyaging to the island, there was also a distinctive orthodox and unorthodox impact from South India on Buddhism in Sri Lanka. A stimulus was given to learning of Pali and Buddhism by scholar monks coming from or through South India.

Changes that occurred in Buddhist philosophy and practice in India after the first century A.D. were gradually introduced into the island either by visiting monks or merchants, who crossed the sea from the mainland. From Sri Lanka, too, spread out Buddhism and Buddhist influences over the seas, especially after the fifth century when the island was connected through expanding maritime trade by sea routes to many ports in Southeast Asia and China. Also, interestingly, after the tenth century, when Buddhism in Sri Lanka had waned owing to unfortunate vicissitudes, the faith in the island was vitalized, especially the priesthood, the *sangha*, by influences that came from Southeast Asian lands, Siam and Burma. The importance of the sea routes and the overseas nexus to the development of Buddhism in Sri Lanka is clear.

Expansion of Buddhism throughout India and beyond occurred simultaneously with the spread of overseas trade. Not only did produce come into the island and go out through sea trade, but so did ideas and practices into and from Sri Lanka. As early as the third century B.C., the Sinhalese had been making long sea voyages along the east coast of India up to the Ganges delta and along the Ganges to Pataliputra. A friendly mission from king Devanampiya Tissa (250-210 B.C.) to the Mauryan court set off the port of Jambukola in north Sri Lanka and reached Tamralipti at the mouth of the Ganges in seven days and up the Ganges to Pataliputra in another seven days.

Owing to the lively commercial and cultural exchange between Sri Lanka and North India, more than one route was used by traders, pilgrims and missionaries. From Pataliputra, there were three routes to the island; one came through Vedisa and Ujjain in Avanti, a large trading centre from early times, to Bharukachcha (Broach) on the western India coast. Then the journey was by ship traversing the western coast to Sri Lanka. During the reign of Asoka, Mauryan culture was introduced to the island via the sea.

Andhra was another area with which Sri Lanka had direct maritime commercial connections. Products from Sri Lanka were sold to Romans through South Indian ports and South Indian ships were used for transport. South Indian Buddhist influence also entered Sri Lanka across the sea.

Seaborne trade between Sri Lanka and Kantakasela, renowned emporium of the Krishna delta, was regular. Goods from Sri Lanka, ivory and tortoise shell, were common in South Indian ports. Again, religious influences accompanied seaborne traffic from southern India. Buddhadatta, a Tamil from the Cola land and Dhammapala from Kancipuram were southern Indian Buddhist scholars who came to Sri Lanka. After the fifth century, the interaction of scholars, monks, nuns and pilgrims grew. They braved the seas to keep alive contact from the mainland with the island.

Nagarjunakonda and Amaravati were active trading centres which had links with Sri Lanka. Mahayana influence came into the island from these places in the later years of the early period.

Cultural and religious intercourse accompanied trade to Sri Lanka from kingdoms in Southeast Asia and from China.[7] Unsettled conditions made the land route via Central Asia insecure, and then the sea route grew even more popular. Sri

Lanka, owing to its central and commanding position in the Indian Ocean, remained crucial in the sea route of traders and travellers. The merchant, the scholar, the pilgrim—all—took to the sea in quest of different values, and in this process they touched Sri Lanka.

Buddhist teachers joined merchant ships to cross the oceans in those early centuries, and there developed a close link between Buddhism and trade. Hardly surprising, since the Buddha himself had received much aid and encouragement from wealthy traders. Missionary efforts coincided with times of lively trade between South and Southeast Asia. The earliest Sailendra inscription of Java, the stone of Kalasan (A.D. 778), bears a Sanskrit reference that the temple was dedicated to goddess Tara who helped creatures to cross the ocean of suffering without fear; perhaps metaphorical yet significant, because it could well be an allusion to the maritime voyages of merchants and pilgrims. Tara meant star; and stars guided the sailors in their voyages.

Javanese Buddhists of the Sailendra period and other parts of Buddhist South Asia enjoyed cultural interrelations. Relations with the Indian subcontinent would have usually been through Sri Lanka, conveniently sited for sailors to halt at, before embarking on the longer voyage across the Gulf of Bengal to the Straits of Malacca.

There is evidence to surmise that Buddhism, like Islam later, spread along trade routes. Nevertheless, trade per se was important as it opened the way for Sri Lanka to maintain closer maritime relations with the West and East. It was a means of contact, before the age of tourism, that linked countries together.[8]

Literary references to relations between Sri Lanka and the Sabaceans and Phoenicians in the second century B.C. abound. These trade relations brought to Sri Lanka merchants who were also purveyors of the culture of their people. Sri Lanka got exposed to cultural influences from both the West and the East. Centrally situated on the transoceanic East-West sea route from Mombasa to the Moluccas, it was a haven to mariners and merchants on long journeys. Also, the fertile isle had a variety of merchandise which lured foreign merchant and mariner alike.[9]

Kufic inscriptions along the coast of Sri Lanka offer evidence of early visitors from Arabia. Sailing ships from Arabia and Persia touched the island, seeking trade or shelter from adverse weather. Midway between the Horn of Africa and the Straits of Malacca, Sri

Lanka became not only a necessary stopover but also an entràpot for the exchange of wares. Mariners, merchants, pilgrims and seafarers mingled, while a brisk exchange of cultures and produce of diverse lands took place.

Arab relations with Sri Lanka date back to the pre- Christian era. At the beginning, the economic motives of trade and commerce impelled the seaborne visitors; thence followed cultural influences. In the second century B.C., trade with Sri Lanka lay in the hands of Arabs. Then came competition from Greeks, Romans and Persians. By the beginning of the seventh century A.D., it was trade with China that grew dominant. While the Arab contact with Sri Lanka is learned from literary sources which are sketchy and incomplete, adequate data are available to support the story of this contact after the birth of Islam in the seventh century.

Contacts of Arabs with Sri Lanka after the rise of Islam show that there were maritime and trading activities of diverse ethno-cultural groups who inhabited large areas west of Sri Lanka, bounded by the shores of East Africa, Southern Arabia and the Persian Gulf. The eastward maritime contacts stretched up to the eastern archipelagos and Canton.

A single monsoon wind was insufficient for travel across from the Persian Gulf or the South Arabian ports to the Indonesian archipelago and beyond. Journeys had to be broken and Sri Lankan ports were frequented by voyaging vessels. Sheltered harbours offered facilities for repairs and servicing of vessels. There also were facilities for replenishing stocks of food and water. The adventurous trader bought valuable products for sale—spices, precious stones, pearls and ivory. Sri Lankan pearls had been sold from pre-Christian times to the wealthy of the Mediterranean and the Near East. The pearl banks of the island were situated off the coast of Mantai, a haven to merchants.

The island's chronicle, the *Mahavamsa,* records a gift of pearls by Prince Vijaya to the king of Pandya at Madura. In the days of Pliny, Sri Lankan pearls were esteemed in Rome. He remarks that the island's pearl fishery was productive while the pearl banks of the Persian Gulf were getting depleted. Ptolemy too, speaks of this pearl trade. He says that pearls had turned the island into a fascinating place for foreign merchants voyaging across the seas for articles of value.

Arabs and Moors seem to have visited the island to take part in the pearl fisheries as divers. In the Arab-Sri Lankan maritime trade, Mantai was a crucial port and premier emporium, till the Cola invasion heralded the decline of Mantai as a thriving port city. Archaeological surveys and excavations have confirmed the significance of Mantai in maritime commerce. Chinese and Islamic pottery ware, glazed ceramics from the Far East, glass from the Near East, glass beads, shells and cowries, copper and iron slags have been found, and remind us of Sunthramurthi Nayanar's sixth-century description of the commercial grandeur that the cosmopolitan port city, Tirukkestisvaram-Mantai, had once witnessed.

Mantai offers ample evidence of maritime contact with several countries and is the most popular port of the island referred to by Cosmos Indicopleustes in the sixth century. A community of Nestorian Christians had settled in Mantai, according to some. Settlements of traders on the coasts of the island were not uncommon, as archaeological finds and inscriptions indicate.

It was through emporia such as Mantai that the oceanic trade of China and the Near East got linked in the island, which offered the venue. Persians, Arabs, Chinese and East Africans took the leading role in sharing the commerce along with Indians from Gujarat in the west and Bengal in the east. The ports of Sri Lanka were used for storing and re-exporting the merchandise of the subcontinent, the eastern archipelago and China.

Arab trading activity in Sri Lanka and Asia after the seventh century got related to the expansion of Islam and Muslim political power. *The Thousand and One Nights* were Arabian tales based on the experiences of navigators composed in the early Abassid period (A.D. 750-800). Sri Lanka, which shared in the mercantile trade of the period, was familiar to navigators and received a place in the Arab tales as Serendib—the land of rubies. On his seventh voyage, Sinbad bore gifts from the king of Sri Lanka to the caliph of Baghdad. The Arab Muslim contact with Sri Lanka was really a continuation of the earlier contact of the Christian (Nestorian), Zoroastrian and Jewish maritime trade. Arab Muslims settled on the island and Muslim mystics came as visitors.

By the thirteenth century, Sri Lankan kings were seeking the friendship of the Arabs. An embassy was sent to the Arab court of Egypt in 1283 and from Yemen arrived an envoy at the court of the Sri Lankan king. The message despatched to Egypt referred to the pearl fisheries, precious stones and cinnamon. Ibn Battuta in A.D.1344 commented on the Arab dominance in the trade of the region and of Sri Lanka.

Maritime trade kept Arab-Sri Lanka relations briskly alive from the pre-Islamic to the post-Islamic period. Colonies of foreign Muslim merchants, beginning from the seventh century, settled along the southwest coast, maintaining cultural and commercial contacts with Baghdad and other Muslim countries. While earlier Sri Lankan-Arab relations focused on trade, later on religious and cultural contacts waxed stronger, reaching their zenith in the fourteenth and fifteenth centuries.[10]

Sri Lanka's maritime contact with China also goes back to an early date. A mission despatched by Wang Mang visited the island at the beginning of the first century A.D.,[11] while Sri Lankan ambassadors to the courts of Caudius at this time commented on the thriving maritime commerce between Sri Lanka and China. Embassies carrying gifts called on China in the first and second centuries. After the fourth century, such visits grew more frequent.[12]

These maritime contacts continued uninterrupted throughout the early centuries. Four Sri Lankan embassies called at the Chinese court during the early fifth century.[13] Eight *bhikkunis* (Buddhist nuns) from the island reached Nanking in 426 and three more in 429; and for the first time, an ordination ceremony of women took place in China. In 456, five Sinhalese monks, one an eminent sculptor, called on the Chinese Emperor. Religion and culture interlinked Sri Lanka and China through the maritime route.

By the second quarter of the sixth century, Chinese vessels and craft from other lands of the Far East brought into Sri Lankan harbours cargoes of silk, which were exchanged for the merchandise of the Persians and Axumites. East and West met at the entràpot of Sri Lanka.

Chinese texts furnish ample references to the exchange of embassies between Sri Lanka and China in the seventh and eighth centuries and maritime religious relations.[14] The records supply incidental references to the maritime intercourse, and occasionally, significant and valuable information on religious, cultural, economic and political matters. Brief references to the transoceanic contacts have been bequeathed by travellers, merchants, geographers and soldiers. The official records of Chinese emperors speak of embassies despatched and received and other political relations. The data from China are buttressed by local evidence, rock inscriptions and coins.

An account from China speaks of an embassy with an image of the Buddha from a Sri Lankan king to the Emperor during 405-418, after ten years' delay en route. Another Sri Lankan king sent a letter along with gifts to the Chinese court in 428; two other embassies from Sri Lanka bearing presents reached China in 430 and 435.

Indications of a fair measure of maritime trade between the countries abound. From China were received, for distribution westward, silk, aloes, clovewood and sandalwood. Gifts from Sri Lanka to China consisted of pearls, gems, filigreed gold and valances. From the Sri Lankan emporia, vessels from western lands collected merchandise landed from Chinese junks. Not only was Sri Lanka a distribution centre in this maritime commercial exchange but also exported its own produce East and West.

Among the series of embassies to China from Sri Lanka during 405 to 762, the envoys of king Silakala (518-31) to China sought trade. An impediment to this rather regular maritime trade and Sino-Sri Lankan cultural relations arose, however, after the mid-eighth century when the Malay empire of Srivijaya grew. It maintained commercial contacts with China severing China's links with Sri Lanka which were resumed only in the fifteenth century.[15]

Sri Lanka also served as a conduit of maritime mercantile relations between China and other lands. Eminent scholars of Mahayana Buddhism visited the island en route to the Far East from India. Gunavarman of the Kashmir royal family and Vajrabodhi, after sojourning in the South Indian Pallava court, visited Sri Lanka and went to China after having enriched their experience. The interest of Chinese scholar pilgrim monks in Sri Lanka often coincided with a ferment of Mahayana Buddhism in the island and the subcontinent.

The *Manasollasa*, an encyclopaedic work composed either by the Hoysala king, Somesvara II (1126-38) himself or during his reign, mentions textiles of Sri Lankan origin together with stuff from China. Foreign merchants from India, Arabia and China frequented the shores of Sri Lanka and established trading posts dealing in articles from diverse lands. According to Idrisi, ships from China and other distant lands called on the island with the wines of Irak (Iraq) and Fars (Persia).

Especially significant is the remarkable episode of the visits of the Chinese Grand Admiral Cheng Ho to Sri Lanka. The Ming Emperor sent out Cheng Ho across the seas to spread the power and prestige of the empire abroad. A demonstration of Chinese seapower would instil pride and confidence among Chinese subjects and demonstrate to foreign lands the prudence of forging friendly relations with the powerful Chinese empire. The many visits of Cheng Ho to Sri Lanka while seafaring abroad were a deliberate and integral aspect of Ming foreign policy.

Cheng Ho endeavoured to intimidate Sri Lanka to accept the supremacy of the Ming Emperor—an aberrant enterprise in the otherwise peaceful maritime contacts between China and Sri Lanka. Following Cheng Ho's maritime ventures, the trilingual inscription at Galle in south Sri Lanka offers significant evidence on the maritime intercourse between Sri Lanka and other countries. The inscriptions in Chinese, Persian and Tamil show that all these communities had braved the seas to trade and do business in Sri Lanka.

After the unusual interlude of Cheng Ho, from 1433 onwards maritime relations between Sri Lanka and China again became regular and cordial. Tribute-taking Sri Lankan missions crossed the seas to China in 1436, 1445 and 1459. Items of tribute included gems, coral, gold, crystals, baby elephants, various kinds of fragrant articles, fine cotton, golden orioles, small bowls and medicines. Not all these were indigenous; some were exotic. The list of articles indicates the island's brisk and lively maritime mercantile activity. Chinese sources make it evident that tribute-carrying missions to China ceased after 1460. Sri Lanka was united, more confident and stronger and saw no need to send any more such missions.

Between 1400 and 1460, Sri Lanka despatched to the court of the Ming Emperor six missions, commencing from 1416 and continuing through 1421, 1433, 1436 and 1445 to 1459. Likewise, Chinese Admiral Cheng Ho visited the island on at least five occasions; first in 1406 and then in 1409, 1411, 1432 and 1439. From 1400 to 1460 there prevailed close and constant political contact over the seas between the two countries. For the first time, it was in this era that China, so far apart, intervened in Sri Lankan politics.

Sino-Sri Lankan relations were also unusual owing to some other types of contacts. Sri Lankan craftsmanship in gold, silver, jade and gems was highly esteemed, and Chinese craftsmen came over to learn the skills. Chinese musical instruments and swords were imported by Sri Lanka. Chinese soldiers served in the army of the Sinhalese king, Parakramabahu III.

As a rule, the use of the seas in these centuries, when the West and the East enjoyed maritime contact with Sri Lanka, was governed by the principle of *mare liberum* and not by the principle of *mare clausum* or *mare nostrum*. Cheng Ho's attempt to assert Chinese overlordship over international waters and maritime relations was a rare exception to the open and free attitude to the use of the oceans and sea.[16]

The maritime routes to Sri Lanka from the East and West were also routes of commerce in the wider sense of communication and social interchange.[17] They conveyed not merely coveted material articles but also equally valuable yet less tangible ideas, myths and legends. They provided the means of communication between diverse peoples and of bringing together various rich civilisations. Through them, the world's major religions like Hinduism, Buddhism and Islam mingled with and influenced one another. Śri Lanka's contacts with other cultures came through the maritime routes; cultural contacts were forged with Greece, Persia, China and Islam. The story of early Sri Lanka illustrates close interconnection between commercial and cultural exchange via the maritime routes. All this mainly peaceful exchange ended, however, when the Portuguese arrived in the sixteenth century, introducing Christianity, commerce and culture through coercion.

Maritime contact with pre-sixteenth century Sri Lanka engendered an exchange of technical, technological and scientific knowhow and a transfer of skills and craftsmanship. Observation and discourse enhanced and enriched knowledge. Much of this activity has gone, unfortunately, unrecorded. Much evidence is available, but what is still unknown of Sri Lanka's maritime relations remains immense. Data on the type of craft, technology practised in navigation and sailing and more information on methods and modes of exchange, on tariffs and taxes, on the machinery and mechanics of the management of ports and maritime intercourse and on repairing and victualling of vessels would be welcome indeed.

The scholar would welcome more investigation to help pursue in greater detail a study of what was then known on scientific nautical matters, cartography, ocean current movements and sea-lanes, and even expeditions to and from Sri Lanka. Also, closer sedulous search and study are needed of crafts, ports and the use of shallow draughts and secure anchorages.

The ports of Sri Lanka, especially Trincomalee no doubt, retained their strategic value even thereafter. The Portuguese used Hormuz, Colombo and Malacca as ports under their control to maintain a monopoly of the seas to the west and east of Sri Lanka. Later, under the British, when Anglo-French rivalry in India prevailed, it was Trincomalee that became strategically more significant. Thereafter, while Galle until the 1870s, and then Colombo, became commercially important ports and were used also in carrying passenger traffic to Australia and beyond, Trincomalee lost lustre, waiting to be resurrected once more as an important harbour in the First and Second World Wars.[18]

More recently, Trincomalee gained importance when India showed serious concern over it because of her own strategic and security interests as evidenced by the Indo-Sri Lanka Agreement of July 1987. Sri Lanka has thus commanded continuous significance in maritime movements in the Indian Ocean, whether commercial or military. Because of this, maritime relations have throughout been important in the island's historical development.

The ports of Sri Lanka, particularly Colombo, remain busy even today. Colombo ties up all the region's business, to the island's profit. Another peculiar purpose served by the ports now, especially in the north of the island, is as conduits for the supply of relief and provisions to people suffering in a protracted ethnic strife. The State's security forces use ports and roadsteads around the island's north and east to wage their war against the Sri Lankan Tamil militants who are clamouring for a State of their own and are locked in a confrontation against the Sinhalese-dominated State. The ports now serve purposes other than they did in the early and medieval times of Sri Lanka's history.

NOTES

[1]See Weerakkody, D.P.M., "The Earliest Greek Notices of Sri Lanka" in *The Sri Lanka Journal of the Humanities,* 10 (1-2), pp. 1-26.

[2]See Weerakkody, D.P.M., "Sri Lanka through Greek and Roman Eyes" in S. Bandaranayake, et al. (eds.), *Sri Lanka and the Silk Road of the Sea,*

Colombo, 1990.

[3]See Roland, Silva, *Mantai—The Great Emporium of Cosmas Indicopleustes*, Colombo, 1990.

[4]See Nicholas, C.W. and S. Paranavitana (eds.), *University of Ceylon, A Concise History of Ceylon,* Colombo, 1961, pp.1-16, 95-121, 159-83, 247-76 and 318-40.

[5]See Roland, Silva, *op. cit.*

[6]See Lorna, Dewaraja, "The Impact of the Sea Route on the Development of Buddhism in Sri Lanka", a paper presented to the Maritime Silk Route—International Seminar, Colombo, 1990.

[7]See J.G. De Gasparis, *Expansion of Buddhism into South East Asia,* Colombo, 1990.

[8]*Ibid.*

[9]See M.A.M. Shukri, *Arab Contact with Sri Lanka—Sindbad and Ibn Batuta,* Colombo, 1990.

[10]*Ibid.*

[11]See K.M.M. Werake, "A New Date for the Beginning of Sino-Sri Lankan Relations" in *The Sri Lanka Journal of the Humanities,* IV (1-2), Peradeniya, pp. 64-73

[12]See John M. Senaveratne, "Chinese-Sinhalese Relations in the Early and Middle Ages" in *Journal of the Royal Asiatic Society,* XXIV (69), 1915-16, Colombo, 1916, pp. 74-105.

[13]See *University of Ceylon, History of Ceylon,* vol. I, parts I & II, Colombo, 1959, pp. 302, 362, 379 & 383 and pp. 5-7.

[14]See Henry P. Abayasekera, "A History of Long, Fruitful Ties", *Daily News,* 1 October 1990.

[15]See G.P.V., Somaratna, "Grand Eunuch Ho and Ceylon" in *Journal of the Ceylon Branch of the Royal Asiatic Society,* New Series, vol. XV, Colombo, 1971, pp. 3-47; Werake, K.M.M., "A Re-examination of Chinese Relations with Sri Lanka during the Fifteenth Century A.D." in C.R.De Silva and Sirima Kiribamune (eds.), K.W. *Goonewardene Felicitation Volume,* Peradeniya, 1989, pp. 89-102; Abayasekera, Henry P., op. cit.

[16]See B.E.S.J. Bastiampillai, *China-Sri Lanka: Trade and Diplomatic Relations Including the Voyages of Cheng Ho,* Colombo, 1990.

[17]See "Sri Lanka as the Mid-point in the East-West Silk Route and the Centre of Convergence of the Cross Currents of Buddhist Philosophy", *Address by Frederico Mayor at the Opening of the Seminar,* Colombo, 1990.

[18]See H.A. Colgate, "The Royal Navy and Trincomalee: The History of their Connection, c. 1750-1958", *Ceylon Journal of Historical and Social Studies,* VII, Peradeniya, 1961, pp. 1-16.

AN ENQUIRY INTO THE PRESENCE OF THE CHINESE IN SOUTH AND SOUTH-EAST ASIA AFTER THE VOYAGES OF ZHENG HE IN EARLY FIFTEENTH CENTURY

Haraprasad Ray

The sudden disappearance of the Chinese from the Malabar coast during the mid-fifteenth century has remained an enigma in the history of Asia's maritime trade. Except for stray references, no serious attempt seems to have been made to study it in depth. What is more, Chinese sources have remained virtually untapped.

This paper examines this question from different angles. First, whether the Chinese disappeared from the Kerala coast altogether; if so, why? Secondly, did Chinese maritime trade in South and Southeast Asia cease altogether? And last, what impact did the cessation of voyages have on Chinese overseas trade?

REFERENCE TO CHINA IN FOREIGN LITERATURE

We have no direct Chinese evidence to indicate the cause of Chinese withdrawal from Calicut or, for that matter, Kerala coast. But we can make some logical assumptions from an analysis and contrastive study of available data.

We do not know of any reference to the Chinese either in Bengali or any other language during and after the fifteenth century, although Bengali literature is full of accounts about the Turks and other Muslims. The only Indian reference is from the testimony of Joseph of Cranganore in Kerala, preserved in the Portuguese accounts discussed in the following pages.[1] Besides, the Dutch captain Nisuhoff, speaking about Quilon, the lower or little Gelan (Quilon) of the Chinese, says that it was known as Coulang China, probably because that was the portion occupied by the Chinese settlement.[2] Similarly, according to Marignolli, (mid-fifteenth century) Cranganore was known earlier as Cynkali, signifying "Little China".[3] Garcia de Orta (1563) mentions a Chinese stone with apparently an inscription, as having been taken away by the Zamorin (Samuttiri) from Cochin. This stone tablet was, obviously, the one sent by Yongle. It consecrated a mountain as "the guardian mountain of the country" and contained a long inscription; a poem appended at the end, is supposed to have been composed by the emperor himself.[4]

The only other reference to Zheng He's voyages to the Indian Ocean, so far as we know, comes from an Arab record included in the Japanese work on Zheng He by Torada Takanobu. It states, inter alia, that the Chinese fleet, which visited the Yemeni court during the reign of Al-Malik al-Nasir of the Rasulid dynasty between 30 December 1418 and 27 January 1419, brought gifts equivalent to 20,000 *miscals,* comprising expensive perfumes, scented wood and Chinese pottery. The Chinese envoy, presumably Zheng He, was accompanied by the Yemeni envoy, Kadi Waqif al-Abdur Rahman bin Zumeir, who escorted him to the court. The Arab ruler sent, in exchange, luxury goods and objects made from corals at the port of Ifranza, wild cattle and asses, domesticated lion cubs, wild and trained leopards. The Yemeni envoy accompanied the Chinese to the port of Aden with the gifts. The Chinese visit to Mecca in June 1432 is also noted by Arab historians. This means that a two-way trade was maintained under the facade of exchange of gifts.[5]

CHINESE WITHDRAWAL FROM KERALA COAST

After 1439, we do not hear of any Indian envoy visiting the Chinese court nor any Chinese ship coming to the shores of Bengal or Kozhikode. When Abdur Razzak of the court of Shahrukh visited Kozhikode in 1442, he noticed many Chinese merchant ships in Ormuz which fell on his way to Kozhikode,[6] but he does not mention the presence of any Chinese on the shores of Kozhikode. His description of Kozhikode people as 'chinibachagan', does not, to our knowledge, refer to 'sons of the Chinese'. The text makes it clear: "The inhabitants of Calicut are adventurous sailors; they are known by the name of *tchinibetchegan (chini-bachagan),* and pirates do not dare to attack the vessels of Calicut."[7] The expression 'chini' is clearly an adjunct describing the inhabitants of Kozhikode, who were brave sailors. In Malayalam, the word *'cina'* means 'large cargo boat'.[8] Hence 'Chinibachagan' (*cinibacagan* or *tchinibetche-gan*) means 'boatmen', ship-boys, i.e. the sailors employed on ships, the ocean-going large vessels. The Chinese would not have shed their Mongolian features so soon; in which case, Abdur Razzak ,who described the Keralites as dark skinned in the same context,[9] would have surely noted their features if they were of Chinese origin, as he had already come across them in Hormuz.

The sudden disappearance of the prosperous Chinese merchants from the Kerala coast would have appeared as amazing as the stoppage of the voyages, but for a chance reference in one of the Portuguese voyages.

There is a reference to the withdrawal of the Chinese from Kozhikode in the reliable testimony of Joseph of Cranganore, dated before 1505, and briefly noted before. It suggests that the Chinese were forced to withdraw from Kozhikode between the thirties and forties of the fifteenth century (about eighty years before the testimony) because of outrages committed against them by the Samuttiri, after which the Chinese gathered a large armada, attacked and pillaged the city, and left for ever.[10] The cause of outrage by the local king is ascribed to the instigation by the Arab traders, who were envious of the competition from the prosperous Chinese.[11] After this fiasco, the Chinese junks occasionally visited Nagapattinam port under the Vijayanagara kingdom.[12] An echo of this incident is also found in the information supplied by Girolamo Sernigi to his Florentine correspondent, after Vasco da Gama's return, about the incursion into Malabar by long-haired warriors, supposedly the Chinese but mistaken by the Portuguese as slaves or Germans, because of their complete ignorance about Chinese presence in the area, and also because the Chinese skin resembled the European.[13]

There is an indirect evidence to confirm Joseph's evidence. So long, scholars have believed that Zheng He died around 1435, when he was Commander of the Nanking Garrison. But some textual evidence, discovered recently, establishes that Zheng He died at Kozhikode.[14] If this is taken as convincing proof—of which the Chinese scholars have no doubt—then the year of his death, which is given as 1433, coincides roughly with the period vouched by Joseph. Could it be that Zheng He's death had a link with the violence incited against the Chinese! Is it possible that he was killed in this violence or during the violent reprisal let loose by the

Chinese, which caused damage to the port? The Chinese Admiral might have been either killed or seriously injured and died on his way back home. The mutual destruction thus caused led to the expulsion of the Chinese, without any trace left for posterity. This incident adds a new dimension to the Chinese presence in this part of the Indian Ocean.

That the Chinese did not visit Kozhikode is proved by Abdur Razzak's evidence also.

THE IMPERIAL BAN AND INTERNAL CONVOLUTIONS

Stoppage of Chinese voyages to South Asia has been related to the stringent ban imposed by imperial order on private as well as official maritime voyages. Among the reasons for the ban are: the rise of the Confucian bureaucracy; their hatred for and opposition to the rise of the eunuchs; the Mongol and other tribal menace on the north and northwest border; the drainage of national wealth due to protracted war with the Annamese (the Vietnamese); expensive and unprofitable tribute trade, encouraged by the eunuchs, but opposed by the officials (during the later stage); and the *Wokou* (Japanese) pirate menace on the coastal areas. All these factors have been analysed extensively by various scholars. The present author, who has discussed them in detail, has a somewhat different tale to tell.[15] Shipping at Quanzhou was shifted to Fuzhou in 1474 during the Chenghua reign.[16] Fuzhou and nearby areas had become a busy port since the third voyage of Zheng He (1409-11). All the ships used to be anchored at Taiping-gang (old name Majiang) in Fuzhou during both the outward and return journeys.[17] This change of trading port, however, adversely affected the silk trade as also the economic condition of the local populace, which continued with their private trade through various clandestine means.[18]

Almost all the ports were infected with this malaise. According to one estimate, tariff obtained by the treasury from Guangzhou (Canton) was insignificant—a little more than forty thousand *liang* a year—while the Chinese officials in the port cities and intimately connected with the private traders reaped enormous profit from the illegal trade they encouraged for their own benefit.[19]

In the reigns of Hongwu (Taizu) (1368-99) and Yongle (Chengzu) (1403-24), the country was ruled by the sword. Imperial power was at its height and many administrative policies were enforced with the vigour of martial law. The entire population across the country was under registration, with each family permanently confined to its registered domicile and occupation. Military power among all the vassalages was successfully terminated, and feudal autocratic rule of absolute monarch was further strengthened.[20]

The court's stringent economic control was not limited to taxation. Materials and services were called for by acquisition. Military supplies such as bows, arrows, and winter garments, and palace supplies such as wax, tea, fresh food, dyes, charcoal, lumber, paper and medicines were all contributed by the people. Basic metals, including copper and iron, were either mined by the State or requisitioned from civilian sources.[21]

This virtually eliminated a great portion of the cost of governmental operation, while aggravating the penury of the people, especially when we consider the frequent embassies visiting in and out of China, covering by road all the distances from the port of disembarkation to the capital and back. All their expenses had to be borne by the people. Silver and other precious metals were forbidden in private transactions. The court rarely paid anyone in gold or silver. Grain payments were supplemented with paper currency, which was neither convertible nor backed up with valuables.[22] In the 1430s, government paper currency as the only legal tender was formally abandoned as it was found unworkable. By 1450, its value had depreciated by one thousand times,[23] so that even the Chinese were reluctant to accept it. The foreigners declined to accept it, demanding silk, porcelain and large sums of copper coins as largesse, and as payment. The Ming government could not compel the foreign envoys to sell the merchandise they imported at arbitrarily low prices, but had to pay the market rates.[24] In 1453, a Japanese embassy brought in supplementary tributary goods. The Board of Rites appraised these at 34,700 strings at the current rate. The price was settled at 44,700 strings of paper notes at the old Xuande rate, but the Japanese demanded 207,000 strings at the current rate.[25] After long haggling, the price was settled at 44,700 strings.[26] In 1464, the Board of Rites reported that the foreign envoys utterly refused to accept the notes, and suggested that they be paid in silk and textiles.[27]

Paralleling the physical decay of the navy, demoralisa-tion of the personnel had gone so low that, according to a report in 1442 , the government troops engaged in defence against the *Wokou* anchored their warships in the ports. Some returned home, others engaged in commerce, trafficked in illicit salt, fished or gathered firewood.[28]

While the rich and powerful families prospered, the poor suffered from the bans on maritime commerce and sea voyages. Demoralisation and desertion set in, in the army also.[29] The fighting personnel were employed on grain transportation on the canal, mostly as stevedores. The practice of rotating the troops to Peking for periodic drills during the Xuande period (1425-35), and their employment now and then as labourers in palace and temple construction, degraded and humiliated them.

In the early Ming period, the navy boys travelling abroad received an additional subsidy to the extent of a third of their pay, and those who went with the voyages were liberally rewarded.[30] By the Chenghua period (1465-87), the subsidy was cancelled, and a system of rotation was introduced, by which the men were remunerated for only six months of work.[31] Moreover, according to a practice instituted in 1435, the men were required to supply at least thirty per cent of the cost of building and repairing ships. Such heavy burden compelled the hapless men to sell their belongings, and even their children, to meet the expenses.[32] A large number had no option but to join the pirates for their livelihood.

CHINESE WITHDRAWAL FROM THE INDIAN OCEAN—A MYTH?

The rich and powerful families, on the other hand, despite vigorous protests of the officials and the curbs imposed by the authorities, increased their landed estates. The influential members of the court, the local magnates and rich merchants accumulated vast amount of wealth.[33] Not only did they engage in such nefarious business as hoarding of goods and manipulation of currency, they also defied the law by smuggling and trafficking with foreign adventurers.[34] The powerful families of Fujian and Zhenjiang, for example, traded with Japanese pirates.[35] Their associates at court protected them and carried out their bidding. Palace attendants outfitted merchant ships and the criminal elements of the coast abetted them in making profits.[36] Honest officials tried to curb them but failed. These corrupt officials were euphemistically called 'pirates who wore caps and gowns'.[37] Wei Juan, the Superintendent of merchant ships at Guangzhou, was an example of eunuchs who prospered from private trade and who misused their official positions to undermine the tributary system.[38]

As the maritime prohibitions were increasingly enforced, the illegal private trade operators joined with pirate ships. Maritime trade was an inevitable trend and a source of income for people in the coastal provinces, as for most of them agriculture was not profitable. From middle fifteenth century onwards, there had been a great spurt in the building of private ships and in non-official intercourse with foreign countries. Zhang Xie, author of *Dongxi Yang Kao* (A Study of the Eastern and Western Ocean) (1618), notes: "During the Chenghua and Hongzhi reigns (1465-1505) there were those among the rich and major families who travelled in large ships to trade abroad".[39] Foreigners continued to come to China for tribute trade, and Chinese traders, especially the coastal residents of Southeast China, began trading with foreign countries in their own private ships.[40] This continued till they were supplanted by the Europeans, who continued to maintain the chain and later monopolised it.

CHINESE TRADE IN SOUTH AND SOUTHEAST ASIA

These traders and many unscrupulous officials invested their capital in overseas commercial ventures and built large ships for foreign trade. The men of the coastal districts, who had a long maritime tradition, sailed these vessels as sailors to avoid starvation. With the introduction of new techniques of cotton processing, and paper and textile manufacture, the rich region of the lower Yangtze had grown richer and, hence, needed foreign markets. Zhejiang and Fujian exported porcelain and many other products. Zheng He's naval voyages had paved the way for a wave of Chinese migration to Southeast Asia and increase in commercial intercourse with this region.[41] The Arab and Persian traders had suffered a setback due to aggressive Chinese naval voyages to the far end of the Indian Ocean, verging on armed trade.[42] The foreigners were no longer required to come to the Chinese ports to obtain Chinese products; instead, the great junk fleets of China now carried Chinese produce into all parts of the continent to contend for commerce in the East. The Chinese traders were also active in the east coast of Tamil Nadu (Vijayanagar kingdom), as confirmed by Joseph of Cranganore as also by some paintings which show Chinese traders along with the Arabs during the sixteenth century in a temple of Tirunelveli district of Tamil Nadu.[43] The evidence of Tomé Pires (early sixteenth century), Mendes Pinto (the mid-sixteenth century Portuguese adventurer), and others, shows that even in the first half of the sixteenth century, Chinese ships were still navigating in the eastern Indian Ocean.[44] Private trade transplanted the official tributary trade that the Zheng He voyages helped to flourish.[45] As it paid huge returns, the rich and influential investors had to safeguard their interest. For them, the eventual ban on foreign travel and trade came as a blessing in disguise.

Recent studies, which are still continuing and hence incomplete, have provided us with evidence which shows the presence of Chinese porcelain ware of different qualities (like white-and-blue porcelain) on the coast of Tamil Nadu . This porcelain ware, belonging to sixteenth-seventeenth centuries, is spread over large areas like Vellore, Golconda and even as far as Fatehpur Sikri. This widely used popular ware was probably brought by the Chinese traders themselves. The possibility of some of it being brought by Indian traders from Malacca, etc., cannot be ruled out. On the other hand, the evidence from the western coast belongs to the thirteenth-fourteenth centuries.[46] A few items, belonging to the seventeenth century and later, may have been brought by Indian or western traders. There is an indirect reference in Sri Lankan literature to the scene of maritime trade shifting from the west to the east coast of India. A poetical work, *Gira Sandesays,* written during the reign of Parakramabahu, probably the sixth (1412-67), describes how the Sri Lankan ruler invaded the port of Adivirama (Adhiramapattanam in Tanjore district) because a ship (presumably a trading ship) he sent there had been plundered by the ruler of the region.[47]

Misgivings regarding continuity or otherwise of trade persist among scholars. But it is a mistake to see China's maritime activity as a part of royal activity only. Commercial activity and mutual trade among nations, after all, have continued from time immemorial more due to individual or group initiative than mere State patronage. State interest originated only when the court saw it as a profitable enterprise enriching the royal coffer. This proves Braudel's significant remark that "although the State was much stronger than society, it was not stronger than the economy"; and the economy was sustained through private initiative only.[48]

State-sponsored trade tends to be stupendous in volume because of regal pomp and show of prowess. It is costly and unwieldy, hence not sustainable for a long period due to contradictory forces, specially when royal patronage is missing.

A rough contour of the entire spectacle is visible now. At the turn of the century, we find the Chinese at the periphery of Asian trade. The Chinese voyages (1405-33) started with limited aim, presumably military, but gradually transformed into mainly commercial venture, with the eunuch Zheng He at the helm; and for a time the Chinese became contenders for a place in Asian trade, the trade missions reaching out to such remote countries as Aden, Mogadishu, Malinde and Mecca. The Arabs saw in it a threat to their interest, and hence, contrived to expel the Chinese from Kozhikode (Calicut) through their powerful clout at the Samuttiri court. Having been forced to leave Kozhikode, they shifted their attention to the Tamil Nadu coast during the mid-fifteenth century. During the early sixteenth century, Tomé Pires finds them concentrated on the Malacca port. It is also possible that before the advent of the Portuguese, the Chinese operated from Semudera (northern tip of Sumatra, adjacent to Achin of the later period) also, since this was a busy *entrepot* during the fifteenth century, as testified by the Chinese.[49] All trading ships stopped there, and the Chinese treated it as a garrison from where parts of the flotilla went to Bengal, Sri Lanka and Kerala.[50] After the Portuguese conquest of Malacca in 1511, they shifted to Patani on the eastern coast of the peninsula. The private traders wanted to avoid risk and expense. They preferred Patani because it was nearer to China, voyages were short and profits larger.[51] This was the safest and best way to thrive under those trying circumstances, with no safeguard from the State. It was presumably from these ports of Southeast Asia that the Chinese transacted their trade with the Coromandel coast.

Once the Chinese traders left the western shores of India, there was no coming back. Local enmity inhibited them. Besides, the voyages to the western coast were very costly, made possible by State financing alone. The traders, once they shifted to the east India coast and thence to the Malayan peninsula, did not feel encouraged to take the long voyages to the west, primarily because trading on the nearer ports was already highly profitable.

It is, however, too early to jump to a definite conclusion. Accepting the limitation of historical evidence, it may nevertheless be pointed out that such a hypothesis is justified, unless disproved by fresh revelations.

SUMMARY OF DISCUSSION

In the discussion that followed, it was pointed out that the Periyar river changed course during 1441, and led to the decline of the port of Kozhikode (Arunachalam). The author pointed out later that Kozhikode is on the Beypore river, and all the areas around it are still existing without being in any way affected topographically. Many such areas, including the present-day Silk Street, carry signs of reminiscences of China. Then, it was remarked that in Batavia and the Philippines the riots against the Chinese did not lead to their desertion of the port (Van Goor). During private discussion, it was pointed out that the Chinese as a whole were not opposed by the local powerful lobbies in these places. The local authorities were not inimical to them; what is more, there was sharp reaction from the Chinese government against these atrocities. Besides, there was no alternative location to fall back upon as a recompense. Hence, there was no question of the Chinese abandoning them; for the Chinese, they were vital ports. On the other hand, Kozhikode palpably did not provide such favourable conditions: neither an imperial umbrella nor local Indian support, so to say, was extended to them. The imperial ban was already in the offing.

NOTES

[1]W.B. Greenlee (tr. and ed.), *The Voyages of Pedro Alvares Cabral to Brazil and India*, London, 1938, p. 109.

[2]D. Ferroli, *The Jesuits in Malabar*, vol. I, Bangalore, 1939, p. 14. Ma Huan and others' accounts of early fifteenth century call it "Little Gelan", see Feng Chengjun (ed.), *Yingyai Shenglan Jiaozhu* (Yingyai Shenglan of Ma Huan annotated), Taipei (Reprint), 1970, pp. 37-8.

[3]H. Yule, H. Cordier, *Cathay and the Way Thither*, vol. III (republished), Taipei, 1966, p. 249.

[4]Ming Taizong Shilu, (Taipei ed., 1961-66), J.183, pp.1b-2b.

[5]Terada Takanobu, Zheng He, Tokyo, 1981, pp.124-5. Text obtained by courtesy of Prof. Zhou Shaoquan of the Institute of Historical Studies, Academy of Social Sciences, China, Beijing. The text was very kindly explained to me by Mr. S.K. Chaudhuri, Reader in Japanese, University of Delhi. The Chinese Mission's visit to Mecca was due to political disorder

in Yemen; K.N. Chaudhuri, "A Note on Ibn Taghri Birdi's description of Chinese ships in Aden and Jedda", *Journal of the Royal Asiatic Society of GB & Ireland,* 1989, p.112.

[6]R.H. Major (ed.), *India in the Fifteenth Century,* 1857, Delhi (reprint), 1975, pp. 5-6.

[7]*Ibid.*, p. 19. Major wrongly translates the expression as "son of the Chinese", following the French translation by Quatremere.

[8]B.C. Balakrishnan (ed.), *Malayalam Lexicon,* vol. V, Trivandrum, 1985, p. 462.

[9]R.H. Major, *loc.cit.*

[10]W.B. Greenlee, *loc.cit.*; for date of the testimony, see p.105; for reliability of his statement, see pp. 95-7.

[11]See K.P.P. Menon, *History of Kerala,* vol. I, Ernakulam, 1924, p. 287.

[12]W.B. Greenlee, *op.cit.*, p.109; see also G. Bouchon, "Les Musulmans du Kerala", *Mar Luso Indicum,* vol. II, 1973, pp. 49-50.

[13]See G. Bouchon, *ibid.*, p. 49.

[14]Zheng Yijun, *Lun Zheng He Xia Xiyang* (on Zheng He's Voyages to the Western Ocean), Beijing, 1985, pp. 335-7.

[15]See my paper "The Eighth Voyage of the Dragon that never was: An Enquiry into the Causes of Cessation of Voyages during early Ming Dynasty", *China Report,* 23(3), 1987, pp. 157-78.

[16]Sa Shiwu, "Ming Chenghua Jiajing Jian Fujian Shibosi Yizhi Fuzhou Kao" (Shifting of the Fujian Office of the Maritime Shipping to Fuzhou during Chenghua Reign), *Yugong* (Chinese Historical Geography Semi-monthly), VII(1-3), 1937, p. 248. Huang Tianzhu, Cheng Peng, "Quanzhou Gudai Sizhiye ji qi chanpinde waixiao" (Quanzhou's overseas trade in silk and other products), *Haijiao shi Yanjiu,* vol. 4, 1982, pp. 25-6.

[17]Sa Shiwu, *loc.cit.*

[18]Huang Tianzhu, Cheng Peng, *loc.cit.*

[19]Zhang Dechang, "Mingdai Guangzhou haibo maoyi" (Maritime trade at Guangzhou in the Ming Dynasty), *Qinghua Xuebao* (Journal of Qinghua University), IX(2), 1932, pp.16-7.

[20]Bai Shouyi, *Zhongguo Tongshi Gangyao* (An Outline History of China), Shanghai, 1983, p. 298.

[21]Ray Huang, "Fiscal Administration during the Ming Dynasty", *Chinese Government in Ming Times: Seven Studies,* Charles O. Hucker (ed.), New York, London, 1969, pp.105-6.

[22]*Ibid.*, p.106.

[23]Liansheng Yang, *Money and Credit in China,* Cambridge, Mass., 1952, p. 67.

[24]Jungpang Lo, "The Decline of the Early Ming Navy", *Oriens Extremus,* vol. 2, 1958, p.155.

[25]Ming Zhengtong Shilu, j.236, p.1. For official rate see Ji Hung, *Xu Wenxian tongkao,* j.10, 2860, col.3.

[26]*Mingshi*, j.322, p. 7.

[27]Ji. Juang, *op.cit.*, j.10, 2861, col.1.

[28]*Ming Dazheng Zuanyao*, j.22, p.24, quoted in Jungpang Lo, "The Decline", *op.cit.*, p.160.

[29]See Jungpang Lo, *ibid.*

[30]In early Ming the monthly pay of a regular in the navy was 1.5 picul of rice (*Mingshi*, j.82, p.17), plus a subsidy of 0.4 picul a month for 'out-to-sea' service, Gu-Yanwu, *Tianxia Junguo Libing Shu* (The Merits and Drawbacks of Different Regions in China), (A.D. 1662), 1879 (reprint), ce.3b, pp. 76, 111.

[31]Jungpang Lo, *op.cit.*, p.161.

[32]Jungpang Lo, *loc.cit.*

[33]Mingshi, j.77, 78, quoted in Zheng Hesheng, Zheng Yijun, *Zheng He xia Xiyang Ziliao huibian* (Collection of Materials on Zheng He's Voyages to the Western Ocean), Jinan, 1980, vol. I, p. 69.

[34]See Ts'ao Yunghe, "Chinese Overseas Trade in the Late Ming Period", *International Association of the Historians of Asia, 2nd biennial conference*, Taipei, 1962, p. 430.

[35]*Mingshi*, j.322, p.12.

[36]*Ibid.*, j.205, p.1.

[37]*Ibid.*

[38]*Mingshi*, j.304, p.18.

[39]*Congshu Jicheng chubian*, ed. bk. 3260, j.7, p. 89.

[40]See also, S. Tsenghsin Chang, "Commodities imported into the Zhangzhou region of Fujian China, during the Late Ming Period A comparative and analytical analysis", *A paper presented at the Symposium on Entrepreneurs' Emporia and Commodities in Asian Maritime Trade, 15th-18th Centuries*, Heidelberg, 1989, pp.1-3.

[41]Lin Renchuan, "Mingdai siren haishang maoyi shangren Yu Ekou" (Private Maritime traders and Japanese pirates during Ming dynasty), *Zhongguo Shi Yanjiu* (Studies in Chinese History), vol. 4, 1980, p.106; Ts'ao Yunghe, *op.cit.*, p. 430.

[42]J.K. Fairbank, "Tributary trade and China's relations with the West", *The Far Eastern Quarterly*, I(2), 1942, p.142.

[43]See S. Hariharan, "Tiruppudaimaruddur Paintings", *South Indian Studies*, vol. II, R. Nagaswamy, Madras (ed.), 1979, pp.167-77.

[44]A Cortesao, *The Suma Oriental of Tomé Pires: An Account of the East from the Red Sea to Japan, written in Malacca and India in 1512-1515, Hakluyt Society*, vol. II, London, 1944, pp. 268-72; John de Courcy, "Chinese Voyaging in the Indian Ocean before the European Influence", *Indian Ocean Newsletter*, VII(3), 1986, p. 6.

[45]J.K. Fairbank, *loc.cit.*, and *Trade and Diplomacy on the China Coast: The Opening of the Treaty Ports, 1842-54*, Stanford, 1969, pp. 23-38.

[46]N. Karashima, "The Chinese potteries excavated on the Malabar

Coast of India", *Museum*, 462, August 1989, pp.17-25 (in Japanese). The author is indebted to Ms. N. Kongari of JNU, New Delhi, for rendering it into English.

[47]Quoted by R.A.L.H. Gunavardana, "Changing patterns of Navigation in the Indian Ocean and their impact on pre-colonial Sri Lanka", in Satish Chandra (ed.), *The Indian Ocean, Explorations in History, Commerce and Politics,* New Delhi/Newbury Park/London, 1987, p. 87.

[48]F. Braudel, *The Perspective of the World Civilization and Capitalism, 15th-18th Century,* vol. III, tr. S. Reynolds, London, 1985, p. 55.

[49]Feng Chengjun (ed)., *Yingyai, Jixing Shi*, p.1, text, p. 27; Xingcha Shenglan, pp. 22-3.

[50]In addition to the above, see also, *Yingyai*, p. 50 (to Maldives), p. 55 (to Aden), p. 59 (to Bengal).

[51]M.A.P. Meilink-Roelofsz, *Asian Trade and European Influences,* The Hague, 1962, p. 265.

THE COMMERCIAL ACTIVITIES OF THE FUGGER FAMILY IN THE SIXTEENTH CENTURY

Rose Marie Gräfin Fugger

The Fugger family came from the village Graben but moved to Augsburg in 1367. That city received its name—Augusta Vindelicorum—from legionaries of Rome who built a fort there in 15 B.C. in honour of Emperor Augustus. It was built originally for military purposes, but through its favourable location at the very end of Via Claudia Augusta, the fort soon became the capital of the province Ratien. It flourished as a bartering place, as an administrative centre from where the Romans directed and built the main roads which brought trade and culture from Italy to Gaul.

With these geographical and historical antecedents, Augsburg was later able to fulfil its task as the trading centre of the western world in the fifteenth and sixteenth centuries. Its long association with Italy had equipped it with the newest business techniques. The nearness of the Tyrolian, Hungarian and German mines provided sources of profit. The majority of the fortunes were made by the famous trading houses dealing in cloth, fustian and silks; they were concerned with the import and distribution of spices; export of silver and copper; and interests in mining.

In 1490, Ulrich Fugger was the nominal head of the family enterprises, but his youngest brother Jakob had taken control of all the important deals. At that time, the firm already differed from other Augsburg firms: Trading and mining enabled Jakob to enter the more dangerous fields of banking and international finance; and like the Italians, he maintained a network of agencies (*Faktoreien*) in all the principal trading centres of the western world.

It was especially Hungary and Tyrol which attracted Jakob Fugger's interest. Until the mines of Spanish America were opened to world trade in middle sixteenth century, these were the world's largest silver and copper producing areas. The transition from buying and selling of metals to mining and refining them was an easy step. Mines were bought or financed; new techniques were developed (for example the Saiger method, with which it became easier to separate silver from copper ore); also pumping stations were installed to enable deeper digging into the mines; foundries and smeltries were brought under single ownership. All this was necessary for Jakob Fugger's price policy. He also made frequent use of his position to form cartel agreements for the purpose of raising the price of copper. By 1498 Jakob had the world monopoly in copper.

The German Reichstag (Diet) attacked private monopolies as examples of godless usury. Nevertheless, the German kings and Emperors (Maximilian I, Ferdinand I, Charles V) secretly pledged themselves to these monopolistic ore contracts to protect the merchants in the hope to better their own desperate need for financial help. In times when the Habsburgs had to concentrate their resources on war, or whenever they were hard pressed for funds, the rich merchants became indispensable. Such times were not rare in Europe, and they coincided with periods of the swift growth of capitalism in importance and power.[1] Even the Popes regularly resorted to international banking houses—with the only difference that, sometimes, they enforced the payment of debts with the threat of excommunication. The mines and their financing were the basis for the trade with India; meaning, the Emperor and also the King of Portugal needed the big trading houses for quick credit to finance the explorations; for equipping the ships for the expeditions; for supply of raw materials and at the same time for taking delivery and distribution of the overseas products.

Besides monopoly, another point of controversy in the Christian community was usury. The ecclesiastical authorities held to the doctrine that trade, though necessary, was dangerous to one's soul.[2] It was argued that money-lending was sinful because 'time' belongs to God; and money-lenders usurp the ownership of time when they demand interest over a period of time.[3]

In the fourteenth century, a Papal Bull ordered that he who defends the taking of interest to be in conformity with Christianity should be punished as heretic. In the fifteenth century, this was slightly modified to admit the rightfulness of taking a moderate profit. Even Martin Luther still equated taking profit with murderers and thieves.

The Fuggers—while good churchmen—were determined to remove the general prejudice of public opinion against interest taking. So in 1514, together with other influential merchants of Augsburg, they employed Dr. Johannes Eck, Professor of Theology at the University of Ingolstadt, to present for debate the thesis of defending the right of a Christian to take interest at a rate of five per cent. The University of Bologna accepted Dr. Eck's thesis. The Universities of Leipzig and Vienna did not agree, but the Imperial Council brought effective pressure on them to give Dr. Eck the wanted certificate.

This implied the civil recognition of the lawfulness of usury and soon it became a common practice.

The first contact of the Fuggers with the ruling house, the Habsburgs, was in 1473 when Friedrich III came to Augsburg on his way to Trier to meet Charles the Bold of Burgundy, to whose heiress he wanted to marry his son. He was so bare of cash that he had to leave the city without paying the bills of the small tradesmen with whom he had dealt. To avoid a scandal, the city council finally lent the Emperor money, taking in pledge his gold and silver table service.[4] An Emperor who could not pay the butcher and the baker obviously was grateful to Ulrich Fugger who let him have on credit the silk, satin and cloth of gold for himself and all his courtiers—so necessary to make a brave show when he was trying to arrange a good marriage for his son. This transaction did not lead to a continuous connection with the Habsburgs, but when Maximilian I came in possession of Tyrol, he re-established contact with the Fuggers. This was in 1492. "As Columbus discovered the New World, so the Emperor discovered his bankers, worth to him much more than Peru." Of all the Habsburgs, Maximilian was known as the worst money manager. When he exhausted his credit and income, he was forced in old age to borrow from the Fuggers "in order to eat".[5] And as the Habsburgs seldom could pay back their loans, they paid with privileges. In the fifteenth century, it was the mining concessions in Tyrol; in the middle of the sixteenth century, the King of Spain offered the security of the American silver mines.[6]

Jakob Fugger's efforts on behalf of Charles of Spain to be Emperor cast the die for the future of the Empire as well as for his own house. Emperor Maximilian was determined in his last years to bring to the throne his grandson Charles, Duke of Burgundy and King of Spain. But Francis I of France and Henry VIII of

England entertained similar hopes, as Germany was not a hereditary kingdom but an elected one. The outcome rested on securing the necessary votes. Patriotism, sense of duty and carrying out the rules as laid down by the Golden Bull were followed by none.

The seven Electors were by no means consistent in their views, and quite a few took bribes from all parties. This election is a long and interesting story, but the details are not relevant to this paper, so it suffices to know that Francis I promised half his year's income (which was thought to be three million livres) to secure the credit of the Fuggers. Complications arose for the Fugger firm in their dealings with the Curia. The Holy See through Cardinal Wolsey held out hopes for Henry VIII. But nobody could outbid Charles; the cost for the Crown being 850,000 florins, of which two-thirds, that is 543,000 florins, were advanced by Jakob Fugger and his brother's sons; 143,000 florins by the Welsers; and 165,000 by Genoese and Florentine merchants. The election was on 28 June 1519. The 'cheques' of the merchants were exchanged by Charles' agents against the election bills of the Imperial Electors.

After Charles V was elected, he broke his solemn promise to repay the loan. As late as 1530, more than half remained to be paid. So Jakob Fugger writes the famous letter to his Emperor:

> ... it is also well known and evident that your Imperial Majesty without me might not have acquired the Imperial Crown, as I can attest with the written statement of all the delegates of your Imperial Majesty. And in all this I have not looked at my profit. For if I had withdrawn my support from the House of Austria and transferred it to France, I should have won large profit and much money which were offered to me. But what disadvantage would have arisen thereby for the House of Austria, your Imperial Majesty with your high intellect may well conceive...[7]

As a security for this loan, by skilful negotiation Emperor Charles was persuaded to give Jakob Fugger the lease of the three Spanish Orders of Knighthood (Maestrazgo). This was highly important, as the mercury mines of AlmadÇn and the silver mines of Guadalcanal were included and it was only with the help of mercury (quicksilver) that silver could be separated from the ore, in which it is usually embedded. So the election of Charles V has a direct bearing on the Indian trade. It was argued that, as transport costs at that time were so enormous and protracted, only the most valuable and durable goods would be shipped—that is, silver from the West to East and spices from East to West.

Jakob Fugger's efforts to secure for Charles V the Crown reinforced the dealings of his firm with the Emperor and King of Spain and made the latter even more dependent on Fugger money; but the dealings with Iberia started much earlier. Originally, Venice was the centre of commerce. Only, the Republic of Venice outlawed any direct trade; goods had to be bartered through Venetian intermediates. Hence, as long as Venice had peaceful relations with the Ottoman Empire, Venice virtually had a trade monopoly. But as war broke out in 1499 between the Republic of Venice and the Sultan Bajesid II, trade was suspended for years. It is fascinating to note with what rapidity the South German merchants moved, first to Genoa and then learned the economic value of the Portuguese and Spanish discoveries and conquests.

The Spanish—except the Catalans—were no experts in commerce. Their fairs were still like medieval marketplaces; there was none of the ease and technique which merchants all over Europe acquired at the cosmopolitan school of Italy. To make up for the deficiency, Spanish merchants had to fall back on foreign helpers, mostly Germans. The people who returned from the Indies were not the rich of Spain[8]

The Welser family of Augsburg was much more adventurous than the more cautious Fuggers; they were born for trade rather than finance. So when Cabot returned from the West Indies with tales of wealth and adventure, the Welsers set off for the exploration of Venezuela and the colonisation of Rio de la Plata. Only once, and doubtless under their influence, the Fuggers contemplated a similar undertaking. They obtained a contract more liberal than ever given a Spaniard. Vido Herrll (Veit Hoërl) was the Fugger agent. He discussed with the "Council of the Indies" the proposals which his superiors had already negotiated with the King. The Fuggers were to obtain the regions between Chincha (where the realm of Pizzaro ended) and the Strait of Magellan and all the islands and the mainland territory as far as 200 leagues (about 1,100 km) from the coast. Beginning with Anton Fugger, they were to bear the titles of Governor and Captain General for three generations. They were to appoint and remove the officers of justice; also, theirs was the right of patronage. Of all the gold and silver they found, the

Crown would receive only one-tenth for ten years. For twelve years, they would not have to pay duties on anything they bought or took in their ships. A clause in the contract further stated ... "the King will be careful that no prohibited person trespasses the land of the Fuggers and that no one goes as a lawyer".

For some unknown reason, this fantastic project was dropped by the Fuggers, although there is evidence that representatives of the firm were in other provinces of Spanish America in subsequent years.

The ties of Augsburg to Lisbon were so strong that the voyages to East India undertaken by the Portuguese were closely studied. Hardly did the first merchant ship arrive at the ports of Portugal and Spain from America and East India, when agents from the great Augsburg trading firms appeared in Lisbon. From the time that the Portuguese fleet began to bring Indian spices to Europe, Lisbon became the leading spice market of the western world. Consequently, the Welsers of Augsburg sent their agent, Simon Seitz, to the court of King Manuel in 1503. On 13 January 1503, a licence contract was signed between the King and the German merchants. The Germans lost no time in outfitting three ships to India: Hieronymus, Raffael and Leonhard. Welsers contributed 20,000 florins, Fuggers 6,000 and 36,000 jointly by the Hochstetters, Imhofs, Hirschvogels and Gossenbrots (all Augsburg merchants). They owned the ships and the cargo, but the Portuguese Crown insisted on a Portuguese captain and crew, who had to be paid for eighteen months. They left Belem near Lisbon on 25 March 1505. The humanist Dr. Peutinger boasted in a letter to Emperor Maximilian, saying: "It was a great thing for the Augsburg firms of the Welsers, Gossenbrot and Fuggers to be the first Germans to see India".[9]

The Germans were allowed to buy as much spices and other goods from India as they wanted, but the contract with the Crown stipulated that they had to pay the King thirty per cent of all imported goods and that they were not allowed to underbid the King's prices for pepper. This system was known as "Indian Contract" and the reselling of pepper was called "European Contract". It became vastly risky for the traders as there were great fluctuations in the prices. The sudden falls in prices produced not a few bankruptcies.

In 1522, Jakob Fugger took the initiative and invested 10,000 ducats in a new undertaking to sail to the Moluccas (no mentioning of the Welsers). Seven ships were to be outfitted. Fugger offered to secure the ships needed and other material like copper, tar, ropes and masts. The fleet under Kommendator Garcia Jofre de Loaysas left La Coruna in July 1525. This undertaking had nothing but bad luck. Loaysas died on the way after they passed the Magalhaes Strait, as did his successor Sebastian Elcano. One of the ships, the Santa Maria de la Victoria succeeded in reaching the spice-island of Tidore at the coast of Halmahera, where a fort was built.[10] Later disagreements started, in which the Spanish held on to Tidore till the Treaty of Zaragoza 1529—when Spain waived its claim to the Moluccas—and the Portuguese held on to Ternate (another island, at that time world-famous for its clove, and seat of mighty Sultans).

Shortly after Loaysas left Spain, another fleet was outfitted to sail to the Spice Islands under Captain Sebastian Cabot. Again, there was German financial participation but neither the Fuggers nor the Welsers backed this enterprise because of the high risk involved. This expedition was, too, a failure, which fully justified their restraint.

It was much laterunder the great-great nephews of Jakob Fugger, namely Philipp Eduard (1546-1618) and Octavian Secundus (1549-1600) that the Fuggers engaged themselves again in the Indian trade. The brothers were, on the whole, a different breed. They received a mercantile education in Amsterdam, and a humanistic one at the Universities of Bourges, Padua and Bologna, with added studies in Rome. Their inclinations, without doubt, tended more towards the acquisition of a solid humanistic education, than being active in commercial activities.

They left the main branch of the Fugger firm in 1578.[11] With their new company, a Pepper Contract was formed in 1580 with Markus, Paul and Mathaeus Welser for the Portuguese East India trade. It stipulated that five ships should bring pepper to Lisbon yearly, for sale at a price fixed by the King. They established five agencies (faktoreien) on the Malabar coast for the purchase of the merchandise and also additional agencies in the Hanseatic-Dutch-English region for selling them. The whole undertaking was full of problems from the beginning. So, after a while the Fuggers loosened their ties with the Welsers. As a consequence, they had to build up their own administration on the west coast of India. The representative they sent overseas was a relative of the Welsers; he was twenty-eight years old, had a good education and was called Kron. In 1587 he established agencies in Goa, Cochin, Cannanore, Calicut and Quilon. He was able in time to establish contacts with all the political and commercially powerful men between the southern coast of Africa and Japan. He got to know the intentions of Dutch and English merchants, of local dignitaries who would cooperate with the Portuguese and also those who did not believe in fair play. He stayed in Asia for over thirty years, his fate alternating in great fortune and equally great disasters. Philip Eduard and Octavian Secundus Fugger wrote countless letters to him, of which copies are still kept in the Fugger archives.[12] They are answers to Kron's letters, in which he noted everything of importance: his impressions of thefor himnew continent; all the quaint and novel experiences, and also about the difficulties he encounteredsuch as the competition of the Arab traders, who traditionally got the best prices and the most valuable goods; the building of seaworthy ships; the procuring of a trustworthy crew; the disorganisation of the Portuguese administration. The Viceroys established most luxurious courts in Goa with the money that was intended to be spent on the Spice Route. As the Portuguese King assented only a low salary to the colonial employees, corruption was rampant. Besides, financial machinations and squandering became the typical characteristic of the Estado da India.[13]

In March 1586, the first fleet of the newly founded company left Lisbon. Instead of the five ships which had left, only two returned home. Instead of the expected 30,000 quantals[14] of pepper, the ships San Thome and Nostra Senora de Conception brought only 10,368 quantals back.

The years 1588 and 1589 brought better results as all ships reached Lisbon safely. Those years the price of pepper was low, therefore Kron tells us that he bought with the extra money additional goods which would sell well in Europe: 1735 tonnes of cinnamon, 1627 tonnes indigo, 289 tonnes rubber, 162 tonnes cloves, 28 tonnes nutmeg, 12 tonnes incense and 20,004 crates with silks and cotton.

The good fortune was short-lived. The ample supply of pepper brought first fluctuations and then sudden fall in prices. Added to this were other losses: it became impossible to bring the goods to their destination in the north of Germany, sailing through

Gibraltar, passing the Spanish and the Portuguese coast at a time when the King of Spain, Philipp II, and Queen Elizabeth I of England were at warespecially, not if you were traditionally on the side of the Spanish kings. After five ships were sunk, the English fleet captured the Augsburg ship Madre de Dios at sea in 1592, loaded with Indian pepper. The Fuggers wrote a reproachful letter to the Queen, demanding the return; they also asked Emperor Rudolf II for intervention. He wrote three letters on their behalf in 1594, 1595 and 1597, but to no avail. The German merchants received no compensation. On the contrary, Francis Drake, the famous pirate, captured in 1589 alone sixty ships from the German traders.

After all those difficulties, the brothers Philipp Eduard and Octavian Secundus sold their Asia Contract in 1591 and, a year later, the Europe Contract. The high risk connected with the spice trade contradicted the aims of their firm, which was to secure safe and profitable investments. Therefore, we can observe in the following years their retreat more and more from business obligations.

It would be wrong to speak of the decline of the Fugger family or firm. It was not only a matter of being unable to stem the flood of loans to the Habsburgs; being unable to compensate for the losses, as the Emperors and kings also kept for their own use the shares of gold and silver belonging to the Fuggers; and the state of bankruptcies and the bottomless pit of the Habsburg finances. It was even more a shift within the members of the Fugger family to different values and aims in life.

While Jakob and Anton Fugger had hardly made use of the titles as counts which they received in 1473, their descendants were not any more solely concerned with hard work, but spent most of their time at court or on their vast estatesestablishing valuable libraries, taking interest in music, architecture, natural science, writing books and not only collecting them, but also becoming patrons of the arts and acquiring more and more land and magnificent residences. At the same time, their social position through marriage into the high aristocracy showed a vertical mobility.

The company continued for another century, but their commercial activities decreased more and more. By the end of the seventeenth century, the firm had lost its internal solidity, but contrary to quite a few famous German merchants, notably the Welsers, the Fuggers never went into bankruptcy, although the

Spanish branch of the Habsburgs has, up to this day, not repaid the millions of florins they owe the Fuggers. The final blow to the economic life of Germany as a whole was then dealt by the Thirty-Year War which, together with the religious and political disunion, brought on an economic decline so great that complete recovery came only after more than a century and a half elapsed. It also put a final end to the active trading activities of the Fuggers. What remained of their wealth was chiefly the land purchases, which Jakob and Anton Fugger had made immune to the vicissitudes of mercantile and commercial fortune. Today the Fugger Bank is flourishing, but the international importance of the family is gone.

NOTES

[1]G. Strieder, "Origin and Evolution of early European Capitalism", *Journal of Economic and Business History*, 1929, p.16.

[2]W. Ashley, *Church and Usury*, Longman, p.36.

[3]A. Gurevic, "Das Weltbild des mittelalterischen Menschen", Beck Verlag, p.168.

[4]P. Van Dyck, *Captain of Industry*, Harpers, January 1910, p.276.

[5]G. Arcienegas, *German Conquest in America*, Macmillan, 1943, p.60.

[6]Some of the occasions are listed here:

1492: Maximilian decided to wage war in revenge against Charles VIII of France, who alienated his already wedded wife Anna of Bretagne;

1492: for the payment of English subsidies;

1493: he needed 84,000 gulden for the reception of his second bride, Blanca Marie of Milan;

1491-94: for fighting the Turks;

1499: for the war with Switzerland;

1505-15: for the Ten-Year War in Italy;

1505: for the Imperial Diet in Konstanz;

1505: for the League of Cambrai;

1515: for the Congress of Vienna;

1515: for the double wedding of his grandson and his granddaughter.

[7]Fugger-Familien Archiv, Dillingen.

[8]G. Arcienegas, *ibid.*

[9]P. Dirr, *Augsburg, Klinkhard und Biermann*, p.75.

[10]D. Hall, *A History of South East Asia*, Macmillan.

[11]R. Hildebrandt, "Die Georg Fuggerischen Erben", Dunckel & Humblot, p. 61.

[12]Fugger Familien Archiv, (F.A. 46.1), Dillingen.

[13]F. Salentiny, "Die Gewürzroute", *Du Mont*, p.142.

[14]Quantal; today about forty-six kilos.

EUROPEAN EXILES, RENEGADES AND OUTLAWS AND THE MARITIME ECONOMY OF ASIA c.1500-1750

G.V. Scammell

For centuries, Europeans were fascinated by rumours and legends of the wealth and wonders of the Orient and by stories of the supposed existence there of realms free from all those tiresome taboos and restrictions that prevailed in the West. Long before the arrival of Vasco da Gama, renegades were serving the Mongols in Iran and Marco Polo had been in the entourage of the Grand Khan himself. The Portuguese pioneers were disconcerted to encounter, in 1501, a certain Benvenuto de Abano, who had spent the previous twenty-five years sailing the seas of Asia, and his contemporary, the Muslim Khoja Safar Salmani, an erstwhile Genoese or Albanian.[1] But this was nothing compared with the flow that followed western penetration of the maritime economy of the East, scattering European adventurers and outlaws throughout the Orient, anywhere from the shores of the Persian Gulf to those of the Pacific Ocean. And very soon these hopefuls were joined by European pirates, some working from ports in their mother countries, some from the Caribbean and North America, and some from bases in the Indian Ocean, of which Madagascar was, according to taste, the most celebrated or the most notorious. Such men, frequently of remarkable skills and fearsome abilities, exercised a considerable influence on the maritime history of the East in the early modern centuries. It is with the origins, aspirations and activities of these elusive—indeed, often anonymousbut nevertheless highly significant figures that this paper is concerned.[2]

Refugees from, or rejects of western society came from many parts of Europe, and not necessarily from its most impoverished or politically turbulent areas. The Jesuits were scandalised by the cosmopolitan throng they encountered at the court of the Mughal emperor Akbar, whilst later the Maratha Admiral, Kanhoji Angre (1669-1729), 'used', it was said, 'many Europeans' to man his formidable squadrons. Such expatriates were mostly deserters from the service of western maritime powers established in the East; and hence, initially, the large numbers from Portugal. Some Portuguese were already employed in Bengal—as soldiers, amongst other thingsas early as 1521.[3] Thereafter, they crop up alike in Thailand, Vijayanagara and the Bay of Bengal—to whose rich pickings 2,000 had been drawn from Goa alone by the late 1500s—and where, as in the Red Sea, they were busily engaged in piracy. They appear in Mesopotamia, at the royal court of Golconda and in the imperial Mughal capital. By the seventeenth century there were Portuguese serving the Persians at Kung or working as seamen in Muslim vessels engaged in evading Portugal's attempted control of the export of pepper from western India. They built fortifications and provided shipping for Shivaji. They supplied gunners to the Mughals, pilots for the Chinese, galley commanders for the ruler of Arakan and constructed men-of-war for the Sultan of Atjeh. Some even got as far as setting themselves up as princelings along the eastern shores of the Bay of Bengal.[4]

By the early 1600s the English were, if less numerous, scarcely less ubiquitous; and this notwithstanding the endeavours of some staunchly Protestant officers of the East India Company to prevent 'the shame' which befell 'our religion' through the conduct of such renegades. The celebrated Will Adams was profitably ensconced in Japan at the beginning of the seventeenth century—deaf to the calls of marital bliss and duty in the home countrywhilst a compatriot was equally happily established in the Celebes.[5] Others were settled in Madagascar shortly after and, as a chance reference in the account of a shipwreck reveals, in Kerala. In the mid-1600s there were those, allegedly encouraged by ill-disposed compatriots, who fled from Surat to join local potentates, and there were enough Englishmen scattered about the countryside around Bombay for the East India Company to urge that they should take up residence in its newly acquired possession. But to little effect, and later in the century we meet their fellows serving by land or sea the rulers of Gujarat, Bengal, Arakan, Golconda and Bantam. Some held high office under the Shah of Persia (Iran). More numerous still were those in Mughal pay—their alcoholic prowess already remarked by the emperor Jehangir—whilst others made a significant contribution to the armed strength of the Marathas. Many more were less ominously employed by local merchants—by those, for example, of

Gujarat and Bengal, or by the Armenians of Madras.[6] Of the numbers involved it is difficult, if not impossible to say, though we hear on one occasion (1654) of twenty-three deserters from Surat. But such was the propensity of the English to decamp that in the late 1670s the East India Company warned all freemen—those trading, that is, under its licence—in and around Masulipatnam that they were to move into Madras and further forbade them to build houses or acquire property elsewhere, or to enter the employment of any Indian prince. So little was the message heeded, however, that in 1680 Charles II of England found it necessary to call home from India all Englishmen in indigenous service there. Meanwhile British pirates, soon reinforced by their brethren from North America, were roaming the Asian seas from the shores of East Africa to the Straits of Malacca.[7]

The story was much the same with the Dutch—or at least with that cosmopolitan labour force employed by the Dutch East India Company—and despite the fact that, on the whole, prosperous and tolerant Holland was a country to which, rather than from which, people fled. One Dutchman was encountered by the English at the beginning of the seventeenth century living it up on an island in the Molucca Sea "with as many women as he pleaseth... he will sing and dance all day long, near stark-naked... and will be drunk for days together".[8] Less hedonistic, or less fortunate compatriots were subsequently employed, or sought employment, in Japan and Gujarat, turned Muslim at Mocha (1647), and like all others flocked to join the Mughals. Indeed such was the scale of their exodus that in the mid-1600s the Dutch East India Company was anxious to reach agreement with the Imperial Court concerning the recovery of these miscreants.

Then, of course, as in Europe itself, and as in the polyglot world of commerce and seafaring anywhere, westerners in Asia commonly migrated, fled or were ejected from the service of their own country into that of some other European power. In the early 1600s, the Portuguese were leaving Sao Tomé by the score to join the Dutch at Pulicat, yet their fleet in action against the English in the Persian Gulf in 1625 had amongst its complement 200 English, Scots, Irish and Dutch 'runagadoes'. The Abbé Carré later met Frenchmen in Portuguese service at Kung, and at Daman (1673) came across a compatriot from Provence waxing rich on the proceeds of commanding indigenous and Portuguese ships whilst his lady, in true

Latin style, pursued a colourful romantic life in his absence.[9] A certain William Carmichael turned up in England in the early 1600s, leaving a wife and family in Goa, having been employed, so he claimed, by the Portuguese in Asia—including Chinafor thirty years.[10] By the middle of the century his fellows were deserting both to the Portuguese in Coromandel and to the Dutch at Surat—to whom one, allegedly of a "perverse and passionate" nature, he thought to take himself when in trouble for his misdeeds, chiefly a reluctance to attend church. Others jumped ship at Goa (1651) and Daman (1652). The garrison drummer at Madras, after some ill-advised exploits, departed (1651) for Goa and ended in Macassar. A contemporary, thwarted in his expectations of undertaking a voyage to Pegu for the influential Mir Jumla, fled to São Tomé and Madras; the matter had to be regulated by an Anglo-Portuguese agreement in 1651.

This cosmopolitan diaspora was part of a far larger movement. Economic disaster, poverty, religious bigotry, intoler-ance, oppression and lack of opportunity at home drove ambitious or disgruntled Europeans not only to Asia but also to flee from their mother countries to neighbouring States, to join the Ottomans in the Levant, to become Muslim corsairs in North Africa, or to take their chance among the Africans of Guinea or the Indians of North America. But no call was stronger and more insistent than that of the Orient. Its major indigenous States neither offered easy access to the agents of European companies or powers nor were much impressed by their claims. The western presence was primarily maritime, with Europeans soon scattered along the routes now worked by their ships from which, as in other waters and at other times, they freely deserted. Expatriates encountered pockets of political instability, providing limitless opportunities for the able and unscrupulous. There was the prospect, whether by trade or plunder, of riches of a staggering order. There were wealthy, powerful and often tolerant rulers willing to pay for the services which westerners could—or alleged they could—provide. In a world now afflicted by the pretensions and rivalries of European States, and far more profoundly by those of newly emergent indigenous powers, various local potentates were persuaded of the advantages that could accrue from the employment of European naval and military technology, then in process of making significant advances. Indigenous shipowners similarly saw the benefits to be gained by hiring western commanders or pilots with inside knowledge or particular skills to take charge of their vessels on commercial routes opened up by Europeans, or on those on which the competition, not to say outright hostility, of western craft was to be expected.

Renegades and their fellows thus came to fulfil a number of clearly defined functions. Many were gunners both by land and sea. Pre-European Asia certainly had its firearms and artillery, but western guns rapidly improved in quality and effectiveness from the late sixteenth century, chiefly as the result of almost incessant warfare, just as the skills needed for their handling became more exacting. Hence European experts, or self-proclaimed experts, in the gunner's art crop up throughout much of Asia from the early 1500s. In 1663 Father Godinho acutely noticed that though the Mughals had a great deal of artillery, their tactics of cavalry raids in open country gave them little occasion to use it. He thought their gunners poor and believed most of them to be Dutch or Portuguese and hardly Europe's finest.[11] But despite this somewhat jaundiced testimony, expatriate influence was clearly considerable. When, for example, Aurangzeb, outraged at the doings of western pirates, decided to have a navy of his own, it was to be under his "Frank gunners". Many of these were in fact English and their exodus from the service of the East India Company is well documented. Thus there were complaints in 1656 that as the imperial siege train made its way to Lahore it was re-inforced, if that is the right word, by drunken English sailors transmuted into artillerymen; and indeed, Emperor Jehangir was of the opinion that the more his English gunners imbibed the better they shot. In 1670, the Company proceeded against one described as a gunner's assistant who was recruiting in Bombay for the Mughals, whilst some years later the imperial representative in Surat was pressing the English for gunners and encouraging crews to desert from Company ships to serve as artillery-men. Some of these specialists are even known to us by name, like Thomas Roach, chief gunner at Agra in 1674 and obviously a man of standing with the Emperor.[12]

Other evidence is patchy but significant. In the early 1500s, the presence of renegade gun-founders in Calicut was one of the many bones of contention between the Portuguese and the Zamorin. Soon after their arrival in the East, the English noticed that the ships of Atjeh carried "very good brass ordnance: semi-cannon, culverins, sakers, minions" or, in other words, a full range of western weapons.[13] The East India Company learned in 1653 that eight of its soldiers had already deserted from Madras to be gunners in local service and two more were on the point of going. Meanwhile in Golconda the influential Mir Jumla was employing French, Italian and English artillery-men and gun-founders, and at the end of the century the notorious former buccaneer Plantain was chief gunner to Kanhoji Angre. In short, there was a close relation-ship between European renegades and nascent indigenous naval power.

Similarly much in evidence were those expatriates who manned or navigated Asian vessels. In 1601, for example, the Dutch met a Japanese craft on passage to Manila under a Portuguese pilotand hopelessly off course. During that brief period from the late 1500s to 1635, in which the shogunate licensed Japanese overseas trade, most of the ships engaged carried Portuguese pilots who were familiar with the routes to be sailed. Mughal vessels in the Bay of Bengal used Portuguese seamen in the 1650s, and in the late 1600s English pirates intercepted a Chinese junk off Malacca with two Portuguese pilots on board. A ship belonging to Mir Jumla, bound for Persia (Iran) in 1650 carried an English pilot, as did one from Bengal which put into Gombroon in 1654. The list might easily be extended.[14]

Almost as numerous were Europeans in command of local vessels. They, too, could offer indigenous owners expert knowledge of particular waters and, in addition, useful contacts in ports where their fellow countrymen were established. In return, they could expect handsome remuneration and attractive partnerships in commercial ventures. Many, however, werelike as not—of that sinister breed, later found in the novels of Joseph Conrad, obliged for various reasons to exercise their skills in regions little frequented by their compatriots. So in the early 1600s, a vessel belonging to the 'princial Moor' of Masulipatnam and under a Portuguese master was intercepted by the Dutch on passage from Tenasserim (Mergudi).[15] Later in the century, Petro Loveyro, known to the English as "an antient Portuguese", and clearly an experienced seaman, commanded Bengal ships working to Sri Lanka and the Maldives. At the same date the Abbé Carré knew Frenchmen who were masters of Indian vessels sailing from Surat and Daman. He met the English commander of a ship belonging to a Surat Armenian, whilst another Englishman subsequently had charge of the locally owned

Welcome of the same port. So ubiquitous were these Europeans that in 1652 Jean-Baptiste Tavernier, a seasoned traveller, came to the unhappy conclusion that their services were in such demand since neither Indians nor Persians had "the least knowledge of navigation".[16] Yet at that very time indigenous ships under indigenous command could be met in harbours throughout huge areas of maritime Asia, whilst—as European pirates were to find to their cost—many such vessels were not only armed but well able to look after themselves.

The renegades, however, whose activities were most apprehensively watched by their compatriots were those engaged, one way or another, in providing or commanding military and naval forces for local rulers. Portuguese experts built, or helped to build, fortifications for Shivaji.[17] Earlier (1615), one of their compatriots had supplied the formidable ruler of Atjeh with twelve "very great galleys", only to come to a depressing end—trampled to death at his royal master's command lest he might perform a similar service for others. At the beginning of the seventeenth century the Japanese, eager to acquire shipwrights who could build them vessels capable of crossing the Pacific, had to make do with such secrets as they could elicit from Will Adams, an English pilot employed by the Dutch East India Company, who was originally detained in the islands and subsequently reluctant to depart from them.

More sinister still were the naval and military *condottieri*—a breed dying out in seventeenth and eighteenth century-Europe—commanding their own forces and serving where the pay or opportunities seemed best. In 1521, the Portuguese encountered in Bengal a fellow countryman with his followers—equipped, it may be noted, as archers and not with the latest weaponry—so integrated into the indigenous world that they had no hesitation in setting about their supposed compatriots. Some years later the colourful Diogo Soares de Mello was fighting for the Burmese in Thailand, whilst in the 1580s and 1590s there were Portuguese mercenaries engaged on both sides in the Thai-Burmese wars. At the end of the century, one set up what was tantamount to his own principality at Siriam, in the Irrawaddy delta; and others were making their presence felt in Laos and Cambodia.[18] In the 1660s, an English officer who had fought on the losing side in the civil wars at home turned up in imperial pay in Persia (Iran) together with several other European experts. He was taken on by the Shah "to discipline his people in the military art"—by no means the first or last to be so engaged—only, like many others after him, to fall on hard times after the death of his master. Meanwhile the King of Arakan had a fleet of galleys fighting somewhat unsteadily (1665) under Portuguese command against the Mughals and, as we have already noticed, Europeans figure largely in the upsurge of Maratha seaborne endeavour under Shivaji and his successor. In 1659 the Portuguese captain of Bassein reported that he had succeeded in the tricky task of attracting to the Lusitanian cause one Ruy Leitao Viegas who was then with his followerssome 340 "Portuguese and Topazes, black and white"—on the point of putting to sea with a flotilla of Maratha war vessels.[19] Some years later the English authorities investigated (1684) the doings of a former officer in an East Indiaman who, having deserted at Goa (1677), compounded his many sins by having in his possession a Maratha commission to command a force of five or six vessels and to raise some English seamen to crew them. And at the end of the century, the erstwhile pirate Plantain, now a Maratha officer, had charge, amongst other things, "of all the affairs of the grabs and gallivats" those formidable small craft propelled by sail and oarsand on the most generous terms.

But there was no surer way to wealth, it was widely believed, than by downright robbery, and in the centuries between 1500 and 1750 piracy flourished as never before, on a global scale. This was the age of the Caribbean buccaneers, the Barbary corsairs, the Japanese wako, the Omanis, the pirates of Malabar and many others besides. But our concern is with the Europeans, amongst whom the British loomed so large that even a compatriot dismissed them as no better than "a nation of pirates". First on the scent of loot in the East, however, were the Portuguese. Barely had they arrived, before royal officers were off chasing indigenous vessels (1519) and by the 1530s, their freebooters were roving the Bay of Bengal. But apart from the ravages of the Portuguese there and in the Red Sea, most western pirates found it more profitable and less hazardous to stay nearer home. In the Atlantic they could hope to pick off Spanish treasure ships returning from the Americas and Portuguese vessels bringing back gold from West Africa: such depredations being seen as much as a godly duty as a speedy way to worldly wealth by ardent Protestants. With any luck, too, they might take Portuguese Indiamen as they struggled home on the last leg of the world's most arduous voyage. Hence, the fate of the *Madre de Deus* which the English captured (1592) with an astonishing lading of jewels, spices and silks worth about fifty per cent of their mother country's annual imports.[20]

Already, however, English interest was shifting further east. Francis Drake's celebrated circumnavigation of the globe (1577-80), in the course of which he acquired a shipload of booty in the Pacific at a time when Elizabeth I was nominally at peace with Spain and Portugal, showed, amongst other things, that such feats could win the sovereign's approval. Indeed, the Queen in effect gave the royal blessing to piracy, setting a precedent followed, albeit far less rewardingly, by her successors. The voyage also showed that the riches of the East were at the mercy of those bold and resourceful enough to seek them. The message was not lost on intransigent Protestants when in 1580 Catholic Spain annexed Portugal and her empire and so appeared to control most of the known world. Following the outbreak of the Anglo-Spanish War (1585) a plethora of schemes was hatched for profitable incursions into Asia. Little was to come of them, though during the second English circumnavigation (1586-88) Thomas Cavendish took a Manila galleon with a cargo of enormous value and at the end of the century the remnants of one expedition found their way to Southeast Asia and the survivors of another plundered Portuguese shipping in the Straits of Malacca. Peace between Spain and England (1604) had little effect other than to let loose into the East a wave of piratical and semi-piratical ventures, now directed to riches whose magnitude was fully understood, and to opportunities whose scope was fully appreciated.

The most tempting prizes, as the Portuguese had long known, were to be found in the Red Sea. From its shores indigenous vessels sailed eastward with ladings which included large amounts of bullion. Towards the holy places of Islam there came, in the time of pilgrimage, vessels carrying the devout of Asia, and more especially those of the Indian subcontinent, with all their valuable finery. They also had on board presents for the keepers of the shrines from such grandees as the Mughal Emperors and their ladies, besides those goods which the pilgrims hoped to sell to cover their expenses and all those many and varied things which were to be marketed at the great fairs held in Arabia during the *hajj*"—all manner of East India goods, and abundance of fine stones for rings and bracelets... china-ware...", or in other words "all the most precious commodities of the three-quarters of the world".[21] Equally attractive was the great commercial bottle-neck of the Straits of Malacca, where indigenous and western shipping passing between India, China and the Philippines could be intercepted and cargoes of silver—including that coming from America via Manila—spices and textiles could be had. Better still, in waters as vast as those of the Pacific and the Indian Ocean the chances of being caught were negligible since no power had as yet either the resources or the will to police them, and many rulers were indeed willing to encourage, or at least condone piracy. And happily, too, islands like those off the coast of East Africa provided safe and well-supplied bases, controlling both indigenous commercial routes and those sailed by European Indiamen.

Early on the scene were the ships of the recently founded English East India Company, in whose establishment and initial policies a vital role was taken by men experienced in and enriched by Atlantic privateering. Hence, although England was allegedly at peace with the joint Hispano-Portuguese empireapart from yet another privateering war in the early 1620s—it was to the accompaniment of skirmishes, pitched battles and the capture of Portuguese prizes anywhere from East Africa to South China that the Company pushed eastward. And local shipping, whose presence or behaviour was not to the liking of its officers, received similar brusque treatment. The policies of the Dutch East India Company were the same, and during a brief period of joint operations (1620-22) the two corporations were engaged in outright piracy. Chinese ships were, for example, captured off Manila, and it was from such prizes that the Dutch obtained much of the silk, so vital to their early trade with Japan.

There were some subsequent isolated piracies by individual East India Company captains, but in general they had other things to do. Private enterprise, however, went from strength to strength. In 1613, the ship carrying an emissary of the English East India Company was threatened by pirates after passing the Cape of Good Hope. It was only saved when its assailants were distracted by the appearance of a vessel, which turned out to be yet another freebooter, homeward bound from Sumatra. Five years later, the celebrated English diplomat Sir Thomas Roe denounced the doings of French, English and Danish rovers in the Red Sea and Persian Gulf. Not surprisingly. Hardly had the English East India Company been chartered than James I was licensing venturers to breach its monopoly, leading to raids on the coasts of Java and Malaysia. Worse was to come. Charles I of England, ever short of money, commissioned Captain Quaile, a well-connected one-time privateer—in whose earlier projects the King, in true Elizabethan style, had invested—to "range the seas the world over" in one of the royal ships in pursuit of prizes. Which he did with a vengeance. The Dutch at Surat reported his arrival in 1631 with "no small store of ducketts", the fruits of his activities in the Red Sea. A further cruise in the same waters yielded at least six indigenous craft with cargoes of "ryce, opium, silk Stuffes, gold and bullone" and his ship, though not Quaile himself, finally returned home with loot valued at £20,000—at a time when in England £5,000 would buy a good vessel.[22] The following years saw French captures of even richer prizes in the Red Sea and the loss to a London pirate of a Surat vessel—which significantly mistook him for a Portuguese or Turkish rovercarrying coins and goods said to have been worth £30,000-£40,000. In 1636, the formidable London entrep-reneur William Courteen, then engaged—amongst other thingsin breaching the monopoly of the English East India Company, despatched a squadron to Asia. Its backers included the King himself and it was commanded by the former privateer and one-time (though singularly unfortunate) East India Company captain, John Weddell. After a voyage which took him to western India and Atjeh he clashed with the Chinese at Canton and eventually turned up in Masulipatnam with a prodigious lading of precious metals. In the 1640s, Courteen was behind another bold project, initially floated by others, to colonise Madagascar. The island, thought the proposed commander in the original plan—Prince Rupert, nephew of Charles I and a future wild cavalry general and dashing admiral—" may easily be made to hold the balance of all the trade between the East Indies and the rest of the world". It could, that is to say, fulfil a similar role to that of the buccaneering bases of the Caribbean. These grand plans speedily foundered, but in the meanwhile European freebooters set about indigenous shipping. True, some never took a prize, and for some the outcome was far from that expected, with one French crew blown into Aden by bad weather (1656) and there seized and forcibly circumcised. But others enjoyed astonishing success, like those desperadoes under the command of a former factor of the English East India Company who wrought such havoc in the Red Sea (1662) as to provoke the Mughals into attempting to create their own navy.

Now the pace became hotter still as pirates and buccaneers, who had long haunted the Caribbean, found it prudent to move on. Settlers in the islands came to see them as obstacles to a rewarding (if illicit) commerce with the Spanish possessions, and in any case defences against their raids were being strengthened and measures to control them were more vigorously enforced. As a result, their efforts were deflected to the East, with appetites further whetted, so it was alleged, by rumours of the loot taken by the English East India Company during the course of its local wars in the late seventeenth century. Some of the buccaneers marched across the Isthmus of Panama, launched themselves into the Pacific in pursuit of the galleons carrying American silver to the Philippines, and then pushed on to the Indian Ocean. Others came through the Straits of Magellan, but the majority followed the old-established route round the Cape of Good Hope, with many improving the shining hour by cruises along the West African littoral to pick off slavers. They attacked Asian seaborne commerce, European and indigenous alike, anywhere from the western shores of the Indian Ocean and the Arabian Sea to the waters of the Pacific. From the mid-1600s they had bases in Reunion and the neighbouring islands, and in particular in Madagascar where, by the early 1700s, there were about 250 of them out of a total pirate community of roughly 2,500.

The majority of these desperadoes were from the West Indies and North America—Boston, Rhode Island, Philadelphia, New York. They were reinforced by mutineers who seized the vessels in which they were serving and by deserters from the various East India companies. Many were of that familiar and unlovable breed of keeper turned poacher—commanders of privateers or men commissioned to round up pirates, who took to piracy themselves. Of such none is better known than Captain Kidd, son of a Scottish Presbyterian minister, husband of a rich colonial widow and one-time privateer against the French, who was hanged for his misdeeds in 1701. Nor should it be overlooked that some pirate vessels were local craft commanded by Europeans. In 1684, for example, one belonging to the King of Thailand, with an English captain, took an Armenian-owned ship from Madras which was promptly refitted to be employed in piracy.

By the closing decades of the seventeenth century European freebooters were capturing Chinese junks in the Straits of Malacca and intercepting vessels bound for Japan or returning from Manila. They plundered Portuguese shipping off Sofala or on passage between Goa and Macao and took English East Indiamen in the waters of Indonesia. In the Red Sea, where very often whole squadrons were operating, they plundered the traffic to and from Mecca, as when on one occasion they took the celebrated *Ganj-i-Sawa'i* laden with "great quantities" of gold and silver and carrying a ruby-encrusted saddle destined as a present to Aurangzeb. Equally staggering was the caputre at Reunion in 1721 of a Portuguese Indiaman taking home the ex-viceroy, Dom Luis de Meneses and a cargo of silks, textiles, porcelain and diamonds. Together with the loot harvested in earlier triumphs this yielded its captors something like one million pound sterling.[23] Nor was this unique. A venture in 1662 allegedly netted twelve million pound sterling.[24] The division of this spoil amongst crews yielded the lucky—and this of course takes no account of the many ventures that failed—from £500 to £1,200 each. Had they persevered as honest seamen at home they might have been paid—always assuming they were paid at all—24 to 25 shillings a month, rising to 55 shillings in wartime, whilst masters of slaves would get £8 and of Indiamen £10.[25] There is perhaps no more eloquent testimony to the value of Asian trade or to the scale on which eastern riches were transmitted to the West by non-commercial ways so easily overlooked.

Handling loot of this order rapidly became a substantial and well-organised business. Some of the takings were shipped directly to the West Indies and North America, where, from the 1670s East Indian goods, mostly the fruits of piracy, were being sold in flagrant contravention of the supposed monopoly of the English East India Company and the terms of the English Navigation Acts. There were other major markets in Dutch Cochin and English Bombay, where the pirates had European accomplices, and in western Indian ports where they dealt with local merchants. Most of the loot, however, changed hands in the Comoros, Madagascar and the neighbouring Ste Marie. The islands gave easy access to the Red Sea and dominated all the most important commercial routes between East and West. They were free from the competition of agents of the great European monopoly companies whilst attracting Arab traders from East Africa. Like the old buccaneering strongholds of the West Indies they offered excellent anchorages, food—rice and cattle especially—and the support of at least some of the local people, not to mention the solace of the sexual favours of their women. As on the eastern littoral of the Bay of Bengal, indigenous political rivalries allowed the enterprising to fish in troubled waters, receiving, in exchange for weapons and assistance, slaves taken in internecine wars. There was indeed a close connection between piracy and slaving, since merchants who came to purchase loot commonly bought slaves for whom there were flourishing markets in Indonesia, and more especially in the western Atlantic settlements whose voracious demands the licensed monopoly suppliers were rarely able to meet. To the islands, and particularly to Madagascar, merchants from the West Indies and North America sent provisions, reinforcements, guns and liquor—much of it lethal firewater—though some ships came out via Madeira to secure choicer vintages. These goods the pirates purchased with precious stones, bullion, spices, oriental textiles and porcelain, mostly taken in the Red Sea. The trade soon became so routine that vessels sailing to and from America carried correspondence, both business and personal, between freebooters and their wives and families—a common theme the explanation of the delayed homecoming of loving husbands and dutiful fathersand American merchants appointed resident factors in Madagascar, some of them former buccaneers.

Hence there flowed from the Indian Ocean to the Americas a rich and variegated commerce ranging from slaves destined for the plantations to the cheaper oriental textiles with which New World merchants could buy blacks in Africa or the Caribbean. Some of the more luxurious items were absorbed by an affluent and growing American domestic market, with the Iberian settlements supplied through such entrepots and Jamaica and Curacao. A great deal, however, of the bullion and oriental goods that reached North America was re-exported to Europe—once again contravening the English Navigation Acts—to help pay for those manufactures the colonies so urgently needed. Of the value of these dealings we know as little as of the smugglers' trade. But there is some hint as to what was going on, and of its significance, in the allegations that at the end of the seventeenth century cargoes (chiefly precious metals) worth anything from £100,000 were being surreptitiously landed in obscure creeks and havens around New York and Philadelphia.

Hardly surprisingly, some pirates were able to set themselves up as princes or even kings in Madagascar, like that improbable pair

Abraham Samuells—offspring of a shipwrecked European sea captain and a Malagasy Queen—and his successor, a one-time ship's carpenter from Wales. Such potentates monopolised the slave trade of their domains, taxed vessels that came within their reach and in general carried on the style of the Portuguese frontiersmen in Burma and elsewhere. So, too, like European and Goan adventurers in East Africa they had armies, slaves and strings of local mistresses, the favourites—notwithstanding that they now bore such homely names as Moll, Sue and Peg—dressed in "the richest silks" and festooned with diamonds. But these regimes were not to endure much beyond the opening decades of the eighteenth century. European naval power grew stronger. Affronts to the rights of property could no longer be tolerated. Piracy sank from being a bold, admired and rewarding expression of bravura and rugged individualism to yet another vice of the lower orders. And now, too, the tentacles of Imperial Government began to reach the remotest corners of the world. The European pirate community in Madagascar died out, or was driven out, though the old traditional ways were for a time pursued by the offspring of local women and the last of the freebooters.

Western pirates, renegades and exiles were recruited from a wide spectrum of the lower ranks of European society and from many parts of the continent and its transatlantic possessions. Thus, of the crew of one ship *c.*1700, forty-three were English, fifty French and the remainder Danes, Dutch and Swedes, besides which complements frequently included non-Europeans and slaves. A handful of adventurers and pirate chiefs were, or claimed to be, men of some social standing. The celebrated Captain Bowen was of "creditable parents" from Bermuda; Captain Kidd was a son of the manse; and the redoubtable Henry Avery, who tried everything from logging in the Caribbean to a spell in the Royal Navy, was a supposed scion of the landed gentry. So, too, of course was that remarkable earlier Portuguese frontiersman, Diogo Soares de Mello. For the rest pirate crews were, like other renegade groups, made up from deserters from the employment of States or trading companies, failed merchants, disillusioned colonists, escaped convicts and runaway indentured servants (white slaves in fact) from the Atlantic settlements. Many, in common with pirates elsewhere, were former professional seamen. They included those who had turned freebooter for no better reason—so they said—than that they had been forced into it by their captors. Some had come on hard times, either shipwrecked or unemployed. There were others who had been packed off to sea by their relatives as dangerous or useless—addicted to "vice and drunkenness"—and were impatiently awaiting some change in their fortunes. And there were plenty who mutinied and seized their ships since they were, or considered themselves to be, ill-treated by their officers, swindled by their employers and persecuted by society—victims, as one put it, of "laws which rich men have made for their own security".[26] Ashore many Europeans, Portuguese especially, found themselves in exotic surroundings for the simple reason that as convicts they had been exiled there. Others, men and women alike, fled, as they did in the Americas, from regimes not to their liking. In 1653 the officers of the English East India Company at Madras feared their troops would disappear if disciplined, whilst an English sailor, captured by the Dutch (1653-54), received so cool a reception after struggling back to Surat that he promptly went over to the Mughals. Men similarly deserted from the Portuguese *Estado da India*, feeling themselves deprived of their rightful rewards by that network of influence, patronage and corruption that controlled preferment, or since they had suffered at the hands of royal officials.

Then there were those who turned pirate or renegade, or disappeared into exile on a drunken whim, or to avoid the consequences of crimes, real or alleged, or to escape their creditors—always a powerful incentive to swift and secret departure to distant places. Emboldened by drink a group of fuddled English seamen set off to join the Mughals in 1656. The colourful career of Diogo Soares de Mello in the Orient began when he was exiled to India for murder and received renewed momentum when he was obliged to flee the consequences of amatory brawls on arrival there. And Father Godinho discovered at the imperial Mughal court in the mid-1600s, all those comfortably ensconced there because of "crimes committed elsewhere".[27]

But Asia offered more than an agreeable refuge for the dispossessed, disinherited or disaffected of the West. Those Europeans who had seen, or heard of the riches of Vijayanagara or the Mughals were no longer content, as the saying went, to eat hay. Pirates flocked to the East. Others were able to enjoy, less arduously and precariously, lives in every way more rewarding than would have been their lot at home. Will Adams showed a natural enough reluctance to leave Japan in the early seventeenth century, where he was set up with an estate, a Japanese wife and (eventually) a Japanese mistress. A fellow countryman in the Celebes at the same date told his would-be rescuers that he had "nothing to live on in his counterye (but was) in the waye of doing himself good here".[28] Some years later yet another Englishman, this time serving the Mughals, wrote with engaging simplicity to his parents "I doe live well" and that—obviously a novel experience—he was now being paid. True, there was the considerable snag that though Mughal munificence was liberal, the real value of wages and gifts was eroded by the need to engage in that conspicuous consumption—that grand and elegant way of living—which, as the missionaries sourly observed, characterised imperial society. Then, of course, there were those entrepreneurs who attempted to have the best of both worlds. Portuguese adventurers in and around the Bay of Bengal in the sixteenth and early seventeenth centuries endeavoured to use the positions they had obtained in indigenous society, or the concessions they had secured from local rulers, to extract rewards and honours from the mother country, just as English pirates, if successful enough, might be transmuted into colonial governors, naval officers or landed squires.

Others meanwhile waxed rich on what Father Godinho succinctly described as "business opportunities". Thus they might be licensed to produce wine in the Mughal realms, which they did cheaply, and then sold their vintages at suitably enhanced prices.[29] They could engage in that infinity of trades that Asia offered, pursuing the same opportunities as were so avidly seized upon by western country traders of assorted nationality, especially those Portuguese and Indo-Portuguese who lived beyond the reach of Lusitanian authority, yet who were never quite either exiles or outlaws. It was, for example, Portuguese renegades, including some who had converted to Islam, who were thought to be behind much of the smuggling of pepper from Konkan ports in the early seventeenth century, to the distress of the *Estado's* few remaining honest officials. Alternatively, they could enjoy the rewards of office, like that one-time buccaneer who became chief gunner of the Maratha fleet and as such was entitled, along with his shipmates, to seventy-five per cent of the value of all prizes taken.

Nor was it merely riches, power or rank that Asia could offer. There was the chance for westerners to escape from those bonds and constraints imposed, however feebly, by the teachings of Christianity and the conventions of European civilisation. There were plenty of expatriates happy enough, then as now, to idle away their days in alcoholic stupor. There were plenty, too, coming from a Europe in whose Protestant realms fornication and its consequences were savagely punished, who were drawn to the apparent delights of societies in which slavery, concubinage and polygamy were widespread and accepted. Now they could live like that inebriated Dutchman we have already encountered or those Portuguese in the Bay of Bengal whose behaviour put a disapproving observer in mind of "wild men and untamed horses".[30] Others rejected the ordained social hierarchy and proposed to conduct themselves according to their own radical convictions. In pirate craft, captains and chief officers were elected by their crews—unthinkable in merchant vessels or men-of-war—and, equally unthinkable, all decisions of any consequence were taken by a mass meeting of the ship's company. Such democratic and unusual ways of proceeding underlay the even more remarkable attempts to establish "a sort of commonwealth" in Madagascar, reinforcing official suspicions that pirates would eventually set up somewhere an "alternative (and seditious) order". There briefly appeared on the island the so-called State of Libertatia, intended as a retirement home for freebooters, but from which slavery was banned and into which freed slaves were welcomed. And elsewhere in Madagascar there emerged, as we have already noticed, various homespun potentates: white skins, surrounded by their Malagasy women and retainers, yet—some at least—ruling their subjects in rude natural dignity.

Some exiles, outlaws and renegades could thus clearly live happily enough in their new environment even though many pirates were willing to accept pardons and there was a constant trickle of other Europeans, long domiciles in the East, back home. Enterprising, unscrupulous or fortunate individuals might become prodigiously wealthy and hence eligible for enthusiastic readmission to the bosom of their parent society. And in the early modern centuries, when the authority of European governments was still so fragile, rulers were in no position to risk the hostility, or to lose the potential services of so many men of proved ability. Thus the English Crown long tolerated the misdeeds of pirates who were, as an ex-rover turned naval officer explained in the early seventeenth century, "the most daring ... in war". Such indeed was the perception about them that Peter the Great of Russia and Charles XII of Sweden, together with many lesser lights, were involved in negotiations—all abortive in the long run—to harness their talents and resources to a variety of commercial schemes.[31] Not all former pirates could, however, become, like the celebrated William Dampier, explorers or naval captains. Many never took a prize, others gambled or drank away theirs Then again, though some Europeans achieved in indigenous service ranks they could scarcely have hoped for at home, none attained an eminence, or exercised an influence comparable to that of the Jews, Greeks, Italians and others in the far more primitive realms of the Ottomans. It was, moreover, the fate of many to come to a sudden and exceedingly unpleasant end—put to death for treachery suspected or anticipated—or at best to be summarily dismissed.

To attempt to strike a balance between the benefits accruing from the activities of European exiles, renegades and outlaws in Asia and the damage they inflicted is neither profitable nor possible. We can, however, see that luckless Portuguese convicts, dumped in out-of-the-way places, were able to provide their compatriots with useful information about local conditions and affairs, particularly in East Africa. More importantly, pirates and footloose Europeans opened up new and valuable trades, notably that between the Indian Ocean and Atlantic America, or—like Will Adams in Japan—facilitated the introduction of westerners into unfamiliar markets. One way or another they encouraged the dissemination of European technology in the East—selling arms, building western-style ships for local magnates—and so, like as not, exacerbated indigenous conflicts. But these were processes already set in train by the very arrival of Europeans in Asia. Again, the settlements made by adventurers, such as those of the Portuguese on the Coromandel coast of India, could provide the basis for the subsequent establishment of a more formal authority by their mother country. In the same way, the depredations of pirates in the Indian Ocean brought the intervention of European trading companies—concerned for the safety of their commerce—with the French, for example, digging in on Mauritius. Furthermore, though expatriates might live on amicable terms with local peoples—a further manifestation of that pragmatic tolerance which could flourish where diverse cultures met—they were just as likely to commit acts of fearsome brutality, with western pirates torturing or murdering the crews and passengers of the ships they took. On European maritime commerce in Asia freebooters inflicted some spectacular if isolated blows—none more remarkable than their capture of Dom Luis de Meneses. On indigenous seaborne trade their impact was more substantial, though not crippling. Their onslaughts in the Red Sea in the late seventeenth century disrupted the commerce of Mocha and, according to the former English chaplain at Surat, "so impoverish'd... some of the Mogul's people that they must either cease to carry on a trade or resolve to be made a prey".[32] Even so, usually working with only a single ship, or in small groups, their ravages were never so serious as those of the North African corsairs in the West in the seventeenth century. They did, however, provoke Mughal retaliation. An imperial fleet was projected and repeatedly in the course of the later 1600s officers of the English East India Company in the subcontinent were arrested, its factories closed, its goods impounded and compensation demanded for the damage done. Like their compatriots who were—at least in European eyes—more lawfully employed in Asia, western adventurers and freebooters had an influence that was locally significant but in general modest, which, given the paucity of their numbers and the vastness of the world in which they were operating, could hardly have been otherwise.

NOTES

[1] G.V. Scammell, *The Great Age of Discovery, 1450-1650,* London, Hakluyt Society, 1982, p. 6.

[2]G.V. Scammell, *The First Imperial Age, European Overseas Expansion c.1400-1715,* London, 1989.

[3]Genevieve Bouchon and Luis Filippe Thomaz (eds.), *Voyage dans les deltas du Gange et de L'Irraouaddy, 1521,* Paris, 1988, pp. 51 & 337.

[4]*The New Cambridge History of India,* I, 1; M.N. Pearson, *The Portuguese in India,* Cambridge, 1987, p. 87; G.V. Scammell, "The Pillars of Empire: Indigenous assistance and the Survival of the *Estado da India* c. 1600-1700", *Modern Asian Studies,* 22 (3), 1988, pp. 437ff at p. 485; Anthony Disney, "Smugglers and Smuggling in the Western half of the *Estado da India* in the late sixteenth and early seventeenth centuries", *Indica,* 26 (1-2), 1989, pp. 57ff at p. 65: *Intrepid Itinerant, Manuel Godinho and his journey from India to Portugal in 1663,* ed. and tr. John Correia-Afonso and Vitalio Lobo, Bombay, Oxford University Press, 1990, pp. 52 and 71; A.R. Kulkarni, "Marathas and the Sea", in K.S. Mathew (ed.),

Studies in Maritime History, Pondicherry, 1990, p. 9; Bouchon, *Voyage dans les deltas*, p. 62.

[5]Derek Massarella, *A World Elsewhere: Europe's Encounter with Japan in the Sixteenth and Seventeenth Centuries,* Yale UP, 1990, p. 105.

[6]Serafim D. Quiason, *English "Country Trade" with the Philippines, 1644-1765*, Quezon City, 1966, pp. 37ff.

[7]A huge fund of information on English and other renegades is to be found in F.C. Danvers and W. Foster (eds.), *Letters received by the English East India Company from its servants in the East, 1602-1617*, 6 vols., London, 1896-1902; W. Foster (ed.), *The English Factories in India, 1670-77, 1678-84,* new ser., Oxford, 1952-5. See also Charles Crey, *Pirates of the Eastern Seas*, 1618-1723, London, 1933.

[8]G.V. Scammell, *The World Encompassed. The First European Maritime Empires c.800-1650,* London, 1981, p. 412.

[9]Lady Fawcett (tr.) and Sir Charles Fawcett (ed.) with the assistance of Sir Richard Burn, *The Travels of the Abbé Carré in India and the Near East 1672 to 1674,* 3 vols., Hakluyt Society, 1947-8, III, 748ff.

[10]G.V. Scammell, "England, Portugal and the *Estado da India* c.1500-1635", *Modern Asian Studies,* 16 (2), 1982, pp. 177ff.

[11]Correia-Afonso (ed.), *Godinho*, p. 71.

[12]Foster et al., *Factories,* passim.

[13]G.V. Scammell, "Indigenous Assistance in the Establishment of Portuguese Power in Asia in the Sixteenth Century", *Modern Asian Studies,* 14 (1), 1980, pp. 1ff at pp. 3-4.

[14]Massarella, *World Elsewhere...*, pp. 81 and 132-3.

[15]W.H. Moreland (ed.), *Peter Floris: His Voyage to the East India in the Globe, 1611-15,* Hakluyt Society, 1934, p. 68.

[16]V. Ball (ed. & tr.), *Jean-Baptiste Tavernier, Travels in India, 1640-67,* revised ed. by William Crooke, OUP, 1925, I, pp. 203-7; cf. K.N. Chaudhuri, *Trade and Civilisation in the Indian Ocean. An Economic History from the Rise of Islam to 1750,* Cambridge, 1985, pp. 139-40.

[17]Kulkarni, "Marathas and the Sea", p. 96.

[18]Pearson, *Portuguese in India*, p. 86.

[19]Scammell, "Pillars of Empire", p. 485.

[20]Scammell, "England, Portugal and the *Estado*," p. 180.

[21]M.N. Pearson, "Pious Passengers' motivations for the Hajj from early modern India", in Mathew, *Studies in Maritime History*, pp. 112-26; see also the accounts of Joseph Pitts (c.1685) and Charles Jacques Poncet (1700-1791) in Sir William Foster, ed., *The Red Sea and Adjacent Countries at the Close of the Seventeenth Century,* Hakluyt Society, 1949, pp. 38 & 158.

[22]G.V. Scammell, "Shipowning in the Economy and Politics of Early Modern England", *The Historical Journal*, XV (3), 1972, pp. 385ff.

[23]Grey, Pirates, passim; C.R. Boxer, "The Count of Ericeira and the Pirates", *History Today,* XXIV, 1974, pp. 854ff.

[24]D.C. Coleman, *The Economy of England, 1450-1750,* Oxford, 1977, p. 133.

[25]Ralph Davis, *The Rise of the English Shipping Industry in the Seventeenth and Eighteenth Centuries,* London, 1962, pp. 136ff.

[26]Marcus Rediker, *Between the Devil and the Deep Blue Sea: Merchant Seamen, Pirates and the Anglo-American Maritime World 1700-1750,* Cambridge, 1987, p. 245.

[27]Pearson, *Portuguese in India,* p. 86; Correia-Afonso (ed.), *Godinho,* p. 209.

[28]Massarella, *World Elsewhere...,* pp. 80-1 and 105.

[29]Correia-Afonso (ed.), *Godinho,* pp. 67-8.

[30]Pearson, *Portuguese in India,* pp. 67-8.

[31]Holden Furber, *Rival Empires of Trade in the Orient 1600-1800,* Minneapolis, 1976, pp. 144-5.

[32]Foster (ed.), *The Red Sea,* pp. 175-7.

TAXATION IN THE COASTAL TOWNS OF WESTERN INDIA AND THE PORTUGUESE IN THE SIXTEENTH CENTURY

K.S. Mathew

The West Europeans' mercantile interest prompted them to attempt opening a direct sea route to the East. This would enable them to purchase the exotic commodities at source, avoid intermediary Muslims and Italian merchants and the exorbitant duties charged by the various rulers dominating the land routes. The Iberian monarchs came forward to sponsor the undaunted navigators, one of whom in search of India landed in the western hemisphere and the other anchored off Calicut on the west coast of India. When actual trade with India commenced after Vasco da Gama's explorative activities, the Portuguese were at a loss to find commodities that the Indian market would buy. Even for fitting out the early voyages they had taken loan from Italian financiers like Bartholomeo Marchioni. Yet Joao da Nova failed to sell the commodities he took with him to Cochin in 1501-2 and could not purchase Indian merchandise since he had neither cash nor precious metals.

The King of Portugal, Dom Manuel I added to his title a new epithet, "Lord of Navigation, Trade and Commerce of India" in 1501. It was decreed next year that all the ships should collect passes (*cartaz*) issued by the Portuguese captain or factor, failing which they would be attacked and confiscated. Though initial payment for the *cartaz* was nominal, the ships were bound to visit the stipulated ports under Portuguese power and pay customs on their cargo.

Unable to cope with the demands of the trade and commerce with India solely out of their own resources, the Portuguese tried to lure merchant financiers from Germany and Italy with liberal privileges and favourable conditions for large investments. The kings resisted for long the attempts of these financiers to obtain monopoly of trade with India. In the meantime, the Portuguese administration took pains to generate funds in India itself through plunder, taxes imposed on areas conquered by, or ceded to them, and by collecting customs at various coastal towns. The present study is intended to highlight taxation in two important regions of the west coast of India, namely Gujarat and Malabar coast, but emphasising Diu and Cochin, during the sixteenth century. Contemporary documents, chiefly in Portuguese, constitute its main source of information.

Jalal Khan, later known as Ahmed Shah II and brother of Mohammad Begada of Gujarat, after capturing the Chinese junks that arrived at Diu from Cochin, built a great mosque and laid the foundation for the port town of Diu.[1] Later Mohammad Begada, impressed by the gallantry and intelligence of Malik Ayaz, assigned the port of Diu to him with a view to developing it as an important port town.[2] Merchants from the Red Sea, Persian Gulf and from all the coastal regions of Arabia and India came to Diu for trade.[3] The customs house at Diu, and Gogla on its opposite side, across the creek, yielded substantial revenue in the early 1530s, and attracted the attention of the Portuguese.[4] They considered Diu "the key to the entire India" and desired to have a foothold there at any cost.[5] Aware of the importance of Diu as a commercial centre, Khwaja Safar, hailing from Albania, later in the service of the Sultan of Cairo, invested 300,000 *crusados* in Diu in the 1520s. At a later date, he had 600,000 *crusados* as his commercial capital at Diu.[6]

Malik Ayaz, under the scheme of developing Diu as an international port, requested Dom Francisco de Almeida, the first viceroy of Portuguese India, to send to Diu ships loaded with spices and copper.[7] Subsequent to the naval battle at Diu, a treay was concluded, and the Portuguese set up a factory at Diu in 1509, with Tristao de Ga as the factor, a writer and four others.[8]

The hallmark of the administration of Alfonso de Albuquerque, the governor of Portuguese India, was the acquisition of territories to bring up men of mixed blood to fight for Portugal and to generate local funds for administrative and commercial enterprises. He allied with Malik Gopi, a powerful merchant governor and king-maker of Gujarat, to have a fortified settlement in Diu. Their incessant attempts, however, bore fruit only about two decades later.

Diplomatic manoeuvring having failed, the Portuguese organised the largest fleet ever sent to India, with Nuno da Cunha as the captain-in-chief and St. Thomas, the Apostle of India, as its heavenly patron. Da Cunha was asked to establish a fortress in Gujarat, preferably in Diu. In order to be closer to the target, da Cunha shifted the capital of Portuguese India from Cochin to Goa in 1530. The Sultan of Gujarat, Bahadur Shah, was involved in a fight with Chitor. Probably, he was also afraid of an attack by the Mughal Emperor Humayun. To keep the Portuguese in good humour, in lieu of Din he surrendered Bassein and the seven islands of Bombay. The treaty between the Sultan and the Portuguese king, concluded on 24 December 1534,[9] gave the Portuguese the right to collect taxes on land and sea at and around Bassein.

Accordingly, all the vessels bound for the ports of the Red Sea or the Persian Gulf regions were bound to collect passes from the captain of the fortress at Bassein; and on their return they were required to visit Bassein to pay customs on their cargo. Vessels from the Straits were also similarly obliged to touch Bassein and pay customs. Refractory ships were confiscated. Horses being an important component of imports from Arabia and Persia, all horses from these regions had to pass through Bassein. Taxes were also collected at Mahim, Mazgaom Mumbaim, Caranja, Salcet and Thana. Betel leaves, oil, opium, vegetables, fish, salt, toddy, flowers and so on in the various villages surrendered to the Portuguese were taxed. Some villages were farmed out to collectors of taxes; some toll places (Caranja, Thana, Mahim) were auctioned.[10]

The Sultan of Gujarat had ceded Bassein to keep the covetous Portuguese off Diu, the most important entrepot of western India. But the huge revenue from Bassein only whetted their appetite for Diu. At last, caught between the more powerful land-based Mughals and the maritime forces of the Portuguese, the Sultan Bahadur opted for what he thought was the lesser evil. He permitted the Portuguese to occupy Diu as a purely temporary concession. The treaty between the Sultan and the King of Portugal, concluded on 25 October 1535, gave permission to the Portuguese to construct a fortress at any place of their choice in Diu. They were also entitled to collect customs on the horses brought from Ormuz and Arabia. The right of *cartaz* and collection of duties was thus shifted from Bassein to Diu.[11]

A new treaty, signed between Sultan Muhammed Shah of Gujarat and the King of Portugal on 11 March 1539, laid down a new system of revenue sharing. Accordingly, both Portuguese and Gujarati officials were posted at the four gates opening to the sea through which passage was permitted. The Portuguese officials were to stay in the city to monitor the movement of the commodities round the clock. All the customs income was received in the chief customs house at Diu. The Portuguese got a third of it and the Sultan the rest. Officials of both parties were to make entries of the income simultaneously; and decisions on specific issues were to be taken by mutual consent. Both the parties counted the cash, ascertained the receipts and kept the cash in a chest. The chest was double-locked, each party having a key. At the end of the month or quarter, the collection was divided. The expenses of the customs house were proportionately shared. Inspection of vessels and appraisal of commodities were done jointly. The Portuguese were entitled to customs on horses imported from the region from Rosalgatt to Ormuz; the Sultan on horses brought from the Arabian coast to Caixam and beyond the Straits.[12]

The Sultan of Gujarat lost Diu to the Portuguese in 1546, when the troops of Khwaja Sofar, who had been trying to retake Diu for the Sultan, were routed. The Portuguese now had all the customs revenue as also revenue from local taxes at Diu.

Horses were charged forty-two *pardaos* as customs. There was also tax on local products like oil, ghee, fish, opium, arrack and betel leaves. Besides the principal customs house at Diu, there were minor ones in Gogla, Vanakbara and Pallarym.[13] It was reported around 1568 that merchants from all over the world were happy to go over to Diu where better security than in any other port was found. As a result, the income of Diu increased by leaps and bounds. If Goa and Bassein had to come to its help in the initial stages by sending about 30,000 *pardaos* annually, around 1568 the income from Diu itself provided for its various expenses and sent regularly more than 30,000 *pardaos* to Goa every year.[14]

The revenue from Diu along with that of the customs house at Daman was farmed out in 1574 for 131,500 *pardaos.* This was a considerable decrease over previous years because no ships reached Diu that year. Even so there was a significant increase in six years. Besides this amount, 3,000 *pardaos* as customs duties from the horses were to be added. Thus the total revenue of 1574, excluding the expected income from the scheduled ships, amounted to 134,500 *pardaos.*[15] The amount usually received by the Portuguese from ships to which *cartazes* were issued was quite huge, especially when they returned from the region of the Persian Gulf and Red Sea. Ships from Mocha carried silver, gold, coral and other items of great value; accordingly, they paid large sums as customs. When Gujarat was annexed by Akbar in 1572 and friendly relations were established with the Portuguese at Diu, it was agreed that Akbar could be given every year a free *cartaz* to send his ship from Surat to Mocha. This implied that the ship on its return trip would not be taxed. It was estimated by Portuguese writers of the period that more than 15,000 *cruzados*(?) were lost to the Portuguese by exempting just one ship a year![16] The total income from Diu around 1581 amounted to 100,000 *pardaos* after deducting the various expenditures incurred for administration.[17]

The attempts made by the Portuguese under various pretexts to collect taxes at the port town of Cochin and the background in which they established themselves there with a settlement of their own, protected by a fortress, speak for their keen interest in generating local funds. Relations with the King of Cochin were much more delicate than those with any other ruler on the subcontinent of India, and there was no ground for the Portuguese to collect taxes at this port. When they were repelled by the Zamorin of Calicut, the King of Cochin permitted them to have a factory there in December 1500, and to commence commercial enterprise. As João de Nova failed to procure commodities from Cochin in 1501-2, on account of lack of funds and difficulty of disposing of the European goods brought by the Portuguese, as noted above, the King of Cochin came forward as a surety for the merchandise supplied by the local merchants on credit. He helped Vasco da Gama in 1503 to come to terms with the merchants regarding the fixation of the prices of commodities, which lasted for several decades.

With a view to extracting permission to build a fortified fortress built of stone against the existing tradition of the land, the Portuguese set fire to their own factory and settlement. The sympathetic King then issued orders to build a fortress of stone in a place of their own choice, throwing to the winds the prevailing tradition of the country. The King of Cochin put up a vigorous fight against the Zamorin for giving asylum to the Portuguese, losing a few of the members of his royal family in the process. He accepted the position of a vassal and took oath of fealty and vassalage to the King of Portugal at the time of his coronation in 1505 by the first viceroy of Portuguese India, Francisco de Almeida. He advanced considerable loans to the Portuguese whenever they were in financial problems. They owed him 10,000 *ducats* in 1513. He also helped them that year to get cargo as they did not have funds.[18] Even though the Portuguese promised not to enter on any friendly relations with the Zamorin without the consent of Cochin, treaties of peace and friendship were concluded with the Zamorin to the dismay of Cochin. He remonstrated in writing to the King of Portugal between 1512 and 1516, but did not in any way reduce his support to the Portuguese.

Against the backdrop of the delicate relations existing from 1500 onwards, the Portuguese King through his officials asked Cochin to become a Christian. He also asked Alfonso de Albuquerque to conquer Cochin. But the Portuguese Governor, though imperialist to the core, wrote back to the King pointing out the unfairness of such a step since Cochin was the only person who had stood by the Portuguese through thick and thin.[19] Cochin permitted them to develop a settlement in Cochin parallel to the town of the local people. This settlement was later raised to the status of a city by John III, the King of Portugal through a charter issued on 12 March 1527. This city grew up as a great urban centre with several institutions not answerable to Cochin. It laid claim to collect taxes and customs duties at the port of Cochin and issued orders to this effect. When Cochin took up the matter with the King of Portugal, they pretended it had been a mistake. After several discussions, a treaty was concluded. Still the Portuguese established their claim for a share of the customs duties and taxes.

Before the sixteenth century, even before the Portuguese came, the King of Cochin obliged everyone to pay customs at Cochin for cloves, nutmegs, maces, cloth from Bengal, sealing wax, and tin (*calaim*), which was brought from Malacca through Coromandel.[20] Details on the rate and quantum of taxation are not available. Since commodities not mentioned above were exempted from taxation, presumably the King was getting a large amount on taxed items. Trade in cloth with Bengal was an important economic activity before the sixteenth century. After establishing themselves at Cochin, the Portuguese continued this. Similarly, after the conquest of Malacca in 1511 the Portuguese developed trade with Southeast Asian countries, Coromandel and Bengal, from their base in Cochin.

A number of merchants from Italy and Germany came and settled in Cochin soon after the direct sea route connecting the Malabar coast with Portugal was opened. Among these were: Leonardo Nardi, a Florentine merchant and agent of Bartholomeo Marchioni, who was in Cochin from 1501;[21] Girolamo Sernigi, Florentine, in the first decade of the sixteenth century, taking active part in trade with the southern India;[22] Giovanni Buonagrazia from Florence, who reached Cochin with Vasco da Gama in 1502: he owned a vessel in Vasco da Gama's fleet;[23] Andrea Corsali, who stayed for a couple of years in Cochin, engaging himself in trade with Southeast Asia and Malabar coast: he was familiar with Persian and Malayalam;[24] Francesco Corbinelli, also from Florence, who was quite active in the trade based in Cochin, along with Giovanni da Empoli, another Italian;[25] Pietro Strozzi, Italian: after a few years of stay, he died in Cochin;[26] Giovanni di Vecenzo Rifolfi, Piero di Giovanni di Dino, Mariotto di Vico da Granaiuolo di Valdelsa, and Filippo Cambini.[27] Three vessels owned by the consortium of Augsburg merchants, Germany, also reached Cochin along with the fleet of Francisco de Almeida. Later a number of German merchants like the Fuggers, Welsers, Hochstetter, Imhof and Hirschvogel sent their agents to Cochin, for trade in pearls, precious metals and pepper. The huge amount of taxes that Cochin was deriving on all the goods passing though it from Southeast Asia, Coromandel, Bengal and Malabar, made the Portuguese King greedy. Even after shifting the political capital of Portuguese India to Goa, Cochin continued to be the commercial headquarters.

To revert to the taxes imposed on Cochin by Portugal, Affonso Mexia, the Comptroller of Finances for Portuguese India, issued an order in the 1520s, whereby the residents of the city of Cochin were asked to pay duties to the King of Portugal on cloves, nutmegs, mace, textiles of Bengal, sealing wax and tin brought to Cochin from Malacca via Coromandel. All other items were exempted from duties, according to long-standing custom. Deprived of a large sum, especially in the wake of unprecedented increase of trade in these items conducted by the Portuguese, the Italians and the German merchants, the aggrieved King of Cochin represented to John III, King of Portugal. He mentioned that the port of Cochin was on land under his jurisdiction. Since he was the ruler of that region, he argued, the right to collect taxes or duties was exclusively his. He requested the Portuguese King to respect his right.

Presumably, convinced of his argument, King John issued an order addressed to Dom Nuno da Cunha, Governor of Portuguese India (1529-39) on 24 February 1530. He instructed the Governor, the Comptroller of Finances and all their successors to observe this order. The King of Portugal reiterated that he was pleased with the long-standing friendship of Cochin and the valuable services rendered by him. The Portuguese officials were asked not to prevent him from collecting taxes on commodities brought to the port of Cochin by the Portuguese Christians. Interference of any sort by the Portuguese officials was forbidden. The successive Governors and Viceroys acknowledged this right and reissued the orderMartim Afonso de Sousa (1542-45) on 12 January 1543, Jorge Cabral (1549-50) on 24 January 1550 and the secretary of Afonso de Noronha (1550-54) on 7 December 1550.[28]

Portuguese officials availed of every opportunity to enhance the income of their part of Cochin. Viceroy Dom Afonso de Noronha issued an order on 2 January 1551, to collect a special tax of one *pardão* each from the Muslim and Canarese merchants interested in conducting trade in the city.[29] Unaware of the order issued by the King of Portugal prohibiting interference by Portuguese officials in the tax affairs of Cochin, Francisco Barreto, the Governor (1555-58) issued an order asking the Portuguese settlers at Cochin to pay customs to the King of Cochin on all commodities brought to Cochin irrespective of the port of origin. The aldermen and officials of Cochin represented to Barreto, presented to him a copy of the order issued by the Portuguese King, and requested him not to change their tax traditions. Excusing himself of not having been aware of the prevailing custom, he issued another order on 3 February 1558 restoring status quo ante.[30]

Dom Antão de Noronha (1564-68), the Portuguese Viceroy was reported to have issued an order asking the married Portuguese settlers of Cochin to pay duties to the King of Cochin on commodities of *all sorts* brought to the port of Cochin as at Goa.[31] This order does not seem to have been protested. Later, the aldermen and officials of municipality of Cochin introduced a new tax of an extra one per cent on all commodities, including food materials, brought to the port of Cochin. This was meant for the construction of ships at Cochin. The Viceroy Dom Antonio de Noronha (1571-73) endorsed the decision and issued an order to this effect on 30 October 1572.[32]

Felippe I, who took over the administration of Portugal in 1580, wrote on 7 September to the King of Cochin confirming all the grants made and the agreements concluded by his predecessors from the time of Emmanuel I. An order issued by a Portuguese Viceroy affirmed the right of the King of Cochin to collect duties on *all* the commodities brought to the port of Cochin by the married settlers of the city of Cochin in the same way on commodities brought by the Hindus and Muslims both for entry and exit.[33] The officers of the King of Cochin argued that this order of the Viceroy was also ratified by King Philip I through his letter of 7 September 1580.

Since the revenue claims made on the port of Cochin by the Portuguese and the King of Cochin had become quite confusing, it was felt necessary to spell out minutely the details of these rights. The friendship and generosity of Cochin, who remained a loyal vassal of the King of Portugal on the one hand, and the laudable services of the Portuguese married settlers on the other, prompted the Portuguese authorities to conclude a contract with all solemnity in 1584 in this regard. The monastery of St. Antony at the City of Santa Cruz, Cochin was the venue. Dom Duate Menezes, the Viceroy (1584-88) represented the Portuguese King. Itiquanach Menon, Captain General and Governor General, represented Cochin. Twenty- four persons elected by the residents of Cochin also participated in the deliberations leading to the agreement signed on 12 December 1584. Others present were the interpreter of the King of Cochin, Attorney General of the Portuguese, and several other officials like the Comptroller of Finances, procurator of the city, the writer of the factory and that of the municipality. The following were some of the provisions of the agreement:

> Both the Portuguese and Cochin renounced whatever rights they had so far enjoyed as regards the collection of revenues at Cochin. Both agreed to accept the terms and conditions laid down in the present document.

A general customs house was established at Cochin for all merchandise brought to Cochin and taken from there by land and water. Bachelors and persons in the service of the King of Portugal were asked to pay six per cent taxes to the King of Cochin and *lagimas* (? perks) to the officials. They were to pay taxes both for entry and exit. The married settlers were required to pay only 3.5

per cent tax to the King of Cochin, and only for entry. Commodities of all sorts were taxed. Both bachelors and married residents were expected to pay one per cent for the city.

The Hindus, Muslims, Jews, Armenians, *Mukkuvas,* Christians, Parava Christians, Venetians, Christians of St. Thomas and local Christians of southern parts were asked to pay customs duties just as before to the King of Cochin. But the Christian residents of the city of Cochin were bound to pay only 3.5 per cent entry tax. All were obliged to pay one per cent to the city.

The Portuguese King was given the right to collect taxes on all commodities which the Portuguese and the officials of the Portuguese, Eurasians (mestizos), Portuguese born in India, and local Christians of the northern regions might send to the port of Cochin. The rate of revenue collection was fixed as six per cent both for entry and exit besides the perks to the officials. One per cent additional tax for the city was obligatory. The married settlers of Cochin were not required to pay perks to the officials. Those in the service of the King of Cochin were expected to pay customs duties to the King of Cochin even though the commodities brought by them were not from the northern parts. In the same way, Christians of the northern part were bound to pay duties to the King of Portugal for commodities they brought from south.

Matters related to the handling of taxes meant either for the King of Cochin or for the King of Portugal were to be settled as a whole in the same customs house jointly by officials of both parties. No handling of such matters outside the customs house was permitted. The King of Portugal was expected to help the King of Cochin in the collection of revenues at the port of Cochin for himself by sending Portuguese officials who would do the work as if it was meant for the King of Portugal. These officials were not to permit the residents of the kingdom of Cochin to go to Goa when they brought their commodities from China, Malacca, Moluccaos, Pegu, Tenasserim, Martaban, Bengal and other parts of the south, without paying customs duties at Cochin.

The expenses related to the surveillance of the port and the persons appointed to keep watch of the customs house and the payment of the officials working there were to be shared by both parties. The respective officials were appointed by the Viceroy of Portuguese India as also the King of Cochin. Those in the service of the King of Cochin, Muslims, Jews, Hindus and others mentioned above were bound to pay exit duties to the King of Cochin for things purchased from bachelors. If the residents of the native town of Cochin (*Cochin de cima*) entered the port of Cochin, they were expected to appear before the customs house. If they did not carry goods other than food materials, and these were of the residents of native Cochin, such as Nairs and others, they were to be permitted to proceed to native Cochin town, according to the orders of the King of Cochin.

If by chance the commodities of the married settlers reached any customs house other than that of Cochin, they could be released with the undertaking that customs duties would be paid to the King of Cochin in view of the appraisal made in that particular customs house.

There was no obligation to pay exit duties on commodities purchased from bachelors by the married residents or those purchased from the latter. Similarly, the married residents were not expected to pay any tolls on the commodities brought by land or river except the stipulated three and a half per cent.[34]

The Portuguese Governor, Manuel de Sousa Coutinho (1588-91) issued an order on 6 April 1590, permitting the officials of the municipality of Cochin to collect half a per cent tax from the residents of the city. This amount was meant for the construction of a new jetty enabling easy movement of the ships.[35]

An order issued by Governor and Archbishop Alexio de Menezes on 11 August 1607 exempted the married settlers of Cochin from paying taxes on the commodities brought from south of Cochin at Goa provided they carried a certificate issued by the officers of the King of Cochin to the effect that duties were paid at Cochin. But they were asked to unload the goods at Goa and show the certificate and proceed further north if they wanted. They were not bound to pay further taxes.[36]

The agreement reached between the Kings of Cochin and Portugal protected the Portuguese married settlers and also the Christian settlers of the town of Cochin under the jurisdiction of the municipality. Only three and a half per cent taxes were levied on them. Similarly, those coming from the regions north of Cochin were brought under the jurisdiction of the Portuguese King. Taxes were imposed on all items, unlike before the arrival of the Portuguese. These settlers were also exempted from paying *lagimas* to the officials. But in practice, the one per cent tax was insisted upon from everyone without discrimination.

The attempts made by the Portuguese to levy taxes from Gujarat and Malabar indicate the need they felt to generate local funds to conduct trade and commerce as also to meet the financial requirements of administration. In the territory of Bassein, the collection of taxes from people engaged in the production of various agricultural and non-agricultural items and from those engaged in exchange activities, surrendered to them by the ruler of Gujarat, could be justified on the assumption that the surrender involved transfer of right over the territory and proprietary possession. But they insisted that all ships moving in the Indian Ocean regions should collect passes from the Portuguese captain of Bassein; and that they should return to the same port or any other port suggested by the Portuguese officials to pay taxes to the Portuguese. Similarly, an obligation was imposed on everyone dealing in horses from Arabia and Persia, that all horses bound for India had to be brought to Bassein and customs duties on them paid to the Portuguese at Bassein. These claims, definitely, were not warranted by the right they got through the surrender of Bassein. They were an encroachment on the freedom to move in the Arabian Sea or Indian Ocean.

After establishing a fortress at Diu after 1535, the Portuguese insisted that all ships plying in the Arabian Sea or Indian Ocean should collect passes from the Portuguese officials at Diu and that they should return to the same port to pay customs. Similarly, all the horses imported to India from the Persian Gulf, Red Sea regions and Sind were to be brought to Diu for paying approximately forty-two *pardaos* per horse. The Portuguese were given only a place to build a fortress, but no territory was surrendered to them at this stage. Therefore, it should be assumed that the claim was not because of their proprietary right on land, but because of their presumed claim of supremacy over the Indian Ocean regions.

By 1539, as we have observed above, the system of sharing of revenues at the ports of Diu and Goghla was accepted. One-third of the total revenue at these ports was appropriated by the Portuguese. With the acquisition of the entire island of Diu, they collected taxes systematically from the cultivators, artisans, craftsmen, merchants and from the vessels plying in the region of Diu and further. Everyone, including the great Akbar was asked to collect *cartazes* from the Portuguese for sending his ships anywhere. In view of the agreement, one free *cartaz* was given annually to the Mughal empire. So, no other reason than their claim for supremacy over the Indian Ocean regions could be found as the basis for their activities in Gujarat.

The same claim was reiterated for collection of tax at the port of Cochin. The ambitious ruler of Cochin, trying to liberate himself from the clutches of a sort of vassalage to the Zamorin of Calicut, fell prey to the Portuguese. Availing themselves of the opportunity, the Portuguese extorted the right to build up a fortress and an urban settlement in Cochin next to the native town of Cochin. They could not get any territorial possession in Cochin other than this. But with the liberal concessions made by the king, they developed a fortified settlement with a number of institutions, both civil and ecclesiastical. The King of Cochin was permitted by the Portuguese to collect taxes only on specified items brought from south of Cochin. Whenever he asserted his right on any other items or whenever the Portuguese Viceroys consented to let him collect taxes on such items by oversight, the Portuguese residents made representations to the authorities concerned and the attempt was withdrawn. On some occasions the Portuguese authorities themselves laid claims for revenues from all the merchandise irrespective of the existing practice. The King of Cochin was not allowed to collect taxes on commodities brought from the north.

The Portuguese went a step ahead. They insisted on a favoured treatment for Portuguese married residents and Christian settlers even for merchandise brought from the south of Cochin. The preferential treatment for their own subjects and co-religionists speaks again for their special claim. Besides, all were asked to pay one per cent additional tax on every item for the Portuguese town of Cochin. Despite the delicate relation they had with the King of Cochin, they acted as if they had proprietary rights over the Indian Ocean regions. The right to collect taxes from territories conquered by, or ceded to them could be explained in the light of their proprietary possession. The claim they laid for the revenues in the coastal towns was presumably based on their assumed supremacy over the Indian Ocean and the Arabian Sea.

The Portuguese claim in the Indian Ocean regions was justified very graphically by a Portuguese historian of the first half of the sixteenth century, João de Barros. To begin with, he buttresses the assumption of the title "*Senhor da Navegação, Conquista e commercio da Ethiopia, Arabia, Persia e India*" (Lord of navigation, conquest and commerce of Ethiopia, Arabia, Persia and India) by Dom Manuel in 1501 and then the subsequent right of monopoly by bringing the various juridical and ecclesiastical reasons into play. The King assumed the title in the wake of the discovery of the sea route by Vasco da Gama and especially after the return of Pedro Alvares Cabral. He took possession of whatever was discovered and was conceded and granted to him by the supreme pontiffs. This grant was made because of the large expenditure incurred by Portugal in terms of bloodshed, sacrifice of lives of the Portuguese, sickness and dangers and works of thousand sorts in discovering the new lands.

Dom Manuel I, King of Portugal, took the title because the supreme pontiffs, beginning with Pope Eugene IV and Pope Nicolas V to Pope Sixtus IV, granted to Portugal everything from Cape Bojador till the end of the East that they would discover. The entire India, islands, seas, ports, fisheries and so on were clearly included in the papal donations. The King ordered Vasco da Gama and Pedro Alvares Cabral to discover three things, which no king of Europe cared for, nor tried to discover. The ruler of Portugal assumed the title over these three essential things of the entire Orient. He discovered the navigation of the unknown seas through which people travelled from Portugal to India in the East; he took possession of the route of navigation by navigating in it. The King discovered the lands inhabited by the idolatrous gentiles (Hindus) and heretical Muslims to be able to conquer and take away these lands from their hands; they being unlawful holders since they denied to God the glory due to him as Creator and Redeemer. Hence the King assumed the title over these lands. He discovered the trade in spices which was dealt by those infidels. Just as he was the lord of the route and of the conquest of the land, it was fitting that he be the lord of trade of that land.

Barros added that there was no need of further justification for these titles assumed by the King than the first apostolic grant. These titles, based on the papal grant, were again confirmed by the right of usurpation or prescription, as the jurist put, of more than fifty or so years of possession as seen in the process of Portuguese history. He referred to the undisturbed and pacific possession of the land for a stipulated period, which gave a proprietary right by the legal title called prescription.

As regards navigation, the power of the Portuguese fleets in the oriental regions was so great that with these fleets Portugal could be the lord of the seas. This made both the Hindus and the Muslims ask for certificate of safe conduct called *cartaz* from the Portuguese officials posted in India so that they could peacefully and securely send their ships. If an infidel from places where there were no Portuguese fortresses or with which the Portuguese had no friendly relations was found, he could be rightfully captured, as in a just war.

Portuguese writers of the time recognised that seas had to be regarded as open to everyone, since there was no other public passage. They held, too, that a Christian through faith and baptism was brought under the jurisdiction of the Roman Church; thereby, he was subject to Roman law. They further opined that the common right of passage in the seas for navigators and the obligation of respecting the property of those navigating in the seas were applicable only in Europe—and that, too, only to Christians. The Portuguese and other kingdoms directly under the Pope observed this law not because they were subject to the imperial law as feudatories, but because these laws were just and agreeable to reason, which was considered the mother of law.

Muslims and Hindus were not privileged to enjoy the advantages of these laws. They were outside the law of Christ, which was the true one to be respected and held in esteem by everyone, under pain of eternal fire. The Hindus and Muslims were not members of the evangelical community, though they were in potency while alive. Evidently, they lost the common right because they did not accept the Christian faith. Further, even those who received that faith were not entitled to this right in the oriental regions because, before the Portuguese entered India, and took possession of it, none of them had acquired any property by way of inheritance or conquest. So, nobody but the Portuguese had any right in India. This state of affairs was based on the natural principle and common law, according to Barros.

As regards title of conquest, Sofala, Quilon, Mombacsa, Ormuz, Goa, Malaccsa and Moluccas with all the islands were under the jurisdiction of the Portuguese King even before the end of the first half of the sixteenth century. The city of Diu and Bassein with the lands attached to them were also in possession of Portugal. Similarly, Chaul, Bhatkal and all those areas where Portugal had fortresses and officials for administration had been under the Portuguese King. Quilon and Mombasa had been given up on account of sickness and lack of any good results. The islands of Socotra and Anjediv, being not essential, were left out. Moreover, there were other areas, and ports which were in friendly relation with the Portuguese and received Portuguese vessels as the Portugal was their ruling power.

The title of trade was also due to the King of Portugal. This was clear because several ships carrying spices and other sorts of commodities used to reach Portugal from India every year. Commercial relations of this nature presupposed the agreement of two contracting parties which entailed peace, friendship and observance or obedience to the contract. Beyond this general convention, Portugal had trade with India in three ways: First, trade was conducted with the conquered areas of the Indian Ocean regions by establishing commercial relations with the local people as vassal with the lord of the vassal, whose revenues for entry and exit belonged to the crown of Portugal. Secondly, the Portuguese concluded permanent contracts with the local kings and rulers regarding the prices of commodities purchased and sold by the Portuguese—as with the kings of Cannanore, Chale, Cochin, Quilon and Ceylon. These were the lords of all the spices available in India. The contract was only for the supply of spices to the officials of the Portuguese King stationed in his factories in India for the annual fleet going over to Portugal. Commodities other than spices were free to be purchased by the Portuguese privateers and local people at any price mutually agreed upon. Thirdly, the Portuguese merchant vessels plied through all the parts of the Indian Ocean conforming to the practice of the place and exchanging commodities with the local people at prices agreed among themselves.[37]

These views and arguments were challenged by other European powers, especially in the wake of the vigorous activities of Protestantism. The first doctrinal and systematic exposition rejecting the Portuguese claims of supremacy over the Indian Ocean regions came from the Dutch scholar Hugo Grotius, who was called upon to find justification for the capture of a Portuguese ship and its confiscation in the East.

Presumably, the wave of Protestant revolution that was rampant in the Low countries, and the inveterate enmity of the Netherlanders towards the Spanish throne, prompted them to call the papal bulls in question and flout Portuguese supremacy. This was aggravated by the fact that the Spanish King, who since 1850 was also the King of Portugal, prohibited the sale of spices to the Protestants. Hugo Grotius, with a view to justify the capture of the Portuguese galleon, *Santa Caterina*, published in 1608 his *Mare Liberum* attacking the monopolist attitude of the Portuguese, and defending the right of Vereenigde Oost-Indische Compagnie.

The English went a step further than the merchant adventurers of the Levant Company. They established the English East India Company and acquired a foothold in the port towns of India. The English mind, too, was not ready to accept the arguments put forward by the Portuguese and the Dutch as a final verdict on the subject. William Welwood published the booklet *An Abridgement of the all the Sea-Laws* in 1613, providing the theoretical background for the British claims to the domination of the sea. John Seldam defended the right of the British Crown to appropriate sea and land and refuted the ideas expressed in Mare Liberum. His tract, entitled *Mare Clausum*, was written in 1617 or 1618. In 1619, Welwood wrote *De Dominio Maris Jurisbusque ad Dominium Praecipue Spectantibus Assertio brevis ac methodica*. This, too, argued against the proposition of Grotius. Seraphim de Freitas, a Portuguese writer and professor at the University of Valladolid, asserted and reaffirmed the right of the Portuguese and published a number of arguments refuting those of Grotius and other theorists. This book, entitled *De Justo Imperio Lusitanorum Asiatico,* was published in 1625. Thus, both Portuguese and Dutch claims for domination of the Indian Ocean and the adjacent areas were challenged by interested parties who vied with each other for free trade in the Indian Ocean region. By the second half of the seventeenth century, the Portuguese were confined to the colonies of Goa, Daman and Diu, giving way to other European powers.

It may be concluded that on realising the need for generating local funds, the Portuguese had recourse to various legal presumptions buttressing their claim for supremacy over the Indian Ocean regions. The levy of taxes from the areas under their jurisdiction such as Goa, Bassein, Daman and Diu in course of time provided them with a sizable amount to cater to the needs of administration and trade. The success achieved by the Portuguese gave incentives to other powers like the French and the English who, too, came to India basically for trade and commerce. The French collected systematically land revenue from the areas around Pondicherry and the eighty villages surrendered to them near Pondicherry by Chanda Sahib of Carnatic in 1749 and later confirmed by Muzaffar Jung, the Nizam of Hyderabad. Further, they collected land revenues systematically from the villages around Masulipatam and the northern Sarkars of Andhra, namely, Mustafanagar, Ellore, Rajahmundry and Chicacole, all of which were granted to them by Muzaffar Jung. As protectors of the Nizam, they collected land revenue from the districts leased out to them. The English went a step ahead of the French. As soon as they won the Battle of Plassey in 1757 they got the zamindari of the Twenty-four parganas near Calcutta, from where they began to collect land revenue. Later, by 1760, they got the zamindari of the districts of Burdwan, Midnapore and Chittagong. After the victory at the Battle of Buxar, they extracted from the fugitive Mughal Emperor Shah Alam II the approval of their right to collect revenues from Bengal, Bihar and Orissa, namely the *diwani.* Thus the Portuguese showed the way for other European powers to collect revenues from India itself, to generate funds locally for trade and commerce and stop the flow of money and precious metals from the home countries. But in claiming supremacy over the merchant vessels plying in the Indian Ocean regions and buttressing their presumed legitimacy based on papal authority and other legal fictions, the Portuguese stand out. The taxation on the port towns was based on legal presumptions that could not stand the test of reasoning and argumentation initiated by the Dutch, the English and the French.

NOTES

[1]João de Barros, relying on the Chronicles of the Sultanate of Gujarat, presumably *Tarikh-i-Bahadur Shahi* of Hussan-ud-din Khan and other contemporary sources, wrote in the first half of the sixteenth century about the rise of Diu. Ref. João de Barros, Da Asia, Decada II, part I, Lisboa, 1778, pp. 213-14.

[2]Gaspar Correa, *Lendas da India*, tomo 1, Coimbra, 1922, pp.746-7; Haji and Dabir, *An Arabic History of Gujarat,* Baroda, 1974, vol. 1, p.34; Tomé Pires, *The Suma Oriental of Tomé Pires,* Nendeln Liechtenstein, 1967, p.35.

[3]Barros, *op.cit.*, Decada II, part I, p. 214.

[4]The anonymous author of "Lembranças das Cousas da India em 1525" gives 4,200 million *crusados* as the annual income from Diu from customs

duties by 1525. Ref. Rodrigo José de Lima Felner, *Subsidios para a Historia da India Portugueza,* Lisboa, 1888, pp. 34-6.

[5]Luciano Ribeiro, "Preamubulos do primeiro cerco de Diu", *Stvdia* no.10, Lisboa, 1962, p.190.

[6]Diogo do Couto, *Da Asia,* Decada IV, part 1, Lisboa, 1778, p.211, Decada V, part 1, p.199, MSS. Archivo Nacional da Torre do Tombo (hereafter ANTT) *Cartas dos vicereis,* Maço unico, no.24.

[7]Fernao Lopes de Castenheda, *Historia do Descobrimento e Conquista da India pelos Portugueses,* Coimbra, 1924, livro II, p. 385.

[8]Correa, *op.cit.,* tomo I, pp. 596-7.

[9]Simão Botelho, "O Tombo do Estado da India" in Rodrigo Jose de Lima Felner, pp.134-8; Diogo do Couto, Decada IV, liv.IX, cap.II, pp.316-9; Julio Firmino Judice Biker, *Collecção de Tratados e Concertos de pazes que o Estado da India Portugueza fez com os Reis e Senhores com que teve Relações nas partes da Asia e Africa oriental desde o principio da conquista até ao fim do seculo XVIII,* tomo I, Lisboa, 1881, pp.63-75.

[10]Simão Botelho, *op.cit.,* pp.138-50.

[11]Simão Botelho, *op.cit.,* folio 180v.

[12]Biker, *op.cit.,* tomo I, pp. 75-83.

[13]Panduronga, S.S. Pissurlencar (ed.), *Regimentos das Fortalezas da India,* Bastora, 1951, pp.268-71.

[14]José Wicki, "Duas relações sobre a situação da India Portuguesa nos annos 1568 e 1569", *Stvdia,* no.8, Lisboa, 1961, p.177.

[15]Jean Aubin (ed.), "Le Orçamento do Estado da India de Antonio de Abreu (1574)", *Stvdia,* no.4, Lisboa, 1959, pp.179-80.

[16]Diogo do Couto, *op.cit.,* Decada IX, pp. 81-5.

[17]MSS ANTT. "Fundo Antigo", no.845. Ref. also Artur Teodore de Matos, *O Estado da India nos anos de 1581-1588,* Ponta Dalgada, 1982, pp.87ff.

[18]Raymundo Antonio de Bulhão Pato (ed.), *Cartas de Affonso de Albuquerque seguidas de documentos que as elucidam* (hereafter Cartas....), tomo III, Lisboa, 1903, pp.396-7.

[19]*Cartas....,* tomo I, pp.367-9.

[20]MSS. Bibliotheca da Ajuda, Lisbon, codex no.51-VII-14 folio 23 and K.S. Mathew & Afzal Ahmad (eds.), *The Emergence of Cochin in the Pre-Industrial Era: A Study of Portuguese Cochin,* Pondicherry, 1990, p.35.

[21]Herman Kellenbenz, "The Portuguese discoveries and the Indian and German initiatives in the Indian trade in the first two decades of the 16th century", *Congresso International: Bartholomeu Dias, sua epoca: Actas,* vol. III, Porto, 1989, pp. 611-12.

[22]Marco Spallanzani, "Fiorentini e Portoghesi" in *Aspetti della vita economica Medievalle, Atti del convegno di Studi nel X Anniversario della morte di Federigo Melis,* Firenze-Pisa-Prato, 10-14 Marzo, pp.321-32.

[23]*Ibid.*

[24]Herman Kellenbenz, *op.cit.*, p. 612.

[25]Virginia Rau, "Un Florentino an Service de l'expansion Portugaise: Francesco Corbinelli" in *Fatti e idee di Storia economica nei secoli XII-XX. Studi dedicati a Franco Borlandi*, Bologna, 1977, in Kellenbenz, p.610 and Marco Spallanzani, *Giovanni da Empoli mercante e Navigatore Fiorentino*, Firenze, S.P.E.S., 1984, p.254.

[26]G. Uzielli, "Pietro di Andrea Strozzi, viaggiatore Fiorentino del secolo delle Scoperte" in *Miscellanea della Societa geografica Italiana*, V, 1895, pp.1-41.

[27]Herman Kellenbenz, p.613.

[28]MSS. Bibliotheca da Ajuda, codex 1, folios 47-8.

[29]*Ibid.*, folio 18.v

[30]*Ibid.*, folio 23r-23.v

[31]*Ibid.*, folio 47.

[32]*Ibid.*, folio 37.

[33]*Ibid.*, folio 48.

[34]*Ibid.*, folio 50v-54.v

[35]*Ibid.*, folio 56.

[36]*Ibid.*, folio 70.v

[37]João de Barros, *Asia*, Decada I, 6th ed. by Hernani Cidade and Manuel Murias, Lisboa, 1935, pp.227-30.

DISPUTE FOR MACAO TRADE BETWEEN EUROPEAN POWERS FROM THE SIXTEENTH CENTURY TO THE NINETEENTH CENTURY

Deng Kaisong

Since Portuguese lease of Macao in middle sixteenth century, Macao had become the commercial entràpot between the West and the East. It monopolised China's foreign trade, resulting in the jealousy of the European powers. With the decline of their hegemonic place in the East since the seventeenth century, the Portuguese had lost their colonial trading posts in Africa and Asia. Seeing this, the European powers attempted to take Macao from the Portuguese, and turned it into a base to invade China. During the two centuries before the breakout of Opium War, Macao had been the strategic point in the 'Trade War' and 'Colony War' between the European powers. This paper will inquire into the course of the fight between the European powers like Portugal, Spain, Holland, Britain and France for Macao trade during this period.

I

In 1535, the Portuguese bribed the Chinese local official Huang Qing into a yearly tribute of a cargo tax of 20,000 taels of silver, in exchange of berthing merchant ships at Macao port, and making trade right on these ships. In 1553, the Portuguese presented their wish to lease the land of Huogen (Macao) to dry in the sun the goods soaked in the sea water when the ship was racked by the waves.[1] The Commander-in-Chief of the expedition from Goa to Japan, Leonel de Sousa, offered a bribe of 1,000 taels of silver each year to Wang Bo, the local officer in charge of the ports in Guangdong Province, to get the permission of berthing the Portuguese merchant ships at Macao port. From then on, Macao was let by lease of land to the Portuguese who tried to use it as the trading post to monopolise China's foreign trade. Busy trade was carried on between Macao and Goa, Nagasaki, Manila and other European and American ports. Large galleons with loads of 600 to 1,600 tons were sailing between Lisbon, Goa, Nagasaki, Manila, Acapulco and Lima, among which the trading line between Goa, Macao and Nagasaki was the busiest. During this period, Macao eventually turned into the exterior port of Guangzhou and the first entràpot between the West and the East. The Portuguese made great profits by using Macao as a port to ship goods in and out. According to statistics, between 1580 and 1590, the shipment of raw silk from Macao to Goa alone had brought the Portuguese a yearly profit of 360,000 taels of silver. In 1636, the profit reached 720,000 taels of silver.[2]

The profit ratio of a particular cargo is even more surprising. For instance, of the twenty-three kinds of cargo shipped from Macao to Nagasaki and Goa, sixteen cargoes had a profit ratio of over 100 per cent. What is more, the Portuguese tried to grab more wealth from China by trading in Chinese coolie (labour force) and opium smuggled to Macao. As early as 1613, they had begun to make profits by trading in innumerable number of men and women yearly in Macao.[3] In the Qing dynasty, they set up 'Pig market' in public, selling thousands of Chinese labourers. According to Portuguese official figures, from 1856 to 1873, the Chinese coolies exported from Macao numbered 182,500.[4] The profit ratio of coolie trade reached as high as 800 per cent, much higher than that of common goods. Besides, the Portuguese were almost the sole trader to export opium to China.[5] At first, "they shipped to China a small amount of opium from Goa and Daman, the Portuguese leased territory in the north-west coast of India".[6] After that, the opium trade was increasingly large. In short, the Portuguese had seized exceptionally great wealth from China by monopolising the trade in Macao. According to a rough estimate by the Portuguese historians, the Portuguese gained a yearly profit of one million Escudo from their colonies in Asia, a large part of which came from the trade in Macao. Portugal's illegal occupation of Macao and the mystically great profits gained from its monopolisation of the West-East trade caused exceedingly great jealousy of the other European colonial powers like Spain, Holland, England and France. They came one after another to Macao, fighting fiercely against the Portuguese.

II

Spain had actively planned its invasion of China ever since its occupation of the Philippines. In 1597, Miguel Logez de Legazpi, Commander of the expedition to the Far East, suggested that the Spanish King should detach a fleet to the coastal areas of China, "to see what's going on there, and accomplish other vitally important missions."[7] In 1586, the Governor of the Philippines reported to the Spanish King, Philip II, by saying that, made up of beggars, the Chinese army could not stand a single blow. The invasions of the coastal China should be speeded up, he suggested.

In 1590, under order of the Spanish King, the Governor of the Philippines sent a warship to Macao to purchase munitions and other commodities. Although the Governor of the Philippines repeatedly expressed his friendly attitude to the Portuguese, the latter feared the coming of the Spaniards would be a threat to their monopolistic place in the trade in Macao. They "were constantly on the alert for the Spaniards,"[8] so that no sooner did the Spanish ship arrive at Macao than it was detained by the Portuguese. To relax the tension caused by the incident, the Spanish King issued an order in 1594, laying an embargo on direct trade between the Philippines, Macao and China. In 1595, the Governor of Goa also declared that they would never allow the Spanish to interfere in Macao's business affairs.[9]

In spite of numerous restrictions placed by the Portuguese, the Governor of Manila tried to break through the Portuguese monopoly of trade in Macao. In 1598, he sent Juan de Zamu-dio to head a warship to Macao for direct purchase of China's iron, aluminium and other goods. On 5 September, the ship "arrived and berthed at Macao port, requesting to trade with China. The local authorities condemned the ship for breaking China's law by intruding China's territory and decided to repel it. The foreign merchants in Macao were told not to make any contacts with the Spanish."[10] In October, the ship sailed to Humen. The Spanish demanded of the local authorities of Guangdong province to make room for Spanish traders to reside in, store up cargo, do business and build a trading port. This caused great panic among the Portuguese. They told the Governor of Guangdong that the Spaniards were gangsters and pirates, and appealed to the Ming authorities to expel them from China. In the meantime they protested against the Spanish. Zhang Panghan, the Deputy Officer of Sea Affairs in Guangdong province, "summoned his soldiers and gave orders to burn the shelters of the Spanish". But the Spanish "did not leave China for the east"[11] until 1 October the following year. Before the Spanish could leave Guangdong, the Portuguese launched a sudden attack on the Spanish flagship. Retreating to Manila with goods from China, the Spanish swore to retaliate. They expelled the Portuguese from the Philippines, monopolised the trade between Manila and Japan and made great profit from it. For a long time thereafter, the Spanish did not revisit Macao until 1744, when the Governor of Manila sent three Spanish warships to harass Macao. As the Chinese authorities had been on full guard against the Spanish, their attempt to scramble for the trade in Macao did not succeed.

III

After the revolution in the Netherlands from the end of the sixteenth century to the beginning of the seventeenth, Holland abruptly gained prominence in Europe. United with Britain, it defeated Spain and became the new maritime overlord after Spain. In 1595, the Dutch sent naval forces to Bantam and made mandatory trade with the natives. Seeing the Portuguese occupy Macao, and make great profit by trading with China, India, Japan and American countries, the Dutch felt envious. They attempted to drive the Portuguese out of Macao at all cost, monopolise the Macao market and grab wealth from China. "Since the Portuguese began to trade in Xiang Shan (Macao) and occupied Luzon, the Dutch had ever been jealous".[12] Since then, the Dutch often came eastward to Macao and fought violently against the Portuguese.

In 1599, the Dutch New Brabant Company put forward a proposal to open China's market. In 1601, the Dutch ships made their first appearance in Macao, "requesting to trade with the Chinese, without any evil intentions".[13] The Portuguese, however, "worried that the real purpose of the Dutch under pretext of mutual trade was nothing but" to occupy Macao. So they expelled the Dutch by force.[14] In the battle, five Portuguese were killed or wounded, twenty Dutch soldiers were captured, of whom seventeen were gibbeted and three were sent to the Strait of Malacca. The Dutch decided to retaliate by plundering Portuguese merchant ships. At the beginning of 1603, the Dutch fleet robbed the Portuguese ships in the Strait of Malacca, taking away artistic works worth 5.7 million silver dollars and lacquerware, pottery and other goods. In July the same year, the Dutch fleet intercepted a Portuguese merchant ship near Macao, looted its cargo and burnt the ship. The loot was much and rich. There were, for example, 2,800 sacks of milk powder, each costing 500 guilder, the total amounting to 1.4 million guilder (equal to two million Chinese silver dollars).

In July 1604, the Dutch merchant vessel, under command of Captain Witbrand Van Wearük, left Dutch East Indies for Macao. They intended to trade with the Chinese, but were forced back by the Portuguese. Then the ship was blown to Pescadores (Penhu) by hurricane, where it met fifty Chinese junks and was forced to go back. In 1607, Captain Malelief commanded a Dutch warship scouting in the sea waters of Macao. He made some contacts with the Chinese local officers and was allured ashore by the Portuguese, who burnt the ship and drove them out of Macao. But the Dutch were never willing to admit defeat in Macao. In January 1614, Jan Pietersoom Coen, the Governor of Indonesia, wrote to the Director of the Dutch India Company suggesting another attack on Macao, to drive the Portuguese out and seize the trade in Macao. He pointed out that if the Dutch attacked and occupied Macao, they could not only replace the Portuguese for the supply of Chinese silk to the Japanese market, but also cut the Portuguese Empire's supply line in Asia so as to get directly China's wealth and resources which the whole world had long thirsted for.[15] If they could not take Macao, they could take Pescadores and Taiwan. He told Kornelies Reyersz that, "if we want to break through the way to trading with China, we must, apart from seizing Macao with the help of God, build castles in a favourite region in Zhangzhou or near Guangdong, and garrison troops in them". "If we can not take Macao (which I don't wish so), we must garrison some fleets around Macao, and send the main force to what is called on the map the Pescadores (Penhu)". "While the main force of the above-mentioned fleets is sailing to Pescadores, we should, whether or not we have taken Macao, immediately send several sailing ships or local vessels to Taiwan and the other islands nearby seeing it there are best harbours and places to build a city on and to assemble troops."[16]

After such busy mobilisations and preparations, the Dutch

despatched seventeen warships (including two English ships) and 2,000 soldiers (among whom 900 were Dutch soldiers, the rest being Malaysian and Japanese) under command of Admiral Kornelies Reyersz. The expedition set out from Indonesia and got to Macao on 20 June. They launched a forceful attack on Macao. But Lopo Sarmento de Learalho, Commander-in-Chief of the Portuguese forces in Macao, had given orders to the fortresses to get ready for the Dutch attack and announced a martial law on all missionaries and citizens. The acting president of the Madre de Deus College (SÉo Paulo), Bruao, ordered his men to move four cannons to SÉo Paulo keeping guard against the Dutch attack. The authorities in Manila sent Spanish troops to the sea waters of Macao, to help the Portuguese. The war for Macao had in fact become a war between Holland and Britain on one side and Spain and Portugal on the other. On 24 June, the Dutch bombarded the city wall of Sao Francisco, through which about 600 to 800 Dutch soldiers landed. Just then, the Portuguese fired four shells at the landing soldiers from the nearby hills of Sâo Paulo. An amunition box was hit and caused a tremendous explosion, which drove the Dutch soldiers into great confusion, who fled in panic. The Portuguese troops lying in ambush then set upon them, landing them into even greater confusion. Some were killed, some drowned and the rest retreated to the ships on the sea. The battle lasted two hours; about 200 to 300 Dutch soldiers were killed or wounded; the captain of the Dutch troops was captured; and four Dutch warships were burnt down.

It look the Dutch some time to forget this fiasco. They attacked again in 1627, and failed again. In 1661, they planned to take another offensive for Macao, but did not succeed. In 1688, the Dutch fleet came to Macao, but was hit by gunfire from Monte Fortress, and was repelled again. Five times the Dutch attacked Macao, five times they failed. Nevertheless, the Dutch admired and valued highly the Macao market, declaring that "we would like to exchange Macao for any of our colonies in the Far East, except for Batavia and Sri Lanka."[17] After these failures, the Dutch by making use of their control of the Strait of Malacca, cut Macao's connection with Goa and Europe, and dealt a heavy blow to the Portuguese trade in Macao. In the eighteenth century, with the decline of the Dutch, Britain, which was on the ascendant, came to Macao for another round of fight against the Portuguese.

IV

The British first came to Macao in 1635. That year, with the purpose of finding a foothold in China and trading directly with China, the British East India Company sent the warship *London* to Macao.

The Englishmen had permission from the Governor of Goa. They were received by the Portuguese in Macao and given a hand in the trade with China. In the same year, the English King, Charles I, despatched a merchant fleet under command of John Weddell, in pursuit of warehouses in China. In 1637, the fleet sailed into the waters of Macao, and anchored at the port of Taipa. Fearing that the Englishmen might seize the business from Macao, the Portuguese refused them permission to land. Failing to disembark at Macao, the English fleet sailed into the mouth of Pearl River, requesting to trade in Guangzhou. The Chinese troops in the Humen fortress fired artillery, trying to stop the fleet. The Englishmen fought back, attacked and occupied the fortress, pulled down the Chinese national flag and took away thirty-five Chinese cannons, which they later returned to China after the protest of the Chinese Government. After returning to England, Weddell put forward to the English King the plan to occupy Hainan island. The plan was not carried out because of the breakout of the English Revolution.

The 1642-48 English bourgeois revolution established bourgeois political power and stimulated its foreign trade and colonial plunder. On 9 August 1644, an English fleet, sent by the British East India Company, made its first appearance in Macao. But the Chinese authorities did not allow them to trade unless they paid a tax of 2,000 taels of silver. The Englishmen bargained for half the price, but were refused. The Portuguese also made trouble for them. So they left for Bantam after five months' stay in Macao. In 1674, the East India Company sent another merchant ship to Macao, but only sold ten bolts of cloth at a very low price. Again in 1688 and 1689, two ships were sent to Macao, but could not bargain on acceptable tax amount.

The Englishmen were greatly discontented with their failures in Macao. In the eighteenth century, they changed tact. In November 1742, an English warship intruded into China's territory, Macao, for the first time. The captain requested to sail into Guangzhou under the pretext of repairing the hull of the ship and getting food supplies. The ship was not a convoy ship to escort cargo fleet, but one taking part in the fighting against the Spanish naval forces in Peru. It had no business to enter Chinese waters. When the Qing government refused the demand, the captain gave an ultimatum that unless his demand was met within twenty-four hours, his ship would force a way to Guangzhou. When the corrupt Qing government made an exception by consenting to the captain's demand, he further demanded that the Qing government should make full preparations for what he needed as soon as possible. "Bread must be baked, pork must be salted", he shouted. What a pirate logic! In 1765, the English Governor of India despatched a warship to Macao, with 100 rupees worth of silver dollars. The Guangdong Customs Macao Office demanded to inspect the ship, but was refused by the captain, who claimed: "If inspection of any ship under my command is demanded, it will not be worth my duty." In fact, the ship was loaded with such contraband as opium. In 1766, the British Royal Navy warship carried a large amount of silver, sailing into Macao. The captain declared, as soon as the ship got ashore: "We swear that there is no opium, nor other cargo. Therefore, China cannot take it for something beyond a merchant ship or a warship." He refused to pay the tax required and threatened the Chinese local authorities that, "If their (Chinese) fortress fires first, they will very soon know that it is useless for such fortress to hold back the attack of a British warship".[18]

At the end of the eighteenth century, with powerful merchant fleets and warships, Britain had become the most prosperous commercial centre and the most powerful colonial country in the world. When so many of its efforts to seek trade in China never succeeded, the Director of the English East India Company wrote to the Governor of India saying that he maintained that the British should replace Portugal for the occupation of Macao and make Macao a big business port in the east. In 1789, the English King George III appointed Charles Cathicari Ambassador to China in the hope of improving Britain's trading affairs in China and being ceded a place or an island to do business. In 1792, George Macartney was sent to Macao and next year he was in Beijing. On the occasion of the eightieth birth anniversary of Emperor Qian Long, he requested permission to dispatch a diplomatic envoy to Beijing, but was refused.

At the end of the eighteenth century, caused by the French Revolution, there were many wars between the European countries, especially England and France. In 1795, the French warship *La Flaria* came to Macao in pursuit of an English ship. France and Portugal were then at war. The Municipal Senate of Macao was about to detain the French ship as captured. The dispute was settled when the magistrate of Xiangshan country intervened. In 1801, the allied forces of France and Spain invaded Portugal. For its own interests in the Indian Ocean, Britain decided to detach troops to assist the Portuguese and help them in defence of Macao. The Governor of India, Marquis Wellesley, sent six warships reaching Macao on 15 February. The Portuguese in Macao did not welcome the visit of the English warships. "The Chinese authorities were surprised at the English expedition's intention to occupy Macao".[19] The Portuguese reported to the Qing government in Beijing and the local authorities in Guangdong Province of the attempted invasion by the English ships, and asked China for protection. Indignantly resentful of the Portuguese attitude, Britain decided to seek revenge. In defence of the visit, it explained that the warships' purpose in coming to China was "nothing but to protect Portugual from being invaded by France". In 1808, 100,000 French troops invaded Spain, causing the breakout of the Peninsular War. The Governor of British India, Lord Minto, sent nine warships and 300 soldiers from Madras, under command of Admiral William O' Brian Druny. Under pretext of helping the Portuguese against the French,[20] they sailed from Madras in India, arrived at the sea waters of Macao and made a forceful landing on 21 September. The troops made a fierce attack on Macao, occupying the fortresses of Guia, S. Francisco and Bomparto.[21]

The Chinese Government took a strong stand against the English invasion of Macao, declaring that Macao was part of China's territory, but not a dependency of Portugal. Therefore, Britain had no right "to protect Macao". It warned the English troops "to withdraw from Macao and sail offshore immediately". If the Englishmen "dared to break China's law again", the Chinese Government would assemble large forces to encircle and supress them.[22] Meanwhile, the Chinese Government disposed troops around the town of Xiangshan and Macao, in full battle array. Under pressure of the Qing government, the Englishmen retreated.

After repeated failures in Macao, the English shifted their attention to Hong Kong, and finally occupied Hong Kong after the breakout of the Opium War.

To sum up, in the two centuries between the middle of the sixteenth century and the beginning of the nineteenth century, the European colonial powers—Portugal, Spain, Holland, Britain and France—waged 'Trade War' and 'Colonial War' in Macao on the pretext of promoting trade. Their real purpose was nothing but to occupy Macao and set up their colonial base, open the enclosed door of China and exercise economic invasion of China. This is by no means historical coincidence, but has deep social and economic roots.

First, the development of the capitalist mode of production of the European colonial countries stimulated these countries to fight for trade in Macao, so as to meet their needs in primitive accumulation of capitalism.

Second, with vast territory, rich resources and large population, China had a strong appeal to the colonial countries in Western Europe. Macao was the gateway to go deeper into China's big market.

Third, the peculiarly favourable natural conditions (shallow water and monsoon climate) of the port of Macao were advantageous to berthing sail-ships of the early colonial countries in Western Europe.

The fight for trade in Macao lasted over two hundred years. The 'Trade War' and 'Colonial War', were not without great influence on both their home economy and China's economy and society.

First, it promoted the rise and development of the capitalist mode of production in Western European countries.

The sixteenth and seventeenth centuries saw the disintegration of the feudal system and the primitive accumulation of capital in Western European countries. The term primitive accumulation of capital has two connotations, i.e., exploitation at home and plunder of foreign countries. Between the middle of the sixteenth century and the beginning of the nineteenth century, the colonial powers Portugal, Spain, Holland, Britain and France came to fight each other in Macao, each intending to occupy Macao. The competition ended in Portugal's illegal lease of Macao, upon which they built a base to carry out trade and loot to interior China, Southeast Asia, America, Europe and Africa. Portugal shipped cargoes from European countries to Macao, by which they transported Chinese goods out to all parts of the world and sold them at a much higher price. From the trade in Macao, especially the savage coolie (labourer) trade and the evil opium trade, ·they made enormous profits. Through the trade in Macao, the Portuguese plundered treasures not only from China but also from Southeast Asia, America and African countries.

On the other hand, in the sixteenth century, the mode of production in Western European countries was at a far lower level than in China. So, these colonial countries chose to trade with China via Macao. In course of the trade with China, the Chinese advanced technology in metallurgy, silk and ship-building was diffused to these countries. It not only promoted the development of the productive force in these countries, but also played an important role in the course of the Bourgeois Revolution in the seventeenth century and the Industrial Revolution in the eighteenth century.

Second, it accelerated the disintegration of the feudal economic structure in China. Owing to the European powers' competition for trade, China's traditional silk, tea and earthware were exported to other countries, in exchange for large amount of silver, which sharply increased the treasure of the Beijing authorities. This was favourable to China's tax system because it changed from tax paid in kind into tax paid in currency. China's production and economy were also promoted to a certain extent. More significant was the development of commodity economy and the rise of handicraft industry in Guangdong Province.

Third, it promoted China's foreign exchange of science and technology and culture. Macao, the exterior port of Guangzhou, had become the entrêpot of this foreign trade and the centre for Chinese foreign technology and cultural exchange. From Macao, China's silk products, porcelain and lacquerware were exported to the rest of the world, and its technique in these handicrafts was consequently followed and studied by the world's people. Likewise, with the foreign traders and missionaries coming to China, western advanced technology in astronomy, calendar, mathematics, physics and medicine, etc. also spread to China and had a great influence on China's social life.

NOTES

[1]Kuo, Fei, *Gazetteer of Guangdong from 1573 to 1620*, vol. 69, Macao.

[2]Deng, Kaisong; Huang, Qichen, *The Rise and Fall of Macau's Foreign Trade in the Ming and Qing Dynasty*, Research of Chinese History, 3rd issue, 1984.

[3]Kuo, Shangbin, *A Report to the Emperor by Guo Gei*, vol. 1, p. 35. See also *A Book of Taxes and Corvèe in Guangdong Province.*

[4]Chen, Hansen, According to the statistics on '*Historical Sources of the Overseas Chinese Labourers*', issue 4, Zhong Hua Book Store, 1982, p. 55.

[5]*Selected Works of Marx and Engels*, vol. 2, p. 136.

[6]Greenburg, *A History of Sino-Britain Trade before the Opium War*, Zhong Hua Book Store, 1964, p. 99.

[7]Jin, Zhuguang, *Gazetteer of Guangdong from 1662 to 1723*, vol. 28, p. 23.

[8]C.R. Boxer, *Macao as a Religious and Commercial Entrêpot in the Sixteenth and Seventeenth Centuries*, Acta Asiatica, 26, 1974, p. 4.

[9]Zhang, Tianzhe, *A Study of Sino-Portuguese Trade*, pp. 105-6.

[10]Zhang, Weihua, *Notes on the Four European Countries in the History of Ming Dynasty*, p. 83.

[11]*Ibid.*

[12]*History of the Ming Dynasty*, vol. 235, Holland.

[13]*Ibid.*

[14]Wang, Lingheng, "A Traveller's Note of Guangdong", *A Study of Invaders*, vol. 3, p. 21.

[15]C.K. Boxer, *Fidaigos in Far East 1550-1770*, Hong Kong, pp. 45-7, 73.

[16]Quoted from Sugi Naojir", *The Story of the Building of the Town by Relanzhe?*

[17]C.A. Montalton de Jersus, *Historic Macao*, Hong Kong, 1984, pp. 5, 6, 7 & 125.

[18]H.B. Mores, *The Chronicles of the East India Company Trading to China 1635-1834*, vol. II, pp. 20-1.

[19]*Ibid.*, vol. III, p. 76.

[20]*Ibid.*, p. 92.

[21]*Historic Materials of Ming Dynasty*, pp. 24-5.

[22]*Historic Facts about the Diplomatic Affairs from 1796 to 1821*, vol. 2.

COASTAL SOCIETY IN BENGAL: MERCANTILE ENTERPRISE AND URBANISATION, 1575-1608

Aniruddha Ray

European travellers in India[1] had theorised that the merchants and the weavers would not leave their areas, although Babur[2] long ago had stated the contrary about peasants. Here, in a brief span of nearly fifty years, end of the sixteenth to early seventeenth century, we would try to analyse the mobility of the people linked with new enterprise and urbanisation. We would analyse the migration of population from the Bhagirathi river towards the Padma river as well as to the west of the Bhagirathi, which had changed the socio-economic situation of coastal Bengal. We would use the contemporary Bengali poems, letters of the contemporary travellers as well as the extant Persian sources translated into English. Interestingly, the rise and fall of Bâro Bhuyians, the twelve semi-autonomous *zamindars* of Bengal are involved in the emergence of a new situation in the background of the Mughal-Afgan contest for supremacy, which had inspired the Bengal nationalist writings from the middle of the nineteenth century.

Before Gaur was abandoned in 1575, it was the principal urban centre in Bengal. Doubts had been raised about the existence of the legendary city of Bengala, which was claimed as the principal urban centre of Bengal. It can now be established that the city of Bengala was Gaur.[3]

Although Gaur was known from the eighth century as Laksmanabati,[4] its phenomenal rise could be traced with the arrival of the Turks in Bengal. It had remained as capital till the fourteenth century when it was shifted to Pandua, about thirty kilometres northwest of Gaur. It is taken for granted that the river had shifted from Gaur, which led to the transfer of capital. We would see how far this hypothesis can be accepted. The account of Ibn Battuta,[5] who came to Bengal at this time, spoke of intense civil war, which would throw a doubt on the shifting-of-the-river thesis. Battuta called Saptagram (Satgaon) a big city and mentioned that the entire area from Saptagram to Gaur was full of urban settlements.

The capital of Bengal had often been shifted in quick succession. By the end of the fifteenth century, Gaur was once more made the capital. In 1563, the capital was shifted to Tanda by Suleiman Karrani, by which time, we are told, the river had shifted away from Gaur. In 1575, the captial was brought back to Gaur by the Mughal General Munim Khan but it was shortly abandoned due to the plague. The capital was taken to Rajmahal, on the other side of the river from where it was brought to Dacca in 1608. It was once more shifted to Rajmahal after 1639; brought back to Dacca after 1659, and shifted to Murshidabad in the early eighteenth century. The shifting of the river could not have been the cause of so many shifts. One may postulate that the politico-economic axis had shifted from one area to another. In this brief essay, we would try to analyse the elements of such a process within a brief time-span.

From the writings of Thome Pires[6] and Duarte Barbosa[7] of the sixteenth century, it becomes clear that Gaur was the principal urban centre of Bengal. Out of approximately 40,000 inhabitants, most of whom were living in huts, there were Bengali merchants who carried goods up to Malacca. Some of them used to live there permanently. The principal items were textile and its products. Yet Gaur was not the overseas port; it was served by another port nearby.

With the coming of the Portuguese in the second decade of the sixteenth century, we get a better view of Gaur. It was estimated that this biggest city of Bengal had 200,000 inhabitants.[8] The number appears exaggerated as we find approximately the same number at Surat at the end of the seventeenth century, then at its height.[9] From the Portuguese descriptions of the city of Gaur, we get the view of a big avenue lined by shops on both sides with people thronging the streets, while the big palaces were on both sides of the avenue. Behind these avenues, there were different quarters earmarked for the sale of different commodities,[10] a picture that was not much different from those of Delhi or Agra of later days.[11]

That Gaur was not an overseas port may be seen from the writings of Le Blanc[12] at the end of the sixteenth century, apart from the Portuguese writings earlier in the century. The merchandise had to be carried to Gaur by the winding Bhagirathi river for nearly twenty miles. During ebbtide, it was difficult for bigger boats to go to Gaur and in full moon, the city used to get flooded. Le Blanc did not get terribly excited by Gaur; he was far more impressed by Calicut or Cambay. Yet Gaur was the wholesale depot where foreign merchants, including the Chinese, the Russians or the Georgians and others carried on commerce even by overland route. It was the wholesale mart of Bengal drawing the surplus of the countryside.

Le Blanc called Gaur the usual Moorish city. We can see this from the extant ruins as well as the description left behind by the English travellers from the end of the eighteenth century. The description of Major Rennel[13] or Creighton[14] would show that the ruins had continued all along the river for fifteen to twenty-five kilometres. Its breadth was only between three to five kilometres. Therefore most of the roads of the city ran parallel with some criss-crossings. There was a brick dam to prevent the city from getting flooded during the full moon. There were small canals to channelise the surplus water on which were bridges, pictures of which adorned the books of Ravenshaw and Creighton.[15] There were *hammams*, inns and mosques—all pointing to the Islamic style of the city architecture, the hallmark of a Moorish city usually found in North India.

The fall of Gaur was not an isolated phenomenon. It was the decline and decay of an entire area or, more properly, a region that had suffered devastation in a long and bloody war. Many of the satellite towns around Gaur, so much praised by Ibn Battuta earlier, also suffered decline at the same time. Despite the frequent changes of the capital, no other city or town could take the place of Gaur. The fall of Gaur was the disintegration of the symbiotic relationship between the metropolis and the satellite, the disruption of the communication between the principal city and its hinterland.[16] To look for the shifting course of the river as the principal motor would take our enquiry away from the contemporary socio-economic structure and its changes within.

It is interesting that the port of Saptagram declined at the same time that the Mughal Emperor gave the Farman to the Portuguese to establish at Hughli, a few miles downstream on the main channel of the river. These three incidents (the fall of Gaur, the fall of Saptagram and the rise of Hughli) were neither isolated nor sudden. The newly appointed Mughal General, Islam Khan, marched on the banks of the Padma river in eastern Bengal in the early seventeenth century, instead of the Bhagirathi banks. It is rather surprising that he went straight towards eastern Bengal than seize the Hughli-Saptagram complex. But in the light of the history of the area, his decision was natural and timely.

Among the satellite towns of Gaur, one finds similarities and dissimilarities. Pandua near Gaur, was once a capital. Buchanon Hamilton,[17] traveller of the late eighteenth and early nineteenth centuries, has referred to it as a big city. He had seen the ruins of an old palace encircled by broken walls. Eleven kilometres from Pandua was Malda.[18] Its rise began with the establishment of the English factory in the seventeenth century. It had been prosperous but the old city had completely vanished long since. Tanta had gained some fame for its mint.[19] Devikot, on the northern border, was a big city in the pre-Mughal era. The author of *Tabaqat-i-Nasiri*[20] had classified it as the second city after Lakhsmanabati. Perhaps its prosperity was due to the overland trade with countries beyond the Himalayas. The old city could not be traced now.

Thus, the rise and fall of certain cities in this area had continued over a long period of time. It only showed that Gaur was not the only urban centre. A large number of smaller towns and cities on the banks of the Bhagirathi had created a complex of urban settlements. Walls, lofty gates, mosques, *hammams*, caravans and *reis* did show a certain social and political connection with northern India. But the further one goes towards the sea, the more this style diminishes. In eastern Bengal, particularly in the coastal areas, this style was rather rare. Therefore, there was no uniform social structure in different areas of Bengal, due to uneven development over time.

One of the oldest cities of India, Saptagram (Satgaon in Irfan Habib's *Atlas*)[21] was famous in the *Rarh* area (modern Burdwan, Howrah, Hughli, Midnapore, Nadia and Twenty-four Parganas). It was a *sarkar* (including the city) during the time of Abul Fazl,[22] which then included Nadia, Hughli and Twenty-four Parganas. At the time of Muhammed bin Tughluq, it was a mint town, issuing its last coin in A.D. 1550.

At the end of the sixteenth century, Mukundaram Chakrabarty,[23] the Bengali poet, expressed his dissatisfaction with the Rarh area but praised the city of Saptagram. He found the banias of Saptagram getting all the wealth by sitting with him. Yet the legendary merchant of the poet, Dhanapati Saudagar, purchased goods for his seven ships at Saptagram and reached the mouth of the sea through the Saraswati river.[24] The river was still navigable and there was no other port between Saptagram and the sea. In that case Saptagram was acting as the principal port of Gaur.

It would be difficult to compute the revenue of Saptagram port since no serious work has been done as yet. From a contemporary Bengali poem of the early sixteenth century, it may be inferred that two Hindus had taken *ijara* of Saptagram for twelve lakh rupees and collected around twenty lakh rupees,[25] a fantastic figure comparable to the revenue of Surat in its heyday.[26] Even assuming that this figure included the land revenue of the dependent villages, the amount appears highly exaggerated. Abul Fazl, at the end of the sixteenth century, had given the figure of slightly more than four lakh rupees for the entire Saptagram *sarkar*,[27] which was obviously based on Tódar Mal's *Bandobast*, which in turn was based on the records of the Afgan period. The description of the contemporary Bengali poet Krishnaram seems to suggest that Saptagram city was extended up to Tribeni, the confluence of three rivers and full of people.[28] While by the end of the fifteenth century, Bibpradas Piplai, the contemporary Bengali poet, had described the prosperity of Saptagram,[29] Nihar Ranjan Ray had detected the gradual silting of the Saraswati river on which Saptagram was located, by a study of the same source.[30]

Around A.D. 1530, the Portuguese were calling Saptagram a prosperous city but its death-knell had already been sounded. Big ships of the Portuguese could not enter the Saraswati river and they had to unlade the goods at Betore on the Bhagirathi to transport it by smaller boats to Saptagram.[31] Around this time, one would notice the existence of Sheths Basaks near modern Calcutta, close to Betore,[32] obviously engaged in trade with the Portuguese. Mentioned by the contemporary Bengali poets, Portuguese writers and travellers, Betore never tried to substitute Saptagram although it helped the port to survive. Yet the silting of the Saraswati may not have been the principal cause of the decline of Saptagram port. Both Surat and Cambay had the same characteristics. The cause therefore lay in the movement of the historical forces of the times.

The struggle for the control of the hinterland of Gaur and Saptagram was the principal historical force at this time. In 1536, after the defeat of Muhammed Shah III at the hands of Sher Khan, Bengal was linked once again to northern India. Although Sher Shah's son, Islam Shah, refused to concede some autonomy to the local chiefs which was granted by Sher Shah, the death of Islam Shah in 1552 allowed Muhammed Shah to take over power in Bengal. The brief Afghan interlude was offset by the Orissa King occupying Tribeni. By 1575, Daud Khan Karrani was killed by the advancing Mughals; and the Afghans, divided into small groups, continued the hit-and-run tactic till the second decade of the seventeenth century. It is interesting that in the midst of this continuous fighting, Emperor Akbar gave the Portuguese the Farman to begin trade at Hughli.[33] His intention to use the Portuguese against the Afghans was not in vain as the Mughal Governor of Saptagram, Mirze Rayat, fled to the Portuguese at Hughli pursued by the Afghans. Even Man Singh, despite winning several battles against the Afghans, could not hold them down, which justified Abul Fazl's comment of *Bulag Khana* (the house of the rebels).[34]

This continuous war from the end of the 1530s had made the banks of the Bhagirathi dangerous and unsafe. Communication was disrupted between the hinterland and the river. Without a proper administration, the merchants did not risk their goods. In the poem of Mukundaram, written around 1579,[35] the *Dihidar* Mahmud Sharif was forcing the survey of the land and claiming revenue on the basis of *zabati* system introduced by Todar Mal, thus replacing the age-old *muktai* system prevalent in Bengal. Their attempts failed and later on Islam Khan introduced it once law and order had been established. The poem of Mukundaram graphically described the uncertainty of the times while he fled to a Hindu *zamindar* in Birbhum. The peasants were trying to desert but forced to stay while the value of the rupee was falling—a clear indication of unusual times.

The silting of the Saraswati and the decline of Saptagram as an overseas port or the plague at Gaur[36] had merely acted as catalysts. The bloody and continuous war for over seventy years had helped the rise of the Portuguese, who managed to build a fort at Hughli far ahead of other Europeans. Needless to say, the Mughals drove the Portuguese out of Hughli within three decades of establishing their power in Bengal in the seventeenth century.

There was no big city in Bengal since the fall of Gaur in 1575. Hughli had not grown so quickly as to become the principal port. Mukundaram, while referring to Garifa (Gouripur) and Halishahr on the other bank in 1579[37] did not mention Hughli. All this resulted in the desertion of Rarh, from where people had begun to move towards Bhati,[38] where new types of urban settlements began, different from those of the Moorish towns of Gaur and Saptagram.

One should note, however, that all the towns on the banks of the Bhagirathi in the Rarh were not of Moorish type. There is mention of small towns like Santipur or Nabadwipa in the Vaishnava literature. The nature of these settlements was different from those of Gaur or Saptagram. Some writers mentioned walls or lofty gates of some houses, which would suggest class division in housing within the city. These were of traders who had brought goods from Benaras, Orissa, Tibet and even Kashmir,[39] although neither Nabadwipa nor Santipur were overseas ports. The trade was obviously based on textile and rice.

Interestingly there is no mention of zamindar or king of these towns in contemporary Bengali literature. Chaitanya had trouble with the Qazi, who was shown as the authority in the town of Nabadwipa in Vaishnava literature.[40] Most of these towns did not have the wall to separate them from the surrounding areas, which in a way, had influenced the cultural life-style of the inhabitants of these towns. Milk food and vegetarian dishes were mostly available, descriptions of which abound in the writings of contemporary Vaishnava poets.[41] These were not much different from the food of the rural area. At the same time, when the cost of sugar was very high, the preparation of sweets would suggest a kind of prosperity that could come only from the integration of rural products and external trade. These are noticeable in the Vaishnava literature, where the merchant and the trader come back again and again, neglecting the zamindar and the peasant. It is no wonder that Chaitanya's movements were limited to these towns, which were of mixed types with no wall to break the urban-rural continuum. Yet the prosperity did not last long. The tumultuous political history in the background of the Mughal-Afghan contest had devastated these areas which coincided with the decline of Saptagram, the fall of Gaur and the beginning of the rise of Hughli by a European power controlling the mouth of the sea. The axis then shifted to Bhati, where new forces had begun to emerge.

From the writings of Mukundaram, it appears that the administration in Bengal was rather relaxed before the imposition of new regulations, particularly in the south Rarh. His description of *mahajan* in the village was not a figment of imagination as Abul Fazl stated that the peasants used to pay revenue in either gold or silver rupees.[42] This would suggest a high degree of cash liquidity, which would be difficult to accept in view of the high credit interest in Bengal compared to that of western India, for example. Besides, the extensive use of cowries for small transactions with lower price level[43] would doubt such availability of fund. In Mukundaram, the peasants were paying revenue to the zamindar or *dihidar* and not to the State directly as stated by Abul Fazl.

In contemporary Bengali literature, the zamindar was not always shown as a devil. He was happy to receive one silver rupee per plough and he was interested in the expansion of cultivation for which he was granting the usual concessions.[44] The development of such unused lands, leading to urban settlements with people migrating with the blessing of the zamindar, was one of the subjects of the poet. The *mahajan* and the zamindar merged into one as he advanced loans to the newly settled peasants, who then were settling the educated Kayasthas in their lands.[45] Here the peasant gradually emerged as small zamindar or *pahi kastha*, which was different from the situation in south Rarh. There the society was far more stratified with the *dihidar* using force to keep the peasants tied to the land.

It is difficult to determine the amount of landholding of the individual peasant, who was forced to pay several taxes and tolls, often unauthorised. The peasant's life was not pleasant, if we believe the view of a modern historian.[46] But the picture was different in the newly settled areas. There peasant did not have to pay any tax for three years and his life depended to a great extent on the zamindar, particularly at a time when there was no settled administration of a centralising authority in the background of a bloody war.

Yet the Saptagram area was not totally deserted. In 1565, the traveller Caeser Fredericki called Saptagram a good city, "a reasonable faire citie for *Cities of the Moors* [italics mine] abounding with all things...". In the port, he found thirty to thirty-five big and small ships lading rice, cloth, long pepper and other sorts of merchandise.[47] Ten years later in 1575, Le Blanc found rice, cloth, sugar, etc. in abundance at Saptagram, which had a Portuguese fort.[48] In a few years' time the trade would pass on to Hughli. Between 1583 and 1591, Ralph Fitch came to Saptagram, where he found many things to buy. But he did not mention any ship in the port. The road between Hughli and Saptagram was full of jungles where dacoits live.[49]

The parcelisation of power in the absence of any central authority was noticeable in the emergence of weekly *huts* or bazaars set up by the local people on the banks of the Bhagirathi.[50] There was no mention of any central market or wholesale distribution centre. The sale of surplus produced in the rural areas had been advantageous to the buyers, as noted by Fredericki. Hughli as a wholesale clearing house could not come up earlier due to the severe Mughal-Afghan contest. The process of urbanisation had already started in Bhati with the emigration of the panic-stricken people of the Rarh.

The excellent map of Joa de Barros (died 1575)[51] showed at least five towns in the lower Sundarban delta. After the fall of the Karrani dynasty in 1575, the process of urbanisation in Bhati had accelerated as their followers had fled to these rather inaccessible areas. Abul Fazl's description of the escape of Sirhari, the treasurer of Daud Karrani, with the treasures of Daud to Katar (Jessore) in the Bhati by a boat was one of such illustrations.[52] Then began the process of the rise of new chieftainship. By 1599, when the Jesuit Fathers had reached Jessore, it was a powerful kingdom with the capital at Chandecan and ruled by Pratapaditya, son of Srihari.[53] The map of Petrus Bertius of 1600,[54] based on the writings of the Jesuits, showed that Chandecan had reached the west bank of the Bhagirathi comprising the deltaic areas vulnerable to the invaders from the sea.

Rarh was not altogether abandoned. The map of Buffin, appended in Thomas Roe's travels,[55] still showed Saptagram with the fort. Yet the shift of the population towards Bhati was unmistakably clear. The ruins of Iswaripur,[56] immortalised in the romantic legends of Bengali nationalist writings, still waited for an archaeologist. But by 1600, Pratapaditya of Jessore had become the leading zamindar of Bhati.[57]

There were also other zamindars in Bhati whose rise could be traced after the fall of the Karrani dynasty in 1575. Isa Khan of Sonargaon, although defeated by the Mughals in 1583, was considered the most powerful zamindar in 1586 and significantly a friend of the Christians by Ralph Fitch during his visit in 1586.[58] Kedar Ray of Sripur and Vikrampur (killed in the battle with Man Singh), Ram Chandra Ray of Bakla (son-in-law of Pratap), Satrajit Ray of Bhusna and others were there with almost independent powers. Some of them concluded treaties independently with the

Portuguese officials.[59] Their capitals were not the Moorish towns like Gaur or Saptagram. These were mixed towns, with no separating walls.

Ralph Fitch saw at Bakla many stores of rice, silk and ordinary cotton. Given the high price of silk, it may be assumed that it was exported. The women of Bakla wore various silver ornaments "ringed with silver and copper and rings made of elephant teeth...".[60] These were imported, which would suggest an overseas trade as well as formation of a certain wealthy class. This was not unnatural as Abul Fazl stated that Bakla touched the sea, so much so that the town was flooded in 1585 and had to remove inland. Fitch must have been in this new town, as he mentioned only one straight street with high buildings on both sides, without referring to the sea. The basis of such wealth appeared to be export of rice and cloth. Its growth might explain the delayed progress of Hughli.

This was not the only town thriving on the export of rice and cloth. Fitch mentioned big storehouses of rice and cotton at Sripur. Twenty kilometres from there was Sonargaon. Fitch found it to be the best place for the finest cotton in the whole of India, which were exported to all parts of India, Pegu, Malacca, Sumatra and many other places. Even the Portuguese then fighting at Ceylon, used to buy there victuals for the army. Fitch also observed that the houses were "very little, and covered with straw and have a few mats round about the walls and the door to keep the Tygers and Foxes" out. Many of the people were very rich and "... they live off rice, milk and fruits...".[61]

Despite the wealth, drawn from a prosperous export trade, Sonargaon was not a city like Gaur. Rather, it resembled Nabadwip, inhabited by bania traders living on vegetarian diet. There was no wall breaking the rural-urban continuum.[62] Fitch did not mention any mosque, caravanserai or *hammams.* The rice and cotton trade from the surplus products of the countryside had helped its prosperity.

The new urban settlements, although of mixed types, so graphically described by Mukundaram in his poem,[63] were made possible by the zamindars of Bhati. That these zamindars had certain wealth may be seen in the Mughal campaign of Islam Khan in the early seventeenth century. In 1608, he collected huge wealth in one night from Dacca region. Pratapaditya sent to him fifty thousand rupees in silver coins. Only when he failed to send the required gold *mohur* and failed to visit him personally, did Islam Khan turn against him.[64]

It would be a mistake to think that all this wealth came from trade. The Mughals had often employed these zamindars to collect revenue. After the death of Kedar Ray, Pratapaditya was asked to collect revenue from Sripur and Vikrampur. It would show that Todar Mal's *Bandobast* had failed and Islam Khan was given wider latitude to collect *peshkash*, which could not be equated with *hastabud jama* laid down by the central government. It was the arbitrary imposition by Islam Khan which was strictly collected by him that led to the final breach with these zamindars. The later survey of the land, as per *zabti*, did not reduce the revenue, which would show that the amount imposed by Islam Khan was higher than that of the Afghan period, reflecting the growing prosperity of these zamindars. This might explain why the new Mughal Subadar, Islam Khan, decided to march straight to Bhati, leaving the beaten track in the Rarh to establish his capital in the lower Sunderban delta at Dacca in 1608.

Without a proper metropolis and without a central authority to mop up the surplus, Bhati developed unevenly given the system of communication and the enterprise of these pioneering zamindars. The mixed towns of Bhati, therefore, had varying growth rates. The areas between these towns were not uniformly developed and many areas were full of jungles, bristling with wild animals and dacoits. The letter of the visiting Father Pimenta made this clear.[65] A contemporary letter of 1599 stated that during the voyage by boat from Chandecan to Sripur, pirates had repeatedly attacked the boat. He was also suffering from high fever, possibly malaria.[66] A letter of early 1600, referring to the journey by boat from Bakla to Chandecan, stated that while on one side of the bank, forest was being cleared and rice and sugar-cane were grown, on the other bank, there was dense jungle, where tigers roamed freely. Actually, a tiger followed the boat for quite some distance.[67] The process of new settlement had started, but before it could develop fully, different circumstances hindered its path.

From the third decade of the sixteenth century, the Portuguese had emerged as a sea-power in the Bay of Bengal. Their control over Saptagram, where they had a fort, enabled them to control communication in the Bhagirathi. The sea and its mouth were infested with Portuguese freebooters, whose attempts at piracy and slave trading often substituted the gradually diminishing Portuguese trade. The description in the letter of Father Fernandes clearly indicates the existence of such pirates at the mouth of the Meghna river and coastal Bengal.[68] The poet Mukundaram immortalised the merchants' fears about the *Harmada* lying in wait at the mouth of the Bhagirathi.[69]

Some enterprising zamindars of Bhati, whose prosperity depended on the mercantile activities, had therefore made compromises with the Portuguese. From the letters of the contemporary Jesuit Fathers, it is clear that many of these zamindars had employed the Portuguese in their armies. Some of them were given *jagirs* within the zamindaris on condition of payment of annual revenue. Many of these Portuguese had continued trading and amassed wealth and power, constituting a separate power block within the kingdom.

These rich and powerful Portuguese welcomed these Fathers, which in turn, led the zamindars to accept them. Isa Khan was considered to be friendly to the Christians.[70] Ram Chandra Ray of Bakla welcomed the Christian Fathers in his court.[71] Pratapaditya went a few steps further. He allowed the Jesuits to build a church within his zamindari, perhaps a little away from his capital, which was inaugurated by him and his eldest son in January 1600. Pratap also allowed the Fathers to make conversions. The church was given the surrounding land and the peasants were asked to pay revenue to the church, proceedings of which were duly recorded.[72] The Mughal Emperor Akbar had also given similar privileges to the Jesuit Fathers, as a result of which churches were built and conversions made within the Mughal Empire.

The growing power of the Portuguese and their increasing privileges created problems within the coastal society of Bengal. A serious riot between the Portuguese and the Afghans within the zamindari of Pratap[73] forced him to encourage other religious groups, including the Vaishnavas. By then the menace of the Arakanese had appeared, which jolted the coastal society.

After the fall of the Karrani dynasty and taking advantage of the Mughal-Afghan contest, the Arakan King Mang Felung (1571-83) conquered the entire Chittagong, Noakhali (sea coast of eastern Bengal) and Tripura. The two-pronged drive through the sea and over land by the Arakanese was successful as they seized almost the entire coastal Bengal, including Sonargaon area.[74] The Mughals managed to halt their progress and the Mughal conquest of Sandwip island, at the mouth of the Bay, saved eastern Bengal from the Arakanese. It was a timely move as the fight for that island had begun earlier, with Kedar Ray twice capturing it under command of his Portuguese captain, Carvalho, and twice losing it. The island became the focal point for the triangular contest.[75] Meanwhile, the Arakan-Portuguese alliance was becoming a serious threat to the Bengali zamindars. One should, therefore, see their attitude towards the Christian missionaries in this particular context.

Despite driving away the Portuguese from Hughli in 1632 and suppressing the zamindars by the second decade of the seventeenth century, the Mughals failed to provide security in the coastal areas of Bengal. In 1640, Father Manrique found the coastal areas deserted due to continuous Arakan raids, who often came up to Dacca to procure slaves.[76] With the establishment of Mughal power in Bengal, people of the coastal areas had begun to move towards the Bhagirathi banks where the growth of the Hughli had attracted the traders and foreign companies. It was only after 1660 that the coastal areas of Bengal began to be populated. Thus one can trace two shifts of population or perhaps three, within a span of one hundred years. Contemporary revenue records of Bengal, so ably analysed by Saba Samiuddin,[77] would show indications of these swings.

Contemporary revenue records show the growth of Bengal's revenue and its uneven development. There is a clear increase of *jama* (revenue estimate) from 1595 onwards. The base of twenty-five crore dams as annual revenue of Bengal, as estimated by Abul Fazl in 1595-96, was on the lower side since the Mughals had not reached eastern Bengal. Actually, most of Bhati areas remained outside the pale of Mughal rule at the time and therefore its revenues could not be properly computed.

As a result, the estimates of the later period showed remarkable increase. This rise could not have been merely an estimate on paper. The consistent and determined imposition of Mughal rule and strict insistence on collection were the hallmarks of Islam Khan's rule that netted larger revenue.

In 1632, Father Manrique put this as over thirty-six crore dams, while Byazid, a court historian (1628-36) put it over forty crores. From 1647, it continued to rise although it was never more than five per cent of the total *jama* of the Mughal Empire.

Abul Fazl's revenue estimate of Gaur and Sharifabad Sarkar showed these to be the highest in Bengal per square mile, viz. 10.6 and 10.7. The latter comprised lands west of Saptagram and west of Bhagirathi, where there was not much fighting. Bakla, Sonargaon and Saptagram had much lower rates, viz. 3.5, 2.6 and 3.0, nearly one-third those of Gaur and Sharifabad Sarkar. Abul Fazl himself mentioned that both Saptagram and Hughli were under control of the Feringhis. One may therefore reasonably conclude that Abul Fazl's estimate was based on information available before the fall of the Karrani dynasty, i.e. before 1575. The coastal areas like Khalifabad had the lowest rate, i.e. 1.0. It may be postulated that the principal revenues came from land; the revenue of the new settlements in Bhati would not have come to Abul Fazl at Delhi so soon. This discrepancy would be clear if we look at Abul Fazl's revenue estimate of urban areas.

In Abul Fazl's estimate, the revenue of urban Gaur was the highest, although by the end of 1575, Gaur had been abandoned and the capital had been shifted elsewhere. This would clearly suggest that the information of Abul Fazl was nearly twenty years old. Gaur had the estimate of eight lakh dams, whereas Jessore, where Srihari had fled with the treasure of Daud, had two lakh dams. One may recall that the Jesuit Fathers during 1599-1600 were calling Pratapaditya of Jessore as the leading zamindar of Bengal. But Abul Fazl's estimate, assuming to be of pre-1575, would show that Jessore was already beginning to rise, which might explain why Srihari had fled there in the first place. Ghoraghat (near Rangpur in Bangladesh now), later a Mughal *thana* for checking the overland trade with the Himalayan traffic, had almost the same *jama* as that of Jessore.

Significantly, Sonargaon, home of the legendary and the most powerful zamindar, Isa Khan, had 50,000 dams in Abul Fazl's estimate. Only by accepting this figure as of pre-1575, we can explain this low *jama*, since Isa Khan's rise took place after the fall of Daud in 1575. One may also recall that Isa Khan's Sonargaon had the largest concentration of foreign merchants at the end of the 1580s. Isa Khan's death robbed Sonargaon of its rise, which might explain why the Jesuit Fathers decided to build their first church in Bengal at Jessore and why the Mughal captain Mirza Nathan was called the leading zamindar of Bengal.

Abul Fazl's estimate, as analysed by Samiuddin, showed the

highest *jama* per square mile in north-western Bengal. Mandaran, for example, doubled its *jama* between 1595 to 1605. This signified that the *jama* increased more as one moved towards Bihar, suggesting naturally the beginning of the population flow to the other side of the Bhagirathi much earlier than to Bhati. As the Mughal stranglehold on Bihar and Bengal increased, this *jama* increased also as the western part did not have the problem of either the Portuguese or the Arakani invasions that had devastated eastern Bengal. Mukundaram's flight to Birbhum on the other side of the Bhagirathi would point to the same. The decline of *jama* in northern Bengal coincided with growth on the other side and population flow to the northwestern Bengal.

Given the circumstances, one would have expected quicker development in eastern Bengal, indicated by the rise of different principalities, like Jessore and Sonargaon. But this did not happen except at a few places like Sylhet. Khalifabad or southern Bengal near the sea coast had the lowest *jama* till 1656, when it began to increase. Certain prosperous places like Bakla did not show any increase. The failure of the Mughals to hold the sea coast against the repeated Arakani attacks by fast moving boats, despite the presence of the Mughal officials at Dacca, devastated the area.[78] The obliteration of the semi-independent zamindars, who used the Portuguese to hold off the attacks of the Arakanese, and the Mughals' disinclination to employ these Portuguese in the army or in the fleets might have been the factors for their failure to keep the Arakanese at bay. The transfer of the capital from Dacca to Raj Mahal by Sultan Shuja after 1639 encouraged the people to leave the devastated eastern Bengal for the peaceful banks of the Bhagirathi. Mir Jumla brought the capital back to Dacca after Shuja's defeat in 1659.[79] But by then the Bhagirathi banks had begun to prosper. The transfer of the capital to eastern Bengal merely reflected Mughal anxiety to hold the coast against the continuous Arakan threats.

But they still failed in this, unable to hold Chittagong on the seaside and Assam on land. Chittagong's *jama* was the nearest to Gaur; and it was the home of the Portuguese pirates in alliance with the Raja of Arakan. Although the Mughals were able to snatch both Chittagong and Assam, including Sandwip island, they could not hold it for any length of time.

Once it was clear that the Arakanese could not be checked in coastal Bengal, the population began to shift towards the Bhagirathi, helped by the expulsion of the Portuguese from Hughli in 1632. The arrival of the English helped this process. In course of time, the capital was shifted to Murshidabad with the increasing trade of the European Companies and growing links with northern India.

From 1575 to 1647, the *jama* of the Mughal Empire had shown a fifty per cent increase. During that period, from 1575 to 1648, the jama of Bengal had doubled, from twenty-five crore dams to fifty crore.[80] The rise of *jama* in northern India was partly offset by a comparative rise in prices, indicating that jama in real terms had not increased that much. For this period, the price list of Bengal is not available; but the later price list would show only negligible increase, suggesting that production continued to match the increasing import of bullion. Certain items like silk would have to be exempted from this hypothesis. In any case, compared to that of northern India, the increase of *jama* in real terms in Bengal becomes quite clear. This would be seen in the collection of enormous fortunes by Shaista Khan and Sultan Shuja, two Subadars of Bengal.

While the banks of the Bhagirathi got separated from the network of the national markets for nearly seven decades, the efforts of semi-autonomous zamindars integrated some of the coastal towns into the national and international markets, although no hierarchic structure similar to that of Gaur is discernible. The localisation of different smaller coastal towns and their integration with the markets and ports outside depended, to a great extent, on the production of a compact unified area, separated under the rule of these pioneering zamindars, who combined in themselves the dual role of landholder and trader-cum-*mahajan*. The Mughal advance shattered this delicate balance. Under the Mughals, a hierarchical centralised system, with Dacca and Murshidabad at its apex, and with links to the systems of northern India rather than Southeast Asia, became effective. The arrival of the Europeans turned it into a different direction. But that is another story.

NOTES

[1]*Archives Coloniales et Nationales*, Paris, Colonie C(2) 72: letter of Pondicherry to Paris, 17 February 1721, f. 52: "...all the riches and the power

imaginable would not be able to transplant a natural Indian to another province, specially the weavers and the merchants..." (my translation).

[2]*Babur-Nama*, tr. from the original Turkish by A.S. Beveridge, 2 vols., New Delhi, 1979, II, pp. 487-90 (reprint).

[3]Article of Aniruddha Ray entitled, "The City of Bengalla in the European Travel Account and Cartography" in *Essays on Indian History and Culture* (Sheikh Ali Felicitation Volume), New Delhi, 1990, pp. 123-34.

[4]For a brief history, see A.F.M. Abid Ali Khan, *Memoirs of Gaur and Panuda*, Calcutta, 1931 (reprint by West Bengal Government), Calcutta, 1986.

[5]H.A.R. Gibb (ed.), *Ibn Battuta: Travels in Asia and Africa, 1325-1354*, London, 1929, 267 post.

[6]Tomé Pires, *Suma Oriental*, 2 vols., I, 1644, pp. 88-91.

[7]Duarte Barbosa, *The Book*, II, pp. 135-48.

[8]De Barros, *De Asie* (quoted by Abid Ali, *op. cit.*, 33). Also see Manuel de Faria e Sousa, *The History of the Discovery and Conquest of India by the Portuguese* (tr.), I, pp. 416-8.

[9]Article of Aniruddha Ray entitled, "The Growth of the City of Surat, 1610-1671", in *Journal of the Asiatic Society of Bangladesh* (Humanities), Dacca, XXIV-VI, 1981, pp. 95-107.

[10]See the descriptions of Gaur by João de Barros and Fernão Lopes de Castenhada in R.B. Smith, *The First Age*, Bethesda, 1969, pp. 130-4; also see an anonymous manuscript, *ibid.*, 134-7.

[11]F. Bernier, *Travels in the Mughal Empire* (tr. & ed. by A. Constable), New Delhi, 1972, p. 245 (reprint).

[12]Vincent Le Blanc, *Les Voyages Fameux*, Paris, 1648, pp.125-6.

[13]James Rennell, *Memoir of a Map of Hindustan*, Indian ed., 1976 (1st ed. 1788), pp. 147-8.

[14]H. Creighton, *The Ruins of Gaur*, 2 vols., II, London, 1817, pp. 1-2; also see the description of the ruins in the 17th century by W. Hedges, *The Diary*, 1681-1687 (Yule ed.), 3 vols., I, London, 1887, pp. 88-9.

[15]J.H. Ravenshaw, *Gaur: Its Ruins and Inscriptions*, London, 1878.

[16]Mirza Nathan, *Baharistan-i- Ghayebi*, tr. by M.I. Borah, Gauhati, 1936.

[17]Abid Ali, *op.cit.*, pp. 141-2.

[18]*Ibid.*, 146 post. See the picture of the ruins of caravanserai (148).

[19]Rennell, *op.cit.*, p. 148. Only the rampart was visible to him.

[20]Minhaj-us Siraj, *Tabaqat-i Nasiri*, tr. into Bengali from Persian by A.K.M. Zakaria, Dacca, 1983, pp. 41-3.

[21]Article of D.A. Crawford entitled "Satagaon or Tribeni" in *Bengal Past and Present*, 1908, vol. III, pp. 18-26. For the location, see Irfan Habib, *An Atlas of the Mughal Empire*, OUP, 1982, 11A.

[22]Abul Fazl, *Ain-i-Akbari*, tr. by Jarret and Sarkar, New Delhi ed., 1978, p. 154.

[23]Mukundaram Chakrabarty, *Kavi Kankan Chandi* (Bengali), Indian Press, Allahabad, 1921. There are disputes regarding different manuscripts. See Sukhomoy Mukhopadhya, *Madhya Yuger Bangla Sahityer Tathya O Kalakram* (Bengali), Calcutta, 1974, pp. 152-4.

[24]*Ibid.*, pp. 201-5.

[25]Krishnadas Kaviraj, *Sri Chaitanya Charitamrita* (Bengali), Basumati ed., 1326 B.S., pp. 288-9. Also see A. Gupta, *Hughli*, Calcutta, 1321 B.S., pp. 62-3 (Bengali).

[26]Article of A. Ray, "Growth...", *op. cit.*, pp. 95-107.

[27]Abul Fazl, *op. cit.*

[28]Quoted in A. Gupta, *op.cit.*, p. 61.

[29]Bipradas Piplai, *Manasa Vijaya*, ed. by Sukumar Sen, Asiatic Society, Calcutta, pp. 142-3. It is doubtful if it was completed by A.D. 1496 as there are references to tobacco and the port of Hughli.

[30]Nihar Ranjan Ray, *Bangalir Itihas* (Bengali), Calcutta, 1948, 2nd ed., 1951, p. 97.

[31]M.M. Chakrabarty and L.S.S. O'Malley, *Bengal District Gazetteer: Hooghly*, Calcutta, 1913. The process has been clearly described by the contemporary traveller Caeser Fredericki (*Purchas*, v, 410-11).

[32]Article of C.R. Wilson entitled "Note on the Topography of the river in the 16th century from the Hughli to the sea as represented in 'De Asie' of D.C. Barros" in *Journal of Bengal Asiatic Society*, 1892, Pt. I, 110-11.

[33]Abul Fazl, *Akbar Nama*, tr. by Beveridge, III, Delhi, 1973, 96 post (reprint).

[34]*Ibid.*, p. 427.

[35]Mukundaram, *op.cit.*, pp. 4-5.

[36]Article by Rakhaldas Bandopadhya entitled, "Saptagram or Satgaon" in the *Journal of the Asiatic Society*, v, pt. I, no. 7, Bengal, 1909, pp. 245-8.

[37]Mukundaram, *op.cit.*, p. 201.

[38]Article by Abdul Karim entitled, "Bhati as mentioned by Abul Fazl and Miraxa Nathan", in *N.K. Bhattasali Commemoration Volume*, Dacca, 1966, pp. 311-22.

[39]Best description in Jayananda, *Chaitanya Mangal* (Bengali), written before the middle of the 16th century, ed. by B.B. Majumdar and S. Mukhopadhya, Asiatic Society, 1971, pp. 11-3.

[40]Sri Bindaban Das, *Chaitanya Bhagavat* (Bengali), Mayapur, Chaitanya Math, 3rd ed., 479 Gourabda.

[41]Jayananda, *op.cit.*, pp. 64-5.

[42]Abul Fazl, *Ain*, II, p. 134.

[43]Mukundaram, *op.cit.*, p. 161.

[44]*Ibid.* See an interesting article by Tapan Raychoudhury entitled, "Revenue Administration in Bengal in the early days of Mughal Rule" in *Journal of Asiatic Society of Bengal*, Calcutta, XVII, (1), 1951, pp. 31-61.

[45]Mukundaram, *op.cit.*, p. 85.

[46]Tapan Raychoudhury, *Bengal under Akbar and Jahangir,* Munshiram Manoharlal, 2nd ed., 1966.

[47]Fredericki, *op.cit.*, pp. 410-11.

[48]Le Blanc, *op.cit.*, pp. 127-8.

[49]Ralph Fitch in *Purchas,* v, pp. 482-3.

[50]Fredericki, *op.cit.*, pp. 410-11; Fitch, *op.cit.*, p. 483.

[51]See fn No. 32.

[52]Abul Fazl, *Akbar Nama*, II, 172; Nizamuddin Ahmed, *Tabaqat-i Akbari* (tr. by B. De), Asiatic Society, Calcutta, II, p. 478.

[53]Fr. Pimenta's annual letter of Goa, 1 December 1600 (tr. by Hosten in *Bengal Past and Present,* 1925, Vol. 30, pp. 52-5). See also S.C. Mitra, *Jasohar Khulner Itihas* (Bengali), Calcutta, 2nd ed., 1965, pp. 473-5, for the letter of Fr. Fernandes to A.R.P. Niccolai Pimenta, Sripur, 15 January 1599.

[54]Susan Gole, *A Series of Early Printed Maps of India,* New Delhi, 1980, T. 11.

[55]Buffin's map appended, *ibid.*, T. 12.

[56]J. Westland, *Report on the District of Jessore,* Calcutta, 1871.

[57]Article of Aniruddha Ray entitled, "Case Study of a Revolt in Medieval Bengal" in *Essays in Honour of Prof. S.C. Sarkar,* New Delhi, 1976, pp. 135-64.

[58]Fitch, *op.cit.*, pp. 484-5.

[59]Article of N.K. Bhattasali entitled, "Bengal Chiefs Struggle for Independence in the reign of Akbar and Jahangir" in *Bengal Past and Present,* 1928, vol. 69, pp. 25-9; no. 70, pp. 135-42; no. 71, pp. 32-50; no. 75, pp. 19-27. For the treaty between Parmananda Ray of Bakla and the Portuguese Viceroy of Goa in 1559, see J.N. Sarkar (ed.), *History of Bengal,* Dacca University, vol. II, pp. 358-9 (portion written by Surendranath Sen).

[60]Fitch, *op.cit.*, p. 484.

[61]*Ibid.*, pp. 484-5.

[62]*Ibid.*

[63]Mukundaram, *op.cit.*, pp. 84-5.

[64]Baharistan, *op.cit.*, p. 142.

[65]Letter of Pimenta, 1 December 1600, *op. cit.*

[66]Letter of Fr. Fernandes, Dianga, 22 December 1599, tr. by Hosten in *Bengal Past and Present,* vol. 30, 1925, p. 59.

[67]Letter of Fr. Fonseca, Chandecan, 20 January 1600, tr. by Hosten in *Bengal Past and Present,* 1925, pp. 63-5.

[68]Fernandes, *op.cit.*, pp. 58-9.

[69]Mukundaram, *op.cit.*, p. 242. Baharistan stated that Pratapaditya submitted because he was unable to oppose the Feringhee and the Arakanese attacks (*op. cit.*, p. 136).

[70]Fr. Pimenta, *op.cit.*, p. 54.

[71]*Ibid.*, p. 62. Also, Fonseca, *op.cit.*, pp. 63-4.

[72]*Ibid.*, pp. 65-7.

[73]Fernandes (*op. cit.*, p. 58) mentioned that the Pathans had killed the Portuguese captain Carvalho but Pierre Du Jarric stated that he was killed by Pratap (*Histoire des Memorables Advenues des Indes Orientales, 1608-14*, 4 vols., Bordeaux, pt. 4, pp. 860-61).

[74]For Arakanese expansion, see D.E.G. Hall (ed.), *A History of South-east Asia*, Macmillan, 1968, pp. 270-6; A.B.M. Habibullah stated that Arakanese invasions of Bhulua and other Mughal districts "roughly coincide with the final destruction of the Bhuyians of Bhati, particularly those of Bakla, Sripur and Bhusna" (in *Journal of Asiatic Society of Bengal*), 1945, XL, pp. 33-8.

[75]For the struggle over the island of Sandwip, see Pierre Du Jarric, *op. cit.*, pp. 848-61; also see R. Chakrabarty and A. Das, *Sandwiper Itihas* (Bengali), Calcutta, 1330, B.S., pp. 36-54.

[76]Sebastian Manrique, *Travels*, tr. by Luard, Oxford, 1877, 2 vols., I.

[77]Unpublished M.Phil thesis of Saba Samiuddin in Aligarh Muslim University, Department of History. I am grateful to Samiuddin for allowing me to cite the figures.

[78]Jamini Mohan Ghosh, *Magh Raiders in Bengal*, Calcutta, 1960.

[79]Sarkar (ed.), *History of Bengal*, 378 post.

[80]Article of Irfan Habib entitled, "The Mansab System, 1595-1637" in *The Proceedings of the Indian History Congress*, 1967 session, p. 238.

SLAVE TRADE IN THE INDIAN OCEAN IN THE SEVENTEENTH CENTURY

S. Arasaratnam

The existence in the Indian Ocean of a commercial traffic in slaves has been well known to historians of commerce but has not received the intensive attention that the other high-profile commodities such as pepper, spices, textiles and bullion have. General histories of Indian Ocean commerce make brief reference to the trade in slaves. Historians of the Indian economy have noted the relationship between famines and food scarcity and the rise of a slave market. Historians of Bengal have looked at the dreadful years of Arakanese, Magh and Portuguese-led terror and kidnapping for slavery of thousands living on the shores of the Ganges delta. The evidence of the slave trade in the Indian Ocean is scanty and periodic, and could reflect the nature of the trade. This paper attempts to look at the trends in the traffic in slaves, as a reflection of demand and supply and as performing a function in the Indian Ocean world economy. I propose to bring together the available evidence on the trade in slaves as a commodity across the Indian Ocean in the immediate pre-imperial period. In this period, the Indian Ocean trading system operated as a viable system, exchanging a variety of commodities over long distances and short hauls. I have taken the seventeenth century as my time period and it will readily be seen that there are huge gaps in the evidence. It might reflect the spasmodic and periodic nature of the trade in slaves but also reflects the sheer lack of information for long stretches of time. Also, though I have taken the entire Indian Ocean region, eastern and western, as the area of study, it will be seen that much of my evidence relates to the eastern more than to the western. This may be indicative of the relative unimportance of this sector in slave trade but may also be the result of the way the evidence has come down over the years.

A few general considerations emerge at the outset. As the period studied is one of intense commercial activity across the Ocean, it is natural that trafficking in slaves should be a consequence of the search for exchangeable commodities in the commercial process. The trade of the Indian Ocean represents an exchange of agricultural, manufactured and extracted goods governed by market forces from a variety of diverse economic and ecological systems to maximise returns. Population being a key element in the resources of a region, it was but natural that human resources should be brought into this exchange mechanism. In this period, well-populated, manufacturing and food-producing areas entered into exchange with sparsely populated but resource-rich areas with extracted and gathered produce desired in overseas markets. India was both an importer and exporter of slaves in this period, in limited quantities determined by a number of factors to be discussed later. Southeast Asia, where bondage and slavery were major forms of relationships embracing a large proportion of the population, had a thriving slave trade, primarily intra-regional but also looking outside the region in times of need.[1]

In the western Indian Ocean along the East African coast northward to the Red Sea and southern Arabia, there had been ancient slave trading sea routes by which Arabs traded in slaves from Madagascar, the Zambesi valley, Mombasa, Kilwa, Sudan and Ethiopia into the Arab and Ottoman states of North Africa and West Asia. This was continuing in our period and it is not the intention of this paper to deal with this phenomenon, except to note the flimsy evidence on the continuing import of slaves into India in the period by re-export from the Arab entrepots of the Red Sea and South Arabia with which Indians traded. In the sixteenth and early seventeenth centuries the Portuguese were continuing to import slaves into India through Goa from their colonies in Mozambique and Mombasa. There is evidence from travellers of the existence of a slave market in Goa but these slaves would primarily have served the needs of the *Estado* for manpower.[2] The slaves imported from West Asia into the Mughal Empire are what are called 'luxury' slaves: eunuchs, personal attendants and palace guards, concubines. Their numbers were small and it may be assumed that this import continued in the seventeenth century, handled mainly by Indian Muslim merchants on the West Asia route.

In the seventeenth century, the quickening of the pace of trade across the Ocean led to some developments in the trafficking in slaves. Certain conditions were created affecting demand and supply of slaves in the maritime region of the Ocean. The growth of the port-city States of Southeast Asia increased the demand for labour and the financial resources to acquire labour from whatever quarter. The State most relevant to our discussion here is the Sultanate of Acheh, which port became, in the first half of the seventeenth century, a major trading entrepot and important terminus of westward trade across the Indian Ocean. Acheh needed labour to expand its pepper plantations and to cultivate its paddy fields for a growing trade and population. Further inland were the tin mines which also absorbed large supplies of labour of a different type. For these puposes, Acheh was locked into the vast Southeast Asian slave trading networks eastward through the straits but was always prepared to take advantage of the international trade routes to satisfy its demands. The expansion of the money economy, accumulation of treasure in the hands of the ruler and the ruling classes created an international market in Acheh for slaves, which entrepreneurs to the west were quick to exploit.

A new element in the trafficking in slaves in the seventeenth century was the demand introduced by the new Europeans who had appeared in the Indian Ocean. Portuguese, as noted above, were heavily involved in the slave trade right from the outset of their appearance in the Indian Ocean. This was facilitated by their early settlements and entrenchment of power in Guinea, Angola, the Cape, Madagascar, Mozambique and other East African ports proximate to major slave markets. But the African slaves brought by them were largely intended for own use in the *Estado,* as labour, domestic servants, fighting men and ship hands. Portuguese officials and casados became major slave owners because of the cheapness of slaves. There was no great market for the slaves they brought outside the *Estado* except for some demand in the Islamic States of western and northwestern India. The major new element introduced by the Portuguese was the expansion of the slave trade in the northeastern Indian Ocean. The unofficial Portuguese presence in the Bay of Bengal grew uncontrolled by, and independent of, the authority of the *Estado.* The bases of this activity were the casado settlements of Hughli, Sandwip, Chittagong, Dianga and, on the Burmese side of the coast, in Syriam.

Development of the slave trade at the end of the sixteenth and beginning of the seventeenth century became tied up with political and military ambitions of powers on the Burma/Bengal land and coastal frontiers. The kings of Arakan expanded westward and established their hold over Chittagong, Noakhali and Tipera by the end of the sixteenth century. A succession of powerful and ambitious rulers continued their hold on the delta lands and waters, terrified local princes and peoples of the coast and arrogated the human and material resources to themselves. They allied with the Magh people of the border areas and used them as their forward troops in plundering and raiding lower Bengal. The presence of the adventurous Portuguese settlers without political authority or permanent territory proved a further weapon in their aims. Arakanese organised and financed combined raids with Maghs and Portuguese to the delta, up the rivulets of the estuary, and kidnapped hundreds, later thousands of Bengalees whom they sold as slaves. Thus the ports of Arakan, Chittagong, Hughli, Tamluk and Pipeli became major slave markets. In this way an activity, which had gone on at a low key for decades, suddenly became, in the beginning of the seventeenth century, a large-scale operation, with its effects on the Indian Ocean trading system.

The other new element was the entry of the Dutch and the English. It was the Dutch who had the major impact on slave traffic, introducing a new demand for slave labour in the settlements that they developed in maritime Asia. The rise of the European port city in areas where wage labour was expensive and difficult to recruit and organise, brought into existence mechanisms for the purchase and sale of slaves either through existing channels or through new transactions. In the early decades of the seventeenth century, the Dutch had decided to annex and found colonies in small spice-producing islands of the Moluccas as well as to establish and develop a port settlement in Java as the capital of their eastern enterprise. Later in the course of the century, the number of these settlements increased through their own logic; and the Dutch found themselves in possession of innumerable forts and little townships surrounding them through extensive parts of maritime Asia. The manpower necessary to construct and maintain these was expensive if recruited by payment of wages. Hence the search was on for outright purchase and ownership of slave labour. The English did not found colonies in the seventeenth century—they could not afford it—but established coastal settlements which expended and consumed labour. They would also find it economical to purchase slaves rather than hire labour. Thus the need of these Europeans was for centralised slave markets with facilities for bulk purchasing, rather than the fragmented and small-scale buying and selling of slaves that had always been the norm.

Another factor in the trafficking in slaves in the seventeenth century was the periodic increase in supply in the Indian subcontinent caused by food shortage and famine. The fine balance between population and food resources that existed in many parts of the subcontinent would be severely disturbed by a succession of failed harvests caused by two or more years of successive drought or cyclonic storms and floods. In districts bordering on the coast, which in the seventeenth century had become increasingly monetised, large groups of the population depended on food grains bought for cash in the market. When their access to cash was interrupted and scarcity led to steep rises in the price of food grains, this section was reduced to starvation, left their villages as entire families, drifted towards the ports and sold themselves into slavery. Historians of traditional India have noted this as a means for the enslavement of people but in pre-colonial periods it would have been an isolated and confined phenomenon and the purchasers of slaves would have been in close proximity to the homes of the enslaved people. The slaves would thus not have been transported to distant places, as was the case in the seventeenth century.

Also, the insatiable demand by Europeans, especially the Dutch, for slaves thus procured on the India coast, appears to have become well known in the interior and offered enslavement as an alternative to starvation during times of scarcity and famine. The areas so affected were not the marginal areas of food production but those which usually produced surpluses. Thus in our period, at different times, slave purchases were made in this way in Bengal, Orissa, the Godavari delta, Chingleput/North Arcot districts, Thanjavur and Madura. One hears of an occasional such instance in south Kerala. Interestingly enough, this phenomenon is not noted in our period on any great scale on the west coast of India. Even during the very severe famine of 1630-32, when grain prices rose sharply and there is evidence of disease and death on a large scale, there is no record of people selling themselves into slavery. Part of the explanation for this may be the attitude of the Mughal State and the tight control it had over trade in its ports. This factor of State policy will be considered later with some evidence of State intervention in the slave trade.

It appears thus, the two sources of the supply of slaves in the Indian Ocean trade centred on India were kidnapping and conquest or voluntary sale to escape famine. For this reason, when the former, that is forceful capture, was controlled, there was, unlike in Africa, no steady flow of slaves to keep a trade going. The picture is more complex in Southeast Asia, where dependence and bondage of various forms were in existence and there were many means by which one could acquire the services of another. But even in Southeast Asia, as will be seen later, the creation of new demands by European colonial powers, specifically the Dutch, resulted in an increase in supply and the rise of slave markets in numerous islands. Consequently, the proportion of the population in some form of slavery or another was very great indeed.

As the Dutch were the major buyers of slaves in this period, it may be appropriate to start with their role in the slave trade. As early as 1615 the Dutch were concerned with the provision of labour for their fortification works in the East, where they found the excessive heat prevented the effective use of their own service personnel in labouring jobs. In a despatch that year the Governor-General notes that one slave can do more work than two of the Dutch nation.[3] The Dutch were already thinking of Madagascar as a possible source of slave labour in the Southeast Asian settlements. In these early decades they sent ships to Madagascar and the Mozambique Channel and located the major slave markets, where they realised that the price of slaves was considerably less than in Asia. The problem of course was the long sea voyage and that mortality on ships was high, as well as the adaptability of these slaves to totally different working and living conditions. In 1684 for example, out of 274 slaves bought in Madagascar only 108 survived the journey to Batavia.[4] After the establishment of the Cape settlement in 1652, it was possible to organise voyages to Madagascar in search of slaves, both for the Cape itself and for Asia. When the need for slaves was desperate, there were even attempts to sail to the west coast of Africa, to Angola and Guinea to purchase slaves, but these were not successful. Whenever the Asian sources of supply dried up, these South African sources were tapped but the poor survival rates did not make this a viable venture. African slaves were used for the more demanding construction labour in the forts and battlements of major cities like Batavia and Colombo. When the Dutch expanded into the west coast of Sumatra and developed pepper plantations and started to work the gold mines, African slave labour was resorted to; and in the 1670s and 1690s we see a resumption of the Madagascar slave traffic. The Africans were not found suitable in agricultural labour but were more effective in the mines.

The most effective source of slave labour for the Dutch through the first half of the seventeenth century was the Arakan/ Bengal coast where the slave labour markets were fed by the slave-raiding activities of the Arakanese, Maghs and Portuguese until the Mughals put an end to them by extending effective control over the Bengal/Burma border and the Delta waters. From 1625, the Dutch realised the immense potential of the Arakan market in satisfying their demand and entered into dealings with the king, who tightly controlled this trade. In 1626 four ships sent to Arakan to buy rice and slaves returned to Coromandel with 250 slaves. Later, another ship brought 130 slaves from the same place. Dutch officials reported enthusiastically on the possibilities of this trade. They said that it was possible to buy 1,000 to 1,500 slaves per year in Arakan. The Arakanese king was able to get about 10,000 slaves by slave-raiding and permitted their sale in his ports or in the Portuguese-controlled ports of Chittagong and Dianga in return for an export tax of twenty-five per cent per slave.[5] The king's licence was needed for purchase and export and he was prepared to grant one to the Dutch. The Dutch thereafter were permitted to export a limited number of slaves, always with the explicit approval of the king.

The eastward expansion of the Mughals and the consolidation of their authority over Bengal and Assam brought them into conflict with Arakan and their coastal allies, the Maghs and Portuguese. The Mughals were aware of the depredation committed by these people and decided to root out this menace. This process lasted over three decades and only ended with the conquest of Chittagong under Shaista Khan in 1666. With the Mughal conquest of Hughli in 1635, this port ceased to be a slave market. In 1645, the king of Arakan forbade the export of slaves and the Dutch noted a reduction in the number of slaves available in that kingdom.[6] The Portuguese occasionally continued to engage in slave-raiding and they sold the slaves in the ports of Pegu and Arakan. This was done by freebooters who had settled in islands of the delta after their withdrawal from Hughli. These raids were undertaken in league with the Arakanese sailing in their armed *jalias*, which sometimes went deep into the Ganges and in Pipeli, robbing and plundering villages. To ensure a supply, the Dutch even went to the extent of entering into a contract with a Portuguese captain to buy up all the slaves they captured at fixed prices and paid out an advance to the Portuguese of Rs. 2,500.[7]

Because of the uncertainty of the slave market in Arakan and the obstacles placed in their path by the king, the Dutch decided to abandon their factory in Arakan in 1647. The increasing need for slaves in Batavia and the Moluccas forced them to make another attempt to re-establish trade in Arakan in 1649 and purchase slaves. The trade was resumed and continued till 1662, when, with reasonable regularity, 150 to 400 slaves were shipped annually to Batavia. From the available records, the following figures can be compiled of slaves shipped from Arakan to Batavia:

1636	216 Slaves	1656	288
1644	600	1658	153
1647	1046 (from Akrakan and Pegu)	1659	407
1654	311	1660	421
1655	200	1662	101

(Source *G.M.* vol. II, III).

Besides the difficulties in procuring slaves in Arakan, another obstacle presented itself. The Dutch were now building up a substantial trade in the Bengal ports of Hughli and Balesore. Their emergence in Arakan as major buyers of slaves was giving them a bad reputation with the Mughal administration in Bengal. On an embassy to the prince Muhammad Shuja the Subahdar of Bengal, in 1653, the Dutch Commissioner Verpoorten met with hostility from Mughal officials at the court, who accused the Dutch of transporting annually 5,000 to 6,000 Bengalees kidnapped by the Arakanese slavers as slaves to Batavia.[8] Again in 1657, Dutch officials in their factory at Pipeli were accused by Mughal officials of buying 1,600 slaves from the Arakanese, of whom 900 were alleged to be Muslims, and shipping them away.[9] They were threatened with expulsion if they continued this practice. A strategy adopted by the Dutch to forestall this was to permit Dutch freeburgher traders to carry on the slave trade in their ships direct from Batavia. Some of them did this successfully and shipped slaves as part of their cargo, which they sold in Malacca and Batavia to the Company or to private buyers.[10] Both the factor of not endangering the growing trade in Bengal and the drying up of supplies in Arakan led to a virtual disappearance of Dutch trade in slaves in Arakan and Bengal after the 1660s.

To what extent the slave markets of Arakan fed the Asian trade is difficult to determine. The Portuguese seem to have shipped slaves from Bengal and Arakan to Acheh where, as seen above, there was always a demand for slaves. There was no demand for Arakan slaves in India but they may have featured in the transhipment to Acheh via Masulipatnam and Porto Novo. Indian merchants trading in Acheh and Burma would have been well aware of the possibilities but it is unlikely that the numbers would have been great. The numbers shipped by the Dutch were considerable and they seem mainly to have been used in Batavia where they were put to work in building construction, agriculture and domestic service. A few seem to have been sent to the Banda islands where again they worked on the nutmeg plantations and in the domestic service of the Dutch planters.

Slave trade by conquest or slave-raiding is thus one isolated episode in the history of commerce, though a powerful one while it lasted. The configuration of political power put an end to that episode and that phenomenon does not raise its ugly head in the Bay of Bengal any further. The second source of slave trafficking was more persistent, if periodicthe voluntary sale into slavery to avoid starvation. Again the Europeans appear as major players in this aspect of the trade. It accompanied every climatic crisis that led to scarcity and famine. A prolonged period of drought followed by famine conditions in 1618-20 in coastal southern India saw the first large-scale export of slaves from this coast in the seventeenth century. The Dutch appeared as the major buyers. In 1622, a thousand slaves were purchased in Coromandel by the Dutch and exported to Batavia. In the following year 700 were shipped again to Batavia and another shipment of 200 a little later.[11] It appears that during this crisis the ports of shipment were Paleacat and Devanampatnam, which indicates that the central Coromandel area was most affected by the famine.

The Dutch saw here a good opportunity to supply their colonies of Amboina and Banda islands and the newly established settlement of Batavia. The limit to their purchase of slaves was only imposed by the shortage of cash. The officials on the coast declared that 2,000 could have been bought if only they had the money. It was a feature of this trade that the supply stopped as soon as conditions eased and regular food cultivation was resumed. In 1646/47 there appears to have been a food crisis in Bengal and the Dutch took the opportunity to purchase slaves. For some years then there was no opportunity to purchase slaves anywhere in India till 1658 saw a succession of war, failed harvest, pestilence and tyrannical regimes in the southern part of Coromandel. The war of Bijapur against the Marathas and Thanjavur, accompanied by the war between Thanjavur and Madura, coincided with a succession of drought and failed harvest and produced the most horrendous famine experienced by the south in this century. The Dutch were once again taking advantage of the opportunity. Contemporary reports speak of families, entire villages and castes from deep in the interior trekking to the ports and selling themselves into slavery. Tuticorin, Nagapatnam, Porto Novo, Devanam-patnam and Paleacat were ports to which these slaves were brought for sale to overseas shippers, Europeans and Indians. Till June 1660, a total of 3,695 slaves were bought at Nagapatnam and shipped to Jaffna in North Sri Lanka. After this shipment, another 4,000 were procured and officials reported that another 2,000 to 3,000 could be bought.[12] Most of these were sent to Sri Lanka because of the ease of transporting them there and subsequently selected numbers were shipped to Batavia. Direct shipments were made to Batavia from Nagapatnam and Paleacat. With the improvement of economic conditions in 1662, the trade stopped abruptly. The trade never assumed this scale in succeeding years. There were small numbers of about 100 a year traded in the Bay of Madura ports during the 1670s, when political unrest in the hinterland and crop failures produced supplies on a small scale. Tuticorin was the major port of export; the slaves were shipped to Sri Lanka and then on to Batavia or to the Cape Colony.

For the Dutch, the Coromandel slave trade was the most useful means of augmenting the supply of labour in their colonies. The Coromandel slaves were reputedly malleable and subject to disciplined control. They were agricultural workers and there was a fair proportion of skilled labourers among them. In the group that was taken to Jaffna in 1660 there were 500 weavers and cloth painters who set up a weaving and dyeing industry in Jaffna. Besides, those traded in the 1660-62 famine were bought as families with numbers of women and children. When they were settled in Sri

Lanka in conditions very similar to the lands they had left, they survived as a community, providing bonded labour to the Dutch to answer to every demand they made of them. Some were settled in the lands around Colombo as agricultural labour to recultivate paddy fields abandoned during the war with the Portuguese and Kandyans. Others were put to work in construction in Colombo, Galle and Jaffna. Still others were sold to the Dutch freeburgher community and even to affluent Sri Lankans. A good number were shipped to Batavia and some to Malacca where they worked in a variety of urban tasks. A few were sent to the Banda islands and Amboina and assigned to Dutch freeburgher planters to whom their docility proved a valuable asset as contrasted to the assertiveness of the African slaves and of some Southeast Asian islanders.

It is interesting to examine the attitude of the indigenous Indian States to this periodic expansion of the slave trade. In the northern State of Golconda, it appears that as long as the Europeans took care not to purchase and enslave Muslim subjects of that State, the rulers turned a blind eye to this trade. Masulipatnam does not appear as a major port for the slave trade, except for transhipment of those brought from Bengal and Arakan. This was probably done from ship to ship without landing the slaves on shore. In the southern ports, the Dutch usually exercised some caution, though Hindu rulers of the far south do not seem to have bothered about those expanded shipments of 1660-62. In fact, there is some evidence that Thanjavur authorities connived at this trade with the Portuguese and even Indian merchants.[13] There is one exception to this, however. When Maratha power expanded into the eastern Carnatic in the 1670s, Shivaji issued an edict in 1678 strictly prohibiting the transport of slaves by the Europeans.[14] After the 1680s, the Dutch were unable to procure any slaves from the Bay of Bengal ports and there was an end to the export of slaves from India eastward to Southeast Asia. Indians already enslaved and settled in Batavia, Malacca, Amboina, Banda islands, Padang, Sri Lanka and the Cape were assimilated into the local population.

As with the Arakan slave trade, there is hardly any evidence to determine the extent of Asian participation in the slaves trade of eastern India. A study of Acheh maintains that there was a direct trade in slaves between Indian ports, especially from the Coromandel coast and Acheh. It points to evidence of the presence of large colonies of foreign slaves maintained by the Sultans and that Indians formed a good part of this slave colony.[15] While Portuguese, English and Danes shipped slaves as part of their cargo, it produces evidence that Muslim and Hindu merchants of Masulipatnam, Nagapatnam and Porto Novo also regularly shipped slaves to Acheh. Because of an acute shortage of manpower in Acheh, the Sultan Iskandar Muda (1607-36) during a period of expansion, encouraged the import of slaves and strictly prohibited their export. Bengal and Coromandel slaves would have been put to work in the pepper plantations and rice fields and as artisan labour in the port. Slaves were thus yet another commodity in the trade exchange between India and Acheh handled by Indian merchants whenever the buying price in India was right and the profit margin with shipping costs and loss due to mortality on board was considered satisfactory. There is some scattered evidence of the export of slaves from the port of Madras, presumably by Indian and English free merchants of that port. It may be speculated that these shipments would have been also to Acheh or to the Dutch in Paleacat who were noted as keen buyers; and again, the supply would have been determined by economic conditions of the hinterland. In September 1687, 665 slaves are registered as having been exported from Madras. The Fort St. George administration imposed an export duty of one pagoda (Rs.3.75) on each slave, a high enough duty that attests to the profitability of the trade to the exporter.[16] There were complaints in Madras of kidnapping children for export and now and then prohibitions on the export of slaves had to be made. Alternatively, strict regulations were promulgated to register slaves with the Justices of the Choultry before export, to ensure that the slaves were not acquired by force. After the Mughal conquest of Golconda, which made them masters of the Madras hinterland, Mughal authorities opposed this trade and in 1688 the export of slaves from Madras was prohibited altogether.[17]

There is scanty evidence on the movement of prices and, because of the fragmented and random character of the markets, it is impossible to make any generalisation on trends.[18] In 1636, the Dutch bought slaves in Arakan at twenty Dutch guilders or sixteen rupees each. In 1655 the price paid in a contract with Portuguese slave raiders in Dianga was on a scale according to the slave's age. Men aged twenty to thirty-six sold for twelve reals (twenty-four rupees), women aged twelve to twenty-five sold for eight and a half reals (twelve rupees), boys of eight to nineteen years for seven and a half reals (fifteen rupees), girls of seven to twelve years for six reals (twelve rupees) and children of three to six years for two and a half reals (five rupees).[19] The data cover the period when the slave markets operated in Arakan and may be taken as a range of prices that operated in these markets. During periods of mass purchase in Coromandel with a raging famine in the hinterland, prices naturally fell dramatically. During the 1660 famine the Dutch reportedly bought slaves at one real or two rupees each. Another random piece of evidence appears in 1703 when a "lusty Coffree", presumably an able-bodied African slave, was offered on sale for twenty-five pagodas or ninety rupees.[20] Remembering that this was after the trade in slaves was prohibited in Madras, this reflects the scarcity value of slaves by that time.

Comparing these prices with those in Madagascar and in the Southeast Asian slave markets is not a very fruitful exercise, but the evidence is presented here for what it is worth. In 1679, the Dutch bought slaves in Madagascar at thirty-six rixdollars or ninety rupees each for men and twenty-four rixdollars or sixty rupees for women. In 1695 the price at Madagascar was somewhat less, fifty-eight Dutch guilders or forty-eight rupees. Thus the prices at Madagascar appear substantially higher, possibly because Madagascar trade was competitive, with European and Arab traders participating. Prices in Southeast Asia fluctuated and slave markets were fragmented and numerous.

In 1676, in Kissar, an island on the northern tip of Timor, the Dutch bought slaves at twenty-two rixdollars (fifty- five rupees) each. In 1678, the price in the southern island off Timor, Roti and Sawar, had risen to thirty rixdollars (seventy-five rupees) for men and twenty-four rixdollars for women (sixty rupees). Purchase prices in the Timor region in the 1670s were steady around that amount. In Nias, off the west coast of Sumatra and a well-known slave supplier, prices fluctuated from thirty-four to forty guilders (twenty-eight to thirty-two rupees) in 1679 to forty-five rixdollars (one hundred and twelve rupees) in 1688. It appears that prices in Southeast Asia were going up, with the Dutch forced to rely solely on that region for its supply of slaves.

The slave trade within the Indian Ocean did not develop as an intrinsic part of the overall trading system because the steady ingredients of demand and supply were absent. Though the demand may be said to have been present, particularly after the entry of the Europeans into permanent positions on the coast, it was not one that was steady or extensive. Supply was even more unsteady, depending on coincidental circumstances determining economic prospects and the configuration of powers determining slave-raiding or conquest. Intermediary mechanisms facilitating the trade could not develop uninhibited because of ideological constraints both in Hindu and in Islamic States. Undoubtedly these constraints were readily overcome when the price was right and profits were substantial. But the constraints were always present in the background, preventing a market-oriented growth of this trade.

NOTES

[1]Slavery and different forms of bondage in Southeast Asia have been well studied. A good summary of the historical situation is in A. Reid (ed.), *Slavery, Bondage and Dependency in Southeast Asia,* St. Lucia, 1983, ch. I, pp. 1-43

[2]Especially Pyrard's account, cited in W.H. Moreland, *India at the Death of Akbar*, London, 1962, pp. 84-5 (reprint)

[3]*Generale Missiven der VOC,* 'S Gravenhage, 1960, I, p. 46 (hereafter *GM*).

[4]*GM,* IV, p. 726.

[5]*GM,* II, p. 185.

[6]*GM,* II, p. 280.

[7]*GM,* III, pp. 49 and 479.

[8]*GM,* II, p. 624.

[9]*GM,* III, p. 132.

[10]*GM,* III, p. 162.

[11]*GM,* I, pp. 121 and 131

[12]*GM,* III, pp. 335 and 355.

[13]*GM,* II, p. 791.

[14]P. Van Dam, *Beschrijvinge van de Oosindische Compagnie,* 'S Gravenhage, 1932, ii.2, p. 114.

[15]T. Ito, The World of the Adat Acheh. A Historical Study of the Sultanate of Acheh. Ph.D. Thesis, Australian National University, 1984, pp. 396-413.

[16]H. Love, *Vestiges of Old Madras,* London, 1913, I, pp. 545-6.

[17]Love, *op.cit.*, I, p. 546.

[18]Conversions have been made at the rate of twenty stuivers to a rupee. It is obvious that there is no relationship in the value of a rupee in places as distant as Madagascar and Nias, off Sumatra.

[19]*GM,* III, p. 48.

[20]Love, *op.cit.*, II, p. 63.

FACING THE CROWD: THE URBAN ETHNIC POLICY OF THE DUTCH EAST INDIA COMPANY 1600-1800

Remco Raben

A salient feature of the colonial cities in Asia was the presence of two or more different racial or ethnic groups within the same urban area. In every colonial city, the authorities would be faced by an Asian crowd which far outnumbered the Europeans. Ethnic relations were moulded into a hierarchical structure in which the European minority ruled over the other, non-European groups. In this 'colonial situation' an antagonistic relationship developed along colour lines, which had its most characteristic efflorescence during the heyday of colonialism, in the nineteenth and early twentieth centuries. Urban societies of pre-modern colonial times certainly foreshadowed the later developments, but have some characteristics of their own as well: the colour lines, for instance, were less strict than in later times due to predominance of religious criteria, the emphasis on commercial gains, or to the lack of European women. The complexity of urban ethnic relations in early-colonial cities in Asia is enhanced by the existence of many local variations.

In the following pages I will reconstruct the urban ethnic policy of the Dutch East India Company. To form a judgement on the determining factors in the emergence of the ethnic and social structure in the Dutch cities, we have to carefully assess the relative weight of the specific functions these cities performed, the aims of the colonisers, and the local conditions. Emphasis will be laid on the ethnic residential pattern in colonial cities. For the Dutch case, two cities will be taken as examples: Batavia and Colombo. Thanks to the existence of unique population censuses, we can determine the extent of ethnic spatial segregation in the two colonial cities. The censuses and their background will be dealt with in some detail. And finally, an attempt will be made to allot the Dutch case a place in the spectrum of the policies of other European colonial authorities in Asia.[1]

The Dutch East India Company has often been brought into disrepute by historians for its obsession with regulation and registration. Only recently the Dutch Indologist J.C. Heesterman wrote disparagingly of "the rationalistic tendency to control by exhaustive rules and regulations."[2] Another Dutchman, J.C. Van Leur in this context wrote about "a mania for accountancy and registration".[3] One of the happy side-effects of this 'aberration' is the availability of many demographic statistics of cities and areas governed by the Company. These certainly deserve some detailed attention, as they are probably unique in early-modern colonial history and are an invaluable instrument for determining the ethnic residential distribution in the towns.

The most outstanding data relate to Batavia. From 1673 up to 1792, almost without any gaps, yearly censuses were compiled by the Dutch authorities. More incidental are censuses of subordinate factory towns such as Kota Ambon, Malacca, Cochin, Jaffnapatnam and Colombo. The only known census extant of this last city is from 1694, but many more seem to have existed.[4] The censuses taken here for comparison are the 1699 census for Batavia, and the 1694 census of Colombo.

The Batavia censuses comprise two annual lists: one of the inner city ṇṇ within the wallsṇṇ and the southern suburb, the other of the surrounding area, comprising both the other suburbs and the immediate countryside. The census was compiled by the blockmasters or district supervisors (*wijkmeesters*). Abstracts were sent to the Directors in the Dutch Republic and are now kept in the archives in The Hague. In their original form probably all households were listed separately by the blockmaster, who went from door to door to register the occupants. This detailed information of the structure of the families or households has been lost in the abstracts sent home. What have survived are long lists of numbers noting the totals of inhabitants in each block. Furthermore, a distinction is made into broad categories of sex (male/female) and age (adults, children younger and older than fourteen), and ethnic group.[5] The records allow scarcely any demographic conclusions, but do give detailed information on the ethnic dispersion of the inhabitants over the various town areas (see Appendix I).

In the census of Colombo also a distinction is made between two parts of the town: the fort and the town proper. The quarters outside the town walls, and the surrounding countryside—which was not yet then greatly developed—are not taken into account. Both Fort and Town are divided into cadastral plots or blocks, just as in Batavia. In the census, the households are listed separately, allowing us to extract the family structure.[6] The results are confusing, as categories are not consistent and the information is full of nuances and subtle variations. The lack of clarity about the ethnic origin of the inhabitants reflects the jumble of colonial society. For the sake of compatibility, the family description is transformed into a list comparable to the Batavia census (see Appendix II).

Apart from problems of interpretation and the unclear categorisation which is characteristic for this 'pre-statistics' period, the censuses are definitely biased. Indeed, as Peter Burke argues, both censuses not only tell us untruths about those enumerated, they can also tell us truths about the compilers: they reveal something about the preoccupations and mentality of the counting authorities.[7] The censuses were drawn up by a group which was politically dominant, but numerically in a minority position. The Dutch authorities lived with a permanent distrust, a good deal of incomprehension, and even fear for the Asian peoples surrounding them. And they probably did not have much sensibility for the subtleties within the Asian communities, or not to the same extent they had for the Europeans. While the mixing of Europeans with Asians was generally registered, miscegenation between Asian groups is never recorded.[8]

What then were the authorities in Batavia and Colombo after? The compiling of the population lists cannot be dismissed as just "a mania for registration", as they served a specific purpose. Illuminating in this respect are the instructions for the newly constituted blockmasters of Batavia, drawn up in 1655: "Because the number of inhabitants of this city ... is increasing from year to year, and because they comprise many different nations, among whom some are not greatly to be trusted, ... this city will be divided into certain blocks and quarters and over these will be placed blockmasters ...". The foremost task of the blockmasters was to keep a record of all dwellings and the number and ethnicity of the inhabitants, and especially of the foreign nations. Thus they were to keep a keen eye on strangers who were possibly residing in town unregistered. Those who were caught, especially "the great many of riff-raff of Blacks,

Mestizos and Portuguese", could be deported "to clear the land of such vagrants".[9] 'Knowledge is power', the authorities must have thought, and knowledge of the composition and whereabouts of their residents meant command over the inhabitants. Of course this created only an *illusion* of control, as people were not to be kept in check merely by counting them, and many inhabitants probably shied away from the blockmasters in their yearly counting rounds. Illegal Chinese labourers, runaway slaves, Catholic priests, Company deserters and all of such ilk, all for their own reasons—be it fear of persecution, justice, or tax gatherers—wanted to avoid registration.

Apart from providing a sense of security, the censuses also served a social purpose. According to both the Colombo and Batavia census instructions, on the basis of their statistics the blockmasters had to keep an eye on the honesty of breadwinning and occupations of the inhabitants. They had to reprimand whoever kept unruly households and who were a danger to the city's peace. They were to assist anybody who was unemployed; in Colombo the blockmasters were licensed to enrol European or Mestizo boys who did not want to learn a craft and to force them into Company service.[10] Special attention was to be given to the conduct of unmarried women. Every case of lapse from the straight and narrow path was to be reported to the police officers or Company authorities. The blockmasters were the eyes and ears of the Government.

Let us now turn from the motives to the results of the censuses. In the presentation of the figures (Appendices I and II) the number of male inhabitants is presented: the ethnic diffusion could be measured only on the basis of the information on the male population. In the census lists, the ethnicity of women and children remains often hidden from sight. Furthermore, in their residential policy the authorities focused mainly on the male inhabitants.[11]

On the basis of the census, Batavia can be divided into five sections, which reflects the ripples on the surface of a pond after a stone has been thrown into it. First, there is the Fort—which is not included in the census. This is purely Company domain, containing the warehouses, barracks and offices, as well as the living quarters of the Governor-General. Secondly, the town within the walls, which is divided into two areas, cut in two by the River Ciliwung. Only five of the multitude of ethnic groups resided in this area: Europeans,

Mestizos, Asian Christians (*Mardijkers*), Chinese and slaves. The Chinese inhabitants constituted the largest contingent (except for the slaves). The eastern part of the city within the walls had the greatest concentration of Europeans. It is evident however that even in the inner city the Europeans formed only a minority. One should be aware though that all Company servants who did not live in the town are not included here. For instance, most soldiers and lower-ranking personnel were accommodated in the Castle, in the guard-houses and in the outposts. The number of Company servants totalled 4,007 in 1699.[12]

The third sector is the suburbs. Except for the southern suburb, which fell under the jurisdiction of the inner city, the boundaries of the suburbs are hard to define. The eastern suburb (roughly block L 14-19) is characterised by a greater diversity of ethnic groups than the inner city, but *Mardijkers* are dominant. The southern suburb has an ethnic mixture comparable to the western inner city. The western suburb was the least developed. There the urban zone did not stretch beyond the city walls and soon gave way to *kampungs* and gardens. In the southern parts of this western suburb though (blocks O 1-5), the Chinese were in the majority. It was there that the Chinese *kampung* was set up after the 'Chinese massacre' in 1740.

In a circule around the suburbs lay the actual Ommelanden, stretching a few miles inland. This was a mixed landscape of gardens, *kampungs*, arable land, and country estates. Here a rough division can be made between the areas within and beyond the outposts, a ring of small redoubts at some distance from the inner city.[13] In the area within the redoubts many concentrations of foreign Asian communities, especially those from the Indonesian archipelago—Buginese, Macassarese, Ambonese, Balinese and others—were to be found.[14] The irregular distribution of the ethnic groups points to the fact that they lived in fairly closed communities. Unfortunately, the cadastral blocks do not indicate individual *kampungs*, but the tendency is clear. The fifth and last area comprises the Ommelanden outside of the outposts. Here there were scarcely any Europeans resident. The majority of the population was made up of Indonesian peoples, mostly Javanese.

The census of Colombo shows us something quite different. The case is most evident for the Fort: here out of the 158 adult men, 132 were European, fifteen Mestizos or Castizos, and of the three men unspecified, two were probably either European or Mestizo. In addition to them, one Topass and five Sinhalese men lived within the confines of the Fort. In the group of women (not included here), the Asian world is far better represented: apart from thirty-nine females of European blood, there were fifty-six Mestizos, one Topass and fifty Sinhalese women (twenty-seven are unspecified). As can be deduced from these figures, the children living in the Fort were mostly of mixed descent. One important difference with the situation in Batavia was that the Fort area was not completely reserved for accommodation of Company personnel and for purely administrative and commercial purposes. Unlike Batavia, it had neatly laid-out streets, where officials lived with their families, and where even freeburghers and Asians could have their homesṇṇat least at that time: residential conditions became restricted after 1758.[15]

In the Town area also, the group of Europeans, Mestizos, Castizos and Topasses, as well as other Asian Christians (bearing Portuguese names) made up the majority of the inhabitants, but less so than in the Fort. Apart from these, there were quite a number of Sinhalese men and many more women to be found, as well as a good score of *Chetties*, from the Hindu traders' caste of *Chettyars* originating from mainland India. Only one 'Moor' (part of a rather mixed group of Muslim indigenous, Bengali and Coromandel traders), one Javanese and a few Paravar men (from the fishers' caste) were living in the town. There was a relatively large section of the population of the Town area, the ethnicity of which cannot be assessed with any certainty, but here again a large proportion was European, Mestizo or Asian Christian. Most of the Dutch inhabitants of Fort and Town were Company servants—208 are registered as such in the census. In 1694 the Company personnel of Colombo numbered 1,622 (of which only these 208 were living in independent households, the rest not being represented in the census and being quartered in the guardhouses and outposts).[16]

Already by 1694, Colombo seemed to be a quite homogeneous society. Hardly any system is detectable in the residential distribution of the population groups within Colombo which is shown in the Appendix. The Fort was primarily, but not exclusively, Company territory: the main administrative, military and commercial buildings stood there and it was clearly and safely separated from its surroundings by walls, a moat and a lake. It is surprising, though, that people other than Company servants were allowed to live within the Fort, but these were only those of 'reliable' descent: Europeans, part-Europeans, and their families. Some of the lower-ranking Company personnel, as well as some Sinhalese and Chettyar families—most of them bearing Portuguese names and professing the Christian faithṇṇhad made their homes in the Town, without much ethnic concentration.

Nevertheless, this image of a homogeneous, mixed society is highly deceptive: the census does not include the area outside the Town confines. This was exactly the place where the quarters of 'Moors' and Chettyars took rootṇṇseparated from each other as well as from the town proper.[17] Unfortunately, we do not know the number of settlers in these fringes of Colombo. Just as in Batavia, the majority of Asian inhabitants—except for the Mestizos and the Asian Christians—have been quite successfully kept out of the core area of the city.

Three conclusions can be drawn from the censuses. First, that around 1700 the authorities in both cities had succeeded to a fair degree in achieving the segregation of population groups, principally along lines of religion, and additionally between the non-Christian groups themselves. Secondly, that the distribution of the population groups over the urban territory took place according to the classification of the colonial authorities: the Europeans, Christians and economically predominant groups occupied the core area, while groups who could not boast any privilege according to their race or faith were grouped on the periphery of the city. A third outstanding fact concerned the difference between Batavia and Colombo: ethnic dispersion in Colombo was definitely less regulated than in Batavia; Colombo's ethnic appearance was more European than in the Company capital; furthermore, in Colombo no group enjoyed the privileges the Chinese in Batavia did.

RACE AND SPACE IN BATAVIA AND COLOMBO

The separation of population groups in Batavia and Colombo cannot be accounted for by a process of self-segregation, although this did occur to a certain degree. The segregation was slowly but surely enforced as the Asian population in the cities multiplied and the Company authorities tried to tighten their grip on urban society. This process differed locally in speed and intensity. It took several decades before a society had developed in which the constituent parts were balanced out and a more or less consistent policy was developed. Once crystallised, the system lasted until the end of the eighteenth century. To account for the similarities and differences of the ethnic composition and organisation of Colombo and Batavia, we have to consider the genesis of the cities, the developments in population composition, the local conditions, and the role of the city authorities in ordering urban society.

BATAVIA

The building up of Batavia started almost from scratch. After the conquest in 1619 most of the former inhabitants fled the neighbourhood. Governor-General J.P. Coen was immediately confronted by the problem of how to populate his urban brainchild and to provide the manpower needed to build up the city structure. He adopted three schemes. The first was to invite, and eventually to force, Asian traders to come and settle in the new town called Batavia. Experience gleaned in nearby Banten had taught that the Chinese were the most industrious urban dwellers to be had, both in terms of being quite a reliable workforce as well as being the predominant sea traders in the Chinese and Indonesian waters. The blockade of the harbour of Banten, the promotion of Batavia as an attractive market, and the forceful seizure of Chinese junks did indeed have its effect: within six months, 400 Chinese had already (albeit temporarily) settled in Batavia.[18] Within ten years their numbers had risen to 3,000.[19] This level was maintained, with ups and downs, until the 1680s, after which the number of Chinese would rise again dramatically.

Coen's second line of policy was to bring in as many slaves as could be bought in Coromandel, Arakan and elsewhere. But, although indispensable to manpower in the years of development, the slaves or their offsprings were not considered to be the mainstays of the new colony. This privilege was reserved for the Dutch settlers, the target of Coen's third scheme. Coen dreamed of a prosperous Dutch settlement colony, but this stranded on the unwillingness of the Dutch to emigrate in great numbers, as well as on the reluctance of the Directors in the Dutch Republic to apportion them part of the Asian trade. In 1628, when the kingdom of Mataram threatened war, apart from the Company personnel only 210 able Dutch men could be mobilised.[20] The main bottleneck in Batavia was the shortage of women. Year in, year out Coen tried to persuade the Directors to send respectable families and nubile girls, but to no great avail.[21]

It soon dawned on the officials in Batavia that, if there was to be a purely Dutch colony in Batavia, it would take a long time. Coen's successors adopted a second-best scheme by which the connubial association of Dutch men and Asian women was to be encouraged. Their Eurasian offspring would be more immune to the pernicious climate and would feel more attached to the Indies than Europeans. In fact, this was only legitimising what was already taking place on a large scale, albeit without the legal bond: from the time of the arrival of the first Dutch ships in Asia, the men had laid their eyes and their hands on Asian women. About the 1640s the Mestizo society was fully authorised by the Governors-General and the Directors. In 1641, Governor-General Antonio van Diemen wrote to his superiors: "If we want to establish something permanent, it will have to be brought about by the indigenous women, just as the Portuguese have been putting into practice."[22]

But whatever the plans and the practice, with the European settlers remaining sparse and most of them dying like flies or happily returning to their homeland, Dutch colonisation never really did get far. The Directors at home did not give colonisation priority. They were businessmen, not empire-builders. The Dutch and Eurasians were to remain a minority. Consequently, Batavia became a predominantly Asian city. As it slowly grew to the status of primate city, it became the destination for a host of temporary or permanent settlers of widely divergent origin, arriving spontaneously, by force or by invitation. These were the traders who were to be met in every coastal trading centre in South and Southeast Asia, including Chinese, Malays, Persians, Armenians, Arabs, Indians and Indonesians. Others were slaves, from the coasts of the Indian Ocean and the Indonesian archipelago. Moreover, there were baptised Indians from the Portuguese territories, often freed slaves; they were known as Topasses of Mardijkers. Then, of course, there were Javenese who were lured by the prosperity of Batavia or who had fled from the neighbouring States. And finally, a countless number of population groups from every corner of the archipelago, including banished princes with their retinues, or bands of fighting men in temporary service of the Company.

The Dutch officials did not view this Asian demographic take-over with indifference. Even though they encouraged the Asian immigration to a certain degree, they nurtured a profound distrust towards the Asian population, whether for political, racial or religious considerationsṇṇand often for a combination of these factors. Javanese and other Indonesian peoples were considered a "murderous and perfidious nation": elsewhere they are called "lazy, thievish and murderous.".[23] All slaves were considered to have a "dangerous disposition", a qualification that did not take a turn for the better after manumission, as even the Mardijkers (who were Christians) were called "black riff-raff... being by nature disposed to the utter idleness, being evil in morals and by upbringing".[24]

During the course of the seventeenth century, an intricate system of control evolved. While the city was still under construction, there had been some attempts to confine the Asian population groups to separate quarters, mainly on the western side of River Ciliwung, which cut the city in two. It seems that both Javanese and Chinese inhabitants lived separately in their own streets, which were barred at night. Other population groups also had their own quarters (Moors, Bandanese, Malays and Malabars). This segregation was not consistently enforced and in the course of several decades, the Asian inhabitants were to be found all over Batavia, although most of them still lived in the western part.[25]

The 1650s brought change. Renewed hostilities with Banten and the influx of large groups of Javanese immigrants, as well as increasing disorder in the countryside (the Ommelanden) spurred the authorities to take measures. Thus in 1651, probably at the instigation of the Directors in the Republic, an ordinance was issued ordering that all "indigenous" (i.e. Javanese) inhabitants should have themselves registered and that they should carry identity papers. They had to stay indoors after 9 o'clock in the evening.[26] The registration system did not function smoothly because, as early as in 1655, the Governor-General had to admit he did not know the number of Javanese inhabitants in the city.[27] Even more important was the decision in 1655, made under the threat of war from Banten, to move the Javanese families out of the walled city and to settle them under strict control on an assigned piece of land outside the gates because: "this people [is] very dangerous for the Dutch State here, as our enemies from outsides collude with them". A head was appointed over them. They were admitted into the town during the day time but only selectively and under certain conditions.[28] New Javanese settlers, arriving from Bantenese territory, were not received with open arms by the authorities, but were admitted only so as to weaken the Bantenese enemy.[29]

Another development in train in these years was the trek of the Asian Christian Mardijkers to the area outside the walls. They jibbed at the obligation and the cost of building their houses in brick, as stipulated for the inner city. This resulted in empty spaces and disorder, especially in the western part of the town, where the Javanese had already been forced to leave their houses. The Government reacted with an ordinance, only giving permission to build houses outside the walls if land there was to be brought under cultivation.[30] But the exodus was not to be curbed and in the subsequent years, a suburb was laid out to the east of Batavia completely in accordance with the Dutch tradition of a grid of wide and straight streets along canals.[31] Here, as can be seen in the 1699 census, was to be the Mardijkers' quarter.

A third event was the arrival of groups and companies of Indonesian auxiliaries in Batavia. These were mainly of Ambonese and Sulawesian origin (called Macassarese, Butonese, Buginese and others). It started with a company of Ambonese soldiers under the command of Raja Tahalele in 1656.[32] From then onwards, there was an Ambonese minority in Batavia which led a peripatetic life, travelling to wherever the Company needed their military skills. In about 1663 a detailed set of regulations was issued for the Muslim Ambonese in Batavia. It was stipulated that the Muslim Ambonese had to settle on the lands appointed to them; they were placed under the command of a captain of their nation called Lebe Hoelang and other officers of lesser rank, and were subject to the supervision of a Dutch official; the Ambonese officers had to administer justice among their countrymen for minor offences; they had to keep permanent register of all their subordinates and give account of them to the supervisor; apart from the enlistment in Company service during expeditions, the Ambonese had to form a militia for emergencies; they were banned from having intercourse with Christian women; at night they had to keep to their own quarter. It was explicitly stated that nobody was allowed to harm them on account of their religion, provided they refrained from public religious acts and attempts to convert Christians. They were not expected to set their hands to the plough: but, if they so wanted, they could get some land suitable for cultivation.[33]

I have dealt with these regulations in some detail, as they set the tone for all subsequent legislation on ethnic groups in Batavia. The essentials are clear: segregation, indirect rule, (conditional) freedom of religious practice and availability for military purposes. The most peculiar features of this legislation were its selectivity and the fact that the object of the segregation laws was not primarily to separate all Asians from Europeans but rather the Asian population groups from each other. Indeed, *divide et impera.*

In the 1680s, this system of regulations was to be overhauled and completed. At that time, peace was at last returning to the Batavian territory after many years of turbulence caused by the wars with Banten and by gangs of robbers. The grip of the Company on the surrounding country, the Ommelanden, was tightened: a polder board and blockmasters were appointed and the Ommelanden were surveyed and mapped. All Asian inhabitants other than Mardijkers, slaves and Chinese, were assigned to areas of land (*kampungs*), under their own headmen. The inhabitants were to be registered on the same footing as was already the practice in the inner city.[34] In 1688 an all-embracing law was issued that encapsulated all previous regulations, fixing place of residence, prescribing registration, introducing identity cards, restricting mobility and so forth.[35] Later still, marriage outside one's ethnic group was prohibited, as was the wearing of clothes other than those of one's own group. Furthermore, to curb the influx of Asian people, the import of slaves was restricted, as was the immigration of Chinese, who were now coming to Batavia in hordes.[36] All this was done "as a very efficient and powerful means to henceforth check the thievery, robbery and murders as well as other evils by daily encroaching Javanese, Malays, Balinese, Macassarese, Buginese, Saleverese, Butunese, Bimanese and similar dangerous Eastern people".[37]

The system of rule was crystallised in about 1700 and remained in existence throughout the eighteenth century. Still, some changes did occur. The first was the gradual erosion of the Chinese privileges through immigration restrictions, prohibition on marrying non-Chinese, the admission of Muslims on to the board of curators (*boedelmeesters*; formerly only Chinese had a seat in this board), and, in 1741, the formal institution of a Chinese *kampung* in the southwestern suburb.[38] The dependence of the Dutch on

Chinese labour, diligence and trade connections remained, but the relationship cooled down considerably, finally resulting in the Chinese massacre of 1740. The second change was the exhortation of the Indonesian inhabitants to engage in agriculture, a tendency which, after the crisis in the sugar industry in the 1720s, was accompanied by a diversification of crops. Their role as military auxiliaries and thus the need to be permanently mobilisable waned. The Company reacted by trying to tie them to the land and transform them into agriculturists. Embryonic sedentary settlements of these Indonesian population groups developed in the Ommelanden, structured around marketplaces and an expanding road network. In the 1750s, the Indonesian peoples were even allowed to buy and possess land. But the system of indirect rule and legal pluralism remained in operation until the early nineteenth century.

COLOMBO

In Colombo, the starting point was quite different from that in Jakarta/Batavia. First, the stage was set by the Portuguese, who had settled in Colombo in 1517. When the Dutch took over in 1656 they did not obtain a locus rasus, but a city styled in the Portuguese fashion. Colombo was a large circumvallated area enclosing streets and gardens laid out more or less at random.[39] The inhabitants of both the city and its neighbourhood were converts to Catholicism.[40] Secondly, the southwestern part of Ceylon had been a Portuguese dominion that was already functioning with regard to the procurement of the valuable products of the island, to wit: cinnamon, arecanuts, pearls and elephants. As the peeling of cinnamon was done by the Sinhalese mainly as service to their overlord, the Company tried to continue the traditional system. The Company limited the social and geographical mobility of the inhabitants as much as possible. Innumerable decrees seem to indicate this: intercaste marriage was discouraged as much as possible, and if it did take place, the resulting offspring was to be classified under the caste most lucrative for Company's interests—usually the cinnamon-peelers or Chalias.[41]

Another difference was that Colombo had to share its role in the maritime trading relations with other places on the island. Galle was to be the point of departure for the Company ships to the Dutch

Republic, and the strategically positioned town of Jaffnapatnam kept its importance as market town for the Indian traders. In contrast to Batavia, where the Company established itself primarily in order to centralise its administration, in Ceylon the VOC came for the riches of the land. In comparison to Batavia, from the start Colombo had a greater role as an administrative centre for a producing hinterland, and played a very modest part in the intercontinental and intra-Asian trading networks.

In the aftermath of Adriaan van der Meyden's occupation of Colombo in 1656, all Portuguese families were evicted from the island. Only a few white people were left in Colombo. As for the remaining Mestizos, Topasses and Sinhalese, they were to be discarded as soon as any suspicion of their betrayal of the Dutch cause might arise.[42] Another event was the depopulation of the surrounding territories and demolition of its villages by the armies of the inland kingdom of Kandy or Kanda uda pas rata. The inhabitants would slowly, and only partly, return during the 1660s and 1670s.

As in Batavia after its conquest, the first priority of the Company authorities was to secure the supply of foodstuffs (especially rice), the restoration of the trading connections, and the provision of labour. To this end large quantities of slaves were imported from Coromandel. Land was granted in fief to the Sinhalese auxiliaries, the Lascarins, and to the slaves, in order to get cultivation under way.[43] Attempts were made to lure Hindu and Muslim Indian traders to Colombo bringing with them the necessary rice, salt and other food articles, but there was little to offer them in return, because the arecanuts, which were in demand with the traders, were not reaching Colombo as a result of the depopulation of the Company districts.[44]

In the meantime, the reconstruction of the city was slowly put in motion. After a short period of indecisiveness about whether or not to turn the city over to the Kandyan king, Raja Sinha, it was decided to put itṇṇat least temporarily, but it proved to be permanentṇṇin a state of defence, to hold it against Portuguese or even Sinhalese attacks.[45] The old extended Portuguese walled town was cut in two. One part was to be the Fort where the Company administration would be housed; the remaining half of the town was to be the Black Town. The old city walls were retained and strengthened to protect the town area which was to serve as a retreat for the indigenous community in the event of war.[16] Only later, the city walls were allowed to dilapidate and were eventually demolished, and only the Fort area remained walled. Telling are the efforts of the Dutch to alter the city structure completely: the rather unplanned criss-crossing pattern of the Portuguese town was immediately supplanted by a rectangular lay-out which had been applied also in Batavia and in the urban extensions in the Dutch Republic.

The curious thing is that at this time, some years after its demise in Batavia, the idea of white colonisation, and its half-brother Mestizo colonisation, resurfaced.[17] Even before the capture of Colombo, Dutch colonisation plans in Ceylon had been approved by the Directors in the Republic and by the High Government in Batavia. But the Dutch freeburghers in Colombo were forced to face up to the same problems as their counterparts in Batavia. Due to the unwillingness of the Company to allow the burghers to open commercial relations to any profitable degree, most of them were destined to live a very modest life. Within a few years many freeburghers trickled back into the Company's ranks.[18] Despite the wishes of the ambitious Governor, Rijklof van Goens, it was soon decided that the colony would be peopled by the 'slow' method, the procreation of children by the married soldiers or *casados*, as they were called by the Portuguese.[19] In 1694, only twenty-eight male freeburghers were registered in the census.

The Company authorities, especially Rijklof van Goens, seem to have nurtured a deep-rooted distrust for the non-Dutch communities such as the Muslims, Chettyars and 'Portuguese'. This last category included hardly any European-born Portuguese, but mainly Asian converts who spoke Portuguese and had embraced the Roman Catholic religion. The majority of them remained on the island after the banning of the 'real' Portuguese, much to the misgivings of the Dutch. They were eventually ejected from the towns "which affords much peace to the State security as well as to the propagation of the true religion".[50]

Nor were the 'Moors' much favoured by the Company. They had been able to dominate much of the arecanut and elephant trade from the island, to say nothing of the essential rice imports. Van Goens wanted to oust these Muslims from the arecanut trade.[51] In his opinion the Moors were the most despicable of all the Asian inhabitants of the island, being of "a very contemptible and vile descent" and having accepted the Muslim faith and embraced the art of piracy as a result of contacts with the Turks.[52] In 1659 the Dutch authorities prohibited Muslims and other non-Christians from possessing any shops and allowed them only to practise a craft under a master and to participate in overseas trade only in cooperation with Dutch participants.[53] In 1665 it was prohibited to sell real estate to the Topasses and natives.[54] The results of the restrictive measures regarding the Muslims were disastrous: in 1669 a famine affected the country and the Company's subjects were said to have sunk into poverty.[55] But the Indian traders proved to be indispensable for the supply of rice, which the island did not produce in sufficient quantities, and for the purchase of the elephants, an important source of Company profits. And Governor Laurens Pijl (1679-92) did concede that the Muslims were essential to the commercial links between Ceylon and the Indian subcontinent.[56] Later the critical attitude to the Muslims assumed more economic overtones. Governor Becker (1707-16) stated in his *Memoir* that "... their presence is very prejudicial to the interests of the Company.... But those who have been permitted for many years to live either here or in the Galle Commandement, and the Chitties and Paruas, are to be permitted to remain on their performing extra services.... Beyond this no Moors may possess any immovable property...".[57]

The distrust of the non-Christian peoples in Colombo, as was the case in Batavia, was translated into a policy of segregation, both from the Christian section of the inhabitants, as well as from each other. Under the governorship of Cornelis Jan Simons (1703-7), the communities of Cettyars, Muslims and Paravar were assigned their own separate residential quarters under their respective heads, supervised by the Dessave of the Colombo district "who keeps a special roll of them, and if necessary could order a good many of them to take their turn at the public works".[58] The Muslims, Chettyars and Paravar had to always carry a certificate to prove the legality of their residence and their obligation to perform the Uliyam or statutory services.[59] In the Muslims' quarter, Governor Simons:

> had the old street cleared in order to root out the kissing and coquetry of all kinds of rabble living there outside streets without their evil being discovered, and made it five Rhineland Roods

> broad and had yet another new street built through this disorderly quarter and commanded the Moors to build their houses with their fronts to the street in an orderly fashion, which was accordingly done.[60]

The Chettyars' quarter was located on the northeastern side of the town along the coast; the Muslims' quarter lay more inland, between the Chettyars' quarter and the lake, towards the Wolvendaal Church. Later, the washermen's caste community also had its own residence on the southern coastal strip. And finally, across the lake on a peninsula, the living quarters of the Company slaves were set up.[61]

Thus Colombo also had its segregation, although the regulation was much less intensive than in Batavia. In Colombo too, the segregation served several purposes: both from the angle of security and for social and economic reasons. Again we see the existence of legal cleavages between Europeans and non-Europeans. Although the religious attitude of the Company authorities was partly influenced by the presence of many Roman Catholics among the islanders, the main demeanour was one of religious tolerance.[62] As we have seen, ethnically the Fort and the Old Town had kept its European appearance to a far larger extent than Batavia. This 'whiteness' was undeniably determined by the size of the town: put simply there were sufficient Europeans to make the town look 'white'. The relative unimportance of Colombo as interregional transit port made the city only a minor destination for (temporary) migrants or trading communities. The resulting urban society was more stable than the perpetual motion of Batavia, and did not call for very rigorous regulation.

The ethnic relations of pre-modern Dutch colonial society are characterised by a jumble of assorted motives and interests. Orders from home on this subject were not very detailed and left the authorities in Asia room to handle matters according to their own judgement and experience.[63] The Dutch did not cast their cities into any readymade straitjacket, and ethnic relations tended to be diverse, depending primarily on the local needs of the Dutch. Thus, Batavia became the laboratory of colonial society. The experience from Batavia was to be applied in other Dutch cities, such as Malacca, Colombo, Cochin and Makassar. Due to its size and the number of inhabitants the urban organisational structure of Batavia was more elaborate than in the other Dutch cities.

Local circumstances did leave their mark on the residential patterns. One of them was the urban morphology. Batavia was planned as a big town, probably in anticipation of the arrival of Dutch colonists. This did not eventuate, so Chinese were tolerated within the walls. The Dutch did not hammer at complete segregation of the Asian peoples from the Europeans. Other local circumstances relate to the specific functions of both cities. The emergence of Batavia as the major port city of the region, and its importance as administrative and military centre certainly enhanced the multitude and diversity of its inhabitants. The concentration on maritime relations rather than on the development of the hinterland during the first century caused the continuous *va-et-vient* and residential unrest which is characteristic of primate port cities. Military interests and the fluctuating population in Batavia called for a specific set of regulations, by which the Asian communities were separated from each other. Colombo had a far more parochial outlook, having more modest commercial aspirations and being primarily the administrative centre of a huge cinnamon plantation.

The paramount factor was of course the weight of commercial interests, which tended to mitigate strictly religious and racial motives. One consequence was the relative subordination of the Church mission to the Company's authorities and interests. Nevertheless, Christianity remained the major touchstone in categorising the urban population, and the Church played an important role in urban society. On the whole, all Christians, whether European or Asian, were subject to the same laws and legal procedures. Asian Christians, especially Protestants, were considered quite trustworthy fellow citizens, albeit of a lower social order. They had right of appeal to the same charitable privileges as the Europeans and Mestizos, although they often received less than European Christians. And just as was the case in the Portuguese *Estado*, Asians and even Mestizos were excluded from service in the Company, except for the lowest ranks.[64]

An official racist attitude was indeed omnipresent but was softened or counteracted by the religious considerations as well as by economic concerns, as was evidenced by the Chinese privileges in Batavia. Similar 'intermediary' groups in Colombo, such as the Chettyars and Muslims, were less favoured, due to the greater self-sufficiency of Colombo. Notwithstanding the partly successful segregation, the social distance between Asians and Europeans could not be absolute because of the continuous practice of intermarriage andṇṇmay be more importantṇṇdue to the economic interests of the Company. The criss-crossing of several interests resulted in a complicated system of social regulations and indirect rule.

COCKTAILING IN ASIA

Let us broaden our perspective and turn to the performance of other European colonisers in Asia. Colonial cities do not seem to have differed very much from each other. Forming (part-) European islands in the Asian stream, they all acted as administrative centres, garrison towns, junctions in the intercontinental as well as regional trading networks, and were the central stage of cultural contact between Europeans and Asians. Nevertheless, they were quite different in morphology, ethnic composition, and social organisation. Every city presented its own peculiar cocktail of ethnic groups, and the authorities adopted different policies in dealing with their Asian inhabitants. The many variations were not only due to the difference in emphasis laid on one of the urban functions or to the variation in local conditions, but also to mentalities stemming from the metropolis. Cities mirrored the ideas of empire that the various colonial powers cherished.

The Spanish colonial efforts were marked by an unmistakable 'imperial' drive, albeit not so much directed at continuous territorial conquest as at the thorough restructuring of the indigenous society. Hispanisation, Christianisation and *reduccion* (resettlement) of the Philippine people were as important as the trans-Pacific trade.[65] Both the metropolitan tradition of urbanisation and the experience acquired as *conquistadores* in the Americas played an important role in the organisation of the city of Manila. Famous, and very characteristic, in this respect are the *Ordenanzas para descubrimientos, nuevas poblaciones y pacificaciones* of 1573, in which King Philip II laid down detailed instructions on the founding, constructing and developing of new towns.[66] One of the most striking consequences of the ordinances was the grid-iron pattern of the streets, crossing each other at regular intervals and thus making rectangular blocks of houses.[67] Another result of the Spanish policies in Manila was the creation of an artificial barrier between the European city within the walls and the Asian or partly Asian suburbs outside the gates. This was done with the intention of reducing the contact between the European rulers and the indigenes, and for reasons of security. No Asian of whatever descent, or even Mestizo, was allowed to have his living quarters *intramuros.* Moreover, the different ethnic groups of Chinese, Japanese, Filipinos and others were allocated their own specific suburbs, although some leniency can be seen in the actual application of this principle.

The Spanish case, with its neatly organised street patterns, its emphasis on Christianisation and Hispanisation, and its strict segregation between Europeans and Asians in the intra- and extramural zones, was to stand alone among the policies of the other European nations. The Portuguese modus, which involved to legally enforced segregation, stands alone at the other end of the spectrum. As John Villiers has pointed out, this was the outcome of a different "concept of empire".[68] The Portuguese attitude was primarily one of accommodation. They were not primarily in pursuit of the conquest of vast territories and a subsequent acculturation by *reduccion* of indigenous peoples. The foremost concern of the Portuguese authorities in Asia was to build, extend and secure the trading network. The missionary activities were certainly applauded by the temporal authorities, but the cross and the sword were not hand in glove as much as was the case in the Spanish Empire.

Central city planning seems to have been completely lacking in the Portuguese territories, and there is no evidence of a segregation policy. In Malacca, 'self-segregation' of the foreign merchant communities was carried over from pre-Portuguese days, and in Goa and Colombo the residential divisions were determined by social factors—but no attempt was made to divide Europeans from the non-Europeans. This is not to say that Portuguese—because they mixed easily with Asians and knew no segregation—were racially and religiously tolerant. Forced Christianisation, demolition of Hindu temples and the setting up of social barriers against non-Portuguese testify to the opposite.[69]

The English, for their part, only slowly engaged themselves in colonial urbanisation, and their efforts are characterised by a flexibility in organising the urban societies according to the local conditions. Here we do not encounter the urge for acculturation that both Iberian colonisers displayed. No strict grid-iron street plans, nor even much trace of city planning; no forced Christianisation; no all-embracing application of English law. Madras, occupied in 1639, was not laid out on the basis of an extensive building programme, and it developed in step with its population growth. A primitive grid form did result, as did a tripartite urban structure of Fort, White Town and Black Town. The Fort was exclusively Company territory. Eurasians and Asian Christians also made their homes, alongside Europeans, in the White Town. Segregation did take place, but occurred largely "spontaneously".[70] Roughly speaking, the same situation prevailed in Calcutta.[71] While in Bombay, the English flexibility in ethnic policy is even more striking, may be under influence of the Portuguese proximity. In order to transform Bombay into a prosperous town, the English—who were to be a very tiny minority for a long time—launched an intensive programme by which Indian occupational groups were invited to settle themselves in the town with the promise of freedom of religion and jurisdiction. The ethnic diversity was thus enhanced by the official policy of accommodation.[72]

The three colonial urban mentalities we have just passed in review differed markedly. Which position did the Dutch occupy in this spectrum of race relations? A striking resemblance seems to have existed between the Spanish and Dutch, both in their segregation policies as in the grid-iron city plan they employed. There is some truth in the observation that the greatest city planners were also the greatest segregators. But this resemblance is deceptive. The segregation in Manila had different overtones to and served partly different purposes from that in Batavia. Their strongest similarity is that both cities were the manifest results of two vigorously led empires.

It is true that while forming their own policy the Dutch did not cast an eye on the urban societies of their colonial neighbours. The example of Manila as a toll-extracting European enclave amidst a ring of Asian communities thrust itself very strongly indeed before the eyes of J.P. Coen.[73] And Portuguese colonial society also exerted a very strong attraction for the Dutch—especially with regard to their capacity for creating a loyal Mestizo population. But the Dutch had not the Lusitanian resilience, nor the Spanish missionary rigidity. It was with the English that the Dutch did share some of the basic colonial aims, namely profits, but until the end of the eighteenth century definitely, John Bull lacked any particular attitude towards city planning and intensive social engineering in the colonies.

The uniqueness of the Dutch Company's performance in Asia cannot be defined in terms of their feeling of racial, religious or cultural superiority—these were common to all colonisers. The most eye-catching feature of the Dutch case is its ambiguity, which was the outcome of the merchant's monopolistic mind, balancing the wish to mould the colonial society to their will and to allot every group its productive role in the Company's system, against the huge costs of doing so. It resulted in a peculiar blend of extreme regulation on the one hand, and a certain reticence to intervene rigorously in the colonised society on the other.

NOTES

[1]Here we are confronting the problem that theorisation on pre-modern colonial cities has hardly yet begun, and comparative analyses are rare. *The Rise and Growth of the Colonial Port Cities in Asia.* Center for South and Southeast Asia Studies, University of California, Berkeley. Monograph Series 25, (1979), repr. Lanham etc., 1985; Gerard J. Telkamp, *Urban History and European Expansion: A Review of Recent Literature Concerning Colonial Cities and a Preliminary Bibliography.* Intercontinental, Leiden, 1978; Robert J. Ross and Gerard J. Telkamp (eds.), *Colonial Cities.* Comparative Studies in Overseas History 5, Dordrecht etc., 1985. Added to these may be Frank Broeze (ed.), *Brides of the Sea: Port Cities of Asia from the Sixteenth to Twentieth Centuries,* Kensington, 1989; contains also contributions on non-colonial cities. An interesting comparative study is John Villiers' "Portuguese Malacca and Spanish Manila: Two Concepts of Empire" in Roderich Ptak (ed.), *Portuguese Asia: Aspects in History and Economic History, 16th and 17th Centuries.* Beiträge zur Südasienforschung, Südasien-Institut, Universität Heidelberg 117, Stuttgart, 1987, pp. 37-57.

[2]J.C. Heesterman, "Warriors and Merchants", *Itinerario* 15, 1, 1991, pp. 37-49, esp. 47.

[3]J.C. Van Leur, "The World of Southeast Asia: 1500-1650" in id., *Indonesian Trade and Society. Essays in Asian Social and Economic History,* Leiden etc., 1983, pp. 157-245, esp. 221.

[4]According to the various instructions to the blockmasters in Colombo, annual lists had to be compiled here too. The instructions have been published recently in the compilation of laws and ordinances of the Dutch *Ceylonese Government, in L. Hovy, Ceylonees Plakkaatboek. Plakkaten en*

andere wetten uitgevaardigd door het Nederlandse bestuur op Ceylon, 1638-1796, 2 vols., Hilversum 1991, pp. 214-7 (1 July 1682), pp. 660-4 (2/5 May 1760) and pp. 873-80 (28 Dec. 1786).

[5]Batavia census: Algemeen Rijksarchief, The Hague, Archives of the Dutch East India Company (hereafter VOC), inv.nr. 1614, f. 891 and 1q078; Colombo census: VOC 1544, f. 820-847. For practical reasons, for Batavia the census of 1699 has been taken. The existence of the censuses has not passed unnoticed earlier, though only recently have historians laid aside their scepticism about the reliability of the statistics. Most important is the article of Frank Spooner, "Batavia, 1637-1790: A City of Colonial Growth and Migration" in Ira A. Glazier and Luigi De Rosa (eds.), *Migration Across Time and Nations: Population Mobility in Historical Contexts,* New York and London, 1986, pp. 30-57. Though very informative at a first glance, the subject-matter (both statistics and qualitative information) is carelessly handled. See also Lenonard Blussé, *Strange Company: Chinese Settlers, Mestizo Women and the Dutch in VOC Batavia,* Dordrecht and Riverton, 1986, pp. 18-19.

[6]In fact, this was done some ten years ago by Gerrit Knaap, 'Europeans, Mestizos and Slaves: The population of Colombo at the End of the Seventeenth century', *Itinerario* 5,2, 1981, pp. 84-101.

[7]Peter Burke, "Classifying the People: The Census as Collective Representation" in idem, *The Historical Anthropology of Early Modern Italy: Essays on Perception and Communication,* Cambridge etc. 1987, pp. 27-39, esp. 27.

[8]It is therefore not surprising that in one instance we have two presentations of the same Batavia census, only the numbers of Europeans and the slaves are the same. These two categories were the most clear cut in the eyes of the Dutch officials. The other categories were blurred. See VOC, inv.nr. 3535, f. 1647-49, Census Batavia 1779; and "Doodlijsten van de stad Batavia van 1759-78", *Verhandelingen van het Bataviaasch Genootschap der Kunsten en Wetenschappen* 2, 2, 1780, pp. 60-4 and pp. 74-9, esp. 74.

[9]J.A. Van der Chijs (ed.), *Nederlandsch-Indisch Plakaatboek, 1602-1811,* 17 volumes; Batavia and The Hague (1885-1900) II, pp. 208-11, 5 Oct. 1655. The instruction was reissued in 1685, see ibidem III, 155-62. In Colombo, the office of blockmaster was instituted in 1673. Instructions were not issued until 1682. Obviously drawn up after the example of Batavia, the tenor of the instructions is the same as in Batavia. See note 4.

[10]Hovy, *Ceylonees Plakkaatboek* I, pp. 214-15, 1 July 1682.

[11]This is confirmed by the prohibitions on marrying outside one's ethnic group and by the law (which is partly in contradiction with the former) that children would assume the ethnic identity of the father. See f.i. *Nederlands-Indisch Plakaatboek* III, p. 565 (5 February 1706) and IV, p.

269 (21 July 1730).

[12]VOC 11544, generale landmonsterrol, 1699.

[13]This distinction in area within and beyond the outposts is not made in the censuses, but derived from "Doodlijsten".

[14]The categorisation in the census falls short of reality. In documents of this period, many more ethnic groups were identified than those included in the censuses. It is probable that they were classified under a common heading, such as the Buginese/Macassarese for all people coming from Sulawesi; and Ambonese for all Moluccans. After the 1750s, the broad categories in the censuses are split up into more specific headings.

[15]Hovy, *Ceylonees Plakkaatboek* II, pp. 608-10, 12 June 1758.

[16]VOC 12372, generale landmonsterrol Ceylon, 1694.

[17]See R.L. *Brohier, Changing Face of Colombo (1505-1972). Covering the Portuguese, Dutch and British Periods* (Colombo, 1984), pp. 53-4. There the author speaks of British times, but traces the quarters back into the Dutch period.

[18]*Nederlandsch-Indisch Plakaatboek* I, p. 599. Elsewhere, Coen, totals them 300-400, see J.K.J. de Jonge and M.L. van Devente (eds.), *De opkomst van het Nederlandsch gezag in Oost-Indi'; verzameling van onuitgegeven stukken uit het Oud-Koloniaal Archief,* 13 vols., The Hague, 1862-1909, IV, p. 190.

[19]*Opkomst* V, pp. 123 and 162.

[20]*Ibid.*, p. 134.

[21]This story has often been told. See f.i. Jean Gelman Taylor, *The Social World of Batavia: European and Eurasian in Dutch Asia*, Madison, 1983, pp. 11-5.

[22]W.Ph. Coolhaas and J. van Goor (eds.), *Generale missiven van gouverneurs-generaal en raden aan Heren XVII der Verenigde Oostindische Compagnie*, 9 vols., The Hague, 1960-88, II, p. 150, 12 December 1641.

[23]*Ibid.* III, pp. 84 and 637, 31 July 1656 and 18 Oct. 1668.

[24]*Ibid.* IV, p. 749, 30 Nov. 1684, *Nederlandsch-Indisch Plakaatboek* III, pp. 147-8; *Opkomst* VII (4), 31 Jan. 1679.

[25]*Nederlandsch-Indisch Plakaatboek* I, pp. 364-5, 4/6 Nov. 1634 and II, pp. 20-1, 31 Jan. 1643. Openbare Bibliotheek Rotterdam, manuscript 86 N ll, Beschryving van de inwoond van Batavia [before 1653].

[26]*Nederlandsch-Indisch Plakaatboek* II, pp. 135-57, Instructions for the Governor-General and Councillors of India, 26 April 1650, esp. 155; ibid. II, pp. 162-4, 9/24 Feb. 1651.

[27]VOC, 677, Resolutions of Governor-General and Council, unfol, 16 March 1655.

[28]*Nederlandsch-Indisch Plakaatboek* II, pp. 203-4 (16 March 1655), p. 207 (13 July 1656), pp. 227-8 (25/29 July 1656); *Generale missiven* III, p. 84, 31 July 1956.

[29]*Generale missiven* III, p. 470 (23 Dec. 1664) and p. 637 (18 Oct. 1668).

[30]*Nederlandsch-Indisch Plakkaatboek* II, pp. 233-4 (29 Dec. 1656/Jan. 1657); *Generale missiven* III, p. 188 (17 Dec. 1657).

[31]Ed Taverne, In *'t land van belofte: in de nieue stadt. Ideaal en werkelijkheid van de stadsuitleg in de Republiek 1580-1680*, Maarssen, 1978.

[32]F. De Haan, Oud Batavia, 2nd ed., Bandung, 1935, p. 372; H.J. de Graaf, *De geschiedenis van Ambon en de Zuid-Molukken*, Franeker, 1977, pp. 147-51; J. Aalbers, *Rijklof van Goens, commissaris en veldoverste der Oostindische Compagnie, en zijn arbeidsveld, 1653/54 en 1657/58*, Groningen, 1916, 123ff.

[33]*Nederlandsch-Indisch Plakaatboek* II, pp. 368-70 (date unknown).

[34]J.A. van der Chijs a.o. (ed.), *Dagh-Register gehouden int Casteel Batavia vant passerende daer ter plaetse als over geheel Nederlandts-India, 1624-1682*, 31 vols., The Hague/Batavia, 1887-1931, 1679, p. 644 (31 Dec. 1679) and 1680, p. 853 (31 Dec. 1680); *General missiven* IV, p. 423 (31 Dec. 1680); *Nederlandsch-Indisch Plakaatboek* III, p. 138 (26 Sept. 1684) and pp. 190-91 (23 July 1686); VOC 701, Resolutions Governor-General and Council, pp. 303-4 (25 June 1686).

[35]*Nederlandsch-Indisch Plakaatboek* III, pp. 236-47, 12/21 Oct. 1688.

[36]*Ibid.*, pp. 262-9 (21/29 May 1690), pp. 517-8 (12/26 July 1701) and p. 565 (5 Feb. 1706); VOC 722, Resolutions GG&C, p. 90 (5 Feb. 1706).

[37]*Nederlandsch-Indisch Plakaatboek* III, 237-47 (12/21 Oct. 1688).

[38]*Nederlandsch-Indisch Plakaatboek* III, 268-9 (21/29 May 1690), pp. 424-7 (12 April/31 May 1697); *Realia. Register op de generale resolutiân van het kasteel Batavia 1632-1805*, 3 vols., Leiden, 1882-86, I, p. 279 (26 Jan. 1717).

[39]Brohier, *Changing Face of Colombo*, pp. 6-12; Algemeen Rijksarchief, The Hague, VEL 941 and 942.

[40]J. Van Goor, *Jan Kompenie as Schoolmaster: Dutch Education in Ceylon 1690-1795*, Groningen, 1978.

[41]See f.i. Hovy, *Ceylonees Plakaatboek* I, p. 110 (15 Aug. 1663) and p. 220 (23 Feb. 1683).

[42]VOC 1215, f. 927r-v, Van der Meijden to G.G. Maetsuiker and Council, 19 Nov. 1656; VOC 1214, f. 479, Van der Meijden to Maetsuiker and Council, August 1656.

[43]VOC 1234, f. 125r-v, Van Goens to Heren XVII, 5 April 1661.

[44]VOC 1215, f. 908, Van der Meijden and Council to Heren XVII, 9 Feb. 1657.

[45]For the indecision, see *Generale missiven* III, p. 83 (31 July 1656) and p. 102 (4 Dec. 1656). It was decided to keep Colombo in c. 1657, see ibid., III, p. 127 (31 Jan. 1657).

[46]Ibid., p. 268 (16 Dec. 1659) and p. 295 (16 Jan. 1660).

[47]K.W. Goonewardena, "A New Netherlands in Ceylon. Dutch Attempts to Found a Colony during the First Quarter Century of their Power

in Ceylon", *The Ceylon Journal of Historical and Social Studies* 2 (2) (July 1959), pp. 203-44. On white colonisation, see f.i. VOC 1233, f.214v, Report of Van der Meijden to G.G. Maetsuiker, 20 Sept. 1660; *Generale missiven* III, p. 793 (31 Jan. 1672). Around 1650, there has been an intensive discussion among the Heren XVII and the Councillors in Batavia about the desirability of extensive colonies with European freeburghers. See VOC 1175, f. 184-230v.

[48]*Generale missiver* IV, p. 294 (13 Feb. 1679) and p. 455 (29 April 1681).

[49]See f.i. *ibid.*, III, p. 329 (16 Dec. 1660) and p. 793 (31 Jan. 1672).

[50]*Ibid.*, 16 Dec. 1659, p. 269.

[51]*Ibid.*, 5 Oct. 1667, p. 591.

[52]Algemeen Rijksarchief, The Hague, Archives Hoge Regering Batavia 542, f. 17, Description of Ceylon by Rijklof van Goens, 29 Sep. 1675.

[53]Hovy, *Ceylonees Plakaatboek* I, 10/17 June 1659, pp. 43-6.

[54]*Ibid.*, 25 July 1668, p. 140.

[55]*Generale missiver* III, p. 695 (17 Nov. 1669) and IV, p. 635 (31 Dec. 1683).

[56]Ibid., p. 695 (17 Nov. 1669); Archives Hoge Regering Batavia, Considerations of Laurens Pijl on Ceylon, 1682.

[57]Sophia Anthonisz, tr. & ed., *Memoir of Hendrick Becker, Governor and Director of Ceylon, for his Successor, Isaac Augustijn Rumpf, 1716*, Colombo, 1914, p. 38.

[58]Sophia Anthonisz, tr. & ed., *Memoir of Cornelis Joan Simons, Governor and Director of Ceylon, for his Successor, Hendrick Becker*, 1707, Colombo, 1914, p. 27.

[59]Hovy, *Ceylonees Plakaatboek* II, 3 Feb. 1744, p. 496.

[60]Sinnappah Arasaratnam, tr. & ed., *Francois Valentijn's Description of Ceylon*, London, 1978, pp. 119-20.

[61]Algemeen Rijksarchief, The Hague, Map Department, VEL 953, plan of Colombo and surroundings by Carel David Wentzel, 1762.

[62]J. van Goor, "Predikanten in de hindu-buddhistische wereld" in idem, *Kooplieden, predikanten en bestuurders overzee* Utrecht, 1982, pp. 109-34.

[63]A very crude assessment of metropolitan instructions can be obtained by glancing through the index on the resolutions of the Heren XVII, VOC 221-4 and on the outgoing letters of the Heren XVII, VOC 345-9.

[64]Asian widows received only three rixdollars from the parish, against the Europeans four. See f.i. VOC 221, Resolutions Heren XVII, 319 (18 Aug. 1634, 11 Sept. 1635 and 16 Oct. 1676); *Nederlandsch-Indisch Plakaatboek* II, pp.133-4 (30 Sept./6 Oct. 1649) and IV, pp. 102 (15 July 1717), p. 119 (15 July 1718), p. 199 (28 Aug. 1727) and VI, p. 646 (12 March 1754).

[65]Robert R. Reed, *Colonial Manila. The Context of Hispanic Urbanism and the Process of Morphogenesis.* University of California Publications in

Geography 22, Berkeley etc., 1978.

[66]See Zella Nuttall, "Royal Ordinances Concerning the Laying out of New Towns", *The Hispanic American Historical Review* 4, 1921, pp. 743-53.

[67]Reed, *Colonial Manila.* See also Robert R. Reed, "The Foundation and Morphology of Hispanic Manila: Colonial Images and Philippine Realities" in Basu (ed.), *Rise and Growth,* pp. 197-204 and the discussion on pp. 221-45 and Robert R. Reed, "The Colonial Origins of Manila and Batavia: Desultory Notes on Nascent Metropolitan Primacy and Urban Systems in Southeast Asia", *Asian Studies* 5, 1967, pp. 543-62.

[68]Villiers, "Portuguese Malacca and Spanish Manila".

[69]Teotonio R. de Souza, *Medieval Goa: A Socio-Economic History,* New Delhi, 1979, esp. pp. 91-3 and 113-5; C.R. Boxer, *Race Relations in the Portuguese Empires, 1415-1825,* Oxford, 1963; Villiers, "Portuguese Malacca and Spanish Manila", p. 46.

[70]Susan J. Lewandowski, "Changing Form and Function in the Ceremonial and the Colonial Port City in India: An Historical Analysis of Madurai and Madras", *Modern Asian Studies* 11 (2), 1977, pp. 183-212; see also Partha Mitter, "Architectural Planning and Other Building Activities of the British in Madras, Bombay and Calcutta (c. 1630-c. 1757)" in Basu (ed.), *Rise and Growth,* pp. 191-5.

[71]P.J. Marshall, "Eighteenth Century Calcutta" in Ross and Telkamp (eds.), *Colonial Cities,* pp. 87-104, esp. 88.

[72]Frank F. Conlon, "Caste, Community and Colonialism. The Elements of Population Recruitment and Urban Rule in British Bombay, 1665-1830", *Journal of Urban History* 11 (2), 1984/85, pp. 181-208; Holden Furber, *Bombay Presidency in the Mid-Eighteenth Century,* London, 1965, 3.

[73]I thank Leonard Blusse for drawing attention to this aspect. See Blusse, *Strange Company,* p. 79, citing H.T. Colenbrander (ed.), *Jan Pietersz. Coen. Bescheiden omtrent zijn bedrijf in Indi'* I, p. 641.

APPENDIX I

POPULATION CENSUS OF BATAVIA, 1699 (MEN)
(in parentheses the percentage of the total free men [tot.fr])

INNER CITY

Block	Eur	Mest	Mard	Chin	MoGe	MaJa	BaMa	tot.fr
EAST								
A	28	1	-	20	-	-	-	49
	(57.1)	(2.0)		(40.8)				
B	17	-	2	35	-	-	-	54
	(31.5)		(3.7)	(64.8)				
C	4	-	-	146	-	-	-	150
	(2.7)			(97.3)				
D	26	1	-	9	3	-	-	39
	(66.7)	(2.6)		(23.1)	(7.7)			
E	20	1	3	28	-	-	-	52
	(38.5)	(1.9)	(5.8)	(53.8)				
F	3	-	-	133	-	-	2	138
	(2.2)			(96.4)			(1.4)	
G+H	8	-	2	70	-	-	-	80
	(10.0)		(2.5)	(87.5)				
I	1	-	-	69	-	-	-	70
	(1.4)			(98.6)				
K	46	5	3	12	-	-	-	66
	(69.7)	(7.6)	(4.5)	(18.2)				
L	28	3	19	36	-	-	-	86
	(32.6)	(3.5)	(22.1)	(41.9)				
Q1	15	-	16	10	-	-	-	41
	(36.6)		(39.0)	(24.4)				

Q2	37	1	10	3	2	-	-	53
	(69.8)	(1.9)	(18.9)	(5.7)	(3.8)			
Q3	19	-	11	10	-	-	-	40
	(47.5)		(27.5)	(25.0)				
Q4	39	3	14	5	-	-	-	61
	(63.9)	(4.9)	(23.0)	(8.2)				
S1	19	2	10	-	-	-	8	39
	(48.7)	(5.1)	(25.6)				(20.5)	
S2	13	6	35	8	2	-	-	64
	(20.3)	(9.4)	(54.7)	(12.5)	(3.1)			
EAST								
Tot.	323	23	125	594	7	-	10	1082
	(29.9)	(2.1)	(11.6)	(54.9)	(0.6)		(0.9)	

Block	Eur	Mest	Mard	Chin	MoGe	MaJa	BaMa	tot.fr
WEST								
A	23	9	106	25	-	2	-	165
	(13.9)	(5.5)	(64.2)	(15.2)		(1.2)		
B	23	11	47	18	20	1	-	120
	(19.2)	(9.2)	(39.2)	(15.0)	(16.7)	(0.8)		
C	22	2	18	142	8	12	8	212
	(10.4)	(0.9)	(8.5)	(67.0)	(3.8)	(5.7)	(3.8)	
D	19	3	36	10	6	27	-	101
	(18.8)	(3.0)	(35.6)	(9.9)	(5.9)	(26.7)		
E	32	2	39	94	6	1	4	178
	(18.0)	(1.1)	(21.9)	(52.8)	(3.4)	(0.6)	(2.2)	
F	4	2	-	288	-	-	17	311
	(1.3)	(0.6)		(92.6)			(5.5)	

G	1	6	40	20	34	13	18	132
	(0.8)	(4.5)	(30.3)	(15.2)	(25.8)	(9.8)	(13.6)	
H	25	-	4	118	4	15	5	171
	(14.6)		(2.3)	(69.0)	(2.3)	(8.8)	(2.9)	
I	7	-	-	146	-	-	-	153
	(4.6)			(95.4)				
K	33	-	2	-	-	-	-	35
	(94.3)		(5.7)					
L	35	-	1	55	-	-	-	91
	(38.5)		(1.1)	(60.4)				
M	13	-	-	28	-	-	-	41
	(31.7)			(68.3)				
N+O	21	2	-	-	-	-	-	23
	(91.3)	(8.7)						
WEST								
Tot.	258	37	293	944	78	71	52	1733
	(14.9)	(2.1)	(16.9)	(54.5)	(4.5)	(4.1)	(3.0)	
Inner city (EAST & WEST)								
Tot.	581	60	418	1538	85	71	62	2815
	(20.6)	(2.1)	(14.8)	(54.6)	(3.0)	(2.5)	(2.2)	
SOUTH								
suburb	43	10	94	81	-	-	7	235
	(18.3)	(4.3)	(40.0)	(34.5)			(3.0)	
TOTAL	624	70	512	1619	85	71	69	3050
	(20.5)	(2.3)	(16.8)	(53.1)	(2.8)	(2.3)	(2.3)	

OMMELANDEN

Block	Eur	Mest	Mard	Chin	Ambo	Moor	Mala	BuMa	BaJa	tot.fr
Outside the posts										
B	-	2	3	46	8	-	-	-	85	144
	(1.4)	(2.1)	(31.9)	(5.6)				(59.0)		
C+D	1	4	19	78	1	3	-	7	1043	1156
	(0.1)	(0.3)	(1.6)	(6.7)	(0.1)	(0.3)		(0.6)	(90.2)	
E	-	-	3	5	1	-	-	-	5	14
		(0.2)	(35.7)	(7.1)				(35.7)		
F+G	2	1	40	114	1	178	-	1	233	570
	(0.4)	(0.2)	(7.0)	(20.0)	(0.2)	(31.2)		(0.2)	(40.9)	
H	4	1	6	80	9	-	5	12	-	117
	(3.4)	(0.9)	(5.1)	(68.4)	(7.7)		(4.3)	(10.3)		
I	3	1	7	9	3	4	60	62	3	152
	(2.0)	(0.7)	(4.6)	(5.9)	(2.0)	(2.6)	(39.5)	(40.8)	(2.0)	
K	1	2	5	1	9	8	69	45	642	782
	(0.1)	(0.3)	(0.6)	(0.1)	(1.2)	(1.0)	(8.8)	(5.8)	(82.1)	
P11-12	-	-	4	50	-	-	-	88	330	472
			(0.8)	(10.6)				(18.6)	(69.9)	
Q	-	-	1	22	3	-	-	870	230	1126
			(0.1)	(2.0)	(0.3)			(77.3)	(20.4)	
R1+2	3	6	22	78	6	5	15	171	310	616
	(0.5)	(1.0)	(3.6)	(12.7)	(1.0)	(0.8)	(2.4)	(27.8)	(50.3)	
Outside the posts Tot.	14	17	110	483	41	198	149	1256	2881	5149
	(0.3)	(0.3)	(2.1)	(9.4)	(0.8)	(3.8)	(2.9)	(24.4)	(56.0)

Block	Eur	Mest	Mard	Chin	Ambo	Moor	Mala	BuMa	BaJa	tot.fr
Within the posts										
L1-10	18	14	255	22	120	-	-	-	-	429
	(4.2)	(3.3)	(59.4)	(5.1)	(28.0)					
L11	14	9	40	31	-	3	1	-	10	108
	(13.0)	(8.3)	(37.0)	(28.7)		(2.8)	(0.9)		(9.3)	
L12-13	4	3	41	10	-	-	7	-	20	85
	(4.7)	(3.5)	(48.2)	(11.8)			(8.2)		(23.5)	
L14-15	8	4	108	11	5	8	3	12	-	159
	(5.0)	(2.5)	(67.9)	(6.9)	(3.1)	(5.0)	(1.9)	(7.5)		
L16-17	8	20	248	10	-	-	-	12	10	308
	(2.6)	(6.5)	(80.5)	(3.2)				(3.9)	(3.2)	
L18-19	9	9	165	29	-	5	-	2	-	219
	(4.1)	(4.1)	(75.3)	(13.2)		(2.3)		(0.9)		
L20	9	-	22	217	-	-	-	31	176	455
	(2.0)		(4.8)	(47.7)				(6.8)	(38.7)	
L21	-	-	160	15	-	-	-	-	26	201
		(79.6)	(7.5)					(12.9)		
L22	1	-	2	15	-	-	-	-	26	44
	(2.3)		(4.5)	(34.1)					(59.1)	
L23-24	-	1	-	19	-	6	3	-	37	66
	(1.5)		(28.8)		(9.1)	(4.5)		(56.1)		
L25	12	6	39	13	-	4	-	-	4	78
	(15.4)	(7.7)	(50.0)	(16.7)		(5.1)			(5.1)	
L26 -27	5	4	2	3	-	-	-	-	-	14
	(35.7)	(28.6)	(14.3)	(21.4)						
L28-35	6	7	1	34	6	-	10	34	93	191
	(3.1)	(3.7)	(0.5)	(17.8)	(3.1)		(5.2)	(17.8)	(48.7)	

M1-2	14 (1.0)	8 (0.5)	3 (0.2)	61 (4.1)	-	4 (0.3)	160 (10.9)	211 (14.4)	1009 (68.6)	1470
M3	3 (0.2)	-	6 (0.5)	158 (11.9)	3 (0.2)	1 (0.1)	313 (23.6)	82 (6.2)	760 (57.3)	1326
M4	7 (3.4)	19 (9.1)	-	21 (10.1)	-	-	-	-	161 (77.4)	208
N	-	-	5 (10.6)	24 (51.1)	-	6 (12.8)	-	-	12 (25.5)	47
O1-5	-	-	1 (1.0)	77 (80.2)	-	6 (6.3)	-	-	12 (12.5)	96
O6-7	6 (0.7)	-	10 (1.2)	318 (39.6)	-	9 (1.1)	18 (2.2)	53 (6.6)	390 (48.5)	804
O8	-	-	5 (1.3)	24 (6.3)	6 (1.6)	-	-	222 (58.0)	126 (32.9)	383
P1-6	5 (2.3)	6 (2.8)	43 (19.8)	85 (39.2)	-	21 (9.7)	-	26 (12.0)	31 (14.3)	217
P7-8	11 (1.2)	5 (0.6)	69 (7.8)	142 (16.0)	-	13 (1.5)	16 (1.8)	435 (48.9)	199 (22.4)	890
P9-10	-	-	4 (5.1)	56 (70.9)	-	-	-	12 (15.2)	7 (8.9)	79
Within the posts Tot.	134	108 (1.7)	1228 (1.4)	1361 (16.0)	134 (17.7)	86 (1.7)	521 (1.1)	1098 (6.8)	3026 (14.3)	7696 (39.3)
Ommelanden tot.	154 (1.2)	132 (1.0)	1339 (10.3)	1878 (14.4)	181 (1.4)	284 (2.2)	680 (5.2)	2388 (18.3)	6000 (46.0)	13036

APPENDIX II

POPULATION CENSUS COLOMBO 1694 (MEN)
(in parentheses the percentage of the total free men [tot. fr])

FORT

Block	Eur	Mest	Topa	Sinh	Chet	Unid	tot.fr
A	11 (84.6)	-	-	-	-	2 (15.4)	13
B	10 (83.3)	2 (16.7)	-	-	-	-	12
C	9 (100.0)	-	-	-	-	-	9
D	31 (79.4)	7 (17.9)	-	1 (2.6)	-	-	39
E	20 (83.3)	3 (12.5)	1 (4.2)	-	-	-	24
F	35 (83.3)	2 (4.8)	-	4 (9.5)	-	1 (2.4)	42
G	12 (92.3)	1 (7.7)	-	-	-	-	13
H	4 (100.0)	-	-	-	-	-	4
Fort tot.	132 (84.6)	15 (9.6)	1 (0.6)	5 (3.2)	-	3* (1.9)	156

* Of these, 1 has a Portuguese name, 2 are probably European Mestizo.

TOWN

Block	Eur	Mest	Topa	Singh	Chet	Parav	Moor	Java	Unid	Tot.fr
A	6	-	-	4	-	-	1	-	20	31
	(19.4)			(12.9)			(3.2)		(64.5)	
B	8	-	-	1	1	-	-	-	-	10
	(80.0)			(10.0)	(10.0)					
C	7	-	-	-	4	1	-	-	6	18
	(38.9)				(22.2)	(5.6)			(33.3)	
D	3	-	-	-	1	-	-	-	-	4
	(75.0)				(25.0)					
E	6	-	-	-	-	-	-	-	2	8
	(75.0)								(25.0)	
FGH	1	-	-	-	1	-	-	-	-	2
	(50.0)				(50.0)					
I	5	-	-	1	1	-	-	1	-	8
	(62.5)			(12.5)	(12.5)			(12.5)		
K	11	7	-	1	-	-	-	-	7	26
	(42.3)	(26.9)		(3.8)					(26.9)	
L	18	-	1	1	6	-	-	-	-	26
	(69.2)		(3.8)	(3.8)	(23.1)					
M	5	-	-	1	5	1	-	-	2	14
	(35.7)			(7.1)	(35.7)	(7.1)			(14.3)	
N	9	1	1	2	1	-	-	-	-	14
	(64.3)	(7.1)	(7.1)	(14.3)	(7.1)					
O	10	-	4	-	-	-	-	-	1	15
	(66.7)		(26.7)						(6.7)	
P	12	2	-	4	9	1	-	-	2	30
	(40.0)	(6.7)		(13.3)	(30.0)	(3.3)			(6.7)	

Q	2	-	-	2	-	-	-	-	1	5
	(40.0)				(40.0)					(20.0)
Town										
Tot.	103	10	6	17	29	3	1	1	41*	211
(48.8)	(4.7)	(2.8)	(8.1)	(13.7)	(1.4)	(0.5)	(0.5)	(19.4)		

* Of these, 22 bear Portuguese names, 1 is Javanese, 3 or 4 probably Sinhalese and 5 European or *Mestizo.*

Total Fort and Town

Block	Eur	Mest	Topa	Singh	Chet	Parav	Moor	Java	Unid	Tot.fr
tot.	235	25	7	22	29	3	1	1	44	367
	(64.0)	(6.8)	(1.9)	(6.0)	(7.9)	(0.8)	(0.3)	(0.3)	(12.0)	

ABBREVIATIONS

Ambo	=	Ambonese
BaJa	=	Balinese and Javanese
BaMa	=	Balinese and Macassarese
BuMa	=	Buginese and Macassarese
Chet	=	Chettyars
Chin	=	Chinese
Eur	=	Europeans
Java	=	Javanese
MaJa	=	Malayans and Javanese
Mala	=	Malayans
Mard	=	Mardijkers
Mest	=	Mestizos
MoGe	=	Moors and Gentiles
Moor	=	Moors
Parav	=	Paravar
Sinh	=	Sinhalese
Topa	=	Topasses
tot.fr	=	total free inhabitants
unid	=	unidentified

SHIVAJI'S NAVAL EXPERIMENT

Madhais Yasin

The lure of water in the form of rivers, lakes and sea has been and still is irresistible and eternal to its coastal inhabitants. The strategic position of the Indian subcontinent in the Orient is obvious. Being in the centre of southern Asia, India overlooks through the expanse of seas around her, Arabia and Africa on the west and Burma, Malaysia, Singapore, Thailand on the east. The Indian peninsula is washed by three seas—Arabian, Bay of Bengal and Indian Ocean. It has been righly remarked: "It is an obvious fact to any student of history that India's security lies on the Indian Ocean".

The impression that India was not a seafaring nation is rebutted by a noted historian, who said: "They developed not only city life but also international trade ... and they knew most of the metals and planets, made pottery, boats and ships".[1] The Harappan civilisation reveals that there was an appreciable amount of maritime activity nearly 3,000 years before Christ. The Harappan skeletal finds prove that they were very intimate with the sea as shell bangles and mother of pearl shells were found on the dead.[2] Even the seals found there bear testimony to this, as some of them have fish and anchor representations.[3] The Harappan was our earliest sailor.[4]

During the Vedic age, i.e., from 2,000 BC to 500 B.C. literature is the living testimony of their maritime activity. The Rig Veda is replete with such instances.[5] *Varun* was termed as the Lord of the Sea, and was exhorted to be tranquil. In the same spirit, the Indian Navy had adopted the *shloka* as its motto.[6]

In Valmiki *Ramayana*, one finds *shlokas*, which mention several countries abroad, taken to be references to places such as China, Java and Sumatra, as likely places where Sita might have been abducted.[7] Similarly, recent research proves that the west coast sea route existed during the Mahabharat Age.[8]

The Hindu period shows that India had a vigorous maritime activity, mainly commercial. India also had established its colonies in Southeast Asia, which was known as the Greater India.[9] After the decline of the Vijayanagar Empire this activity was not sustained. It is a historical truth that any nation which neglects its naval power loses its sovereignty. The same happened with India. Complacency in maritime activity made her subject to the rule of Muslim kings.

Though there was a Naval Department in the Mughal period, in truth they did not clearly appreciate the importance of seapower: "The Mughals' lack of aspiration and foresight regarding mastery of the seas after consolidating their empire on land, resulted in the neglect of seapower; this is a lesson of history. Their continental outlook paved the way for the ingress of the European powers which resulted in directly influencing India's destiny".[10]

In South India, sovereign powers like Yadavas of Devagiri did not aspire to rule the waves.[11] Due to their neglect of the sea, foreigners dominated the Indian Ocean. The sovereignty of the sea had been effectively dominated and exercised by the Portuguese. No merchant dared to launch his bark on the Arabian Sea or the Indian Ocean without first purchasing the permission of the Government of Goa. Even sovereign powers like Golconda and Bijapur had to undergo this humiliation.[12]

It was left to Shivaji, the founder of the Maratha Empire, to create a navy and naval bases. His teacher, Shri Samarth Ramdas had rightly remarked about his disciple.[13]

GENESIS OF THE MARATHA NAVY

After gaining control over the towns of Kalyan and Bhivandi in A.D. 1658, and three years later on the south Konkan coast, Shivaji realised that it would not be possible for a power to dominate the Deccan without a navy of its own. It would not only protect his kingdom, but also lead to economic uplift.[14]

To protect the rich products of peninsular India from the Europeans, a strong navy was the need of the hour. Besides the Europeans, the Abyssinian Siddis were a thorn in his flesh. They were not only like "mice in the house", a nuisance, but also a plague.[15] Janjira was their stronghold, a Gibraltar of the Muslims. It occupied a strategic position, and from there Siddis imposed levies on the vessels coming into the Konkan coast. Wherever there was a source of revenue within his grasp, Shivaji wanted to lay hands on it himself.[16] Evacuation of Janjira from the Siddis was Shivaji's life ambition.[17]

Though no definite date is on record on the formation of his navy, A.D. 1659 is an important date in the military and naval history of the Marathas, for it witnesses both the discomfiture of Afzal Khan's expedition and the beginnings of the Maratha navy.[18]

Shivaji desired that Indians should have control of overseas trade so as to bring prosperity to the State. For this, a mercantile marine was the first necessity.[19] His nationalism challenged him to wrest the revenue from the European traders, when his people were living on the slender resources of his sterile motherland. It would also vindicate their honour, who had to buy passports from the Portuguese at Goa for plying in the Indian Ocean. It would also help him in consolidation of his naval scheme. For this purpose a mercantile marine was the first necessity, which is the nursery of a fighting navy.[20] "Prudence therefore dictated and foresight suggested that he should equip a fighting fleet of his own to protect his people, to punish his enemies, to provide for the prosperity of his ports and to secure for himself and his subjects a share of the maritime trade".[21]

During his struggle against the Deccan powers and Aurangzeb, he had understood that his enemies might try to starve him into submission by stopping provisions from their country.[22] Bahadur Shah actually did so. If command of the sea was in his hands, he could get an abundant supply from the ports of the South even when the usual trade routes of the country were blocked to him by his enemies.[23]

According to local law and usage of the age, all flotsam and jetsam and the cargo of ships wrecked in the neighbouring sea belonged to the ruler of the coast land. Only the possession of a fleet of his own could have enabled Shivaji to enforce this right.[24]

MARINE FORTS OF SHIVAJI

It has been rightly remarked about Shivaji: "It was a great mercy that Shivaji was not a seaman, otherwise he might have swept the sea as he did the land, with the besom of destruction. Even as it was he was nearly doing so. He liked the sea but the sea did not like him".[25]

The Konkan coast is hemmed in with a network of forts. They are of three types, inland, headland and island, which have played an important role in the history of the Konkan. They were an adjunct to the navy. In times of war they served as supply depots and places of refuge to the navy. The warships replenished their resources from the fort depots.[26] During the rough season the Maratha navy anchored in some good port overlooked by a fort.

All of Shivaji's forts were of uniform pattern.[27] Vijaydurg, popularly known as *Gheria*, was rebuilt by Shivaji. It was the most perfect example of a coastal fortress.[28] Also known as the Gibraltar of Konkan, it has successfully withstood attacks of the Europeans and the Siddis for over half a century.

Kolaba fort was constructed by Shivaji in the last year of his life, when all his attempts to conquer Janjira from the Siddis had failed. The fort was well equipped with storing arrangement for grain, oil, ghee, sugar and the other necessities. The magazine house at the southern end of the fort was separated by a good distance from the granary, etc., to avoid hazards.[29]

Sindhudurg fort was constructed by Shivaji at the southern end of Ratnagiri district when all his attempts to take the island fort of Janjira proved futile. The fort was one of Shivaji's greatest achievement.[30]

Ratnagiri contains a series of fortifications on the high land at the west end of the north arm of Ratangiri harbour.[31]

Anjanwel occupies a commanding position south of the Jog river. It was counted as a strong sea-fort.

Yashwantgad fort protects the Jayatpur harbour inside the creek. It used to be one of the chief ports of the Konkan. The fort has seventeen bastions and a moat to the north.[32]

After his failure to capture Janjira, Shivaji planned to take Khanderi in order to keep control over the English at Bombay. The foundation stone of Khanderi fort was laid on 27 August 1679.[33]

ADMINISTRATION OF FORTS

Shivaji paid great attention to the administration of forts. In general it was the joint responsibility of many officers to administer and protect the fort. The work was entrusted to a chain of officers from the highest to the lowest. In every fort there were three officers of the same status and of joint authority. The *havaldar* was the chief of these officers and head of the garrison. The *sabnis* was in charge of accounts and the muster roll. The *karkhanis* was mainly responsible for commissariat work.

Shivaji allocated 175,000 *hons* for the building and repair work of important forts. Sindhudurg, Vijaydurg and Suvarndurg were allotted ten thousand hons each for their annual upkeep and maintenance.[34] Besides, Shivaji often tempted workmen from Bombay with offers of better wages.[35]

NAVAL ADMINISTRATION

There was no independent naval department. There was a naval *subha* consisting of 200 ships. The officer in charge of a *subha* was the *subhedar.* Land was assigned for the maintenance of the navy. Normally its cost of maintenance was not defrayed from other sources of income.[36] *Ajnapatra,* a manual for the naval administration, gives the following guidelines. The naval men should patrol the seas and keep watch on the enemy. They should always replenish the supplies and ammunition of the naval forts. Complaints from the keepers of the naval forts should be reported to the King. The naval men should be vigilant. Foreign vessels without a permit should not be allowed to pass unnoticed. Foreign merchants should be given every possible encouragement to maintain friendly relations and carry on trade with one's own country.[37]

Shivaji was very strict in the execution of his orders. In the naval battle of Khanderi against the English, he threatened his men on the island that he would behead their wives if they surrendered against his orders.[38] Shivaji severely reprimanded Subhedar of Prabhavalli for not executing his orders promptly for the supply of corn and cash to the naval commanders, Daulat Khan and Daryasagar at Padamdurgh. He also accused him of being a possible victim of Siddi's bribe.[39] It is truly said about of him that he created a new order of things.[40]

NAVAL FLEET

WARSHIPS

Shivaji's fleet consisted of *gallivats* and *ghurabs,*[41] besides *tarande, taru, shibbad, pagar* and others. J.N. Sarkar lists *tarande, taru, shibbad* and *pagar* under mercantile marine, while B.K. Apte puts them under fighting ships.[42] His contention is that any ship which was armed or equipped with a gun could be termed as warship in the Maratha period. Hence, there was no hard and fast distinction between a warship and a mercantile ship.[43]

Big *ghurabs* weighing about 300 tons had three masts, and those weighing 150 tons had two masts. *Gallivats* were large row-boats built like *ghurabs* but of smaller dimensions, the largest rarely exceeding seventy tons with two masts, of which the mizen was very slight.[44]

MERCANTILE SHIPS

In the source material of the Maratha period a merchantman is often called *sahukari tarande. Sahukari* means a merchant and *tarande* a vessel. Similarly *machava, jahaj, batela, taru, shibbad* and *mahagiri* generally denoted merchantships.

Balav or *Balyava* was a small fishing craft peculiar to the Konkan coast.

Machava of the small size was employed for fishing and was known as *kola* or *kali machava.* The biggest with guns on board could be turned into a warship.[45]

The term *mahagiri* or *mahangiri* included both the warships and the cargoships of the Maratha period. It functioned as a mail-carrier and ferried the creeks. It transported building material like mortar, sand, bricks and stone.[46]

There are different versions about the numerical strength of Shivaji's fleet. According to Sabhasad there were two squadrons of 200 vessels each. Orme says that in 1875 Shivaji's fleet consisted of fifty-seven sails (fifteen *graphs* and forty-two *gallivats*), all crowded with men.[47] Fryer saw on his way to Kharepatan thirty small ships and vessels, the Admiral wearing a white flag aloft.[48] According to J.N. Sarkar the Maratha chronicles give the total number including war vessels and mercantile marine as 700 vessels. The English factory reports never put the number of Shivaji's fighting vessels about 160 and usually as sixty only.[49] S.N. Sen says that the total numerical strength of his navy "may be reasonably put at 200 ships, big and small."[50] This is exclusive of his mercantile merchantship.

Most captains of Shivaji's fleet were Muslims by faith. Each squadron was under command of an Admiral, Daria Sarang, and a Mai Naik.[51] There was another Admiral, Daulat Khan by name, but he was an officer distinct from Daria Sarang. The bulk of the common crew probably consisted of Kalis and Bhandaris, who were hardy races of fishermen.[52]

Shipbuilding was an indigenous calling handed down from father to son. Shipwrights of Konkan were mostly illiterate. Their knowledge of shipbuilding was not scientific. They could not put on paper the plan of the ship to be built though they could copy a model to its minutest details. No revolutionary changes were introduced in the craft.[53]

NAVAL EXPLOITS

Shivaji's 'show the flag' forays along the west coast created panic and concern among the alien powers, notably the English and the Portuguese. They presumably thought 'What if he repeats his exploits at sea with similar tenacity and purpose as he has carried out his lightning campaign on land.' He would have had, had he men like Palkar and Malusare, Kank and Pusalkar for his admirals.[54] The Portuguese, a decadent power at that time, saw straws in the wind and remained submissive to Shivaji . . . their arrogance of the yesteryears had eclipsed.[55]

Shivaji's relations with the English were not happy. The two loots of Surat in 1664 and 1670 made the English realise the impotency of Mughal power, and hence there was an illusory peace between the two.[56] Still the British were pragmatic enough not to break off the peace treaty.[57] English goods were denied entry into the Maratha land, but were forced to sell them at the port. The English ships had to pay customs, whereas they did not pay it at other ports.[58]

The English factors praised Shivaji for encouraging trade and commerce of his people with the same tenacity as he formerly did for plunder.[59] His trading vessels loaded with goods traded with Persia, Basra and Mucha (in Western Arabia), etc. He had not only salt boats but also regular 'May Fleet' which plied between his ports and those of Arabia and Persia.[60]

NAVAL ENGAGEMENTS

BARCELORE PLUNDER

Of Shivaji's naval expeditions only three are important. The first, in 1665 was the plunder of Barcelore or Basrur, which was the chief port of the Bednur kingdom. He managed with a good plunder, as his attack was most unexpected. He sent back his fleet except twelve frigates. When he reached Karwar, he was challenged by Sher Khan. Shivaji sent a message to Sher Khan to deliver the British merchants up to him or to permit him to capture them himself. To this blackmail the British contributed £112 or 8,000 *hon* to save Company's property. Shivaji returned disappointed, saying that "Sher Khan had spoiled his hunting at the Holi, which is a time he generally attempts some such design".[61]

NAGAON EXPEDITION

In November 1670, Shivaji assembled a vast fleet of 160 sail at Nagaon and mobilised a considerable army. The expedition was organised on a very elaborate scale, and caused much anxiety and speculation at Surat and Bombay, but it ended in smoke.[62]

JANJIRA

But the enterprise which was Shivaji's life ambition, the genesis of his naval exercise, was the conquest of Janjira from the Arabian Siddis. The war against the Siddis began as early as 1648[63] and continued up to his death, having been marked in the interval by some very stiff engagements. Siddi was also helped by the East India Company against Shivaji. Once to Shivaji victory of Janjira was in sight, when Fateh Khan, fed up with incessant warfare thought of surrendering Janjira to Shivaji.[64] But his three Abyssinian slaves took up the command, imprisoned Fateh Khan, and changed allegiance from Bijapur to the Mughals.[65] In 1671 they recovered Danda Fort from Shivaji, who was planning to capture Janjira, but failed even to retain Danda.[66] The only consolation Shivaji could have was the occupation of Khanderi.[67] Nevertheless, the conquest of Janjira remained an unfulfilled aspiration. It obviously proved the superiority of the Siddi's fleet over that of Shivaji.[68]

SNAGS

Shivaji's naval policy is formulated by *Ajnapatra*, which says that land should be assigned for the maintenance of the navy. *Ajnapatra* expresses concern that if income from customs is allotted to the navy there is every possibility that the burden of taxation would fall upon the merchant community, which would ruin trade and prosperity.[69] An appraisal of this policy makes it shortsighted and indiscreet, which hampered the growth of the Maratha power. Portugal, Holland, England and France prospered because of their overseas trade. Their navies were not only self-sufficient economically, but contributed to the national wealth. Trade was the life-blood of these navies.[70]

The Maratha navy also suffered from technical flaws. The construction of medium sized *ghurbs* recommended by the *Ajnapatra* was well-suited to the shallow waters of the Konkan. But when called upon to face the heavy, well-equipped European ships they were bound to be sunk like lead. It also focuses the defects in the naval policy in economising expenditure on it. This was the reason of Shivaji's failure in capturing Janjira from the Siddis. A historian says: "All his brilliant victories seem to be eclipsed by this single failure of his life. The causes of this lifelong disappointment are to be traced to his inferior navy and artillery".[71]

Shivaji had no cannon-foundry, no factory for making first-class gun powder in his kingdom. All his naval ornaments and superior munitions had to be purchased from the European traders, who gave him rejected material. Thus in gun-powder his largest vessels were inferior to the third-rate English or Portuguese fighting ships.[72]

Shivaji's sea battles merely followed the tactics of land-fighting. The marksmanship of his gunners was poor and slow.[73] Thus the new technology of naval warfare was not developed. Shivaji depended more upon numerical strength than tactics. In a naval warfare Shivaji's side always suffered heavy casualties.[74] The navy was clearly not a Maratha institution as the army was.

Shivaji's first love was his land forces. He did not give the navy the senior service rating, which was given to it by the European countries. Shivaji, who remained unruffled and unbeaten on land, felt uncomfortable in sea voyage.[75]

With all shortcomings and snags, Shivaji deserves the credit for establishing a navy to restore the prestige of India at sea, which was dominated by the alien powers. He was engaged throughout his life in a deadly warfare first against Bijapur and afterwards the Mughal Empire, so that he had no time to give the navy its due.

"His far-reaching aims were not understood after his death by any of his successors, and the empire of the sea and the naval instrument for wielding it were given up, uncontested and unchallenged".[76]

NOTES

[1]R.C. Majumdar, *Ancient India,* Delhi, reprint, 1968.

[2]Sir M. Wheeler, *The Indus Civilization*, Cambridge, 1968; Sir John Marshall, *Moohenjo-Daro and the Indian Civilization,* 3 vols., London, 1931.

[3]*Ibid.*

[4]K. Sridharan, *A Maritime History of India,* New Delhi, 1982, p.14.

[5]Rig Veda 1.25.7, *Taitriya Upnishad*, Durga Suktam.

[6]*Ibid.*

[7]Virahmihara, *Bharat Samhita*, ch. V and VII.

[8]T.S. Shej Walkar, *The Mahabharat Data for Aryan Expansion,* published in the Deccan College Research Institute, Bulletin, II (2 & 3) and IV.

[9]R.D. Bannerjee, *Prehistoric Ancient and Hindu India,* Delhi, reprint, 1979, pp. 277-8.

[10]Sridharan, *op.cit.*, p. 55.

[11]Surendra Nath Sen, *The Military System of the Marathas,* New Delhi, 1958, p.152.

[12]*Ibid.*, Lok Rajya, Chattrapati Shivaji Maharaj 300th Punyatithi special number, April 1980, "Shivaji Maharaj—A Sea King" by V.G. Khobrekar.

[13]"His determination is loftier than the mountains, he is the sole supporter and saviour of his people, he is resolute in the pursuit of his ideals, he lives like an ascetica truly great yogi."

[14]Sir J.N. Sarkar, *Shivaji and his Times,* reprint, Delhi, 1973, p. 225; *Lokrajya*, "Meghadambri Special Number vol. 40, 16 April 1985; "Random Thoughts on Raigad, Shivaji and Shivaji's Navy", by Vice Admiral M.P. Awati:

> Shivaji would not let Konkan be overridden by those inimical to Maratha policy. As we shall examine in a little while, his interest in the navy was the result of his concern for the safety and security of the coastal tract in his rear. One has to look for the genesis of his navy in this strategic fact.

"Marathas and the Sea", a paper read by A.R. Kulkarni at the International Symposium on Maritime History, Department of History, Pondicherry University, Pondicherry, 1989.

[15]S.R. Sharma, *Founding of Maratha Freedom,* Poona, 1964, p. 222.

[16]Govind Sakharam Sardesai, *New History of the Marathas*, vol. I, Bombay, 1968, p. 290.

[17]N.S. Takakhav, *Life of Shivaji*, reprint, Delhi, 1985, vol.I, p. 213.

[18]S.N. Sen, *op.cit.*, p. 156.

[19]Sir J.N. Sarkar, *op.cit.*, p. 246.

[20]*Ibid.*

[21]S.N. Sen, *op.cit.*, p. 154.

[22]Factory Records, Surat, vol. 88, fols. 216-17.

[23]S.N. Sen, *op.cit.*, p.154.

[24]Sir J.N. Sarkar, *op.cit.*, pp. 246-7.

[25]James Douglas, *Bombay and Western India,* vols.I & II, London, 1893.

[26]B.K. Apte, *A History of the Maratha Navy and Merchantships*, Bombay, 1973, p.15:

> Forts mounted with guns of good calibre could effectively repulse enemy ships from entering the rivers on which they stood. A well-defended estuary could thus help keep the enemy armada at bay. However, if the fort-guns failed, the armada of the land-power anchoring in the creek of the river was always in danger of being destroyed without action as it could not escape into the sea ... ships in the creeks and in the ports under the cover of fort-guns were always from an attack.

[27]Sir, J.N. Sarkar, *op.cit.*, p. 247:

> The site chosen is usually a cliff or a spot of land more than half surrounded by the sea. The whole top of the hill or the end of the promontory is surrounded by a wall which is relieved by numerous bastions. There is seldom more than one entrance to the fort, and this is generally the strongest part. The outer gateway is thrown forward and protected by a bastion on each side and often by a tower—above.... Inside the main wall there was generally an inner fortress or citadel (bala gila in Persian and Marathi), and surrounding this were the various buildings required for the accommodation of the troops, and also magazines, tanks and wells.

[28]*Bombay Gazetteer*, vols. I, II, p.74; vol. X, p. 380.

[29]*Bombay Gazetteer*, vol. X, p. 338.

[30]B.K. Apte, *op.cit.*, p. 23.

[31]Sir J.N. Sarkar, *op.cit.*, p. 248; *Lok Rajya*, 1 April 1980; Shivaji Maharaj, *op.cit.*

[32]*Gazetteer of the Bombay Presidency*, vol. X, pp. 341-84.

[33]Factory Records Surat 87, Surat to Bombay, 22 April, vol. 106, May 1672; Orme Manuscripts, p.116; Factory Records, Surat 4, Consultations 4 & 15, September 1679, *Bombay Gazette*, vol. XIII, pt.II, p.478; Orme, *Historical Fragments of the Mogul Empire*, etc., London, 1805, pp. 80-1.

[34]*Lok Rajya*, 16 April 1985; *Marine Forts of Shivaji* by Suresh Vasant Jadhav.

[35]Factory Records (1671-72).

[36]P.N. Joshi, *Ajnapatra*, Venus Prakashan, Poona, 1960, pp. 40-4.

[37]*Ibid.*

[38]B.K. Apte, *op.cit.*, p.176.

[39]*Lok Rajya,* Chhatrapati, Shivaji Maharaj 300th Punyatithi Special Number, Nature and Significance of the New Order Created by Shivaji by J.V. Naik.

[40]*Ibid.*

[41]Shankar Narayan Joshi, *Krishnaji Anant Sabhasad Virachit Chhatrapati Shri Shivaji Raja Yanchi Bakhar,* Poona, 1860.

[42]B.K. Apte, *op.cit.*, p.120.

[43]*Ibid.*, p.141.

[44]R. Orme, *Military Transactions in Indostan,* 2nd ed., vol. I, pp. 401-2.

[45]G.S. Sardesai, *Selections from the Peshwa Dafter,* Bombay, 1933, pp. XVI, 47.

[46]*Gazetteer of the Bombay Presidency,* vol. XIII, pp.1-345.

[47]S.N. Sen, *op.cit.*, p.158.

[48]Crook Fryer, *A New Account of the East Indies and Persia,* Hakluyt Society, p.145.

[49]Sir J.N. Sarkar, *op.cit.*, p. 259.

[50]S.N. Sen, *op.cit.*, p.158.

[51]Rajwade, *op.cit.*, *Marathyanchya Itihasachi Sadhane,* vol. VIII, p. 27.

[52]S.N. Sen, *op.cit.*, p.161.

[53]B.K. Apte, *op.cit.*, pp.168-70.

[54]Lok Rajya, *op.cit.*, 16 April 1985.

[55]S.R. Sharma, *op.cit.*, p. 235; Sir J.N. Sarkar, *op.cit.*, pp. 350-54.

[56]Diary of W. Hedges, ed. by Yule, Hakluyt Society, vol. II, p. CCXXVI gives Surat to Company, 20 November, 1670; Dutch Factory Records, Translations, vol. 29; Surat to Directors, 14 November, 1670; *Ibid.*, vol. 29, Letter No. 763 and vol. 27, No. 719; Akhbarat-i-Darbar-i-muala, for many years (London and Jaipur MSS), 13-10; Factory Records, Surat, vol. 88, p. 227, 7 September, 1674.

[57]*Robert Orme Manuscripts,* vol. 114, Section 3, 15 September, 1674, pp.186-8.

[58]Factory Records, vol. 87, pp.196-7, 1 September, 1674.

[59]*Ibid.*, vol. 88, p. 227, 7 September, 1674.

[60]*Ibid.*, Bombay, vol. 6, pp.14-15, 13 April, 1670; Sir J.N. Sarkar, *op.cit.*, pp. 259-60; Sen, *op.cit.*, p.158; Factory Records, Surat, vol. 86, 12 March, 1664/5, p.170.

[61]Factory Records, Surat, vol. 104, Karwar to Surat, 14 March, 1665, Sabth 70-71.

[62]*Ibid.*, vol.105, fol. 72 Orme, *Historical Fragments*, p. 207.

[63]Sardesai in his *New History of the Marathas*, vol. I, p. 290, gives the date 1657.

[64]Factory Records, Surat 105, Hubli to Surat, 17 July, Bombay to Surat, 16 October, 1669.

[65]Orme, *Historical Fragments*, p. 87.

[66]Factory Records Surat 87, Surat to Bombay, 22 April, vol. 106, 1 May, 1672; ibid., Surat 4, Consultations, 4 September, 15, 1679; Orme, *Manuscripts*, p.116.

[67]*Gazetteer of Bombay Presidency*, vol. XI, p. 325. Khanderi has been mentioned as the island of Cheul, measuring "a falcon shot long and arquebus shot broad".

[68]D.R. Banaji, *Bombay and the Sidis*, London, 1932, p. 31.

[69]P.N. Joshi, pp. 40-44.

[70]B.K. Apte, p.174.

[71]Bal Krishna, *Shivaji the Great*, reprint, Delhi, 1985.

[72]Sir. J.N. Sarkar, p. 255.

[73]*Ibid.*

[74]Orme, *Historical Fragments*, pp. 77-78.

[75]D.F. Karkara, *Shivaji*, p.129.

[76]*Ibid.*, p. 131.

COMMODITY COMPOSITION OF THE ENGLISH TRADE ON THE COROMANDEL COAST (1611-1652)

S.Babu

When the demand for the spices of the East increased highly in the home market, the English East India Company came to the Asiatic regions for procuring them directly first on the western coast of India. But the Company was not able to get the much desired spices. At the same time, the Company had witnessed the indigenous merchants' commercial operations with the Southeast Asian countries, a congenial centre for different sorts of spices. They used the cotton fabrics from India chiefly from the Coromandel coast to barter for the spices of the Indonesian archipelago. Following this, the English Company used the cotton fabrics from the Coromandel coast to exchange for the spices to supply for domestic consumption. In the early stages the English Company exported indigo and saltpetre from the Coromandel coast to England. But, when the demand for Indian textiles, especially from the Coromandel coast was felt, they were taken in considerable volume. As a result of this change, the Coromandel coast attained greater importance in the commercial activities of the Company. The change of interest in the commodities of export from the coast boosted production in the primary and secondary sectors to meet the demands. This study tries to throw light on the commodity composition of the English trade on the coast and its impact. Mostly contemporary sources are used in the preparation of this study.

Since the time of the second voyage, the factors in the East informed the Directors of the Company of the need to substitute Indian cotton piece-goods for bullion, if pepper and other sorts of spices were to be purchased most profitably in the Southeast Asian markets.[1] The factors after their arrival at Bantam realised and reported that European goods were not to be sold in large quantities in Java, Sumatra or Moluccan Islands, the chief supplier of pepper and other spices, and that it was not profitable to conduct trade in these commodities for cash. They had seen the indigenous trading system of exchanging textiles for spices.[2] The textiles from the Coromandel coast had enjoyed a traditional market in that region. Therefore, the factors recommended that trade on the eastern coast of India, known as Coromandel coast should be attempted. In the first voyage of James Lancaster it was found that the Portuguese carrack captured by him was loaded with a large quantity of calicoes, which he successfully exchanged for pepper at Bantam.[3] It proved how useful that commodity was to procure pepper and other spices.

The natives in these quarters were gifted with the art of painting on calicoes to the highest pitch of perfection, and these products were in great demand in the Southeast Asian region.[4] Besides this, many other factors motivated the English Company to initiate its commercial activities on the Coromandel coast. The availability of varieties of cotton textiles at a cheaper rate than at Surat, its nearness to the Southeast Asian region (Spice Islands) which was the centre of spices, the existence of seaports surrounded by a good number of weaving centres and the desire to be free from the difficult and troubled commercial atmosphere of the western coast were some of the important considerations.

Considering the importance of Coromandel piece-goods, in 1630 the Council at Bantam recommended their Honourable Masters in London to send out £67,500 per annum in specie to Masulipatnam to be invested in country cloth. This could be exchanged in Bantam for spices to the value of £1,35,000.[5]

The demand for the textiles in Southeast Asian countries to barter for pepper and other spices was varied and a large volume of cotton fabrics was sent there. By and large the export from the Coromandel coast was woven piece-goods, the produce of the weavers' community. Calicoes, muslins and dress materials or fancy goods were in greater demand.[6] Calicoes were produced in almost all manufacturing centres on the coast. It was plain, either bleached, unbleached or dyed in different colours and generally called *baftas.*[7] The demand for textiles in the Southeast Asian region was so specialised that particular varieties were supplied only by the weavers of certain Indian villages according to the taste of the market.[8]

Among the textile products exported from the Coromandel coast to the Southeast Asian countries, the most important items were *salempuris* and *muris* of finer to coarser quality in many colours.[9] The next item of export was *muri*, both of finer and coarser quality. The *chintz* made out of *muri*, was in great demand in the Southeast Asian markets.[10] The painting work on *muris* was done by skilled craftsmen in the villages of Pulicat, Nellor, Arni, Chenglepet and Cuddalore.[11]

Percallas, a high quality plain cotton cloth produced at Pulicat was also exported.[12] Another type of cloth which was woven from cotton thread and dyed in bright colour with stripes and checks, was called Guinea cloth. It was worn by the tribal population in the Southeast Asian region and the Company exported in large quantities.[13] Besides, *kaingulong* (rolled cloth, *chelas, medaphons, drongangs, dupatta, ginghams,* handkerchiefs and piece-goods were exported by the Company.[14] *Sucatoons* were heavy cotton cloth used as blankets and also for packing.[15]

From the above-mentioned fine cotton fabrics a beautifully painted cloth was manufactured. This was known as *pintado* or painted, and was in great demand in Moluccan Islands.[16] Moreover goods such as shirts, trousers, *matafon, allejaes, baftas,* red *beathilles,* Golconda *beathilles, sarassamalaya* and sailcloth were exported to Southeast Asian countries.[17] Textiles were the major export item of trade because of their low price, durability and attraction achieved through the expertise in dyeing, painting and printing.

Diamonds from the Golconda mines constituted an important item of export from Masulipatnam. The quality of diamonds was reportedly good and orders were issued by the officials of Bantam to procure as many as possible. Diamonds were in great demand in Achin.[18] The extracted products like saltpetre and gunpowder were other exports of the Coromandel coast.[19]

Animal skins were also exported to Bantam for local consumption though on a limited scale.[20] The other aspect of the English trade was the export of slaves from the Coromandel coast to the Southeast Asian countries but not on a regular basis.[21] It was usually at the time of famine or devastation caused by prolonged warfare, that a number of people offered themselves for sale. This human cargo was mostly shipped to Achin or Tennasserim for sale to work in plantations or for domestic use.[22]

In addition, the Company exported agricultural products, and extracted as well as processed goods. Indigo (Tamil: *averier* or *neelam*) was in great demand and was exported to Pegu and Tennasserim. It was produced in different degrees of refinement and the price differed accordingly.[23] Rice from the Coromandel coast was too exported. But it depended on the surplus. Further, tobacco, sugar, ginger (dry and green) and opium were the other agricultural products of the region that were exported.[24]

The available data on the volume of trade show that textiles constituted the major items of export from the Coromandel coast. In the year 1614 nearly 12,500 pieces of cotton textiles, worth £2,802 were exported. Within ten years the figure had gone up to the value of £6,193 and nearly 907 bales (90,700 pieces) cloth.[25] The increase in the volume of export shows the growing importance of the trade on the Coromandel coast. Further, in 1621 the total volume of goods was £8,423 and it increased to £14,217 in 1650.[26] Again it shows the gradual development of trade.

In the early stages the English Company exported cotton fabrics both from the west coast (Surat) and east coast to barter for the spices of the East Indies. But gradually there was a change in the demand of textiles in the Southeast Asian markets. The English merchants discovered that the Coromandel piece-goods were better sold and were in great demand at Bantam than the textiles from Gujarat.[27] There developed a great demand for Coromandel *pintdados* or painted goods in the markets at Moluccas, Macassar, Bantam and Jambi.[28] The change in the demand for the products of India in the archipelago made the Coromandel cotton goods replace Gujarat textiles in 1630s. In the meantime the devastating famine of 1630 further disrupted supplies. As a result the Company now chose fully Coromandel as an alternative source for textiles to the eastern markets.

The English Company trading with Southeast Asian countries procured spices and sent to England. Some amount of pepper, nutmegs, cloves, mace and many other sorts were brought to the Coromandel coast.[29] In addition, the Company imported natural products like sandalwood, ebony, elephants, *collombacke* or sweetwood and Chinese dishes, silk, porcelain, gumlac, eaglewood and redwood.[30]

Regarding the volume of imports from the Southeast Asian region to the Coromandel, one can observe that only a small amount of spices and other natural products were brought back. The maximum value of these products was just £7,965 for 1647.[31] The value of imports from the Southeast Asian region was only one-third the value of exports. Therefore, we can say that the fundamental idea of the English Company was to procure the spices from the Southeast Asian islands for the Coromandel textiles. Thus the textiles of India played two important roles in the English Company's commercial activities. On the one hand they helped to exchange for the spices of the Southeast Asian region and on the other they became a link for the operation of 'triangular spice trade', i.e., Coromandel-Southeast Asia-England.

The existing contemporary records of the period show that in the early part of this study most of the cargoes despatched from the coast were taken to Spice Islands. But only a small amount of goods was taken to Europe by the English Company. At the initial stages the principal commodity acquired by the English Company for the European market on the coast was indigo; later, saltpetre was added to it.[32]

Though the Company procured the fine varieties of indigo from Biana and Sarkhej in Gujarat, the very low price of Coromandel indigo attracted the Company and it was exported in a limited quantity. The production process of indigo was carried on in the Deccan and along the eastern coast, i.e. in villages near the seaports.[33] When indigo replaced woad as a dye-stuff in the woollen industry it had attained great importance and demanded very much. For example, in 1640 the Company supplied 500 *candies* or 2,000 cwt of indigo from the Coromandel coast.[34] But in the second half of the seventeenth century the export of indigo was gradually reduced in view of the better sort imported from the West Indies. Besides, the English merchants had quickly discovered that calicoes could be sold in large quantities in the home market and in Western Europe.[35] Thus, the Company gradually shifted its attention to the export of calicoes from the coast, when it had found a great fascination in European markets.

The export of saltpetre was a new development in the history of the English Company's maritime trade on the Coromandel. There was an ever-increasing demand for it in Europe.[36] It was an essential commodity for the manufacture of gunpowder. Though it was prohibitive because of its bulk and weight for seaborne trade, the growth of an extensive munition industry in Europe and the use of artillery, made Indian saltpetre a strategic raw material and a profitable article of commerce. In England, the demand for saltpetre was closely connected with national political and military considerations especially due to civil war between Charles and Parliament.[37]

Saltpetre was obtained from various parts of India. The Coromandel coast was the first region to be exploited.[38] Due to its low price saltpetre from this region was in great demand and fetched high profits to the Company. The following quantity of export shows the gradually increasing demand of the product: 1625—45 tons;[39] 1643 to 1650—200 tons.[40] In the early stages indigo and saltpetre were mainly shipped for England via Surat.

The cotton fabrics procured by the English East India Company from the coast were very useful in two different ways: (i) In the early stages, the cotton textiles of Coromandel coast were used to barter for the spices of the East Indies and in turn exported to England. (ii) The discovery of the existence of market for Indian textiles in Europe had initiated the direct export from the Coromandel to England, a later development.

The textiles sold by the Company in London market consisted of different kinds which differed from each other in size, quality, texture and colour. The prices of each type differed naturally according to its quality and texture. Cotton goods, both plain and designed had found a favourable demand in England. The plain textiles of India displaced the more expensive linens imported from Holland and Germany for household use. The patterned or designed varieties were very much used for hangings and decorative purposes in houses. So, in 1624, the Governor of the Company declared that England saved annually a quarter of a million sterling by the substitution of Indian calicoes for foreign linens through the eastern trade.[41] In the early stages calico was in demand in England only as table cloth, coverlets, napkins and wall-hangings.[42]

The first attempt of the English Company to supply calico from the Coromandel coast to England was made in 1621.[43] Afterwards, the ships which were leaving Surat for England regularly carried a part of textiles from the Coromandel coast. The indication of the prevalence of a European market for the Coromandel cloth comes from the letter of Thomas Ivy written in 1647, which was intended for re-export to the continent.[44]

The names of these different types of calicoes, which were sent to England were *percallas, muris, salampuris* and *chintz*.[45] Longcloth, especially that manufactured at Madras, was a notable item in great quantity both in the East and West, either in the form of plain dyed or figured *chintz*. It was the highly demanded calico in the London market in the mid-seventeenth century. The one from Madras was considered the best.[46]

Salampuris from the Coromandel coast with bright colours were in great demand in Europe as bed spreads and furnishings.[47] *Muris* were blue cloths used for painting on it (to produce *chintz*) and they enjoyed a good market not only in England but also in France and other foreign lands.[48] Besides, many other varieties of textiles were collected by the English Company and exported for European consumption. They were *beathilles*, Golconda beathilles, *izzarees, allejaes, dungarees*, sail-cloth, *ginghams* (striped cloth), *gobar* (curtain cloth) and *sarassas* (multi-coloured cloth).[49] The sales of textiles were ordinarily made by piece or by *corge*.[50]

In the meantime, the sudden outbreak of famine in 1630 in Gujarat and in the north brought down the production of textiles and supplies were disrupted. The Directors of the English Company sought to find out some other avenues to get supplies when the west coast (Surat) failed to meet the increasing demand in the home and in the European markets.[51] At this juncture, the factors stationed on the coast reported that they could procure large quantities as desired by the Company.[52] So the Company started sending indents directly to the Coromandel coast to get supplies of textiles to suit the taste of European markets. The first instance of direct shipping from the Coromandel coast to London was started in 1649, when a consignment of 18,225 pieces of textiles and other commodities was despatched from Fort St. George by the ship *Bonito*,[53] the first ship to go home directly from the new settlement.

The increased demand for the Coromandel piece-goods led the Company to write in February 1650, to the President at Surat that the Coromandel textiles were very much preferred to any of the Surat cloth in France and other foreign markets.[54] Further, the volume of trade also shows the increased demand for textiles. In 1621, nearly 12,500 pieces[55] and in 1639, 18,225[56] pieces were taken by the Company from the coast. It had gone up to 52,000 pieces in 1652.[57] Thus, calico became a useful item for all classes and its use as a soft and lighter inner garment began to be realised. In the second half of the seventeenth century Madras replaced Surat as the principal supplier of textiles.

When cotton textiles of the coast fetched a high price in the

European markets, the importance of the Coromandel coast increased in English maritime history and it began to supersede Gujarat as the source of supply.[58] The calicoes from Madras were more suitable for European markets than those of Gujarat and were sold at considerable profit.[59] The other development was that while in 1650 there was depression in European markets it was recorded that the sales consisted chiefly of goods from the Coromandel coast. The shift in the seventeenth century European trade in India from Surat to Coromandel and the price structure of the cotton goods suggest that the character of the textile market in Europe underwent a notable change. Thus, during the latter part of the first half of the seventeenth century the Coromandel coast occupied a prominent place in the English Company's East India trade.

Besides cotton textiles, a large number of commodities such as raw cotton, cotton yarn, sugar, turmeric, pearls (from Tuticorin), diamonds (from Golconda), sugar-candy, rice, tamarind, opium, gumlac and the spices like ginger, cardamom, pepper, mace and cloves were sent to the redistribution centres of London.[60] Further, the diamonds from Golconda too found a place in the invoices of the Company.[61]

The English Company made huge profits on the sale of Indian commodities in England, especially cotton textiles. For example, "in 1630s a piece of cloth bought in India for seven shillings sold in London for a pound sterling, i.e. a profit of about 300 per cent. A pound of clove or nutmeg bought in India for eight to nine pence sold in England for six shillings at a profit of about 800-900 per cent".[62]

The imports of the English Company from England to the Coromandel consisted of a number of goods directly or via Bantam. Since there was not much demand for European goods in the East, precious metals (specie) occupied an important position among the imports from England. But the nationalists had criticised the drain of bullion from England by the Company to procure the eastern commodities. Therefore, the English Company was forced to take certain European goods to avert criticism at home.

The English Company brought lead, tin, copper, quicksilver, ivory, coral, gilded mirrors, blades, knives, sword-blades, arms and ammunition to the Coromandel coast from England.[63] Besides, woollen goods, stammels, Venice reds, broadcloth, kersies, embroideries; luxury goods like velvets, damasks, satins, taffetas and curiosities like toys, combcases, spectacles, pictures and looking glasses were imported to Coromandel.[64] Since the demand for the European goods was insignificant in India they were mostly given as *peshkash* or gifts to the local rulers or merchants to get their help.[65]

The change of interest in the commodities of export on the Coromandel coast shown by the English Company gave a new direction to the maritime trade on the region and production was boosted. In the early stages indigo and saltpetre were given much importance in the exports of the Company; later the interest was shifted to textiles. As a result, villages in large numbers took advantage and production was increased. This is clear in the volume of trade.

Agricultural production on the coast was boosted in tune with the increasing demand for cotton and textiles of different sorts in the markets of Southeast Asia and Europe. It is clear from the increase of weaving activities in villages in this region. Cotton cultivation was given a push to furnish the necessary raw material for weaving. We may conclude that the intensification and expansion of cotton cultivation was effected on this region. Thus the initial process of commercialisation of agriculture was brought about to keep pace with the developing maritime trade on the coast.

The increasing demand generated by the English Company geared up production in the secondary sector. A large number of villages were engaged in weaving and other activities connected with textile production. It seems that a considerable change had taken place in the seventeenth century. The artisans became dependent on those who advanced money and became 'contract producer'.

The English commercial contact with Coromandel coast affected its economy, too. The Indian indigo replaced woad, a traditional raw material in the European dyeing industry. The export of saltpetre from the coast activated warfare methods in England. Indian textiles replaced the foreign linens in the English domestic market and a new pattern was initiated in consumption. As a result, the English economy had some impact.

To conclude, it may be said that the growth of English trade on the Coromandel coast brought about considerable changes in the agrarian and non-agrarian sectors of production. These changes also had their impact on the socio-economic conditions. The interest shown by the European Companies, especially the English in the export of textiles, could be considered the chief reason for the emergence of the Coromandel coast as a significant region in the world market in the mid-seventeenth century. The hold of merchant capital in the production, too, should be counted.

NOTES

[1]*Letters received by the East India Company from its Servants in the East* (transcribed from the Original Correspondence Series of the India Office Records), W. Foster (ed.) (henceforth, *Letters*), vol. I (1602-1613), London, 1896, pp.xxxii, 78.

[2]K.N. Chaudhuri, *The English East India Company: The Study of an Early Joint Stock Company, 1600-1640,* London, 1965, p.14; Tapan Raychaudhuri and Irfan Habib (eds.), *The Cambridge Economic History of India,* vol. I, c.1200-c.1750 (henceforth C.E.H.I.) (reprint), New Delhi, 1984, pp.407-10.

[3]*The Voyages of Sir James Lancaster to Brazil and East Indies, 1591-1603,* W. Foster (ed.), Hakluyt Society, London, 1904, p.107.

[4]*Letters*, vol. I (1602-1613), pp.10-15.

[5]William Foster, *English Factories in India* (henceforth *E.F.I.*), vol. IV (1630-1633), Oxford, 1910, p.111; W.W. Hunter. *History of India*, vol. VII (reprint), New Delhi, 1987, p. 223.

[6]Vijaya Ramaswamy, *Textiles and Weavers in Medieval South India*, Delhi, 1985, pp.131-2.

[7]A commercial name for ordinary calico. *E.F.I.*, vol. I (1618-1621), p. 61. For details of textile dimension, ref. S. Babu, "Textile Trade of the Coromandel Coast and the English East India Company (1611-1652)", in the *Journal of the Institute of Asian Studies*, VII (2), Madras, March 1990, pp.159-60.

[8]*C.E.H.I.*, vol. I, p.296.

[9]*Letters*, vol. II (1613-1615), pp. 32, 88; vol. V (1617), p. 258; *E.F.I.*, vol. II (1622-1623), pp.102-3; Vijaya Ramaswamy, *op.cit.*, Glossary I.

[10]*Letters*, vol. I (1602-1613), p. 88.

[11]Vijaya Ramaswamy, *op.cit.*, p. 215.

[12]*E.F.I.*, vol. I (1618-1621), p.266; vol. III (1624-1629), p. 6.

[13]W.H. Moreland, *From Akbar to Aurangzeb: A Study in Indian Economic History*, London, 1923 (reprint), Delhi, 1972, p. 55.

[14]*E.F.I.*, vol. I (1618-1621), p. 61; S. Arasaratnam, *Merchant Companies and Commerce on the Coromandel Coast, 1650-1740,* Delhi, 1986, p.100.

[15]Arasaratnam, *op.cit.*, p.101.

[16]*Letters*, vol. II (1613-1615), p. 32; vol. VI (1617), p. 258; *E.F.I.*, vol. II (1622-1623), p.103.

[17]Tavernier, *Travels in India*, V. Ball (ed.), Vol. I (reprint), Delhi, 1974, pp. 50, 76, 118 and 171. A white muslin mostly made on the coast or at Masulipatnam, name is supposed to be connected with Portuguese *beatilha*—veli'; *E.F.I.*, vol. II (1622-1623), p.103; *Letters*, vol. II (1613-1615), p. 88; *E.F.I.*, vol. II (1622-1623), p.107.

[18]*E.F.I.*, vol. I (1618-1621), p. 75; vol. III (1624-1629), p. 92.

[19]*E.F.I.*, vol. III (1624-1629), p. 92.

[20]*Letters*, vol. IV (1616), p.18.

[21]*Letters*, vol. I (1602-1613), p. 71; Arasaratnam, *op.cit.*, p.104.

[22]*E.F.I.*, vol. I (1618-1621), p.141.

[23]Shafaat Ahmad Khan, *The East India Trade in the Seventeenth Century*, London, 1923, p.12.

[24]*Letters*, vol. V (1617), pp. 60, 237. Demand of the Agency (Bantam) and the supplies from its factories at Masulipatnam, Pulicat and Madras.

[25]*Letters*, vol. I (1602-1613), pp. 40, 135; *E.F.I.*, vol. II (1622-1623), pp.118, 238.

[26]*E.F.I.*, vol. I (1618-1621), p. 264; vol. VIII (1646-1650), p. 320.

[27]*Letters*, vol. I (1602-1613), p. 270.

[28]Moreland, *op.cit.*, p. 32; Vijaya Ramaswamy, *op.cit.*, p.131.

[29]*Letters*, vol. I (1602-1613), pp. 47, 74; vol. IV (1616), p. 60; *E.F.I.*, vol. II (1622-1623), p.136; vol. III (1624-1629), p.151.

[30]*Letters*, vol. I (1602-1613), p. 74; vol. II (1613-1615), p. 315; vol. IV (1616), p. 74; vol. VI (1617), p. 73; *E.F.I.*, vol. II (1622-1623), p. 23; vol. III (1624-1629), p.151.

[31]*E.F.I.*, vol. VIII (1646-1650); p.136.

[32]H.H. Dodwell, *The Cambridge History of India: British India*, vol. V (1847-1858), Cambridge, 1929, p. 92; Moreland, *op.cit.*, p. 98.

[33]Moreland, *op.cit.*, p.110.

[34]*E.F.I.*, vol. VI (1637-1641), p.119. One *candy* was equal to twenty *maunds*. One *maund* varied from 27 lbs (pounds) to $32^1/_2$ lbs. See, *E.F.I.*, vol. V (1634-1636), p. 40; Chaudhuri, *The English East India Company*, p.175; *Letters*, Vol. I (1602-1613), p. 336; *E.F.I.*, vol. III (1624-1629), p. 245.

[35]Moreland, *op.cit.*, p.100.

[36]Dodwell, *op.cit.*, Vol. V, p.106.

[37]Khan, *op.cit.*, p.13; C.E.H.I., vol. I, Talboys Wheeler, Early *Records of British India—A History of the English Settlements in India*, Delhi (reprint), 1972, p.150.

[38]*E.F.I.*, vol. II (1622-1623), pp. xi, 90, 336; vol. VII (1642-1645), pp. 205, 256; vol. VIII (1646-1650), pp.186-7; Moreland, *op.cit.*, p.120.

[39]*E.F.I.*, vol. III (1624-1629), p. 92.

[40]Moreland, *op.cit.*, p.120.

[41]Dodwell, *op.cit.*, vol. V, p.92.

[42]*Letters*, vol. I (1602-1613), p. 28; Vijaya Ramaswamy, *op.cit.*, p.136.

[43]Moreland, *op.cit.*, p.128; Vijaya Ramaswamy, p.136.

[44] *E.F.I.*, vol. VIII (1646-1650), pp.163-4.

[45] *Letters*, vol. II (1613-1615), p.136; Arasaratnam, *op.cit.*, pp. 98-102.

[46] *E.F.I.*, vol. IX (1651-1654), p. 250.

[47] Arasaratnam, *op.cit.*, p. 99.

[48] *E.F.I.*, vol. II (1622-1623), p.102; Vijaya Ramaswamy, *op.cit.*, p.137.

[49] *E.F.I.*, vol. I (1618-1621), p. 264; vol. III (1624-1629), pp. 92-5; Arasaratnam, *op.cit.*, pp. 98-102; Vijaya Ramaswamy, *op.cit.*, pp.130-40.

[50] '*Corge*' perhaps derived from the Telugu '*Khorjam*', a term used for a bale of twenty pieces. See, Arasaratnam, *op.cit.*, p. 98; Five *corges* formed a bale; *E.F.I.*, vol. I (1618-1621), p. 265; Chaudhuri, *The English East India Company*, p.197.

[51] *E.F.I.*, vol. V (1634-1636), p. 57; Chaudhuri, *The English East India Company*, p.197.

[52] K.N. Chaudhuri, *op.cit.*, p.197.

[53] *E.F.I.*, vol. VIII (1646-1650), p. xxx; Moreland, *op.cit.*, p. 98.

[54] *E.F.I.*, vol. VIII (1646-1650), p. 297.

[55] *E.F.I.*, vol. I (1618-1621), p. 209.

[56] Moreland, *op.cit.*, pp.129-30.

[57] A.I. Chicherov, *India, Economic Development in the 16th-18th Centuries Outline History of Crafts and Trade*, Moscow, 1971, p.122.

[58] Moreland, *op.cit.*, p.131.

[59] *Ibid.*, p.103.

[60] *Letters*, vol. II (1613-1615), p.136; vol. V (1617), pp. 60, 223; *E.F.I.*, vol. I (1618-1621), p. 61; vol.II (1622-1623), p.192; K.N. Chaudhuri, *Trade and Civilization in the Indian Ocean An Economic History from the Rise of Islam to 1750*, New Delhi, 1985, pp. 20-30.

[61] W. Noel Sainsbury, *Calendar of State Paper Colonial Series, East Indies*, vol. I (1513-1616) (henceforth *Calendar of State Papers*), London, 1862, p. 384.

[62] Chicherov, *op.cit.*, p.122.

[63] *E.F.I.*, vol. III (1624-1629), p.180.

[64] *Letters*, vol. I (1602-1613), pp. 28, 192; vol. II (1613-1615), pp.117, 193; vol. VI (1617), p. 251; *E.F.I.*, vol. II (1622-1623), p.180; vol. III (1624-1629), pp. xxxiv, 357-8; vol. IV (1630-1633), pp. 5-6.

[65] *Letters*, vol. II (1613-1615), p.193; *E.F.I.*, vol. II (1622-1623), pp.102, 103, 118.

THE DUTCH EAST INDIA COMPANY AND THE PEPPER TRADE BETWEEN KERALA AND TAMILNAD, 1663-1795: A GEO-HISTORICAL ANALYSIS

Mark Vink

Here (from the Indian Ocean's Billows Hoare)
Discerned is of Mountains a long Rowe
Serving for Nat'ral Walls to Malabar,
Inroads of those of Canara to bar

Gate the Countrey's Natives call this Ridge
From foor whereof starts out a narrow Down
Which (back't by that) is by a natural Siege
Of angry Seas affronted...

-Luiz de Camões, The Lusiad, or *Portugals Historicall Poem,* Richard Fanshaw tr. London: H. Moseley 1655, p. 140.

In the wake of the great voyages of discovery of the fifteenth century, the African, Asian and American continents were opened for exploitation by Europe. As a result, the productive resources of the newfound worlds were incorporated into that of the old in what was to become the so-called "European world-economy".[1] In Asia, the "Vasco da Gama era", starting with the arrival of the famous Portuguese explorer at Kozhikode (Calicut) in 1498, ended only with the withdrawal of British forces from India and of the European navies from the Straits of Formosa in 1949. During this period, Portuguese, Dutch and English fleet subsequently dominated the main thoroughfares of the Indian Ocean.[2]

At the turn of the seventeenth century the Dutch, combining their erstwhile dispersed efforts in the United East India Company or Verenigde Oostindische Compagnie (VOC), began to challenge the supremacy of the Portuguese Estado da India in eastern waters. By 1630 they had secured their position in the region east of Malacca and next shifted their attention to the heartlands of their politico-commercial enemies in the west. In a prolonged and systematic military campaign, the Dutch supplanted the Portuguese in Malacca (1641), coastal Sri Lanka or Ceylon (1638-56), Nagapattinam in Tamilnad or the Coromandel coast (1658), and Kerala or Malabar (1658-63).

Kerala (Malabar), or the west coast of India extending from Mount Deli in the north to Kanniya Kumari (Cape Comorin) in the south, was the last of the Dutch acquisitions taken from the Portuguese and of great commercial and political importance to the VOC. Commercially, the high-quality, albeit more expensive, pepper from Malabar was held to be a welcome addition to the lower quality, and therefore cheaper supplies in Sumatra and elsewhere in the Indonesian archipelago.[3]

According to the VOC, however, merely securing an economical supply in itself was only half the point. The other half was to seal off the rest of the market and command self-determined prices. As Jacob Hustaert, the Dutch Governor of Ceylon (who also commanded the VOC establishments in Malabar until 1669), wrote to his subordinates in March 1664:

> Considering that the pepper trade is the bride around which everything dances, we recommend Your Honours to bend your best efforts to bring great quantities of Malabar pepper into Company hands every year... while at the same time you should prevent the indigenes from transporting [it] elsewhere by sea or land in secret.[4]

This ambitious scheme was based on the optimistic reports produced by Rijckloff van Goens, the Governor of Ceylon between 1662-63 and 1665-75. In his *Beschryvinge van de Oostindische Compagnie* ('Description of the East India Company'), for instance, Pieter van Dam, the *advocaat* (counsel) of the Company (1652-1701), reported: "The said Van Goens constantly professed, that Ceylon could not only support itself by its own revenues and profits, but would also be able to raise a pretty penny, which testimony he also gave with regard to Malabar...".[5]

Other, political, factors which made the Company directors in Europe, the Gentlemen Seventeen or *Heeren XVII*, willing to support the schemes of Van Goens were the peace negotiations then progressing between the States-General and King Pedro VI of Portugal against the backdrop of the Anglo-Portuguese marriage between Charles II and Catherine of Braganca—which, in the words of Van Dam, was considered to be "an irretrievable blow to the Company".[6]

It was rumoured that an English fleet was ready to take over the Portuguese possessions in Asia and that all of them (and not merely Bombay) were part of her dowry. A military confrontation with the rising power of the English naturally seemed less attractive to the Company than a further undermining of the already weakened Portuguese.

Five costly expeditions were necessary before the objective of ousting the Portuguese from Malabar was attained. In early 1663, however, the Company could call itself master of the forts at Cochin, Quilon, Cranganur and Cannanur and had taken over the smaller factories and stations elsewhere, as at Pallipuram (Aya kotta), Tengapatanam, Kayamkulam and Purakkad. For more than a century, until 1795, these establishments would remain under Dutch control.

The European presence on the Malabar coast had severe political, socio-religious, and economic implications for local society, such as the continuation and promotion of the political fragmentation or 'Balkanisation' of the country, the Latinisation of the indigenous Christian Church, and, apart from the commercialisation of the economy, the re-routing of trade.[7]

While the commercialisation of the economy was, in part, the result of the introduction of new exotic products, such as cashew nuts, tobacco and guava, and the more extensive cultivation of such old indigenous products as, among others, coconut, pepper, wild cinnamon, cardamom and ginger.[8] The re-routing of trade from the Indian Ocean to the South Asian subcontinent itself was a logical consequence of the Company's effort to monopolise the most lucrative branches of Malabar's external trade. In a communication to Pieter de Bitter and Cornells van Valkenburg, chiefs of Malabar, Van Goens wrote in March 1663:

> [the principle that the Company has in mind] is to keep all pepper and wild cinnamon under its control, not only according to the ancient right, which we have conquered from the Portuguese by force of arms, but also the binding contracts

> in which we have been confirmed by the king of Cochin and the subordinate rajas. Out of these, the heavy expenses which the Company has borne for such a long time, and which it is still forced to carry, have to be paid. To this concept also belongs the exclusion of all opium imported by private persons....[9]

There was, however, a price tag attached to this aggressive policy in the form of numerous guard posts on land and a powerful fleet at sea.[10] And even with heavy expenditures success was anything but guaranteed. As early as January 1668, Commander Isbrand Godske questioned the feasibility of Van Goens' ambitious scheme:

> It seems that this cannot be achieved without great difficulties and estrangement. After all, ..., the Honourable Company must be willing to effectuate this work by force of arms—as the Portuguese have done (not without heavy expenses) by maintaining a large number of frigates at sea and considerable armies on land. In this manner they forestalled the possibility of any import [of opium] or export of pepper... But this has led to the practice of pepper being exported overland, which as we have been told, did not amount to much previously.[11]

Nine years later, Godske's doubts were shared by Hendrik Adriaan van Reede tot Drakensteyn. In March 1677, the Dutch commander of Malabar wrote to his successor Jacob Lobs: "...And when it appeared that the coast was so well guarded and no unauthorised persons could slip through the dragnet, everything was transported overlandexactly what one had sought to prevent at sea with such great expenses and hazards. All the while, the indigenes ridiculed us for our lost labours.[12]

In June 1681, for example, Commander Marten Huijsman estimated that only one-third of the pepper production of Malabar, which he set at 15,000 candies or seven and a half million pounds, was exported by sea. Seven decades and many disillusions later, Commander Frederick Cunes assessed the output of the "black gold of Malabar" to be ten shiploads or between eight and nine million pounds, of which he believed half was transported to Coromandel, the north and the Deccan, and thence further into Hindustan.[13]

For comparison: whereas the English East India Company

valued Malabar pepper output between 1833 and 1836 at 54,698 candies or twenty-seven million pounds, the Portuguese in the early seventeenth century put the pepper production in southwest India from Honavar (Onor) to Travancore at a minimum of 258,000 quintals or ca. 13 million pounds. Of this, some 20,000 to 30,000 quintals was brought by the Portuguese to Lisbon, the remainder being either consumed locally or exported overland to Tamilnad, and North by sea to Gujarat.[14]

The overland trade between the west and east coast of India, so frustrating to the Company, was embedded in such natural and human structures as landform, climate, vegetation and soils, land use and agriculture, social hierarchy, and infrastructure. In Braudelian terms, these *structures* formed an "upper ceiling" or "limit of the possible".[15] The resulting human-environment system is the outcome of a two-way process of adoption and adaptation between man and his natural environment.[16]

As far as landform is concerned, the most important determinant were the Western Ghats (from Hindi *ghat*, landing-place, mountain pass or entrance), the peninsular massif from lat. 20° north of Bombay, to lat. 12° near Kozhikode (Calicut). The Ghats proper are only a few miles wide as a rule and generally 2,500 to 3,000 feet (760 to 915 metres) high, with culminations up to 4,500 feet (1,370 metres). Farther south, the dissected belt is higher and wider, consisting of a number of discontinuous elevations—the Nilgiris (Blue Mountains) with a summit level of 6,000-8,000 feet (1830 to 2,450 metres); the Anaimalai with Anaimudi (8,874 feet or 2,695 metres) the highest peak of the peninsula; the Palnis; and in the south, the Cardamom Hills.[17]

Although they provided Malabar with a natural defence against potential influences from the East, the Western Ghats were no unsurmountable barrier. Time and again, the rulers on the west and east coast, such as the Venad kings of Travancore and the Vijayanagar emperors and their self-appointed heirs the Nayaks of Madurai extended their influence beyond the mountains.

Apart from military purposes, however, the mountain passes also served more productive and peaceful ends, for Indian merchants tended to use the same paths as their military counterparts. In March 1677, for instance, Commander Van Reede distinguished no less than twenty to twenty-four of these military and commercial highroads:

> Malabar is being separated like a wall from the countries of Madurai by high mountains. These mountains lie, so to speak, back-to-back against one another. Nevertheless, these two countries maintain communications by twenty to twenty-four routes or big roads, namely two in Travancore, three in Kayamkulam, two in Kundara, six in Tekkumkur, two in Vadakkumkur, three in and behind the lands of Cochin, two in the domains of the Zamorin, and two in the countries of the Kolathiri or Raja of Cannanur.[18]

Van Reede, however, was talking about trails or major routes not about passes. The number of actual *ghats* was more limited. From north to south, the most important ones were the Perambadi Gap to Coorg, the Periyar and Tamarasseri Gaps to the Malabar Wynaad and Mysore, and, in the Travancore area, the Bodinayakkanur, Kambam, Aryankavu, and Aramboli Gaps.[19]

One should not, however, think too highly of these passes. Describing the "very rude" condition of the country's infrastructure prior to their take-over at the turn of the nineteenth century, the British called the Periyar Gap, leading to the deadly atmosphere of the malarious Wynaad ("Land of the Swamps") jungle, "the worst ghaut in the south of India, being so steep as to be nearly impracticable for laden cattle, and totally so for wheeled carriage; neither is it capable of much improvement, the declivity being in many places one in three feet".[20]

The most important pass of all was the Palghat Gap, a large opening in the Ghats, 20 miles wide and not more than 970 feet (296 metres) high. It was through this gap that the bulk of the overland trade between Kerala and Tamilnad took place. It was not without reason that the British considered this strategic highroad "the key to the west coast".[21]

The climate of South Asia is determined by the monsoon regime (from the Arabic *mausim*, or Portuguese *monção*, or season), which is characterised by a seasonal shift of winds and subsequent change in precipitation.[22] Although there are but two monsoons, the southwest and the northeast, three seasons are recognised in South Asia: the rainy season (June to October) is a time of high temperatures and abundant moisture, bringing seventy-five per cent of Malabar's total annual rainfall. The most intense precipitation (100 to 200 inches), however, does not occur at the sea coast or at the foot of the mountains, but at intermediate elevations, normally 2,000 to 3,000 feet in the Ghats. The cool season (November to February) is a time of the northeast monsoon and—especially after the end of December—prevailing dry weather. The hot season (March to May) is a period of inconsistent and low intensity winds, with convectional showers bringing as much as ten to twenty inches of rainfall in the southern and eastern coastal areas of South Asia.

It was between January and May that the bulk of the trade took place when the 'gathering season' (December and January) was followed by the 'festival season' (January to April/May).[23] As Commander Godefridus Weijerman of Malabar explained to his successor Cornelis Breekpot in February 1765:

> since the harvest of this popular fruit [pepper] does not take place before late December, when it has come to its full ripeness and is picked and dried, it is no sooner available than the end of January... until well into the middle of April. At the end of this month, this grain is rising still a little in price, not only because of scarcity, but also because the pepper buyers are afraid of the uncoming bad weather [i.e., the rainy season].[24]

Land use and agriculture in Malabar were (and still are) characterized by the cultivation of labour-intensive food and cash crops—rice, coconut, and its derivatives—in the populous coastlands, and labour-extensive cash crops, in particular such spices as pepper, wild cinnamon, and cardamom, in the interior.

In the low alluvial and marine coastland of Malabar wet-rice is easily grown under natural inundation. The normally early arrival of the rains permits a first crop to be planted in April or May and harvested in September; the prolonged season of rains often allows for the planting of a second, less abundant rice crop, which is harvested in January. On the inland laterite terraces and hills, either upland rice or *ragi* is grown without inundation during the rains. In 1677, for instance, Adolff Bassingh, the Dutch resident at Tiruchinapalli (Trichinopoly), observed:

> The country belonging to this nayak of Madurai [Chockanatha] from the river Coleroon to the places in the west between the mountains [the Western Ghats] consist principally of agricul-

> tural lands. The *nelli* [from Telugu and Tamil *nelli*, 'rice-like'] and other field crops in these regions are harvested twice a year in greater abundance than anywhere else because of providence and nature. The rivers and smaller streams make the soil extremely fertile because of their timely flooding. Moreover, these people have used their ingenuity by capturing the excessive water in tanks or ditches. When needed, this water can be transported via canals or artificial waterways to the dry fields in order to bring the sown crops to full maturity....[25]

In 1743, Commander Stein van Gollenesse lyrically described the abundance of rice which was grown in Nanjinad, a small principality beyond Kayamkulam: "it [Nanjinad] produces so much of this grain that the king [of Travancore] levies tolls every year amounting to 300,000 gallioons [Travancore fanams, or ca. 360,000 guilders]".[26]

Little rice, however, was exported from Malabar since it was needed to support its dense population. The major export area for rice, therefore, was Kanara, the region north of Malabar, which was called by the Company "the granary or bread chamber of the entire coast of India and Arabia".[27]

In addition to the rice fields, nearly every homestead had its own garden patch with numerous vegetables—primarily for home use, but, in case of a surplus, also for sale at the local market—among which were mango, jac, lime, orange, plantain, betel leaf, arecanuts, and so forth.

After rice, coconut was the second most important crop of Malabar, growing typically in the sandy coastal strip. With more careful preparation it could also be cultivated on alluvial loams on the interior laterites. In the lowland, the acreage of coconut groves locally equalled or exceeded that in rice.

The lavish green of the coconut trees would be the first thing to catch the eye of a visitor to the Malabar coast, and normally would make a big impression. As Wouter Schouten, a merchant in the service of the VOC (1658-65), observed in his *Oost-Indische Voyagie* ('East Indian Voyage'):

> The Coconut or Lagnes-tree is one of the most excellent trees of India. It grows abundantly in many countries and kingdoms of Asia, but in particular along the entire coast of Malabar,

> where they stand in innumerable numbers in countless and pleasantly shaded groves.[28]

Even Philippus Baldaeus, the Reformed Minister in Company service (1655-66), had an eye for the worldly beauty of the region. In his *Naauwkeurige Beschryvinge van Malabar en Coromandel* ('Exact Description of Malabar and Coromandel'), he observed: "The whole country is densely covered with coconut trees, which stand there in countless numbers and give the whole region a delightful appearance".[29]

The coconut was not merely an aesthetic but also an economic acquisition for the region. Van Linschoten, for instance, enumerated the high commercial value of the coconut tree, of which almost no part was wasted: the wood was used for heating and cooking, the coir fibre from the husk of the shell for ropes and matting, the leaves for sails and thatch, and the fruit for food, and dried for oil as well. This dried meat or copra was also used to make toddy and arrack, "which", Linschoten added, "is very good wine and is the wine of India".[30]

Between 1833 and 1836, the English East India Company estimated the average production of coconuts in Malabar to be 300 to 400 million annually, in addition to which 1.3 to 1.6 million pounds of copra were exported. Moreover, in June 1681, Commander Huijsman of Malabar set the quantity of arrack produced in Malabar at 15,000 candies or 7.5 million pounds.[31] No wonder that Linschoten considered the coconut to be "the most profitable tree of all India".[32]

Although economically the coconut tree and its derivatives may have been the most important cash crop of Malabar, historically the most interesting one has been pepper. The "moeny of Malabar", as it was called, requires much moisture and hence thrives best in the deep valleys of the Western Ghats. The most famous production areas were Tekkumkur and Vadakkumkur, the latter of which was known to the Portuguese as Piementa or "pepper kingdom".[33]

The pepper of south Malabar was bigger and heavier than the northern variety. As Baldaeus testified: "Although Cochin produces much pepper, the heaviest comes from the lands of Cannanur in the interior.... In Calicut, on the other hand, pepper is smaller of grain and less plentiful than in Cannanur and

Cochin...".[34]

The trailing plant which produces pepper is propagated by planting a cutting at the root of the jac, the mango, or other tree having rough bark, up which the vine climbs. After it has been planted, it requires no great trouble or attention, the cultivator having little more to do than to collect the produce in the proper season. When the fruit is intended for black pepper, it is not allowed to ripen, but is collected green, and becomes black on drying. That which is intended for white pepper, is left to ripen thoroughly, in which state the berries are covered with red pulp, which, being washed off, leaves the peppercorn white, and requiring merely to be dried for the market.[35]

Other labour-extensive products of the interior besides pepper were cardamom and wild cinnamon. Like so many other spices, the seed capsule or seed of cardamom was used both in medicine and in food processing. The best variety of cardamom was grown in the hilly country of Kottayam. In the kingdom of Cochin another, greatly inferior, kind was found, which, according to Commander Adiraan Moens, "is smaller and of which the peel or rind becomes brownish in time, while the other or northern kind is yellow and better to look at".[36]

Cardamom was produced spontaneously in the woods of the high lands, the care given to it being merely the cleaning of the ground from trees where they were observed to spring naturally. In 1801 the English East India Company estimated the annual produce of cardamom in Malabar to be 76,800 pounds.[37]

Another spice gathered in the forests of Malabar was wild cinnamon or *canela do mato.* Compared to the cinnamon produced in Sri Lanka (Ceylon), however, the wild cinnamon of Malabar was of inferior quality. "The places where cinnamon grows", Linschoten observed, "are most and best on the island of Ceylon, where there are whole forests full of cinnamon trees. On the coast of Malabar there grows likewise great store and some woods of cinnamon, but half as good and lesser trees, the bark being greyer and thicker, and of small virtue...".[38] Other forest products were ginger—mostly from Calicut and Cannanur—wax, a little lac ("poor and woody"), and various sorts of timber, like teak and sandalwood.

In March 1677, Commander Van Reede drew up an elaborate list of the Company settlements on the Malabar coast along with the products that could be procured *in situ.* Tengapatanam, on the coast south of Trivandrum, gave iron, fine coir, jute, yarn, cotton piece-goods, tanned and untanned leather, parchment, raw sugar (candy), blue stone and flooring-slab, and provisions. Compared to Tengapatanam, Quilon was rather unimportant, at least from the Dutch commercial point of view, giving only a small quantity of pepper. In Kayamkulam, halfway between Purakkad and Quilon, on the other hand, a variety of commodities could be procured: pepper, wild cinnamon, arrack, dried cow hides, and gun fuses. Kallikkattu Tura (Morenbril), a *pagar* or fenced stronghold north of the outlet to the sea of Kayamkulam Lagoon, gave some coconuts. Purakkad produced pepper, wild cinnamon, arrack, and timber. Cochin gave pepper, cardamom, coconut oil, and fuses. Cannanur, finally, gave cardamom, pepper, arrack, masts, and "many other comforting items".[39]

Having dealt with the natural setting of the overland trade, it is now time to look at its human "limitations", such as the social organisation and the regional infrastructure. As almost everywhere else in India, the social structure in Malabar was based on the Hindu caste or *varna* system. This meant that status was expressed in the traditional hierarchy of Brahmans—priests, Kshatriyas—rulers and warriors, Vaisyas—traders, and Sudrasservants. Those who had no place in this scheme were Pariahs, or "outcastes, untouchables". The French sociologist CÇlestin BouglÇ has characterised the system by three tendencies: rejection, hierarchy, and hereditary specialisation ("répulsion, hiérarchie, spécialisation héreditaire").[40]

To understand how this theoretical scheme operated in practice, however, one should not overestimate the importance of the traditional *varna* divisions. For the concrete social structures what matters is how the system operated in a certain social community. Such a community was made up by a multitude of sub-castes, the so-called *jatis*, or grouping of households characterised by commensality and endogamy.[41]

In addition to the Nambuthiris, who may be termed 'indigenous', there were two other classes of Brahmans who, though domiciled since early times in Malabar, were quite distinct in race, customs, and appearance from the Nambuthiris and were looked down upon by them (the feeling was mutual), as inferiors and foreigners: the Empranthiri or Konkani Brahmans from Kanara, and the Pattars or Tamil Brahmans from the east coast.

Like the Muslims in north Malabar and the small but ancient Jewish colony in Cochin, the Konkani and Tamil Brahmans were involved in wholesale trade. It is hardly surprising that none of these four groups originally came from Malabar since the native Malabar castes had only a limited radius of action. Even the Nambuthiris could not leave Malabar without losing status. Moreover, their wealth was tied up to the ownership of land.

Whereas the Muslims, Jews and Konkanis were largely oriented to the westward maritime trade, the overland trade to Tamilnad or the Coromandel coast was the virtual monopoly of the Pattars, or Tamil Brahmans. Although there were large colonies of Pattars from Tinnevelly, Thanjavur (Tanjore), and Coimbatore spread throughout the country, their main habitat was in and around the country of Palghat. Wherever they settled permanently they would live in *gramams*, or villages with houses built contiguously to one another in straight streets, while the Malabaris themselves lived in dispersed settlements, in detached houses surrounded by gardens. In other places where their residence was only temporary, the Pattars were collected under *Samuha madhams*, or houses belonging to the community.

The Pattars enjoyed several commercial privileges. In his *Mallabaarsche Brieven* ('Letters from Malabar'), Jacobus Canter Visscher, the Dutch chaplain at Cochin (1717-1724), observed:

> The rajas of Malabar have granted certain commercial privileges to the Pattars. The first is almost complete exemption from customs: they pay only half the usual duty for the loads they carry on their heads, and nothing for those they carry on their backs. As a result, you can generally see them laden with two packages. They are restricted, however, to such goods as they can carry overland themselves. Their second privilege is an allowance of free food at any pagoda [*Uttuparas* or choultries were usually attached to pagodas] they visit as long as they stay there. In return they are bound to sweep and clean the building when required. They enjoy the same privilege at the courts of several rajas where they appear in great numbers on festival days, during which they take the opportunity to eat voraciously. On these occasions they will also receive a few fanams. Their third privilege consists of the right to carry loads being confined to men of their own caste and nation, an arrangement by which

> many thousands of their poor are supported, since no other race is allowed to have any share in their profits.[12]

An almost identical description is given by Van Reede, who reported the existence of large companies or societies among the Pattars, enjoying a virtual monopoly in the carrying trade: "In this manner all things that are imported in and exported from Malabar are carried by these Pattars on their heads and shoulders, and sometimes whole armies of them can be found on the up-country roads".[13]

Below the rank of the Brahmans, the social structure of Malabar differed greatly from the traditional four-caste division. For one thing, there were very few Kshatriyas, with the exception of the Cochin ruling family and a few petty chieftains, and no Vaishyas at all. Although the numerically predominant Nayars of Malabar may be classified as Sudras, it should be remembered that their position in the caste hierarchy was quite different from that of their counterparts on the east coast, where both Kshatriyas and Vaisyas were well represented. As a result, a mere third-rank category in the *varna* hierarchy in theory, they came second to the Brahmans only and hence enjoyed a higher status in Malabar than in Tamilnad.

The Nayar community of Malabar consisted of three main divisions: (i) the Samanthas or ruling castes, to which the leading royal families, such as that of the rajas of Calicut, Vaddakumkur, Alanggadu (Magat), and the vast majority of minor chiefs belonged; (ii) the large class of agriculturists which constituted the militia of Malabar and (iii) the lower classes, such as barbers, washermen, potters, and weavers. Though they were all Nayars, western writers generally confined the term to the first two of the arms-bearing *jatis*.[14]

In theory, the Christians of Malabar should have been outside the caste system, but in practice they were Indians who had merely undergone a process of Christianisation and had remained part of the traditional *varna* hierarchy. They were Christians in faith, but Indian in all else including their conception of their community as a caste.[15] As Visscher observed:

> Their dwellings are separate from those of the other inhabitants, consisting of hamlets or villages in which they live together,

> the houses being small and mean. It seems that they keep very strict genealogical records and they will neither marry nor in any way intermingle with the new low-caste Christiansbeing themselves mostly *casta de nairos*, that is, nobility of the Nayar caste, in token of which they generally carry a sword in the hand, as a mark of dignity.[46]

According to local tradition, the Indian Christians had been made converts by the Apostle Thomas on the coasts of Coromandel (Tamilnad) and Malabar (Kerala) in the first century A.D. The St. Thomas Christians, as they were subsequently designated, lived mainly in the interior, in the region which the Portuguese called the Serra, or mountains. In the two centuries between 1580 and 1780 their number probably doubled from *circa* 75,000 to 150,000.[47] "Driven out of their country," Van Reede wrote in March 1677, "they subsequently multiplied themselves and have become a great mass of people or crowd, occupying more than fourteen hundred villages and one hundred and fifty churches".[48]

While there is relatively little uncertainty in qualitative matters, there is more confusion concerning the livelihood of the St. Thomas Christians. In January 1668, for instance, Commander Godske called them "all impecunious persons, being more pedlars than merchants". Thirteen years later, in June 1681, Commander Huijsman provided a more generous assessment, styling them "mostly merchants and practitioners of the important handicrafts, who also carry the rifle". Finally, in May 1698 Commissioner Hendrik Zwaardecroon spoke of "pepper farmers, who are mostly St. Thomas Christians".[49]

At first glance, these observations appear to be totally incompatible. In fact, all of them carried an element of truth. In their quality of pseudo-Nayars, the St. Thomas Christians were recruited into separate companies for warfare by some chieftains. At the same time, it seems that they were, for the most part, pepper farmers of the Malabar hills, selling their crops in small quantities in the vicinity, in most cases the local *bazaar* or market. It was this ideal combination of merchant and warrior (not unfamiliar to the VOC), which made Visscher propagate the conversion of the St. Thomas Christians to the Dutch Reformed religion.[50]

It should be noted, however, that although the Hindu and Christian Nayars were known as farmers, the actual cultivation of their lands was done by outcaste agricultural labourers, such as the Pulayars, Cherumars, or Parayas.[51] The Nayars themselves were averse to manual labour of any kind, which they considered to be highly degrading and contented themselves with mere supervision. As Linschoten observed: "The Nayars wear the nails of their hands very long, whereby they show that they are gentlemen...".[52]

The poor infrastructure of Malabar was a great obstacle to a smooth course of the overland trade, for roads were in a very poor condition indeed. The situation was further hampered by the political fragmentation and the incessant state of warfare. Apart from impeding trade, native rulers were highly apprehensive of creating highways for invading armies. As a result, little or nothing was done to improve the situation, that is, with the exception of the avenues of trees (Salai) of Mangammal, the Queen-Regent of Madurai (1689-1704), in Tinnevelly and Madurai, and the gun roads of Tipu Sultan, the ambitious ruler of Mysore (1782-99), centred on Seringapatam.[53]

The improvements they made, however, were haphazard and had no long-lasting effects, for they were merely unmetalled tracks, very ill-suited to cart traffic in any but the finest weather. Thus, when the British took over Malabar in the late eighteenth century, they had to start almost from scratch. In their own words: "The problem was not one of maintenance, but one of construction".[54]

While wheeled traffic was well-nigh impossible, horses were hardly an alternative. As Visscher asserted:

> I have never seen a Malabari on horseback, and even their princes do not possess steeds. Indeed, they would be of no use in the low flat lands where the ground is much broken and very marshy, and intersected with streams. Besides this, there are no beaten roads, the whole country being covered with bushes and underwood.[55]

Therefore, the only means of transportation was provided by the Pattars. Apart from the strength of their own muscles, they also relied heavily on animal power, that is, pack-oxen. One bullock or *boi* was able to carry the same weight as five men, or circa 220 pounds. This heavy reliance on animal power earned the Pattars the name of *boieiros*, or bullock-team drivers.[56]

The overland trade was a large-scale enterprise, handling

millions of pounds of pepper (and other commodities) a year. Apart from the "large armies" of Pattar carriers, it also involved large numbers of pack-oxen. In 1519, for instance, Hector Rodrigues, the avaricious Portuguese captain at Quilon, seized 5,000 bullock-loads of pepper (*ca.* 1100,000 pounds), which certain traders of the east coast had collected in barter for 5,000 bullock-loads of rice. In November 1677, Bassing reported the existence 250 years earlier, of a very rich *boieiro* owning over 20,000 oxen, engaged in the pepper and arrack trade from Malabar to the countries of Carnatica and Madurai.[57]

In his *Six Voyages*, Jean Baptiste Tavernier (1605-89), the famous French traveller and jewel trader, reported: "...it is a wonderful thing to see ten or twelve thousand Oxen at a time all laden with Rice, Corn and Salt, in such places where they exchange their commodities...". In addition, Tavernier mentioned a great inconvenience for travellers, "that when they meet with these numerous Caravans in streight places, they are forc'd to stay two or three days till they are all past by".[58]

In 1677 Bassing estimated the annual volume of trade at the three markets or *pettai* (from Tamil *pettai*, "extramural suburb of a fortress, or the town attached and adjacent to a fortress) near Tiruchinapalli, an important regional distribution centre: one hundred *bahar* (48,000 pounds) copper, sixty *bahar* (28,800 pounds) tin, forty *bahar* (19,200 pounds) spelter, and thirty *bahar* (14,400 pounds) lead. In addition, 6,000 *bois* (1320,000 pounds) of pepper, 6,000 *bois* (1320,000 pounds) of boiled arrack from Malabar, 1,400 *bois* (308,000 pounds) of Ceylon arrack, and one hundred *bois* (22,000 pounds) of long pepper. "The amount of other commodities cannot be estimated, since they are sold only on occasion, but the said commodities are for the most part purchased and used by everyone".[59]

Exchange and distribution took place via a hierarchy of markets, from the small weekly *bazars* in the localities to the large annual fairs. The function of the smaller units was to assist the larger centres in the distribution of the imports and the collection of the exports.[60] In 1677, for example, Bassing reported that the pepper, which had been carried to Tiruchinapalli was from thence transported to the north to Ariyalur, Tanjore, Mangalore (twenty-two miles west of Vriddhachalm), Gingi, and Vellore, all the way to Tirupati, or a distance of ninety Dutch miles.[61]

TABLE 1

VOLUME OF TRADE AT THE THREE MARKETS OUTSIDE OF TIRUCHIRAPALLI ACCORDING TO BASSING, 1677

Commodity	Amount	in pounds
Copper	100 bahars	36,000 pounds
Tin	60 bahars	21,600 pounds
Spelter	40 bahars	14,400 pounds
Lead	30 bahars	10,800 pounds
Pepper	6,000 bois	1320,000 pounds
Malabar arrack	6,000 bois	1320,000 pounds
Ceylon arrack	1,400 bois	308,000 pounds
Long Pepper	100 bois	22,000 pounds

Source: Bassing, "Eenige Verhalinge...", [ff. 9-10], in James Ford Bell Library, Minneapolis, Minn., B 1738 Mos., Manuscript Papers relating to Dutch Trade in India, Negapatam, 1738.

In 1743, Stein van Gollenesse mentioned the existence of several *bazaars* in the "pepper countries" of Tekkumkur and Vadakkumkur: "Most of the pepper [of Tekkmkur] is brought up-country to the *bazaars* of Kun [Kunnakulam?], Serepilly [Cheruvalli?], Irataperha [Eratupetta?], Erunalur [Iramallur?], and Irruny [Erumeli?], and from there it is fetched by Pandyan merchants with their oxen...". The Dutch commander also mentioned the "great territory of Kismalanaddu [in Vadakkumkur], in which lies the well-known *bazaar* Toddopale or Caricotty [Karikkad]".[62]

The flourishing pepper export to the east coast was viewed with consternation and frustration by the Dutch. On the one hand, they considered this flow of spices outside their control as smuggling, as it, in their opinion, clearly ran against the monopolistic treaties with the various indigenous rulers on the west coast. On the other hand, they came to realise they were in no position to stop it. The reasons for their impotence can be grouped under four headings: military, sociological, economic and political. Taken together, they explain the relative autonomy of the east-bound, continental from the west-bound, maritime trading system.

Although the Dutch were not to be outgunned on the coast, they were certainly outmanned in the interior. Their limited base of operation was clearly understood by Van Reede and Godske. Both commanders of Malabar stressed the necessity of native 'collaborators'. In March 1677, a desperate Van Reede had asked, not without some sense of drama: "What means could one think of to close or block those [inland] roads for us, who merely occupy the extreme banks or beaches of Malabar? And who could or would be willing to do that...?"[63]

Nine years earlier, in January 1668, Godske had already provided the only answer possible by advising his successor Lucas van der Dussen to appease the rajas most important to the Company, such as those of Cochin, Vadakkumkur, and Tekkumkur. To which he added:

> Especially the raja of Tekkumkur should be caressed because of the great quantity of pepper that region produces, lest the Company be deprived of it in case of discord. For his estates are well-situated with regard to the overland export, since Madurai is almost to the rear of them. Therefore, Your Honour would do better—as I have usually done—to cultivate his friendship more than all others. The more so, since his country is very populous, and, as a result, we could effect little or nothing against his lands by force of arms in case of estrangement.[64]

Both Van Reede and Godske, however, realised they were asking the impossible and that the appeasement policy was predestined to failure. For various reasons, a native ruler had little to gain and much to lose by preventing pepper being 'smuggled' to the east coast. For what it was worth, he might have won the respect of the Dutch, but at the same time, and more importantly, would have lost that of his subjects and hence run the risk of losing his kingdom as well. Thus, maintaining checkpoints on his borders in order to prevent the outflow of grain was a dubious policy, to say the least.

For one thing, strict observance of the monopolistic agreements would be highly unprofitable. Although the treaties stipulated that half of the 'illegal' pepper intercepted would be for the local raja, the financial liabilities were clearly outweighed by the expenses needed to maintain the necessary men and material. He would damage his own purse even more, because land tolls were on the average much higher than sea tolls.[65]

In addition, strict enforcement of these treaties would have been close to political suicide and clearly not within the power of a ruler. The monarchical concept in Malabar was not the idea of the *cakravartan* as ruler of a universal State, but instead reflected the notion of limited royal authority. The rights and duties of rulers were delineated according to tradition, which was believed to have been effectuated by the legendary Cheraman Perumal, who was held to have ruled the whole of the country in the early ninth century.[66]

In a description which bears close resemblance to the 'social contract' of Rousseau between rulers and subjects, Commander Stein van Gollenesse in 1743 explained:

> Although the king and princes exercise great authority over their subjects, affairs are so regulated by the laws of Cheraman Perumal that their rule can in no way be called despotic. Subjects obey their king ungrudgingly as long as he remains within the limits of the law, and even if a chief were to wrong a few individuals, the whole community would not take up the quarrel. However, if he were to issue orders calculated to injure the interests of the whole community, they would not be obeyed. I draw attention to this in special connection with pepper... Having examined the subject more carefully, I have come to the conclusion that their power in this matter is small if they do not wish to bring the hatred of the whole nation upon their head.[67]

The economic reasons which guaranteed the autonomous existence of the overland trade system were a logical consequence of the mercantile policy of the Dutch. The idea behind the VOC's monopolistic agreements with indigenous rulers was to maximise profits by minimising purchase prices and increasing selling prices. The ensuing huge margins of profits were needed to make up for their expenditures on forts and garrisons.

Steengaard's internalisation of protection costs can therefore hardly be considered an advantage. As the Dutch historian Marie Meilink-Roelofsz has put it: "It was precisely where the Company had commercial dealings with its Asiatic counterparts that it was at a disadvantage because of its maritime, military and administrative apparatus. It then attempted to meet its Asiatic competitors by adopting redistributive tactics".[68]

Exclusive treaties with native rulers were an indispensable means in the cut-throat competition with the Asian merchants, with whom the Dutch could not compete on even terms. Since, however, these contracts were generally disregarded by the 'untrustworthy' rulers and the VOC lacked the means to correct them, the Dutch faced an unequal fight.

In January 1668, Commander Godske came with what he believed would be the 'egg of Columbus', when he recommended a shift from military to mercantile means to stop the pepper 'smuggling': "In my opinion, the best and the cheapest way to divert the pepper and opium smugglers from the sea and land routes is to sell the opium here at, or a little below, market price. Thus, we would further our trade, improve our finances and receive larger quantities of pepper than ever before."[69]

Godske's views were supported by Van Reede. In November 1691, the Dutch Commissioner asserted "that it was in the power of the Company to take over the entire commerce [of Madurai] from the Pattars and natives, since they cannot compete with the Company, because to travel by land is more expensive than to travel by sea".[70] Bassing actually provides some figures on the costs of overland trade based on Tiruchinapalli. Unfortunately, we cannot compare these figures with the cost of maritime commerce, if only because ships cannot sail over land. But it is clear that Godske's solution was only a castle in the air, for it would have undermined the very structural foundation of the Company. As early as October 1654, the Gentlemen Seventeen had already concluded: "In comparison with the Moors and other indigenous nations, our carriages and expenditures run too high. Therefore, we cannot compete with them."[71] Their negative view was confirmed by Stein van Gollenesse. In 1743 the Commander of Malabar declared that

> to follow the market is well-nigh impossible because an ordinary merchant, who had to defray no expenses of any importance, is better off with twenty-five per cent profit on pepper than the Hon'ble Company with one hundred per cent, inasmuch as the latter has to bear the considerable burden of so many establishments on this coast.[72]

TABLE 2

COSTS OF TRANSPORTATION (FREIGHTAGE AND TOLLS) PER BOI AND DISTANCE FROM TIRUCHINAPALLI ACCORDING TO BASSING, 1677

From Tiruchinapalli to	Cost*	Distance
Porto Novo and Cuddalore	47 fanams	N.A.
Tengapattanam	40 fanams	N.A.
Paleacatte	57 fanams	40 Dutch miles
Nagapattinam	16 fanams	35 Dutch miles
Tuticorin	22 fanams	67 Dutch miles
Ariyalur	8 fanams	15 Dutch miles
Thanjavur	10 fanams	11 Dutch miles
Velliyakundam	11 fanams	N.A.
Mangalore	12 fanams	N.A.
Gingi and Vellore	> 12 fanams	36 Dutch miles
Tirupati	48 fanams	90 Dutch miles

*In November 1681, after much confusion, the Governor-General and Council at Batavia decided to value the pagoda "henceforth at six guilders and five stuivers for each fanam of which twenty-four go in the pagoda". See: W.Ph. Coolhaas (ed.), *Generale Missiven IV*, p. 485. The rate of conversion thus became: 1 fanam = 1/24 pagoda or five stuivers (fl. 0, 25).

Source: Adolff Bassing, "Eenige Verhalinge van de Voornaamste Coopluijden van Petten off Marten Buijten de Stad Trichenapallij...", [ff. 6-7, 9, and 20], in: James Ford Bell Library, Minneapolis, Minn., B 1738 Mos., Manuscript papers relating to Dutch Trade in India, Negapatam, 1738.

The political factors which ensured the relative autonomy of the overland trade were the extreme fragmentation of Malabar and the limited powers of the rulers. Ironically, it would seem that the Company's very divide-and-rule policy worked against her. The VOC, however, did not have much of a choice. This lack of an alternative became painfully clear with the rise of Travancore and Mysore in the eighteenth century. After 1730 and 1760, respectively, both native States vigorously set out to enlarge their territory and tried to establish a government monopoly in the country's staple products, such as pepper, cardamom, tobacco, and so forth. When the Dutch intervened and tried to bring Marthanda Varma, the ambitious ruler of Travancore (1729-58) into line, their forces were checked and defeated at Coalachel in August 1741.[73] Although the Battle of Coalachel was little more than a skirmish, it made the VOC realise that

> On the one hand [wars only serve] to reveal the impotence of the Europeans against the natives of the country if they have to be brought to reason by force of arms; on the other hand, to impose a great and unbearable burden on us, rather than to bring the Company something substantial, proportionate to the great hazards, inconveniences, burdens and crosses which it has brought on itself by the wars.[74]

By the Treaty of Mavelikkara, concluded in October 1748 and ratified in August 1753, the VOC not only gave up its former monopolistic designs, but also its self-appointed guardianship over its client States. In article nine of the Treaty, the Company promised Marthanda Varma "that the Company shall renounce all alliances with the other chiefs and nobles of Malabar with whom His Highness might desire to wage war and shall not thwart him in this matter in any respect".[75]

By this time, the Company, fed up with Malabar, was rapidly sinking into a financial morass as it was faced with mounting competition from other European nations and corruption among its own servants. In his *Reize van Zeeland* ('Travel from Zeeland'), Johan Splinter Stavorinus, the Dutch rear-admiral visiting Malabar betwen 1775 and 1778, summarised a conversation that had allegedly taken place between Governor-General Jacob Mossel (1750-61) and Stein van Gollenesse, the former commander of Malabar and now Director-General at Batavia:

> From the time that it was conquered to a few years ago, the Malabar coast has been one of the heaviest burdens of the Company in India. Therefore, when Director-General Stein van Gollenesse maintained that Malabar, where he had long been stationed as a commander, was one of the most important

possessions of the Company, Governor-General Mossel had a different opinion and replied instead that he rather wished that the ocean had swallowed up the coast of Malabar one hundred years ago.[76]

Eventually, after many years of financial hardships, the Company was freed from the 'heavy burden' to be sure, albeit not the way it wanted. Having sold its forts at Cannanur, Cranganur, and Pallipuram, the VOC in 1793 stopped doing business in Malabar altogether, though retaining a low-profile presence in the form of its forts at Cochin and Quilon.

Thus, when the French invaded the Dutch Republic in 1795, the exiled Stadtholder William V fled to England and, by the so-called 'Letters of Kew', requested of all Dutch governors and commanders overseas that "His Brittanic Majesty's troops shall be admitted and take possession of the forts in our colonies, and that they are to be considered as the troops of a kingdom in friendship and alliance, in case these colonies should be summoned by the French".[77]

In the confused political situation that followed, however, the VOC Directorate hesitated to confirm the appeal. Thereupon, Cochin's Commander, Jan Lambertus van Spall, initially refused the English call upon him to surrender. Men o' war were brought into position by the English Commander George Petrie, and after a brief bombardment, Cochin's powder magazine was struck and blown up. Cochin, together with Quilon, passed into Dutch history on 20 October 1795.[78]

NOTES

[1]Immanuel Wallerstein, *The Modern World System I. Capitalist Agriculture and the Origins of the European World-Economy in the Sixteenth Century* (Studies in Soical Discontinuity), New York: Academic Press, 1974, pp. 87-108.

[2]Carlo M. Cipolla, *Guns, Sails and Empires. Technological Innovation and the Early Phases of European Expansion, 1400-1700,* Manhattan, Kansas: Sunflower University Press, 1985, p. 5.

[3]Kristof Glamann, *Dutch-Asiatic Trade, 1620-1740,* Copenhagen/ The Hague: Danish Science Press and Martinus Nijhoff, 1958, p. 81; T.I. Poonen, *Dutch Hegemony in Malabar and Its Collapse, A.D. 1663-1795,* Trivandrum: Department of Publications, University of Kerala, 1978, p. 22.

[4]"Instruction of Jacob Hustaert to Commander Ludolph van Coulster and Council of Malabar, 6.3.1664" in Hugo Karel 's Jacob, *De Nederlanders in Kerala, 1663-1701. De Memories en Instructies Betreffende het Commandement Malabar van de Verenigde Oost-Indische Compagnie* (Rijks Geschiedkundige Publicati'n [RGP]), Kleine serie nr. 43, The Hague: Martinus Nijhoff, 1976, p. 26. *Idem*: "De VOC en de Malabarkust in de 17de en 18de Eeuw", in Marie Antoinette Petronella Meilink-Roelofsz (ed.), *De VOC in Azi'*, Bussum: Fibula-Van Dishoeck, 1976, p. 85.

[5]Pieter van Dam, *Beschryvinge van de Oostindische Compagnie*, F.W. Stapel (ed.) (RGP), Grote serie nr. 76, The Hague: Martinus Nijhoff, 1932, p. 296.

[6]*Ibid.*, p. 321.

[7]A. Sreedhara Menon, *A Survey of Kerala History*, Kottayam/ Trivandrum: C.M.S. Press and St. Joseph's Press, 1967, p. 225.

[8]*Ibid.*, K.M. Panikkar, *Malabar and the Portuguese. Being a History of the Relations of the Portuguese with Malabar from 1500 to 1663*, Bombay: D.B. Taraporevala Sons & Co., 1931, p. 206.

[9]'s Jacob, *op.cit.*, pp. 5-6. For the monopoly treaties with the various native rulers, see: Jan Ernst Heeres (ed.), *Corpus Diplomaticum Neerlando-Indicum II*, The Hague: Martinus Nijhoff, 1931, *passim*.

[10]For the financial results of Malabar between 1661-62 and 1793-94, see: George D. Winius and Marcus P.M. Vink, *The Merchant-Warrior Pacified. The VOC (The Dutch East India Company) and its Changing Political Economy in India*, New Delhi: Oxford University Press, 1990, pp. 169-72.

[11]"Memorandum of Commander Godske to his successor Lucas van der Dussen and Council of Malabar, 5.1.1668", In 's Jacob, *De Nederlanders in Kerala*, p. 51.

[12]"Memorandum Van Reede, 14.3.1677", In :'s Jacob *op.cit.*, pp. 182-4.

[13]"Annotations on the Memorandum of Van Reede by Commissioner and Commander Huijsman and Council of Malabar to the Governor-General and Council, 28.6.1681", in : 's Jacob, *op.cit.*, p. 163; *Memorie door den Afgaanden Commandeur Fredrik Cunes aan desselfs Vervanger den Weledelen Heer, Aankomende Commanderur Casparus de Jong, overgegeven de dato laatsten December 1756* (Selections from the Records of the Madras Government, Dutch records no. 3), Madras: Government Press, 1908, p. 2; K.P. Padmanabha Menon, *History of Kerala. A History of Kerala written in the Form of Notes on Visscher's Letters from Malabar*, New Delhi: Asian Educational Services, 1984, I, p. 364.

[14]Michael Naylor Pearson, *The Portuguese in India* (New Cambridge History of India 1.1), New York/Cambridge, 1987, pp. 44-6; Edward Thornton, *A Gazetteer of the Territories under the Government of the East India Company and of the Native States on the Continent of India*, London:

William H. Allen, 1854, III, p. 376.

[15]Fernand Braudel, *Civilisations Matérielle et Capitaisme (XVe-XVIIIe Siècle) I. Le Possible et l'Impossible: les Hommes face á leur Vie Quotidienne*, Paris: Librairie Armand Colin, 1967, pp. 15-6.

[16]Peter Haggett, *Geography: A Modern Synthesis*, San Francisco: Harper & Row, 1983, p. 15.

[17]Norton Ginsburg (ed.), *The Pattern of Asia*, Englewood Cliffs, N.J.: Prentice-Hall, 1958, pp. 483 et seq; O.H.K. Spate and A.T.A. Learmouth, *India and Pakistan. A General and Regional Biography*, London: Methuen, 3rd ed., 1967, pp. 14 ff.

[18]"Memorandum Van Reede, 14.3.1677", in :'s Jacob, *op.cit.*, p. 158.

[19]F.B. Evans (ed.), *Madras District Gazetteers. Malabar and Anjengo*, Madras: Government Press, 1908, I, pp. 4, 264 et seq; W. Francis (ed.), *Madras District Gazetteers. The Nilgiris*, Madras: Government Press, 1908, I, pp. 1-3, 113, 223, 227, 230-3; W. Francis (ed.), *Madras District Gazetteers. Madura*, Madras: Government Press, 1906, I, pp. 2, 155 and 312; Sreedhara Menon, *A Survey of Kerala History*, p. 5.

[20]*A Gazetteer of the... East India Company*, II, p. 21.

[21]*The Imperial Gazetteer of India*, Oxford: Clarendon Press, new ed., 1908, XIX, p. 358: *A Gazetteer of the... East India Company*, II, p. 2.

[22]The following is largely based on: Spate and Learmouth, *India and Pakistan*, pp. 46-52; Ginsburg, *The Pattern of Asia*, pp. 453-500; *A Gazetteer of the... East India Company*, III; p. 376; *Madras District Gazetteers. Malabar and Anjengo*, I, pp. 223 and 270.

[23]*Madras District Gazetteers. Malabar and Anjengo*, I, p. 223; *Madras District Gazetteers. Tiruchinapalli*, I, p. 20.

[24]*Memorie door den Afgaanden Commandeur Godefridus Weijerman aan desselfs Vervanger den Weledelen Heer Aankomende Commandeur Cornelis Breekpot overgegeven de dato 22 Februarij Ao. 1765 Gecopieerd door den Wel Eerw. Heer P. Groot* (Selections from the Records of the Madras Government—Dutch Records No. 12), Madras: Government Press, 1910, p. 26.

[25]Adolff Bassing, "Eenige Verhalinge van de Voornaamste Coopluijden van Petten off Marten Buijten de Stadt Trichnapallij...", [ff. 14-15], in: James Ford Bell Library, Minneapolis, Minn, B 1738 Mos., Manuscript Papers Relating to Dutch Trade in India, Negapatam, 1738.

[26]A. Galletti, A.J. van der Burg and P. Groot, *The Dutch in Malabar* (Selections from the Records of the Madras Government Dutch Records No. 13), Madras: Government Press, 1911, p. 54.

[27]"Memorandum Van Reede, 14.3.1677", in 's Jacob, p. 192.

[28]Wouter Schouten, *Oost-Indische Voyagie*, Amsterdam: Jacob Meurs and Johannes van Someren, 1676, p. 279.

[29]Philippus Baldaeus, *Naauwkeurige Beschrvvinge van Malabar en Coromandel,* Amsterdam: Jansonius van Waasberge and Johannes van

Someren, 1672, p. 100.

[30]*The Voyage of John Huyghen van Linschoten*, II, p. 49.

[31]*A Gazetteer of the East India Company*, III, p. 379; *Madras District Gazetteers. Malabar and Anjengo*, p. 223; "Annotations on the Memorandum of Van Reede by Commissioner and Commander Huijsman, 18.6.1681", in :'s Jacob, *op.cit.*, p. 163.

[32]*The Voyage of John Huyghen van Linschoten*, II, p. 43.

[33]Padmanabha Menon, *History of Kerala*, II, p. 123; Panikkar, Malabar and the Portuguese, p. 15; *A Gazetteer of the East India Company*, III, p. 376.

[34]Baldaeus, *Naauwkeurige Beschrvvinge van Malabar en Coromandel*, p. 99.

[35]*A Gazetteer of the East India Company*, III, p. 376.

[36]"Memorandum Moens, 18.4.1781", in Galletti, Van der Burg and Groot, *op. cit.*, p. 215.

[37]*A Gazetteer of the East India Company*, III, p. 379.

[38]*The Voyage of John Huyghen van Linschoten*, II, p. 77.

[39]"Memorandum Van Reede, 14.3.1677", in :'s Jacob, *op.cit.*, p. 156. Van Reede's data have been supplemented by those given in the "Memorandum of Moens, 18.4.1781", in: Galletti, Van der Burg and Groot, *op.cit.*, p. 53 ff.

[40]Célestin Bouglé, *Essais sur le Régime des Castes*, Paris: Presses Universitaires de France, 4th ed., 1969, p. 3.

[41]Louis Dumont and David Francis Pocock, "Commented Summary of the First Part of Bouglé's Essais", in: *Contributions to Indian Sociology* 2, 1958, p. 52. See, for instance Nieuhof's comments on the eating habits of the 'tribes' in Malabar. Nieuhof, *Zee-en Landt-Reize*, p. 144.

[42]Visscher, *Mallabaarsche Brieven* in: Padmanabha Menon, *op.cit.*, III, p. 9.

[43]"Memorandum Van Reede, 14.3.1677", in: 's Jacob, *op.cit.*, p. 98.

[44]'s Jacob, *op.cit.*, p. xxvi; Panikkar, *op.cit.*, p. 20. In March 1677, Commander Van Reede estimated the total number of Nayars at a minimum of one and a half million. Although one should not attach too much faith to the accuracy of these figures, they do, however, indicate how many Nayars every *nad*, or group of hamlets, had to deliver in times of war. "Memorandum Van Reede, 14.3.1677", in: 's Jacob, *op.cit.*, pp. 90-6.

[45]Brown, *The Indian Christians of St. Thomas*, pp. 3-4, 81 and 173.

[46]Visscher, *Mallabaarsche Brieven*, in: Padmanabha Menon, *op.cit.*, II, p. 42. See also: "Memorandum Moens, 18.4.1781", in: Galletti, Van der Burg and Groot, *op.cit.*, p. 171.

[47]Brown, *op.cit.*, pp. 2, 15, 36, 93, 121 and 176; Padmanabha Menon, *op.cit.*, III, p. 421.

[48]"Memorandum Van Reede, 14.3.1677", in: 's Jacob, *op.cit.*, p. 164.

[49]"Memorandum Godske, 5.1.1668", in 's Jacob, *op.cit.*, p. 49; "Annotations to the memorandum of Van Reede by Huijsman, 28.6.1681",

in idem, p. 165; "Memorandum of Commissioner Hendrik Zwaardecroon to Commander Magnus Wichelman and Council of Malabar, 31.5.1698" in *idem*, p. 291.

[50]Visscher, *Malabaarsche Brieven.* in Padmanabha Menon, *op.cit.*, II, p. 43.

[51]*Idem*, III, pp. 332, 423 and 476-7.

[52]*The Voyage of John Huyghen van Linschoten*, I, p. 282.

[53]*Madras District Gazetteers.* Madura, pp. 54-5 and 154; *Madras District Gazetteers. Malabar and Anjengo*, p. 264.

[54]*Madras District Gazetteers. Tinnevelly*, pp. 240-1.

[55]Visscher, Mallabaarsche Brieven. in Padmanabha Menon, *op.cit.*, III, p. 3.

[56]Adolff Bassing, "Eenige Verhalinge...", [f.5]; Pearson, *Malabar and the Portuguese*, p. 47; 's Jacob, *op.cit.*, p. 206, n. 47.

[57]Krishna Ayyar, *A Short History of Kerala*, p. 88; Panikkar, *op.cit.*, p. 96; Padmanabha Menon, *op.cit.*, I, p. 287; Adolff Bassing, "Beschrijvinge van den Oorspronk der Nayken van Madura...", [ff. 4-5], in James Ford Bell Library, Minneapolis, Minn, B 1738 Mos., Manuscript Papers relating to Dutch Trade in India, Negapatam, 1738.

[58]Jean-Baptiste Tavernier, *The Six Voyages of John Baptiste Tavernier through Turkey into Persia, and the East Indies. Travels in India*, London: R.L. and Moses Pitt, 1678, pp. 27-8.

[59]Bassing, "Eenige Verhalinge...", [ff. 9-10].

[60]*The Imperial Gazetteer of India*, XVI, p. 299; *Madras District Gazetteers. Tinnevelly*, p. 216.

[61]Bassing, "Eenige Verhalinge...", [ff. 6-7, 20].

[62]"Memorandum Stein van Gollenesse, 1743" in Galletti, Van der Burg, and Groot, *op.cit.*, p. 57.

[63]"Memorandum Van Reede, 14.3.1677" in 's Jacob, *op.cit.*, p. 160.

[64]"Memorandum Godske, 5.1.1668" in *idem*, p. 49; an almost identical (copied?) line of argument can be found in, Van Dam, *Beschryvinge van de Oostindische Compagnie*, p. 291.

[65]See, for example "Memorandum Godske, 5.1.1668" in 's Jacob, *op.cit.*, p. 50.

[66]According to legend, the Perumals or rulers were elected for a twelve-year period by the Nambuthiris from the adjoining countries of Cola, Pandya and Cera. All in all, there were reputed to have been twenty-five of them between A.D. 216 and 825. The legend is probably a euphemistic reform of recording the conquest and subjugation of Malabar by the Cera, Cola and Pandyan kings.

[67]"Memorandum Stein van Gollenesse, 1743" in Galletti, Van der Burg and Groot, *op.cit.*, pp. 51-2. Compare with: "Memorandum Van Reede, 14.3.1677" in 's Jacob, *op.cit.*, p. 160.

[68]M.A.P. Meilink-Roelofsz, "The Structures of Trade in Asia in the

Sixteenth and Seventeenth Centuries. Niels Steensgaard's 'Carracks, Caravans and Companies'. The Asian Trade Revolutions. A Critical Appraisal", in *Mare Luso-Indicum* 4, 1980, pp. 23 and 39-40. For a discussion of the Steensgaard-Meilink-Roelofsz controversy and the Dutch policy in Malacca, see: Marcus Vink, "Passes and Protection Rights. The Dutch East India Company as A Redistributive Enterprise in Malacca, 1641-1662", in *Moyen Orient and Ocean Indien (Middle East and Indian Ocean) xvie-xix* S, 7, 1990, pp. 73-101.

[69]"Memorandum Godske, 5.1.1668" in 's Jacob, *op.cit.*, p. 53.

[70]"Instruction Commissioner Van Reede, 23.11.1691", in *idem*, p. 236.

[71]Algemeen Rijksarchief (ARA) The Hague, Archief VOC, f. 345v, Missive Gentlemen Seventeen to the Governor-General and Council in Batavia, 8.10.1654.

[72]"Memorandum Stein van Gollenesse, 1743", in Galletti, Van der Burg and Groot, *op.cit.*, p. 72.

[73]Winius and Vink, *The Merchant-Warrior Pacified,* pp. 143, 145-6.

[74]K.M. Panikkar, *Malabar and the Dutch. Being the History of the Fall of Nayar Power in Malabar*, Bombay: D.B. Taraporevala Sons & Co., 1931, p. 118.

[75]ARA, VOC 2834, OBP 1755, fls, 30-37, Peace concluded with Travancore, 15.8.1753. See also: T.I. Poonen, *Dutch Hegemony in Malabar*, p. 117.

[76]Johan Splinter Stavorinus, *Reize van Zeeland over de Kaap de Goede Hoop en Batavia naar Samarang, Macasser, Amboina, Suratte, enz. ...2nd Part, Eerste Boek,* Leiden: A. and J. Honkoop 1798, pp. 205-6.

[77]O.C. Kail, *The Dutch in India,* New Delhi: Macmillan, 1981, p. 192.

[78]ARA, 2.01.27, Comité tot de Oost-Indische Handel en Bezittingen, 1791-1800, inv. nr. 58, fls. 189-92, Capitulation of Cochin, 20.10.1795.

THE TRADE ACTIVITIES OF THE BANYANS IN MOZAMBIQUE: PRIVATE INDIAN DYNAMICS IN THE PANEL OF THE PORTUGUESE STATE ECONOMY (1686-1777)

Luis Frederico Dias Antunes

The presence of Asians in East Africa has been recorded from the tenth century. Masoudi (tenth century), Alberuni (A.D. 1030), Al-Idrisi (A.D. 1154), Ibn Battuta (A.D. 1331) and Ibn Al Werdi (fifteenth century) refer to the existence of trade exchange between southern Arabia (Oman) and India and East Africa.

The archaeologist R.W. Dickinson, in explorations done in 1961 and 1972, found various ceramic pieces of the fourteenth-fifteenth centuries, in Sofala and in the estuary of the river Save which did not in any way belong to the Swahili civilisation that at the time predominated the East African coast. This pottery, according to Dickinson, had many similarities with that of the Gulf of Cambay. Authors like Roger Summers admit the possibility of help by Indians in gold mining in the sixth century in present-day Zimbabwe. Summers asserts that there are many technical similarities used in these mines and in South Indian mines, which were abandoned in the fourth century.[1]

Arab and Indian influence made itself felt in East Africa through the introduction of new food plants, such as rice, banana, coconut, mango and citrus trees.

In the art of navigation as well, strong Arab, Indian and even Malayan influences are noted in East Africa. Even today, in Mozambique and in the Bay of Luanga, *caiques* exist. These are boats derived from Indian or Arabian *pangaios,* well known from remote times in the northern and central coasts of Mozambique. Very similar to these are *inchos* or *almadias* which are still found in Cape Delgado. The name comes from Arab *almadia,* which means canoe. Other boats, like the *mutumba* of Port Amelia, *cangaia* of Relampazo and the *cumpulo* of Muendage, have two floats which stabilise the boats, a likely Indonesian influence.[2]

When the Portuguese arrived on the East African coast, they found a network of Arab cities and establishments between Mogadoxo and Sofala, of which the most important were Kilwa, the islands of Querimba, island of Mozambique, Angoche and Sofala, where an intense commercial activity was developed with the Sultanate of Oman and Cambay. The importance of these cities and coastal establishments, normally built on the seaside or a river valley easily accessible from the interior, was in the facility of trade exchanges with the natives. The trade consisted in the exchange of varieties of cotton cloth from Cambay, and beads for the ivory, slaves and gold of Sofala, and for amber, wax and resin. Several Portuguese records attest that Islam was predominant in the East African coast and that the exports from Cambay to the region comprised, for a long time, items preferred by Muslims.

In 1505, D. Francisco de Almeida, the first Viceroy of India, passed the Regulations (Regimento) in order to boost the trade between the East African coast and Cambay. The Regulations said that the goods from Cambay "are very advantageous to Sofala" and so the trade contacts with it needed to be reinforced.[3] In 1508 Duarte Lemos wrote to the King that Sofala "wanted only pieces of cloth from Cambay and beads from Milinde". Every year, he wrote, Indian ships arrived at Angoche loaded with about 100,000 pieces of cloth from Cambay in exchange for ivory and gold.[4] Duarte Barbosa, in 1516, explained well how trade was conducted between the East African coast and Cambay, mentioning in detail the areas, the traders and the products.

Commercial activity in Mozambique thrived after the Portuguese arrived, with a vast commercial network along the East African coast up to Oman and Cambay. Commercial activity developed according to the nature of the monsoon, in a triangle that had its vertices in Sofala, Oman and Cambay.

In the closing years of the eighteenth century, however, the Portuguese State of India was in unmistakable administrative and economic decline. The hope of redemption was seen only in the economic prospect of the port of Diu, the rivers of Cuama and the fortress of Mombasa. Diu was seen as a possible source of redemption not only because it was a good port situated in the textile area of Cambay, which was the central producer of a great variety of cloths very much in demand in East Africa but also because it boasted of the dynamic presence of the Banyan merchants, who showed a capacity to enlarge their commercial activities and had adequate experience and capital.

The counterparts of Diu, which had the capacity to reactivate the commerce on the other side of the Indian Ocean, were the rivers of Cuama and the Mombasa fort. The rivers of Cuama were an area rich in gold and ivory; Mombasa had a harbour to export ivory and a fortress which guaranteed security on the coast between the Querimba islands and the Lamu archipelago. The picture of abundance and wealth in the rivers of Cuama and the economic potential of Mozambique, described for us in the middle seventeenth century, is so eloquent and graphic that perhaps it was a deliberate exaggeration meant to influence, decisively, the thinking of the Crown about solving, through the creation of the Banyan Trade Company of Diu, the commerical crisis that the Portuguese Empire was facing.

THE BANYANS IN MOZAMBIQUE (1686-1700)

The founding of the Banyan Trade Company of Diu, in 1686, opened the way to a new style of trade administration between Gujarat and the East African coast. Its main achievement was to accumulate substantial capital in the Mozambican markets. Until then, external trade between India and East Africa were the exclusive monopoly of the Governors of the several Portuguese coastal settlements in India. Mozambique's internal trade was decided by the administration in the colony. If trade was the monopoly of the Crown, it was in the hands of the Board of Trade of Mozambique and rivers; if more liberal, it was conceded to the Governor of Mozambique by contract. If trade was open, any subject of the Crown could participate in it.

The Banyans' trade practices, on the other hand, were oriented towards maintaining their commercial monopoly on the basis of market forces and a position of privilege. Part of their expertise was in efficient market administration. In Gujarat textiles, they had expert knowledge of the commercial value of different varieties, their availability, a hard head for costs and benefits, and a thorough grasp of banking practices. They dabbled in politics only to the extent that it served their economic quest, bribing several economic agents, public and private, and plotting with the power brokers to manipulate the administration to suit their interests.

When, in the last quarter of the seventeenth century, the Portuguese authorities made the Banyans sole concessionaires to trade in East Africa, both external and internal, they founded the Banyan Trade Company. The Banyans had been, throughout, striving to attain such a monopoly. This would help them reap huge returns in terms of reduced freight, reduced wages to the crew, and from price differentials of various commodities (cloths, beads, food, ivory, gold and slaves) in the different markets.

When the Count of Alvor gave the Banyans of Diu monopoly only over the so called "ship of Mozambique", the head of the Banyans, representing the shareholders of the Company, added the demand that they should be allowed larger participation in the trade circuits of the East African coast. Under the protection of the Jesuits, the Banyans, particularly the contractors of the Mozambique voyages, managed to obtain more prerogatives, such as: custom rights as enjoyed by the Portuguese rulers of Diu; non-interference by the Portuguese administration in their production activity of "bertangil" cloth, particularly from the tax collector of indigo; freedom to choose their crew; freedom to choose their freight; prohibition on non-members of the Company from transporting in the ships more butter, oil, wheat and beads than those loaded by members; compulsion of immediate payment for merchandise bought from them, so that they were not strapped for finances, and preference of clearance and repair of their ships.[5]

In January and February, during the winter monsoon, representatives of the bigger shareholders of the Company, together with other Banyans, as servants and cooks, and a crew mainly composed of *lascars* of Muslim origin, left the Portuguese settlements of Diu, Chaul and Damâo for Mozambique, in boats laden with all kinds of goods (cloths, beads, etc.). On arriving at Mozambique, they bought and rented warehouses and shops and started operating the business of the *mahajan* of Diu and Cambay.

Security of the Banyans' investment in their cargo was assured since the Governor of Mozambique and the Royal Treasury were bound to buy it. Part of the shipment of textiles was despatched to the account of the Governor on credit. In exchange, he was obliged to buy a fixed amount of cloth on the account of the Royal Treasury. The Banyans were also assured continuous access to credit, thus virtually subordinating the Portuguese administration to the economic interests of the Banyans. The Banyans also transported, on their own account, a significant amount of cloth and beads. Part of it was sold, for huge profits, in Mozambique; the rest was shipped for trade in secondary ports of the colony.

The Crown had instituted the system of a price list to protect its own interests. This price list was to act as a guide list to regulate the Mozambique market. But the Banyans and the local Portuguese bureaucracy seems to have exploited it to deplete the Royal Treasury and line their own pockets. Under the prevailing arrangement, the Crown was bound to buy cloth from the Banyans. The price to be paid for each "*corja*" of cloth (twenty pieces of cloth) was fixed after meetings and debates in the custom house in the presence of the Governor of the settlement, all the customs officers, the merchants and the captain of the crew of the Banyans. It was natural that the legal prices, determined in a meeting where the only people present were those with private interests in commerce, and those who owned large quantities of cloth to sell to the Royal Treasury, were high. After seeing to the portion of cloth to be sold to the Royal Treasury, the merchants agreed among themselves to lower the prices of the goods only to the extent that they would make a handsome profit on their sale of cloth to the natives but not drive up the prices of ivory and gold inordinately.[6]

In the prevailing conditions of liberal trade in the rivers of Cuama, the Banyans, the 'canarins' and other small Asian and Portuguese merchants flooded the market with cloth, pushing prices to rock bottom, but increasing the price of gold (by about fifty per cent) and that of ivory. All, and "mainly the natives of India" entered the river region in search of gold and ivory, bypassing fairs where prices used to be fixed, to make quick profits.[7] In the face of rising demand and short supply, large quantities of fake gold and ivory of doubtful quality began to be circulated.[8] Before things got too far out of hand, the government closed the rivers to trade. It is probable that this closing of the rivers to trade, between 1690 and 1694, curtailed the Banyans' activities in Mozambique. The scanty information available about their presence in this period appears to confirm this supposition. The government had, by now, acquired better control of the situation. Generalised smuggling was now under better control, curbs on trade in the river region had raised the prices, and custom taxes had enabled better control of movements in the ports. While this increased the income of the Crown, in the same measure it depleted the profits of the Banyan merchants.

In 1691, the Banyans threatened to cease trade with Mozambique because the dealers in gold and ivory bought these cheap from the Banyans and sold them for a disproportionate profit. The Overseas Council (Conselho Ultramarino) then intervened, but not to the advantage of the Banyans. Since free trade was the norm, it said, the matter was entirely between the Banyans and the dealers. The Council also suggested that the Royal Administration should, in all business affairs with the Banyans, deal as on an entirely private basis.[9] The result of this intervention was that while the Banyans suffered a loss of income, the gross income of the Royal Treasury, obtained from the Banyans' contract for Mozambique, was, between March 1691 and March 1695, 152,334 xerafins, 4 tangas and 44 reis—not a discouraging figure.[10] The income would have been even larger, had not the war with Changamira, which was at its height in 1694 and 1695, impeded the collection of a large part of the revenue.[11] Much of this income came from the dealers in Mozambique—about twenty-nine per cent, while income from the dealers of Sena was only nine per cent; income from the dealers at Sofala did not even reach one per cent.[12]

The Banyans were, indeed, having a hard time of it. Because of the boycott by the Portuguese, between 1693 and 1695, they could recover only about 17.4 per cent of the 40,139 xerafins invested in 1694 on the purchase of cloth.[13]

Worse was to follow. In 1695, the General Company of the Commerce of India was founded. Its General Board decided, as a means of rapidly making up its capital, to lower, outside the market laws, the price of cloth by about one-third of the real value. By this means, the Company meant to keep the profits which had been going to the Banyans. In addition, payment for this cloth was to be made by means of promissory notes, and not in ivory or gold. With this measure, the Banyans suffered a total loss of about 20,000 xerafins.[14]

The Banyans then retaliated. The Banyans' three-year contract, worth 6,662 xerafins, 3 tangas and 20 reis for voyages to Mozambique, which limited the kind of items they could transport to the East African coast, had expired. But the Banyans sent their ship to Mozambique loaded with all sorts of merchandise.[15] They calculated, perhaps, that if the merchandise was placed in the market, the sale proceeds would cover the risk; and even if things fared badly, they would gain in other ways.

Hardly had the ship, chartered by Xama Ricabo and Mado Hargy, touched the island, when it was raided and all its cloth forcibly acquired at the prices ruling at Cambay. This loss, resulting from the difference in price and non-recovery of the expenses of transport, the Banyans had been prepared for.[16] As they had calculated, when this merchandise flooded the market, it ruined the Portuguese competition.[17] Compounding the Banyans' calculated move was the inability of the Portuguese to concentrate on economic matters, because of the political difficulties they were having in the last decade of the seventeenth century, such as the war in the rivers, attack by the Arabs of Oman on Mozambique and the loss of Mombasa. Prices, which since 1691 had been on the upswing, fell dangerously, while the prices of gold and ivory rose.

This was a premediated disrespect by the Banyans to elementary market laws. At a time when there were signs that commerce was slowing down, and it was necessary to curtail supply, the Banyans did exactly the opposite, as a challenge to the General Company of Commerce of India, which aimed for a monopoly of the markets. The Banyans also played coy when the Company asked them to be its shareholders. To the several solicitations, the Banyans of Diu regularly responded with promises of heavy funds but letting the matter rest there. While the Banyans of Diu promised to invest 80,000 xerafins, their clan in Goa, Damâo and Chaul remained silent.[18] But not wishing to dare the Portuguese authorities openly, the Banyans played the game of symbolic gestures. After much insistence by the Portuguese authorities, the Banyans Vitula Comoty, Deudas Gandy and Aria Parbu, in the name of all Banyans residing in Portuguese India, invested about 161,463 xerafins, a ridiculous amount considering their financial capacities. The amount offered was about 18.7 per cent of the initial capital of the Company.[19] The dissolution of the Company in 1698 closed the first phase of the Banyan presence in Mozambique.

DOMINATION OF COASTAL COMMERCIAL ROUTES: THE BEGINNING OF THE EXPANSION OF THE BANYAN MERCANTILE CAPITAL (1701-22)

The period 1701-22 marked the beginning of the Banyans' attempt to dominate the commercial flow of Mozambique with the secondary ports of the colony, namely, Inhambane and Angoche.

At the end of 1699, the Board of Commerce was re-formed with the intent to try to limit, even more firmly, all possibility of introducing goods in the rivers.[20] Yet ironically, though commercial activity on the rivers of Cuama came down a great deal, there was no one, not even the Dominican priests, who "entered the rivers poor and did not leave rich.".[21] On the Swahili coast, north of Cape Delgado, Arab boats freely navigated and dealt in ivory and amber.[22]

To recover from the relative economic failure of the General Company and restore the confidence of the Banyan merchants, the Board of Commerce sought to restrict the smuggling activities of the customs officers, by paying them in cash rather than cloth, paying them promptly, and fulfilling promptly commercial obligations, including the settlement of old debts and payment for cloth sent from Cambay.

The curbs on the commercial activities of customs officers, which reduced competition for Banyan activities, restored in them enough confidence to resume their trade with Mozambique.[23] The fall of Mombasa and Kilwa, in 1698, to the Arabs of Oman, was also a turning point. Until then, the people north of Zambezi, particularly the Yao, used to take ivory and slaves from the remote interior to the coastal cities. But with the change of rule, this market gradually closed down. From 1702, the relationship between the Arabs of Oman and the African merchants of Mombasa and Kilwa cooled, and this market was strangulated.[24] According to Alpers, the direction of trade turned towards Mozambique at the beginning of the eighteenth century, not only because the ports of Kilwa and Mombasa were abandoned, but also because the Arabs failed to provide these ports with regular supplies of cloth and glass beads to attract merchants in the hinterland of Africa.[25]

Mozambique, which had good contacts with other coastal communities of the East African coast and with India, then became an attractive alternative to trade with the ports on the Swahili coast, benefiting the Banyan merchants, who were there in an appreciable number. In 1706, Soirea Sinai, Vitula Cammotim, Aria Purbu, Arba Sinay, Vitogy Sinay and Santoja were some of the Banyans who immensely benefited from the commercial activities in Mozambique. They were enough comfortably placed that they could raise a loan of 100,000 xerafins "to conquer the island of Timor".[26] Also, trade between Diu and Mozambique should have been profitable enough not to discourage the Banyans Macandagi Sacar, Pacavar Pareca and Valabo Gocal, contractors of Diu, with the loss of their ships with cargo by sinking, in 1702 and 1703; not only did they maintain their trade with Mozambique, but tried to acquire one more cargo ship from the Royal Treasury.[27]

Unfortunately for the Portuguese Crown, it did not have sufficient economic clout to control market movements. This it sought to achieve by resort to legal means. But the officials of the Board of Commerce and the Banyan merchants made sure that their private interests prevailed against those of the Crown.

Thus it was that, in 1700, the Board lowered the price of ivory sold in Mozambique to 550 cruzados, lower by 50, 150 and even 250 cruzados to its current prices on land. In 1721, the price difference actually increased to 300 cruzados![28] Such price differentials were justified as a weapon against smuggling by the residents of Mozambique, in Makuana, and as being for the benefit of the Crown by reducing the price of cloth. In reality, the interest of the Board was a more private one. By this means, the members sought to obtain good quality cloth cheaper and in larger quantities than those acquired for the Royal Treasury, to later sell these, in Sena, at higher prices. The small quantity of ivory entering Mozambique and the heavy demand of the Indian merchants for it, who tried to obtain it by any means, gave a fillip to the smugglers' market.

With these underhand dealings, the loss to the Crown was tripled over the years. It lost in the obvious difference in the prices of ivory; it lost because it could not realise profits on the meagre quantities of cloth which arrived in Sena in a bad state; and it lost because the smuggling could not be prevented.

The Banyans, in contrast, benefited all round. They benefited from the huge price difference of cloth and ivory in the Indian and African markets. They also profited because they were paid in gold.[29] Unlike ivory, which was a fragile product, perishable and subject to great price fluctuations, gold did not depreciate in value with time.

An indication of the growing power of the Banyans in Mozambique in this period was the leasing by them of various Mozambican ports. Calcanagi Valabo, for example, leased for three years, the ports of Inhambane and Angoche, for 11,000 cruzados each, which took away their commercial control from the Royal Treasury. With these leases, the Banyans could resell to these ports the cloth found in the bazaars of Mozambique, and purchase ivory and gold outside the tight limits of the administration of Mozambique.

In 1722, Baxira Mocaly bid for the lease of the Mozambican market against Valabo. Mocaly was the favourite of the Board of Commerce, and Valabo was preferred by the Governor. Baxira won the lease. It may be noted that the bidding was limited to Indian mercantile capital, Baxira being a Muslim hailing from India, who had come to Mozambique with the son-in-law of his boss, probably a Banyan.[30]

Ironically, the King had prohibited the lease of Angoche and Quelimane, and of the Mozambique settlement, to non-Catholics. But the orders came too late.

The weak structure of Portuguese commerce, with its incapacity to accumulate and reinvest capital in Mozambique, was partly on account of the mode the Crown adopted to govern the colony. It was an economic and social pattern heavily dependent on State protection. Every Portuguese was a Crown officer in this system, paid mostly in cloth. The social hierarchy determined everyone's standing in commerce. Evading the customs, defrauding the State, was the norm. The Banayans, frequently despised and oppressed for their religious beliefs, were another community, apart from the Portuguese in the colony, who maintained close economic ties with the Crown.

Smuggling, an important feature of the parallel economy, was an important activity for everyone, particularly the Banyans. Smuggling plagued every administrative and political hierarchy of Mozambique. As the Board of Commerce pointed out in 1722:[31]

> All who go to that port of Mozambique, from the castellan, or superintendent till the smallest lascar came from there rich, each bringing considerable fortunes, according to the positions they held, which shows it was not only superintendents, factors and other officials, but also private, and religious people who all returned with large fortunes.

Smuggling was intimately connected with the geographic diversification of the Banyan mercantile capital. An old necessity, now stimulated by the action of the Banyans, the smuggling was, in great part, effected by the poor of Mozambique, who used as a cover the prerogative to trade with Makuana. A great part of the ivory which left Makuana was not from this region, but from Sofala, Sena and

Quelimane. The tusks from the ships were transhipped before arriving in Mozambique, at various points of the coast, such as Mongincual and Angoche, and also at land points. At times, the smuggling became so pervasive that the Crown found its revenue slashed by over forty per cent in entry duties and freight duty. Mozambicans put together the smuggled ivory with the little amount of legally acquired ivory and sold it at below market prices. The existence of smuggling, within the limits of tolerance, was implicitly accepted since the Portuguese writ did not run in the Mossuril and the Cabaceiras.[32] Smuggling also took place on a large scale in the interior, on voyages to secondary ports of the East African coast and en route to India. This phenomenon was confined mostly to the lascars and other Muslims, who made up the greater part of the ships' crew.[33]

Members of the Board of Commerce found another way of defrauding the Treasury under cover of commercial monopoly. They acquired, on behalf of the Royal Treasury, more cloth than needed at below market prices, dumped it for a long time in the warehouses, and sold it as new for high profits.[34] Not surprisingly, between 1710 and 1718, the Mozambique settlement incurred heavy debts to the Banyan merchants of Diu, totalling 223,122 cruzados, not counting old debts, all for cloth acquired and not paid for.[35]

Pilferage was another problem. When the huge loads of ivory acquired on the way finally arrived at Mozambique, they were not even enough to load the small ship *S. Tiago*; nor could they pay for the rice to be loaded in exchange, without which the dealer of Sena could not carry on the trade.[36]

Feeling himself out of his depth, the Viceroy, D. Filipe de Meneses, lamented "that the orders ... sent to Mozambique and the rivers, were not obeyed, no matter how correct they were".[37] For better control, from 1720, the ships from Mozambique, Diu and Damâo were forced to take copies of registers of cloth and ivory that they transported; the customs officer was similarly expected to send lists to the Rector of the Jesuit College of Mozambique.[38] For internal commerce, the Viceroy dissolved the Board of Commerce and leased the monopoly to the Governor of Mozambique, just like "mercê de Sofala".[39]

This change lasted hardly two years. In 1722, the Board of Commerce was again reinstated.[40]

PASSAGE TO THE HINTERLAND AND COMMERCE WITH THE MAKUAS AND THE YAO: CONSOLIDATION OF BANYAN MERCANTILE CAPITAL (1723-70)

The period 1723-70 saw the progressive consolidation of Banyan mercantile capital in Mozambique's economy. The Banyans, Hindus and Muslims, having gained control of the coastal trade, attached themselves to the hinterland and by establishing solid commercial relations with the Swahilis, Makuas and Yao, extended their influence to Makuana and to the routes which conducted the commerce with the interior in the north up to Niassa. This they did by strengthening the connection between mercantile Baynan capital and Portuguese political power and economy, by the general use of credit and usury and by their hold on trade of goods much in demand, such as cloth, beads, ivory and slaves. The Banyans also actively struggled against the commercial economy which the Portuguese wished to establish with the Makuas and Yao.

The foundation of the good relations between the Banyans and Swahili was the Banyans' secular and non-racial outlook and the harmonious collaboration between Hindus and Muslims in Diu which was reflected on the African shores as well.[11] The relations between Banyans and Africans were in fact better than the Africans' relations with the Portuguese. The Makua chiefs "respected the gentiles (Banyans) with more attention than the Portuguese". Some Banyans not only lived among the Africans in the villages but also took the native women as concubines.[12]

In 1723, the Portuguese administration granted to the Muslim Indian Baxira Mucali the privilege to establish himself in the continent and be escorted by armed lascars. He was motivated to invest in extensive palm groves and construction and repair of housing both in the coastal areas and the hinterland. Two Banyan workers, probably carpenters, attended to the repairs of houses. Baxira had endeared himself to the Royal Treasury by offering always "with all his wealth to assist in payment in the settlement".[13] Similar prerogatives were conceded, in 1727, to Ahmed Souly, Caliangi Valabo and other Banyans. The intention was that they could attract the capital of rich Indian merchants to Mozambique.[14]

It was not always a love relationship. The Portuguese had to pamper to the Banyans, knowing well that they could in no way compete commercially with the Banyans, which also brought in an element of suppressed hostility. The Portuguese resented the fact that they were completely dependent on the Banyans' presence for generating greater customs revenue which sustained the garrisons. Without the Banyans, there was no way of paying the salaries of the administrative and military personnel.

This resentment showed itself, for example, in the severe accusations against Baxira Mucali by the Portuguese residents of Mozambique. The year after the Governor Alvaro Caetano de Melo (1721-23) left, Mucali, who had enjoyed special favours of the Governor, was accused of enriching himself with the undue advantages granted by the Governor and of other irregularities. It was said that, supported by various orders from Goa, Mucali took advantage of his position as financier of the settlement of Mozambique to negotiate cloth prohibited in the closed ports, to acquire many slaves, to speculate in seized properties, to collect ivory of the best quality, usury and price monopoly.[15]

There must have been an element of truth in these accusations. For though the deliveries of ivory sent from Sena to Mozambique between 1717 and 1727 showed a recovery to the previous levels of dispatches of ivory, in the period 1721-22 the lowest quantities of ivory were registered.[16] The cause was said to be Caetano de Mello's smuggling of ivory in league with the Banyans. In 1721, the Governor concealed the cargo of his cloth in the hold of the ship, which produced a profit of eighty-three ivory tusks. The following year, he forced the ivory warehouses of the Royal Treasury to be opened and hid hundreds of tusks in Calinagi Valabo's house. If anyone dared to oppose him, he pursued them relentlessly, stopped their ships and had them robbed by customs officers on the pretext of inspecting the cargo.[17] Between 1723 and 1730, the deliveries of ivory from the rivers increased slightly, reflecting a slack in smuggling.

In 1727, the position of the Royal Treasury improved at least to the extent that it could pay off part of the old debts to the merchants, to keep them interested in continuing business dealings in Mozambique. Of the twelve creditors considered, four were Banyans and the rest Portuguese. But while the total loan outstanding from the Portuguese was about 55,000 cruzados, the value settled with the Banyans was 240,080 cruzados, almost five times the former.[18]

Looking for financial alternatives, the principal preoccupation of the Royal Administration was to enhance income from customs. The success of coastal and overseas navigation, the smuggling, the robberies and the diminution in the quantity of goods traded brought down the income.[49] The administration was closely dependent on the volume of goods transacted by the Banyans for its customs income. Thus, between 1724 and 1727, income from customs from the entry of five ships from India laden with cloth and other goods doubled over the previous years.[50]

In 1744, coinciding with the dissolution of the Board of Commerce of Mozambique, urgent consultations were held to restructure and improve the administration and economy. About fifty reports appeared on the subject, all of them pointing to the need for strengthening the customs positions. Monopoly on commerce, tax increase on goods most in demand in the trade with India and reduction of warehouse charges and freight were some of the measures suggested, and later implemented by Francisco de Mello de Castro.[51]

Mozambique's income from customs grew between 1754 and 1756. Making a decisive difference to the tax collection was a payment of 77,796 cruzados for the entry of cloth from Cambay and the export of ivory, mats, rhino horns and slaves. The tax, paid by the Banyans of Diu and Damão, was about fifty-eight per cent of the total customs taxes.[52]

The Banyans, who had a monopoly of the cloth trade, became a strong pillar of Mozambique's economic activity. Their credit activities supported an extensive commercial chain that linked Goa, Damão and Diu to the East African coast. The goods which the Indian merchants transported in ships, which annually docked in Mozambique, were exchanged for ivory.

The cloth had two destinations. One part was supplied, at credit, by the Royal Treasury to the different dealers of the secondary ports. These kept a part for payment of salaries and delivered the other part, on loan, to private merchants who ventured in the commerce of the rivers. Business risk was great and the results were known in India, the starting point of the chain, only three years later. Any merchant who ventured to negotiate the cloth on consignment in the interior without sufficient funds to meet business failure, faced bankruptcy.

The other part of the cloth was transacted in the island by the Banyans, who controlled the entire wholesale commerce. They charged higher prices from the Portuguese than from fellow Indians or Swahili merchants, who only transacted retail commerce. The

Portuguese merchants were, therefore, obliged to sell the cloth to the Africans at the current market price. The Banyans, on the other hand, could negotiate at much reduced prices, without unduly sacrificing on profit. For the Portuguese merchants the inevitable result was debt, which made them uneasy about renouncing their possessions of land, houses, palm groves, cattle and slaves in favour of the Banyans.[53]

A look into the accounts of the General Board of Commerce between 1716 and 1745 gives a glimpse of the Banyans' financial power. About sixty-one per cent of all the individuals who loaned money to the Board were Banyans, the merchants of Diu and Damão. Seventy-seven per cent of those indebted referred to debts to the Banyans. The Banyans' loan practices pointed to usury. From loans granted to the Board they earned an income of about eighty-eight per cent of the loan amount.

The total debt to the Indian merchants of Diu and Damão, which was four times above the debt of the Portuguese merchants, would be more voluminous. Unfortunately, the relevant documentation was concealed and purposely destroyed.[54] We know, however, that the debts of the Royal Treasury to the Banyan merchants of Diu, between 1700 and 1718, were about 223,123 cruzados.[55]

In middle eighteenth century, the Banyans' debt situation seems to have worsened. Deuchande Seuchande, the Procurator of the Mahajan community of Diu in the fortress of Mozambique accused the dealers of Sena, Sofala and Inhambane of crooked dealings. He demanded an investigation of the account books to verify all the debts of the dealers.[56] The debt figure in 1745 amounted to 300,443 cruzados and 245 reis; in 1754 it increased to 75,214 cruzados and 30 reis.[57]

The importance of the economic intervention of the Banyans in East Africa was especially felt in terms of the products they dealt in. All kinds of cloth from Cambay and Surat, and beads from Balagate and from Portugal, constituted a base of commerce with the Africans. In the rivers of Cuama and in Inhambane these products were the current exchange, and in the Mozambique they were the main products in commercial relations with Makuas and Yao. In the mid-eighteenth century, when the Mozambique trade was Crown monopoly, the consumption of Indian cloth was about 350 to 400 bars, equivalent to 120,000 to 160,000 pieces of cloth per year. The volume of business doubled when free commerce prevailed.[58] The acquisition of Indian cloth was a way of accumulating wealth, in association with the acquisition of women.[59] Dependence on this prestige item for social prestige also made the Africans dependent on those who had the commercial means to supply and deal in it. To reduce this dependence, the Africans commenced, from the mid-seventeenth century, local production and sale of 'machiras', roughly woven and much more resistant than the Indian cloth.[60] In 1728, there were "many cotton plantations in the rivers of Sena, where cloth was manufactured which they called machiras". Together with the cloth of Pate, this posed a stiff competition to the Indian cloth and induced grave losses to the Board of Commerce.[61] Cultivation of cotton was prohibited by an order of the Crown, but the order could be implemented only in the 'prazos' of the Crown and did not have any practical effect in the vast lands which were out of the domain of the Crown.[62]

Beads from Balagate were another product in great demand in East Africa. The Mozambique market consumed between 25,000 and 30,000 bundles of beads a year, the greater part of which came from Portugal, originally from Venice. The Portuguese derived their profits from this business only as dealers, and had no control on production and price factors. When the Mozambique trade was the Crown monopoly the price of the bundles varied between 4 cruzados and 300 reis and 5 cruzados and 100 reis. In the regime of free trade this could reach 6 cruzados 200 reis and even 7 cruzados. Apart from negotiating in beads of Balagate, the Banyans sought, in auctions in Mozambique, to stall the supply of beads from Portugal.[63]

Ivory was, from the end of the seventeenth century and during the eighteenth century, together with gold and slavery, Mozambique's product of greater interest for commerical transactions. Just as gold was important for the dominating Shona elite, ivory represented to the Maraves, Makuas and Yao one of the main founts of wealth. As a result, the development the elephant hunting organisation promoted a big flow of weapons and contributed to widening the social division of work and to strengthening the power of the native chiefs.

At the end of the first quarter of the eighteenth century, the Arab merchants of north Kilwa who used to traffic in slaves along Niassa and Cape Delgado, spread their area of operation, together with the Makua and Yao chiefs, from the regions further inside Lake Niassa, and more to the south, from the rivers of Cuama up to the coastal zone between Quelimane and Rovuma.[64] After following, mostly, the routes of ivory trade, the greater part of the slaves who left Mozambique and the Quelimane were supplied the Oman sultanate and, in a greater scale, to the French islands of the Indian Ocean. In 1721, the first chance contacts were made by the French merchants with the East African coast to obtain slaves for the Island of Mascarenhas. Only after 1733, contacts with these islands became more frequent by intensification of the traffic of slave labour to work in the coffee, sugar, cotton and indigo plantations, in exchange of food supplies, weapons and ammunition. Zanzibar also was an important slave market, mainly after the introduction on the island of clove and coconut plantations.

Slave traffic in Mozambique was illegal, disallowed even to foreign ships docked in any coastal port, except in cases of extreme necessity. These exceptional cases, however, became frequent, transforming the commerce of necessity into commerce of profit. The main reason of the Portuguese opposition to slave traffic was that this traffic was controlled by the Swahili, who had established solid commercial nets with the interior. The Swahili, the Portuguese merchants of Mozambique and the Banyans who possessed many slaves, were very active in this trade.[65] The estimated numbers of slaves leaving Mozambique for the Indian Ocean islands showed that, between 1736 and 1750, about 6,000 were transported.[66] In the fiftieth decade, the slave traffic of Mozambique to the islands of Mascarenhas proceeded without any necessary justification, since food became short.[67]

This traffic, which assumed great importance from 1771, provoked deep internal alterations in Macua society. The practice of kidnapping young girls for marriage, which was used to solve the problems of demographic equilibrium and to assure the reproduction of the social group, became, through the intensification of the slave traffic, more common.[68] The process of introducing weapons and ammunition started by elephant hunting, registered, by the influence of the slave commerce, a significative increase.[69] Similarly, the flow of weapons brought by the French, Swahili, Portuguese and Banyans, contributed to the appearance of strong Makua leadership, of which those of Murimuno and Micieira were most prominent.[70]

The import of Indian cloth increased after a concession, in 1757, of free commerce to all Portuguese Crown subjects in India to negotiate in the different Mozambique ports. But the Banyans their intensified commercial relations with the Makuas and Yao, significantly reducing the margins of profit of Portuguese merchants, who operated in Mozambique and in Mossuril and Cabaceiras.[71] Once established in the continent, the Banyans sought to avoid all Portuguese intermediaries. They created their own circuits, established direct contacts with the native merchants and Swahili, or used the *mossambazes*, a type of African travelling salesmen who crossed the interior to sell their merchandise in Sena and Tete. When they suffered price losses on account of excess supply of beads and cloth, they sold the goods in the fair of Zumbo for high profits; this induced them "to do the same with the king of Changamira, with an aim to make themselves lords of gold produced in the mines of Abutua".[72] In this way, the competition of the Africans and the Banyans against the Portuguese not only reduced the official customs revenue, but also the private commerce of the Portuguese residents of the rivers of Cuama and Mozambique.

The competition for control of the traffic of Makuana ended, in 1766, when the Portuguese residents of Mozambique created the Makua and Yao Company of Commerce. Intending to wipe out all advantages the Banyans enjoyed in the territory, the Governor, David Marques Pereira, by proposition of the Holy House of Mercy, prohibited about 300 Banyans from trade in the territory, and from owning "houses, palm groves and ships" in the continent. He ordered the sale of their properties within three months and limited their presence in the island to twelve establishments. The reason given for this drastic measure was that the Banyans had strong control of trade, which was the only support of the Mozambique residents and the only motive for the Yao and Makuas to move to Mossuril and Cabaceiras.[73]

Just as in 1694, when the Portuguese intended to obliterate the activity of the Banyan Trade Company of Diu, the Banyans once again reacted in apparent submission. They accepted the Governor's orders who, in turn, authorised them to go to the continent to cover their debts.[74]

Control of the Makuana commerce, a coastal strip the limits of which were not very precise, with probably Memba constituting its northern extremity and Angoxe in the south, had previously been the object of great disputes and quarrels between the Africans, Swahilis and Portuguese. In 1753, and between 1756 and 1758, the blockade of transit of caravans of the Yao merchants, which were composed of many slaves and thousands of loaders of ivory, disturbed considerably all the commerce of Makuana. This blockade prejudiced the interest not only of the Swahili of Sancul and Quitangonha in slave traffic, but also of the Yao, to whom were destined the larger parts of the bead trade, and of the Portuguese and Banyans in the traffic of food, ivory and slaves. The Portuguese expeditions to unblock the transit of merchandise and to punish the native Makuas, Murimuno and Mauruça rulers ended in a military rout.[75] The slave commerce with the Querimba islands and the ivory from Mombasa was also prevented.[76]

The Mozambicans' campaign against the commercial monopoly of the Banyans in Makuana became more subtle in 1759, when the Portuguese authorities attempted to know the source of wealth of the latter and tried to control this accumulation, by making inventories of inheritance. But the Jesuits came to a most forceful defence of the Banyans. The Jesuit interest was, among others, in safeguarding the income from renting the houses and warehouses of their constituents. They claimed that the Register of Wealth for inheritance was never maintained in Goa, Damão and Diu, or even in Mozambique where, since 1700, eighty-eight Banyans and Muslims had died. They also argued that these harassing attitudes were unexecutable and damaged the interests of the Royal Treasury. It was the Banyans, after all, who promoted the growth of the customs income, supported the war against the Marathas in India, contributed to the purchase of food, loaned money, paid the troops, lent slaves and spent large sums in charity, they contended.[77]

The government repeatedly sought to make the Banyans to leave the territory, reduce their commercial presence, impose transfer of properties and limit their accumulation of capital; with little consequence, however.[78] The economic weight of the Banyans was such that, in 1758, the income of the customs of Mozambique "was supported by the customs which were contributed by the Banyans and merchants of Diu, Damão and Goa".[79] Of thirty-seven shops and warehouses existing in Mozambique, between 1762 and 1765, thirty belonged to Banyans and seven to Muslims.[80] Ponja Valgy, the owner of one of them, was the principal merchant of Mozambique and Diu, had loaned ships, supplied cloth by consignment and paid for the food for the fortress of Mozambique, and claimed the right to go about in a palanquin.

As earlier, the Makua and Yao Company of Commerce could not withstand the combined force of the Banyans. Heeding the complaints of the merchants of Diu, Damão and Goa, who alleged that the activity of the Company contravened the regime of free trade in force, and the general instructions of 1761, the Crown ordered its dissolution in 1769.[81]

THE PASSAGE OF BANYANS TO THE RIVERS OF CUAMA: THE CONCLUSION OF THE EXPANSION OF THE COMMERCIAL ACTIVITY IN MOZAMBIQUE (1771-77)

In 1771, the final phase of expansion of Indian mercantile capital commenced. After having taken possession, gradually of coastal commerce, the traffic with the Makuas and Yao in Makuana, and having enlarged their commercial influence in areas close to Niassa Lake, the Banyans started to act, personally, in the rivers of Cuama. Many Banyans and some Swahilis installed themselves in Sena, where they built new shops and warehouses and developed their commercial network in the rivers of Cuama, in the Monomotapa fairs and in the Orange and Botanga regions.

It was only after 1771 that the Banyans obtained passports from the Portuguese authority authorising them to move about, for short periods, to the river to collect their debts. Taking advantage of this concession they attached themselves to Sena, starting to sell in their establishments both the usual Indian merchandise—cotton and silk cloth, trinkets, sugar, crockery, spices and beadsand African merchandise, especially preserved food, wines and liquors. The Banyans frequently sent their slaves to meet the *mossambazes* who were at the service of the richer merchants of the Monomotapa fairs, for cheap exchange of cloth, and receive large quantities of ivory and gold. At other times they supplied woven cloth to the *mossambazes* who traded ivory in the Marave lands, in Bororo and also in Manica, an area of scarce economic resources which, being close to Sena was preferred by the poor.

The alteration of the market rules by the direct and various types of intervention by the Banyans in the commerce of the whole region of the rivers of Cuama and by the intensification and diversification of the products traded, resulted in great losses in the price of cloth and the ruin of many Portuguese merchants.[82]

Though the first legal authorisation was given to the Banyans to move to the area of Sena in 1771, their presence in this area dates from at least 1767. In that year, a Banyan goldsmith in Sena was prohibited from continuing that professional activity and all his tools were seized from him. Only boilers were allowed there, but not even the judge of Sena believed that this Banyan complied with this sentence as "with his profession as a boiler he could earn very little and rob much less".[83]

Very likely, the Banyans participated, at this time, in the ivory trade with Manica and Orange and gold from Abuta and Zumbo.[84]

In the meantime, while the Banyans in Mozambique managed to install themselves with their shops in the area of Sena and sought successfully to widen their commercial network to the interior lands of Marave, their countrymen in Diu were not particularly happy with the way trade in Mozambique was going. In 1773 and 1755, the Mahajan community, contractors of voyages to Mozambique, and some Banyans of Diu sought a number of measures to facilitate their commercial activity. They asked for protection from the Goan authorities against the favouritism of Governor Pereira de Lago, who conceded gunpowder and arms to the French trade in the ports of Mozambique and Querimba and against the obstacles which he put against their trade.[85] Curiously, it was the Banyans of Mozambique, involved in the slave trade, food trade, arms and *patacas* with the French in the Mauritius islands, who defended Pereira de Lago.[86]

The Banyans' presence in Mozambique, even after the extinction of the Banyan Trade Company, in 1777, was economic and socially solid. In 1780, there were six commercial ships in Sena where sixteen Banyan merchants worked and only one shop was owned by two Muslim tradesmen.[87] In spite of the big competition and the disturbances they caused to the Portuguese trade in the area of Sena, the Banyans were considered indispensable.[88] Also, the presence is recorded in 1793 of thirteen rich Banyan merchants in Mozambique. They owned several shops and warehouses. There were also a large number of other Banyans and Indian Muslims who supplied slaves to the regular Portuguese troops.[89]

GLOSSARY OF PORTUGUESE TERMS

Almadia	Canoe, quick boat. Frequently used in Portuguese records concerning the Indian Ocean.
Alfandega	Custom-house.
Bertangil	Indian Cloth.
Canarim	Indian Christian, usually from Goa.
Estado da India	State of India, the name applied to the Portuguese possessions east of Cape of Good Hope, of which Mozambique formed a part until 1752.
Estanque	Monopoly.
Fazenda Real	Royal Treasury.
Junta do Comèrcio	Board of Trade.
Lascar, lascarim	From the Persian vocable *lashkar*. The first meaning 'sea soldier or sailor' and the second 'ground soldier'.
Machira	A rough, durable cotton cloth woven by the people of Zambesi.
Mahajan	A body governing in commercial matters people engaged in a particular occupation. Also a city-wide body regulating all commercial matters.
Mossambazes	An African or mulatto trading agent, usually a slave, who travelled in the interior on behalf of his master on the coast.
Pangaio	Medium-sized lateen-rigged sailing vessel.
Praça	Portuguese settlement.
Santa Casa da Misericoridia	Holy House of Mercy, a charitable brotherhood.
Velorio	Glass trade beads, usually Venetian.

WEIGHTS

Arratel	0, 459 kg.
Arroba	32 arrateis, 14.688 kg.
Bar	20 faraçolas, 247.860 kg.
Bar	4 quantals, 234.900 kg.
Candil	about 460 kg.
Corja	20 pieces of cloth, 1/20 bar.
Faraçola	27 arrateis, 12.393 kg.
Maina	1/12 faraçola, 1.03275 kg.
Oitava	1/8 onça, 0.0036 kg.
Onça	1/16 arratel, 0.0287 kg.
Quintal	4 arrobas, 58.725 kg.
Rubo	1/14 maina, 0.25819 kg.

CURRENCIES

Real (pl. reis/reales)	Smallest monetary unit. Worth about 1/16 of a penny in the 19th century.
Cruzado	A silver coin to equal 400 reis, worth about 4 shillings in English money at the beginning of the 17th century.
Matical	Measure of gold based on the Syrian dinar, equivalent approximately to 4.25 g.; in the seventeenth century worth 1.5 xerafins or 6 tangas.
Pataca	Spanish silver coin to equal 6 cruzados.
Tanga	Coin worth about one-sixth of matical.
Xerafim	An Indo-Portuguese coin equal to 300 reis.

MOZAMBIQUE TRADE REGIMES (1686-1786)

1686-90	Free commerce to all subjects of the Crown.
1690-94	Board of Commerce of Mozambique and Rivers.
1694-98	General Company of the Commmerce of India. Period of commercial identification.
1699-1720	Board Commerce of Mozambique and Rivers .
1720	Mercé de Sofala.
1720-44	Board of Commerce of Mozambique and Rivers.
1744-57	Customs Council of the State of India.
1757-61	Free Commerce to all subjects to the Crown.
1761-86	Free Commerce through the Regulations of 1761.

NOTES

[1]António Rita Ferreira, "Moçambique e os naturais da India Portuguesa", in Luis de Albuquerque e Inácio Guerreiro (org.), *Actas do II Seminário Internacional de Historia Indo-Portuguesa,* Memorias, Estudos de Historia e Cartografia Antiga, 25, Centro de Estudos de História e Cartografia Antiga, Instituto de Investigaçáo Cientifica e Tropical, Lisboa, 1985, p. 617.

[2]Armando, Reis Moura, "Barcos do littoral de Moçambique", in Monumenta, Lourenço Marques, 8, 1972, p. 15.

[3]António da Silva Rego (pref. em colab.), *Documentos sobre os Portugueses em Moçambique e na Africa Central (1497-1840)*, Centro de Estudos Historicos Ultramarinos, vol. I, p. 156.

[4]*Ibid.*, p. 276.

[5]Treslado do "Alvará do Sr. Conde Vice Rey Francisco de Távora, sobre a Companhia dos Baneanes, e seus privilégios, Diu, 27 de Março de 1686", Diu, 14 de Março de 1733, pub. por Jerónimo José Nogueira de Andrade, Do Estado em que ficavão os Negocios da Capitania de Moçambique nos fins de Novembro do Anno de 1789 com algumas Observaçõens e Reflecçõens sobre a causa da decadência do Commercio dos Estabelecimentos Portugueses na Costa Oriental de Africa (1790), Arquivo das Colónias, Lisboa I, 1917, pp. 281-6.

[6]"Copia da carta do General Pedro Saldanha de Albuquerque", Moçambique, 12 de Agosto 1783, pub. por Jerṭnimo José Nogueira de Andrade, pp. 232-3.

[7]"Moçambique em 1688" in G.M. Theal, IV, pp. 436-440.

[8]"Carta do Vice-Rei para o Rei", *A.H.U.*, India, CX. 34, Doc. 142, 29 Out. 1688; Carta do Rei para o Vice Rei, 20 Març. 1690, in G.M. Theal, *R.S.E.A.*, vol. IV, pp. 447-9.

[9]*Ibid.*

[10]"Parecer do Conselho Ultramarino sobre vários capitulos de uma carta regia", *A.H.U.*, Cx. 37, Doc. 13, India, 9 Març. 1693.

[11]"Orçamento do lucro que teve a Fazenda Real correndo por sua conta e contrato de Moçambique e Sena no decurso de 4 anos, começados em Março de 1691 e findos em outro tal mês de 1695: abatidas as despezas que se fizeram na administraçao do dito contrato e os 33.000 cr. de pensao anual de paga do Presidio de Moçambique, do Zimbahoé, da mercé de Sofala, e todas as mais ordinarias", *A.H.U.*, Cx. 4, Doc. 5, Moçambique, 3 Jan. 1700.

[12]"Carta da Junta Geral do Comércio de Moçambique para o Rei", *A.H.U.*, Cx. 4, Doc. 5, Moçambique, 7 Jan. 1700.

[13]"Orçamento do lucro ...", *A.H.U.*, Cx. 4, Doc. 5, Moçambique, 3 Jan. 1700.

[14]"Copea da Petição que fizerao Xama Ricabo e Mado Hargy guzarates mercadores e moradores na fortaleza de Dio ao Vice Rey o Conde de Villa Verde", *A.H.U.*, Cx. 40, Doc. 30, India, 23 August 1699.

[15]*Ibid.*

[16]"Carta do Vice Rei para o Rei", *A.H.U.*, Cx. 40, Doc. 30, India, 15 Dez 1696.

[17]"Carta de Camara Coutinho para os Mazanes de Diu", *Filmoteca Ultramarina Portuguesa,* Livro de Diu 1, 3ș, Banda, 23 Dez. 1698; "Carto deo Vice Rei para o Rei", *A.H.U.*, Cx. 40, Doc. 30, India, 15 Dez. 1696.

[18] "Carta do Vice Rei para o Rei", *A.H.U.*, Cx. 40, Doc. 30, India, 15 Dez. 1696.

[19]"Proposta dos moradores dos Rios de Cuama ao Senhor V. Rey", in *Boletim do Governo do Estado da India,* 51, 1865, pp. 318-19; "Proposta da Camara e mais moradores de Moçambique ao Senhor V. Rey", in *Boletim...*, 52, pp. 328-9, 53, pp. 336-7.

[20]Panduronga Pissurlencar, *Assentos do Conselho de Estado,* vol. V, p. 62; "Carta do Vice Rei para os baneanes da fortaleza de Diu", *F.U.P.*, Livro de Diu 1, 2ș Banda, 22 June 1699; "Carta do Vice Rei para o Rei sobre o estado do comércio", B.N.L., Cod. 4406, fols. 155v-156, 21 Jan. 1718.

[21]"Livro de Registo das consultas e mais cartas feitas pela Junta do Comércio ao Vice Rei", in *Arquivo Português Oriental,* nova serié, IV, 2, 2, 29 Out. 1699, p. 130.

[22]"Carta da Junta Geral do Comércio de Moçambique para o Rei", *A.H.U.*, Cx. 4, Doc. 5, Moçambique, 5 Jan. 1700; "Carta do Vice Rei para o Rei", *A.H.U.*, Cx. 44, Doc. 62, India, 30 Dez. 1700.

[23]"Carta do Vice Rei para o Rei", *A.H.U.*, Cx. 44, Doc. 62, India, 30 Dez. 1700.

[24]"Carta da Junta Geral do Comércio de Moçambique para of Rei", *A.H.U.*, Cx. 4, Doc. 5, Moçambique, 5 Jan. 1700.

[25]Panduronga Pissurlencar, op.cit., p. 76.

[26]Edward A. Alpers, *Ivory and Slaves in East Central Africa,* Heinemann Educational Books, London, 1975, p. 70.

[27]J.H.C. Rivara, *O Chronista de Tissuary,* vol. II, Jan./Dez., p. 176.

[28]"Carta do Vice Rei para os baneanes contratadores da viagem de Moçambique", *F.U.P.*, Livro de Diu 1, 6º Banda, 9 Jan. 1703; "Carta do Vice Rei para o capitão dos baneanes de Diu", *F.U.P.*, Livro de Diu 1, 6⁰ Banda, 9 Jan. 1703; "Carta do Vice Rei para os contratadores da viagem de Moçambique", *F.U.P.*, Livro de Diu 1, 8⁰ Banda, 20 Out. 1703; "Carta do Vice Rei para Pacavir Pareca e Valabo Gocol, Contratadores do barco de Moçambique", *F.U.P.*, Livro de Diu 1, 10⁰ Banda, 6 Fev. 1705.

[29]G.M. Theal, vol. V, pp. 30-1.

[30]"Copia da carta do Ouvidor de Moçambique Joseph Moreyra Freyre que se acha nesta Secretaria da Junta Geral do Comércio de Moçambique", *A.H.U.*, Cx. 4, Doc. 19, Moçambique, 13 August 1721.

[31]"Carta do Vice Rei para Calliangi Vellabo", *F.U.P.*, Livro de Diu 1, 80 Banda, 28 Abr. 1708; G.M. Theal, 18 Fev. 1709, p. 145.

[32]"Copia da carta do Feitor de Moçambique Pedro de Mello Pinheiro

que se acha na Secretaria da Junta Geral do Comércio de Moçambique", *A.H.U.*, Cx. 4, Doc. 19, Moçambique, 15 Ag. 1722.

[33]"Consulta da Junta Geral do Comércio de Moçambique sobre uma carta do Vice Rei", *A.H.U.*, Cx. 4, Doc. 20, Moçambique, 17 Out. 1722.

[34]G.M. Theal, 26 Jan. 1719, pp. 57-60.

[35]"Carta do Vice Rei para o Rei, sobre o estado do comércio da India", B.N.L., Cod. 4406, 21 Jan. 1718, fols. 154-6.

[36]"Memorandum do Desembargador Duarte Salter de Mendonça", Lisboa, 7 Dez. 1751, pub. Fritz Hoppe, *A Africa Oriental Portuguesa no tempo do Marquês de Pombal (1750-1777)*, Lisboa, Agencia Geral do Ultramar, Apenso II, Doc. 1, p. 338;

"Carta do Vice Rei para a Junta do Comércio de Moçambique e Rios", Goa, 3 Jan. 1720, pub. G.M. Theal, p. 73.

[36]"Carta do Vice Rei para o Governador de Moçambique", Goa, s/d, pub. G.M. Theal, pp. 57-9.

[37]"Carta do Vice Rei para o Junta do Comércio de Moçambique e Rios", Goa, 3 Jan. 1720, pub. G.M. Theal, p. 73.

[38]"Carta do Vice Rei para a Junta do Comércio de Moçambique e Rios", Goa, 10 Jan. 1720, pub. G.M. Theal, pp.82-3.

[39]"Carta do Vice Rei para o Junta do Comércio de Moçambique e Rios", Goa, 20 Jan. 1720, pub. G.M. Theal, p. 90.

[40]"Informaçao de Francisco de Mello de Castro, Governador de Moçambique, para o Rei sobre o comércio dos Rios de Cuama", *A.H.U.*, Cx. 8, Doc. 42, Moçambique, 20 Nov. 1753.

[41]"Carta do Governador de Moçambique para o Vice Rei sobre o mau procedimento de 4 religosos jesuitas", *A.H.U.*, Cx. 5, Doc. 26, Moçambique, 16 Nov. 1734.

[42]"Carta dos Irmãos da Santa Casa da Misericordia de Moçambique para o Rei, sobre os prejuizos causados pela presença dos baneanes na dita praça", *A.H.U.*, Cx. 16, Doc. 4, Moçambique, 2 Jan, 1759.

[43]"Còpia da carta de Duarte Salter de Mendonça para o Rei", *A.H.U.*, Cx. 4, Doc. 22, Moçambique, 3 Set. 1723.

[44]"Còpia da Provisão Real sobre Amade Souly poder negociar nas terras firmes da Macuana", *A.H.U.*, Cx. 4, Doc. 37, Moçambique, 10 Marc. 1727.

[45]"Carta do Juiz Conservador do Tabaco para o Vice Rei", *A.H.U.*, Cx. 4, Doc. 26, Moçambique, 15 Jan. 1727.

[46]"Certidão do Livro das Receitas e despezas do feitor da Junta Geral Anttnio Pereira", *A.H.U.*, Cx. 4, Doc. 36, Moçambique, 15 Jan. 1727.

[47]"Ctpia da carta do feytor de Mossambique Pedro de Mello Pinheiro que se acha nesta Secretaria da Junta Geral do Comersio de Mossambique e Rios", *A.H.U.*, Cx. 4, Doc. 19, Moçambique, 15 Ag. 1722; "Cópia da carta do Padre Frey Franmcisco de Nossa Senhora que se achq nesta Secretaria da Junta Geral do Comercio de Mossambique e Rios", *A.H.U.*, Cx. 4, Doc. 19, Moçambique, 15 Ag. 1722.

[48]"Certidão do Livro das Receitas e despesas do feitor da Junta Geral António Pereira", *A.H.U.*, Cx. 4, Doc. 36, Moçambique, 15 Jan. 1727; "Certidao das dividas contraidas pela Junta Geral do Comércio através dos Livros de Receita e despesa do feitor António Pereira", *A.H.U.*, Cx. 4, Doc. 42, Moçambique, 12 Ag. 1728.

[49]"Carta do Vice Rei para o Rei sobre os meios para se restabelecer o comércio de Moçambique e Rios", *A.H.U.*, Cx. 5, Doc. 7, Moçambique, 14 Jan. 1733.

[50]"Carta do Juiz Conservador do Tabaco para of Vice Rei", *A.H.U.*, Cx. 4, Doc. 26, Moçambique, 30 de Jun. 1724; "Certidão dos Rendimentos da Alfândega de Moçambique, no tempo do feitor Antonio Pereira", *A.H.U.*, Cs. 4, Doc. 40, Moçambique, 16 Ag. 1727.

[51]"Collecção de manuscritos originaes acerca do Estado e decadencia da India entre os annos de 1744 a 1746", B.N.L., Cod. 4180.

[52]"Extracti do Rendimento da Alfãndega desta Ilha e Fortaleza de Monssabique do tempo de 3 annos comessados no de 1754, e acabados no de 1756", *A.H.U.*, Cx. 10, Doc. 47, Moçambique, 1756.

[53]"Carta dos Irmãos da Santa Casa da Misericordia de Moçambique para o Rei, sobre os prejuizos causados pela presença dos baneanes na dita praça", *A.H.U.*, Cx. 16, Doc. 4, Moçambique, 2 Jan. 1759; "Carta do Governador de Moçambique para o Rei, sobre o Bando que lançou sobre os baneanes", *A.H.U.*, Cx. 14, Doc. 39, Moçambique, 10 Ag. 1758.

[54]"Dividas que fica devendo a Junta Geral do Comércio de Monssabique às partes na forma de ordem assima pela maneira seguinte 1716-1744", B.N.L., Cod. 4179 e 4180, Goa, 12 Jan. 1745.

[55]"Memtria de Luiz de Meneses, Conde da Ericeira, sobre o comércio de Moçambique", *A.H.U.*, Cx. 5, Doc. 3, Moçambique, 4 Nov. 1730.

[56]"Representaçao de Deuchande Seuchande, Procurador da Comunidade dos Mazanes de Diu, na fortaleza de Moçambique, ao Rei", *A.H.U.*, Cx. 7, Doc. 33, Moçambique, 27 Nov. 1752.

[57]"Consto do que a Fazenda Real devia aos baneanes desde 1746 até 1751", *A.H.U.*, Cx. 7, Doc. 33, Moçambique, 27 Nov. 1752; "Carta do Padre Phelippe de Macedo, Reitor do Colègio jesuita de Moçambique e Juiz Conservador dos Mazanes na Ilha, para o Rei", *A.H.U.*,Cx. 7, Doc. 34, Moçambique, 28 Nov. 1752; "Extracto da importancia geral das carregaçoens que se mandarao por conta da Fanda Real para as feitorias de Senna, Sofala, e Inhambane, e Resgatte que veyo de cada huma dellas com a reducção a cruzados, moeda corente na terra, desde Abril de 1746 athe Agosto de 1754", *A.H.U.*, Cx. 10, Doc. 20, Moçambique, 10 Nov. 1754.

[58]Alexandre Lobato, *Evolução administrativa e economica de Moçambique (1752-1763)*, I Parte, Fundamentos da criaçao do Governo Geral em 1752, Agência Geral do Ultramar, Divisão de publicações e Biblioteca, 1957, p. 258.

[59]"Extracto da importancia geral ...", *A.H.U.*, Cx. 10, Doc. 20,

Moçambique, 10 Nov. 1754.

[60]"Descripção dos Rios de Senna feita por Francico de Mello de Castro no ano de 1750", Nova Goa, Imprensa Nacional, 1861, p. 17.

[61]*Ibid.*

[62]*Ibid.*

[63]"Certidão por que se arrematou o vellorio que veyo por conta da Fazenda Real na nao N. Senhora da Conceyção e S. Antṭnio de Padua no Leyllão que se fez delle", *A.H.U.*, Cx. 10, Doc. 33, Moçambique, 18 Nov. 1754; "Collecção de manuscritos originaes (...) entre os annos de 1744 a 1746", B.N.L., Cod. 4180.

[64]José Capela e Eduardo Medeiros, *O tráfico de escravos de Moçambique para as Ilhas do Indico (1720/1902)*, Nc̤leo Editorial da Universidade Eduardo Mondlane, 1987, pp. 7-8.

[65]"Carta de Francisco de Mello de Castro para o Vice Rei sobre os mouros disporem de escravos", *A.H.U.*, Cx. 8, Doc. 40, Moçambique, 18 Nov. 1753; "Carta de Francisco de Mello de Castro para o Vice Rei, sobre a concessâo de liberdade para que os capitães e restante tripulaçao das naus pudessem embarcar escravos", *A.H.U.*, Cx. 8, Doc. 51, Moçambique, 29 Nov. 1753; "Informaçao de Frei João de Nossa Senhora, Administrador Episcopal, sobre assuntos religiosos", Cx. 9, Doc. 3, Moçambique, 20 Dez. 1753.

[66]José Capela e Eduardo Medeiros, pp. 24-5

[67]"Carta do Governador de Moçambique para o Rei sobre o comércio com os franceses", *A.H.U.*, Cx. 10, Doc. 28, Moçambique, 15 Nov. 1754.

[68]José Capela e Eduardo Medeiros, p. 98.

[69]"Lista da carregação que vay para as Ilhas de Quirimba no Hyacte, S. Anna e S. Francisco de Paulla a cargo do Escrivão delle Joaquim Mexia, e do Manoel Jozé Vieyra, para entregar ao Capitam e Juiz dellas Manoel de Souza Britto", *A.H.U.*, Cod. 1310, fol. 3, 22 Jul. 1753; "Carta do Governador de Moçambique para o Rei, sobre o Bando que lançou sobre os baneanes", Cx. 14, Doc. 39, Moçambique, 10 Ag. 1758; "Bando de Pedro Saldanha de Albuquerque, Governador e General de Mossambique, sobre os moradores da Ilha de Moçambique, do Mossuril e Cabaceiras comerciarem armas com os Macuas", Cx. 1, Doc. 51, Moçambique, 5 Set. 1758.

[70]"Informação de Francisco de Mello de Castro, Governador de Moçambique, para o Rei sobre o comércio dos Rios de Cuama", Cx. 8, Doc. 42, Moçambique, 20 Nov. 1753, fols 9v e 11; Breve noticia da infelicidade que teve a nossa expedição de Moçambique primeira que fez El Rey N. Senhar D. José I destruida pello Rey dos Macuas ...", in *Arquivo das Colonias,* vol. II, 8 Maio 1754, pp. 106-12; "Carta de Francisco de Mello de Castro para o Rei, acerca do nosso dominio na Macuana", in *Arquivo das Colonias,* vol. IV, 16 Nov. 1754, pp. 62-3.

[71]"Resposta do Dezembargador Procurador da Coroa do Estado da India a um requerimento do Dezembargador André de Souza de Vasconsellos", *A.H.U.*, Cx. 11, Doc. 35, 6 Ag. 1754; "Copia do Alvará, por que

se fez publica a ordem de Sua Magestade pella qual manda que os portos, de Senna, Sofala, e Inhambane sejao livres, para todos os seus vassallos, moradores de Goa, e das mais partes, e terras da Azia, sugeitos ao seu Real dominio", *A.H.U.*, Cx. 13, Doc. 47, Moçambique, 9 Ag. 1757; "Carta do Vice Rei para o Rei, acerca do comércio de Moçambique", *A.H.U.*, Cx. 14, Doc. 44, Moçambique, 15 Ag. 1754.

[72]"Carta do Capitão-general Pereira do Lago ao Secretrio dos Negocios da Marinha, e de Dominios Ultramarinas Francisco Xavier de Mendoça Furtado", pub. Fritz Hoppe, 15 Ag. 1766, pp. 349-51; "Ctpia dos estatutos da Companhia do Comércio com os Mujaos e com os Macuas sancionados pelo capitão-general Pereira do Lago", pub. Fritz Hoppe, 11 Marc. 1766, pp. 353-61.

[73]"Bando dado por David Marques Pereira a limitar a presença dos baneanes em Moçambique", *A.H.U.*, Cx. 14, Doc. 17, Moçambique, 11 Maio 1758; "Carta do Governador de Moçambique, sobre o Bando que lançou sobre os baneanes", *A.H.U.*, Cx. 14, Doc. 39, Moçambique, 10 Ag. 1758.

[74]"Carta dos mercadores baneanes da Ilha de Moçambique a David Marques Pereira sobre o Bando por este lançado", *A.H.U.*, Cx. 14, Doc. 17, Moçambique, 22 Maio 1758.

[75]"Breve noticia da infelicidade ...", in *Arquivo das Colónias,* vol. II, 8 Maio 1754, pp. 106-12; "Carta de francisco de Mello de Castro para o Rei, acreca do nosso dominio na Macuana", in *Arquivo das Colónias,* vol. IV, 16 Nov. 1754, pp. 62-3.

[76]"Carta de Francisco de Mello de Castro ao Rei sobre o comércio de Cabo Delgado e Mombaça", *A.H.U.*, Cx. 10, Doc. 37, Moçambique, 20 Nov. 1754.

[77]"Representaçao de Baneanes e Mouros ao General e Governador de Moçambique sobre se fazerem inventários dos bens dos defuntos", *A.H.U.*, Cx. 16, Doc. 6, Moçambique, 2 Jan. 1751.

[78]"Bando de João Pereira da Silva Barba proibindo que baneanes e mouros pudessem passar ao continente", *A.H.U.*, Cx. 23, Doc. 25, Moçambique, 31 Jan. 1763; "Carta onde baneanes e mouros pedem ao Rei uma Provisao para que os inventários dos seus defuntos fiquem a seu cargo", *A.H.U.*, Cx. 25, Doc. 15, Moçambique, 11 Marc. 1765.

[79]"Certidão da quantia de direitos que tem pago os Banianes, e homens de chapeo de Moçambique", *A.H.U.*, Cx. 25, Doc. 14, Moçambique, 2 Ag. 1758.

[80]"Rellação das Boticas, e Lojas dos mercadores, e ourives desta ilha que hao-de pagar a Fazenda Real annualmente com principio em 18 de Junho de 1762, e acabado em 17 de Julho de 1764, a rezao de 15 cruzados cada anno", *A.H.U.*, Cx. 24, Doc. 89, Moçambique, 1762-64; "Rellação das Boticas abertas dos mercadores, e ourives desta Ilha que pagâo a Fazenda Real annuaçmente 15 cruzados cada botica principiado a 18 de Junho de 1764, e acabo (sic) a 18 de Março de 1765", *A.H.U.*, Cx. 24, Doc. 89, Moçambique,

1764-65.

[81]"Cópia dos estatutos da Companhia do Comércio com os Mujaos e com os Macuas sancionados pelo capitao-general Pereira do Lago", pub. Fritz Hoppe, 11 Març. 1766, pp. 353-61.

[82]"Bando dado por Antonio de Mello de Castro, Governador dos Rios de Sena, sobre o comércio dos baneanes e mouros nesta villa", *A.H.U.*, Cx. 30-A, Doc. 41, Moçambique, 25 Ab. 1780; "Carta de António de Mello de Castro para o Governador de Moçambique", *A.H.U.*, Cx. 33, Doc. 52, Moçambique, 22 Març. 1780.

[83]"Carta do Juiz ordinário da vila de Sena para o Governador de Moçambique", Cx. 27, Doc. 7, Moçambique, 20 Jan. 1767; "Carta de Pereira do Lago para o Vice Rei sobre os ourives baneanes falsificarem o ouro", *A.H.U.*, Cx. 28, Doc. 88, Moçambique, 20 Ag. 1768.

[84]"Oficio de Inacio de Melo Alvim a dar noticia de grandes resgates do Zumbo e Manica", *A.H.U.*, Cx. 27, Doc. 68, Moçambique, 10 Jul. 1767; "Carta de Frei Manual José de Santa Anna, padre beneditino, para Pereira do Lago", *A.H.U.*, Cx. 27, Doc. 114, Moçambique, 24 Set. 1767.

[85]"Petição dos Mazanes de Diu, contratadores das viagens de Moçambique Ö Junta do Comércio", B.N.L., Cod. 8841, 21 Dez. 1773; "Carta dos Mazanes na India a queixarem-se das obstruçaes que Pereira do Lago fazio ao seu comércio com Moçambique", *A.H.U.*, Cx. 30-A, Doc. 11, Moçambique, 25 Nov. 1775.

[86]"Atestado do Corpo de Baneanes sobre o comércio dos franceses nos portos de Moçambique", *A.H.U.*, Cx. 30-A, Doc. 25, Moçambique, 15 Ag. 1778.

[87]"Rellação dos comerciantes banianes e mouros autualmente existentes nesta villa de Senna com caza, e Loge aberta com declaraçâo dos Passaportes com que passarao para estes Rios Rios", *A.H.U.*, Cx. 32, Doc. 130-A, Moçambique, c. 1779.

[88]"Carta de António de Mello de Castro para o Governador de Moçambique sobre o prejuizo que causam os baneanes ao comércio dos Rios", *A.H.U.*, Cx. 33, Doc. 57, Moçambique, 30 Març. 1780; "Bando dado por Antonio de Mello de Castro sobre o comércio de baneanes e mouros em Sena", *A.H.U.*, Cx. 30-A, Doc. 41, Moçambique, 25 Ab. 1780.

[89]"Rellação dos Banianes, que tem suas Cazas nesta Capital, em que rezidem, e outras para recolherem as suas fazendas", *A.H.U.*, Cx. 65, Doc. 17, Moçambique, 19 Set. 1793; "Rellação das pessoas que se achão em Mossambique, e tambem as do Mossoril, que dao Escravos para o expediente da guerra, segundo a ordem do Illustrissimo, e Excelentissimo Senhor Cappitam General", *A.H.U.*, Cx. 70, Doc. 80, Moçambique, 12 Maio 1795.

EARLY COMMERCIAL ACTIVITIES OF THE FRENCH IN PONDICHERRY: THE PONDICHERRY AUTHORITIES, THE JESUITS AND THE MUDALIARS

Ajit Neogy

Their ignorance of Indian society—its manners, customs, character and language—prevented traders of the European trading companies from directly contacting the indigenous merchants, weavers, dyers, artisans and producers. They overcame this difficulty by recruiting local people who acted as go-between. These were either leaders of caste, or local merchants having some business acumen, and were variously known as *banians*, agents, *dubash*, etc.

When Pondicherry was founded, the French too had to depend on such intermediaries. The contribution of one of the earliest Pondicherry families which worked for three generations for the development of French commerce in Pondicherry still remains obscure and unassessed. The Pondicherry branch of this family was headed by Lazare de Motha Tanappa Mudaliar. For three generations he and his successors acted as *dubash* with rare distinction and unparallelled competence. Unfortunately, this family has not left behind any memoir or journal like Ananda Rangapillai, or preserved the letters and correspondence exchanged between them and the Company. Some oblique references to them are found here and there but not adequate for reconstructing the history of the family. Jaganou Diagou, the present incumbent of the family, has written a small monograph entitled "Les Premiers Modeliars de la Compagnie de l'Inde Orientale", which is more of a narrative.

The Mudaliar controlled the commercial affairs of the Company. He acted as the chief intermediary between the Company and the merchants, weavers, fishermen and artisans who supplied to the Company merchandise for export and bought the imports.[1] He was the Company's broker and exercised his moral authority and economic power over the inhabitants. All orders were conveyed and carried out by him. He brought workers, recommended craftsmen and gave loans.[2] He drew up and signed contracts on behalf of the Company and stood as the guarantor of Indian tenants, local farmers and entrepreneurs vis-a-vis the Company. The Mudaliar also fixed the prices of commodities bought and sold by the Company.[3] No business could be transacted without him. He was also the Dubash of the Governor because he acted as his Tamil interpreter. The first Mudaliar was a Christian called Lazare whose family was in active service of the Company since the time of François Martin.

François Martin was among the first few Frenchmen who came to Pondicherry in early 1674. Accompanying him was the trusted Lazare de Motha Tanappa Mudaliar.[4] Tanappa Mudaliar, a merchant of Pounamalli near Madras, was a Vellaja (Vellala)[5] by caste and had good business contacts with Mylapore (San Thomé). The Jesuit Abbé Carré was so much impressed by his honesty and integrity that he recommended him to Blanquet de la Haye and François Martin.[6] The French position was then precarious in San Thomé. The Dutch had besieged the place and food supply was completely cut off. Tanappa Mudaliar earned the confidence of the beleaguered French by supplying them food. François Martin soon made him his Dubash—the first Dubash of the Company (not Naniappa Pillai, as claimed by Rose Vincent).[7] Tanappa worked with Martin for the development of Pondicherry where there were only a few hundred fishermen's hut. The Danes, who had been there earlier, failed to develop the place. But Pondicherry had all the pontential for development as a trading outpost. It "was easy to defend, having natural obstacles on three sides against surprise attack—the river Ariancoupam on the south, marshes and sand-dunes on the north and sea on the east, where shallow roadstead prevented the close approach of men-of-war.[8] Its location in a cottonngrowing area contributed to its unbounded commercial importance. Weavers lived around in good number and fabrics could be bleached in the abundant waters.[9] A few thousand fishermen "who could be most conveniently utilised for the loading and unloading of ships" also lived around the place.

The early French Governors of Pondicherry realised that the first thing necessary to transform Pondicherry into a trading outpost was to patronise the local trade. The newly arrived French in Pondicherry had no knowledge of the local people and society.

Tanappa Mudaliar played here a crucial role. He invited more fishermen to settle in Pondicherry. He contacted the weavers of the surrounding places and induced them to settle in different parts of Pondicherry. Export from Pondicherry of the textile produced by them would save the carrying cost. Dyers and artisans also were invited to settle in the new place. Tanappa Mudaliar's endeavour paid off, and traders and craftsmen started clustering around the fort of Pondicherry from the time of its foundation. New roads were constructed and people of different castes and communities were urged to build their houses along the roads. Coral and pearl merchants, who were mainly Armenians and Jews, were invited to establish commercial links with Pondicherry. Grain merchants and sellers of fruits, spices, betel leaf and tobacco set up shop. By 1709 the population rose from 20,000 to 30,000.[10]

Tanappa was also instrumental in building magazines for housing the merchandise coming from and going to France. Ivory, precious stones, textile—mainly cotton and silk—were bought on the Coromandel coast. Muslin, saltpetre, camphor and spices, specially pepper, were exported to France. Painted cloth of Pondicherry, despite Colbert's ban, was very much in demand in France.[11] The English bought 'Pully-cherry cloth' from the French.[12] From France came clocks, hats, good wine, hardware and luxury goods. Pondicherry's speciality was the dyeing of raw cotton in blue.[13] Craftsmen were busily doing their jobs—"smelting iron, tanning leather, weaving and dyeing cloth which foreigners so loved to buy".[14] The weavers received special consideration and they were attracted to settle here on promise of exemption of all taxes for one year. Traders were offered favourable conditions, which provided the stimulus to many merchants of Madras to emigrate to Pondicherry. Pondicherry's subsequent development as the centre of export and import in the Bay of Bengal was largely due to the services rendered by Tanappa Mudaliar. Martin made him his Dubash and the Company rewarded him by making him its 'courtier' and 'Chef des Malabars.'[15]

Tanappa died in 1691. After his death, the Dutch captured Pondicherry and pillaged the town, forcing the merchants and artisans whom Tanappa had installed to leave the place. The task of rebuilding the town, reviving its trade and commerce and bringing back the weavers, artisans and merchants fell on Mutiapa Mudaliar, successor of Tanappa. He started a tortuous negotiation with them to return to the town and offered them advantages.[16] But a Christian Mudaliar was not to the liking of François Martin's successor Hébert, "an avaricious and a brutal man", as Governor of Pondicherry. Hébert was anti-Jesuit. He believed that the Mudaliar had not given sufficient proof of his competence in the sale of coral; the prices of coral had fallen and the Company's interests had suffered.[17] The Governor also accused the Mudaliar of having divulged an important piece of information to the Jesuits about a confidential negotiation with the Raja of Gingi. Hébert dismissed Matiappa in December 1708[18] and appointed Naniapa Pillai, an honest and capable Hindu merchant from Madras, as Dubash.

But the Jesuits were annoyed. A Hindu Dubash was anathema to them and they started conspiring for the removal of the Governor and the Mudaliar. Naniapa's appointment marked the beginning of the declaration of war between Hébert and Père Buchet, the Jesuit Supérir.[19] The Jesuits had also taken umbrage at the construction of Hindu temples near their church. The Jesuits had a good deal of influence at the court of Louis XIV, whom they pressurised to recall Hébert. They also wanted it resolved that the Mudaliar should be a Christian and that Naniapa should be immediately dismissed. Versailles recalled Hébert and appointed Dulivier to succeed him. The Conseil du Roi also decided on 14 February 1711, that the post of Mudaliar (who would be Chef des Malabars) would be given only to an Indian Christian.[20] Though orders were given, for Naniapa's immediate dismissal, the Directors of the Company, realising the far-reaching consequences such a step would have on the Company's business operation, decided to go slow; six months were given to Naniapa to embrace Christianity or be sacked. To appease the Jesuits, orders were passed banning all types of instrumental music accompanying the Hindu marriage parties.[21]

This mixing up of religion with trade and commerce had fatal consequences on the Company's commercial activities in Pondicherry. The new Governor obliged the Jesuits by acceding to their demand to demolish some Hindu temples, but drew the line at dismissing Naniapa, whose services had become indispensable to the Company. In a long letter (18 July 1714) he explained why Naniapa had to be retained.[22] His dismissal would cripple French trade in more ways than one. It might result in the farmers, the toddy contractors and anyone who was directly or indirectly connected with the business of the town leaving town. Further, two vessels had already left Saint Malo in 1713. The Mudaliar was in charge of loading the vessels with textiles and other merchandise for their return journey. Four more vessels were to follow. A man of Naniapa's experience could alone do the job of loading them. Moreover, his relations with the Muslim rulers were friendly. The Nawab of the Carnatic had demanded from the French either the retrocession of some villages given earlier to them or payment of a huge amount; he had actually despatched a cavalry to realise the demands. Naniapa intervened and brought about an amicable compromise.

But the Jesuits were so obstinately demanding Naniapa's removal that the Conseil Supèrieur had to appoint one Savari as co-Mudaliar. Savari was a Christian, but not a man of the Jesuits. The Jesuits also demanded that on days of Christian festivals public Hindu ceremonies should be prohibited and even celebration of Hindu festivals on these days should be banned. This was done. There was strong reaction among the people against this arbitrary policy and they decided to leave town. An organised agitation started (November 1714) and the Governor imprisoned a few leaders. Some others were threatened with dire consequences. In February 1715, when Dulivier did not permit observance of the Masi-Magha festival,[23] half the population left Pondicherry, including big and small merchants, fishermen, washermen and coolies (porters). The collection of rent and revenue fell.[24] Trade came to a standstill, with the shops and magazins were shut. Food became unavailable and the town wore a deserted look. The two French ships were stranded in the port. The administration requested Naniapa to call back the people who had left town. The Jesuits, however, held Naniapa responsible for all that was happening in Pondicherry and hardened their attitude.[25]

Hébert during his first term of office in Pondicherry had plunged French trade in a mess by his intolerant and shortsighted policy. Dulivier rescued the situation by his honest endeavours. He declined to yield to the pressures of the Jesuits in so far as French business interests were concerned. French trade began to prosper after a period of recession. This is evident from the fact that in 1714 Dulivier had loaded *l'Auguste, lex Deux Couronnes* and *le Lys Brillac* with merchandise which fetched seven million pounds. In 1715, *le Saint Louis, la Mercure, le Jazon, le Venus, la Grade Paix, le Franáois d'Argouges* and *le Chasseur* were loaded with merchandise which was sold at eighteen million pounds.[26] This brisk trade was possible because of Naniapa. He also started negotiations with the Nawab of Arcot for giving to the French the right of striking coins. This right was formally accorded later when Canagraya was Mudaliar.

Meanwhile, Hébert was in financial distress in France and sought to return to India. He compromised with the Jesuits, who agreed to support him on condition that he agreed to dismiss Naniapa and appoint a Christian Mudaliar. According to Martineau, the Jesuits were so hostile towards Naniapa because they knew that their interests would continue to suffer so long Naniapa remained Mudaliar.[27] Already the Jesuits had become hateful to people. Naniapa's continuance as Mudaliar would stand in the Jesuits' way of getting new converts. But Hébert consented to the Jesuits' conditions, and through their intervention the Directors of the Company made Hébert 'General de la Nation' on 16 January 1715—an exceptional and unheard of title.[28] This was a position superior to Governor. Hébert's son was made a member of the Conseil Supérieur and accorded the second position in the settlements. An ambitious man and backed by the Jesuits he realised that it was necessary to cripple the power of Dulivier to crush Naniapa and he followed a systematic policy of usurping the power of Dulivier.

The Directors of the Company of Saint Malo held a high opinion about Naniapa and they trusted no one else in money matters.[29] Unable to dislodge Naniapa, Hébert tried to enrich himself by fraudulent means. He urged local merchants to hike the prices of cloth by twenty to twenty-five per cent for the merchants of Saint Malo. He calculated that the merchants of Saint Malo would refuse to pay the full hike but would compromise at fifteen per cent, which would be his profit.[30] Naniapa strongly opposed and rejected this underhand deal. Baffled in his attempt, Hébert brought false charges of corruption, embezzlement and the like against the Mudaliar. On his refusal to pay money which Hébert demanded for hushing up the charges, he was arrested on 19 February 1716, chained, and locked up in an unhealthy vault. He was denied treatment. A kangaroo trial found him guilty. His household goods were sold out at throw away prices, and bought by Hébert. Naniapa died a broken man, physically, mentally and materially. The vengeful Hébert did not stop there. A number of big merchants—merchants of Malabar—who had been friendly with Naniapa

(Ramananda, Amavachetty, Andiapa, Tiruvangadam) were also arrested, dispossessed and publicly humiliated.[31]

Shocked at these misdeeds of Hébert, many Hindu businessmen left the place. Commercial activity was paralysed. Imprisonment of persons and confiscation of property desolated the place. Such was the horror prevailing that merchants of other nations felt no inclination to come to Pondicherry for doing business.[32]

The Directors of the Compagnie de Saint Malo, when they were apprised of the goings-on in Pondicherry, told the King and the Conseil de Marine that if the Hébert father and son were not removed from Pondicherry, they would not send any ships to India.[33] The Compagnie des Indes not having ships, only the ships of Saint Malo were being used as the means of transport since 1709. The threat of withdrawing their vessels from India, therefore, had the desired effect. The two Héberts were arrested and deported to France in 1717.

The temporary Governor, who followed, failed to transfuse vitality into Pondicherry. Canagaraya, who belonged to Tanappa Mudaliar's family was made Mudaliar. But his relations with the temporary Governor were far from satisfactory and he was dismissed. More often than not, the Mudaliars had to incur the displeasure of Pondicherry Governors, and this ultimately clogged the business enterprise of the French Company.

The company created by the Royal Act of 24 February 1685 consequent upon the liquidation of the Royale Compagnie de France des Indes Orientales, facing various types of interruptions and seizure of Pondicherry by the Dutch, suspended all trading activities. It also suffered from shortage of funds. In 1709 the Company made a treaty with the shipowners of Saint Malo. The latter tried to activate the moribund trade of the Company, but the Jesuits' interference nullified their efforts. It was against this background that the merchants of Saint Malo finally merged in 1721 with the Compagnie d'Occident founded by law, paving the path for the creation of Compagnie des Indes.

NOTES

[1]Jaganou Diagou, "Les Premiers Modeliars de la Compagnie de l'Inde Orientale", p.5.

[2]Rose Vincent, *The French in India,* p.42; "Zenith in Pondicherry"

by Rose Vincent.

[3]*Revue Historique de Pondicherry*, vol. XVI, 1989-90: "The Organisation of French Trade in India", by B. Krishnamurthy, p. 42.

[4]Henri de Closets d'Errey, "Institutions Religeuses et Artisanales de l'Inde", p.59.

[5]They are cultivators as well as landholders.

[6]Jaganou Diagou, p. 38.

[7]Rose Vincent, p. 38.

[8]S.P. Sen, *The French in India: First Establishment and Struggle*, p. 335.

[9]Rose Vincent, p. 28.

[10]*Ibid.*, pp. 30-32.

[11]Rose Vincent, pp. 33-5.

[12]G. Jouveau-Dubreuil, Dupleix, p. 52.

[13]*Ibid.*, p. 35.

[14]Rose Vincent, p. 42.

[15]Henri de Closets d'Errey, p. 60.

[16]*Ibid.*

[17]*Ibid.*, p. 61; Jaganou Diagou, p. 8.

[18]Paul Olangier, *Les Jesuits A Pondicherry (Société de l'Histoire des Colonies Françaises)*, introduction by A. Martineau, p. 8.

[19]*Ibid.*, p. 9.

[20]*Ibid.*, p. 354.

[21]Marguerite V. Labrendi, *Le Vieux Pondicherry*, p.115.

[22]Paul Olangier, p. 357.

[23]The Masi-Magha festival is generally celebrated on the full-moon day in the month of Magha which corresponds to the English months of February-March. (P.V. Jagadisa Ayyar, *South Indian Festivals*, p. 37).

[24]Marguerite V. Labrendi, p.115; Y.V. Gaebele, *Histoire de Pondichéry*, p.22.

[25]Paul Olangier, p.363.

[26]*Ibid.*, p. 369.

[27]*Ibid.*, p. 16, introduction by A. Martineau.

[28]*Ibid.*, p. 370.

[29]*Ibid.*, p. 371.

[30]*Ibid.*

[31]*Ibid.*, p. 380.

[32]*Ibid.*, p. 398.

[33]*Ibid.*, p. 399.

SOCIAL CONDITIONS AND TENSIONS ON BOARD THE EIGHTEENTH CENTURY EAST INDIA SHIPS

Karel Degryse

East India trade from the southern Netherlands, undertaken by the Ostend Company and its predecessors between 1715 and 1735, has always had a good reputation regarding the social and material conditions on board the East India ships. There was a rather low mortality of eight per cent during the voyage. In the other companies, the mortality figures averaged between fifteen and twenty per cent. Food for the sailors was not abundant and surely monotonous, but the number of calories provided was sufficient, even for the heavy ship's labour. Desertion did not much occur among the crews of the Ostend ships.[1] We get the impression that conditions on board were rather good also when reading the ship's journals, written by the captains or navigating officers. These contain technical information concerning navigation; for the rest they mention only some minor problems concerning the crew.

We have found some other sources, documents not easily accessible, that give a completely different idea of the social conditions on board. These exceptional sources are some juridical dossiers—especially the *Van Pruyssen* case, a well-documented sodomy case dating from 1727-28[2]—and the journal of Gerard de Bock.[3] De Bock officially was a writer on board the *Saint-Elisabeth*, a Chinaman that left in 1724, but in fact he was a spy for the Directors of the Company. He kept a secret diary where he noted everything that went wrong during the voyage. His main job was to trace any fraud at the expense of the Company; but he also recorded the continual social tensions that made the life of the sailors nerve-racking and hard.

The most important tensions on board the East-Indiamen were, according to these sources, between the Flemish and the British part of the crew; between merchants and navigating officers/captain; between navigating officers/captain and the common sailors. The Flemish-English tension mainly occurred during private expeditions, before the erection of the Ostend Company in December 1722. Many of the captains and a substantial part of the crew were then British, and a common complaint by the Flemish sailors and officers was that they were treated unjustly vis-a-vis their British colleagues.[4] After 1722, almost all the captains were Flemish, and complaints, of discrimination diminished substantially.[5]

Tension between the merchants and the naval officers came of having two sets of masters on board—the captain and the supercargo. On board every East-Indiaman there were merchants, appointed by the Company, who were in charge of the merchant-goods and the silver that was brought to the East Indies. These merchants, called supercargos were the real leaders of the expedition—certainly so once the ship had arrived in the East Indies. The head-supercargo was the best paid servant of the Company. His prestige was higher than the captain's; he sat at the head of the first table. The captain was the undisputed master of the ship at sea, as far as nautical or disciplinary matters were concerned, but he had no jurisdiction over the merchants, some of whom made a nuisance of themselves with excessive drinking at table and drunken brawls. The fact that the first supercargo very often was a British (Peter Spendelow, Robert Hewer, Alexander Hume...)—even under the Company—while the captain was Flemish, was also a source of discord. These tensions were bad for the general atmosphere on board.[6]

The most serious tension was that between the common sailors and the navigating officers, including the captain. This came of a very strong class segregation. The two groups lived almost completely separated from each other. The officers and the merchants dined rather richly at the first and second tables, while the sailors had a much more sober meal on deck. The first group was housed in more or less private cabins and had the disposal of some decent lavatories; the second had to sleep in hammocks between-decks and used the galleon of the ship or the barrels of the guns to ease nature. In the juridical court material mentioned earlier the common seaman is often described as the scum of the nation, to imply that statements or accusations coming from ordinary sailors were not trustworthy.[7]

The captains and the officers consequently were not on familiar terms with their crew, and those who behaved otherwise were considered by the Directors of the Company as unfit for the job.[8] The captain had to maintain order and discipline on the ship and he usually ruled there with a mailed fist. The punishment meted to seamen was sometimes out of all proportion. De Bock, although he was a writer and not a sailor, was perplexed to see how a ship's carpenter was immediately beaten and half killed by captain Roose. The only reason for this was that the sailor had protested verbally against a superior over some minor affair. He was further put in chains for the rest of the journey.[9] Another horrifying case occurred in 1728 on the Chinaman *The Eagle.* There the second captain, Dominicq Bracq, stabbed the boatswain's mate with his sword, only because the latter had refused to leave the captain's room. The mate died a few days later. The second captain was pardoned for this manslaughter; he was even praised by the Directors for his behaviour as he was the only one who had kept discipline on board of *The Eagle,* the other officers being too lax. He was later promoted and was in 1729 appointed captain by the Company.[10] Such an unpunished brutality, combined with the class segregation and the haughty behaviour of the officers, who besides were mostly drunk, caused a growing animosity on board between the two groups. A clear illustration of that hostility was the phenomenon of the 'blind spirit' (de blinde geest' in Dutch), that seems to have been well known on East-Indiamen. According to de Bock, this consisted of the crew taking revenge on the officers if they could do so with impunity. So, when the lights went out by accident at night, the officers ran the risk of having some heavy things thrown at their heads. This throwing in the dark was called "the blind spirit".[11]

Another reaction against the harsh discipline and the brutality of the commanders was the robust solidarity among the common sailors. This was particularly obvious in the sodomy case I have studied.[12] Two sailors, accused of sodomy, were put in chains for the rest of the voyage, to be judged when the ships were back home. As sodomy was a capital crime they had to be judged by a higher court. A third person involved also had to appear before the same court but he was not incarcerated because he was a supercargo. Nevertheless, it was the two prisoners who managed to escape and at the end only the supercargo was brought to trial. The first sailor broke out of his chains and swam ashore while the ship was anchoring near Kanton. He did this in broad daylight, but when the crew was interrogated by the captian, they declared to have seen nothing at all. The second escaped when the ship was already anchoring in the roadstead near Ostend. He had clearly received help from outside to break the lock on the door and break loose of his chains. The first case was one of passive solidarity: nobody wanted to declare anything about his escape. In the second case the solidarity was more active: some sailors effectively helped their colleague to escape.

Before coming to some general conclusions, I have to mention two recent studies that reached me shortly after I had finished my small study concerning the social conditions of sailors during the eighteenth century. They both deal more or less with the same subject. In 1986 N.A.M. Rodger published "*The wooden world. An anatomy of the Georgian Navy*". He studied shipboard life on the ships of the English Navy during the Seven Years' War (1756-63). His remarkable conclusion was that the traditional view of the Navy, as an institution with a harsh, oppressive and tyrannical discipline, and with sailors drawn from the dregs of society, was wrong. According to Rodger, the discipline was rather lax, the officers worked rather by persuasion than by command and there was no division of class on board. The strength of the Navy at that moment was formed by the unity of the crew, high and low; they were "bound by mutual ties of dependence and obligation".[13]

One year later, in 1987, Marcus Rediker published his book *Between the Devil and the Deep Blue Sea. Merchant Seamen, Pirates and the Anglo-American Maritime World, 1700-1750.* He also came up with a remarkable conclusion. Rediker dealt with the common seamen who worked on the merchant ships in the transatlantic trades. He especially studied them as employees, as workers. What he says on discipline on board is striking.[14] He describes it as very harsh, brutal and he also discovered a very strong class division between the common crew and the officers. So his conclusions are exactly the opposite of what Rodger concluded.

How is that possible? From the first part of my paper it is obvious that my findings concerning the Ostend Company completely support the thesis of Rediker, but it would be too simple to say that Rediker is right and Rodger wrong. I think that the solution to their contradiction lies in the fact that the sailors they studied, worked and lived in totally different circumstances. Rodger calculated that the larger men-of-war from the Navy were at sea only forty-one per cent of their time during the Seven Years'

War. The rest they spent in harbours; and when the ships put out to sea it was seldom for long periods. When the men-of-war were anchoring in the harbour or even in the roadstead, the sailors could easily receive leave.[15] The seamen that worked on the merchant ships, on the other hand, especially those involved in the transatlantic trades in the East India trade, were at sea for very long periods. Rediker has pointed out that the number and the importance of the conflicts on board, and hence the need for strong discipline, not only depended on the size of the ship but especially on the length of the voyage. In a recent article he states: "The length of the voyage ... was crucial because the close and isolated quarters of the shipwith its food shortages, monotony, and frustrations of confinement—bred conflict and animosity like a hot-house".[16] If the Navy ships had more and longer voyages during the Seven Years' War, there would have been exactly the same problems as on the merchant ships mentioned. That is indeed what happened at the end of the century. The year 1797 was the year of the great naval mutinies, and one perceived on the ships "class interests at work which united lower deck (the crew) and quarter deck (the officers) against each other".[17] Rodger gives no clear answer for this phenomenon, but I think that the fact that the men-of-war were coppered at that time and stayed much longer at sea, was a crucial factor.[18]

To conclude, let us return to the East India trade. If the length of the voyage was the most important factor in originating conflict and calling for harsh and brutal repression, this certainly must have been the case in the East India trade. The East-Indiamen were away from home for about eighteen months. All that time an average of a hundred men (sometimes more, when there were soldiers on board) had to live and work together in a vessel that was about 33 metres long, 10 metres large and 4 metres deep, if it was a ship of 400 tons. Considering that alone, I think, it is clear why tensions, stress and conflicts could rise to explosive proportions on board those ships. A journey to the East Indies in the eighteenth century certainly was no pleasure trip.

NOTES

[1]K. Degryse, "De maritieme organisatie van de Oostendse Chinahandel (1718-1735)". Mededelingen van de Marine Academie, XXIV, 1976-77,

pp.19-57; R. Baetens, "De voedsel-rantsoenen van de zeevarenden: de theorie getoetst aan de werkelijkheid", Bijdragen tot de Geschiedenis, 60, 1977, pp.273-309; *idem* "Les conditions sociales Ö bord des navires flamands vers l'Orient (résumé)" in "Seamen in Society Gens de Mer en Société (Comm. Intern. d'Hist. Marit., Boucarest, 11-12 Aug. 1980)", Parthes, 1980, pp.207-9; C. Koninckx, "Voeding op zee in de 18de eeuw. Een kwantit-atief en vergelijkend onderzoek" Mededelingen van de Marine Academie, CCV, 1978-79, pp.1-32; *idem* "Ziekten op zee. Pathologie van de ziekten in de grote vaart in de achttiende eeuw" Mededelingen van de Mrine Academie, XXVI, 1980-82, pp.33-54. See also K. Degryse and J. Parmentier, "Maritime aspects of the Osten trade to Mocha, India, Bengal and China (1715-1732)", in "Company and Shipping", Leiden, Center for the History of European Expansion (in press).

[2]State Archives Ghent, Raad van Vlaanderen nr. 22997.

[3]City Archives Antwerp, Generale Indische Compagnie nr. 5689 bis. See also K. Degryse "Sociale en sexuele spanningen aan boord van de Oostendse Oost-Indiâvaarders (1715-1734)", Collectanea Maritima IV, Brussel, 1988, pp.69-79, concerning the above-mentioned sources.

[4]J. Mertens "Oostendse schepen naar Kanton (1719)", Ostendiana IV, 1982, pp.19-37, gives examples of that opposition.

[5]K. Degryse and J. Parmentier, "Maritime aspects of the Ostend trade...".

[6]The journal of De Bock illustrates those tensions very well: notes of 30.4, 16.5, 29.6.1724 and 24.5.1725.

[7]See the "Van Pruyssen"-case: K. Degryse "Sociale en sexuele spanningen...", pp. 74-9.

[8]F. Prims, "De reis van den Sint-Carolus", Antwerpen, 1926, pp.33-4.

[9]City Archives Antwerp, GIC nr. 5689 bis: 21.8.1724.

[10]City Archives Antwerp, GIC nr. 5601: the Bracq-case.

[11]City Archives Antwerp, GIC nr. 5689 bis: 29.6.1724.

[12]State Archives Ghent, Raad van Vlaanderen nr. 22997.

[13]N.A.M. Rodger, "The wooden world. An anatomy of the Georgian Navy", (Fontana Press ed., 1988), p.11 and ch. VI (especially pp. 205-7).

[14]M. Rediker, "Between the Devil and the Deep Blue Sea. Merchant Seamen, Pirates and the Anglo-American Maritime World, 1700-1750", Cambridge 1987, see especially ch. V: "The seamen as the spirit of rebellion. Authority, Violence and Labour Discipline", pp. 205-53.

[15]N.A.M. Rodger, "The Wooden World...", pp. 37-9.

[16]M. Rediker, "The Common Seamen in the Histories of Capitalism and the Working Class", International Journal of Maritime History, I (2), December 1989, pp. 343-6.

[17]N.A.M. Rodger, "The Wooden World...", p. 206.

[18]*Ibid.*, p. 346.

THE DUTCH EAST INDIA COMPANY AND THE TRADE OF THE CHULIAS IN THE BAY OF BENGAL IN THE LATE EIGHTEENTH CENTURY

Bhaswati Bhattacharya

Monopolisation versus liberalisation of various branches of Asian trade was a much discussed subject at different levels of the Dutch East India Company's (*VOC*) administration throughout the eighteenth century. Naturally the debate touched upon the trade in the Bay of Bengal in which the *VOC* had been participating since its early years. In spite of its monopolistic claims over different items and routes of trade in the region, the *VOC* was facing increasing competition from other groups of merchants involved in the port-to-port trade of the Bay of Bengal. This essay seeks to look at the challenge offered by a section of Asian traders, namely the Chulia merchants of the Coromandel coast to the activity of the *VOC* in the Bay of Bengal in the later middle decades of the eighteenth century. It will be shown that the Chulias, operating side by side with European and other Asian traders, posed a serious threat to Dutch monopolistic claims on the main branches trade to and from the coast. In this paper I shall concentrate on Chulia trade with the ports in Southeast Asia though this group of merchants traded with Malabar and Sri Lanka as well. It is interesting to note that while the *VOC* insisted on maintaining its monopoly, its agents on the Coromandel coast were in favour of liberalisation of trade in the region. The *VOC* retained its monopoly though in practice it was violated by Chulias and others alike. As the century was drawing to its close, the ineffectiveness of the monopolistic claims of the *VOC* became more and more clear and finally, the Anglo-Dutch Treaty of 1784 marked the end of the monopoly of the *VOC* and declared free trade in the region. The period marked the emergence of English private traders as the predominant group of merchants in Asian trade. The Chulias adjusted themselves with the new situation and continued to trade.

Before discussing the trade of the Chulias and the Dutch reaction to it, it is perhaps worthwhile to say a few words regarding the Chulias and the regulations imposed by the *VOC* on the trade to and from the Coromandel coast. Among all the rivals of the Dutch, the Chulias are of special interest to us as they were the remnants of independent overseas traders the coast had seen in the previous century. In the seventeenth and eighteenth centuries they were to be found in Cuddalore, Porto Novo, Karaikal, Nagore, Nagapatnam, Adirampatnam, Tondi and Kilakarai. The origin of these Muslim traders goes back to the Arab merchants of the ninth and tenth centuries who had settled along the coast and intermarried with local Tamils.[1] The Muslim community on the coast had four subdivisions,[2] and the wealthy and the prosperous merchants were usually called the Maraḳkayars.[3] In her recent studies on Islam in South India, Susan Bayly has suggested that in the early nineteenth century, the Marakkayars of this region who were Shafis (thus distinct from the Hanafis), were very conscious of their Arabic origin and would usually intermarry with Shafis from Malabar, Sri Lanka and Southeast Asia.[4] This seems to have been a result and continuation of the commercial and cultural contacts established by the Chulia merchants of Coromandel with ports in Southeast Asia in the seventeenth and eighteenth centuries.[5] Muslim traders from Coromandel traded regularly at Perak in the early eighteenth century and were held in high esteem in that Malay state.[6] It has also been suggested that the Nagore-Acheh trade route was one of the most important trade routes in the Bay of Bengal in the eighteenth century.[7] It is thus clear that in course of their long-standing relationship with the Southeast Asian countries, the Marakkayars had established commercial and cultural links with the ports in the region where many of them had settled.

Dutch participation in the port-to-port trade of Asia was bound to affect the trade of the Chulias as the former had tried to restrict Coromandel trade and shipping to Southeast Asia with their control of Malacca and the adjacent straits. Not only, the *VOC* also claimed a monopoly on the trade in various kinds of cotton cloth, the chief item of export from the coast. Traditionally these textiles were exchanged in the Malay-Indonesian ports for spices, minerals, metals, elephants and Chinese goods which were not termed as 'monopoly goods' by the *VOC* with the effect that trade in these items was forbidden for others. Arasaratnam has shown that after an initial setback resulting from this monopolistic attitude of the *VOC* the indigenous traders reappeared on the scene already in the late seventeenth century taking advantage of the gaps in the system established by the *VOC*. Thus the fall of Malacca to the Dutch had resulted in an increase in the Coromandel merchants' trade to Acheh, Johore, Kedah, Bantam and Macassar. After the capture of Bantam by the Dutch in 1682 and the naval blockade in the Java Seas, indigenous merchants of Coromandel concentrated on ports like Kedah, Perak, Johore and Acheh on the western shores of Southeast Asia.[8] This orientation on part of the Coromandel merchants continued till the late eighteenth century. But they seem to have stopped sailing to Johore in this period. Acheh and Kedah were now the most frequented ports in the region.

The main centres of activity of the Chulias on the Coromandel coast were Porto Novo and Nagore. Nagore, situated about five kilometres north of Nagapatnam, was a centre of free trade under the King of Tanjore. Due to the tax concessions given by the district officials merchants were attracted to the port, which began to flourish from about the beginning of the eighteenth century.[9] To Muslim merchants coming from other regions Nagore had another attraction. There were several *dargahs* or mosques, of which the most important in the eighteenth century was the *dargah* of Shahul Hamid Naguri. As a site of these mosques, Nagore developed strong religious and cultural links with Batticaloa in Sri Lanka and the Indonesian islands. Nagore was also a centre for shipbuilding.[10] For all these reasons the port seems to have been a refuge for all those traders who wanted to evade the monopolistic regulations of the *VOC*.

Under the direct rule of the nawab of Carnatic, Porto Novo was another major centre attracting private European and Asian traders. Many rich Hindu and Muslim merchants lived here carrying on trade to Acheh, Kedah, Pegu and Arakan. Both Nagore and Porto Novo were frequently visited by Chulia merchants settled at ports in Southeast Asia. Till the 1770s, the Dutch at Nagapatnam tried to attract this traffic of Nagore to their port by various means. First the customs duty at Nagapatnam was lowered in order to match that at Nagore. This measure proved ineffective.[11] They would also try to persuade rich merchants of Nagore to come to settle at Nagapatnam. This attempt was successful once when the two rich Marakkayar brothers—Sala Poele and Seijdoe Poele—

moved from Nagore to Nagapatnam in the early 1740s.[12] A similar attempt was made in 1777 when it was hoped that Mahomed Cassiem, one of the principal merchants of Nagore with an extensive network of trade with overseas ports, would come over to Nagapatnam. This time the plan did not work out, since Nagore soon passed under the control of the English and Mahomed Cassiem was more interested in cultivating the friendship of the English.[13] In spite of all these measures, Nagore continued to be a 'thorn in the flesh' of the Dutch on the coast who were of opinion that destruction of Nagore was necessary for the benefit of the Company's trade.[14]

The Chulias were not the only traders posing a challenge to the Dutch Company trade in the Bay of Bengal. Armenians were another group of Asian merchants competing with the Dutch. They were indispensable in the sense that most of the European private and company trade to Manila was carried on under Armenian cover. They were also taking part in the trade to Syriam, Pegu and Martaban.[15] The middle decades of the eighteenth century witnessed a shift of attention on the part of the English private traders from the western Indian Ocean to the Bay of Bengal resulting, in the words of Furber, in "commercial revolution" in the Bay of Bengal.[16] The close contact between the Portuguese of Macao and the English country traders has been studied by B. Souza. Portuguese trade was of considerable importance to the English East India Company for the customs paid by those Macao traders on imports from China at Madras.[17] While sailing from Goa to Macao, they would stop at Port Novo, Pondicherry, Fort St. David or Madras to take in textiles and opium for Southeast Asian ports and China. They brought sugar from Macao much to the detriment of the *VOC*'s interest.[18]

Growing activity of the French private traders was another area of concern for the *VOC*. The French were the main rivals of the English in the 1730s and 1740s.[19] During and immediately after the Anglo-French wars French trade to the East Indies received a serious setback. This trade was gradually coming up again in the late 1760s. They were exporting textiles from the coast directly to France, to the Red Sea and to their Asian colonies.[20] This trade further increased following the opening of the East Indies trade by the French Crown for private traders in 1769.[21] In 1777 the Directors of the *VOC* at Amsterdam had the information that 3,86,614 pieces of textiles had been imported to Europe that year via France and

Denmark. This quantity did not include the goods freighted by the French, the amount of which was unknown. Four more French ships were expected to arrive in France from Bengal, Coromandel and Malabar with textiles among other goods the same year.[22]

The most important development of the Malay-Indonesian world in the eighteenth century was the rise of the Bugis of Celebes. The Bugis were fierce warriors and traded to all parts of the archipelago. They first invaded Johore and established their political power in that kingdom. They also controlled Selangore and Kelang, the former tin-areas of Johore. Riau under the Bugis grew as an important centre of trade. They smuggled spices in small parcels from the eastern kingdoms to ports like Kedah, Perak and Acheh from where these were taken to the Coromandel coast by private European and indigenous traders.[23]

The Danes at Tranquebar were noted to be the principal carriers of textiles to Europe on private account. They were also carrying private freight from Porto Novo to Pegu, Kedah, Acheh and, from 1745 onwards, to Manila.[24] Tranquebar thus offered a typical example of the combination of European and Asian interests vis-a-vis the monopolistic regulations of the *VOC*.

Naturally, the employees of the *VOC* on the coast, who saw in these developments an opportunity to widen their own network of trade, did not want to remain idle viewers. Even before Gustaaf Willem van Imhoff presented before the Directors of the Company his famous considerations regarding free trade in Asian waters, the Governor and Council at Nagapatnam had taken initiative in this regard. The Batavia Council, on the basis of the suggestion of the Nagapatnam Council, decided to free the trade from the coast "to Bengal along the coast of Pegu up to Malacca and to Achin and other places lying on the north and northwestern coast of the island of Sumatra... where the Company has not signed monopoly treaties...".[25] This privilege was meant for burghers and inhabitants of the country, subjects of the Company or the indigenous kings or the allies of the Company. With the Company's pass they would be able to despatch their vessels from such places on the coast as were under the Company's jurisdiction or at least where the Company had a factory and to certain places mentioned in the pass which would be issued at Nagapatnam for a round year. Everyone who had the pass could import and export, without hindrance, slaves and all kinds of goods except copper, tin, spices, vermilion, quicksilver,

Bengal goods like single and double armozijns, mombanis, taftas and bandanoes which the Company imported to the coast, or guineas, salempores or parcallas raw, bleached or blue of the quality, length and width that was procured by the Company, provided he paid the customary export and import duty. Ships or vessels sailing with the Company's pass were not permitted to load or unload at any port belonging to other European Companies or indigenous rulers. Violation of any of these conditions would result in confiscation of goods and vessels. Those who had the permission to carry on trade in this way, could also freely sail to Sri Lanka for purchasing chanks and other permitted goods and import and export these goods without having to seek further permission.

The Nagapatnam Council assumed that implicitly the notice extended the freedom of trade to the Western Indian Ocean also as the *VOC* had to compete with other traders at Surat, Mocha, Jedda and other places.[26]

The Nagapatnam Council welcomed the limited freedom of trade granted by the notice of 1740. "This change in the policy was necessary in order to check the rivals", they wrote. The Council further commented that freeing of the trade to both sides of Malacca could not be any more detrimental to the despatch of the Company's textiles to those regions than it already was, since those places were regularly visited by a great number of private European and Muslim traders. The Council added:

> It is not possible to put a stop to this trade. As regards the import of goods over there, it has been rightly noted by the officials that due to the closeness of Nagore where everyone is welcome and the newly emerged Karikal where everything is brought for sale, this trade will remain unchanged whether we allow free trade at Nagapatnam or not. The only difference is that the latter does not hinder the things in the least while the Company is deprived of the profit that it could otherwise make from the import and export duties. The profit from customs duties at Company's places would have been greater than that at other European ports had the Company allowed indigenous trade at ports under its jurisdiction.[27]

This shows that the *VOC*'s officials on the Coromandel coast were aware of the implications of the developments that were taking place in the Bay of Bengal trade vis-a-vis the *VOC*'s policy regarding Asian trade. They also proposed that the prohibition on the import of tin be lifted as this would affect the trade with Perak and Kedah where the only product was tin.[28] Their other recommendations included a total revision of the toll-list at Nagapatnam according to the prevailing rates at neighbourhood ports and a change in the pass policy. They pointed out that the Danes at Tranquebar did not bother about the pass and carried freight goods belonging to indigenous merchants.[29]

The notice of 1740 was renewed in 1741. In the latter year van Imhoff placed before the Directors in Amsterdam his suggestions regarding freedom of trade in Asia. He argued that since the Dutch did not have command over all branches of Asian trade, it was impossible for them to control this trade. He pointed out that apart from the trade in spices and Japanese copper in which the *VOC* had a monopoly, their trade was insignificant compared to that of the English and French. So, it would be logical if the *VOC* gave up monopoly in all trades except in Japanese copper and spices in the region west of Batavia and developed Batavia as the centre for all Asian trade.[30] van Imhoff's proposals were accepted by the Directors at their meeting of 2 April 1742. Soon after he reached Batavia as the Governor General of the Indies (1743-50), the Council there took resolutions to throw open the trade in the region west of Batavia.[31] The resolution was meant specially for the burghers of Batavia, but Asian traders also could take part in this trade. The Nagapatnam Council was asked to send order to all the subordinate factories to extend all possible help to the burghers in their trade so far as it did not affect the Company's trade. However, the *VOC* retained its monopoly on copper, spices, tin, pepper, opium and coarse textiles.

This change of policy was hailed by the Nagapatnam Council. They made some suggestions which included that private merchants should not be allowed to call at a port of any other nation on the coast before the cargo of their ship had been examined at Nagapatnam or any other of the Company's factories. Otherwise it would be impossible to watch if these vessels carried contraband goods.[32]

At a meeting in 1745 it was stipulated that all vessels sailing to the Coromandel coast must call at one of the Dutch factories in order to show that they were not carrying any contraband goods.

They would be required to pay a three per cent duty ad valorem on imports if the cargo was unloaded at that port. A similar three per cent was to be paid on goods transported from the Company's factories. The Nagapatnam Council was asked to send a copy of the resolution to all subordinate factories.[33]

The Nagapatnam Council thought, however, that it would not be advisable in the Company's interest to introduce a three per cent export duty at Nagapatnam. It would discourage merchants coming from Batavia and other places to buy anything of considerable value at Nagapatnam and they would sail to the neighbouring Muslim port, Nagore, where they had to pay about one per cent duty on goods exportedan amount very little and much lower than the charge payable at Nagapatnam. This measure, the Nagapatnam Council wrote, would only give Nagore another chance to prosper at the cost of Nagapatnam and its inhabitants whereas just the opposite had been desired in 1741 when the Nagapatnam Council had decided to fix the customs duty at that place at a rate little lower than that at Nagore to attract the trade and powerful merchants of that place. For the same reason the Council now suggested that only an import duty of three per cent be introduced in addition to the fee payable to the farmer of the mouth of the river. This import duty would be collected from vessels coming from Batavia and not from vessels coming from Pegu, Tenasserim, Kedah, Acheh and other places as these vessels would then sail to Nagore.[34]

Initially, the Batavia Council insisted on the payment of three per cent both on export and import. Finally, at the insistence of the Nagapatnam Council, the export duty payable at Nagapatnam was totally abolished "in view... specially of the changed circumstances".[35]

It is thus evident that Dutch officials on Coromandel were in favour of freedom of trade in the Bay of Bengal. As Nagore and Porto Novo continued to flourish, they tried to attract the attention of their superiors to the growing necessity of encouraging free trade in the region.

Specially *VOC*al in this regard was Pieter Haksteen, the Governor of Coromandel (1765-71). Being informed by the Coromandel officials that the failure of the *VOC* in getting the required quantity of textiles was due to a tough competition in that trade, the Batavia Council had passed a resolution on 12 August 1760 forbidding the import of any kind of textiles to Batavia on private account before the Company's demand for the Fatherland and the Indies had been fully met.[36] Haksteen related the thriving trade at Porto Novo and Nagore carried on by Coromandel Muslims, Muslims of the "opposite coast" and English and other European private traders in the 1760s to this interdiction on private trade in textiles. If private traders were allowed to export textiles from Nagapatnam, Haksteen argued, many merchants and weavers would settle at that port and bring prosperity to the port. If merchants were allowed to buy and sell freely at Nagapatnam, they would not go to Nagore or to ports under the English and French where these merchants could freely import any commodity that suited them.[37] In view of the circumstances, Haksteen advised to throw open the import trade to Batavia in all goods including even spices.[38] Though the *VOC* retained its monopoly on spices till the end, the interdiction on private trade in textiles was withdrawn in 1771. Except for ordinary bleached, raw and brown blue guineas, salempores, parcallas and baftas which the *VOC* required for its trade to the Eastern Kingdoms, the Cape, Timor and some other places, the other varieties were thrown open to private trade.[39]

Frequent references to the prosperity of Porto Novo and Nagore, and the concern of the Dutch on the coast regarding freedom of trade at ports under Dutch control bear evidence to the fact that the waves of the commercial revolution in the Bay of Bengal had reached the shores of Porto Novo and Nagore. It is also evident that though the English private traders were forcing their way to the forefront, the Chulias both from the Coromandel coast and ports on the opposite coast had played an important role in the trade of the region at least till the late 1770s. A considerable part of the trade between Coromandel ports and Kedah, Acheh, Malacca on the opposite coast was in the hands of either the Chulias of Coromandel or their counterparts on the other side of the Bay. A report sent from Malacca in 1755 mentioned that an English private ship and seven Muslim ships from Pondicherry, Porto Novo and other places had arrived before the river (at Malacca) with textiles and other goods which they sold for elephants, arecanuts, gold, tin and wax.[40] This trade seems to have reached its peak in the 1760s. A report sent from Nagapatnam to Batavia in 1762 mentioned that twelve ships had come that year from ports on the opposite coast to Porto Novo.[41] These merchants were buying mainly coarse textiles, which resulted in an increase in the cost price of textiles, and the Company's merchants could not procure as many as 260 bales against the demand for Company's trade.[12] They brought spices in small parcels, which they used to collect at Kedah and Acheh. Coming to the Coromandel coast they bought whatever textile was available "without bothering about the length and width of the cloth". As many as twenty vessels were reported to have come from Pegu, Kedah, Malacca and Acheh in 1764 to Porto Novo alone. Consequently, a large quantity of textiles was being sold at Nagore and Porto Novo. The Nagapatnam Council noted that their presence made it impossible for the Dutch to procure textiles.[13] A report sent in the following year noted that side by side with the English, French and Danish merchants, merchants settled at the other side of the Bay featured regularly in the Coromandel trade.

> The English are powerful rivals, not to speak of the French and the Danes. The English carry on a considerable private trade in these regions. They take a huge quantity of textiles to the Malay coast, the Straits of Malacca and the west coast of Sumatra over and above what they 'smuggle' directly into the Company's places . . . people from the opposite coast also fit out their ships more and more for this coast, specially for Porto Novo and Nagore, from where they despatch a considerable quantity of textiles to the detriment of the Company's and its subjects' interest.[44]

In 1766 again twenty ships and vessels belonging to the Muslims of the opposite coast came to Porto Novo. The Nagapatnam Council expressed their concern regarding this regular source of impediment to their trade.[45] These "Moors" carried on their trade with Coromandel during the remaining years of the decade.[46]

This trade received direct encouragement from the rulers of different Southeast Asian states. Specially, the kings of Kedah and Acheh were sending ships to Coromandel. In 1739 the Dutch reported the arrival of a ship belonging to the King of Kedah at Cuddalore with eleven elephants.[47] In 1748 another ship belonging to the King of Kedah, also with elephants on board, was reported to have been captured by the English at Fort St. David.[48] The same year Ananda Ranga Pillai, the *dubash* to the French Governor at Pondicherry noted that six to seven ships belonging to the King of Acheh and five or six ships belonging to the King of Kedah were sailing to Porto Novo, Nagore and Nagapatnam.[49] The King of Siam also took part in this trade.[50]

Chulia trade continued in the 1770s. The early years of the decade saw the *VOC* trying to obtain Nagore from the King of Tanjore. The attempt ended in a failure.[51] Already in 1769 the Company's demand for textiles from the coast had been remarkably reduced.[52] Still the officials were anxiously trying to attract the merchants of Nagore to Nagapatnam.[53] Contemporary accounts clearly show that Chulias from Nagore and Porto Novo were still sending out ships to Acheh, Mergui, Siam and the eastern coast.[54] Thomas Forrest, who sailed to the Mergui archipelago in the late eighteenth century, noted that every year twelve to fifteen Chulia vessels weighing about 200-300 tons regularly traded at Acheh. In 1772 the King's merchant at Acheh was a Chulia.[55] Chulia trade to Kedah seems to have received a serious halt after 1771 when the Bugis under Raja Haji attacked Kedah, leaving the port totally devastated.[56] It was the period when the English East India Company and English private traders concentrated their activity at Southeast Asian ports where they stopped over on their way to China, sold opium and textiles and bought tin for China. English private trade increased considerably following the Anglo-Dutch Treaty of 1784 which ended the monopoly of the *VOC* and allowed free trade in the region. But Chulias seem to have adjusted to the situation and continued to trade. That they still played an important role in the politics and trade of Kedah is clear from the fact that in the early 1780s a Chulia named Jemmal was the merchant and minister of the King of Kedah.[57] Chulias also traded at the newly founded settlement of Penang where many of them had settled. Out of the twenty-four ships and vessels that left the Coromandel coast for Penang in 1788, eight vessels were owned by the Chulias.[58] At the beginning of the nineteenth century they were settled at Kedah and trading at Mergui.[59] Every year eight to ten vessels of 150-200 tons were visiting Acheh from Coromandel, mainly with textiles.[60]

NOTES

I am grateful to Prof. Ashin Das Gupta, Prof. S. Arasaratnam, Prof. B. Arunachalam, Prof. J. Van Goor and Mr. Raja Mohammad, research scholar, Pondicherry University for their valuable comments and suggestions.

This study is based mainly on the Overgekomene Brieven en Papieren series of the records of the Dutch East India Company preserved at the General State Archives, The Hague.

[1]S. Arasaratnam, *Merchants, Companies and Commerce on the Coromandel Coast, 1650-1740,* Delhi, 1986, pp. 218-9.

[2]*Ibid.*

[3]E. Thurston, *Castes and Tribes of Southern India,* Madras, vol. 5.

[4]S. Bayly, "Islam and State Power in pre-colonial South India" (unpublished), paper presented at Yogjakarta in 1986 as a part of the Cambridge-Leiden-Delhi-Yogjakarta project on India and Indonesia.

[5]S. Arasaratnam, *op.cit.*

[6]B. Watson Andaya, *Perak, the abode of grace, a study of an eighteenth century Malay State,* Kuala Lumpur. 1979.

[7]S. Bayly, *op.cit.*

[8]S. Arasaratnam, *op.cit.*

[9]Memoir of Governor Jacob Mossel, 20 February 1744, *VOC* 2631.

[10]This assumption is based on information available in Dutch records referring to a ship belonging to a Marakkayar merchant. This three-masted ship, 42 1/4 cobidos long over the keel (1 cobido = 18 inches, thus about 64 feet) was built at Nagore; Political meeting at Nagapatnam, 7 January 1745, *VOC* 2652, pp. 431-3.

[11]Memoir of Governor Jacob Mossel, *op.cit.*

[12]Political meeting at Nagapatnam, 31 August 1742, *VOC* 2574, p. 417.

[13]Nagapatnam-Batavia, 17 October 1777, *VOC* 3482, p.108;
Nagapatnam-Batavia, 25 September 1778, *VOC* 3512, p. 300.

[14]General Letter, Governor Generalthe Directors, 30 December 1758, *VOC* 2912, p.468.

[15]S. Arasaratnam, *op.cit.*, pp.169, 200.

[16]H. Furber, *John Company at Work: A Study of European Expansion in India in the late 18th Century,* London (second printing), 1951, pp.160-68.

[17]G.B. Souza, *The Survival of Empire: Portuguese trade and society in China and the South China Sea, 1630-1754,* Cambridge, 1986, p. 223.

[18]*Private Diary of Ananda Ranga Pillai,* tr. and ed. by Frederick J. Price assisted by K. Rangachari, vol. 1, p. 226; vol. 4, p. 83; Nagapatnam to Batavia, 14 October 1766, *VOC* 3164, pp.141, 364; RFSG, D/E, vol. 12, 5 October 1737, p.79; 5 September 1740, p.113.

[19]RFSG, D/E, vol. 12, 22 January 1737, p.25; vol. 15, 15 February 1745, p.39.

[20]Nagapatnamthe Directors, 11 December 1766, *VOC* 3164, p. 94.

[21]Provisional demand for piece-goods for the year 1779 and the response of the Coromandel officials, *VOC* 3513, p. 561.

[22]*Ibid.*

[23]Nagapatnam-Batavia, 11 December 1766, *VOC* 3164, p. 419.

[24]Manuscript of A.C. Visscher written C.1750 (private papers). I am grateful to Dr. H.W. Van Santen for drawing my attention to these manuscripts. Also see H. Furber, *Rival Empires of Trade in the Orient, 1600-1800,* Minneapolis, 1976, pp. 287-8; O. Feldbaek, *India Trade under Danish Flag,* Copenhagen, 1969, pp.17-8.

[25]Notice regarding free sailing, Nagapatnam 23 July, 11 August 1740, *VOC* 2506, pp.450-3; also *VOC* 4472 not foliated.

[26]Nagapatnam-Batavia, 9 October 1742, *VOC* 2556, pp.706-24.

[27]*Ibid.*

[28]*Ibid.*

[29]*Ibid.*

[30]The considerations of G.W. Van Imhoff 24 November 1741, ed. with introduction by J.E. Heeres, BK ITLV, vol.LXVI.

[31]Resolutions of the Batavia Council, *VOC* 780, pp. 388-9.

[32]*VOC* 2631, pp. 625-7.

[33]Nagapatnam-Batavia, 13 October 1746, *VOC* 2677, pp. 250-1.

[34]*Ibid.*

[35]Batavia-Nagapatnam, 27 June 1747, 4 August 1748, HRB 308; pp. 51, 84-5.

[36]Extract, Batavia-Nagapatnam, 13 September 1760, HRB 309, pp.167-8.

[37]NagapatnamBatavia, 18 August 1765, *VOC* 3135, pp. 401-2.

[38]Memoir of Pieter Haksteen, 1771, HRB 344.

[39]Extract, Circular letter, Batavia-Nagapatnam, 3 December 1771, HRB 310, pp.137-9.

[40]Report submitted to the Governor General regarding the trade to Trengganu, Kedah and other places, by Gerits Zeeman Carga, Malacca, 19 June 1755, *VOC* 2861, p.24.

[41]Nagapatnam-Batavia, 11 December 1762, *VOC* 3043, p.135.

[42]Political meeting at Nagapatnam, 18 November 1762, *VOC* 3044, pp. 481-3; 17 February 1763, *VOC* 3078, pp. 81-2.

[43]Nagapatnam-Batavia, 14 October 1764, *VOC* 3107, pp. 251-2.

[44]Nagapatnam-The Directors, 18 December 1765, *VOC* 3135, p. 917.

[45]Nagapatnam-Batavia, 24 July 1766, *VOC* 3164, p. 206.

[46]See e.g. Nagapatnam-Batavia (Secret) 6 March 1768, *VOC* 3229, p.10; Nagapatnam-Batavia (Secret) 22 December 1770, *VOC* 3289, pp. 50-1.

[47]*VOC* 2505, p.1534.

[48]RFSG, C.C. 1748, No. 59, pp. 24-5.

[49]Private Diary of Ananda Ranga Pillai, *op.cit.*, vol. v, p.104.

[50]*Ibid.*, vol. I, p. 269; B. Harrison, "Malacca in the 18th Century: Two governors' reports", *JMBRAS*, vol. 27, part I, May 1954, p. 29; RFSG, D/CB, vol. 90 (1760), 20 May, pp.171-2.

[51]Political resolutions, Nagapatnam *VOC* 3373, 10th October 1773,

pp. 275-91; 21 October 1773, pp. 366-77.

[52]Demand for Returns for the year 1769, dated 14 October 1767, *VOC* 178. As reason the Directors stated that they were dissatisfied since the Coromandel officials failed to supply the textiles in desired quantity and quality.

[53]See note 10 above.

[54]Abbe Raynal, *A Philosophical and Political History of the settlements and trade of the Europeans in the East and West Indies*, London, 1798, Vol. I, p. 279.

[55]T. Forrest, *A Voyage from Calcutta to the Mergui Archipelago lying on the east side of the Bay of Bengal,* London, 1792, p. 41. Forrest saw 12 and 7 Chulie vessels in the years 1762 and 1783 respectively at Acheh. See pp. 25, 45, 60.

[56]B. Watson-Andaya, pp. 301-2.

[57]T. Forrest, p. 48.

[58]Shipping list of the Prince of Wales Island (Penang). I owe this information to Mr. Reinhout of Utrecht University who kindly allowed me to consult his collections from the IOLR, London.

[59]W. Milburn, *Oriental Commerce*: containing a geographical description of the principal places in the East Indies, China and Japan with their produce manufactures and trade, London, 1813, vol. 2, pp. 290-7.

[60]*Ibid.*; also see W. Marsden, *The History of Sumatra:* containing an account of the government, laws, customs and manners of the native inhabitants with a description of the natural productions and a relation of the ancient political state of that island. Reprint of the third edition introduced by J. Bastin, Singapore, 1986, p. 399.

ABBREVIATIONS USED

BKITLV	-	Bijdragen tot de Koninklijke Instituut van Tall-Land en Volkenkunde
C.C.	-	Country Correspondence
D/CB	-	Diary and Consultation Book
D/E	-	Despatches to England
HRB	-	Hoge Regering Batavia
JMBRAS	-	Journal of the Malayan Branch of the Royal Asiatic Society
RFSG	-	Records of Fort St. George

WILLEM BOLTS; INDIA REGAINED AND LOST: INDIAMEN, IMPERIAL FACTORIES AND COUNTRY TRADE (1775-1785)

John Everaert

The Ostend Company, which had been too successful for her rivals, was sacrificed as the peace offering in the cold war between Austria and the anti-Habsburg league. The octroi, initially suspended (1727) for a period of seven years, was finally withdrawn in 1731. Nevertheless a few ships, clandestinely fitted out in Càdiz, sailed under false colours (Prussia, Poland). In this manner the active trade of the Austrian Netherlands to the East Indies was provisionally brought to an end. From then on, the Ostend Company confined itself to passive investments, stopping its activities altogether only in 1774.

The Company had only just got dissolved, when the so-called "Asiatic Association" was established in Antwerp (1775). This trading partnership was a truly international organisation. The initiator was the Dutch-born Willem Bolts, veteran of the English East India Company in Bengal, but fallen into disgrace because of his egregious behaviour, especially after the publication in the early months of 1772 of his "Considerations on Indian Affairs...", a pamphlet in the form of a sustained and copiously documented attack on Clive, his associates and his successor. Bolts now set up a combine with an unscrupulous Antwerp promoter, the merchant-banker Count Charles de Proli, son of a former director of the old Ostend Company. Bearing in mind his own rehabilitation, Bolts sought to reopen an indirect East India trade for the Austrian Netherlands under the imperial flag. The use of Trieste and Leghorn as home ports meant a mere cover-up to bypass the Anglo-Austrian agreement prohibiting the revival of the Ostend Company.

Bolts intended to integrate the Asiatic Association as quickly as possible under the rivalling European trading companies. His sound experience in the service of the East India Company led him to a double strategy: first he would try to obtain a firm footing in East Africa (Delagoa Bay), on the Indian westcoast (Malabar) as well as on the Nicobar islands; next, from these points of support he was going to participate in country trade. Meanwhile Bengal and China remained in the background, until further notice anyway.

Fitted out under the imperial flag, the *Joseph & Theresia* left the Toscan port of Leghorn in September 1776. Bolts not only acted as captain of the ship but also as commander—holding the grade of lieutenant-colonel—to the twenty-five Austrian soldiers on board. In his rank of Imperial Officer the Indian princes were supposed to hold him considerably more official respect and he also would be guaranteed a certain diplomatic immunity by the British. Franáois Ryan accompanied them as supercargo.

We do not have a clear picture of the real apparel costs, since in the bookkeeping as such they are combined with accommodation expenses during the voyage. Bolts himself did not provide any capital: he exclusively brought in merchandise supplied by the Austrian Government, for the greater part guaranteed by the Proli Bank.

The outward cargo—of which there are no invoices to be found—was highly diverse: heavy metals (iron and steel, copper, lead in blocks and plates) from the State mines in the Austrian Succession Lands. Firearms were genuine "strategic" merchandise, since they were used as exchange money in order to obtain concessions from the Indian authorities. The imperial arsenals supplied nearly 14,000 "fusils de garnison" of moderate quality and Bolts laid hands on still another lot of 4,000 rifles and 132 cannons, as well as ammunition and gunpowder. At the intermediate stop at Càdiz silver coins were presumably stocked.

The *Joseph & Theresia*, facing an exceptionally long voyage of fifty-six months, first headed for Surat. The Cambay Gulf was reputed to be a zone with comparative freedom of trade. To Bolts' detriment, however, the British influence was quite strong, since the East India Company had put him on the blacklist, seeking by all means to boycott his plans. The local 'nabab' counted very little and the Marathas controlled the hinterland. For the time being, they showed a pro-English attitude. Surat however was of some importance as storage yard for calicoes and as bridgehead for trade with the Persian Gulf.

In Surat, Bolts and his wife were for about five months the guests of the French Consul Anquetil de Briancourt, while sick officers and sailors were accommodated in the countryseat, the so-called French Garden. Carrying consular letters of recommendation Bolts first took his ship to Gogha (in the Gujarat peninsula) where he was warmly welcomed, making him decide to choose it for his future residence. He concluded a commercial agreement with a certain Ch. Williams, who anyway afterwards deserted to Muscat and Persia, leaving Bolts with a financial bleeding of 200,000 rupiahs. Gogha came under the authority of Ahmedabad, in turn depending upon the Marathas. For that reason in November-December 1777 Bolts travelled to the court in Poona to obtain a concession. Since the French too were anxious to possess a factory in Gogha, Bolts negotiated in Poona in concert with the French emissary. Bolts, his mother-tongue so to speak being English, was fluent in French, Persian and Urdu as well. So he was able to negotiate personally without the help of an interpreter. His approach failed, however, and he returned empty-handed via Bombay to Surat. Next Bolts sent a delegate (Jean ClÇment) to the isle of Sandy (southward from Surat). This representative obtained commercial rights as well as a territorial concession; nevertheless these privileges were never valorised.

Now Bolts, after a short halt in Bombay, sailed to Goa. The Portuguese granted him commercial facilities at their key points Damão and Diu, where Bolts had left some agents. The incident in the African Delagoa Bay, however, next to diplomatic pressure by the English, made this agreement null and void.

From now on, Bolts' principal target was the coast of Malabar, producing spices (pepper, cinnamon), dye-wood (sandal and sapanwood), ebony, rice and betelnut. On the coastline there were a few small kingdoms to be found, under the hegemony of Haider Ali Khan of Mysore. This sultan was strongly opposed to foreign preponderance, lived on bad terms with the English and closely superintended the European coastal factories. Bolts nevertheless realised that commercial bases were indispensable; factories could stock goods—Indian products delivered by contract and by means of advances—as well as European merchandise, pending a favourable market. Thus the ships had to anchor only for a very short period.

Bolts, having thoroughly prospected the whole west coast between Gogha and Calicut, considered the constellation to be favourable: Bolts and the Sultan found the English to be an opponent they had in common. Bolts had firearms and munition at his disposal, these being highly in demand among the sultan's European mercenaries. Equipped with imperial letters of recommendation and at the invitation of Ali Haider Khan himself, Bolts went to negotiate in Mysore.

The mission was a success. His "Compagnie allemande" gained three "firmans" (farmans) in which equality with the remaining companies and, above all, areas for trading posts were granted. Bolts exclusively aimed at commercial concessions and from the very start excluded every possible military garrison. The imperial main factory was set up in Mangalore, a busy town, home port of Haider Ali's navy, a staple for rice and, above all, supplying the very best of pepper. This trading post was equipped with a warehouse, a chapel and disposed of a small sloop. There was a resident to be found, a writer and a chaplain. The second concession was located at Karwar. This was distinctly larger but further away from the sea; a house was built there for the resident. The third factory was situated in Baliapatam (south of Mangalore) and it was founded in order to produce cane sugar and rum, for which the necessary presses and kettles were brought over from Europe.

Meanwhile the *Joseph & Theresia*, without Bolts on board, had sailed to the Nicobar isles to take possession of the archipelago. From there she set off for Madras on the Coromandel coast. Here, too, the European presence was intensive and highly diverse. Bolts intended to call upon foreign commission merchants. To find a convenient return freight, he aimed at Pondicherry and further on Chandernagore in Bengal. Exactly as in Surat he drew the French card. In the course of the years 1779-80 the ship once more touched at Goa, Bombay, Trankebar, Madras, Calcutta and Madras again, this time with Bolts aboard.

During his stay in India, that lasted over two years, Bolts organized a number of maritime campaigns which, roughly, covered two fields: country trade as such, and the sometimes indirect return trade to Europe.

In agreement with a Portuguese salaried supercargo and with the help of French and English captains, about five fittings-out were organised from Surat and Bombay to East Africa (Mozambique and the Baseruto isles). Rice and brandy were bartered for negro slaves, sold on Mauritius and in the Cape Colony. From the imperial factory in the Delagoa Bay, ivory, pearls, tortoise and other shells were brought back to Surat, Bombay or Damão. From Madras a small unit was sent via Pegu to the Nicobar isles, but this mainly turned out to be a storeship.

In league with Andrew Reid, former governor of the English factory in Bombay, Bolts sent a big ship (700 tons) to China. After a fake sale and with Reid on board as supercargo, the ship sailed to Canton under the English colours. There the imperial flag was hoisted. The Asiatic Association was only moderately implicated in the operation (10.4 per cent of the fitting-out costs) while nearly ninety per cent was financed by means of bottomry bonds. This money was raised in Bombay by so-called agency houses—among which Hunter specialised in illegal money transfer to Europe. Bolts, in lack for liquid means after the Williams affair and the equipment of the factories, gained seventeen per cent freightage on his "port permis" (free transport). Next to that, he probably received bribes. Indeed, the imperial flag was misused to camouflage an English fitting-out, in turn repatriating personal capital disguised in bottomry bonds. After an intermediate call in CÖdiz of one month and a half, the ship arrived at Leghorn with a load of Chinese and Indian goods, among them calicoes and raw Bengal silk. The enterprise ended with a small deficit (1 1/2 per cent), but in order to avoid any legal proceedings the Proli group took over all the bottomry bonds as well as the company share.

A variant of this operation was worked out in Madras, this time the destination being Bengal. Again the Asiatic Association was only moderately interested, with a little more than ten per cent of the return cargo, consisting of merchandise at freight transported for third parties. Presumably, this was just another cover-up for a sophisticated transfer of private fortunes in behalf of "servants" of the western companies. For its own account the Asiatic Association unloaded in Leghorn Bengal saltpetre, piece-goods and dye-wood.

Still more suspicious was the fitting out from the Hooghly river, an operation essentially already planned in 1776 under the Toscan colours. By order of Bolts, his supercargo Rr. Ryan sent a former "country-ship" with an English captain and manned by Indian sailors to Europe. The load belonged for the greater part to Bolts, who had borrowed money there for that purpose. Other interested parties were the directors of the Dutch and Danish factories, located respectively in Chinsura and Frederiksnagore (alias

Serampore). The home-cargo consigned to Leghorn and Càdiz, also consisted of saltpetre (used as ballast), calicoes and dye-wood. The ship was seized, however, into Isle de France (Mauritius) and could only be recuperated after many years of proceedings.

Eventually the *Joseph & Theresia*, together with Bolts, returned to Leghorn. Again the home-freight consisted of saltpetre, calicoes from Madras, ebony and dye-wood, but strangely enough no Malabar pepper, except for a few drugs (cardamom). And once more the Asiatic Association showed hardly any interest at all (10.8 per cent), and almost the whole of the cargo came as freight for the account of business companies from Leghorn and of English and French firms, among others a house from Pondicherry, with a branch in Lorient. Because of the chaotic accountancy, the ultimate balance cannot be figured out at all.

Dissatisfied with Bolts' performances, the Antwerp stockholders, by common agreement, took over the East Indian possessions of the Asiatic Association in August 1781. With these they paid their deposit in a remodelled "Asiatic Company", a bookkeeping trickery so to speak. One year later, at Nantes, a ship was fitted out with China as the ultimate destination, but with the mission also to provision on the outbound voyage the factories on the coast of Malabar and the settlement at Nicobar. Among the passengers was an inspector, the military captain Willem Immens, accompanied by about ten new servants, in view of reinforcing the factory staff. In Mangalore brandy and some Bordeaux wine were unloaded. The larger part was, however, discharged in Goa (brandy, wine, oil and cheese) and Bombay in particular, where bars of iron, clothes, marine stores, gunpowder, munition and a few guns were consigned to D. Scott, an Englishman. Immens, who behaved like an inexperienced supercargo, delayed the sale till the rainy season, a decision that cost them three months storage rent and thirty-seven per cent minor value.

Worse still was the situation in the factories as such. In spite of a raise in wages, the staff remained as envious and discontented as before. Some even deserted to join the English or the Indian nawab. The final blow occurred when the neutral imperial factories got entangled in the military conflict between, on the one hand the English troops, and on the other hand the sultan of Mysore and his son Tipu, together with their French allies. The English general Matthews occupied Mangalore and seized the firearms found in the factory warehouse. The staff evacuated to Goa. Karwar too was taken in, but here the personnel stuck to their post. The factory was reinforced by additional staff, although it repeatedly lacked funds. After Bolts' departure, the Baliapatam post had taken up smuggling, among others for the account of the English and consequently appeared to be left in peace. But the rajah of Chaircal looted and demolished the place, and the captured resident was released only for a heavy ransom.

In early 1784 Sultan Tipu reconquered Mangalore from the English. Inspector Immens went to negotiate in Caula about the restoration and maintenance of the factories. He reached an agreement with the sultan, on condition of substantial supply of arms (300 cannons and 600 guns) and the sending of armourers to Mysore. Nevertheless the maritime traffic under the imperial flag to the Malabar coast remained insignificant, which eventually roused the nawab's suspicion.

In his final report (December 1785), Immens pointed out the poor chances of the factories surviving at all. He put forward the following three arguments: because of the English occupation having violated the imperial neutrality, the war situation had been taken little advantage of; chronic lack of funds and quarrelling employees paralysed the efficient functioning; only the vague prospect of at least two company-ships per year could prevent bankruptcy.

Bolts himself had put a lot of energy and money into acquiring the trading bases. He considered them to be a springboard for a lucrative country-trade. But in applying himself to organising clandestine transfer of capital in collaboration with English, Dutch and Danish company servants, he neglected the purely East Indian commercial activities of his own company. Pursuit of self-gain and lust for revenge against the East India Company were his main motives. Bolts still fought a couple of rearguard actions against the newly established Asiatic Company, which was applying itself to China trade, but he did not play an active role any more.

INDIAN PORTS AND BRITISH INTERCONTINENTAL SAILING SHIPS: THE SUBCONTINENT AS AN ALTERNATIVE SOURCE OF CARGO, 1870-1900

Lewis R. Fischer
&
Gerald E. Panting

INTRODUCTION

About the middle of the nineteenth century, one of history's most important revolutions began to take shape. This transformation had no concrete beginning or discernible end, nor was it marked by widespread military adventures or political upheavals. Instead, it was at once both more prosaic and more sweeping. The revolution to which we refer was the birth of a recognisably modern international economy. While there are long-standing debates about the causes which underlay the creation of this new economic order, there is at the same time a remarkable consensus about the range of preconditions that were necessary to bring it about: an exponential increase in the pace of technological innovation; the accumulation of large pools of capital and the development of relatively efficient markets to facilitate its transfer to areas of high demand; the growth and shift of world population; the discovery and exploitation of new deposits of natural resources; and the changing role of governments, especially the almost universal movement towards some degree of economic liberalism in the second half of the century. The evolving international economy was characterised particularly by increasing economic integration and dependence. Perhaps the most visible evidence of this was the exponential increase in the volume and velocity of transnational trade, which expanded on a per capita basis by about sixteen times between 1850 and 1913. To put this figure in perspective, over the same period real output per head grew only by about ninety per cent.[1]

This revolution had important implications for shipping. Since intercontinental trade accounted for an estimated eighty per cent of the growth of international commerce, the most obvious was the need for more tonnage. Shipowners around the world responded by increasing carrying capacity by about 279 per cent between 1850 and 1910.[2] At the same time, owners began to invest in a new technology which promised faster, more punctual, and presumably more efficient operations. At mid-century, the sailing vessel still reigned supreme over the world's seas. While steamers were no longer uncommon, limitations imposed by the need to devote scarce storage space to the carriage of coal, as well as the continuing inefficiency of steel-plate and boilers, restricted them to short routes and precluded them from active participation in long-distance carrying trades.[3] These evolutionary difficulties were also reflected in the low share of steam tonnage, in even the most technologically advanced fleets: Belgium and Britain, which had by 1850 made the greatest commitment to steam, still had only four and three per cent of their maritime investments, respectively, in steamers. But if steam was marginal at mid-century, it gradually became dominant. By 1890, five nations had more than sixty per cent of their carrying capacities in steam. In 1910 steamers comprised more than ninety per cent of carrying capacity in several national fleets.[4]

It was within the context of these wrenching economic and technological changes that shipowners had to make operational decisions in the late nineteenth century. This is particularly true of those who decided to continue operating sailing vessels. The perfection of steam propulsion did not automatically mean an end to the utility of sail. Indeed, sailing vessels continued to find profitable employment until World War I, particularly on long-distance trade routes.[5] But especially after 1880, shipowners began to encounter difficulties in obtaining sufficient cargo. In large measure, this was because in the last two decades of the century, the supply of tonnage outstripped the demand for cargo space. This was, in turn, reflected in freight rates, which plummeted by almost half between 1879 and 1896.[6]

As sailing vessels became less able to compete in the lucrative North Atlantic trades, they were increasingly shifted into longer routes. In particular, there was a noticeable diversion of sail into the Pacific. Since even in 1913 almost two-thirds of the world trade touched upon Europe, this area was among the most remote from the centre of the world trading system and hence the last to be penetrated by steam. If owners of sailing vessels could not find profitable employment for their assets in this region, it is unlikely that they could do so anywhere. Ironically, one of the outbound cargoes almost always available to sailing vessels headed for the Pacific was bunkering coal to feed the ever-expanding maws of steamers.[7]

Yet even in one of its last refuges, ever more frequently sailing vessels had difficulties in procuring full cargoes even here.[8] The problem basically was that while shipowners could procure full cargoes from Europe easily enough, there was insufficient demand for cargo space on the return leg.[9] The problem was not confined to this region, but was endemic to late nineteenth-century shipping. Nonetheless, it was particularly acute in the Pacific.[10] This led to an odyssey that Frank Broeze had appropriately dubbed the "search for alternatives".[11] The term refers to a pattern in which tramp sailing vessels returning to Europe were forced to make calls at a variety of ports in order to secure sufficient cargo to fill their holds.

When Broeze looked at the routings taken by sailing vessels from Australia he found a range of "alternatives", most of which were in Oceania or Southeast Asia. In this paper we are concerned with whether India fitted into the picture. We know that by the last few decades of the nineteenth century, Indian overseas commerce was dominated by steam liners.[12] Nonetheless, we also know that a large number of sailing vessels continued to call at Indian ports. What we want to know—and what the existing literature is silent about—is whether owners of sailing vessels used Indian ports as a way of ensuring full holds for the return trip to Europe in the transitional years 1870-1900.

The analysis in the paper shows that Indian ports were indeed important components of this trading system. The data to be presented show that even in the 1870s, when the challenges from steam and an increasing tonnage glut were only just beginning, Indian ports represented an important cargo option for sail. It also demonstrates that the manner in which Indian ports fitted into this system changed and became more complex as the century drew to a close. In short, the evidence points to the conclusion that India occupied an important, if shifting position, in the late nineteenth-century maritime trading system.

METHODOLOGY

Since our methodology differs significantly from other attempts to examine "alternatives", a brief discussion of the approach we have taken and the sources used is necessary. We are interested here only in voyages made by British Empire vessels which called at Indian ports on the return leg to Europe. While it would be possible for us to examine steamers, our sole focus is on sail, since this type of vessel was by far the most likely either to engage in tramp voyages or to need to search for an alternative port in which to top up its cargo. Similarly, while we could examine the role that ports in the subcontinent played for outbound cargoes, we believe that to do so in a single paper would make the discussion too complex to be easily grasped.

Our sources, while not perfect, are fairly well suited for the task we have in mind. To examine voyage patterns we have used the British Empire "Agreements and Accounts of Crew" which are housed at Memorial University of Newfoundland.[13] Among other things, these documents are superb for tracing voyage patterns. This is because they had to be carried onboard the vessel; whenever the craft put into a port, the documents were handed over to the shipping master or the British consul for safe-keeping. When returned prior to departure, the official affixed a port stamp, showing the dates of arrival and departure. This makes these records better than any other in the world for tracking precisely the movements of vessels. In the 1970s and 1980s, when we were both members of the Atlantic Canada Shipping Project, we used these crew lists to examine the rise and decline of the eastern Canadian merchant marine. As part of this earlier study we computerised all voyages made by vessels registered in four eastern Canadian ports as well as a "one per cent sample" of all non-Canadian, British Empire voyages in our archive.[14] These data sets, extended by subsequent additions specifically designed to capture data on vessels entering Indian ports, form the backbone of this study.

Unfortunately, while the crew agreements are superb sources for tracing voyages, they provide no information on cargoes. We thought briefly about trying to use the annual Trade and Navigation Statements for India, a selection of which has been computerised by Kenneth McPherson, Peter Reeves and Andrew Pope.[15] While this source would have been useful, in the end we decided against employing it here. Our main objection has to do with the fact that thus far our Australian colleagues have only computerised five-yearly samples, one segment of which are for years ending in "5". This makes them less useful for our purposes, since we hold a few agreements for these years and hence cannot match data from the two sources.[16] As an alternative, for this paper we are using a source called the London "A" bills. These are printed documents which list all points of departure and cargoes for vessels entering into selected British ports. Since the ports listed changed during the period of this study, we have limited our data collection only to those ports for which we would derive a consistent time series: London, Liverpool, Bristol, Hull and Southampton.[17] The principal disadvantage of this source compared to the Trade and Navigation Statements is that they only allow us to examine cargoes going into the United Kingdom. Since we know, however, that the U.K. was a much more important destination than the European continent, we are not overly concerned with this limitation.[18] In this analysis, our only concern with these bills is for information on cargoes.

Because of the time involved in data collection and analysis, we have also had to adopt a few practical measures in manipulating the data. Because we are interested here in observing trends and patterns, we have grouped the voyage data from the crew lists by decades (1870s, 1880s and 1890s). For information from the customs records, we have only taken a ten-yearly sample (1870, 1880, 1890 and 1900). While it would of course be possible to go back and fill in the gaps, we are reasonably confident that this procedure does not distort reality. As well, we doubt that a more comprehensive study would add much to what is revealed in the analysis below.

VOYAGE PATTERNS

We can begin our analysis by establishing the number of voyages involved. At present, our data set includes 206 voyages made using Indian ports on the way back to Europe in the 1870s, 187 voyages for the 1880s and 199 in the 1890s. When we compiled our data set from the London "A" bills, we looked for voyages listed as entering from a port in Ceylon, Asia, Oceania, or Austraila with an intermediate Indian port-of-call on the homeward passage. We also looked to see if any of the cargo was loaded in an Indian port. By applying these criteria, we came up with seventy-one voyages in 1870, sixty-two in

1880, thirty-eight in 1890, and twenty-seven in 1900. It is these voyages that we can now examine for patterns.

The first question we asked concerned the regions from which the sailing vessels entered Indian ports. To facilitate comparisons, we have used roughly the same regional breakdown as that employed by McPherson, Reeves and Pope. As Table 1 shows, in the 1870s tonnages entering from Ceylon and Asia were about equal. Those from Oceania accounted for about a third as much tonnage, while vessels from Australia (including New Zealand) and other places were relatively unimportant. By the 1880s, the Ceylonese share had increased by about a third to fifty one per cent. The Asian component had halved in proportional terms while entrances from Oceania increased by almost fifty per cent. The other categories remained identical to the 1870s. In the 1890s, the proportion of entrances from Ceylon declined by about fifteen per cent, the Asian share continued to decline, while Oceania's contribution grew. Once again, there were no significant differences in the shares accounted for by the last two categories. All of this suggests a clear long-term decline in the importance of Asia as a previous port of call and an even more noticeable increase in the significance of Oceania. Ceylon, on the other hand, was more variable, although the long-term trend is clearly positive. Indeed, a regression run on entrances from Ceylon shows an annual increase in tonnage entering of 2.7 per cent per year.[19]

TABLE 1
PREVIOUS IMMEDIATE PORT OF CALL FOR VESSELS ENTERING INDIAN PORTS BOUND FOR EUROPE, 1870-1900

(% of Tonnage)

Year	Ceylon	Asia	Oceania	Australia	Other
1870-79	38	36	12	8	6
1880-89	51	18	17	8	6
1890-99	43	16	30	6	5

Notes: Australia includes New Zealand; other includes a variety of ports where it was clear that vessel was proceeding directly to Europe.

Source: Board of Trade, B.T. 99, "Agreements and Accounts of Crew", 1870-1900.

Yet, as is often the case when examining trading patterns, first impressions can be somewhat misleading. One advantage in using crew agreements as a source is that they allow us to determine not only the port of call immediately preceding an entrance into an Indian port but also the pattern previous to that. We have calculated all the various pairings possible. But given the fact that Ceylon was by far the most important previous port for the period as a whole, in Table 2 we present one view of the trading pattern for those vessels that entered a Ceylonese port immediately previous to calling in India.

These data at once clarify, yet at the same time confuse the picture. If we make the reasonable assumption that the overwhelming majority of these vessels called at an Indian port to pick up rather than to deposit cargo (an assumption which will be demonstrated to be correct later in the paper); the clear implication of these data is that the trading system became more complex over time. In the 1870s, over half of all vessels calling in Ceylon prior to India stopped nowhere else in the Pacific or Indian Oceans on the same voyage. Of those that needed to make multiple ports-of-call to obtain cargo, the majority preceded from a port in Oceania, overwhelmingly from harbours such as Manila and Batavia. The importance of Australia is also heightened by this analysis. But perhaps most striking is the fact that only eight per cent called in two or more regions prior to Ceylon.

TABLE 2

PERCENTAGE OF VESSELS ENTERING EACH REGION BEFORE ENTERING CEYLON PRIOR TO CALLING AT AN INDIAN PORT

(% of Tonnage)

Year	No other Region	Asia	Oce-ania	Aust-ralia	Other	2 or more Regions
1870-79	52	7	22	11	2	8
1880-89	34	9	29	12	1	15
1890-99	10	12	35	16	1	26

Notes: See Table 1.
Source: See Table 1.

In the 1880s, we can see that the picture became more complex. Only about a third of all passages were simple Ceylon-India-U.K./Europe routes. An additional twenty-nine per cent involved at least two of the regions in addition to Ceylon and India. By the 1890s, the system had evolved even further. Only ten per cent of all passages were simple Ceylon-India-U.K./Europe while over a quarter involved at least two regional ports *before* entering Ceylon.[20]

CARGOES

If, as we have already seen, Indian ports were part of this increasingly complex set of "alternatives", what cargoes did vessels procure in these entrepots? To answer this question we can examine a data set derived from the London "A" bills (see Table 3).

TABLE 3
PROPORTION OF SAILING VESSELS ENTERING BRITISH PORTS FROM INDIA CARRYING VARIOUS COMMODITIES, 1870-1900

(% of Tonnage)

Year	Cotton	Textiles	Grain	Jute	Dyes	Tea	Other
1870	58	4	10	5	7	1	18
1880	48	10	44	10	4	3	15
1890	44	22	56	18	5	11	19
1900	30	19	52	56	4	22	41

Notes: Ports of London, Liverpool, Hull, Bristol and Southampton only. Jute included manufactured jute products. Other includes a wide variety of products, of which hides, either raw or tanned, were the most common. Rows can equal more than 100 per cent since many vessels carried more than one Indian commodity.

Source: Great Britain, Customs, London "A" Bills, 1870-1900.

What Table 3 depicts parallels our findings above in the discussion of voyage patterns: that things became more complex over time. In 1870, almost three-fifths of the sailing vessels entering

British ports after an intermediate call in a port on the subcontinent carried raw Indian cotton. No other commodity except grains reached even ten per cent. To underscore the relative simplicity of the pattern in this first year, adding the percentage of all the various commodities only yields a sum of 103 per cent. This rough measure suggests that most vessels calling at an Indian port were able to fill their holds satisfactorily by loading only a single cargo.

In 1880, no single commodity was as dominant as cotton was ten years previously. But we can see the rise of grain almost to the level of raw cotton. This finding has an importance beyond the purely maritime dimension. It is standard wisdom among Indian economic historians that the British and European markets for Indian grains were effectively created by the opening of the Suez Canal.[21] Perhaps this is true, but given the importance of grains as a cargo for sailing vessels—which were banned from the canal—it is at least worth rethinking this explanation. Equally important for our purposes, the growing diversity of cargoes is indicated by the fact that the row for 1880 reached 134 per cent, which likely reflects the greater difficulty in obtaining single cargoes in Indian ports.

By 1890, we can see a continuing decline for raw cotton as a cargo but an equally significant rise in the proportion of cotton textiles and jute products. Grain was now the single most important commodity for these vessels: a majority carried at least some Indian grain. The proportion carrying tea also jumped significantly. And the trend toward diversity continued, reflected both by the rising proportion of "other" cargoes and the row total of 175 per cent.

Finally, the data for 1900 underscore the long-term trend toward cargo diversity. The "other" category had reached forty-one per cent and the row total was a staggering 224 per cent. For the first time, jute was the most common cargo, and the proportion carrying tea also showed a sharp rise. All the other commodities were less prevalent with the exception of the ubiquitous "other".

CONCLUSIONS

The preceding analysis makes several points worth highlighting. First of all, it is clear that Indian ports were part of a much larger maritime trading system for sailing vessels than has been imagined previously. To the accepted list of "alternatives" for tramp sailing craft we need to add ports on the subcontinent. While vessels beginning their loading for the return voyage in Ceylon were especially prone to visit Indian ports, maritime trade from every part of the Pacific was increasingly connected with India. Second, it is equally apparent that this trading system was becoming more complex as the nineteenth century drew to an end. The maritime commercial network that we have described was more likely to comprise multiple ports-of-call, even prior to any entrance into Indian ports, in the 1880s and 1890s than previously. Third, this more intricate trading network was paralleled by a growing diversity of cargoes loaded in Indian ports. In 1870, it appears to have been typical for a vessel to have required only a single cargo to top up its hold. But from 1880 this became more rare, and by 1900 the data suggest that it was almost impossible.

While this paper has focused in a preliminary way principally on the development of a trading system, it also has implications for Indian economic history. As we pointed out above, the fact that so high a proportion of sailing vessels carried grain to the United Kingdom calls into question the accepted generalisation that the opening of the Suez Canal was an integral factor in the establishment of markets for Indian grain in Europe. But there are other points to ponder as well. Additional vessels calling at Indian ports meant increased revenues from port dues, lighterage fees, and the like. It also implied greater opportunities for a wide range of spin-off occupations. Finally, the need to fill unutilised space on sailing vessels very likely provided Indian producers with access to a broader range of markets than would otherwise have been the case. While it is impossible at present to prove this latter speculation, it is worth remembering that after independence many newly created nations, including India, expanded a good deal of scarce capital to try to establish national shipping lines, in part to provide subsidised access to additional markets. The irony, of course, is that conditions in the maritime sector in the late nineteenth century provided something akin to this kind of access for free sailing.

NOTES

[1]Calculated from data in Simon Kuznets, "Quantitative Aspects of the Economic Growth of Nations: X-Levels and Structures of Foreign Trade, Long-term Trends", *Economic Development and Cultural Change*, II (1967); W.S. and E.S. Woytinsky, *World Commerce and Governments*, New

York, 1955, pp. 66-71; P. Lamartine Yates, *Forty Years of Foreign Trade,* London, 1959, especially pp. 32-3.

[2]This figure makes no adjustment for the additional efficiency of steam. If we make the appropriate adjustments, it would appear that shipping investment grew at just about the same pace as international trade over the period as a whole. Significantly, however, it grew much more rapidly during the 1880s and 1890s. See Lewis R. Fischer and Helge W. Nordvik, "Maritime Transport and the Integration of the North Atlantic Economy", in Wolfram Fischer, R. Marvin McInnis and Jürgen Schneider (eds.), *The Emergence of a World Economy 1500-1914,* Wiesbaden, 1986, II, pp. 519-44.

[3]The best general discussion of the evolution of steam technology is Robin Craig, *Steam Tramps and Cargo Liners 1850-1950,* London, 1980.

[4]See Fischer and Nordvik, "Maritime Transport", esp. Table IV.

[5]Yrj" Kaukiainen, *Sailing into Twilight: Finnish Shipping in an Age of Transport Revolution, 1860-1914,* Helsinki, 1991; Eric W. Sager and Gerald E. Panting, *Maritime Capital: The Shipping Industry in Atlantic Canada, 1820-1914,* Kingston, 1990, esp. ch. 6; Lewis R. Fischer and Helge W. Nordvik, "From Broager to Bergen: The Risks and Rewards of Peter Jebsen, Shipowner, 1864-1892", *Siofartshistorisk Arbok 1985,* Bergen, 1986, pp. 37-68; Lewis R. Fischer, Eric W. Sager and Rosemary E. Ommer, "The Shipping Industry and Regional Economic Development in Atlantic Canada, 1871-1891: Saint John as a Case Study", in Lewis R. Fischer and Eric W. Sager (eds.), *Merchant Shipping and Economic Development in Atlantic Canada,* St. John's, 1982, pp. 33-53.

[6]L. Isserlis, "Tramp Shipping Cargoes and Freights", *Journal of the Royal Statistical Society,* CI, 1938, pp. 53-134. But see the important correctives in Fischer and Nordvik, "Maritime Transport", and C. Knick Harley, "Ocean Freight Rates and Productivity, 1740-1913: The Primacy of Mechanical Invention Reaffirmed", *Journal of Economic History,* XLVIII (4), December 1988, pp. 851-76.

[7]The obvious exceptions to this generalisation include the nitrate trades from the west coast of South America and some of the so-called "niche trades", in which bulk cargoes were unavailable.

[8]Lewis R. Fischer, "New York, Rio or Batavia?: The Deployment Patterns of the Canadian and Norwegian Fleets, 1860-1900" in Lewis R. Fischer and Helge W. Nordvik (eds.), *Across the Broad Atlantic: Essays in Comparative Canadian-Norwegian Maritime History, 1850-1914,* St. John's, 1992, shows this problem most clearly.

[9]The best theoretical statement of the problem is C. Knick Harley, "Issues on the Demand for Shipping Services, 1870-1913: Derived Demand and Problems of Joint Production", in Fischer and Sager (eds.), *Merchant Shipping,* pp. 65-86.

[10]For examples elsewhere in the world, see C. Knick Harley, "North

Atlantic Shipping in the Late Nineteenth Century: Freight Rates and the Interrelationship of Cargoes", in Lewis R. Fischer and Helge W. Nordvik (eds.), *Shipping and Trade, 1750-1950: Essays in International Maritime Economy History, 1750-1950,* Pontefract, England, 1990, pp. 147-80; Lewis R. Fischer, "A Flotilla of Wood and Coal: Shipping in the Trades between Britain and the Baltic, 1863-1913", in Yrj" Kaukiainen (ed.), *The Baltic as a Highway for Shipping,* Kotka, Finland, 1992 (forthcoming).

[11]Frank J.A. Broeze, "British Intercontinental Shipping and Australia", *Journal of Transport History,* IV (4), 1978, pp. 189-207.

[12]J. Forbes Munro, "Suez and the Shipowner: The Response of the MacKinnon Shipping Group to the Opening of the Canal, 1869-84", in Fischer and Nordvik, (eds.), *Shipping and Trade,* pp. 97-123.

[13]On these documents, see Lewis R. Fischer, "Sources in Canadian Maritime History, 1850-1914: The International Dimension", in Fischer and Nordvik (eds.), *Across the Broad Atlantic,* forthcoming; Keith Matthews, "Crew Lists, Agreements and Official Logs of the British Empire, 1863-1913", *Business History,* XVI (1), January 1974, pp. 78-80; Rupert C. Jarvis, "Sources for the History of Ships and Shipping and Seamen", *Maritime History,* II (2), September 1972, pp. 168-88; V.C. Burton, "Counting Seafarers: The Published Records of the Registry of Merchant Seamen, 1849-1913", *Mariner's Mirror,* LXXI (3), August 1985, pp. 305-20.

[14]Lewis R. Fischer and Eric W. Sager, "An Approach to the Quantitative Analysis of British Shipping Records", *Business History,* XXII (2), July 1980, pp. 135-51.

[15]See Kenneth McPherson, Peter Reeves and Andrew Pope, "Modern Indian Shipping and Maritime Trade: An Exploratory Study of Developments in the Period c. 1870-1935", in Fischer and Nordvik (eds.), *Shipping and Trade,* pp. 289-352.

[16]When Memorial took the crew agreements, we received only eighty per cent. The remainder were given to repositories in the United Kingdom. The most important of these was the National Maritime Museum in Greenwich, which decided that for research purposes it wanted ten per cent of all agreements. To facilitate the selection of this sample, it was simply decided to give the Museum all agreements for years ending in "5".

[17]Fischer, "Sources in Canadian..."; Edward Carson, "Customs Bills of Entry", *Maritime History,* I (2), September 1971, pp. 176-89.

[18]In 1875/76, for example, McPherson, Reeves and Pope indicate that 889,345 tons of sail shipping cleared Indian ports for the U.K. with cargo compared to 95,978 tons for Europe. Ten years later, the figures were 675,053 and 31,825, while in 1895/96 the numbers were 137,891 and 128,777. While superficially this suggests that in the latter years Europe was "catching up" with the U.K., an examination of the data presented by the authors suggests that the 1895/96 data for Europe are almost certainly erroneous. McPherson, Reeves and Pope, "Modern Indian Shipping",

appendix II.

[19]This growth rate was calculated by a regression equation of the form Log Y = a + b.

[20]The analysis using regions other than Ceylon, while different in certain respects, confirms the argument about the growing complexity of the system.

[21]See, for example, K.N. Chaudhuri, "Foreign Trade and Balance of Payments (1757-1947)", in Dharma Kumar (ed.), *The Cambridge Economic History of India*, Cambridge, 1983, II, p. 850.

WORLD RECESSION, INDIAN OPIUM, AND CHINA'S OPIUM WAR

Man-Houng Lin

One expert on China's Opium War made the synoptical statement: "Chinese officials and scholars unanimously attributed the trouble to the drain of the treasury resulting from the import of opium".[1] An Indian scholar has also claimed that opium importation had caused China's Opium War, 1840-42.[2] This essay will try to reconsider whether the importation of Indian opium was actually the ultimate economic cause for the silver drain the fiscal impact of which brought China to war.

START AND TREND OF THE SILVER DRAIN FROM CHINA

Many scholars have relied on the East India Company record kept by H.B. Morse, a Commissioner of China's maritime customs in the late nineteenth century, to determine the year in which the shift to a balance of trade unfavourable to China took place. Because Morse's data are scattered and sometimes inconsistent, 1825, 1826, 1827 and 1830 have all been given by scholars using Morse data as the date.[3]

The first year that India recorded a surplus in its silver trade with China was 1813-14, as seen in Tables 1 and 2. Data in Table 1 came mainly from the manuscripts of the *Aberdeen Papers* kept in the British Museum for the records of the years between 1814-15 and 1826-27, and from the *Blue Books* for the years between 1830 and 1844. The units used were Chinese tael (37.58 gram of silver in the form of shoes) or Mexican dollars. Data in Table 2 were provided by the Customs House of London in 1859. The unit used was British pound.

The Indian record used here totals the figures recorded at customs in Bombay, Calcutta and Madras. Since the silver smuggled from China was not imported illegally into India, the Indian record includes the smuggled portion which can be missed by the East India Company record as surveyed by H.B. Morse. But it is still unclear whether 1813-14 marked the onset of China's silver outflow. In 1809, the Chinese Government at Canton announced a prohibition against silver outflow; in 1814, the Senior Vice Minister of its Board of Revenue proposed a strict ban on the smuggling of silver taels abroad by merchants.[4] The East India Company's Canton Court Letters also indicate that 1808-15 were possible years for China's silver to have flowed into India.[5] Hence, the first year silver flowed from China is more likely to be around 1809, rather than around 1825.

Silver flowing into India represents almost all of China's total trade deficit. China had in general favourable trade with Asian countries including Burma, Tibet, Cochin China, Japan and Korea.[6] Among European and American countries, in addition to Belgium and Denmark which had negligible favourable trade balances with China, all others had unfavourable trade with China (see Table 3). Although China usually had a favourable balance of trade with both England and the United States, its unfavourable balance of trade with India was much greater than the total of the former balance. England usually had her trade deficit with China paid by India's trade surplus with China. China had unfavourable trade with India throughout the period of 1813-1850 (Table 2). China's deficit with India was also used to pay for the trade deficit with the United States as partial payment for England's deficit, due to British purchase of cotton from the United States.[7] Therefore, silver flowing into India represents almost all of China's total trade deficit.

Aside from the outflow to India, there was a small amount of silver flowing from China to Singapore to buy opium there, and to England to pay for the war indemnity, as shown in Table 1.

Though 1809-14 were also possible years for silver to have flowed from China to India, from Tables 1 and 2 it can be seen that the silver outflow from China had increased from one to two million tael, to three to six million tael in the 1820s, and further increased to eleven million tael in 1844. Therefore, although the silver outflow problem for China can be traced back to 1809-14, it was most desperate in the period between the 1820s and the 1840s.

THE MAGNITUDE OF THE SILVER OUTFLOW

The total silver outflow to both India and other countries in the period 1814-50 was 150 million Mexican dollars.[8] China was not a silver-abundant country. There was, however, an expansion of silver use from the seventeenth century onward. Up to the nineteenth century, silver comprised 97.16 per cent of the total value of regular revenue and all the officially cast copper coins in 1842.[9] In addition to public transaction, silver had been used in China for wholesale exchange. For the retail exchange, copper coins were used. If we take the total silver value of the period around 1850 and divide it by the total silver and copper coin value of that year, we get 76.4 per cent.[10] That is to say, silver constituted about three-fourths of the total money value, while copper coins shared only some one-fourth. Though there was more use of silver tael (silver shoes recast from the imported silver coins) in the north, while in the south silver coins were used (imported silver dollars) in the south, the use of silver was nationwide.[11] China's silver outflow of the early nineteenth century comprised thirteen per cent of the total silver supply and eleven per cent of the total money supply.[12] Such decreases in the silver or money supply had a tremendous impact on China and paved the way for the Opium War. The question here is whether opium importation into China was the ultimate economic factor to shift the trade balance.

THE IMPORT OF INDIAN OPIUM INTO CHINA

Opium was introduced to China in the late fifteenth century by Arab merchants. In the sixteenth century, it was imported as a kind of medicine. By 1700, Portuguese merchants imported 200 piculs of it annually from India into China. Due to a lack of capital, the Portuguese merchants were replaced by British merchants. The British private merchants started to import opium into China in 1757. From 1773 onward, the East India Company also participated in the opium trade, and opium smoking became prevalent at the same time. Though the marketing of it for smoking was prohibited in 1729 and 1780, its import was not prohibited until 1796. Before 1729, an import level of 200 piculs had been maintained; by 1767, this level had increased to 1,000 piculs.[13]

Figure 1 shows the increasing trend of the quantity imported into China from 1798 to 1888. From Figure 1, we can see that in the twenty-five years before 1824, an opium import level of 3,000 to 4,000 piculs had been maintained. From 1824 onward, it increased to more than 10,000 piculs. In the course of the years between 1824 and 1838, it increased up to more than 40,000 piculs, and from 1840 to 1854, another jump was made to more than 70,000 piculs.

Opium was an expensive commodity. Its unit price was close to silk, and about one-fifth that of silver in the early nineteenth century.[14] A picul of opium was valued at about $600 in 1847. At the same time, a family of ten in Canton could get food, clothes and shelter for $400 annually.[15] Commissioner Lin estimated in 1838 that a poor man's annual cost of living was about an opium smoker's daily opium expense.[16]

FIGURE 1
OPIUM IMPORTED INTO CHINA

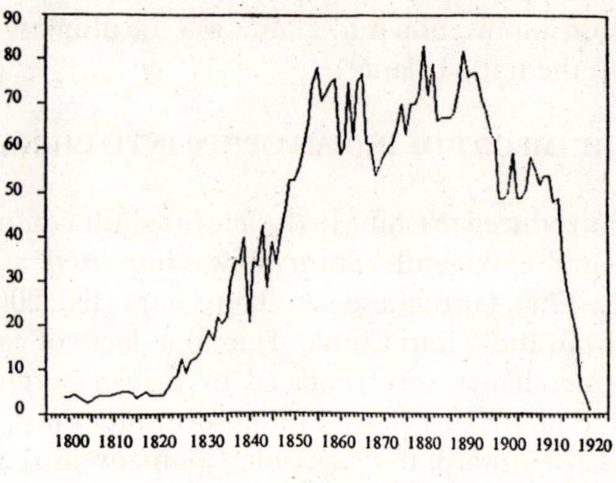

UNIT: 1,000 PICULS

Sources: 1795-1839: H.B. Morse, *International Relations of the Chinese Empire*, 3 vols. (Shanghai: Kelly & Walsh, c.1910-18), vol.I, p.209-10; 1840-60: Yü En-te, *A History of China's Opium Prohibition* (in Chinese) (Shanghai: Chung-hua shu-chu, 1934), p.330; 1861-66: *British Parliamentary Papers*, vol.9, p.217, Report from Hankow; 1867-1916: Hsiao Liang-lin, *Foreign Trade Statistics 1864-1949*, (Cambridge, Mass.: East Asian Research Center, Harvard University, 1974), pp. 52-3, Table 2: Principal Imports of China, 1867-1941. The unit used by Morse was the chest. One chest was around 140 pounds, and it sometimes decreased with seasons and type (see Chang Hsin-pao, p.19). One picul is 133.3 pounds. Since sources other than Morse used picul as the unit, Morse's data in units of chest have been converted to the picul for comparison.

In terms of silver dollars, the early nineteenth-century import value of opium was about 3.7 million dollars a year for before 1818; about 4.6 million between 1819 and 1822; about 7 million between 1822 and 1828; about 11 million between 1828 and 1832, and about 14 million between 1833 and 1838. In terms of British pounds, the value of opium exported from India to China was between £0.34 million and £0.71 million in 1813-20, between £0.81 million and £1.79 million in 1820-30, between £1.47 million and £3.93 million in 1830-39; between £3.5 million and £5.54 million in 1843-50. In addition to a slight drop in the Opium War period, it shows a rapid growth since the 1820s onward, and an acceleration in the 1830s and 1840s.

Such a pattern of increase synchronised well with that of the silver outflow. That is to say, both increased rapidly from the 1820s onward, and accelerated in the 1830s and 1840s.

OPIUM IN CHINA'S FOREIGN TRADE BALANCE

Opium constituted, furthermore, an important role in China's silver outflow because China had a favourable trade balance with almost all countries except India; and other than cotton, China mainly imported opium from India.

Take 1847, for example. In this year, China imported ten million dollars in goods from England, and exported twenty million dollars in goods there, leaving a trade surplus of ten million dollars for China. The United States exported three million dollars in goods to China, and imported nine million dollars in goods from

China, leaving a six million dollar surplus for China. British India exported twenty-three million dollars in opium, and five million dollars in raw cotton to China, while importing two million dollars in raw silk from China, leaving a twenty-six million dollar trade deficit for China. Merchants of the United States and England bought drafts from opium merchants to pay for their debts to China. Even after paying sixteen million dollars to England and the United States, British India still had a ten million dollar surplus with China which was to be paid in silver.[17] Table 4 shows that in India's exports to China during 1813-50, except two years in which cotton shares were larger, opium constituted the chief export.

A QUESTION POSED FROM THE DEVELOPMENT DURING 1850-1888

So far opium seems to be still the only economic variable for the silver outflow. When we look at Figure 1 again, however, we notice that up to 1852 the opium imported annually into China never surpassed 60,000 piculs. Within the forty-three years between 1853 and 1895, with the exception of four years, annual import of opium maintained a level of over 60,000 piculs. And for twenty-two years within this period the level reached over 70,000. In the period between 1879 and 1888, it even surpassed 80,000 piculs. Table 5 shows that the value of the imported opium in the years between 1868 and 1906 was between 38.93 and 55.55 million dollars annually. The average of these thirty-nine years was 45.62 million dollars, with the dollar value very steady in this period.[18] The value of the opium imported annually between 1868 and 1906 was much higher than the 3.7 million dollars of 1818 and the twenty-one million dollars of 1847 previously mentioned.

Yet, following the silver outflow of 150 million dollars in the period 1814-1850, there was a silver inflow of 724 million dollars in the period 1850-86 (see Table 6), even though opium was imported much more heavily in this period. Since the trend of the value of imported opium did not synchronise with the trend of the silver movement in the late nineteenth century, it poses a question whether the importation of opium was the ultimate economic cause for the silver outflow of the period 1814-1850.

The movement of silver in and out of China was mainly determined by the commodity account in the international balance of payments since there were negligible foreign loans and expenses in China in this period. Opium shared from 46.9 per cent to 69.4 per cent of the total import from the British Empire in terms of value in the years between 1834 and 1850.[19] In the decade of the 1850s, such a share increased steadily to 71.1 per cent. From the decade of the 1860s onward, although opium was the main import, it cannot be held responsible for the transition from silver outflow to silver inflow into China around 1850. To explain the swift changes in the trade balance around 1850, we must look at the changes in the export of silk and tea.

THE EXPORT OF CHINA'S SILK AND TEA, 1850-1886

The share of tea export in the total export value of the goods exported by the East India Company was around ninety per cent in the early 1760s and the decades from the 1780s to the 1830s. Only in the late 1760s and early 1780s, this share dropped to between fifty-five per cent and seventy-three per cent as the silk share rose from twenty-three per cent to 37.7 per cent.[20] Tea returned to a share of ninety per cent of the total export value in the late 1830s, early 1840s, and late 1860s. From the late 1840s to the early 1850s, this share was between 37.6 per cent and 72.2 per cent.[21] The share of export value of tea in the total export value dropped from fifty-three per cent in 1872 to thirty-five per cent in 1887.[22] The drop of the share of tea in the total export was due to the increase of silk exporting. From 1872 to 1895, the share of silk export value in the total export value remained between thirty per cent and forty per cent.[23]

The fluctuation of tea and silk export with the change of the other producing areas and with the change of the consumption pattern can be seen in Figures 2 and 3.[24] Yet, Figures 2 and 3 also show an increasing secular trend of tea export from 1850 to 1881 and of silk export from 1850 to 1895.

FIGURE 2

QUANTITY OF TEA EXPORTED FROM CHINA, 1825-1885

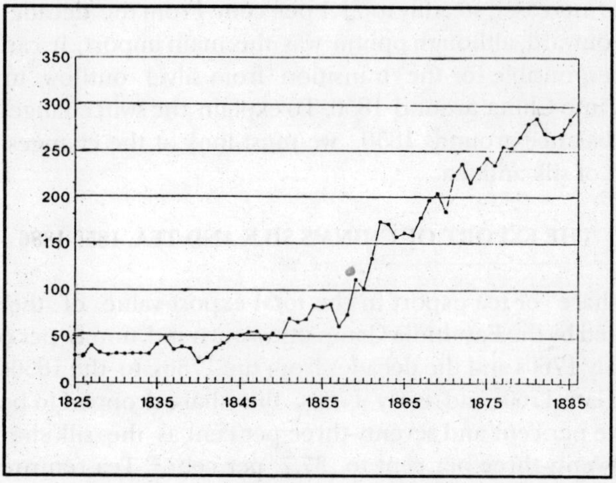

Unit: million lbs.

Sources: 1825-1858: Drawn from data given in John A. Messenger, *India and China (Exports and Imports)*, Office of the Inspector-General of Imports and Exports, Custom House, London, 15 June 1859. The House of Commons, Printed 21 June 1859, p.7; 1859-1886: Chen Tzu-yü, *The Development of Tea Industries in Modern China and the World Market* (in Chinese) (Taipei: The Institute of Economics, Academia Sinica, 1982), p. 324.

FIGURE 3

QUANTITY OF SILK EXPORTED FROM CHINA, 1825-1885

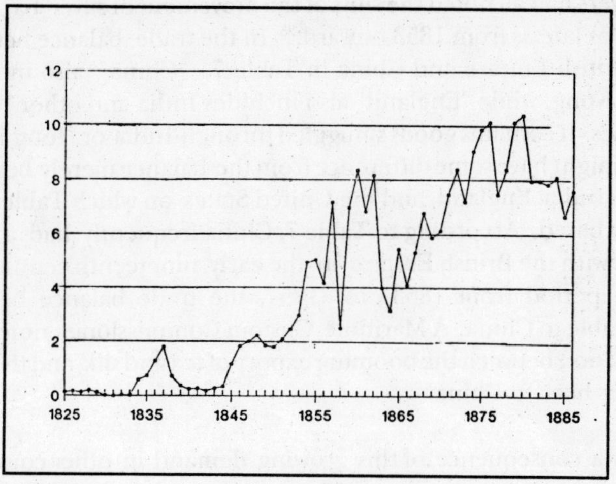

Unit: million lbs.

Sources: 1825-1858: Messenger, p.7; Robert Y. Eng, *Economic Imperialism in China,* the Institute of East Asian Studies, University of California, Berkeley, Center for Chinese Studies, 1986, p.31; 1867-1886: Hsiao Liang-lin, *China's Foreign Trade Statistics,* p.102.

The rapid increase of tea and silk export from 1850 to 1881 or 1895 had caused silver to flow back to China around 1850. The late nineteenth-century Chinese scholar-official Feng Kuei-fen, the *North China Herald,* the British *Blue Book,* and other western observers had all noted the shift of the movement of silver back into China as late as from 1853 onward.[25] In the trade balance between the British Empire and China in Table 7, "China" also includes Hong Kong, while "England" also includes India and other British colonies. It contains goods smuggled through India or Hong Kong. Yet, it might have some difference from the balance merely between China, India, England, and the United States on which Table 2 was mainly based. According to Table 7, China frequently had a trade deficit with the British Empire in the early nineteenth century, yet in the period from 1853 to 1857, the trade balance became favourable to China. A Maritime Custom Commissioner noted the connection between the booming export of tea and silk, and the flow of silver back to China:

> As a consequence of this growing demand in other countries for the tea and silk of China, a most interesting reversal occurred in that movement of bullion which had played so large a part in deciding the Government of China in 1838 to attempt the suppression of the opium trade.[26]

WORLD ECONOMIC BOOM AS A BACKGROUND

There were internal reasons for the increasing export trend of tea and silk. Due to the lack of silver, a barter trading system had been developed in 1847 to exchange tea and silk for opium. The export of tea and silk was hence increased.[27] When the Taiping Rebellion occurred in the period of 1850-68, the silk weaving industries in the main producing area were destroyed by the civil war. Consequently, a great deal of the raw silk turned from the domestic market toward the foreign market for processing.[28] In 1873, steam filature had been imported to increase silk productivity.[29] Yet, without a thriving foreign market, the tea and silk export could not be increased.

Up to 1871, before the rise of tea exports from Japan, India and Ceylon, China provided eighty-five per cent of the world's tea.[30] Prior to the 1870s, when Japan had not yet developed its modern silk trade, China played a crucial role in the world silk market.[31] Precisely because tea and silk were luxury commodities, their increasing export trend must have been backed up by a booming world economy. A survey of China's silk export pointed out:

> In addition to the opening of treaty ports, the silkworm disease in Europe, and the harvest of each silk-producing areas in the world, the export of China's silk was also closely related with the general price of the world market. To take 1872, 1882, 1891, 1901 for example, as these were years of economic recession, China's silk price also decreased.[32]

Chinese Maritime Custom Reports and the British Parliamentary Papers further leave records to illustrate that the favourable world market was partially responsible for China's rapid expansion of tea and silk export. One of them mentioned, "It is remarkable that even in spite of the fact that at the close of our present period (1843-58) this terrible and ruinous civil war was at its height, so much progress in foreign trade has actually to be recorded".[33] In 1863 and 1864 when the Taiping Rebellion reached its climax of chaos and destruction in the silk-producing districts of Kiangsu and Chekiang, exports of silk fell almost to one-third of the previous level, while in 1865-73, these regions regained their production capacity in raw silk.[34] For Taiwan's tea export in the 1860s and 1870s, the British Consuls kept mentioning that there was no need for technological improvement of tea production. The chief tea-exporting province, Fukien, also simply enjoyed the favourable market without any improvements in technology or organisation.[35] There was technological improvement in the silk production in the development of the steam-driven silk reeling machine, yet it did not occur until 1873.[36] Thus, the sustained growth of tea and silk export for about three decades is primarily due to foreign causes.

There were actually a drastic change in international trade at the turn of 1850. Trade liberalism replaced protectionism. Meanwhile, railroads, the telegram, navigation, and banking made great progress.[37] With all these favourable developments, without the supply of money, trade could not have proceeded.

Silver and gold were the chief currency in the world at this time. Before 1870, most countries still employed a monetary system based on the silver standard. Only England had adopted the gold standard in 1816. The United States and the Latin American countries employed a bimetallic standard of gold and silver.[38] The discovery of gold in California in 1848-50 and in Australia in 1851-56, as well as the production increase of existent mines by one-third, led to a jump in the world's gold production. It increased from 1,762,000 ounces in 1841-50 to 6,313,000 ounces in 1851-60 (see Table 8).[39] The world's silver production also began to pick up again after 1850 (see Table 8). From 1850-73 the economic cycle changed to a period of rising prices and economic growth.[10]

A great deal of silver and gold had flowed into Europe and the Americas to purchase their goods. To take China's chief trading partnerEnglandas an example, its export increased by eighty-five per cent in the period 1851-1860, and fifty-six per cent in the period 1861-70.[41] Though there was short-term economic stress in the years 1854, 1858, 1861-62, and 1867-68 due to the Crimean War and the American Civil War, on an average, the British people increased their income after taxes by six per cent in the period 1842-52, and twenty per cent in the period 1853-61. The upper class experienced population growth in the period 1854-70. In the sixteen years between 1854 and 1870, the total of those earning an annual income of £300-1,000 increased by sixty-one per cent, and the total of those earning an annual income of 1,000 increased by sixty-three per cent. Prime Minister Gladstone claimed that the wealth increase of England at this time had been "intoxicating".[12] The increase of wealth in England enhanced England's ability to purchase China's tea and silk. Export trade from China and the overall trade between China and the West increased as a consequence.

Table 7 shows that the import trade with England had greatly improved in 1853 over the 1840s. The trade value with China's second trading partner, the United States, also shows an increase in the period 1850-70 (see Table 9). China's exports to the United States and England were both exceeding her imports from these countries.

The total silver influx in the thirty-seven years between 1850 and 1886 had been 704 million dollars, contrasting with the silver outflow of approximately 150 million dollars in the thirty-seven years between 1814 and 1850. The above evidence shows that other than the import of opium to absorb China's silver in the early nineteenth century, we have to ask why the export of China's tea and silk in the period 1814-50 could not be as thriving as that in 1850-

86 to offset the rising opium import and resulted in the silver outflow of the early nineteenth century.

THE WORLD RECESSION IN THE EARLY NINETEENTH CENTURY

By contrast with the economic boom of the late nineteenth century, there was an economic recession in the early nineteenth century. Wholesale prices fell in general in England, Spain, France and Germany in 1810-1840 (see Figure 4 for England as an example).[43] In England, bankruptcy amounted to 160 cases between 1823 and 1850. The substitution of factory workers for handicraft workers had already increased unemployment, which was further exacerbated by the recession. It filled the last quarter of the early nineteenth century with industrial crises and paved the way for the 1848 revolution.[44]

FIGURE 4

WHOLESALE PRICES IN ENGLAND, 1800-1887

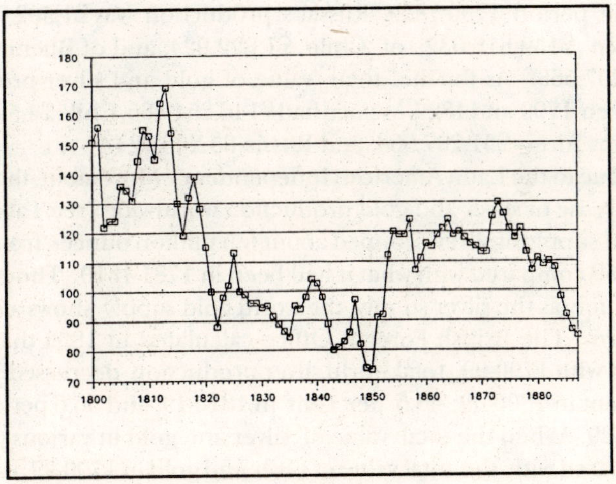

Sources: B.R. Mitchell, *European Historical Statistics, 1750-1970* (Columbia University Press, 1975), p. 388.

Scholars have pointed out that real wages had a fifty per cent increase in the period of *1810* to offset the unemployment rate of probably less than fifty per cent and left some net increase of workers' income.[15] What was crucial for the development of the recession was not, however, the net decrease of income, but the lower growth rate of net income.[16] Though the exact change of per capita income in nineteenth-century England is not known, we can observe its lower growth rate of export. By contrast with the increase of export value by eighty-five per cent in 1851-60, by fifty six per cent in 1861-70, the export value in 1821-30 was lower than that of 1811-20 by twelve per cent, that of 1831-40 was only twenty-four per cent higher than the previous decade, and that of 1841-50 was only twenty-seven per cent higher than the previous decade. In 1825 and 1839, England even had a gold outflow because of the trade deficit.

The improvement of industrial technology in Europe, particularly in England, could certainly have lowered the prices of manufactured goods. But the prices of almost every kind of product fell. The decrease of money supply was still the main reason for the recession.

The world's chief money at this time—silver and gold—came mainly from Latin America and Russia, especially Latin America. In the period 1790-1829, Russia's production was £1,502,981; of Mexico £139,818,032; of Chile £1,822,924; and of Buenos Aires £31,207,568. As for the total value of gold and silver produced between 1790 and 1829, Mexico had £146,254,485, Chile £4,591,412, Buenos Aires £31,207,568, and Russia 85,206,724.[17]

Due to the Latin American Independence Movement, there was a decrease of silver and gold production worldwide (see Table 8).[18] World supply of silver dropped about ten million ounces from 1811 to 1850 compared with what it had been in 1781-1810. Though not as acutely as the silver supply, the world gold supply shows a similar pattern. The British Foreign Office calculated in 1833 that compared with 1790-99, total world silver production decreased by 6.6 per cent in 1800-09; 49.5 per cent in 1810-19; and 56.6 per cent in 1820-29. When the total value of silver and gold in various years is compared with the total value of silver and gold in 1790-99, it is seen that there was a decrease of 4.8 per cent in 1800-09, and 49.7 per cent in 1810-19.[19]

Though paper notes had been issued as a kind of money, as their issue had to be backed up by gold or silver, their issue also was affected by the decrease of gold and silver supply. To take the Bank of England for example, its paper notes issue in 1820-50 was lower than in the 1810s and 1870s.[50] The production of gold and silver was not equal to the amount of gold and silver used as money, and as hoarding tends to be exacerbated in a recession, there was a worldwide decrease in the growth rate of money with the decrease of gold and silver production. To take the United States for example, its money growth rate dropped from 125 per cent in the 1800s to 22.5 per cent in the 1820s, price increase fell from fifteen per cent in the 1800s to .45 per cent in the 1820s.[51] The whole economy had hence fallen into a trough in 1814-49 after the peak of 1789-1814 as given by N.D. Kondratieff.[52]

WORLD RECESSION AND CHINA'S SILVER OUTFLOW

The dull economy in England affected China's silk and tea exports and conditioned her few purchases of British products, as reported by the British Consul at Canton:

> The continued and increased exports from China to Great Britain of tea and silk last year, *at a juncture when the shippers knew almost to a certainty that these articles must leave a loss,* (emphasis added)..., it seems to be very doubtful whether we shall be able, under the most favourable circumstances, to extend our commercial transactions with China beyond their present limits, even availing ourselves to the full extent of all the advantages held out by the treaties.[53]

The Canton British Consul reported again in 1848 that the failure of the import trade was due to "*a restricted circulation of money, and low prices both in this and the market at home, where the stock of commodities had been accumulating for some time*" (emphasis added).... It was also because extensive failure among the native dealers made them "inclined to hold back their funds when required for general trading purposes". The export of tea slackened in 1848 compared with 1847 because of "the accumulated stocks and the low prices which continue to prevail in the European markets". The decrease of both import and export trade also decreased the demand for shipping. The same report said, "A falling off in the shipment of exports at this season of the year, while it hampers in some degree the import trade, naturally also diminishes the means of employment for British shipping, the supply of which is more than sufficient for the present wants of the trade".[54]

The slackening tea export from China to England was not only the situation of 1846, 1847 and 1848. China's tea and silk export had been sluggish in the early nineteenth century compared with the late eighteenth or late nineteenth centuries.

The price of tea exported from China through the East India Company had been lower in the early nineteenth century than in the late eighteenth century. It was 2s 10d to 3s 10d in 1783, 1789; while it was only 2s 8d in 1839, 1s 1d to 2s 3d in 1842, 10d to 2s 4d in 1844, 8.5d to 2s 1d in 1846.[55] The tea value in terms of silver taels exported from China through the East India Company increased by 400 per cent in the forty years between 1760 and 1799, while it increased only by about twenty per cent in the years of 1817-1833.[56]

As compared with the late nineteenth century, the records left by the London customs reveal that the annual growth rate of the quantity of tea exported from China to the British empire averaged 3.73 per cent in the years between 1825 and 1848, while it was 5.91 per cent in the years between 1849 and 1886.[57] The average annual growth rate of the quantity of silk exported from China was 0.48 per cent in the years between 1825 and 1848, and 9.37 per cent in the years between 1849 and 1886.[58] Meanwhile, though the absolute quantity and value of opium imported into China almost doubled in the period between 1849 and 1886, the annual growth rate had been lowered to 1.24 per cent on average, while this rate was 9.05 per cent in the period 1825-48.[59] If the export of silk in 1825-48 was as favourable as that of 1849-86, the silver used to buy opium could still be offset by the silver earned by selling silk. The slower increase rate for the export of tea and silk in the early nineteenth century, however, could not pay enough for the drastically increased import of opium.

The Governor of the chief tea-exporting province noted the impact of this depression in 1846 without knowing the exact reason: "(Fukien province) is not a silver-producing place. Only when the tea and timber merchants came to trade would silver be carried here. After all the comings and goings, there however, remains little silver here".[60]

The worldwide decrease of gold and silver not only slowed down the Euro-American market's purchase of China's silk and tea, it also accelerated the import of opium into China. The British Blue Book observed: "Since 1821, the opium import has increased.... *The difficulties in getting silver dollars were highly related to the abrupt increase in the opium imports"* (emphasis added).[61]

The study by W.E. Cheong pointed out one connection between the worldwide silver shortage and the increase of opium imports into China. From 1565 onward, a Spanish company had used galleons to sail across the Pacific Ocean to exchange Latin America's silver with Chinese or British Indian textiles in Manila. Due to the emancipation movement in Latin America, this Spanish company had lost its trade monopoly. The decrease of silver and gold production in Latin America also disturbed the progress of such trade. Many shareholders of this Spanish company shifted to engage in opium trade from 1827 onward. Some of them were British and American merchants, the most famous being the Jardines and the Mathesons.[62] Those merchants who engaged in trade between China and England and the United States could also be affected by the silver shortage or the general economic recession and engaged in the illegal yet lucrative opium trade, as the *Blue Book* passage indicates.

The import of opium into China also coincided well with the silver outflow and worldwide decrease in silver and gold production. Silver production slowed down from the 1810s onward. The first year for China to start silver outflow was between 1809 and 1814. Though the worldwide shortage of precious metals started in the 1810s, the 1820s saw the ebb. In China, it was not until the 1820s that the officials noted the connection between opium importation and the silver outflow.[63] It was also not until the 1820s that the entrepot to carry opium into China moved from some area more within the jurisdiction of the Ch'ing Government such as Canton, Huangpu to a spot called Lintin, which was fully out of the Government's control.[64] The quantity of opium imported into China had also decreased to more than 10,000 piculs in the 1820s in contrast with previous records which remained less than 4,000 piculs. And the East India Company noted that China had silver outflow around 1825.

In fact, opium was used not only to absorb China's silver but its gold as well, though China had very little gold. One Chinese censor reported in 1838, "The gold price in Kiangsu has recently increased abruptly because opium vendors have carried gold abroad".[65]

When Adam Smith wrote the *Wealth of Nations* in 1776, the same unit of silver exchanged for more gold in China than in Europe. The same unit of silver also had a higher interest rate in China, with the yearly compound rate being 18-20 per cent.[66] The benefits of exporting precious metals to China, due to their higher prices there, disappeared as the western countries came to be in need of such metals themselves. The British Consul noted that the silver price in terms of gold in Canton in 1849 was almost the same as in England.[67] China had fully felt the worldwide shortage of precious metal and economic recession.

CONCLUSION: THE INVISIBLE WORLD

The connection between the world economy and China's silver outflow around the time of the Opium War had both been neglected by the Ch'ing scholar-officials and contemporary scholars. One Ch'ing scholar used 'historical force' to describe the incomprehensible reason behind the unprecedented increase of the price of silver due to the silver outflow.[68] Mainly based on the sources provided by the Ch'ing scholar-officials, contemporary scholars have naturally followed their perspective.

Furthermore, between the end of the East India Company monopoly in 1833 and the Chinese Maritime Customs' establishment of a statistic system from the late 1850s onwards, there is a lack of sources dealing with China's foreign trade history. Without the data provided from India and London and historical background for the global economic cycle, and the abundant economic record kept in the Chinese Maritime Publications and British Parliamentary papers for the development of the late nineteenth century as used by this paper, it is very difficult to perceive the impact of world economy on China's silver outflow in the period 1810-50.

Particularly, as perceived by previous scholars, the export of tea and silk still had some growth prior to 1833. Without a deep understanding of the role played by tea and silk in China's money supply and of the possible effect of the lag of the money supply growth rate behind the economic growth rate in the recession, it is logical for them to focus merely on the importation of opium.

Around 1800, about seventy-five per cent of China's monetary exchange (in terms of value) was made with silver, and about fifty per cent of such silver came directly or indirectly from Latin

America by the export of silk and tea. Though China started to import silver from Latin America from the seventeenth century onward, Japan was the main supplier for China's silver in the seventeenth century. From the eighteenth century onward, imports from Japan greatly decreased and Japan's share in China's silver imports became insignificant. China relied instead on Latin America to provide the silver that she needed. With the old Spanish, Portuguese and Dutch navigation powers declining in the early eighteenth century, it was not until the rise of the power of Britain to expand the China trade that silver was imported on a much greater scale from Latin America. Such increasing import of silver together with China's population increase stimulated China's commercialisation and reinforced her demand for silver.

The sluggish development of China's tea and silk export in the early nineteenth century slowed down the foreign supply of silver for China. It is true that even in such a case, if there were no opium importation, there would have been no silver outflow. But, there would still have been the problem that the money supply fell behind the economic demand for money. This problem was actually a very fundamental economic reason for the Opium War. On the other hand, if there were only opium importation and there were no world recession to slow down China's tea and silk export, the outcome would possibly have been like what late nineteenth-century China had: the gains from selling tea and silk could offset the loss from purchasing opium. Furthermore, the drastic increase of the importation of opium into China from the 1820s onwards had been stimulated by the world recession at this time. World recession is hence more a key factor in the economic background of China's Opium War than the importation of Indian opium.

The connection between the Latin American supply of precious metals and the early modern European societies has long been noted by European scholars. When Fernand Braudel underscored this connection, he added that before the fifteenth century such a connection would not stand as there was then tense competition between metals.[69] In pointing out the connection between the global shortage of precious metal and China's silver outflow in 1810-50, this study is not attempting to copy blindly the western studies about the impact of the precious metals from the New World upon European societies.

For Japan, there might not have been such a connection in the late eighteenth and early nineteenth centuries, as Japan was then a silver producing country and did not rely upon Latin America to supply her chief monetary materials. Where England and China, both relying upon Latin America to provide their chief money, had simultaneously upward price trends in the eighteenth century and downward price trends in the early nineteenth century, Japan had steady or even downward price trend in the eighteenth century and an upward price trend in the early nineteenth century.[70] The common reliance upon Latin America for chief monetary materials between the European-American countries and China makes China's connection with the world economy in this period deserving of more attention.

TABLE 1

THE NET SILVER OUTFLOW FROM CHINA (1814-1850)

Years	Net Silver outflow to India (liano)[1]	Net Silver outflow to Singapore (liano)[2]	Other	Outflow (Mexican dollars)
1814-15				
1815-16	1,324,940			
1816-17	1,068,436			
1817-18	2,021,493			
1818-19	2,549,068			
1819-20	3,614,671			
1820-21	985,944			
1821-22	1,359,661			
1822-23	1,098,014			
1823-24	1,045,960			
1824-25	1,447,722			
1825-26	1,615,289			
1826-27	3,072,012			
1827-28	2,372,382			
1829-30				
1830-31				
1831-32	2,771,809			
1832-33	1,614,152			

Years	Net Silver outflow to India (liano)[1]	Net Silver outflow to Singapore (liano)[2]	Other	Outflow (Mexican dollars)
1833-34	1,690,610			
1834-35	3,755,807		18,873	
1835-36	3,474,410		101,465	
1836-37	3,760,357		79,762	
1837-38	3,556,238		22,929	
1838-39	4,999,907		17,274	
1839-40	6,139,477		176,022	
1840-41	816,523		369,722	
1841-42	2,630,153		330,956	
1842-43	5,677,118		328,373	
1843-44	6,233,310		519,740	
1845-46	11,648,178			
1846-47				8,915,042[3]
1847-48				8,800,000[4]
1848-49[5]				
1849-50				10,000,000[6]
Total	82,343,641		1,965,116	27,715,042

Total of the above silver outflow - 149,962,739 (Mexican dollars)[7]

Sources:

1. The figures for the silver outflow to India were taken from Yen Chung-p'ing (1955), p.34.
2. The figures for the silver outflow to India were taken from Yen Chung-p'ing (1955), p.35. These figures are based on a report of England's Lower House.
3. A portion of the outflow was the indemnity China paid for the Opium War. The whole amount paid was twenty-seven million dollars. Other than the portion used in China, there still remained 12.8 million dollars which flowed to India and London [Yü Chieh-ch'iung, p.23]. In the record of silver flowing to India, 2,679,282 *liang* in indemnities had been included in silver to India in 1839-43 [Yen Chung-p'ing, *ibid.*, p.34]. On p.25 of Yü Chieh-ch'iung, *ibid.*, one *liang* was

computed as 1.45 dollars. 2,679,282 *liang* was equal to 3,884,958 dollars; 12.8 million dollars minus 3,884,958 dollars leave 8,915,042 dollars, the amount which might have flowed to London.

4. Yen Chung-p'ing had no record for the silver outflow to India for 1845. Here, Yü Chieh-ch'iung p.24, record for the 1845 silver outflow from China is used. Yü's record comes from the *British Parliamentary Papers.*
5. For 1846, 1848 and 1849, for which no records were available, Yü Chieh-ch'iung assumed that 1846 had the same trade balance as 1845, and that 1848 and 1849 had the trade fairly balanced (p.24). According to T.R. Banister, "A History of the External Trade of China, 1834-81", whether the trade balance of these years was favourable for China or not is very difficult to say (p.32). This author does not attempt to estimate figures for these years.
6. Hamashita, p.393 got this figure from British Consul Alcock's estimation.
7. The result of multiplying 1.45 by the total of the silver outflow to India and Singapore and then adding the other sources of silver outflow.

TABLE 2

TRADE BALANCE BETWEEN CHINA AND INDIA (1813-1850)

Year	China-> India (A)	Unit: £ India-> China (B)	-> import Balance (B-A)
1813-14	432,528	1,324,067	891,539
1814-15	573,315	1,580,212	1,006,897
1815-16	532,986	1,461,400	928,414
1816-17	704,727	1,591,065	886,138
1817-18	808,363	1,593,216	784,853
1818-19	834,063	1,397,730	563,667
1819-20	731,786	804,022	72,236
1820-21	760,364	2,252,507	1,492,143
1821-22	960,856	1,742,322	781,466
1822-23	734,039	2,070,480	1,336,441
1823-24	478,120	1,690,386	1,212,266

contd.

Year	China-> India (A)	Unit: £ India-> China (B)	-> import Balance (B-A)
1824-25	532,967	1,994,760	1,461,793
1825-26	728,853	2,411,043	1,682,190
1826-27	685,293	2,518,618	1,833,325
1827-28	757,807	2,912,527	2,154,720
1828-29	726,774	2,274,200	1,547,426
1829-30	822,078	2,453,730	1,631,652
1830-31	810,865	2,463,530	1,652,655
1831-32	480,765	3,181,659	2,700,894
1832-33	453,356	2,616,965	2,163,609
1833-34	541,922	3,558,938	3,017,016
1834-35	515,328	2,868,408	2,353,080
1835-36	536,150	4,428,500	3,892,350
1836-37	525,544	5,442,062	4,916,518
1837-38	440,066	4,095,225	3,655,159
1838-39	461,005	4,255,142	3,794,137
1839-40	201,188	1,004,539	803,351
1840-41	629,272	2,176,659	1,547,387
1841-42	566,805	2,883,794	2,316,989
1842-43	572,362	4,397,942	3,825,580
1843-44	638,985	5,724,786	5,085,801
1844-45	804,316	5,552,081	4,747,765
1845-46	733,514	6,508,696	5,775,182
1846-47	666,892	5,231,082	4,564,190
1847-48	1,014,595	4,241,844	3,227,249
1848-49	831,361	6,526,290	5,694,929
1849-50	809,801	6,401,846	5,592,045

Source: Calculated from Messenger, p.11.

TABLE 3

AMERICAN-EUROPEAN TRADE WITH CHINA (1848)

Unit: Spanish dollars

Countries	Import into China	Export from China
United States	2,034,004	6,207,378
France	18,184	110,561
Holland	110,351	679,006
Belgium	13,340	9,314
Denmark	41,687	15,934
Sweden	41,255	265,362
Germany	93,094	261,291

Source: *British Parliamentary Papers,* 1847-48, pp.1-15.

TABLE 4

IMPORTS FROM INDIA INTO CHINA

Unit: £

Year	Opium	Cotton	Other Products	Total Value
1813-14	557,128	625,395	141,344	1,324,067
1814-15	711,776	697,120	171,316	1,580,212
1815-16	580,691	749,394	131,315	1,461,400
1816-17	685,638	779,537	126,070	1,591,065
1817-18	633,157	785,595	174,464	1,593,216
1818-19	685,084	542,566	170,080	1,397,730
1819-20	349,819	272,663	181,540	804,022
1820-21	1,180,063	834,821	237,623	2,252,507
1821-22	965,067	638,937	138,318	1,742,322
1822-23	1,389,805	438,480	242,195	2,070,480
1823-24	940,473	557,352	192,561	1,690,386
1824-25	815,764	882,687	296,309	1,994,760

Year	Opium	Cotton	Other Products	Total Value
1825-26	1,196,283	1,042,387	172,373	2,411,043
1826-27	1,387,380	975,192	156,046	2,518,618
1827-28	1,793,119	937,918	181,490	2,912,527
1828-29	1,262,943	806,260	204,997	2,274,200
1829-30	1,392,617	894,703	166,410	2,453,730
1830-31	1,479,516	833,210	150,794	2,463,520
1831-32	2,326,349	732,262	123,048	3,181,659
1832-33	1,804,011	776,620	36,334	2,616,965
1833-34	2,272,080	1,118,690	168,168	3,558,938
1834-35	1,909,553	738,816	220,039	2,868,408
1835-36	2,866,025	1,345,868	216,607	4,428,500
1836-37	3,934,459	1,287,984	219,619	5,442,062
1837-38	2,904,284	1,025,947	164,994	4,095,225
1838-39	2,791,132	1,235,555	210,455	4,255,142
1839-40	191,422	696,803	116,314	1,004,539
1940-41	1,267,887	707,839	200,933	2,176,659
1841-42	1,839,401	829,013	215,380	2,883,794
1842-43	2,820,352	1,377,630	199,960	4,397,942
1843-44	4,229,542	1,279,164	216,080	5,724,786
1844-45	4,133,591	1,181,459	237,031	5,552,081
1845-46	5,541,735	820,620	146,341	6,508,696
1846-47	4,271,320	863,504	97,158	5,231,082
1847-48	3,507,804	626,120	108,920	4,241,844
1848-49	5,345,719	1,013,512	167,059	6,526,290
1849-50	5,543,588	741,504	116,754	6,401,846

Source: Calculated from Messenger, p.11.

TABLE 5

VALUE OF THE OPIUM IMPORTED ANNUALLY BETWEEN 1868 AND 1906

Unit: Million Mexicon dollars

Years	Value	Years	Value	Years	Value
1868-69	38.93	1880-84	42.98	1895-99	46.43
1870-74	41.01	1885-89	43.54	1900-04	55.55
1875-79	44.21	1890-94	46.12	1905-06	51.10

Source: Man-houng Lin (1985), p.158 gets this five-year average from Hsiao Liang-lin, pp.52-3. The original unit was the tael used by the Chinese customs. Each such tael is converted to 1.45 Mexican dollars for the years between 1868 and 1886, and for the years between 1887 and 1906, it is converted to 1.54 Mexican dollars according to the exchange rate recorded in each year's Chinese Maritime Custom Report.

TABLE 6

SILVER MOVEMENT IN AND OUT OF CHINA

Unit: million Mexican dollars

Years	Inflow	Outflow
1721-1740	68	
1752-1800	105	
1814-1850		150
1850-1866	220	
1868-1886	504	

Sources: 1721-1740, 1752-1800, 1850-66: Yü Chieh-ch'iung (1940), p.36; 1814-50: adjusted from Yen Chung-p'ing, p.34; 1850 and 1866: Yü Chieh-ch'iung, p.27; 1868-86: Calculated from Lin Man-houng, "A comparative study of the trade pattern of Mainland China and Taiwan, 1860-1894" (in Chinese), *Bulletin of the Graduate Institute of History, National Taiwan Normal University* (Taipei: National Taiwan Normal University, 1978), 6:35, p.211 which is calculated from Chinese Maritime Custom Reports.

TABLE 7

TRADE BALANCE BETWEEN CHINA AND BRITAIN (1827-1857)

Unit: £

Year	Import from England into China (A)	Import from China into England (B)	Trade Balance (B-A)
1827	3,743,392	4,855,165	1,315,800
1828	5,576,476	4,208,161	1,083,209
1829	1,893,148	4,049,359	900,643
1830	2,714,313	4,043,148	978,710
1831	3,791,998	3,687,771	-104,072
1832	3,184,050	3,660,713	476,663
1833	4,211,159	3,808,382	-402,777
1834	3,743,392	4,022,257	278,865
1835	5,579,268	5,100,916	-478,352
1836	6,995,690	5,948,440	-1,047,250
1837	4,903,163	4,973,757	70,594
1838	5,576,476	4,770,970	-805,506
1839	1,893,148	4,179,106	2,285,958
1840	2,714,313	3,017,941	303,628
1841	3,791,998	3,531,484	-260,514
1842	5,427,130	4,528,562	-898,568
1843	7,474,173	5,270,529	2,203,644
1844	7,940,830	6,369,906	-1,570,924
1845	9,023,566	6,554,456	2,469,110
1846	7,158,644	7,309,556	150,912
1847	5,840,088	7,717,128	1,877,040
1848	8,061,744	6,650,040	-1,411,704
1849	7,991,213	6,980,473	-1,010,740
1850	7,976,090	6,838,394	-1,137,696
1851	10,756,470	8,895,650	-1,860,820
1852	10,178,669	8,579,714	1,598,955
1853	8,511,489	9,065,952	554,463
1854	7,467,250	100,040,089	92,572,839
1855	7,855,949	9,534,307	1,637,358
1856	9,855,718	10,021,320	165,602
1857	11,872,011	12,364,497	492,486

Source: Calculated from Messenger, pp. 8-9, 11.

TABLE 8

WORLD SUPPLY OF GOLD AND SILVER (1741-1910)

Unit: 1,000 ounces

Period	Gold	Silver
1741-1760	791	17,100
1761-1780	665	21,000
1781-1800	572	28,300
1801-1810	572	28,700
1811-1820	368	17,400
1821-1830	457	14,800
1831-1840	652	19,200
1841-1850	1,762	25,000
1851-1860	6,313	26,500
1861-1870	6,108	39,000
1871-1880	5,472	66,800
1881-1890	5,200	97,200
1891-1900	10,165	161,400
1901-1910	18,279	82,600

Source: Vilar, p.331; Hayasaka Kiichiro, *Silver Prices and Silver Exchange* (in Japanese), Tokyo, 1925, p.53.

TABLE 9

TRADE VALUE BETWEEN CHINA AND THE UNITED STATES

Year	Import	Export	Total
1821	4	3	7
1825	6	8	14
1830	1	4	5
1835	2	6	8
1840	1	7	8
1845	2	7	9
1850	2	7	9
1855	2	11	13
1860	9	14	23
1865	3	5	8
1870	3	15	18

Source: U.S. Department of Commerce, Bureau of the Census, *Historical Statistics of the United States, Colonial Times to 1970,* U.S. Government Printing Office, Washington D.C., 1975, pp. 904, 907.

NOTES

[1]Chang Hsin-pao, *Commissioner Lin and the Opium War* (New York, 1964), p.46.

[2]Tan Chung, *China and the Brave New World: A Study of the Origins of the Opium War 1840-42,* (North Carolina: Carolina Academic Press, 1978); Tan Chung, *Triton and Dragon: Studies on Nineteenth Century China and Imperialism,* (India: Gian Publishing House, 1986), ch.2.

[3]For 1825, see: Yang Tuan-liu, *A Manuscript of Monetary and Finance History of Ch'ing Period,* (Peking: San-lien shu-tien, 1962), pp.263-5, which was calculated from H.B. Morse, *Chronicles of the East India Company,* (Oxford, The Clarendon Press, 1926-29), vol.III, pp.328-9, 365-6, 383-4; vol.IV, pp.21-2, 67-8, 84-6, 99-100, 118-9, 139-40, 158-9, 181-2, 195-6, 248-9, 271-2, 339-40, 369-70. For 1826, see: Yang Tuan-liu, p. 261. For 1827, see: Yü Chieh-ch'iung, *Estimated Imports and Exports of Silver in China during the Period 1700-1937* (in Chinese), (Changsha, the Commercial Press, 1940), p. 20; Yen Chung-p'ing, *Copper Administration of the Ch'ing Dynasty* (in Chinese), (Shanghai, 1948), p.33, (Yen also referred to Latourette's United States' Relation with China); Sasaki Masaya, *Chinese Currency prior to the Opium War* (in Japanese), *To-ho-gaku* (Oriental Studies) 8:94-117 (June 1955), p.112; Otake Fumio, *Researches on Modern Chinese Economic History* (in Japanese), Tokyo, 1932, p.121. For 1830s, see: Hamashita Takeshi, "Foreign Trade Finance in China, 1810-50", in Linda Grove and Christian Daniels (ed.), *State and Society in China, Japanese Perspectives in Ming-Qing Social and Economic History,* (Tokyo: University of Tokyo Press, 1984), p.389.

[4]Yang Tuan-liu, pp. 203, 208.

[5]W.E. Cheong, "The Beginning of Credit Finance on the China Coast: The Canton Financial Crises of 1812-1815", *The New Zealand Journal of History* (Auckland), 5(1) (April 1971), pp.77, 80.

[6]*British Parliamentary Papers,* 1849, vol. 39, p. 46.

[7]Hamashita Takeshi, pp. 393-4.

[8]Aside from the fragmentary silver outflow records provided by the Chinese scholar-officials, another more complete series of documentation is H.B. Morse's *Chronicles of the East India Company.* Yü Chieh-ch'iung, basing his findings on Morse's data, estimated 133,721,830 dollars for China's silver drain during the years 1827-49. Yü Chieh-ch'iung, p. 24. Morse's data had a shorter period coverage of 1817-34, and included only what had been reported to the Canton customs; it did not include the portion smuggled. For the years with no silver outflow record, Yü used some fragmentary annual records. Hence, the outflow records are not as complete as the Indian records.

[9]For detailed calculation process for such percentages, see: Man-houng Lin, "Currency and Society, Monetary Crisis and Political-economic

Ideologies, 1808-1854", Ph.D. thesis, 1989, Harvard University, p. 267.

[10]Detailed calculation, see: Man-houng Lin (1989), p. 267.

[11]Man-houng Lin (1989), pp. 91-9.

[12]For detailed calculation process for such percentages, see: Man-houng Lin (1989), notes in Table VI.3 and VI.4, and p. 219.

[13]Man-houng Lin, "A Supply Side Analysis of the Prevalence of Opium Smoking in Late Ch'ing China, 1773-1906" (in Chinese), Ph.D. dissertation of the Graduate Institute of History, National Taiwan Normal University, 1985, pp. 59-69 had an evidential research to negate a common opinion saying that opium was introduced into China in the seventh century. For the other historical backgrounds of the importation of opium into China, refer also to: Joseph Edkins, *Opium: Historical Note* (Shanghai: Presbyterian Mission Press, 1889), collected in the Inspectorate General of Chinese Customs, Special Series, No.13, pp.14-15; Yano Jin'ichi, "The Opium Problems of China" (in Japanese), *Kindai Shina no seiji oyobi bunka* (Modern China's Politics and Culture), Tokyo, Yiteya shoin, 1926, pp.371-3, 385, 782-3; *International Opium Commission* (Shanghai, 1909), II:320.

[14]For silk, see Man-houng Lin (1985), p.8; for silver, Chang Hsin-pao, p. 44 said that the silver price in 1833-73 in New York was $1.30 per ounce. One pound is 16 ounces. One chest is 140 pounds. 140 pounds of silver is worth $2,912. *British Parliamentary Papers*, 1850, p.120 and $500 to $630 for the Patna opium and $485 to $1,100 for the Malwa opium of 1847. If we take $600 as an average, the opium price is 20.6 per cent that of silver.

[15]M. Martin, *China: Political, Commercial, and Social* (London, Preface dated 1847), vol.II, p. 279.

[16]Chang Hsin-pao, p. 37.

[17]*British Parliamentary Papers*, 1849, vol. 39, p. 73.

[18]One Haikwan tael was 1.45 Mexican dollars before 1860 and around 1.52 dollars between 1887 and 1895. See: Man-houng Lin, *Export Industries of Late Ch'ing Taiwan* (in Chinese), (Bank of Taiwan, 1978), pp.18-19.

[19]*British Parliamentary Papers*, 1859, Sess 2, XXIV, 1871, L. Returns as to Trade of India and China. Cited from Ch'en Tzu-yü, "China's nineteenth-century foreign trade from the perspective of the China-India-England triangle trade" (in Chinese), *Symposium on China's Maritime History* (Taipei, The Sun Yat-sen Institute of Social Sciences and Philosophy, 1984), pp.144-5.

[20]Yen Chung-p'ing, *Selected Statistical Data for China's Modern Economic History* (in Chinese), (Peking, K'e-hsueh ch'u-pan-she, 1955), p.14.

[21]Chen Tzu-yü (1984), pp.144-5.

[22]Man-houng Lin (1978), p.4.

[23]The Inspector General Customs, *Decennial Reports*, 1922-31, fifth issue, synopsis of external trade, 1882-1931, pp.120, 190.

[24]Chen Tzu-yü (1982), p.327; Shih Ming-shong, pp.379-83, Man-houng Lin (1978), pp. 23, 24, 27 have detailed incidents to fluctuate China's export of tea and silk.

[25]Yen Chung-p'ing (ed.), *China's Modern Economic History,* 1840-1894 (Bejing, 1987), I: 363-4.

[26]T.R. Banister, "A History of the External Trade of China, 1834-81", in Chinese Maritime Customs, *Decennial Reports,* 1922-31, p.22.

[27]Yen Chung-p'ing (1987), vol.I, p. 357.

[28]Yen Chung-p'ing (1987), pp. 362-3.

[29]Shih Ming-shong, *China's Silk Industry* (in Chinese) (Taipei, 1968), p. 38.

[30]Man-houng Lin (1978), p.4.

[31]Shih Ming-shong, "Production and Trade of Silk in the Late Ch'ing Period (1843-1911)", in Hou Chi-ming and Yu Tzong-shian, *Modern Chinese Economic History* (Taipei: The Institute of Economics, Academia Sinica, 1979), p.379.

[32]Ch'en Chen (ed.), *Materials for China's Modern Industrial History* (in Chinese), (Beijing: San-lien, 1961), Series 4, vol.1, pp.122-3.

[33]Banister, p. 23.

[34]Shih Ming-shong (1979), p. 381.

[35]Ch'en Ts'u-yü (1982), p.245.

[36]Shih Ming-shong (1979), pp. 370-4.

[37]Tukang, *Cyclical Industrial Crisis* (Chinese translation of a Russian book whose author's name cannot be identified), (Beijing, Commercial Press, 1982), p.95; James Foreman-peck, *A History of the World Economy* (Wheat Sheaf Books, 1983), pp.73-5.

[38]Man-houng Lin, "Depreciation of silver and its effects on the trade and prices of China, 1874-1911" (in Chinese), *Chiao-hsueh yü yen-chiu* (Teaching and Research) 1:30, (Taipei, 1979), p.151; Yang Tuan-liu, p.151.

[39]Pierre Vilar, *A History of Gold and Money,* 1450-1920 (Judith White, trans.), (London: Verso, 1984), pp. 324-7.

[40]Vilar, p. 320.

[41]Vilar, p. 320.

[42]Tukang, p. 102.

[43]For the price trend of Spain, France and Germany, see: Mitchell, p.388.

[44]Tu Kang, pp.14, 38, 46, 47, 363.

[45]Peter Lindert and Jeffrey Williamson, "English Workers' Living Standards During the Industrial Revolution: A New Look", *The Economic History Review,* 36 (1) (February 1983).

[46]Kerry W. Doherty and Dennis O. Flynn, "A Micro Economic Quantity Theory of Money and the Price Revolution", in H.G. Van Canwenberghe (ed.), *Precious Metals, Coinage, and the Changes of Monetary Structures in Latin-America, Europe, and Asia* (Leuven University Press, 1989) also

emphasised the increase of growth rate of money supply rather than the net increase of money to discuss the relationship between the American precious metals and the European price revolution.

[47]*British Parliamentary Papers*, 1836, vol.37, p.427.

[48]Pierre Vilar, *A History of Gold and Money, 1450-1920*, tr. Judith White (London, 1984), p.34.

[49]*British Parliamentary Papers, 1836*, vol.37, p.427.

[50]Mitchell, pp.355-7.

[51]Ravi Batra, *The Great Depression of 1990* (Chinese translation) (Taipei, 1990), p.105.

[52]N.D. Kondratieff, "The Long Waves in Economic Life", Review, II.4, Spring, 1979; Solomos Solomou, Phases of Economic Growth, 1850-1973, *Kondratieff Waves and Kuznets Swings* (Cambridge: Cambridge University Press, 1987) has somewhat revised the Kondratieff Waves, but has not criticised the early nineteenth century portion of such waves.

[53]*British Parliamentary Papers*, 1849, vol. 39, p.10.

[54]*Ibid.*, p.3.

[55]Chen Tzu-yü (1982), pp.10, 19.

[56]Calculated from Yen Chung-p'ing (1955), p.14.

[57]Calculated from the sources for Figure 2.

[58]Calculated from the sources for Figure 3.

[59]Calculated from the sources for Figure 1.

[60]*Palace Museum Archives*, National Palace Museum, Taipei, Taokuang reign, 26.6.28.

[61]Chung-kuo jen-min yin-hang tsung-hang tsan-shih shih jin-jung shih-liao tsu, *Material on History of Currency in Modern China* (in Chinese), 2 vols., (Peking: Chung-hua shu-chü, 1964), p.37.

[62]W.E. Cheong, "Trade and Finance in China: 1784-1834", *Business History*, VI(1) (June 1965), p.45.

[63]Pao Shih-ch'en, *Four Notes on the Anwu County of Anhwei Province* (in Chinese) (1846), 26:4-5.

[64]Man-houng Lin (1985), p.63.

[65]*The Veritable Records of the Ch'ing Dynasty*, Taokuang reign 18.12.10.

[66]P'eng Hsin-wei, *Chinese Monetary History* (in Chinese) (Shanghai, 1958), p.540.

[67]*British Parliamentary Papers*, 1849, Canton.

[68]Wang Ch'ing-yun, *Literary Collections of Wang Ch'ing-yun* (in Chinese) (1890), 5:11b.

[69]Fernand Braudel, On History (tr. by Sarah Mattews) (Chicago: University of Chicago Press, 1980), p.45.

[70]Man-houng Lin, "From Sweet Potato to Silver: The New World and Eighteenth Century China as Reflected in Wang Hui-tsu's Passage About the Grain Prices", *The European Discovery of the World and Its Economic*

Effects on the Pre-Industrial Society, The Xth Economic History Congress, Leuven, Aug. 20-24, 1990 (Germany: Franz Steiner Verlag Stuttgart, 1990), pp. 322-4.

THE AMOY RIOTS OF 1852—COOLIE EMIGRATION AND SINO-BRITISH RELATIONS

Ng Chin-Keong

INTRODUCTION

Large-scale shipments of Chinese coolies under contract to foreign lands began soon after the opening of five ports (Canton, Amoy, Fuchou, Ningpo and Shanghai) to foreign trade under the Treaty of Nanking signed between Britain and China in 1842. The first shipment was sent from Amoy in 1845 to the Isle of Bourbon (Reunion Island) in a French vessel. Since then, Amoy had supplied the largest portion of contract emigrants until this flourishing human trade shifted to other locations in the early 1850s.

Despite the illegality of such activity under Chinese law, the export of Chinese labourers from Amoy was operated in the open with the connivance of local Chinese and British consular officials until the outbreak of riots in 1852 against the abuses of the trade. The coolie trade in Amoy declined drastically after the incident. During the period, Chinese emigration from Amoy was conducted by British local agencies. Up to August 1852, seventy-three per cent of the emigrants were shipped by British vessels, and the rest by ships under Spanish, French, American and Peruvian colours.[1]

The public fury of 1852 has been touched upon in a number of Chinese and English documents. Tien Ju-k'ang wrote in 1957 about the Amoy riots and saw this event as another example of injustice imposed on Ch'ing China by western imperialists. He was critical of both the western imperialists and the corrupt and incompetent Chinese officials, while seeing the riots as a righteous and heroic response of the Amoy people against exploitation and repression. On the other hand, Yen Ch'ing-hwang in his work reconfirmed the conventional image of Chinese officials as being timid and self-preserving. The organisational aspect of the Chinese coolie trade and the abuses in general were described by Wang Sing-wu in his book published in 1978.[2]

Drawing its sources mainly from the British Foreign Office documents, including the seldom used Amoy Consular Records which also contain Chinese-language correspondence, this essay intends to reconstruct the event seen from the local and treaty-port perspectives and re-examine the stereotyped images of the Chinese and British officials in their handling of the matter.

EMIGRATION AND ABUSES

Dr. Charles Winchester, first assistant of the British Consulate in Amoy, provided an eyewitness account[3] of the emigration from this locality during the period. According to him, the Chinese emigration from this port was conducted under both the native and foreign contract systems. It was estimated that the annual exodus from Fukien province involved some 50,000 able-bodied men. The great majority of them left through the Chinese own arrangements, which were either voluntary or conducted by contract. In both cases, the emigrants would work under the prosperous Chinese who had established themselves in the Malay archipelago. The native system had been in existence long before the foreign engagement in the export of Chinese labourers and had facilitated the commencement of emigration under foreign contracts. Until August 1852, the total number of emigrants who left under foreign contracts were estimated to be 6,255. They were shipped to Havana, Demerara, Isle Bourbon, Australia, Sandwich Islands, Batanhas in the Philippines, California and Peru.

The emigration can be attributed to both the push and pull factors. To begin with, the average wages of all labour in the city and the surrounding countryside were very low. They amounted to less than 100 cash per day, or less than two dollars per month for an able-bodied man. The wages of a skilled artisan or agricultural labourer might double this amount. With food provided, the wages would be five-eighths less in money. It ought to be pointed out that jobs were not always available. In the rural sector, as the landholdings were fragmented, they were usually cultivated by the owner or his sons. Under such difficult circumstances, many job-seekers fell easy prey to native crimps (coolie brokers) employed by foreign agents. The foreign contract guaranteed them a fixed income. For example, a Cuba contract stipulated that the emigrant would be paid three dollars per month, in addition to the provision of food. The wages under a Sydney contract were two-and-a-half dollars with rations. Moreover, the prospective emigrants cherished the dream of getting rich in foreign lands. One illustration was given by Dr. Bowring, the Acting Superintendent of British Trade in China, when he said that the representations of the boundless wealth of the golden mountain (California) "have almost fanaticised the people".[4]

Overseas demands for coolies gave employment to a number of crimps. It was a general practice for a European merchant who was engaged in coolie export to employ one or two of them. The latter controlled their subordinate agents, who in turn acted as touts and sent out their own scouts to go around the towns and villages in the neighbourhood to induce the poor and idle. The reputation of the Chinese coolie brokers was very low. The local community accused them of engaging in a trade of "selling men" to English merchants. They practised all the arts of recruiting and were paid fifty cash daily for each man mustered. They also demanded a usurious interest for the money they lent. Their remuneration on each coolie ultimately shipped was one dollar.

The conveyance of Chinese coolies was mainly in the hands of British businessmen, whose main concern was profit. They would try to keep the cost of transportation low. Consequently, the welfare of the emigrants on board was neglected and the mortality rate caused by sickness was high. The condition could turn worse as a result of the cruel and despotic conduct of the ship commander. This explains the rather frequent revolts of the Chinese passengers during their journeys. One such case was the *Robert Bowne* incident. This American ship left Amoy for San Francisco on 20 March 1852, loaded with 410 Chinese emigrants. After ten days at sea the Chinese mutinied and killed the captain, two officers and four seamen. They then took possession of the ship. The surviving crewmen later regained control of the vessel and brought it back to Amoy.[5] A great number of coolies who escaped from the *Robert Bowne* and other vessels brought back the news to their countrymen about the ill-treatment and cruelties to which they were subjected. This had caused great resentment towards the emigration agents within the community.[6]

Despite their awareness of the illegality of organised emigration, the British Consulate in Amoy connived at the involvement of their subjects in such activity because they felt powerless or were unwilling to interfere. For instance, when James Tait, an English merchant and the principal shipper of coolies, applied to the Consulate for a licence to export coolies, Officiating-Consul John Backhouse replied that he had no orders from Her Majesty's Government to do so and therefore, he did not intend to have anything to do with it.[7] Backhouse's response was based on a despatch from Bowring in which he said, "I have had no instructions [from the Foreign Office] either to assist or in any way to interfere with these vast Plans of Emigration".[8]

Meanwhile, the abuses of the foreign contract system and the cupidity of the shippers of coolies had drawn the attention of the British Foreign Office. A despatch to Bowring from the Earl of Malmesbury, the Principal Secretary of State for Foreign Affairs, dated 21 July 1852, stated that "Her Majesty's Government are not ignorant of great irregularities having been committed in the transport of coolies from China in British ships".[9] This letter mentioned especially two notorious cases involving the British vessels *Lady Montague* and *Susannah*. The mortality on the *Lady Montague* in 1850 reached a shocking height of 66.66 per cent.[10] However, the Foreign Office found that the existing state of the British law "unfortunately precludes any effectual interference with transactions of this kind".[11] The British Government considered framing some kind of enactment to provide for such cases; and they expressed their wish that "the British authorities in China should pay close attention to the proceedings of British ships engaged in transporting coolies, and should adopt all legal means in their power to check abuses".[12] In response, Bowring pessimistically foresaw the great difficulty in introducing such legislative enactments. As no aid or cooperation could be relied on from the Chinese authorities and as abundant places of shipment were spread along the coast, where there was no consular representative, he was afraid little could be done to check the frauds and irregularities. Moreover, the British authorities had no control over other foreign ships.[13]

Bowring expressed his anxiety in his despatches to Backhouse on 22 October and 22 November. It came to his notice that Amoy was full of vessels arriving from different parts of the world and loading with emigrants for the Spanish and British West Indian colonies. Several ships had also arrived from Australia seeking agricultural labourers. This pointed to the rise of Amoy as one principal source for the supply of Chinese coolies. He was alarmed by the many abuses that existed as to the manner in which coolies, particularly lads, had been seduced from their families. Coercion had also been resorted to and great desertions had taken place after coolies had been hired.[14] The recruitment system had become outrageous also as a result of the insensitivity of the British agents. They were so notorious and paid such little respect to the local authorities that they built their barracoons by the side of the Amoy Customs House. Bowring himself witnessed the arrangements for the shipment of coolies at Amoy. There "hundreds of them gathered together in barracoons, stripped naked, and stamped or painted with the letter C (California), P (Peru), or S (Sandwich Islands), on their breasts, according to the destination for which they were intended".[15] All this was an eyesore to the local community. The abuses, in Bowring's words, "are not far from placing the coolie emigration in the category of another Slave Trade".[16] But "the authority possessed or exercised by the consuls had been wholly inoperative to check such abuses".[17]

THE OUTBREAK OF RIOTS AND ANGLO-CHINESE DIALOGUES

The irregularities and abuses which were connected with coolie emigration eventually resulted in the outbreak of a riot in Amoy on 21 November 1852. It could be due to the chaotic and confusing situation that it took almost a week for the man on the spot, Acting Consul Backhouse, to send his first report to Bowring. Still, this official did not seem to have grasped the actual occurrence at the time of his writing.[18] He described the disturbance and disorder as "an atrocious outrage" committed by an armed party of Chinese soldiers. According to him, on that evening when a clerk, E.J. Mackay, in the house of Tait and Co., was passing by the street in front of a police court, he was attacked with stones by a group of soldiers. Some of them struck him on the head. They allowed him to leave only after giving him a blow over the head with the sharp edge of a spear, which inflicted a wound about two inches in length. Soon after, the chief mate of an English ship *Australia*, Richard Vallancey, was passing by the same place in company with a friend.

They too were attacked by the soldiers. The friend managed to escape, but Vallancey received cuts over each temple, one spear-thrust in the upper part of his left arm, five or six wounds in his thigh, one in the abdomen, and some other, besides sustaining much injury from the blows inflicted on his head with sticks or stones. He was thus dangerously hurt. Next day, news of the disturbance had spread all over town. All the shops were closed. At the same time, the town became flooded with vagabonds from the neighbourhood, who, united with the bad characters of the town, soon were determined to plunder the hongs of the foreign community, as well as robbing their own countrymen. Backhouse requested commander J.S. Ellman of HM's steam-sloop *Salamander* to bring the ship into the harbour as close to the hongs as possible for the protection of the lives and property of British subjects. Furthermore, a party of fifteen or twenty men was asked to be sent on shore to act as guards.[19] On the forenoon of the 24th, the atmosphere was so threatening that, upon the request of Backhouse, a very strong party of men was landed from the steamer.[20] But the crowd was rapidly increasing and they were pelted with stones by the mob. At length Lieutenant Smith, who was in command of the marines and seamen, gave order to fire. Four of the crowd were killed and five wounded. According to Backhouse, the local authorities fully approved of what had been done by the British and considered that it would be highly imprudent for the marines to be withdrawn from the hongs. He also said the Chinese authorities did not attempt to deny the culpability of their soldiers.

The above gave a cursory glance at Backhouse's early perception of the incident as written in the despatch of 27 November. Interestingly, Backhouse added further information in a private letter accompanying the despatch. He stated in it that he believed "the riots were attributable to an attempt made by Syme... to rescue a coolie broker from the hands of the Chinese authorities".[21]

Two days after the first riot, Backhouse officially communicated to Taotai (Intendant) Chao Lin, the most senior Chinese civil official in Amoy, a formal complaint about the assaults and a demand for the latter's immediate action. On the same day, he communicated again with the official, citing Article I of the Peace Treaty which stated that British subjects should enjoy full security and protection for their persons and property in China. Now there was unrest in the locality and the authorities were unable to suppress the mob. He had no choice but to request the landing of the British marines from the steamer to provide protection.[22]

Taotai Chao, however, had a different story to tell. According to his own source of information, three Englishmen were walking in the street that evening. One of them, being under the influence of liquor, was quarrelling with some soldiers and the crowd outside a police court about some Chinese coolies "whom the English had purchased." He had also commenced bullying them and a scuffle ensued. To substantiate his analysis of the outbreak, the Taotai cited a joint petition presented to him by the gentry, elders and businessmen immediately after the outbreak of disturbance. The petitioners blamed the abusive system of emigration for the outrage and said peace could only be secured to the community when the root cause had been removed. So long as the villainy was tolerated, awful disasters would be the result. They further alluded particularly to the vile impositions which were daily practised upon the people by a class of reprobates, who, under false pretences and delusive offers, had succeeded in enticing them from their homes and sold them to the English. The petitioners mentioned a recent case. It was a day or two ago when one of the *ketou* (brokers in these transactions) called Lin Huan had violently kidnapped an unfortunate man and taken him for sale to the English. Lin Huan was a notorious figure in the local community. He paraded the streets along with bands of armed kidnappers by profession. Murder and plunder had been the order of the day. The people were enraged at this atrocious way of behaving. They seized this infamous broker and sent him as a prisoner to the marine magistrate (Haefang) to be tried and punished. But the petitioners regretted that their authorities had not yet imposed punishment upon him. They conceived that the mandarins had an undoubted right to judge Chinese offences and punish crimes committed by their own people. Unless the authorities condemned the offender to severe punishment, the streets of Amoy, the resort of business and trade, would become unsafe and the interests of the community would be seriously affected. Upon receipt of the petition, the Taotai immediately sent orders to the marine magistrate to cooperate with the military in the seizure of the offenders.

Based on this information, Taotai Chao accused Backhouse for having distorted the picture. He pointed out that Backhouse was vague on several key points and demanded the latter's explanation. He asked "what induced that Englishman to go out on a dark night and in a drunken fit to assault the soldiers and others, what the subject of their quarrel was, who was wounded, and by whom and where". He requested Backhouse to obtain with as much accuracy as possible these various particulars to enable him to proceed with the investigation of the case and deal with it accordingly. Finally, he observed that "a party of troops was landed from the steamer. As this is the first time on record that this has occurred at Amoy, I shall make no comment upon it at present until I have reported the subject officially to their excellencies the Governor-General and Governor of the Province, who will bring it officially to the notice of the Plenipotentiary of your honourable country".[23]

While Chao was engaging in the debate with Backhouse, he received a report from Acting Marine Magistrate Wang on the violent clashes between local people and Englishmen on the 24th. Wang said three Chinese were shot dead by the English and two others were wounded in the affray. He requested his superior to write officially to the British Consul for a joint inquest on the bodies. He also claimed that, having been informed of the clash, he proceeded in person to the spot and succeeded in quelling the row and dispersing the mob.[24]

On the 27th, Backhouse wrote to the Chinese officials to convey the fears of the British merchants for the safety of their hongs and he charged the local authorities responsible for the protection of their property. The marine magistrate and the colonel of the local garrison at once consented to place about six or eight men under petty officers at each of the outlying hongs. These measures apparently did not please the Taotai who, in a despatch sent two days later, was highly critical of the improper wording of the Acting Consul's letter. He reprimanded the latter for shifting the entire responsibility to the Chinese authorities. In his view, the local authorities and their people together with the British officers and their merchants should render each other assistance for the preservation of peace and the maintenance of good feeling between the two parties.[25]

Taotai Chao's tough stance on the issue did not show signs of softening when he communicated again with Backhouse on 2 December. Coming straight to the point, he directed the Consul's attention to the abuses practised by the English hong merchants in their recruitment of coolies through the crimps. "These proceedings", he said, "have given rise to considerable general discontent, and are undoubtedly the origin of the affray in which life has been lost". He warned the Consul that the minds of the people were far from being pacified, nor should they be deceived by the apparent quietness. As the English merchants had not dropped the fatal commerce, there was no telling when a similar affray, such as the last, would again break out. On the part of the Chinese authorities, the marine magistrate had issued orders to make seizure of all the crimps and punish them with a degree of severity. This would "effectually cut off the soil at its root". At the same time, he requested the Consul to give strict injunctions to those hong merchants and others, prohibiting them from entering into arrangements with any agents or contractors for the kidnapping or hiring of coolies.[26]

In reply, Backhouse proposed discussions to be held between the two parties on the drafting of preventive regulations; but he asserted that this step could be taken only after the Chinese authorities had complied with his requests to conduct an investigation into the disturbance and punish the instigators of the riots.[27] To this Taotai Chao responded on 10 December by saying that a joint inquest had been conducted both on the bodies of the four deceased and the wounds received by Vallencey and a Chinese. Steps were also being taken for the apprehension and punishment of the guilty parties who wounded Vallancey. On the other hand, he demanded that orders should be given by the Consul to bring those Englishmen, who unjustifiably fired upon the people. Of coolie traffic, the Taotai said there was a positive law against the emigration of Chinese. Should any natives be found guilty of infringing this law, the authorities would subject them to the extreme penalty of the law. There was no need to formulate new regulations.[28]

In Hong Kong, Bowring had received the report from Backhouse and further information from unofficial quarters. He sensed the gravity of the affair and knew that the exportation of Chinese labourers and the misdoings of the agents had adversely affected what he considered the amicable relations between the British and Chinese subjects. He thought it desirable to send the Secretary and Registrar in the Superintendency of Trade, Frederick Harvey, to investigate the causes of the outbreak and the manner in which coolie emigration had been carried on at Amoy. The latter came on board HM's steam-sloop *Hermes* commanded by Captain E.

Gardiner Fishbourne and arrived in Amoy on 12 December. Whilst at Amoy, Harvey visited the acting marine magistrate twice, the second time being accompanied also by Captain Fishbourne. The mandarin expressed indignation with respect to coolie emigration in general and coolie brokers in particular. As a man-of-war was sent up, he thought the present occasion propitious for putting an end to the illegal traffic in Chinese coolies which had been carried on by British merchants. On the Chinese side, they had been actively and severely dealing with those nefarious brokers.

As to the marines who had fired on the people, the marine magistrate demanded their punishment by the British authorities. When he was told that the mob gathered at the gate of the English hong for plunder and that the English soldiers were justified in protecting British life and property, the magistrate denied that people went there to plunder. Their hatred was directed against the coolie broker who had done so much harm and had ensconced himself inside the hong. Moreover, these people were unarmed. Others were at a great distance from the crowd; some in their boats, others on their balconies, and in particular a babe still in arms, had been innocently involved. He said it was the intention of the Chinese authorities to punish the men who speared and wounded the English mate; but he required from the British Government the trial and punishment of the individuals who had killed the Chinese subjects.

During the interview Captain Fishbourne, R.N. expressed to the marine magistrate the British Government's desire to correct certain abuses which had crept into the system of emigration and their wish for the cooperation of the Chinese authorities in effecting their purpose. The mandarin said he would proceed with unmitigated rigour against all the coolie brokers, but he bitterly complained that those wicked coolie brokers were protected by the English hongs. He then strongly protested against the interference of the English merchants, naming Syme and Tait, who had on every occasion of an arrest, either sent in their cards with messages for the release of such brokers or come themselves to get them out. This, he said, had lowered the mandarins' position and dignity in the eyes of their own people. Harvey later commented in his report on this practice adopted by the English merchants that he considered such habit as "unauthorised and irregular mode of proceeding unheard of at any other port". He trusted means would be found to put a stop to it as soon as possible.

To the proposal whether a petty officer might be appointed by the Chinese authorities to inspect each emigrant ship as it left, for the purpose of satisfying himself that no coolies were carried out of the country against their will, the magistrate smiled at the idea and said, certainly not. He stated that there was a general prohibition in the code of the laws against emigration of Chinese subjects. To regulate would be to recognise the propriety of emigration and contrary to Chinese law. He counter-proposed that the English merchants should be prevented from encouraging more to emigrate. In his reply, Fishbourne said what they could do would be to prevent English subjects from sending Chinese subjects out of their country against their will. To do this effectually they must be informed by the Chinese authorities of any such circumstances.[29]

QUEEN VERSUS SYMEBRITISH JUDICIAL INQUIRY

While Bowring was sending Harvey to investigate the affair, he also instructed Acting Consul Backhouse to hold a formal judicial investigation on what had occurred.[30] After Harvey's arrival in Amoy, a Consular Court of Inquiry was held from 13 to 17 December. It was presided over by Backhouse, Harvey and Commander Fishbourne. During the sessions, the whole of the small British mercantile community were summoned to testify in court. Other witnesses included English and American missionaries and several Chinese. The procedure was recorded in the Minutes of Evidence at the Court of Inquiry, which shed interesting light on several obscure aspects of the riots.[31]

The causes of the riots were closely examined by the court. In the testimony, Syme's assistant, William Cornabe, admitted that the excitement was not the usual manner in which Europeans were treated at Amoy and that there must have been something wrong in the Chinese broker's conduct of his business. The Rev. William Chalmers Burns, an English missionary, believed that they had arisen from excitement in the public mind aroused by the exportation of coolies. There was a general impression among the Chinese community that the coolies had been carried away against their will. To substantiate his observation, the Reverend cited a government proclamation which appeared several months earlier. It was issued by Acting Marine Magistrate Wang, stating that coolie brokers were deceiving and selling poor people. In doing so they had committed a serious breach of law. The proclamation declared that strict orders had been given to the police for the apprehension and severe punishment of these guilty persons.[32]

Reverend Burns mentioned in his testimony two placards which appeared on 23 November. One was written in the name of the scholars and merchants. It made a general reference to the "buying and selling of men" which was carried on at this port for a number of years. Then it went on to complain that of late several tens of native people had joined together for the purpose of obtaining persons to be exported and that they had several hundreds in their employ who were going in all directions, using every pretext by which they might get hold of persons to suit their purpose. The placard then strongly warned the people against being imposed upon by such persons. The other placard, written in the name of the eighteen wards of the town, was of a more violent character. It reacted strongly to what they called the human trade and targeted specifically against the hongs of Syme, Muir & Co. and Tait & Co. These placards were posted up throughout the town and apparently had caused a huge stir among the people.[33]

On forced detention, Francis Darby Syme denied the charges and argued that the coolies in the sheds were most decidedly free agents and at liberty to go in and out at pleasure. Several other witnesses, however, testified to the contrary. Reverend Burns mentioned a specific case about a fortnight before the disturbance arose, in which his Chinese servant begged him to do what he could to have a young man released and restored to his friend. His servant told him that he had gone to the shed in front of Syme's hong, along with the young man's relatives from his village who wished to have him released. According to these relatives, the young man had been deceived and was confined against his will. When summoned to testify before the court, the servant described the shed as being "a very bad place". The men had nothing but the damp ground, with mats spread upon it, to lie down. They were all found with trousers, but otherwise naked. He was positive that the coolies so kept were not at liberty to leave, or in his words, "they could go in, but they could not come out". A similar case was brought up by another English missionary, Dr. J.H. Young, during his testimony. It was about how his Chinese teacher was asked by a female relative from the country to help in seeking the release of her nephew from the coolie ship.

During the inquiry, six coolies from Syme's emigrant depot were brought to testify and they all said they were promised work at Amoy, but on arriving at Syme's hongs, they were pushed into the coolie sheds and were not allowed to leave. Seven other witnesses from Tait & Co.'s coolie depot also testified to the same effect. Other witnesses recollected occasions of personal violence being committed by Syme, who seemed to be fond of carrying a stick and using it to strike at the coolies in the sheds. A couple of eyewitnesses said they had seen the coolies bleeding from the mouth after being beaten by Syme.

As the court proceeded, some missing links of the affair on 21 November also fell into place. It became clear that, in the evening of the 21st, Syme, accompanied by Cornabe as his interpreter, made a visit to a police court with the intention of ascertaining whether one of the men belonging to his hong was being detained, and, if so, liberating him. The mandarin told them the detainee was not their broker. They left subsequently, but were told by someone that this official had deceived them. Syme and Cornabe went back for the second time. It was during this second visit that people, upon recognising Syme, made the assault upon him and his clerk, Cornabe. The broker they were looking for was Lin Huan. Lin had entrapped a man in Amoy and was seized by the people, who turned him to the police court. Both Syme and Cornabe, as well as Lin, managed to escape from the scene amid the confusion and under cover of twilight. Lin took refuge in Syme's hong.[34]

But the anger of the people was aroused and displayed upon Mackay, a clerk with Tait & Co., who arrived at the place shortly after. Lin Huan in his deposition said both the hongs of Syme and Tait came to claim him. Mackay explained his presence differently in his testimony. He said he visited the place wanting to find out what had happened and that he could have been mistaken for Syme by the mob. After Mackay's departure, Vallancey and his companion Arthur Malthew, both from the coolie ship *Australia* appeared on the scene. In their testimonies they did not explain why they went there and what caused their involvement in the fight.

Syme's coming to Lin Huan's rescue had greatly antagonised the local people. The placard issued on the 23rd in the name of the whole community was the outcome of their anger. In it they expressed their determination not to transact with the hongs of

Syme, Muir & Co. and Tait & Co. They threatened that, if people among themselves should trade with these hongs, their houses would be pulled down, their goods plundered and their lives taken. Trade would be resumed only after the escaped coolie broker had been surrendered to their authorities for punishment.

It seems that after the outbreak of the 21st, the mandarin of the police court was disciplined for the incident. This action caused disaffection among the people and led to the closing of their shops from the 22nd until the dispersion of the mob. The act was taken to exonerate this mandarin from blame in regard to the circumstances which occurred between him and Syme. These people, said to be from 3,000 to 6,000, petitioned the Taotai that this official should not be demoted. They were resolved to keep their shops closed until the officer was restored to his former position, and until the coolie broker had been given up to the authorities.

During the examination, the Court of Inquiry also shed light on the obscure areas of the second outbreak on the 24th and the mob's motivation. That morning, about 1,500 men, mainly the Amoy people, assembled in front of the foreign hongs. Consequent on the shootings by the British marines and sailors, as later estimated by Harvey, seven or eight were killed and between twelve and sixteen wounded. In addition to the casualties among the rioters, four others who had nothing to do with the rabble were accidentally killed by stray shots; amongst these a child at her mother's breast.[35]

One witness, the acting-mate of HM's steam-sloop *Salamander*, William Hugh Nurse, told the court that the mob had plundered the outhouses in front of Syme's hong. When he was asked to describe what these outhouses contained, he said there were household utensils for the use of coolies. Then the court reminded him of the fact that these outhouses were only the coolie sheds. Nurse agreed that no direct attempt was made to break open the dwelling-houses and godowns in order to plunder.

Commenting on the intention of the mob, British merchant Robert Jackson considered their object as being twofold: vengeance against the outrage committed by the foreigner, and plunder. But upon being questioned by the court, he agreed that the mob did not at all appear about other hongs, such as those owned by Captain McMurdo and Captain Helm. Other witnesses also admitted that the original gathering of the mob was to obtain delivery of the coolie broker, certainly not for plunder. The crowd's feelings seemed to centre towards Syme's hong only; therefore, plunder generally could not have been their object.[36]

The question of motivation was also addressed to Syme. He was asked to explain why his house became the target of the attack. Syme said it was for plunder. He was then questioned how he would reconcile his claim with the message brought to him by an American missionary, the Rev. John V.N. Talmage, that, if the coolie broker was given up to the authorities and no future decoying of men by brokers would be practised, the people would be sufficiently satisfied and the affair would then come to an end. On this occasion, Talmage was deputed by a group of respectable Amoy residents to call on Syme concerning the matter. In his response, Syme did not fully agree with the court's view that the placards, the circumstances and the exasperation of the people against the coolie broker were sufficient to identify the riots with the recent coolie emigration. He insisted that the crowd who gathered in front of his hong were there merely for plunder. He could not account for the fact that only his hong and that of Tait & Co. were mentioned in the hostile placard.

After the inquiry had ended and sufficient evidence was collected, Backhouse held a Consular Court on 18 December to try Syme and his clerk for offences committed on 21 November. Syme showed his defiance at the trial and did not plead guilty. Nevertheless, the court found that, contrary to the Treaty existing between Britain and China, Syme visited a police court on the subject of a coolie broker, with a view to obtaining his release, and that he had been therefore guilty of a breach of the Treaty. He was fined 200 dollars. Cornabe also was charged for the same offences that caused a riot, in which two British subjects were assaulted. He pleaded guilty. He was fined a smaller sum of twenty dollars because he had acted upon the instructions of his employer. A summons had likewise been served on Connolly, a partner in the firm of Tait & Co. He was to have been tried for "misprison" in confining coolies against their will on board the *Emigrant* depot ship; but the coolies who would have been the witnesses in this case made their escape from the consular jail. The court could only give him a warning as to his future proceedings in regard to the shipment of coolies.[37]

VALLANCEY VERSUS THE CHINESE AUTHORITIES —CLAIMS AND CHINESE COUNTER-CLAIMS

During Captain Fishbourne's interview with Marine Magistrate Wang in December 1852, Vallancey's case was brought up. The former told the Chinese official that, by the custom of England, this English victim claimed an indemnity of 5,000 dollars. Wang said it was not the practice in China to pay money as compensation for wounds inflicted, but that by the laws the case should be thoroughly investigated and the offenders punished. He also reminded his British visitor of the cases in which innocent Chinese had been shot or wounded. These persons were at a distance out of the crowd. He said their relatives had not yet claimed compensation for the tragedies.[38] Harvey later conveyed his thought to Bowring that it would be very difficult to obtain the compensation for Vallancey.[39]

In late December, Bowring had received four petitions from Amoy calling on his intervention in the case of innocent persons who lost their lives from the firing of the marinestwo from the brothers, one from the widow, the fourth from the mother of persons shot. He asked Backhouse for a formal report and suggested the fines levied on Syme and Cornabe be distributed among the families of the victims. So far, Backhouse had not reported Vallancey's claim to Bowring and was, thus, asked by the latter to send him advices.[40] Bowring reported Vallancey's claim and the Chinese petitions to Malmesbury on 27 December. As to the latter case, he stated that such claims were rigidly enforced by Chinese laws against Chinese who were the cause of the accidental death of others.[41]

Backhouse replied in mid-February 1853. He said he had informed the petitioners that Her Majesty's Government could in no way be held responsible. He was far from convinced of the innocence of those who fell victim. The marines only fired when it became absolutely necessary for the protection of their own lives as well as the property which they were placed to guard. If the victims were partakers in the disturbance, their own temerity was alone to blame. Even when they were spectators of an affray in which armed parties were opposed to each other, they should have been sensible to the danger which they incurred. The Acting Consul believed his decision was supported by the laws of his own country under similar circumstances. As to the distribution of the amount of the fines among the relatives of the victims, he requested the cooperation of the Chinese authorities in the matter, but had not yet received any reply. Regarding Vallancey's claim, Backhouse considered it to be exorbitant. He would be willing to support a more reasonable demand.[42]

The final decision on the case was not immediately made pending instructions from London and also due to the unstable local condition which in the latter part of the year led to an uprising and the occupation of Amoy by a body of local rebels for six months. Foreign Secretary Clarenton in the despatch of 20 February 1854 inquired of Bowring about the development of the case. In his despatch of 13 April 1854, the latter directed Consul D.B. Robertson in Amoy to investigate thoroughly the facts of the case, ascertain whether the injuries were inflicted by Chinese soldiers, and how far Vallancey had exercised the necessary prudence in the situation. Having satisfied himself on these particulars, he might suggest to the mandarins the payment of a sum not exceeding 1,000 dollars as compensation. The Consul was empowered to threaten recovery of the sum by levying on the customs dues controlled by the Consulate.

In his reply, Consul Robertson cast some doubts on the claim. To determine who was responsible for the damage incurred, he found it necessary to examine the attendant circumstances. He said Vallancey unfortunately ventured into the streets of the town at a moment when there was great excitement among the people, in consequence of a general belief that British merchants had been engaged in kidnapping Chinese to fill their coolie ships. The visit was also made within an hour or so of a similar attack made on the persons of certain British merchants. Moreover, Syme earlier in the same evening had rescued his coolie broker from the hands of the Chinese authorities and was thus involved in a fight. The situation rendered it dangerous for foreigners to go into the streets.

Having examined the records, Robertson found every witness cognisant of and admitting their knowledge of the state of public excitement which existed at the time of and previous to the attack made on Vallancey, but he did not come across in the voluminous documents any inquiries being directed to the claimant whether he was aware of it. His own statement led to the supposition that he landed and entered the town completely not knowing of the troubled condition of affairs. Robertson found it rather improbable, taking into consideration the excitement which existed and that Vallancey was an officer on board one of the coolie ships, "which were shipping the cause of the dissatisfaction viz. the coolies". If a person persisted in placing himself in danger, it must be upon his own responsibility, as neither Her Majesty's Government nor the Chinese could guarantee security to life or property unless the person himself did all in his power to avoid or prevent danger to either.

Moreover, Vallancey appeared to found his claim on the assumptions that injuries were inflicted by Chinese soldiers. According to Robertson, "this may or may not have been the case". Knowing the facility with which a Chinese mob armed themselves, they might be mistaken by a stranger for military men, but Robertson inclined to the belief that they were not so. Certainly, in the records, there was no evidence provided by any witness except for the claimant and his companion to prove or establish that fact. Even their own depositions did not throw much light on the subject.

Consul Robertson was also of the view that the timing of lodging the claim might not be appropriate. Since the local uprising in the past months, the Amoy authorities had been in shortage of funds. Due to the stagnation of trade, no native customs duties were received and the mandarins were in great distress. He feared that pressing the claim under such circumstances would be considered unfriendly by the mandarins. This would be very injurious to British permanent interests. Finally, he said, of the mandarins holding office at the time of the attack on Vallancey, one only was still in Amoy. He was the Haekwan (customs superintendent), whose duties were unconnected with the military or civil administration of the place.[43]

Bowring agreed to Robertson's observations and gave directions to the latter not to put forward the claim of Vallancey for the present. The Foreign Secretary later also approved of Bowring's suspending the demand. Clarendon asserted, however, that the claim should not be abandoned, and it might perhaps be advisable to make the claim, but not to press it on the Chinese authorities.[44] At the end of the year, the case was thus brought up again to the Taotai by the British consular authorities at Amoy for the purpose of "carrying out the spirit of the Earl of Clarendon's directions".[45]

BRITISH SELF-APPRAISALS

After his on-the-spot investigation, Harvey was able to piece together the picture and gave his appraisal on the affair.[16] He first adverted to the causes of the riots. His report confirmed that the outbreak was attributable to Syme's "unauthorized and irregular proceedings" and that some of the English merchants at Amoy were much to blame for the reckless manner in which coolies had been obtained. These merchants employed men of the lowest possible character to supply emigrants. Abuses, fraud, deception and, in some instances, kidnapping were the natural consequences of the premium paid for every man obtained. Harvey was also critical of what he thought "a disgusting and obnoxious shed", or rather "barracoon", in front of Syme's hong, built for the reception of coolies, or "what Mr. Syme calls 'Applicants for Emigration'". He saw this as a disgrace to the British name and character at Amoy and pressed on Bowring the adoption of every legal means for its removal.

Another appraisal, which was even more sympathetic towards the Chinese case, came from Captain Fishbourne. He said the public mind had been for some few months festering under the accumulated wrongs perpetrated by savage Chinese brokers, with whom their employers were associated in the people's thinking. The illegal interference of Syme to stay the course of justice undertaken by the authorities sparked off at last a revolt at the instance of an indignant and outraged people. The people felt defeated in their legal remedy by the rescue of the broker. When they found out that the broker had hidden himself in the premises of Syme, they determined to take the law into their own hands.

Fishbourne also revealed that various meetings were held by the respectable inhabitants, at which attacking the English hongs, the ships and other extreme measures were proposed. Significantly, such proposals were all rejected, knowing well their triumph would only be shortlived, as steamers would be up from Hong Kong to revenge any attack upon persons or property. Eventually, they marked their detestation of the prevailing coolie system by selecting the coolie shed as their target of attack. They partially demolished it and liberated its inmates.

In the commander's view, Syme "ought to be tried for misprison, if he were not prosecuted under the 2nd clause of 6 & 7

Victoria, cap. 98, of the Slave Act". He found the moral perception of so many in the coolie trade to be so much impaired that they were unable to see they were violating law as well as the commonest moralities. It was in vain to try to enlighten these coolie merchants. He personally saw a man escaping from Syme's shed and being "chased by a set of barbarous harpies who seized him by the tail, arms, and legs, as if he had been a wild animal". Fishbourne was especially critical of Syme's defiant bearing in the Consular Court, saying that the latter had no softening at the thoughts of the deaths. The captain continued, "if he (Syme) did not eventually embroil the two countries, he would eventually destroy all friendly relations between our people and the Chinese at Amoy".[47]

Now, Bowring was ready to make the first report on the case of the Amoy riots to the Foreign Office. Bowring observed in his despatch of 27 December that "the public peace was seriously compromised, large amounts of property placed in jeopardy, and the amicable relations between the subjects of Great Britain and China likely to be interrupted by the misdoings of the instruments and agents engaged in the collection and exportation of Chinese labourers". With reference to the barracoon in front of the foreign hongs he completely concurred with Harvey's opinion that it must be taken down. He had desired "private intimation to be given to Mr. Syme that he had better quietly remove this cause of offence, and I hope that this may be effectual".[48]

On 29 December, Bowring stated his view to Backhouse that their merchants had been in the habit of disregarding and suspending the Consul's authority and had established, independently of the Consulate, direct intercourse with the mandarins. He saw this as one of the primary sources of mischief and one of the abuses which had taken place. Therefore, he instructed the Acting Consul to call the attention of the British community to the provisions of Article XIII of the General Regulations of Trade which stated that, "(w)henever a British subject has reason to complain of a Chinese, he must first proceed to the Consulate and state his grievance... . If an English merchant has occasion to address the Chinese authorities, he shall send such address through the Consul, who will see that the language is becoming...". He required Backhouse to strictly enforce by punishing any infraction. As to assaults, sometimes of a brutal character, being committed upon Chinese subjects by British subjects, Bowring told Backhouse that, "if, on the one hand, we call upon the Chinese authorities to punish their people for their offences against British persons and property, it is equally our duty to see that no outrages committed upon the subjects of China go unpunished". The latter was then reminded of the power of summary jurisdiction. Therefore, the consular authorities had the means of enforcing the obligations of Treaties in this particular, and causing the law to be respected.[49]

It was also on this occasion that Bowring commented on a protest note sent by Backhouse to the Chinese authorities. On the morning of 24 November, Backhouse found out that the broker, Lin Huan, was hiding in Syme's hong. He demanded Syme to deliver the broker to him. On his way to the Consulate, Lin was intercepted and taken away by officers sent by the marine magistrate. Backhouse communicated a strong protest to Taotai Chao against what he considered to be an act of great insult to the British Government.[50] Bowring, however, reminded the Acting Consul of the existing guidelines as regards the right of the British to abstract Chinese subjects from their own authorities and the authority of their own tribunals. He said it was decided before by the Crown lawyers that they had no right to interfere with the legal authority which the Chinese Government exercised over its subjects.[51]

In January 1853, Backhouse reported to Bowring from Amoy[52] that "affairs at this port have entirely resumed their former peaceful aspect, and that the foreign residents can, as heretofore, move amongst the native population without danger of molestation or insult". He attributed the restoration of peace partly to "the inoffensive disposition of the inhabitants, who were aroused to a display of anger and indignation at the hardships to which they were undoubtedly submitted". Due to the abuses of the coolie system, "even the most peaceful and forbearing will be excited to resistance and the endeavour to right their own wrongs".

The calmness of the situation was also attributed by Backhouse to the disappearance of the main cause of excitement. From the outbreak of riots to the end of the year only three vessels left Amoy with coolies. Other ships had proceeded to Namoa, another opium station in the Swatow region, to ship them. By early January 1853, scarcely a single coolie was obtainable at Amoy. The local authorities had taken means to deter the brokers. The latter were forced to discontinue their malpractices for fear of severe punishment. Voluntary emigrants to Singapore and Sydney, however, still embarked from this port.

THE LIMITS OF LOCAL DIPLOMACY

In analysing the Amoy affair, the imperialism-versus-patriotism approach does not reveal much beneath the surface. And the image of the Chinese officials as being timid and incompetent in their conducting of local diplomacy is more a distortion than the whole truth. The event has to be seen both from its local context and broader perspective to convey a fuller picture.

The coolie emigration was conducted in the manner of private enterprise involving both Chinese and English parties. These agents were acting on their own initiatives without permission from or sponsorship of their respective authorities. The English merchants treated the emigrants as human cargo and conducted the business with full entrepreneurship. Profit maximisation, not ethics, governed their business policy and management.

Although Chinese law prohibited outright emigration of their subjects to foreign lands, there was a practical limit to the arbitrary authority of the local government. In the first place, the officials did not have authority to negotiate for amendments to the existing law or treaties; on the contrary, they were bound and were required to abide by both. Still, when they encountered their British counterpart, they were able to stand on their dignity and argued firmly against the latter for the Chinese rights under the Treaty. Viewing it from this angle, these officials had performed a reasonably fair job. Moreover, as Winchester observed, the population pressure in years of scarcity occasioned great anxiety to the local authorities and often led to their disgrace; for any commotions which arose from famine were almost certainly attributed to their neglect or mismanagement. The mandarins knew well that emigration relieved the pressure of surplus population on the supplies of food and deported wild and lawless vagabonds to foreign lands, not to speak of the pecuniary interest which some Chinese officers always contrived to find in the continuance of a forbidden practice.[53] The local authorities were also realistic enough to understand their limited capacity to stop such trade. Their duty and concerns were the maintenance of law and order. They interfered when crimes connected with the system were continued and then made arrests of the subordinate Chinese crimps and agents.

Realising the practical constraints they were confronted with, both the officials and the Amoy community acted with restraint and did not wish to let anti-foreignism influence their actions and excite further disturbances. A case in point was the occasion on 25 November when Acting Marine Magistrate Wang issued a proclamation "to reassure the native population, to calm all foreign merchants, and rigorously to prohibit ill-disposed persons from seeking occasion to foment disturbances". He informed the general public that the broker, Lin Huan, had now been delivered up to justice and punished, all animosities were at an end and trade would proceed as before. Wang issued another proclamation two days later, prohibiting unauthorised publication of placards, with a view to putting an end to "the circulation of fabricated tales, and the inflaming of men's minds thereby", so that "natives and foreigners reside together in Amoy in mutual peace and harmony".[54] As to the Amoy community, despite the great fury, they made an effort to impose self-restraint on themselves and declared in their proclamation issued on 23 November that they did not want any dispute with the whole foreign community. Even the mob during the riots had their justified grievances and found their target accordingly in the persons who were thought to have connections with the abusive system.

On the British side, their consular authorities were fully aware of the illegality of the emigration activity. As Bowring himself had pointed out to them, being the Treaty enforcer at the port, they enjoyed the power of summary jurisdiction and had the means of enforcing the obligations of treaties and causing the law to be respected. Nevertheless, they did not have jurisdiction over other foreign vessels at the ports. Even the control of their own subjects often encountered diplomatic complications. For example, Tait, a British subject, had "all the advantages and influence which his being Spanish, Dutch, and Portuguese Consul gives him".[55] Consequently, the British officials could not take initiatives at will to ease the appalling abuses of the coolie exportation and even thought it unadvisable to do something about it without instructions from their superior authorities. Not surprisingly, they chose to connive at the ongoing activity, although they felt strongly against the misdoings. The British authorities in Hong Kong were also faced with a dilemma between suppressing and condoning the abuses of the coolie system. Their initial reaction had been sluggish until the outbreak of the riots which they could no longer ignore.

The moral sentiments and tenets held by the British officials on the China coast in this incident were genuine and admirable; but they eventually had to give way to considerations of broader British interests. While the British authorities in Hong Kong and Amoy were carrying out a post-mortem on the Amoy affair and making earnest self-examination, Bowring was required to ponder upon the policy implications of a despatch, dated 20 October, from the Earl of Malmesbury on the subject of promoting immigration of Chinese labourers into British Guiana and Trinidad or any another West Indian colonies. At this juncture, the Colonial and Foreign Offices had decided to appoint a Government Emigration Officer to superintend the procedure and ensure the best selection of labourers.

To justify their engagement in the coolie exportation, the British Government argued that a very extensive emigration had for some time been taking place from China and that the Chinese Government had not taken steps to enforce the law or to interfere with the emigration which was actually taking place. The British Government had not forgotten their principles that no official agent should organise within the territory of a friendly State a system in opposition to the laws of the land, but, in the question of emigration from China, the British Government justified an exception to the general rule by arguing that the Chinese prohibition law was dormant, or a tacit consent was given to its violation. Under such circumstances, the British Government viewed that their duty was to place the emigration system on a healthy footing and the Chinese authorities could not consider themselves justified in raising objections to a measure which was to the advantage of the Chinese emigrants and to prevent the recurrence of the lamentable events on board emigrant vessels.

Still, the British Government at this point of time hoped to avoid a head-on clash with their Chinese counterpart, not to speak of the undesirability of having the coolie issue as the source of conflict. Therefore, they imposed the guideline that, should the Chinese Government resolve to adopt a new course and enforce its then inoperative law against emigration from the ports to which the British had access by Treaty, the British Consuls at such ports were bound to act in strict conformity with the Treaty and not in any way aid or abet the shipment of Chinese subjects destined for British colonies. In such a case, the operations of the agent must be restricted to the British territory of Hong Kong. But, the Foreign Office was quick to add if Chinese subjects should, of their own free will, risk the penalty and embark, without the aid of the Consul or of the agent, for any place within the British dominions, the Consul was not bound either to prevent, or even to be ostensibly cognisant of such acts for it was the duty of the Chinese Government to enforce its own laws.[56] This situation had certainly created a difficult dilemma for Bowring concerning the shipment of coolies from ports and places, principally the opium stations, where, under Article IV of the Supplementary Treaty, the British were prohibited from trading. He saw the treaties were part and parcel of the law of England. Therefore, it became a matter how far they might be authorised to allow or sanction the violation of their own engagements.[57]

But there was not the slightest doubt that, whatever the rhetoric or moral and legalistic concerns were, when the different considerations clashed, morals and legality gave way to national interests. At this point, inconsistencies, double standards and hypocrisy crept into the actions of the British authorities. The British Government and its officials stationed in China always stood firm throughout on the question of protecting their subjects and interests. They were never slow to show force and use threat to achieve such purposes. Their actions were, thus, no longer guided merely by morals and legality. Understandably, in the eyes of the Chinese officials and civilians in Amoy, this was clear evidence that the British authorities were interested only in protecting their crooked coolie traders and the abusive system and showed no respect for the Chinese laws.

NOTES

[1]Note prepared by Dr. Charles Winchester, in FO 663/9, enclosure 3 in no.127, 26.8.1852.

[2]See T'ien Ju-k'ang, "I-pa-wu-erh nien hsia-men jen-min tui ying-kuo shang-hang lueh-mai hua-kung teh fan-k'ang yun-tung" (The opposition of the Amoy people to the seizing and selling of Chinese labourers by the English commercial firms in 1852), in T'ien Ju-k'ang, *Chung-kuo fan-ch'uan mao-i he tui-wai kuan-hsi shih lun chi* (Collected papers on the

history of China's junk trade and foreign relations) (Hang-chou: Che-chiang jen-min ch'u-pan she, 1987), pp.214-21; Yen Ching-hwang, *Coolies and Mandarins: China's Protection of Overseas Chinese during the Late Ch'ing Period, 1851-1911* (Singapore: Singapore University Press, 1985); and Sing-wu Wang, *The Organization of Chinese Emigration, 1848-1888: With Special Reference to Chinese Emigration to Australia* (San Francisco: Chinese Material Center, Inc., 1978).

[3]See fn. 1.

[4]FO 228/153, no.2, Bowring to Malmesbury, 17.5.1852.

[5]*Ibid.*; also FO 663/9, Abbott Laurence, US Minister in London, to Malmesbury, 9.9.1852. On mortality and mutiny, see Wang, *Organization*, ch. 6.

[6]FO 228/153, no.4, Bowring to Malmesbury, 16.7.1852; also no.9, Bowring to Malmesbury, 1.10.1852.

[7]FO 663/54, no.14, Backhouse to Tait & Co., 25.8.1852.

[8]FO 663/9, no.36, Bowring to Sullivan, 3.8.1852.

[9]FO 228/153, no.3, Malmesbury to Bowring, 21.7.1852.

[10]Wang, *Organization*, p.212.

[11]FO 228/153, no.3, Malmesbury to Bowring, 21.7.1852.

[12]Ibid.

[13]FO 228/153, no.8, Bowring to Malmesbury, 25.9.1852.

[14]FO 663/9, Bowring to Backhouse, 22.10.1852 and 22.11.1852; also FO 663/58, no.59, Backhouse to Bowring, 20.11.1852.

[15]FO 228/153, no.2, Bowring to Malmesbury, 17.5.1852; and no.5, 3.8.1852.

[16]FO 228/153, no.13, Bowring to Malmesbury, 24.12.1852.

[17]FO 228/153, no.12, Bowring to Malmesbury, 20.12.1852.

[18]For the report, see FO 663/58, no.60, Backhouse to Bowring, 27.11.1852.

[19]FO 663/55, no.34, Backhouse to Ellman, 22.11.1852.

[20]FO 663/55, no.36, Backhouse to Ellman, 24.11.1852. Lieutenant Smith landed with an armed party of officers, eight marines and thirty-seven seamen to protect the house of Syme, Muir & Co. and English merchants. See FO 228/153, Appendix F in inclosure 8 of no.14, Smith to Commander Ellman, 25.11.1852.

[21]FO 228/153, no.14, Bowring to Malmesbury, 27.12.1852.

[22]FO 663/57A, nos.20 and 21, Backhouse to Chao, 23.11.1852.

[23]FO 663/51, Chao to Backhouse, 24.11.1852. The translation of this Chinese despatch can be found in FO 663/5, Chao to Backhouse, 24.11.1852.

[24]FO 663/51, Chao to Backhouse, 25.11.1852. The English translation is in FO 663/5, Chao to Backhouse, 25.11.1852.

[25]FO 663/55, no.39, Backhouse to the British merchants, 27.11.1852; FO 663/57A, no. 24, Backhouse to Chao, 27.11.1852; FO 663/56, no. 19, Chao to Backhouse, 29.11.1852; and the translation of Chao's reply

in FO 663/5, Chao to Backhouse, 29.11.1852.

[26]FO 663/56, no.20, Chao to Backhouse, 2.12.1852.

[27]FO 663/57A, no.28, Backhouse to Chao, 3.12.1852.

[28]FO 663/56, no.21, Chao to Backhouse, 10.12.1852.

[29]For the interviews, see FO 228/153, inclosures 9 and 10 in no.14. See also FO 228/149, inclosure 1 in no.3, Fishbourne to Captain Massie, 15.12.1852.

[30]*Ibid.*; and inclosure 3 in above, Bowring to Harvey. See also FO 663/9, no.61, Bowring to Backhouse, 9.12.1852.

[31]For the Minutes, see FO 228/153, inclosure 8 in no.14.

[32]Wang's proclamation is in FO 228/903, p.149 with a translation in FO 228/153, inclosure 12 in no.14.

[33]For the two placards, see FO 228/903, pp.146-47, the English translations of which are in FO 228/153, Appendices A and B of inclosure 8 in no.14.

[34]FO 228/153, inclosure 8 in no.14, the minutes of Syme's and Cornabe's testimonies; for Lin Huan's deposition made to the Chinese police court, see FO 228/903, p.148b. The translation of this Chinese document was presented to the consular court of inquiry. See FO 663/9, inclosure 15 in no.177 of 1852.

[35]FO 228/153, inclosure 7 in no.14, Harvey to Bowring, 22.12.1852.

[36]Jackson also was involved in the exportation of coolies, but he had not become a target of attack. According to his explanation, he resorted to fair means for the obtaining of coolies. He received those who were perfectly willing to emigrate. However, a Chinese called Lin San, who was brought from Jackson's coolie depot in the town by Harvey and Commander Fishbourne, stated to the court his unwillingness to emigrate. He said he did not ask to come out because he saw others beaten when asking to leave.

[37]FO 228/153, inclosure 7 in no.14, Harvey to Bowring, 22.12.1852; and inclosures 5 and 6 in no.14, Minutes of Consular Court at Amoy, 18.12.1852.

[38]For the minutes of the two interviews, see FO 228/153, inclosures 9 and 10 in no.14. See also FO 228/149, inclosure 1 in no.3, Fishbourne to Captain Massie, 15.12.1852.

[39]FO 228/153, inclosure 7 in no.14, Harvey to Bowring, 22.12.1852.

[40]For the petitions, see FO 228/903, pp.149-50. The English translations are in FO 228/153, inclosures 5-8 in no.17.

[41]FO 228/153, no.14, Bowring to Malmesbury, 27.12.1852.

[42]FO 228/153, inclosure in no.22, Backhouse to Bowring, 16.2.1853.

[43]FO 663/58, no.29, Robertson to Bowring, 8.5.1854.

[44]FO 228/164, no.35, Bowring to Clarendon, 18.5.1854; and FO 228/169, no.103, Clarendon to Bowring, 5.8.1854.

[45]FO 663/58, no.89, Parkes to Bowring, 30.12.1854.

[46]FO 228/153, inclosure 7 in no.14, Harvey to Bowring, 22.12.1852.

[47]FO 228/149, inclosure 1 in no.3, Fishbourne to Captain Massie, 21.12.1852.

[48]FO 228/153, no.14, Bowring to Malmesbury, 27.12.1852.

[49]FO 663/9, Bowring to Backhouse, 29.12.1852.

[50]FO 663/57A, no.23, Backhouse to Chao, 25.11.1852.

[51]FO 663/9, Bowring to Backhouse, 29.12.1852.

[52]FO 663/10, no.5, Backhouse to Bowring, 11.1.1853.

[53]See fn. 1, note prepared by Winchester.

[54]Wang's two proclamations are in FO 228/903, pp.146-47. The English translations of these documents are provided in FO 228/153, inclosures 13 and 14 in no.14.

[55]FO 228/153, no.5, Bowring to Malmesbury, 3.8.1852.

[56]For the British policy directives as explained above, see FO 228/139, no.67, Malmesbury to Bowring, 20.10.1852. For Bowring's responses, see FO 228/153, no.12, Bowring to Malmesbury, 20.12.1852 and inclosure in the above, circular to Her Majesty's consuls in China, 16.12.1852.

[57]FO 228/153, no.13, Bowring to Malmesbury, 24.12.1852.

MALWAN: PORT TOWN AND ITS HINTERLAND—A SOCIO-ECONOMIC STUDY (NINETEENTH CENTURY)

A.R. Kulkarni

GEOGRAPHICAL SET-UP

The Maratha country is fortunate in having a long coastal line, covering a distance of about 720 kilometres from Daman in the north to Bhatkal in the south of the west coast. Unlike other coasts of India, the west coast has numerous small inlets.

One of the natural divisions of Maharashtra comprising the coastal lowland is the Konkan, the other two being the Maharashtra plateau, called the *Desh* and the Western Ghat. The Konkan lowland is not plain though it has some of the features of a plane of marine erosion. The lowland, 530 kilometres long and 50-80 kilometres broad, is much broken by hills, some of considerable extent and elevation.

It is subdivided into northern Konkan comprising the modern Thane and Raigad (the old Kolaba) districts and southern Konkan comprising the Ratnagiri and Sindhudurga districts. Southern Konkan has no coastal plains unlike the north.[1]

Malwan is in south Konkan. The dominating laterite landscape makes the region agriculturally unproductive. Paddy, the staple crop, is grown in the riverine plains and mango orchards are planted on the slopes of the valley. Amba, Kundalika, Savitri, Vashisti, Gad, etc. are the principal rivers. Their course is no longer than 100 km and in spite of heavy rainfall, the rivers run dry as the rain water is easily and most expeditiously disposed of to the sea. The riverine plains are narrow and cultivation is limited to the narrow riverside terraces of about 50 km and the coastal plains near the river mouths. This natural phenomenon speaks for the hard life and proverbial poverty of the people of Konkan.[2]

Malwan district, known as *Sindhudurg*, came into being on 1 May 1981. The old Ratnagiri district, of which Malwan was a taluk, had become too big, particularly after the merger of the erstwhile princely State of Sawantwadi in it in 1949. It was, therefore, split up into two parts and designated as Ratnagiri and Sindhudurg districts.

Sindhudurg district, comprising seven taluks, is bounded up by Ratnagiri district to the north, Kolhapur district and a part of Karnataka state to the east, the state of Goa to the south, and a long strip of the Arabian Sea to the west. Its principal ports are Devgad, Malwan and Vengurla; all the seven taluks, parts of Ratnagiri district and Karnatak state form its hinterland.

HISTORICAL BACKDROP

Konkan, also called *Aparanta*, the land of Parshuram, has a long history. Its long coastline played a major role in shaping its history and its social and economic life. The early settlers came mainly by sea route, as travel by sea was not prohibited at least up to the thirteenth century. The Buddhist monks during the period of Asoka (273-36 B.C.) penetrated into this area, and their remarkable cave temples bear eloquent testimony to their influence on Konkan. The descendants of immigrant Parsis, Jews (Bene Israelis), Abyssinians (Habshis or Siddis as they are known in Konkan) and probably Arabs were among the early settlers. The European powers like the Portuguese, the English, the Dutch and the French started their early commercial activities on the west coast from the fifteenth century onwards. The region in parts was ruled by the Mauryas, the Shilaharas, the Muslims, the Portuguese, the Mughals and the Marathas in the long course of its history. Shivaji, the founder of the Maratha kingdom, had his capitalthe fort Raigadin the Konkan. The Peshwas, who dominated the eighteenth century of Indian history, and who considered themselves as descendants of Parshuram, hailed from the Konkan. This historic milieu shaped the character of the people of Konkan, who were certainly different from the other parts of the Maratha country, in their way of life, language and literature. It was perhaps due to this distinct culture, particularly of the south Konkan, that the people of the region did not wholeheartedly join the 'Maratha movement' of the seventeenth century. We often find them in league with the Portuguese or the Mughals in their conflict with the Marathas of the Desh region.

The port town of Malwan, which is also referred to as Melundi, came to prominence in the seventeenth century with the rise of Maratha power. Earlier, the port of Malwan was notorious for the depredations of the pirates, who were known to the British as *Malwans*, on the coast.[3] Piracy prevailed, it is claimed, to an extent unknown before on the coast, which induced the English to send an expedition in 1765 to reduce Malwan.

Malwan was a well-fortified harbour. Besides the fort of Sindhudurg, it contains the forts of Rajkot and Sarjekot on the mouth of the creek, and Padamgad or Pandavgad in front of the main fort.[4] The Portuguese ships sailing from their North Province, Bassein to Goa had to pass through the Maratha territory at Malwan where the Marathas occasionally demanded *dastaks* or permits from their captains; but they used to maintain that they were exempted from these formalities by the earlier treaties of friendship between the two powers.

The Portuguese in the past claimed supremacy over the Indian Ocean and demanded that all the coastal powers—Indian and non-Indian—should get *cartazes* from them for plying their ships on the Indian Ocean. Shivaji the Maratha king, however, not only refused to ask for *cartazes*, but also insisted that they should seek his permission while passing through his territory. The officers in charge of the checking stations of the ports were instructed to follow this rule strictly. He carried his first naval expedition from Malwan against Shivappa Naik of Basrur in 1665, who was supported by the Dutch and the Portuguese.[5]

Malwan was under the Chhatrapatis of Kolhapur since 1713. The Portuguese complained that the naval and civil officers of the Marathas at Malwan always treated them roughly. It was the contention of the Portuguese that their ships sailing from Bassein towards Goa, passing through Malwan, need not obtain *dastaks* from the Marathas, according to the terms of treaties between the two powers. Yet the Maratha Subhedars and Havaldars stopped their ships, arrested and plundered the travellers, and treated them badly. This Maratha act was regarded as a revolution against the Portuguese.[6]

The Maratha-Portuguese dispute over *dastaks* continued for a long time, and finally it broke out in a war in 1768 when the Marathas captured a Portuguese merchant ship sailing from Africa to Goa, and refused to restore it to them. In the fierceful contest, which lasted hardly for a week, the Portuguese succeeded with minimum losses.[7]

The Sindhudurg fort was captured by the British in 1765 from the State of Kolhapur, but the State kept trying to regain it.[8] The conquest of Malwan was the result of a wanton aggression made by the joint command of Major Gordon and Captain John Watson of the Bombay Marine. The fort was renamed Fort Augustus. The acquisition proving unprofitable, they proposed to destroy the works, but this plan also was abandoned as too expensive.[9] They, therefore, returned it to the Kolhapur State, through a treaty concluded in 1766. The treaty promised not to molest British ships or trade, to give security for the future good conduct, and to indemnify them for losses and expenses.[10]

They evacuated Malwan in May 1766 and it remained politically undisturbed nearly for twenty-five years thereafter. But the Marathas' internal feuds compelled the British to fight for Malwan against the Poona Government of the Peshwa and establish control over it. Mountstuart Elphinstone, the Resident at Poona, exploited the disturbed political situation in western Maharashtra and forced the Chhatrapati of Kolhapur to cede Malwan. A treaty concluded between them in October 1812 put an end to Maratha political power on the west coast.[11] Malwan remained with the British till the transfer of power in 1947.

SOCIAL STRATIFICATION

The geographical set-up and the course of its history have naturally influenced the structure of society in the coastal villages of Malwan. According to the statistics for Ratnagiri district for 1872, the Brahmans, numerically less but socially more influential, were subdivided into eight sub-castes, of which the Chitpavans and the Shenavis were more dominant. The Shenavis or Saraswats no longer append the suffix *brahman* these days. Kayastha Prabhu families were few and were mostly engaged in the clerical professions in the British Company or government.

A report of 1812 by L. Smith on the general state of Malwan and Vengurla, which were by then ceded to the East India Company, gives some details about the population. The six sub-castes of Brahmans residing at these two places were Chitpavan, Karhada, Sastekar, Shenavi, Kudalkeskar and Bardeskar brahmans. The Karhada *brahmans* acted as priests or *upadhyes* of the village communities.[12] The total Brahman strength was: houses 103, men 141, women 182, children 173, totalling 496.

The Census of 1872 categorises the population of Malwan as traders, cultivators, manufacturers and artisans. The trading community comprised six classes, including Vani, Jain, Lingayat, Gujar, Bhatia and Marwadi. The last three must have come long back as traders and shopkeepers and settled down permanently. The Vanis (local traders) seem to have predominated. Malwan had thirty Vani households and 162 members. The Rajputs and Gujars together had three house-holds with eight members (four male, two female and two children). It may be noted that in the entire Ratnagiri district, there were five Marwadis and three Gujars in 1872, and no Marwadi family in Malwan in 1812. The sex ratio among the Gujars and Marwadis seems to have been the lowest. The Rajputs were messengers and constables; the Gujars may have been wholesale suppliers to the Vanis, the retailers. Lingayats, who also were traders, had four families with twenty-one members. They must have come mainly from the neighbouring Karnataka region.[13]

Cultivators were of nine classes, namely Kunbi, Maratha, Bhandari, Shinde, Mali, Pharjan, Ghadi, Meet-gavada and Gavada.[14] The Kunbis were tillers; so were most of the Marathas, a slightly higher caste. The Bhandaris are mainly found in coastal society. Besides cultivating land, they worked as fighting men of the pirates. Their predecessors must have been guards of the royal treasury—*bhandar*—hence the name. They were rated as *shudras.* Among the class of cultivators, they predominated numerically in 1812, with 347 households and 1,423 members (males 423, females 578 and children 422). Shindes were descendants of the female slaves, known as kunbinis, of the zamindars or the influential persons of the village. The Chedvas of Goa also fall in the same class. The Shindes, though originally illegitimate, must have acquired social status equivalent to the Marathas in course of time. Pharjan seems to be a corruption of the Persian *farjan.* Pharjan in Marathi is specifically used for progeny born out of wedlock. In Marathi documents, a distinction has been made between *lekare* (legitimate progeny) and *farjand.*[15] In the Census of 1872, Pharjans and Shindes were shown together.

Ghadi seems to be Gadi anglicised, meaning labourer. Gavada is a subcaste of the Kunbis; Meet-gavadas were engaged in salt manufacture. Malis were gardeners. The cultivators' population in

Malwan area in 1812 seems to have been 2,549, which included Marathas, Bhandaris and Gondees (perhaps a corruption of Gavada).

Manufacturers comprised Teli (oil presser and vendor), *Kosti, Sali* and *Sangar.* The last three were spinners and weavers, but belonged to different castes. *Sangars* wove coarse woollens and may be equated with Dhangars, the blanket weavers. Telis predominated in this category, perhaps because coconuts-their stock in trade—were available in plenty in the Konkan. They had twenty households (thirty males, forty females and thirty children).

Artisans comprised twelve classes, *Sutars* (carpenters), *Sonars* (goldsmiths) and *Lohars* (blacksmiths) being the most important. Carpenters and blacksmiths were required, besides agriculture, for shipbuilding. Goldsmiths were required mainly for assaying the coins received from merchants of different nationalities trading with Konkan. The statistics for 1812 show ten houses of carpenters with forty-five members, and twenty-six houses of goldsmiths with 216 members. *Kasars* (coppersmiths) had seven houses with twenty-two members. Their services were needed for making copper utensils.

Maratha country had a special phenomenon called *balutedar* in its village social structure. There were, usually, twelve types of these village servants—hence the term *barabalute* (twelve *balute*). They rendered all sorts of service to the village throughout the year for a share, called *baluta,* of agricultural produce. Pot makers, carpenters, barbers, blacksmiths, washermen, temple dancers (*kalavantin*), temple priests (*gurav*), priests (*joshi*), *mahars,* goldsmiths, coppersmiths, cobblers, etc. were members of the village communities participating in all social and economic functions, including the administration of justice at village level, as a matter of right. *Baluta* system prevailed throughout Maratha country even under the British.

Bhavin and Devli are institutions characteristic of Konkan society. Devli were the male offsprings of the female servants of the petty chiefs or zamindars and were found mainly in the port towns of Vengurla, Malwan and Devgad. The Bhavin received a piece of land from the master and was generally dedicated to the service of the village deities. One female offspring of the Bhavin was dedicated to the services of the village temple. The dedication ceremony consisted of pouring oil from the temple lamp on her head. The rest of the girls were free to prostitute themselves. In the Malwan region, there were twenty-six houses of *Bhavins* with thirty-three males, forty three females and forty children. *Devlis* earned their living as servants of the village temples, drummers and actors. Kalavantin's main profession was dancing. If she was attached to a temple for dancing and singing she was even endowed with a land grant from the village and was treated as a full-fledged member of the society. There were fourteen houses of Kalavantins in the Malwan region (two males, fifteen females and seventeen children) in 1812. Those who were not attached to temples may have been prostitutes.

There were more Christians than Muslims (in Malwan), because of the religious activities of the Portuguese in the Konkan region. In 1812, there were fourteen Christian households and only five of Muslims. In the Muslim community of Konkan, one finds a strong blending of both Arab and Persian blood. The Arabs came to the west coast even before the advent of Islam. By the tenth century they settled in large numbers in Konkan and married local women. They belonged to the four groups of Muslims namely, Syeds, Sheikhs, Mughals and Pathans. Konkani Muslims may be Jamatis (pure Muslims) or Daldis (converted Hindus, probably from the *Koli* community and from the descendants of the immigrants and slave girls). Daldis are fishermen. The Muslims were mainly associated with shipping activities. Shivaji's chief admiral was a Muslim. Christians also were involved in shipping and fishing. In the Ratnagiri district, there were four Parsi families who were mostly concerned with the shipbuilding industry located in the ports of Malwan, Ratnagiri, Jaytapur and Vengurla.

When the British took over Malwan from the Chhatrapatis of Kolhapur in 1812, it had 1,137 households with 4,846 persons (1,492 male, 1,840 female and 1,514 children). The population of the entire district of Ratnagiri was 88,185. According to Census 1981, the population of Ratnagiri district was 2,111,321 and of Malwan 17,328. With the coming of the British and particularly the disappearance of commercial activities from the Malwan harbour, the pattern of society was changed.[16]

	1872	1901	1911	1931	1981
Male	321489	654497	553382	609309	943395
Female	365129	712577	650250	693218	1167916

The advantageous position of the females in the sex ratio has been consistently fortified. This may be attributed to the lack of avenues of employment in the Konkan. The pressure on land, mostly barren, is increasing and males have to migrate to Bombay or other urban areas in search of jobs, leaving their families to look after whatever meagre landholding they possess and the old members and children who cannot be accommo-dated in the big cities. This situation explains the predominance of women in almost every class of population of south Konkan.

Villages of the Konkan are slightly different from villages of the Desh region. Morphologically, a village in the Deccan is not a stereotype settlement and its characteristics vary from the rainy Konkan to the dry interior. A village in Konkan is a small cluster of houses, situated on the plateau, the coast or along a river entrenched in the plateau. The plateau villages are often large and usally located along the roadside. The coastal villages and the estuarine settlements represent the typical rural settlements.

A coastal village, if it is an agricultural settlement, is located on a flat alluvium-covered littoral platform or on a river mouth plain. It has scattered houses with groves of bamboo, jack-fruit, mango and arecanut. The house, known as *agars*, are constructed in the midst of groves, backed by a rising valley side. The houses are scattered and well spaced. The open space between two houses is filled up with trees, the coconut and arecanut line the margins of the paddy fields. Rice is grown in small patches.

The villages located on promontories overlooking the sea are fishing villages. Here the houses are built in tiers with terraces. The individual houses are raised on a plinth with mud or laterite walls and tiled roofs.[17]

ECONOMY OF MALWAN

Konkan, which is known for its poverty, has seen better days. In ancient and early medieval times, its ports had flourishing trade. The decay of Konkan began with the coming of the western powers and tightening their control over the west coast.

The geography of Konkan does not encourage agriculture. With a thick and extensive cover of laterite, deeply entrenched drainage, a greater degree of inaccessibility and isolation, farming here cannot be substantial. The poor Kunabi of Konkan had no alternative but to seek employment elsewhere within or without Konkan.[18] According to the 1951 Census, a little more than a fifth of the total population of Malwan was engaged in agriculture. The figures are: agricultural classes, 5,276; non-agricultural classes, 24,575; total 29,851.

The Konkan soil may be (a) paddy soil in the narrow riverine plains of the valleys; (b) *warkas* soil on the slopes of the hills; yellowish red and of poor fertility. *Ragi* is the principal crop. Suitable for mangoes and cashewnuts; (c) garden soil at the bottom of the hill ranges; fairly fertile; coconut and arecanut gardens are grown; (d) coastal alluvium. Coconut and arecanut trees are grown; (e) salty soil, locally known as *khar* or *khajan*. The entire western strip washed by the sea, including Malwan, Devgad and Vengurla is salty.

Rice, *ragi*, small millets and *vara* are the cereals and *kulith, udid, moog* and *chavali* are the pulses produced during the monsoon as *kharif* crops. Among the winter (*rabi*) crops, rice, wal, etc. are produced in irrigated areas, in addition to vegetables. Alphonso variety of mangoes are produced at Devgad, Malwan and Vengurla; they have a good market outside India. Cashew-nut plantations also are found at Malwan. Mangoes and cashew-nuts are the major cash crops of Malwan region.

TRADE

Konkan's share in overseas trade in the early period of Indian history was significant. The major ports of Konkan have the peculiarity that they are not on the seashore but in the interior on the creeks. Such construction gave protection from the sea pirates. Besides, the creeks were navigable; the thick forests of Sahyadri protected them from erosion. The cargoes could sail smoothly on the waters of these deep creeks.[19]

Of the fifteen ports on the coast of south Konkan, only seven are useful for trade, as cargo steamers could call at these ports only. All the three ports of the Malwan region, namely Devgad, Vengurla and Malwan fall in this category. As these ports do not possess wharfing and landing facilities, they can admit vessels with a maximum capacity of 200 tonnes only. Devgad, a land-locked harbour, is at all times perfectly smooth. It was the only sheltering place for ships during the southwest monsoon on the west coast. It was taken over by the British in 1819 who converted it into a lighthouse and an observatory. Vengurla, also referred to as Fingurla or Mingrela in the foreign records, was a flourishing trade centre in the seventeenth century, when the Dutch had established their trade settlement there. It is a large town stretching half a league along the coast, with one of the best sea routes in India. All the vessels from Batavia, Japan, Bengal and Ceylon, and vessels inward or outward bound from Surat, Hormuz and the Red Sea anchored here because both the water and rice available here were excellent.[20]

Malwan ports were flourishing trade centres from the medieval period to the nineteenth century. They had trade relations with Arabia, Malabar, Bombay, Cutch, Kathiawar, Goa and some other ports on the west coast. The chief exports in the nineteenth century were rice, linseed, walnut, hemp, cashewnut, mango, dried rind of kokam, coir, coir-rope, coconut, sugar, bamboo, blankets, salted fish, salt, fish, betelnut. Imports were husked rice, cleared rice, gram, oil, English cloth piec-goods, grain, groundnut, tiles, timber, molasses, tobacco, chillies, etc. The exports were partly local and partly from the princely State of Sawantwadi and different parts of Ratnagiri. The imports, mostly for local consumption, came from Bombay, Goa, Karwar and other Konkan ports, Cochin, Calicut and Mangalore. The traders were local Vanis, Gujars, Shenavis, Bhandaris and Gabits. Business in trade was transacted partly with own capital but mainly with borrowings from the Marwadis. Local shipping, consisting of *machvas, phatemavis*, etc. was generally used for trading; they sailed to Bombay, Karwar, Karachi in the north and Cochin in the south.[21]

Trade figures for the nineteenth century, when the Malwan division was under the complete control of the British, would give an idea of the volume of trade transacted here.[22]

Year	Vol. Trade	Year	Vol. Trade
1840	£10,775	1873	£81,639
1850	£13,274	1874-75	£77,683
1867	£99,619	1878-79	£88,574
1871	£81,154		

The exchange rate was approximately Rs.10 per sterling.

Malwan was a centre of great activity right from the sixteenth century. The British opened their factories at Malwan in 1766 and 1792, and finally the port along with its dependencies was ceded to them by the Chhatrapatis of Kolhapur in 1812. The Malwan Residency gives details of the inland customs on exports and imports as they were prevailing in the nineteenth century.[23] The goods were carried mostly by bullock load or head load. Among exports subject to land customs were salt, coconut kernel, betelnut, dry dates, coir, wood, sugar, black pepper, ginger, sandalwood, turmeric, almond, dry fruit, dry walnut, etc. Customs *ad valorem* at three per cent was charged on exports of cloves, nutmeg, mace, silk thread, lead, copper, iron, etc. Duty on the export and import goods by sea was charged at two per cent of the valuation or upon the market price of Malwan. The import duty on Bombay salt was higher than export duty on Malwan salt, to protect the domestic salt industry.

Land custom imports on gram, moog, black gram, *tur*, *udid*, peas, etc. were charged at $4^1/_1$ anna per bullock load. Higher rates were fixed for costly and luxury goods like sandalwood, black pepper, cotton thread, saltpetre, coarse cloth, chilly, jaggery and tobacco.

Some details of the value of export and import trade for 1819 are available.[24] They are:

Total value of trade	: £ 28,570	(Rs.285,790)
Exports	: £ 5,283	(Rs.52,830)
Imports	: £ 23,296	(Rs.232,960)

Details of Exports and Imports from Mr. Hale's Diary of 1819

Exports :	Coriander seeds	: £	502
	Clarified butter	: £	554
	Hemp	: £	1,749
	Piece-goods	: £	793
	Total	: £	3,598
Imports :	Coconut kernel	: £	838
	Grain	: £	1,645
	Piece-goods	: £	2,269
	Rice	: £	12,855
	Total	: £	17,607

These figures include items from Vengurla as well.

The Marathas exempted from customs certain persons under special circumstances. The Kolhapur State had instructed its customs officers of Konkan that the bullocks carrying loads of tobacco should not be obstructed for customs, on their way to Sindhudurg and also on their return from there loaded with some goods.[25] Such exemptions, it appears, were not granted by the British to anybody.

PIRACY

Foreign travellers and geographers have complained about piracy on the west coast, prevailing right from ancient times. According to them, it was freely practised on the Konkan coast south of Malwan, which had become the nest of pirates.[26] In the seventeenth and early eighteenth centuries, Malwan was the headquarters of pirates known as Malwanis. The Portuguese and the English branded Kanhoji Angre, the admiral of the Marathas, as pirate as he was capturing their ships and obstructing their trade.[27] They even accused the Chhatrapati of Kolhapur, who had fitted three kinds of vessels, *galivats, shibars* and *garabs* to ply on the sea under the pretext of patrolling the coast, but mainly for seizing the merchant ships.

> They sailed with no written commission and with instructions to take any vessel they could master except such as had English colours and passes. Sometimes they seized boats under English protection evading the open assault by sending on some boats, who examined the pass, contrived to steal or lose it, and make off. Soon after, the rest of the pirates came up and seized the trader. In many cases restitution was demanded by the British Government and made without demur.[28]

"The Portuguese historians have always described Indian Admirals and seamen who fought the war of national resistance as pirates. Barros found it necessary to defend the Portuguese conduct with elaborate theological legal casuistry that he was aware of the piratical character of his countrymen." The Portuguese were determined to ruin the seaborne trade of India by force and not by fair commercial competition, according to Nambiar, to whom the Portuguese were no less than pirates. The seas, which were free for all to navigate, were declared by them as under their control according to a Papal bull, and forced the merchants to buy cartazes, i.e. permits to ply on the seas, from their captains. Those who did not obtain the permits were punished by capturing their merchant ships. This act of the Portuguese was nothing else but piracy.[29]

Piracy was not easy to suppress as it was difficult to make a distinction between a pirate and a merchant.[30] In those days the pirates were always found on the seas, keeping an eye on cargo ships. They would surround such ships, plunder them, take away persons and children on the ships as hostages, and would release them on payment. They did not belong to any particular caste, religion or nationality. On the west coast, Hindus, Arabs, Negroes from the Persian Gulf and Europeans were found involved in piracy. The Arab pirates had their guilds at Muscat.[31]

In a letter addressed to Sir John Shore, the Governor General in Council, Fort William in 1793, the Bombay Government of the Company narrated the background of their actions against the Malwan port. The report mentions that besides "the Northern Pirates"[32] called the Gabits (fishers and sailors) of Colaba, the Angres, the Peshwa's Government, the Raja of Kolhapur and the Bhonsle chieftain of Sawantwadi was involved in piracy. The Company planned an expedition for the protection of their trade on the west coast against the Malwans, the pirates. But finding it difficult to retain Malwan and its fort, the Company agreed to restore it to Kolhapur on payment of compensation and promise to stop piracy. But piracy remained unchecked. The British, therefore, thought the trade would not be safe unless they held some forts and harbours near Malwan. The Kolhapur State was compelled to cede the harbour of Malwan and the fort of Sindhudurg and its dependencies in 1812. The Raja also agreed to give up piracy, to allow no armed vessels to leave or to enter his ports, to restore wrecks and to help vessels in distress. The chief of Sawantwadi made over the port of Vengurla to the British and agreed to put down piracy. He also conceded several other things like ceding the ports of Nivti and Redi if he failed to check piracy; to pass duty-free all articles required for the British troops; to allow British merchants free passage to and from his territory. The British civil and military control over Malwan and Vengurla put an end to piratical practices on the west coast.[33]

COMMUNICATION

Though Malwan region is best suited for sea traffic because of its fordable creeks at low waters and navigable rivers, land routes are equally important for getting supplies for trade from the hinterland. But because of the rugged and broken belt of coast land and numerous hills, road transport is not only difficult, but also time-consuming. The demand for a railway line has not been met so far.

The principal ghats or passes connecting Ratnagiri district to its hinterland, namely Kolhapur district and parts of Karnataka state, are Bhaitwada, Karul, Phonda, Hanumant, Amboli and Ramghat. For Malwan and Vengurla trade, Phonda and Amboli or Parpoli passes are very important.

The sea traffic is conducted partly by steamers and partly by sailing vessels. Ferries are used on the navigable rivers for transporting goods and passengers. Sailing vessels may be foreign or local. The Foreign ships of the Arab model, carrying cargoes from 75 to 150 tonnes are owned by Arabs and Indian Muslims of the west coast. They generally come from Arabia to Jaytapur, a port of Ratnagiri district, by the end of October bringing dates, raisins, almonds, mats, etc.; after two weeks' stay they sail away with loads of walnut, hemp, turmeric, groundnut, etc. to Bombay or Malabar en route to their homeland.

The local sailing crafts are the *shibadi, phatemari, mhangiri, machva, padav* or *balav, ulandi, pagar* and *don*. The *shibadi* is a large vessel from 100 to 300 tonnes burden. The *phatemari*, a deep narrow vessel, with a great speed and excellent sailer, is twenty-five to forty-five feet long and twenty-five to hundred tonnes burden. The *mhangiri* is like the *phatemari*, but smaller and of ten to twenty-five tonnes burden. The *machvas* and *padvas* or *balavs* are of a broader and flatter build, twelve to twenty-five feet long and of $2\,^1/_2$ to ten tonnes burden. The smaller *machvas* are often used for deep sea-fishing. About fifty-one types of vessels are mentioned in the Marathi records.[34]

These vessels are owned by Bhatias, Gujars, Musalmans, Parsis and fishermen of Gabit, Koli and Kharvi classes of Hindus and Daldi classes of Muslims. Brahmans are also found in the business either as owners of vessels or money-lenders to fishermen.

The *shibadis* have a strength of twenty to twenty-five crew besides the captain; a *phatemari* has fourteen to eighteen, a *mhangiri* has eight to ten, and *machava* has five to seven hands as crew. The seamen were Kolis, Bhandaris, Gabits, Bhois, Kharvis or Musalmans, and came mostly from Vengurla side. These vessels work only during the fair season and are laid up during the southwest monsoon.[35]

The seamen's wages in the beginning of the nineteenth century were: *tandel*, Rs. $7^1/_2$, *sar tandel*, Rs.10, and a sailor (*khalashi*), Rs. $4^1/_2$ per month. The wages on a merchant ship were: *tandel* Rs. 5 to 6, *sar tandel* Rs. 6 to 8 and *khalashi* Rs. 4 to $4^1/_2$ per month, in addition to ration which included ghee, rice, gram, etc. The vessels started sailing on an auspicious day, as suggested by the Brahman after consulting the almanac. He was paid fees for this job up to Rs. 5 in cash plus rice, coconuts, betelnuts, betel leaves, etc. in kind. If the vessels came across temples and mosques called *shunyalaya* on their route, they stopped there for worship and out of respect.[36]

SHIPBUILDING

Shipbuilding or ship repair was done at Malwan by the Hindu carpenters and *Panchkalasis* (a caste) helped by *Cabits* (fishermen) and by the Muslims and the local Christians. The chief boat-building towns in Ratnagiri district in the nineteenth century were Ratnagiri, Jaytapur, Malwan and Vengurla. The teak wood used for shipbuilding has been described by foreigners as the Oak of India.[37] In 1830, the teak forests were transferred by the government to the Khots, the zamindars of the Konkan. This made shipbuilding an important industry at least for a while. When the teak timber stock got reduced, teak wood from Malabar was imported. The local wood of *nana*, jack and mango trees was also used for shipbuilding. An auspicious day was chosen to begin construction of a boat; while launching on the sea, it was decorated with flags and flowers. Muslims used *sabja* leaves for decoration. The vessels were named as Laxmi Prasad, Gangaprasad, Daryadaulat, Bhavani, Sadashiva, Sawai Vetal, Narnag, Bhaskar, Salamati, Bahiri, Sardari, Samser, etc.[38] The vessel was set on a trial trip with music and a company of friends, who were treated to toddy, drink, and betelnuts. Brahmans were given gifts and the shipbuilder was honoured with a turban.

The vessels lasted forty to fifty years.[39]

FISHERIES

Associated with the coast is the industry of fishing. The wealth of the seas influences the economic and political development of nations, as can be seen from the history of European powers like Spain, Great Britain, etc. and Japan, an Asiatic power. The fisheries of western India have great potential. The Konkan fishing community under the Marathas in the seventeenth and eighteenth centuries had shouldered the responsibility of developing the naval power on the west coast. It had relieved, to a great extent, the pressure of population on the land by supplying alternative fish food. The west coast has better fishing grounds and a better variety of fish.[40]

Maharashtra occupies the second position among the maritime states of India. It produces 330,000 tonnes of marine products every year, from 300,000 hectares of water-spread area of numerous reservoirs, tanks, ponds and rivers. It has registered a production of 27,000 tonnes of fish every year. Its fisherman population residing in 375 villages amounts to 232,000.[41]

Malwan and Vengurla ports are known for the production of the oyster variety of shell fish, which is the most highly prized on account of its taste and food value. In the 120 coastal villages of this region, the estimated fish catch is about 350,000 maunds per year. The fisheries face many problems, like lack of finance, inadequate transport and market facilities. Fishery techniques are not fully modernised. Mechanisation would develop this industry appreciably.

MINERAL RESOURCES

South Konkan is rich in minerals. It has large deposits of iron, manganese, bauxite and silica. Iron ore is found at many places in Vengurla taluk. In the area around Redi, it is estimated that there is a reserve of forty-four million tonnes of iron ore. Manganese ore occurs on Vengurla side. There is every scope for the full exploitation of these mineral potentialities.

INDUSTRY

Konkan is very poor in modern-day industries. Big industries are not likely to be set up for various reasons, but there is every scope for developing small industries like fruit and fish canning and processing of cashewnuts by using the raw material locally avilable. Mangoes and cashewnuts are dollar-earning products of the Konkan. Fruit canning has a big market in Bombay, Gulf areas and parts of Europe. The processing of cashewnuts and the extraction of liquid from the cashewnut shell are economically profitable activities. If more area could be brought under mango and cashewnut cultivation in Malwan, Vengurla and Devgad region, it would earn rich dividends.

The economic development of Konkan in general and Malwan region in particular has been arrested for various reasons. The peculiar geographical position of the region is mainly responsible for the poor development in agriculture, trade, industry and transport. The rocky and rugged soil, lack of rich and fertile lands and irrigation facilities, absence of adequate means of transport and communication, non-availability of adequate electric power and capital resources, the deficit in food grains are the main factors which make the region backward. Power, transport and capital are the three major needs of the South Konkan.[12]

The old coastal society of the medieval period started disintegrating in the nineteenth century when the British took over Malwan, Vengurla, Devgad and other parts of the south Konkan from 1812 onwards. Malwan and Vengurla ports last their importance as big centres of trade. The overseas trade declined and the harbours were ill maintained. The Sindhudurg fort of Shivaji is in a dilapidated condition and is now only of historical significance.

NOTES

[1]O.H.K. Spate, *India and Pakistan: A General and Regional Geography,* London, 1953, p.606.

[2]Malwan (16°.00 N, 73°.25 E). In a bay entirely blocked by rocking reefs, there were formerly three small islands, two of them about a quarter of a mile from the shore, and the third separated from the mainland by a narrow channel. On the larger of the two outer islands stands the famous fort of Sindhudurg, and on the smaller, the ruined fort of Padamgad, now at low tide, connected with the mainland by a neck of sand. On what

once was the inner island, and now part of the mainland, lies almost hid in palms the old town of Malwan. Malwan was a place of considerable trade in medieval times. It has been referred to by different names by different people such as Milandi, Mali, Malia, Molundi, etc. *Maharashtra State Gazetteers* (New Series) *Ratnagiri District,* Bombay, 1962 (henceforth *Ratnagiri Gaz.*), pp. 770-1.

[3]Grant Duff (ed.) *History of the Maharattas,* S.M. Edwardes, London, 1921, vol. I, p.478. In the seventeenth and early years of the eighteenth centuries, Malwan was the headquarters of the pirates known as *Malvanis,* a very cruel race according to Grant Duff, the most active and desperate of all the coast corsairs. *Ratnagiri Gaz. op.cit.,* pp. 774-5.

> Shivaji had experienced the most determined and successful opposition to his arms from the fortified islands of the pirates on the coast, especially at Danda Rajpuri, held in Jagir and defended by the Habshees or the Abyssinian slaves of the emperors of Delhi. Anxious to possess a similar fortified island to protect his vessels and be a stronghold in adversity, he ordered a survey of the coast to his Sardars. After much research, the mass of rocks opposite to Malwan was fixed as the site of Sindhudurg.

Balkrishna, *Shivaji the Great,* vol. I, part II, Kolhapur, 1931, p.118.

4Shivaji laid the foundation of the Sindhudurg fort on an island called Kurte at a distance nearly a mile away from the Malwan port town on 25 November 1664 and completed its construction in three years with the help of the Portuguese engineers.

> "On a low island about a mile from the shore, it (Sindhudurg) is very extensive, a little less than two miles round the ramparts. The walls are low, ranging from twenty-nine to thirty feet. They are on an average twelve feet thick, and have about fifty-two towers from forty to one hundred and thirty yards apart. The western side of the outer wall is now broken by dashing waves which have caused a breach of twenty feet in it."

Ratnagiri Gaz., op.cit., p. 773. See also G.S. Sardesai, *Marathi Riyasat: Shakakarta Shivaji* (2nd ed.), Bombay, 1975, pp. 99-100 and 238-9 and his *Shivaji Souvenir,* Bombay, 1927, p. 92 (Marathi part).

[5]T.S. Shejwalkar, *Shri Shiva Chhatrapati,* Bombay, 1964, p.113.

[6]S.S Desai (ed.), *Marathyancha Itihasachi Sadhane* (Marathi translations of Portuguese Sources), vols. 1-5 Wai, 1968, pp.19, 95-6, 101-5.

[7]P.S. Pissurlencar, *Portuguese Marathe Sambandha,* Poona, 1967, pp. 264-5; A.G. Pawar (ed.), *Jijabai Kalin Kagad Patre,* Kolhapur, 1975, pp.157-8, 162, 223-5.

[8]Pawar, pp.119 and 203.

[9]Duff Grant, vol. II, p.235.

[10]Pawar, pp.210 and 323. See also S.S. Desai, *Karveer Chhatrapati and Portuguese,* Kolhapur, 1978, p. 90.

[11]By this treaty of Karvir, "The Raja ceded the harbour of Malwan, which included the forts and island of Malwan or Sindhudurg and its dependencies; he also agreed to renounce piracy to permit no armed vessels to be fitted to the British Government and to restore wrecks, as well as to assist vessels in distress" Duff Grant, vol. II, p.422.

[12]R.D. Choksey, *Malwan Residency,* Pune, 1956, p.18.

[13]*Ibid.*, p.18.

[14]*Ratnagiri Gaz.* (New Series), pp.201-6; Old—vol. X, pp.313-14.

[15]V.K. Rajwade (ed.), *Marathyanchya Itihasachi Sadhane,* Dhule, 1912, vol. XV, letter 279.

[16]*Ratnagiri Gaz.* (New), pp. 201-6; Choksey, p.18.

[17]K.R. Dikshit, *Maharashtra in Maps,* Bombay, 1986, pp.137-8.

[18]*Ibid.*, p.160.

[19]T.S Shejwalkar, *Konkanchya Itihasachi Parshwabhumi,* Pune, 1961, p.21.

[20]*Bombay Gazette,* vol. X (old) (henceforth *Bombay Gaz.*), p. 377; *Ratnagiri Gaz.* (new), p.153. See also A.R. Kulkarni, *Maharashtra in the Age of Shivaji,* Poona, 1969, p. 212.

[21]*Bombay Gaz.*, pp.185-6.

[22]*Ibid.*, pp.177-8.

[23]Choksey, pp.13-14.

[24]*Bombay Gaz.*, pp. 348-9.

[25]V.P. Pingulkar, *Sawantwadi Samsthanacha Itihas, 1911,* p. 73, letter No.94 dated 19 November 1759.

[26]B.K. Apte, *History of Maratha Navy and Merchant Ships,* Bombay, 1973, p. 29.

[27]*Ibid.*, pp.74-9.

[28]*Bombay Gaz.*, pp. 351-2.

[29]O.K. Nambiar, *Portuguese Pirates and Indian Seamen,* Mysore, 1955, pp.i, ii (Preface), 11, 46. Observations of a Dutch Governor, Anthony Van Dieman on Portuguese pirates deserve some attention in this respect. He says, "Most of the Portuguese in India look upon this region as their fatherland, and think no more about Portugal. They drive little or no trade thither, but content themselves with the port to port trade of Asia, just as if they were natives thereof and had no other country." Ashin Das Gupta and M.N. Pearson (eds.), *India and the Indian Ocean,* OUP, 1987, p.78.

[30]*Ibid.*, p.22.

[31]D.G. Dhabbu *Kulabkar, Angre Sarkhel* (Marathi), Bombay, 1939, p.416.

[32]*Pune Archives,* Rumal No. 47, File No. I, Narrative No. 7 (unpublished).

[33]*Bombay Gaz.*, p.198.

[34]Dhabbu, pp. 378-79.

[35]*Bombay Gaz.*, pp.166-74.

[36]Dhabbu, pp. 401-2

[37]B.G. Paranjape (ed.), *English Records on Shivaji*, Poona, 1931, vol. II, letter 110.

[38]Dhabbu, p. 401.

[39]*Bombay Gaz.*, pp.173-4. The observations of a Frenchman about the quality of the Indian vessels of the year 1811 are worth quoting here:

> In ancient times the Indians excelled in the art of constructing vessels and the present Hindoos (A.D. 1811) can in this respect still offer models to Europe so much that the English attentive to everything which relates to naval architecture, have borrowed from Hindus many improvements which they have adopted with success to their own shipping. The Indian vessels unite elegance and utility and are models of patience and fine workmanship.

Quoted in Dhabbu, *op.cit.*, p. 378.

[40]C.D. Deshpande, *Western India: A Regional Geography*, Dharwar, 1948, p. 33-4.

[41]*Glimpses of Maharashtra*, Government Publication, p. 25.

[42]*Ratnagiri Gaz.* (New), pp. 529-33.

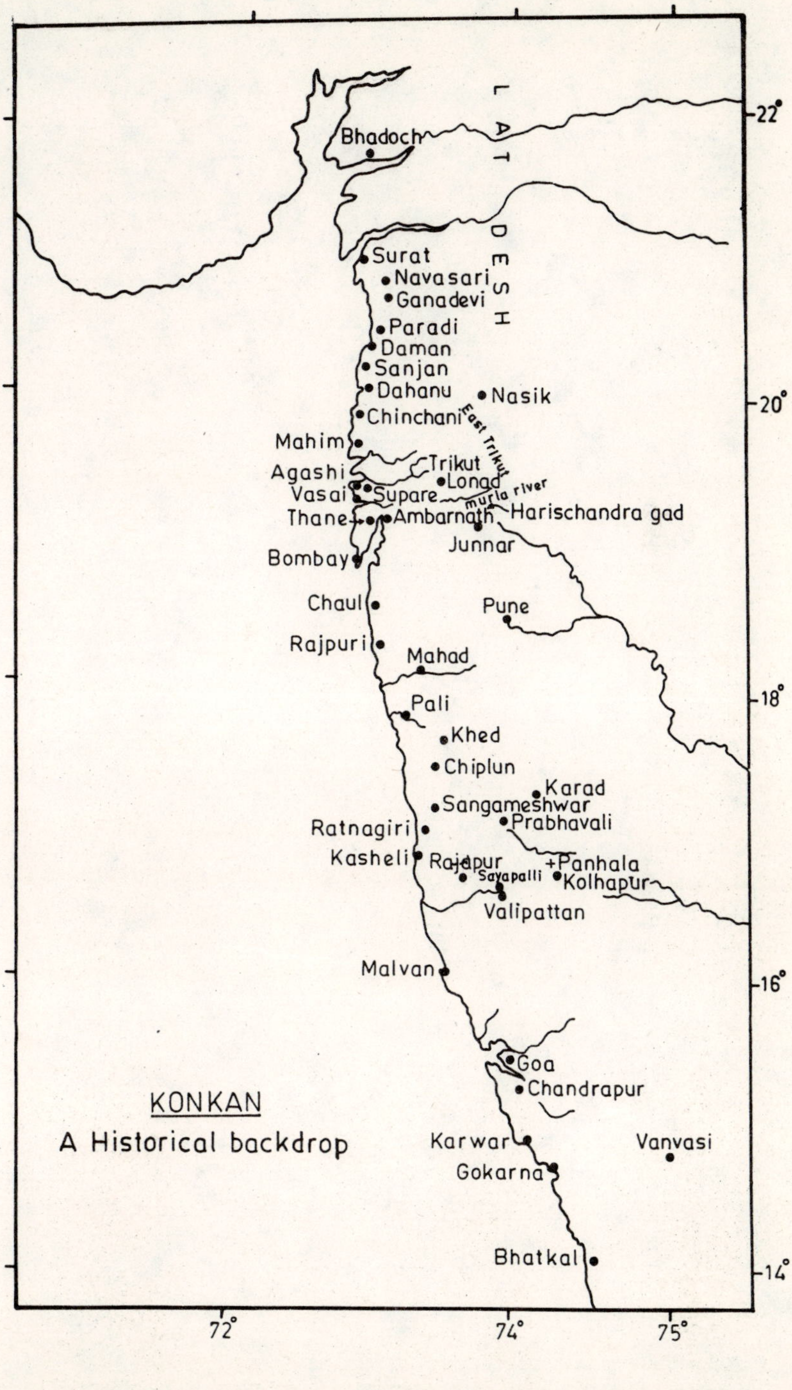
LAT DESH
Bhadoch
Surat
Navasari
Ganadevi
Paradi
Daman
Sanjan
Dahanu
Nasik
Chinchani
East Trikut
Mahim
Trikut
Agashi
Lonad
Vasai
Supare
murla river
Thane
Ambarnath
Harischandra gad
Junnar
Bombay
Chaul
Pune
Rajpuri
Mahad
Pali
Khed
Chiplun
Karad
Sangameshwar
Ratnagiri
Prabhavali
Kasheli
Rajapur
Panhala
Sayapalli
Kolhapur
Valipattan
Malvan
Goa
Chandrapur
KONKAN
A Historical backdrop
Karwar
Vanvasi
Gokarna
Bhatkal
22°
20°
18°
16°
14°
72°
74°
75°

INDIA AT THE CROSSROADS IN THE INDIAN OCEAN

Mihir Roy

> History has shown that whichever power controls the Indian Ocean has, in the first instance, India's seaborne trade at its mercy and in the second, India's very independence.
>
> Jawaharlal Nehru, *INS Mysore*, March 1958

India has a rich maritime heritage dating back to the Vedas and Puranas, which are replete with references to ships, seafarers and sea voyages. The *sombuqs* of the Arabs, jehazi of East Africa, *baghalahas* of the Gulf, *kotias, grabs* and *gullivates* of India and the *fukien junks* of China were long established sailing vessels engaged in commerce, migration and piracy. Navigators from the Orient were also the inventors of the 'kamal' (forerunner of the sextant) and the 'matsya yantra' (fish machine) which was a wet compass enabling mariners to sail the shortest routes across the open seas and not hug the coast.

In spite of such seafaring expertise, the littorals of the Indian Ocean failed to grasp the collateral advantages of sea force. The South Indian dynasties of Satavahanas, Pallavas, Chalukyas, Kalinga, Pandya and Cola used the sea more for making cultural inroads into Malaya, Champa (Siam), Kambuja (Cambodia) and Annam. The Colas and Srivijaya extended their suzerainty over Sri Lanka, Java and Malacca. The Chinese Admiral Zheng He made seven voyages to the Indian Ocean—primarily to glorify Emperor Yung Lo than for any predetermined strategy of colonisation or establishing trading outposts.

It was the Europeans who, in their search for the exotic lands,—which the Book of Genesis described as the 'Garden of Eden'—opened up the Orient for commerce, conversion and colonisation. Pope Calixtus III, by the Treaty of Tordesillas conferred on Portugal the exclusivity of the Indian Ocean. This resulted in fierce rivalry between the European powers culminating in Pax Britannica ensuring Rex Nullius (closed seas) of the Indian Ocean. Britain exploited her sea force for carving out an empire on which the sun never set and made sure that the ingredients of sea-power remained her monopoly. The Indian army was used to subdue the subcontinent, which in turn strengthened the landlocked psychosis which had been earlier evolved by the invaders pouring in through the Himalayan passes. The natural barriers of the northern mountain ranges, as also the 'kalapani' separating India from other countries were therefore more effective in keeping Indians inside the subcontinent than for keeping out invaders!

None the less, this embayed ocean containing one-third of the world's population, three-fourths of the earth's oil resources, two-thirds of its strategic minerals and almost the entire reserves of jute, tin, rubber, cashew and groundnut, continued to be the poorest and least developed segment of planet Earth. Gandhiji aptly described it as "a rich area with poor people". Hence the Indian Ocean region is a mix of poverty and power, intellectuals and illiterates as also messiahs and missiles, with India standing at the crossroads in the emerging economic and new world orders.

The Muslims, on the other hand, were encouraged to cross the seas for performing Haj at Mecca. Hence, Islam leap-frogged from Mauritania to Manila. Today, Islam is perhaps the fastest expanding religion in the world with the total touching 800 million. The Central Asian States of Uzbekhtan, Kazakhistan as also the smaller States of Turkmenistan, Kirghistan and Tadjikhstan are now keen to fashion their own identity and revive their ancient historical, cultural, geographical and religious links with Turkey, Iran, India, Pakistan and China. The cities of Samarkhand, Tashkent, Bukhara, Kiefe, Khwarizn and Alma Ata continue to be entwined with India's folklore of Babar's beloved Ferghana Valley and Adijan city and his uncle Ulugh Beg's observatory in Samarkhand. These Central Asian States also feel close to Turkey through their erstwhile Ottoman links and linguistic affinity. Khirghistan and Kazakhistan on the other hand are closer to China's Muslim population, which may grow into a sensitive dimension with the creeping advance of fundamentalism. Tadjikhstan had close links with Iran and Afghanistan.

The Arabs also are showing an interest in these States. The Saudis have made a beginning by inviting State-recognised muftis and mullahs to join Rabitaal-Alami and by sending millions of copies of the Holy Quran for distribution. Scholarships are also being provided to young mullahs to study religion in Pakistan and Saudi Arabia. Turkey had mooted a Black Sea Economic Union which would have an outlet by sea to the rest of the world.

This transnational Islamic fundamentalism, spreading across the Islamic Crescent, poses more of a challenge in Central and Inner Asia than perhaps to the countries where Islam was introduced by sea, such as Indonesia, Malaysia, Laccadives and Maldives, where the oceans played a coalescing role in amalgamating societies. These Central Asian republics, however, appear to be once again coming into their own as major players in Asia's geopolitics—whether it is South Asia, West Asia, Southeast Asia or the Middle East. India can play an important role by being an experienced midwife in reconciling the past with the present, as Asians already outnumber Arabs during the Haj pilgrimage. Nevertheless it is important that India, with the second largest Muslim population, remains secular in order to be a melting pot for the various political, social, cultural and religious groups. It can only be hoped that the strife between Azerbaijan and Armenia does not turn into a Christian versus Muslim tension. This creeping movement of fundamentalism, whether it is Islam, Buddhism or Hindu reaction, will have significant repercussions in the emerging world order.

NEW OCEAN REGIME

The earlier chaos in the management of the Blue Planet gradually gave way to a new ocean regime on 30 April 1982 after fourteen years of discussion and debate among 160 sovereign States. This quiet revolution radically changed mankind's ways of using and sharing the earth's greatest single resource—its oceans and seas. The Law of the Sea Convention created a new legal regime by dividing the oceans into three separate jurisdictional zones: National, International and Foreign Ocean. Each coastal State has sovereign right over its Territorial Sea (twelve nautical miles from the coastline) subject to the right of innocent passage. In the Contiguous Zone (twelve nautical miles to twenty-four nautical miles), coastal States were authorised to exercise control as necessary to prevent infringements of their fiscal, immigration, sanitation and customs regulations. The Exclusive Economic Zone of 200 miles added 2.2 million square miles to the jurisdiction of New Delhi, which is almost two-thirds of the land area. In the EEZ, the littorals have jurisdiction over both living and non-living resources as also the establishment of artificial islands and installations.

These oceanic activities, paradoxically, added new tension spots such as the demarcation of maritime boundaries, rivalry for seabed resources, narco-terrorism, island grabbing, smuggling, poaching and gun running and environmental warfare such as oil slicks and oil fires. The Indian Ocean, which had hitherto been a neglected ocean, became a sea of strategic contention. For example, the world's military and social expenditure for 1990 identified seventeen conflict areas, of which fourteen were in the Indian Ocean. The popular revolts in Madagascar, Mayotte and the attempted coups in the Seychelles, Maldives and Comoros as also the Sri Lanka insurrection highlighted the brittleness of the political and economic framework in this neglected backyard of the southern Indian Ocean. Further, the Arabian Sea and the Bay of Bengal rapidly became the refuse bin for oil spillage, detergents and seepage disposal. Again global warming, if not controlled, may lead to a rise in sea levels leading to the flooding of low-lying countries such as Maldives, Bangladesh, Lakshadweep and Nicobar islands.

In the International Zone, the mining of seabed minerals is governed by the rules and regulations of the International Seabed Authority (ISA), while living resources need to be exploited within prescribed ecological parameters. The resources of the Foreign Ocean Zone can, however, be exploited only through bilateral agreements.

These extended zones ushered in a number of new factors such as surveillance, surveys, exploration and exploitation of ocean resources and provision of infrastructure for eleven major, twenty intermediate and one hundred minor ports. The application of new technologies such as aquaculture and mariculture and the development of energy from the sea such as waves, wind, and ocean thermal energy conversion (OTEC) also gave a new dimension to the management and development of ocean resources which have wide national and international ramifications.

There have consequently been rapid and unexpected advances in the technology for using the ocean as a source of energy, food, pharmaceuticals, minerals and transportation. This quantum jump in scientific knowledge used for remote sensing, position fixing and dramatic advances in computing, data processing, acoustic and electronic sensing along with the use of moored and drifting instruments, submersibles, robotics and new diving systems has vastly expanded the areas of research in marine geology and biology, physical oceanography and pollution control. These technologies are, however, highly capital-intensive and so a possible way out could be regional cooperation for Indian Ocean littorals. But groupings such as ASEAN, SAARC and GCC are still fragile with many of the States such as Iraq, Iran, Afghanistan and Myanmar being unrepresented. India must, therefore, necessarily play the role of a harmoniser between the North and South as also for South-South cooperation. While the North is evolving a more homogeneous entity, the Indian Ocean States are still in the throes of internal conflicts, religious fundamentalism, ethnicity, casteism and continuing backwardness. After Iraq's defeat, the focus also appears to be shifting from the subcontinent to West Asia. The Soviet States of Azerbaijan, Kazakhistan, Uzbekistan, Turkmenia, Tadjikhstan and Khirgistan, which contain fifty million Muslims, have added yet another dimension in international relations.

Pressure from land and vessel-source pollution and other potentially harmful activities has also brought about increased sensitivity towards the uses of the oceans, especially in the more fragile coastal areas. The convention lays obligations on States to protect and preserve the marine environment and to take all measures necessary to prevent, reduce and control marine pollution. There is also provision for cooperation between States, global and regional, directly or through competent international organisations for formulating rules, standards and practices for the protection and preservation of the marine environment. The Indian Ocean, through which sixty-five per cent of the world's oil passes, is particularly vulnerable to ship borne pollution. This adds another facet to ocean management problems, with peninsular India geophysically dominating this ocean area.

The Indian Ocean States are drawn together by their past experience of population movements, socio-cultural and religious exchanges, and post-colonial history. Mutual cooperation would benefit all of them. But cooperation is easier when societies are similar, or at a complementary level of techno-economic development. The trend hitherto had been to seek techno-economic inputs from the West or from the Soviet Union. Both sides offered these in the perspective of their own strategic needs and economic perceptions. As a result, such 'inputs' or 'aid' have, in most cases, distorted the growth process in the receiving countries. Haltingly and hesitatingly, they are now feeling their way towards mutual cooperation. The South-South dialogue is yet in its infancy, with India at the crossroads between her relationship with the West and her Treaty of Friendship with the erstwhile Soviet Union.

The small island States are the less developed countries of the Indian Ocean. Although varied in their geography, geology, physiography and climate, they share similar constraints to development like limited access to capital markets, poor terms of trade, heavy external dependence and insufficient skilled manpower. Their special problems are density of population, diminishing land for agriculture, low levels of industrialisation, unsatisfactory communications, poorly developed infrastructure and fragile ecosystems, unpredictable weather, and separation by vast stretches of water from their markets.

The task of management of marine affairs is both complex and sophisticated. Interrelated issues arising from UNCLOS must be harmonised and resolved over a wide spectrum. Indian Ocean States, therefore, need to move away from the traditional or dispersed approach to a more coordinated and cohesive management of the oceans. National marine policies need to be formulated in the context of overall development strategy. They should include the national objectives, and appropriate instruments and allocation of resources to achieve these objectives. Expertise must, in turn, be developed to implement these policies. Human resource development is an important prerequisite for resource exploitation.

India must reassess her maritime policy to meet the needs of the emerging macro-economic global balance with Australia, Indonesia and a multi-racial South Africa taking a more corporate interest in this hitherto neglected ocean. She must debate and formulate a 'National Maritime Policy'. Its implementation, however, depends on many ministries with different functions such as fishing, shipping, defence, offshore drilling, and seabed mining, besides several autonomous agencies with blurred linkages, such as the Coast Guard, port and pollution boards, surface transport, and science and technology. There is a need to coordinate these overlapping activities to avoid duplication and wastage of scarce resources. Such a 'Coordination Committee' could well be a 'Council for Ocean Affairs' chaired by the Prime Minister, who is already overseeing related departments like Ocean Development, National Development Council and the Island Development Authority.

IMPLICATIONS OF THE END OF THE COLD WAR

The end of the cold war in 1989 and Iraq's defeat in 1991 saw a diminution in the clash of ideas and ideologies, thereby changing the perceptions of the strategic and security parameters which had held sway for more than four decades. The management of change in itself has become the major challenge, with allies and adversaries interchanging places. The cliche that 'there are no permanent friends and enemies, but only permanent interests' is more valid than ever before, with good governance being a relative value and not necessarily linked to human rights.

With the end of the cold war, the earlier United States policy of containing communism, whether in Korea, Vietnam or Afghanistan, has given way to the vision of a New World Order where the pre-eminence of economics and internal stability offset the short-term gains of a military adventure. Again, the end of the cold war and disintegration of the Soviet Union have brought to an end the system of checks and balances between the two superpowers. This has ushered in an era of unpredictability, with new groupings, such as a refurbished ASEAN, Black Sea Economic Zone, SAARC, unified Europe, American Free Trade Zone encompassing Canada and Mexico and the cheque book powers of Japan and Germany, striving for ascendance. Thus, the post-cold war period has brought in its wake both conflict and cooperation in the search for a New World Order.

CHINA'S EMERGENCE

India and China had a remarkable understanding over centuries, cemented by ancient civilisations and anti-colonial ideologies. In view of their geo-strategic location and massive resources, India and China, with one-fourth of the world's population, are destined to play a global role not only because of their size but also in view of the large markets they provide for goods and services, capital and technology.

They have drifted apart after the occupation of Tibet, followed by the boundary skirmish of 1962. This was further aggravated by

Sino-Pakistan collusion fuelled by superpower confrontation which led to the China card being an ace trump in the trilateral relationship between USA, USSR and PRC. But during the 1980s, a more cooperative relationship with the United States was built up, particularly with the liberalisation of the Chinese economy, its successful modernisation and significant economic growth, which was implemented by a disciplined administrative structure. China's relationship with India also improved after Rajiv Gandhi's visit to Beijing in 1990. This accelerated border talks, including meetings between the military commanders in their pertinent sectors. Detente with the erstwhile Soviet Union in the late 1980s was demonstrated by a $720 million commodity loan from China in March 1991, Moscow agreeing to sell twenty-four high-performance Flanker combat aircraft for $700 million, and border agreements on most of the disputed areas. It appears that China has walked out of the 'age of ideology' and entered the 'age of imageology'.

China's image has improved also because of her economic success. Her external trade touched $110 billion, which was nearly one-third of her GNP, with 16,000 externally aided units. Her agricultural production quadrupled. Her external debt, which was zero in 1959, having risen to $50 billion in 1990, China has developed a stake in the stability of the capitalistic system. It was, therefore, no surprise that 80,000 students went to the United States for training in science and technology. With such a strong political and economic base, China has come out of her isolation. This is demonstrated by her participation in international conventions. As against only eight international conventions in 1970, she has to date taken part in 126 international conventions. China is also a member of eighty-seven inter-governmental organisations, including the World Bank, IMP, IDA, IFC and Asian Development Bank. She is, therefore, poised to be a major actor in the emerging political and economic world orders.

With the Tiananmen Square incident, China partly withdrew from the international scene. Her sense of insecurity was further aggravated by the disintegration of the Soviet and East European blocs, coupled with the dissolution of the Warsaw Pact. The about-turn in the Russian political-economic ideologies, the Western interpretation of intellectual property rights and hegemonistic divides between North and South have led to a policy reassessment by China. Accordingly, she has tended to be the spokesman for the

Third World countries, particularly for North-South issues such as environmental degradation and Uruguay Round of Trade Negotiations, but only if they are touched in general terms. Although China reiterates that she is a developing country and hence entitled to all the concessions and privileges that such countries enjoy, she has refused to join any group of developing countries, possibly to retain a degree of flexibility in international forums, in view of her being a permanent member of the Security Council.

These interlocking factors between domestic and external imageology have possibly led to her signing the Nuclear Non-Proliferation Treaty (NPT), but as a nuclear weapon power. Nevertheless, she supplied fissionable material and other ingredients for weapon development to Pakistan, maintaining that nuclear weapons are more political and psychological tools than military weapons. She expects support from India on her concept of human rights, but has kept away from India's principled stand both on the discriminatory NPT as also intellectual property rights. China also transferred missiles both overtly and covertly to Pakistan, Iran, Myanmar, Syria and Saudi Arabia in spite of her discreet support of the Australian Club on chemical weapons and the Missile Technology Control Regime. From time to time, she raised a muffled voice against the new hegemony. At the same time, she extended soft loans to Burma, Sri Lanka, Thailand and other Indian Ocean littorals for strengthening their military forces. All this makes her relationship with South Asia more translucent than transparent.

In the recent past, China appears to be uneasy with the emerging trends of ethnicity, self-determination, political and religious ideologies and sub-national separatism, which are raising their heads both in Russia as also in Tibet and Sinkiang. Although China has resolved most of her border disputes with the former Soviet Union, there are still some left-overs in Russia, Kazakhistan and Tazikhstan. Border settlements with India that are yet to be resolved are in the Skahsgam valley, Aksai Chin, Himalayan central sector and Arunachal Pradesh.

China is well versed in the use of arms transfers as a powerful instrument of foreign policy. The disintegration of the Soviet Union has opened up more opportunities for China to supplant Russia in the international arms bazar. China has supplied six patrol craft to Sri Lanka; twenty-four Hegu, Hainan and Shanghai attack patrol craft to Bangladesh; twenty-eight Huang fen, Hegu, Hainan,

Huchnan and Shanghai fast attack craft to Pakistan in addition to aircraft, guns, tanks and transfer of production technology. Recently, China has entered into an agreement with Thailand for defence deals amounting to $1 billion. Her export of arms to the Third World is in the region of $1.8 billion annually, which accounts for nearly 6.4 per cent of global arms exports to developing countries. Western restraint in itself has given China a strong leverage to extract concessions.

Recently, China has been articulating a three- dimensional strategic frontier which extends her domain in space, at sea and on land. This merits careful analysis, in order to understand China's role in maintaining global peace. Such perceptions may suggest the continuing need for China to modernise her defence forces to meet a wider range of political objectives and military options.

In view of her maritime seaboard, China can be considered a Pacific power. In this strategic scenario, there are issues across the seas extending to the future status of Taiwan and Hong Kong, the sovereignty of Parcels and Spratley islands in the South China seas as also Pascadores and Prates. Her dispute with Japan over the Senkaku islands is still to be resolved. China has recently claimed a degree of responsibility even over her adjacent waters extending into Southeast Asia. There has been a qualitative as also quantitative expansion of her Navy, with the Northern fleet under Vice-Admiral Qu Zhenmon based at Quingdon; Southern Fleet under Goa Zhejia, based at Canton; and the Eastern Fleet under Nie Kuiju, based at Shanghai. These fleets comprise fifty-nine destroyers and frigates, fifty-three nuclear and conventional submarines with nine submarine depot ships and 700 fast attack craft. There are reports ιt China is probing the pόssibility of acquiring an aircraft carrier from Russia and has bought the aircraft carrier *Melbourne* from Australia. China is also designing and building Han-class nuclear-powered submarines with SLBM, underwater weapons and sensors, and advanced missiles fitted with sophisticated electronics and satellite communications.

MYANMAR'S PRISONER OF ZENDA

China has been a major arms supplier to Islamabad for years. Pakistan was also a major conduit for Chinese military hardware destined for the Mujahideen in Afghanistan. The Karakoram

Highway, completed in 1982, also provided China with a direct road link to the Indian Ocean.

Burma, on India's eastern flank, began to develop into an important Chinese ally from about August 1988 when the two countries signed an agreement establishing official trade across the common border. The present Burmese junta, which seized power on 18 September 1988 after crushing a nation-wide uprising for democracy, clearly saw in China a potential ally, especially when the leaders in Beijing staged a similar action against the pro-democracy activists in June the following year.

Since the signing of the border trade agreement in 1988, Burma has become China's chief foreign market for consumer goods. China in turn is a major importer of Burmese timber, forestry products, minerals, seafood and agricultural produce. World Bank analysts estimate that nearly $1.5 billion worth of goods are exchanged along the Burma-China frontier, not including a flourishing trade in narcotics from the Burmese sector of the Golden Triangle.

A high-powered defence delegation, which included Major Gen. Tin Yun (Chief of the Burmese Air Force) and the directors of ordnance and defence industries paid an unpublicised visit to Islamabad in March 1989 and concluded an arms transfer agreement. This included an initial delivery of 150 machine-guns with 50,000 runs of ammunition and 5,120 mm mortar bombs.

The recent influx of Myanmar Nagas into India, the exodus of Rohingya Muslims into Bangadesh and the presence of thousands of refugees in Thailand and elsewhere are pointers to the misdeeds of the junta in power in Rangoon.

Bert Linter, who represents the *Far Eastern Economic Review*, also made several less reported observations in the international press, such as the ongoing construction of a major naval base on Haingyi island on the Bay of Bengal with Chinese assistance, a sevenfold increase in the number of battalions posted along the border with India and Bangladesh, and signing of a $1.4 billion military hardware deal between China and Myanmar. The deal includes the supply to Myanmar of jet fighters, radar installations, light machine-guns, rocket launchers, etc. China has about twenty military advisers in Myanmar. Some of the hardware supplied by China has been deployed along the border with India and Bangladesh. Moreover, the strength of the Myanmar army has gone up from 190,000 men in

1988 to nearly 300,000.

According to Linter, the junta are doing everything to retain power and had gathered a "lot of toys" to play around with. This had led to minimal insurgency of little consequence but continued attacks on Rohingya Muslims and Myanmar Nagas. These developments are affecting the security of the region. Bangladesh has appealed for assistance to the United Nations in view of the refugees pouring in from Arakan.

Myanmar is also the biggest illicit producer of narcotics in the Golden Triangle and the drugs are spilling over into Manipur and other states in India. The estimated production of 2,200 tonnes of narcotics is twice the production of four years ago. The ruling State Law and Order Restoration Council (SLORC) has entered into treaties with drug barons in various States resulting in a symbiotic relationship. Probably, the SLORC feels that it is better to get Myanmar youth high on drugs than on politics!

While there is little room for optimism with the junta well entrenched, there is nevertheless a glimmer of hope that the manifestations of maintaining a grossly oversized army could lead to conditions which put a severe strain on the junta. In such an eventuality, other factors could intervene and help restore democracy in the country.

The Sino-Burmese border trade agreement of 1988 slipped into temporary oblivion when a nation-wide uprising for democracy shook the country. The National League for Democracy (NLD) was spearheaded by Su Kyi, daughter of Aung San (hero of Burma's independence) and she was promptly put under house arrest. Su Kyi still symbolises the Burmese people's hope for a change and a freer society. The 1991 Nobel Peace Prize winner, in a fashion, makes the future of the SLORC uncertain.

Internally, Myanmar has been a hotbed of intrigue and political turmoil since 1989. It is rapidly becoming a source of instability for the entire region. India, with her goodwill and leverage in Myanmar, is perhaps the best hope for the freedom-loving people of Burma.

FRANCE STEPS INTO THE INDIAN OCEAN

The maritime powers of Portugal, Holland and Britain, who had established large colonies in the East, have completely withdrawn from the Indian Ocean. But France continues to maintain her commercial, cultural and military infrastructure, in the southwest centred in the Reunion Islands and northwest with Djibouti as the focal point, which enables her to claim the status of an Indian Ocean State.

Sovereignty over these islands has added eleven million square kilometres to France's Exclusive Economic Zone, which catapulted her to the position of the third largest maritime nation from the forty-fifth position. France has emerged as a major trading partner of, and a primary weapon supplier to, South Africa and the Gulf. In addition, she is an important source for the transfer of technology, particularly to developing countries. Francophone Indian Ocean islands, however, are characterised by socio-economic disparities, unbalanced development, rapid population growth, unemployment and chaotic urbanisation. President Albert Rene of Seychelles went to the extent of stating that "French presence in the Indian Ocean is an anachronism, which history will eliminate sooner or later". All the same, France continues to be the most important donor country to Seychelles (twenty-seven per cent of her foreign aid), Mauritius (forty-three per cent), Malagasy (thiry-five per cent) and Comoros (thirty-two per cent).

FRENCH SOUTHWEST AND NORTHWEST TERRITORIES

Reunion Islands, which have no pre-colonial history, are situated 240 km to the southwest of Mauritius, 960 km from Malagasy (Madagascar), 2,560 km from the United States military base at Diego Garcia and 2,160 km from the African mainland. French is the *lingua franca* and her influence pervades the financial, commercial, cultural, religious and other aspects of southwest territories, which are a mosaic of several ethnic groups—European, African, Asian and Malgach. Reunion Islands are currently an Overseas Department of France, with her 'plantation economy' being transformed into an 'assisted economy'. France pumps 6.4 billion francs into the health, social and family welfare schemes of the islands.

In the summer of 1972, a popular revolt spearheaded by Malgach students drove away the ailing President Tsiranana, who had ruled Madagascar since 1960. The French naval forces, which were formerly based at Diego Suares, were relocated at Reunion albeit on a French fleet tanker (*La Charent*), which has a flight-deck to operate short take-off aircraft, with a consort of three frigates to give the Rear Admiral commanding the Indian Ocean fleet a modicum of mobility. The air base has also moved to La Montagne, which is north of St. Denis, and is currently the inter-armed force headquarters for France's South West Indian Ocean Military Command (FAZSOI). The French forces stationed in this area have, therefore, the triple responsibility of deterring aggression, safeguarding French territories, and if required, intervene to protect French political and economic interests. With the end of the cold war, France proposes to increase her naval strength in the Indian Ocean.

The second cluster of French-administered islands in this region is the Comoros archipelago covering 2,200 sq km, with a population of 300,000 who are unevenly distributed over the islands of Asjouen (270 sq km) and Moheli (290 sq km). The 'confetti' of the French possessions are the Eparse islands consisting of Glorious, Juan de Nova, Europa and Bassa de India which, in spite of their handkerchief size, are the strategic choke points in the Mozambique channel.

The third cluster of islands are the southern and Antarctica islands (TAAF) which includes Saint Paul, Crozet, Adelie, Karguelen (a likely alterative site to Mururoa nuclear testing site in the Pacific) and Amsterdam islands. The Antarctica cluster, besides being rich in krill (similar to protein-rich shrimp) is said to have reserves of forty-five million barrels of oil, 34.5 trillion cubic metres of gas and other strategic minerals which will be significant in view of the depleting resources in the Indian Ocean.

The territory of Afars and Issas (FTAI) in the north-west, stretching over an area of 23,000 sq km, is currently the Republic of Djibouti situated at the head of the Gulf of Aden at the entrance to the Red Sea, which is across the Babel-Mandeb Straits. Djibouti, which has a population of 200,000 including 10,000 French nationals, of which 6,300 are military personnel, is enclaved between the two warring nations of Ethiopia and Somalia. This French stronghold commands the choke point to the Gulf of Aden to which several pipelines are linked, especially after increasing the depth of the Suez Canal in order to accommodate medium-size tankers.

PAKISTAN'S OCEAN POLICY

Pakistan has a 700 km coastline with about 250,000 sq km of Exclusive Economic Zone (EEZ). Her mercantile marine of 366,059 tonnes has shown a decline over the years. Pakistan does not possess any island territories nor has any large offshore assets. None the less in the last five years, Pakistan has almost doubled her Navy, with assistance from the United States by the addition of six Gearing-class (Fram 1) destroyers with SSM Harpoon missiles, four Garcia-class frigates with sixteen standard SA-M-16 and anti-submarine weapons. Two Leander-class frigates and one large country-class destroyer with Seacat missiles from Britain were commissioned into the Pakistan Navy in 1988. Twenty-eight fast attack craft with SSM Hai Ying missiles from China were added to the Pakistan Navy in 1980. The two Agosta and four Daphne class submarines were petro-fitted to carry both torpedoes and SSM sub-Harpoon missiles. Her six newly acquired P-3C Orion maritime aircraft armed with ASM Harpoons and four Breguet Atlantic patrol aircraft retrofitted with Exocet missiles have sufficient endurance to patrol the major segment of the Arabian Sea.

Within a short span of five years, Pakistan's sixteen missile warships, ten maritime aircraft with ASM missiles, and six submarines with Harpoon missiles, have doubled her naval strength in the Indian Ocean. This overnight expansion merits careful monitoring, particularly with the casus belli for Indo-Pakistan conflict remaining not only unresolved but being fuelled with calculated violations of the Shimla Agreement.

INDIA - A REGIONAL POWER

The everyday responsibilities of the Indian Navy are spread over two million square miles of EEZ, 7,000 km of coastline, 1,284 islands and islets and widely dispersed sealanes of communication (SLOC). The expanding multidisciplinary spectrum of ocean activities has created additional tension spots such as demarcating maritime boundaries, narco-terrorism linked to ideologies, oil pollution, island grabbing, rivalry for seabed exploration, poaching, environmental degradation and safety of ships and seamen. In addition, the security of high-value offshore structures such as Bombay High, which has multiplied to eighteen platforms, seventeen rigs, thirty-two supply vessels and 600 km of submarine pipeline to provide twenty-seven million tonnes of oil is indicative of the expanding oceanic requirements involving the Navy, Coast Guard, merchant shipping, fishing, oceanography and other agencies for harvesting both living and non-living resources.

The expanding responsibilities for navies are in addition to the need to update technologies , which affects the composition and construction of warships. India has two small aircraft carriers, sixteen major surface combatants, fifteen submarines and eight long range maritime aircraft. Assuming that two out of three ships will be operational, she will require at least eight surface ships in each of her three fleets (with the completion of the new naval base at Karwar). The Indian Navy will need to double the number of surface ships and long-range maritime aircraft in an acceptable time frame to patrol an operational radius of 1,500 miles. But, as Admiral Stanfield Turner aptly remarked, "it is more than just a numbers game".

While it was earlier possible for India to buy ships, submarines and aircraft from the USSR on rupee payment spread over fifteen years at low interest rates, it has now become financially suicidal to continue the same in hard currency and at greatly increased prices. Further, the earlier option of "buying security and not building self-reliance" had in a way marginalised the growth of Indian industries and consequently encouraged the brain drain of Indian scientists and engineers to the West. India has, however, now decided to liberalise her economic policies, and integrate with the mainstream of the world economy in order to restore macro-economic balances, which requires her to retain creative technologists and dynamic managers.

India also appears to be at the crossroads between 'import substitution' and 'exports'. According to the Stockholm Institute of Peace Research (SIPRI), arms sales are currently galloping at $1,000 billion per annum, of which China and even Pakistan are well-known exponents. China, a late entry, already accounts for $2 billion, not taking into account the recent surreptitious sale of missiles and nuclear components to Pakistan, and possibly Iran. Hence India must necessarily get over its Nehruvian philosophy and instead export defence items, which will not only rationalise the comparatively small defence budget but also expand the military-industrial complex within the country and thereby create employment and incomes for the rapidly growing industrial labour force. A start has recently been made to fill the void due to the relative scarcity of Russian hardware in Third World countries. This will in turn require some sort of symmetry in defence spending, which for the Indian Navy has been pegged at thirteen per cent of the defence budget (Army fifty-seven per cent, Air Force thirty per cent). At the same time, any additional funds for R&D or for updating maritime ingredients are viewed as expansionist by developed countries. Others at home view it as reducing the allotment to relieve poverty, housing, food subsidies, water and sanitation, which by themselves are perhaps more relevant to the 'Heartlanders' who see the seas as distant luxuries!

But defence and development are inexorably the two sides of the same coin. The expansion of India's maritime ingredients such as shipping, fishing and exploitation of non-living resources are mandatory to alleviate poverty and backwardness. The steps initiated by Japan, South Korea, Taiwan and China merit careful study in order to implement a coherent maritime policy.

If the declining trend in investment in the seas is not arrested, it will inevitably affect the number of vessels available for combating smuggling and thereby checking parallel black market economy and international money laundering. Failure to do so will further confirm India as a 'soft target'. for smuggling gold, silver, narcotics and contraband. In the same vein, poaching for prawns, lobsters, turtles and salt-water crocodile will become lucrative to fishing trawlers even from the Pacific, resulting in additional loss of income for the Indian littorals. Indiscriminate fishing in the breeding grounds with finer mesh nets will also have a long-term adverse effect on the living resources of the Indian Ocean.

The lack of an adequate sea force in the Indian Ocean for effective policing will encourage the surreptitious dumping of chemicals and nuclear wastes as also flushing out of oil bilges from ships, which impinges on the health of the coastal States. The consequences of oil fires in the Gulf, which have added to the 6,000 million tonnes of carbon dioxide being pumped into the atmosphere every year are also a measure of the harm being caused to the environment. This will accelerate global warming and rise in sea levels, endangering low-lying islands in the Indian Ocean such as the Maldives, Laccadives and Nicobar.

NUCLEAR PROLIFERATION

The Nuclear Non-Proliferation Treaty, which consists of various national, littoral and multilateral regulations, trade embargos and sanctions, has undergone a basic change. The 'balance of terror' between the superpowers was, in reality, a 'balance of technological supremacy'. Although arms control measures have contributed to the lowering of global tensions, the arms race continues. The fifteen to twenty-five per cent reduction in the Soviet-American strategic weapons over a period of seven years has been counterbalanced by the exemption of emerging modern weapon systems from future limitations. These new systems will carry more powerful, more reliable and more accurate warheads. The United States is planning to produce an estimated 3,500 new weapons in the next five years, including 'high microwave bombs' and strategic 'earth-penetrating warheads'. Technology has therefore become 'a principle of war' and should be a prime mover in both national development and national security.

Again, the earlier submarine-launched ballistic missile, which was the primary second-strike deterrent, has been overtaken by an array of precision-guided conventional missiles. The repertory of such first-strike weapons includes microprocessed, thermal imaged, laser guided, satellite vectored and electro-magnetically manoeuvred, for a single short kill. So much so, weapons today are called 'dumb' if they are unguided, 'smart' if they incorporate guidance relying on outside sources and 'brilliant' if they are self-guided. Technology will therefore affect the composition and architecture of sea-power, which so far has been out of the superpower accords. A ditty expresses this aptly:

> 'Put the missile out to sea
> Where the real estate is free
> And it is far away from me...'

The reluctance of developed nations to transfer defence technology to Third World countries makes it more important for India to rely on an indigenous system, which may not be as good as the systems available in the international arms bazar. One must, however, not automatically yield to the temptation of resorting to 'licensed production' or 'outright purchase' as this is tantamount to killing the hen to conserve on the chicken-feed.

A practical offshoot of such a policy could be the creation of a 'Department of Aerospace and Missiles'; a Ship Building Authority to reduce losses in shipyards as also the rationalisation and reorganisation of the major seaports and communication infrastructure in order that India is not left behind in the emerging economic world order.

India must invest more than the present two per cent of the GNP in the ingredients of maritime power. For example, although Indian shipping is less than two per cent of the world's tonnage, her 439 ships, with 100 being at sea at any one time, earn nearly Rs. 76,000 crores. The present lop-sided subsidies being extended to a vociferous farmers' lobby in view of their voting strength, at the expense of the coastal community, cuts into the development of ocean-based activities. It reflects a tragic lack of understanding of the potential of the warm, ice-free ocean for rapidly expanding the employment and incomes of the people living in this region.

MARITIME BALANCE SHEET

The Orientals, with the exception of Japan, paid a heavy price for not understanding the collateral advantage of using the seas for defence and development. It is, therefore, necessary to identify the emerging ingredients of maritime power, be it shipping, fishing, drilling, dredging, mining or even gunboat diplomacy, in the new relations between the sea and the State.

The smaller nations will perforce have to look to a friendly regional power, which has the capability and capacity to assist them during national disasters, maritime boundary disputes, island grabbing, offshore exploration, human resource development and so on. India has still not understood the spectrum of options available to a sea force because of interlinking oceanic borders. The controversy with Bangladesh over Moore Island is an example of the need to be purposeful on maritime issues in the international arena. The gradual induction of protective sea forces during the Iran-Iraq conflict was apparently not taken into cognisance when Indian tankers including *Ambedkar, Ras Viswamitra, Varuna* and *Jalpari* were hit by missiles. New Delhi's continued reluctance to escort her unarmed merchantmen to enforce the right of innocent passage during the Gulf conflict was again shown up when the Shipping Corporation vessel transporting refugees and foodstuffs with the approval of the United Nations was stopped, boarded and searched on the high seas in flagrant violation of international norms. Even so, not a whimper of protest was heard from South Block—a sad testimony to the Indian taxpayers' investment in a three-dimensional navy which is but a tool of the nation just as the hammer is a tool of the carpenter, and is therefore, required to be used deliberately and purposefully.

Non-provocative defence should take into account the forces and factors that help or hinder India's maritime capacity of not only being a credible policeman but also eliminate her neighbours' fears. Conversely, she should have the maritime and political strength to deter or defuse the factors that attract the attention of external powers to intervene against the country's national interests. The emerging role of India, standing at the crossroads in the Indian Ocean, may well change the very basis of the strategic, economic and environmental perceptions in this ice-free link ocean. It will be opportune for India, sandwiched as it were between a new economic order and an emerging world order to look ahead and plan so that she may stride purposefully into the twenty-first century, and not remain becalmed in the Ocean of Destiny. So, to conclude with the Sanskrit saying:

'Sam no Varuna'
(May the seas be auspicious to us).